AMERICAN DECORATIONS

VOL II

AMERICAN DECORATIONS

❧

A List of Awards of the
Congressional Medal of Honor
the
Distinguished-Service Cross
and the
Distinguished-Service Medal

AWARDED UNDER AUTHORITY OF THE CONGRESS
OF THE UNITED STATES

1862-1926

❧

*Compiled in the Office of The Adjutant General of the Army
and published by order of the Secretary of War*

UNITED STATES
GOVERNMENT PRINTING OFFICE
WASHINGTON
1927

WAR DEPARTMENT

Document No. 18a

OFFICE OF THE ADJUTANT GENERAL

Printed and bound by Antony Rowe Ltd, Eastbourne

TABLE OF CONTENTS

	Page
Extracts from statutes	V
Explanatory notes	VIII
Congressional medal of honor, awards of	1
Distinguished-service cross, awards of, to—	
Americans	125
British	650
French	653
Distinguished-service medal, awards of, to—	
Americans	669
Belgians	791
British	794
French	804
Italians	829
Japanese	833
Citizens of other countries	834
Members of the Army, in lieu of the certificate of merit	835

EXTRACTS FROM STATUTES AUTHORIZING THE CONGRESSIONAL MEDAL OF HONOR, THE DISTINGUISHED-SERVICE CROSS, AND THE DISTINGUISHED-SERVICE MEDAL

A resolution to provide for the presentation of "medals of honor" to the enlisted men of the Army and Volunteer Forces who have distinguished, or may distinguish, themselves in battle during the present rebellion.

Resolved by the Senate and House of Representatives of the United States of America in Congress assembled, That the President of the United States be, and he is hereby, authorized to cause two thousand "medals of honor" to be prepared with suitable emblematic devices, and to direct that the same be presented, in the name of Congress, to such noncommissioned officers and privates as shall most distinguish themselves by their gallantry in action, and other soldier-like qualities, during the present insurrection. And that the sum of ten thousand dollars be, and the same is hereby, appropriated out of any money in the Treasury not otherwise appropriated, for the purpose of carrying this resolution into effect.

Approved, July 12, 1862.

An act making appropriations for sundry civil expenses of the Government for the year ending June thirty, eighteen hundred and sixty-four, and for the year ending the 30(th) of June, 1863, and for other purposes.

*   *   *   *   *   *   *

SEC. 6. *And be it further enacted,* That the President cause to be struck from the dies recently prepared at the United States mint for that purpose, "medals of honor" additional to those authorized by the act (resolution) of July twelfth, eighteen hundred and sixty-two, and present the same to such officers, noncommissioned officers, and privates as have most distinguished, or who may hereafter most distinguish, themselves in action; and the sum of twenty thousand dollars is hereby appropriated out of any money in the Treasury not otherwise appropriated, to defray the expenses of the same.

*   *   *   *   *   *   *

Approved, March 3, 1863.

[Extract from the act making appropriations for the support of the Army for the fiscal year ending June 30, 1919, approved July 9, 1918]

Medals of honor, distinguished-service crosses, and distinguished-service medals.—That the provisions of existing law relating to the award of medals of honor to officers, noncommissioned officers, and privates of the Army be, and they hereby are, amended so that the President is authorized to present, in the name of the Congress, a medal of honor only to each person who, while an officer or enlisted man of the Army, shall hereafter, in action involving actual conflict with an enemy, distinguish himself conspicuously by gallantry and intrepidity at the risk of his life above and beyond the call of duty.

That the President be, and he is hereby, further authorized to present, but not in the name of Congress, a distinguished-service cross of appropriate design and a ribbon, together with rosette or other device, to be worn in lieu thereof, to any person who, while serving in any capacity with the Army of the United States since the sixth day of April, nineteen hundred and seventeen, has distinguished, or who shall hereafter distinguish, himself or herself by extraordinary heroism in connection with military operations against an armed enemy.

That the President be, and he is hereby, further authorized to present, but not in the name of Congress, a distinguished-service medal of appropriate design and a ribbon, together with a rosette or other device, to be worn in lieu thereof, to any person who, while serving in any capacity with the Army of the United States since the sixth day of April nineteen hundred and seventeen, has distinguished, or who hereafter shall distinguish, himself or herself by exceptionally meritorious service to the Government in a duty of great responsibility; and said distinguished-service medal shall also be issued to all enlisted men of the Army to whom the certificate of merit has been granted up to and including the date of the passage of this act under the provisions of previously existing law, in lieu of such certificates of merit, and after the passage of this act the award of the certificate of merit for distinguished service shall cease; and additional pay heretofore authorized by law for holders of the certificate of merit shall not be paid to them beyond the date of the award of the distinguished-service medal in lieu thereof as aforesaid.

That each enlisted man of the Army to whom there has been or shall be awarded a medal of honor, a distinguished-service cross, or a distinguished-service medal shall, for each such award, be entitled to additional pay at the rate of $2 per month from the date of the distinguished act or service on which the award is based, and each bar, or other suitable device, in lieu of a medal of honor, a distinguished-service cross, or a distinguished-service medal, as hereinafter provided for, shall entitle him to further additional pay at the rate of $2 per month from the date of the distinguished act or service for which the bar is awarded, and said additional pay shall continue throughout his active service, whether such service shall or shall not be continuous; but when the award is in lieu of the certificate of merit, as provided for in section three hereof, the additional pay shall begin with the date of the award.

That no more than one medal of honor or one distinguished-service cross or one distinguished-service medal shall be issued to any one person; but for each succeeding deed or act sufficient to justify the award of a medal of honor or a distinguished-service cross, or a distinguished-service medal, respectively, the President may award a suitable bar, or other suitable device, to be worn as he shall direct; and for each other citation of an officer or enlisted man for gallantry in action published in orders issued from the headquarters of a force commanded by a general officer he shall be entitled to wear, as the President shall direct, a silver star three-sixteenths of an inch in diameter.

That the Secretary of War be, and he is hereby, authorized to expend from the appropriations for contingent expenses of his department from time to time so much as may be necessary to defray the cost of the medals of honor, distinguished-service crosses, distinguished-service medals, bars, rosettes, and other devices hereinbefore provided for.

That whenever a medal, cross, bar, ribbon, rosette, or other device presented under the provisions of this act shall have been lost, destroyed, or rendered unfit for use, without fault or neglect on the part of the person to whom it was awarded, such medal, cross, bar, ribbon, rosette, or device shall be replaced without charge therefor.

That, except as otherwise prescribed herein, no medals of honor, distinguished-service cross, distinguished-service medal, or bar, or other suitable device in lieu of either of said medals or of said cross, shall be issued to any person after more than three years from the date of the act justifying the award thereof, nor unless a specific statement or report distinctly setting forth the distinguished service and suggesting or recommending official recognition thereof shall have been made at the time of the distinguished service or within two years thereafter, nor unless it shall appear from official records in the War Department that such person has so distinguished himself as to entitle him thereto; but in case an individual who shall distinguish himself dies before the making of the award to which he may be entitled, the award may, nevertheless, be made and the medal or cross or the bar or other emblem or device presented within three years from the date of the act justifying the award thereof to such representative of the deceased as the President may designate; but no medal, cross, bar, or other device, hereinbefore authorized, shall be awarded or presented to any individual whose entire service subsequently to the time he distinguished himself shall not have been honorable; but in cases of officers and enlisted men now in the Army for whom the award of the medal of honor has been recommended in full compliance with then existing regulations but on account of services which, though insufficient fully to justify the award of the medal of honor, appear to have been such as to justify the award of the distinguished-service cross or distinguished-service medal hereinbefore provided for, such cases may be considered and acted upon under the provisions of this act authorizing the award of the distinguished-service cross and distinguished-service medal, notwithstanding that said services may have been rendered more than three years before said cases shall have been considered as authorized by this act, but all consideration of and action upon any of said cases shall be based exclusively upon official records now on file in the War Department; and in the cases of officers and enlisted men now in the Army who have been mentioned in orders, now a part of official records, for extraordinary heroism or especially meritorious services, such as to justify the award of the distinguished-service cross or the distinguished-service medal hereinbefore provided for, such cases may be considered and acted on under the provisions of this act, notwithstanding that said act or services may have been rendered more than three years before said cases shall have been considered as authorized by this act, but all consideration of and action upon any said cases shall be based exclusively upon official records of the War Department.

That the President be, and he is hereby, authorized to delegate, under such conditions, regulations, and limitations as he shall prescribe, to the commanding general of a separate army or higher unit in the field, the power conferred upon him by this act to award the medal of honor, the distinguished-service cross, and the distinguished-service medal; and he is further authorized to make from time to time any and all rules, regulations, and orders which he shall deem necessary to carry into effect the provisions of this act and to execute the full purpose and intention thereof.

That the President is authorized, under regulations to be prescribed by him, to confer such medals and decorations as may be authorized in the military service of the United States upon officers and enlisted men of the military forces of the countries concurrently engaged with the United States in the present war.

EXPLANATORY NOTES

The number following name is the Army serial number.
(*) Indicates posthumous award.
R—Residence at entry into service.
B—Place of birth.
NR—No record found in War Department.
G. O. No.—, W. D.—War Department general orders in which citation is published.

The rank in each instance is that held at time of act or service for which the decoration was awarded.

Errors or omissions should be immediately reported to The Adjutant General of the Army by those concerned.

The Distinguished-Service Medal

659

PHABETICAL LIST OF AWARDS OF THE DISTINGUISHED-SERVICE MEDAL IN NATIONAL GROUPS

AMERICANS

[irded for exceptionally meritorious and distinguished services, in a position of great responsibility, under the provisions of the act of Congress approved July 9, 1918, except as otherwise indicated]

)T, FREDERIC V.
R—Willetts Point, N. Y.
B—Massachusetts.
G. O. No. 15, W. D., 1921.

Brigadier general, U. S. Army.
For services in the organization of engineer troops and the procurement of enlisted men for the service in the war. His zeal was untiring and the success of his effort marked.

ER, ALBERT H.
R—Grove City, Pa.
B—Greenville, Pa.
G. O. No. 95, W. D., 1919.

Colonel, Corps of Engineers, U. S. Army.
As commanding officer of the 4th Engineers he contributed materially to the successes of the 4th Division in the Aisne-Marne offensive and in the Meuse-Argonne operations. By his skill in the construction of roads and bridges, he ably assisted in the operations of his division. His ability as a leader was shown in the efficiency of the 4th Engineers, both as a technical and as a combat unit. Later he showed the same rare qualities when he commanded the 27th Engineers.

MS, EMORY S.
R—Manhattan, Kans.
B—Manhattan, Kans.
G. O. No. 16, W. D., 1923.

Colonel, Infantry, U. S. Army.
As adjutant, Base Section No. 5, Brest, France, from Dec. 10, 1918, to Dec. 20, 1919, he displayed exceptional administrative and executive ability, sound judgment, uniform courtesy and unremitting devotion to duty, contributing markedly to the successful accomplishments of Base Section No. 5, upon which was placed among other duties the responsibility for the repatriation of more than a million American soldiers.

MS, HARRY M.
R—Omaha, Nebr.
B—Comanche, Iowa.
G. O. No. 35, W. D., 1919.

Director of inland traffic service, War Department.
His responsibilities have been great in supervising the utilization of railroad facilities and the immense movement of troops and supplies during the war. His excellent judgment and marked ability have contributed materially to the successful and orderly movement of troops and supplies to the ports of embarkation and for the Army overseas.

MS, JOHN H.
R—La Porte, Ind.
B—Chicago, Ill.
G. O. No. 38, W. D., 1922.

Lieutenant colonel, Quartermaster Corps, U. S. Army.
For services as assistant chief, and later as chief of the Subsistence Division, Office of the Quartermaster General. His keen foresight and able grasp of the problems at hand made him an invaluable aid during those days when the all-important work of organizing the food supply was under way. By his tireless energy and marked ability he conducted his duties in the procurement and supply of subsistence stores, as to meet satisfactorily the all-important needs of the Army. In both positions he demonstrated marked business ability, good judgment, and carried to a successful conclusion each project presented to him.

MSON, GEORGE E.
R—Sherman, Tex.
B—Collinsville, Tex.
G. O. No. 56, W. D., 1922.

Captain, Adjutant General's Department, U. S. Army.
As confidential secretary of the Commander in Chief, American Expeditionary Forces, and later of the General of the Armies, he has worked untiringly and given proof of marked ability and resourcefulness. In the multifarious details connected with his duties he has at all times displayed keen judgment, tact, unfailing courtesy, and loyalty. In the office of the Commander in Chief, American Expeditionary Forces, where there devolved upon Captain Adamson a great volume of work and a mass of detail, he handled each new problem which confronted him in an able and masterful manner and rendered invaluable services to the American Expeditionary Forces in a position of great responsibility and in times and circumstances of the gravest importance.

IS, EMMETT.
R—Youngstown, Ohio.
B—New Haven, Conn.
G. O. No. 56, W. D., 1922.

Colonel (Cavalry), General Staff Corps, U. S. Army.
He served with marked ability as Assistant Chief of Staff, G-3, 38th Division, during the early days of its organization and training. As an instructor at the Army General Staff College, American Expeditionary Forces, he displayed high professional attainments, and unfailing energy, performing service of inestimable worth in connection with the instruction and training of officers for General Staff duty. Later in the Office of the Provost Marshal General he again demonstrated those splendid characteristics which have at all times been outstanding features of his service.

RIGHT, OWEN S.
R—Memphis, Tenn.
B—St. Louis, Mo.
G. O. No. 35, W. D., 1920.

Lieutenant colonel, Signal Corps, U. S. Army.
In command of field signal battalions at the front, as an instructor at corps schools, and as division signal officer of the 2d Division, he rendered services of great value to the American Expeditionary Forces.

EN, HERBERT W.
R—Detroit, Mich.
B—Vermont.
G. O. No. 77, W. D., 1919.

Lieutenant colonel, Ordnance Department, U. S. Army.
For services first, as American engineering representative at the conference called to design the Anglo-American Mark VIII tank, and later as being directly responsible for the design of a new, valuable, and easily obtained implement of mechanical warfare, the fast 3-ton tank, susceptible of production in America in such quantity as to constitute a most material contribution to the effective fighting power of the United States Army.

669

ALESHIRE, JOSEPH P
R—Washington, D. C
B—Fort Custer, Mont.
G. O. No. 56, W. D., 1922.

Major, Quartermaster Corps, U. S. Army.
As Assistant Chief of Staff, G-3, 81st Division, from October, 1918, until March, 1919, by his marked ability, high professional attainments, and loyal devotion to duty, he rendered valuable assistance in the staff work in the Vosges during the Meuse-Argonne offensive, thereby contributing materially to the success of his division in those operations.

ALEXANDER, ROGER G
R—Paris, Mo.
B—Paris, Mo.
G. O. No. 59, W. D., 1919.

Colonel (Corps of Engineers), General Staff Corps, U. S. Army.
As chief of the topographical division of the intelligence section he organized and administered, with exceptional ability, the topographical and sound and flash ranging services of the American Expeditionary Forces. Due to his foresight and energy our armies in the field were at all times supplied abundantly with excellent maps of the theater of operations.

ALLEN, CHARLES C
R—Philadelphia, Pa.
B—Philadelphia, Pa.
G. O. No. 43, W. D., 1922.

Lieutenant colonel, Infantry, U. S. Army.
As G-2 of the 33d Division from August, 1917, to June, 1918, and from September to November, 1918, he displayed sound judgment and exceptional ability in the organization, administration, and operation of that section of the division staff. By his tireless energy, military attainments, and unceasing devotion to duty he contributed greatly to the successes of the division during the Meuse-Argonne offensive and the operations in the Woevre Valley from September to November, 1918.

ALLEN, HENRY A
R—Chicago, Ill
B—Madison, Wis.
G. O. No. 89, W. D., 1919.

Colonel, Corps of Engineers, U. S. Army.
He served with distinction as commanding officer of the 108th Engineers and as engineer officer of the 33d Division. By his technical skill and untiring energy in supervising the construction of bridges across the Meuse River he proved himself an important factor in the successes gained by our troops in their operations along the right bank of that stream during the Meuse-Argonne offensive.

ALLEN, HENRY T
R—Sharpsburg, Ky.
B—Sharpsburg, Ky.
G. O. No. 12, W. D., 1919.

Major general, U. S. Army.
In command of the 19th Division he had the important position of conducting the right flank at the St. Mihiel salient. The brilliant success there gained and later repeated in the Argonne-Meuse offensive showed him to be an officer of splendid judgment, high attainments, and excellent leadership. Later he commanded the Eighth Army Corps with skill and judgment.

ALLEN, ROBERT H
R—Buchanan, Va.
B—Buchanan, Va.
G. O. No. 87, W. D., 1919.

Colonel, Infantry, U. S. Army.
As commander of the 356th Infantry during the Argonne-Meuse offensive he proved himself a skillful tactician. Resourceful and energetic, he was at all times equal to any emergency which arose, showing qualities of rare leadership. Subsequently during the march into Germany and the occupation of the enemy territory his administrative ability was reflected in the high standard of excellence consistently maintained by his regiment, rendering services of signal worth.

ALLIN, GEORGE R
R—Iowa City, Iowa.
B—Iowa City, Iowa.
G. O. No. 31, W. D., 1922.

Brigadier general, U. S. Army.
As executive officer and director of training in the office of the Chief of Field Artillery from Mar. 21, 1918, to Sept. 1, 1918, by reason of his high professional attainments, ability, foresight, and judgment, he rendered invaluable aid in solving the many complex problems confronting his arm of the service.

ALLISON, JAMES B
R—Yorkville, S. C.
B—Yorkville, S. C.
G. O. No. 3, W. D., 1921.

Colonel, Signal Corps, U. S. Army.
For services in the organization and training of technical troops of the Signal Corps, while commanding officer of the Signal Corps Training School, Fort Leavenworth, Kans., and commanding officer of the Franklin cantonment, Camp Meade, Md.

ALLISON, NATHANIEL
R—St. Louis, Mo.
B—St. Louis, Mo.
G. O. No. 50, W. D., 1919.

Colonel, Medical Corps, U. S. Army.
As chief of the orthopedic work in the zone of the Army, he personally directed in a most efficient, conscientious, and painstaking manner splinting and orthopedic work, which resulted in the saving of many lives and greatly relieved suffering among our wounded.

ALMY, EDMUND D
R—Altamont, Ky.
B—Wellsville, N. Y.
G. O. No. 116, W. D., 1919.

Commander, U. S. Navy.
For services as force engineer officer, in which position, by his untiring energy and close cooperation with the Army authorities, he successfully equipped a large number of Army and Navy transports.

ALVORD, BENJAMIN
R—Washington, D. C.
B—Fort Vancouver, Washington Territory.
G. O. No. 87, W. D., 1919.

Colonel, Adjutant General's Department, U. S. Army.
As adjutant general of the American Expeditionary Forces during the beginning of its organization his long experience, good judgment, and breadth of vision were of great value in the establishment of the innumerable activities of the adjutant general's department of the American Expeditionary Forces.

ANDERSON, ALEXANDER E
R—New York, N. Y.
B—New York, N. Y.
G. O. No. 56, W. D., 1922.
Distinguished-service cross also awarded.

Major, Infantry, U. S. Army.
He served with the 165th Infantry throughout all its operations, displaying military attainments of the highest order. By his fearless bravery and splendid leadership he at all times inspired a notable spirit among the members of his command. His unflagging energy and resourcefulness in overcoming the numerous adverse conditions which confronted his command marked him as an officer of splendid soldierly qualities. By his sound tactical judgment, keen foresight, and aggressive fighting spirit he proved himself an important factor in the successes of his regiment and division. He rendered services of conspicuous worth to the American Expeditionary Forces.

ANDERSON, ALVORD V. P. R—Montclair, N. J. B—New York, N. Y. G. O. No. 49, W. D., 1922.	Colonel, Infantry, U. S. Army. As commander of the 312th Infantry throughout its organization, training, and all its active operations he displayed marked efficiency, unflagging energy, and military attainments of the highest order. In the attack on Grand Pre, during the Meuse-Argonne offensive, by his prompt conception and brilliant execution of a skillful and successful attack on that strong and dominating position, he contributed largely to our successes in that great operation.
ANDERSON, EDWARD D. R—Jasper, Tenn. B—Jasper, Tenn. G. O. No. 18, W. D., 1919.	Brigadier general, U. S. Army. For services in initiating and executing plans for the mobilization of enlisted personnel of the Army during the war.
ANDRESS, MARY VAIL. R—New York, N. Y. B—New Jersey. G. O. No. 70, W. D., 1919.	American Red Cross. On her own initiative she organized and efficiently developed and administered the work of the American Red Cross at Toul, France. Under her wise supervision this work grew from the ministering and supplying of small comforts to soldiers passing through in hospital trains to an undertaking of extensive proportions, which has aided and cheered thousands of men in the service. In the performance of her exacting tasks, she has displayed marked foresight and sound judgment, with untiring personal devotion to the interests and comfort of those whom she served.
ANDREW, ABRAM PIATT. R—Gloucester, Mass. B—La Porte, Ind. G. O. No. 59, W. D., 1919.	Lieutenant colonel, Ambulance Corps, U. S. Army. Coming to France at the beginning of the war he showed remarkable ability in organizing the American Field Service, a volunteer service for the transportation of the wounded of the French Armies at the front. Upon the entry of the United States into the war he turned over the efficient organization he had built to the United States Army Ambulance Service, and by his sound judgment and expert advice rendered invaluable aid in the development of that organization. To him is due, in a large measure, the credit for the increasingly valuable work done by the light ambulances at the front.
ANDREWS, AVERY D. R—Massena, N. Y. B—Massena, N. Y. G. O. No. 12, W. D., 1919.	Brigadier general, U. S. Army. As assistant chief of staff, American Expeditionary Forces, he has rendered most efficient service in connection with the organization and administration of the transportation department of the American Army in France and as deputy chief of utilities in the services of supply. Later, with marked ability, he headed the important administrative section of the general staff of the American Expeditionary Forces.
ANDREWS, JAMES M. R—Schenectady, N. Y. B—Saratoga Springs, N. Y. G. O. No. 31, W. D., 1922.	Colonel, Infantry, U. S. Army. For services as commander of the 105th Infantry throughout the active operations of the 27th Division in Belgium and France, during the Ypres-Lys and Somme offensives, his energetic and zealous qualities of leadership demonstrated in battle were conspicuous.
ANDREWS, LINCOLN C. R—Seneca Falls, N. Y. B—Owatonna, Minn. G. O. No. 31, W. D., 1922.	Brigadier general, U. S. Army. He originated in military training the analysis and study of the qualities of military leadership and the psychology of military training, and by his lectures and writings did much to make possible the successful training of thousands of civilians into efficient military leaders. He served in turn as organizer of the 304th Cavalry, as commander of the 172d Infantry Brigade, as assistant to assistant chief of staff, G–5, General Headquarters, American Expeditionary Forces, and as deputy provost marshal general, in all of which capacities he held positions of great responsibility and rendered exceptionally meritorious services.
ANDREWS, SCHOFIELD. R—Philadelphia, Pa. B—Governors Island, N. Y. G. O. No. 4, W. D., 1923.	Lieutenant colonel (Infantry), General Staff Corps, U. S. Army. As assistant chief of staff, G–3, 90th Division, from July, 1918, until June, 1919, he displayed sound judgment and exceptional ability in the administration and operation of that section of the division staff. By his loyal devotion to duty, marked tactical ability, and excellent military attainments he contributed materially to the success attained by the division in the St. Mihiel and Meuse-Argonne offensives.
ANSELL, SAMUEL T. R—Coinjock, N. C. B—Coinjock, N. C. G. O. No. 18, W. D., 1919.	Brigadier general, U. S. Army. For services as Acting Judge Advocate General of the Army, whose broad and constructive interpretation of law and regulations have greatly facilitated the conduct of the war and military administration.
ARMSTRONG, FRANK S. R—Jeffersonville, Ind. B—Jeffersonville, Ind. G. O. No. 59, W. D., 1919.	Colonel, Cavalry, U. S. Army. With painstaking efforts he reorganized and placed the Remount Service upon an efficient basis, overcoming innumerable difficulties and finding ways and means of supplying combatant divisions with animals when the sources of supply were very limited. In this great task he showed qualities meriting the highest praise.
ARNOLD, LESLIE P. R—New London, Conn. B—New Haven, Conn. G. O. No. 14, W. D., 1925. Act of Congress Feb. 25, 1925.	First lieutenant, Air Service, U. S. Army. Lieutenant Arnold as assistant pilot of airplane No. 2, the Chicago, and adjutant and finance officer of the U. S. Army Air Service around-the-world flight from Apr. 6, 1924, to Sept. 28, 1924, displayed rare organizing ability, initiative, and resourcefulness in carrying out these duties, in addition to the alternate piloting of airplane No. 2 throughout the voyage. His technical skill, broad vision, business experience, high personal courage, and untiring energy contributed in a very decided manner to the successful accomplishment of this pioneer flight of airplanes around the world. In the splendid performance of these arduous and trying duties he conspicuously contributed in an accomplishment of the first magnitude of the military forces of the United States.

ARTHUR, ROBERT
R—Webster, S. Dak.
B—Webster, S. Dak.
G. O. No. 16, W. D., 1923.

Lieutenant colonel (Field Artillery), Coast Artillery Corps, U. S. Army
He commanded the 121st Field Artillery during the Aisne-Marne, Oise-A
and Meuse-Argonne offensives with distinction. In addition he serve
chief of heavy artillery of the 57th Field Artillery Brigade in those offens
His high professional skill, sound judgment, leadership, and devotion to
were material factors in the successful operations of the artillery forces
which he served.

ASHFORD, BAILEY K
R—Washington, D. C.
B—Washington, D. C.
G. O. No. 3, W. D., 1925.

Colonel, Medical Corps, U. S. Army.
As director of the Army Sanitary School, by his individual energy, ability
vision, he placed at the disposal of the American Expeditionary Force
experience and training facilities of the medical services of the French A1
and of the British Expeditionary Forces in France. He organized a sy
for the training of officers of the medical service of the Army of the U1
States in their duties at the front which contributed to a remarkable d
to the success attained in the treatment and evacuation of battle casua

ATKINS, JOSEPH A
R—Atlanta, Ga.
B—Atlanta, Ga.
G. O. No. 49, W. D., 1922.

Lieutenant colonel (Infantry), General Staff Corps, U. S. Army.
He served with the 3d Division as assistant chief of staff, G-3, from Decen
1917, until March, 1918; acting chief of staff and G-3, from March, 191
May 27, 1918; G-3, from May 28 to June 11, and from Sept. 1 to 19, 1918;
as G-3, 36th Division, from September, 1918, to March, 1919. By his tir
energy, devotion to duty and high military attainments, he contribute
a large measure to the successes attained by the commands with whic
served.

ATKISSON, EARL J
R—Fowler, Calif.
B—Broken Bow, Nebr.
G. O. No. 59, W. D., 1919.

Colonel, Engineers, U. S. Army.
He organized and trained the 1st Gas Regiment in a type of warfare ne
the American Army and directed the operations of that regiment with ma
distinction during the St. Mihiel and Argonne-Meuse offensives of the
American Army.

ATTERBURY, WILLIAM W
R—Radnor, Pa.
B—New Albany, Ind.
G. O. No. 12, W. D., 1919.

Brigadier general, U. S. Army.
As director general of transportation, in the face of almost insurmoun
obstacles he organized and brought to a high state of efficiency the tran
tation service of American Expeditionary Forces. The successful oper
of this most important service, upon which the movements and supply o
combat troops were dependent, was largely due to his energy, foresight,
ability.

*AUBERT, LILLIAN
R—Shreveport, La.
B—West Baton Rouge, La.
G. O. No. 9, W. D., 1923.

Chief nurse, Army Nurse Corps, U. S. Army.
As assistant superintendent, Army Nurse Corps, in the office of the Sur
General during the World War, she rendered services of the highest o
By her devotion to duty and great efficiency at a time when members o
Army Nurse Corps were being enrolled, equipped, and assigned to
overseas and home service she made an invaluable contribution to the
of the Medical Department in caring for the sick. She was taken ill v
on duty Oct. 2, 1918, and died Oct. 6, 1918, of pneumonia, in line of dut
a result of overwork.
Posthumously awarded. Medal presented to mother, Mrs. Grace Aubert.

AULTMAN, DWIGHT E
R—Pittsburgh, Pa.
B—Allegheny City, Pa.
G. O. No. 59, W. D., 1919.

Brigadier general, U. S. Army
As Chief of Artillery of the 5th Corps in the operations against the enen
November, 1918, by his exceptional skill as an artillerist he was la
responsible for the rupture of the enemy's position and the breaking c
resistance.

AUSTIN, ELMORE F
R—New York, N. Y.
B—Roadout, N. Y.
G. O. No. 15, W. D., 1923.

Colonel, Coast Artillery Corps, U. S. Army.
He served as assistant to, and at intervals as the coast defense comma1
coast defenses of eastern New York from August to December, 1917; in
mand of the 57th Regiment, Coast Artillery Corps (155 G. P. F.),
December, 1917, until Oct. 16, 1918, taking part in the St. Mihiel and M
Argonne offensives; and then in command of Replacement Battalion
Army Artillery, from Oct. 17 to Nov. 17, 1918. He displayed at all t
sound judgment, great energy, and a thorough knowledge of his dutie
of which were manifested in the high degree of efficiency attained b;
regiment in organization, training, and active operations.

AUSTIN, FRED T
R—Boston, Mass.
B—Hancock, Vt.
G. O. No. 30, W. D., 1921.

Brigadier general, U. S. Army.
For services while in command of Camp Zachary Taylor, Ky., and particu
during the period that said camp was subject to a severe epidemic of influe

AXTON, JOHN T
R—Salt Lake City, Utah.
B—Salt Lake City, Utah.
G. O. No. 69, W. D., 1919.

Major, chaplain, U. S. Army.
In organizing and administering numerous welfare activities connected
the port of embarkation, Hoboken, N. J., and New York City, whe
provision was made for the comfort and pleasure of enlisted men.

AYRES, LEONARD P
R—Washington, D. C.
B—Niantic, Conn.
G. O. No. 87, W. D., 1919.

Colonel, General Staff, U. S. Army.
His services as chief of the division of statistics, Council of National Def
as chief of the statistics branch of the General Staff, and chief statistical o
of the American Commission to Negotiate Peace have been conspicu
He established the statistical division at General Headquarters, Ame
Expeditionary Forces, and the statistics branch at Headquarters, Se
of Supply, American Expeditionary Forces.

BABBITT, EDWIN B.
R—Washington Territory.
B—Watervliet Arsenal, N. Y.
G. O. No. 19, W. D., 1920.

Brigadier general, U. S. Army.
He commanded the 4th Field Artillery Brigade from its organization to the close of hostilities, participating with marked distinction in the actions on the Vesle River and in the St. Mihiel and the Meuse-Argonne offensives. The skillful manner in which he pushed forward the artillery units in support of the infantry was a material factor in the successes of these campaigns. In the Meuse-Argonne offensive he had under his command, in addition to the 4th Artillery Brigade, the 10th Field Artillery, the 18th Field Artillery, the 205th French R. A. C., and the 2d Battalion, 308th French R. A. C.

BABCOCK, CONRAD S.
R—New York, N. Y.
B—Stonington, Conn.
G. O. No. 87, W. D., 1919.

Colonel, Cavalry, U. S. Army.
As post commandant at general headquarters, he served with distinction. Later he commanded the 354th Infantry throughout the successful operations against the St. Mihiel salient and those of the Argonne-Meuse in which his regiment participated and subsequently when it formed part of the Army of Occupation. At all times he displayed military attainments of the highest order. His unflagging energy and marked tactical ability were demonstrated in the successful accomplishment by his regiment of all missions assigned to it even under the most trying conditions. His service was of great value to the American Expeditionary Forces.

BABCOCK, WALTER C.
R—Boston, Mass.
B—Boston, Mass.
G. O. No. 87, W. D., 1919.

Colonel, Infantry, U. S. Army.
In command of the 310th Infantry he displayed marked ability alike in its organization and training and in the field. In offensive operations against the enemy he led his command with exceptional judgment and tactical ability, showing himself always possessed of a full grasp of the situation and its needs, and keeping his higher commanders at all times informed of the conditions as he learned them by personal reconnaissance. He was untiring in energy and devotion to the important tasks assigned him, acting unhesitatingly and successfully in times of emergency.

BACH, CHRISTIAN A.
R—St. Paul, Minn.
B—St. Martin, Minn.
G. O. No. 70, W. D., 1919.

Colonel, Cavalry, U. S. Army.
As chief of staff of the 4th Division since its organization he has performed his duties with the utmost loyalty, excellent judgment, and tireless energy, both during the training period and in actual combat. To his energy and military ability is due in no small degree the excellent record of his division in the fighting on the Vesle River and during the Meuse-Argonne offensive.

BACON, RAYMOND F.
R—Pittsburgh, Pa.
B—Muncie, Ind.
G. O. No. 56, W. D., 1922.

Colonel, Chemical Warfare Service, U. S. Army.
As chief of the technical division, Chemical Warfare Service, he displayed untiring energy, marked scientific attainments, and a comprehensive technical knowledge in the organization and operation of the laboratory units and proving-ground tests, thereby aiding materially in the success of the American Expeditionary Forces.

BACON, ROBERT.
R—New York, N. Y.
B—Boston, Mass.
G. O. No. 59, W. D., 1919.

Lieutenant colonel, Infantry, U. S. Army.
He served with great credit and distinction as post commandant of General Headquarters and as aid-de-camp to the Commander in Chief. By his untiring efforts as chief of the American Mission at British General Headquarters he has performed with marked ability innumerable duties requiring great tact and address.

BACON, ROBERT LOW.
R—Westbury, Long Island, N. Y.
B—Boston, Mass.
G. O. No. 27, W. D., 1922.

Major, Field Artillery, U. S. Army.
As assistant to the Chief of Field Artillery from Feb. 8, 1918, to Jan. 2, 1919, he planned, instituted, and supervised the system by which an adequate number of properly qualified officers were secured for the Field Artillery.

BAER, JOSEPH A.
R—Reading, Pa.
B—Kutztown, Pa.
G. O. No. 59, W. D., 1919.

Colonel, Inspector General's Department, U. S. Army.
During the active operations of the armies in the field in the St. Mihiel salient and in the Argonne offensive he revealed marked ability in the inspection of conduct and methods and showed military tactical knowledge of a high order.

BAGBY, PHILIP H.
R—Richmond, Va.
B—Richmond, Va.
G. O. No. 49, W. D., 1922.

Lieutenant colonel (Infantry), General Staff Corps, U. S. Army.
He served as intelligence liaison officer between British General Headquarters and American General Headquarters from September to December, 1918; as director of Army Intelligence School, Langres, France, December, 1918, and January, 1919; as assistant, G-2, Third Army, February to July, 1919; then as Assistant Chief of Staff, G-2, American Forces in Germany. Charged at all times with duties of a most important nature, in the performance of which he manifested steadfast loyalty and military ability of a high order, rendering services of signal worth. His comprehensive grasp of all important phases of interallied relations, as well as his unusual ability in delicate and vital matters, were of the greatest value. His rare powers of discernment, his tact and sound judgment contributed materially to the success of the commands with which he served.

BAILEY, CHARLES J.
R—Jamestown, N. Y.
B—Tamaqua, Pa.
G. O. No. 70, W. D., 1919.

Major general, U. S. Army.
He commanded the 81st Division with distinction throughout its operations, beginning Oct. 1, 1918. The excellent conduct of this division was due, in a large measure, to his great military knowledge, energy, and zeal. He has shown qualities of able leadership and has rendered services of great value to the American Expeditionary Forces.

BAILEY, PEARCE.
R—New York, N. Y.
B—New York, N. Y.
G. O. No. 11, W. D., 1921.

Colonel, Medical Corps, U. S. Army.
As chief of the division of neuropsychiatry, Surgeon General's Office, in which capacity he displayed exceptional zeal, foresight, and good judgment in organizing, developing, and directing neuropsychiatric work in the Army on a high plane of efficiency.

BAIRD, CLAIR W.
R—Punxsutawney, Pa.
B—Burton, Ohio.
G. O. No. 16, W. D., 1923.

Colonel, Coast Artillery Corps, U. S. Army.
As assistant to the Chief of Coast Artillery during the entire period of the v and as chief of the personnel section from Sept. 24, 1918, he displayed foresig excellent judgment, and marked ability in the preparation and execution plans for the effective accomplishment of the duties assigned to the Co Artillery Corps in the operations in France, thereby rendering services great value to the Government.

BAKER, ASHER CARTER.
R—Matawan, N. J.
B—Cedar Rapids, Iowa.
G. O. No. 89, W. D., 1919.

Captain, U. S. Navy, retired.
Voluntarily returning to active service after retirement, he served with c tinction as naval representative with the Transportation Departme Through his extensive naval experience, untiring zeal, and intimate kno edge of the French language and customs, he rendered services of inestima value to the American Expeditionary Forces.

BAKER, FRANK C.
R—Washington, D. C.
B—Washington, D. C.
G. O. No. 59, W. D., 1919.

Colonel, Medical Corps, U. S. Army.
As commanding officer of Evacuation Hospital No. 6, at Chateau-Thierry, fr June to August, 1918, Colonel Baker so promptly arranged his hospital un most difficult conditions and with great resourcefulness and good judgm made such use of the inadequate means at his disposal that he was able receive and evacuate after splendid treatment and in perfect order a la number of wounded from the Marne offensive at a time when that sectior France was greatly demoralized.

BAKER, WALTER C.
R—Chester, Pa.
B—Chester, Pa.
G. O. No. 16, W. D., 1923.

Colonel, Coast Artillery Corps, U. S. Army.
As assistant and executive assistant to the Chief of Transportation Service fr Apr. 15, 1918, to Oct. 4, 1920. In this position he demonstrated unusual exe tive and administrative ability, sound judgment and untiring energy, a contributed in a marked degree to the successful operations of the Transpor tion Service.

BALDWIN, KARL FERGUSON.
R—East Liberty, Ohio.
B—Macksburg, Iowa.
G. O. No. 124, W. D., 1919.

Lieutenant colonel, Coast Artillery Corps, U. S. Army.
For especially meritorious and distinguished service while serving as milit attaché at Tokyo, Japan.

BALL, WILLIAM G.
R—Chillicothe, Ohio.
B—Blanchester, Ohio.
G. O. No. 38, W. D., 1922.

Colonel, Quartermaster Corps, U. S. Army.
In organizing and directing the bakery service of the Quartermaster Cor American Expeditionary Forces, including the personal supervision of ː chanical bakeries at Is-sur-Tille, Bordeaux, Brest, and St. Nazaire, Frar By his experience, initiative, and unremitting efforts he brought this imp tant service to a high degree of efficiency in training of personnel, equipm of units, and the prompt supply of soft white bread to the armies of the An ican Expeditionary Forces in France, thereby contributing materially to success of the American Expeditionary Forces.

BALL, WILLIAM L.
R—Woburn, Mass.
B—Woburn, Mass.
G. O. No. 16, W. D., 1923.

Major, Adjutant General's Department, U. S. Army.
As executive officer, statistical division, Adjutant General's Office, Gen Headquarters, American Expeditionary Forces, he displayed outstand administrative and executive ability coordinating the work of various dep ments of that division and maintaining liaison with the personnel adjuta of the various headquarters of the American Expeditionary Forces and w the central records office in Bourges, France. With tireless energy and remitting devotion to duty he met the grave responsibilities of his diffi position with signal distinction, contributing markedly to the succes operations of the Adjutant General's Department, American Expedition Forces.

BAMFORD, FRANK E.
R—Omaha, Nebr.
B—Milwaukee, Wis.
G. O. No. 62, W. D., 1919.

Brigadier general, U. S. Army.
As its commanding officer he organized and successfully conducted the Sec Corps school. Successively in command of a battalion, regiment, brig and division, he participated in the operations of American troops fi Cantigny to those of the Meuse-Argonne. He later commanded the Ai school at Langres, at all times bringing to bear upon his duties his so judgment, high military attainments, and untiring zeal.

BANDHOLTZ, HARRY H.
R—Constantine, Mich.
B—Constantine, Mich.
G. O. No. 59, W. D., 1919.

Brigadier general, U. S. Army.
He served in turn as chief of staff of the 27th Division, as commander of 58th Infantry Brigade, and as provost marshal general of the Ameri Expeditionary Forces, in all of which capacities he displayed exceptic ability. His foresight, broad experience, and sound judgment resulted the efficient reorganization and administration of the important Pro Marshal General's Department.

BANKER, GRACE D.
R—Passaic, N. J.
B—Passaic, N. J.
G. O. No. 70, W. D., 1919.

Signal Corps, U. S. Army.
She served with exceptional ability as chief operator in the Signal Corps change at General Headquarters, American Expeditionary Forces, and l in a similar capacity at 1st Army headquarters. By untiring devotio her exacting duties under trying conditions she did much to assure the suc of the telephone service during the operations of the 1st Army against the Mihiel salient and to the north of Verdun.

BARBER, CHARLES W.
R—Woodbury, N. J.
B—Woodbury, N. J.
G. O. No. 70, W. D., 1919.

Colonel, Infantry, U. S. Army.
As assistant chief of staff, G-1, and later as Chief of Staff, Base Section N during the period of its reorganization he displayed exceptional adminis tive ability and was in a large measure responsible for the efficient or ization created for the repatriation of troops through the port of Borde rendering services of signal worth.

DISTINGUISHED-SERVICE MEDAL 675

BARBER, JAMES FRANK
R—Philadelphia, Pa.
B—Haddonfield, N. J.
G. O. No. 56, W. D., 1922.

Colonel, Corps of Engineers, U. S. Army.
While commanding the 304th Regiment of Engineers of the 79th Division, during the Meuse-Argonne offensive, by his marked ability and tireless energy his regiment was enabled to further the combat operations of his division, frequently building roads and bridges under fire. Charged with the duty of removing enemy mines and traps in front of the right of the 1st Army, he successfully accomplished a difficult and dangerous duty immediately following the Armistice, thereby rendering services of great value to the American Expeditionary Forces.

BARE, WALTER E.
R—Gadsden, Ala.
B—Lexington, Va.
G. O. No. 53, W. D., 1921.

Lieutenant colonel, 167th Infantry, 42d Division, U. S. Army.
For services while in command of the 167th Infantry, operating near Cote-de-Chatillon and Landres-et-St. Georges in the Meuse-Argonne offensive during the month of October, 1918.

BARNES, HARRY C.
R—Guthrie, Okla.
B—Little Rock, Ark.
G. O. No. 133, W. D., 1919.

Colonel, U. S. Army.
As commander of the 30th Artillery Brigade he planned and directed the operations of that unit with great skill and ability during the Meuse-Argonne offensive. As chief of staff of the Railway Artillery Reserve he rendered valuable services in the organization and operations of the Railway Artillery units.

BARNES, JOHN B.
R—Highland, W. Va.
B—Pennsboro, W. Va.
G. O. No. 49, W. D., 1922.

Lieutenant colonel, Infantry, U. S. Army.
While serving successively as G–3 of the 5th and 80th Divisions from June until November, 1918, and then as G–3, 9th Army Corps, he rendered services of great value. By his tireless energy, foresight, sound tactical judgment, and intelligent cooperation he contributed largely to the successes of the operations of those units.

BARNES, JOSEPH F.
R—Washington, D. C.
B—Washington, D. C.
G. O. No. 89, W. D., 1919.

Colonel, Field Artillery, U. S. Army.
As corps adjutant of the 2d Army Corps, by his able management and complete knowledge of all details of the Adjutant General's Department, he established and operated with remarkable success the numerous branches of the Adjutant General's Office. Later as adjutant general, First Army, he organized with rare initiative and administered with marked ability the operations of his important office, rendering services of inestimable value.

BARNEY, JAMES P.
R—Townsend, Va.
B—Dayton, Ohio.
G. O. No. 19, W. D., 1922.

Lieutenant colonel, General Staff Corps, U. S. Army.
As assistant chief of staff, G–1, of the 92d Division, he organized the entire system of supply for the division. Due to his administrative ability, exceptional foresight, and tireless energy, he handled numerous difficult problems of supply and transportation with great efficiency and success.

BARNHARDT, GEORGE C.
R—Norwood, N. C.
B—Gold Hill, N. C.
G. O. No. 9, W. D., 1923.

Brigadier General, U. S. Army.
As commander of the 28th Infantry, he handled his regiment so brilliantly under severe conditions during the St. Mihiel offensive, Sept. 12 and 13, 1918, and during the battle of the Meuse-Argonne, Oct. 1 to 11, 1918, that the regiment demonstrated an unusually high degree of efficiency and morale. He repeatedly displayed superior tactical judgment, and by his exceptional ability, leadership, and devotion to duty, he effectively executed the most difficult missions assigned to his regiment. Later, in command of the 2d Infantry Brigade and then the 178th Infantry Brigade, he again displayed high efficiency and military attainments, thereby rendering with all his commands important services to the American Expeditionary Forces.

BARNUM, MALVERN-HILL.
R—New York, N. Y.
B—Syracuse, N. Y.
G. O. No. 59, W. D., 1919.

Brigadier General, U. S. Army.
He commanded with marked success the 183d Infantry Brigade from its organization to the close of active operations. The conduct of his brigade in the St. Die and Marbache sectors was indicative of his good leadership. As a member of the interallied armistice board he has performed his many exacting duties with marked ability, address, and sound judgment, rendering services of the highest character to the Government.

BARRY, THOMAS H.
R—New York, N. Y.
B—New York, N. Y.
G. O. No. 73, W. D., 1919.

Major general, U. S. Army.
As department commander, central department, he handled many difficult problems arising in that department during the war with rare judgment, tact, and great skill.

BARUCH, BERNARD M.
R—New York, N. Y.
B—Camden, S. C.
G. O. No. 15, W. D., 1921.

Director, War Industries Board.
For services in the organization and administration of the War Industries Board and in the coordination of allied purchases in the United States. By establishing a broad and comprehensive policy for the supervision and control of the raw materials, manufacturing facilities, and distribution of the products of industry, he stimulated the production of war supplies, coordinated the needs of the military service and the civilian population, and contributed alike to the completeness and speed of the mobilization and equipment of the military forces and the continuity of their supply.

BASH, LOUIS H.
R—Peoria, Ill.
B—Chicago, Ill.
G. O. No. 59, W. D., 1919.

Colonel, Infantry, U. S. Army.
He supervised with tact and sound judgment the establishment of the important base ports of St. Nazaire and Brest. Later, while he was adjutant general of the Services of Supply, his splendid knowledge of administration, his energy, and personal attention to duties were shown by the efficiency of his office, which met fully the diversified demands made upon it.

BASKETTE, ALVIN K R—Nashville, Tenn. B—Nashville, Tenn. G. O. No. 59, W. D., 1919.	Colonel, Quartermaster Corps, U. S. Army. He organized and coordinated the several activities of the salvage depot at St. Pierre de Corps, which was the largest and most important of such depots in the American Expeditionary Forces. By his zeal, tact, and ability in solving the various labor problems that arose in connection with the employment of many French civilians, he produced a high degree of economic efficiency in the operations of the Salvage Service.
BATTLE, MARION S R—Tarboro, N. C. B—Edgecombe County, N. C. G. O. No. 60, W. D., 1920.	Colonel, Coast Artillery Corps, U. S. Army. As artillery information officer of the First Army, he efficiently operated this important service. Later, he commanded with distinction a regiment of artillery in the Army of occupation. Subsequently, as provost marshal of Paris, he performed duties of a most difficult nature with unfailing tact, efficiency, and sound judgment. He has demonstrated organizing ability and executive capacity to a marked degree, and he has been a contributing factor toward the raising of the morale and efficiency of the American Expeditionary Forces in Paris. He has rendered services of particular merit to the American Expeditionary Forces.
BAYNE, HUGH A R—Bronxville, N. Y. B—New Orleans, La. G. O. No. 15, W. D., 1923.	Lieutenant colonel, Judge Advocate General's Department, U. S. Army. As assistant judge advocate of the services of supply, as counsel for the United States Prisoners of War Commission, judge advocate of the 80th Division and 9th Army Corps during combat operations in France, he displayed untiring zeal, rare professional ability, and intellectual qualities of a high order. His special knowledge of the French language and the laws of France enabled him to render the Government services of immeasurable value and contributed markedly to the successes of the American Expeditionary Forces.
BEACH, WILLIAM D R—New York, N. Y. B—New York, N. Y. G. O. No. 9, W. D., 1923.	Brigadier general, U. S. Army. As commanding officer, 176th Infantry Brigade, 88th Division, he displayed organizing and training abilities of the highest order, and by the sound judgment, constant initiative, resourcefulness, and indefatigable energy, abundant tact, and thorough understanding of men which characterized his performance of duty as brigade commander, he contributed materially to successful operations of that brigade and the 88th Division.
BEACHAM, JOSEPH W., Jr R—Brooklyn, N. Y. B—Brooklyn, N. Y. G. O. No. 9, W. D., 1923.	Colonel (Infantry), General Staff Corps, U. S. Army. As assistant chief of staff, G-1, 42d Division, from May 10 to Aug. 25, 1918, by his extraordinary energy, initiative, exceptional executive and administrative ability, he rendered valuable services in overcoming many difficult problems of supply under most trying conditions, contributing largely to the successes of the division. Later, as chief of staff, 6th Division, from Aug. 26, 1918, until May 25, 1919, by his intimate knowledge of staff duties, his clear conception of the requirements of troops of the line and by his devotion to duty and marked ability he contributed in a large measure to the progress of the division, thereby rendering valuable services to the American Expeditionary Forces.
BEARSS, HIRAM I R—Peru, Ind. B—Peru, Ind. G. O. No. 89, W. D., 1919. Distinguished-service cross also awarded.	Colonel, U. S. Marine Corps. He commanded with distinction the 102d Infantry, achieving notable successes in the active operations in which that regiment was engaged. By his untiring energy and dauntless courage in overcoming the numerous difficulties confronting him he gave proof of military leadership of a high order.
BECK, ROBERT McC., Jr R—Wickford, R. I. B—Westminster, Md. G. O. No. 59, W. D., 1919.	Colonel, Infantry, U. S. Army. He showed extraordinary efficiency in directing the staff work of the 32d Division at the Second Battle of the Marne and in the operations near Soissons and north of Verdun, France, from July to October, 1918. In the preparations for battle and in the reorganizations between battles, he ably handled the many difficult situations that presented themselves.
BECKHAM, DAVID Y R—Bardstown, Ky. B—Bardstown, Ky. G. O. No. 49, W. D., 1922.	Colonel (Coast Artillery Corps), Adjutant General's Department, U. S. Army. As officer in charge of war risk insurance in the War Department, he organized, perfected, and directed in a highly efficient manner the system of handling insurance and other relief features of the war risk insurance act. To his tact, vision, marked ability, and loyal devotion to duty is largely due the success attained in the handling of a tremendous amount of business and the insuring of more than 90 per cent of the United States Army.
BEEBE, ROYDEN E R—Burlington, Vt. B—South Burlington, Vt. G. O. No. 59, W. D., 1921.	Lieutenant colonel, Infantry, U. S. Army. For services as chief of staff, 82d Division; assistant chief of staff, G-3, 2d Division; and assistant chief of staff, G-3, 1st Army Corps.
BEEUWKES, HENRY R—New York, N. Y. B—Jamesburg, N. J. G. O. No. 59, W. D., 1919.	Lieutenant colonel, Medical Corps, U. S. Army. He rendered especially valuable services as inspector of hospitalization of troops in the field. By tireless energy in the performance of his duties he assisted greatly in raising the efficiency of this service and in bettering the facilities for the care and evacuation of the wounded of our armies.
BEHN, SOSTHENES R—Havana, Cuba. B—St. Thomas, A. W. I. G. O. No. 50, W. D., 1919.	Lieutenant colonel, Signal Corps, U. S. Army. He served in turn as liaison officer with the French Department of Posts and Telegraphs, as executive to the chief signal officer, as commander of a field signal battalion, and as assistant to the chief signal officer, First Army. In all of these capacities he demonstrated marked ability and performed exceptionally meritorious service.

BELKNAP, CHARLES, Jr.
R—Concord, Mass.
B—Maryland.
G. O. No. 116, W. D., 1919.

Commander, U. S. Navy.
For services in connection with the Naval Overseas Transportation Service. His successful organization and administration of this service contributed greatly to the successful operation of the American forces abroad.

BELL, GEORGE, Jr.
R—District of Columbia.
B—Maryland.
G. O. No. 59, W. D., 1919.

Major general, U. S. Army.
He led his command, with distinction, in the offensive operations with the British which resulted in the capture of Hamel and Hamel Woods, and in the fighting on the Meuse that gained the villages of Marchéville, St. Hilaire, and a portion of Bois d'Harville. He displayed a high order of leadership in the Argonne-Meuse offensive, when his division attacked and captured the strongly fortified Bois-de-Forges. The successful operations of the division which he trained and commanded in combat were greatly influenced by his energy and abilities as a commander.

*BELL, J. FRANKLIN
R—Shelbyville, Ky.
B—Shelbyville, Ky.
G. O. No. 73, W. D., 1919.
Medal of honor and distinguished-service cross also awarded.

Major general, U. S. Army.
For exceptionally meritorious and distinguished service during the war as division, cantonment, and department commander.
Posthumously awarded. Medal presented to widow, Mrs. J. Franklin Bell.

BELLINGER, JOHN B.
R—Charleston, S. C.
B—Charleston, S. C.
G. O. No. 56, W. D., 1921.

Colonel, Quartermaster Corps, U. S. Army.
As department quartermaster, Philippine Department, a position of great responsibility, he administered the services of transportation and of the supply of the troops serving in the Philippines and China in a markedly successful manner. He originated and executed the supplying of the Siberian American Expeditionary Forces and the purchasing of foods in the Orient, and aided the Philippine government in its problems. He rendered services of much value.

BENDER, LOUIS B.
R—Charleston, Wash.
B—Highland, Kans.
G. O. No. 56, W. D., 1922.

Lieutenant colonel, Signal Corps, U. S. Army.
He served in the office of the Chief Signal Officer, American Expeditionary Forces, as assistant director of supplies from July, 1918, until December, 1918, and director of supplies from December, 1918, until September, 1919. By his sound judgment, unfailing energy, and unusual ability he rendered services of the greatest value in both capacities. He met the many military commercial problems which confronted him with a broad vision and solved them with unvarying judgment and skill, thereby contributing materially to the success of the American Expeditionary Forces in positions of great responsibility.

BENEDICT, JAY L.
R—Hastings, Nebr.
B—Hastings, Nebr.
G. O. No. 73, W. D., 1919.

Colonel, Infantry, U. S. Army.
In the organization and administration of the procurement and discharge section of the personnel branch, his energy, intelligent application, and good judgment have contributed greatly to the solution of the many difficult personnel problems pertaining to the procurement and discharge of officers, and the building up of the Officers' Reserve Corps.

BENNION, HOWARD S.
R—Vernon, Utah.
B—Vernon, Utah.
G. O. No. 56, W. D., 1922.

Lieutenant colonel, Corps of Engineers, U. S. Army.
As chief camouflage officer, American Expeditionary Forces, from October, 1917, until February, 1919, in a position of great responsibility he rendered conspicuous service in an entirely new field of endeavor. By his tireless energy, sound judgment, and marked technical ability he organized and placed the work of the camouflage section on a practical and highly efficient basis and directed its functions in a most satisfactory manner, thereby contributing materially to the success of the American Expeditionary Forces.

BENSON, WILLIAM SHEPHERD.
R—Macon, Ga.
B—Macon, Ga.
G. O. No. 116, W. D., 1919.

Admiral, U. S. Navy.
As Chief of Naval Operations, his close cooperation and assistance in that position did much toward the successful outcome of the combined operation of the Army and Navy overseas.

BENTON, GUY POTTER, Dr.
R—Burlington, Vt.
B—Kenton, Ohio.
G. O. No. 19, W. D., 1920.

Director, Educational work in American Expeditionary Forces.
As director in charge of the educational work undertaken in the Third Army of the American Expeditionary Forces, by his marked ability, untiring energy, and loyal devotion to his task, he contributed in a large measure to the successful results obtained in this vast undertaking. Through his great work among 10,000 illiterate soldiers over 8,000 of them were taught to read and write. By his efforts he has rendered services of particular worth to the American Expeditionary Forces.

BERRY, HARRY S.
R—Hendersonville, Tenn.
B—Nashville, Tenn.
G. O. No. 4, W. D., 1923.

Colonel, 115th Field Artillery, 30th Division, U. S. Army.
As commander of the 115th Field Artillery during its organization and training he displayed marked efficiency, great resourcefulness, and military attainments of a high order. He commanded a grouping of his regiment and other French and American Artillery units in the Meuse-Argonne offensive; also a grouping of his regiment and other 155-millimeter howitzers in the operation of the Second Army, and by his skilled and energetic handling of his command played an important part in the success of these operations.

BETHEL, WALTER A.
R—Smyrna, Ohio.
B—Smyrna, Ohio.
G. O. No. 12, W. D., 1919.

Brigadier general, U. S. Army.
As judge advocate of the American Expeditionary Forces he organized this important department and administered its affairs with conspicuous efficiency from the date of the arrival in France of the first American combat troops. His marked legal ability and sound judgment were important factors in the splendid work of his department, and he at all times handled with success the various military and international problems that arose as a result of the operation of our armies.

BEVANS, JAMES L.
　R—Decatur, Ill.
　B—Platteville, Wis.
　G. O. No. 87, W. D., 1919.

Colonel, Medical Corps, U. S. Army.
　He served with distinction as chief surgeon of the Third Army Corps, where he solved important problems of sanitation and evacuation with conspicuous success. He showed marked administrative ability during the final phases of the Argonne-Meuse offensive, when, through his sound judgment and efficient supervision of the medical and sanitary services under his direction, many lives were saved, thereby rendering valuable service to the American Expeditionary Forces.

BIDDLE, JOHN.
　R—Grosse Ile, Mich.
　B—Detroit, Mich.
　G. O. No. 59, W. D., 1919.

Major general, U. S. Army.
　In command of American troops in England, by his tact and diplomacy in handling intricate problems, he made possible the successful transshipment of many thousands of men to France. To his executive ability the efficient handling, control, and dispatch of casual troops through England is largely due.

*BIDDLE, NICHOLAS.
　R—New York, N. Y.
　B—Fort Whipple, Ariz.
　G. O. No. 9, W. D., 1923.

Lieutenant colonel, General Staff Corps, U. S. Army.
　For services as intelligence officer, in charge in the city of New York during the entire period of American participation in the World War. His ability as an organizer, his broad experience in large affairs, contributed largely to the failure of the enemy to thwart our military efforts in the city of New York by espionage, sabotage, and propaganda.
　Posthumously awarded. Medal presented to widow, Mrs. Nicholas Biddle.

BILLINGS, FRANK.
　R—Chicago, Ill.
　B—Iowa County, Wis.
　G. O. No. 69, W. D., 1919.

Colonel, Medical Corps, U. S. Army.
　For services in the organization and administration of the division of reconstruction of the Medical Department.

BINGHAM, ERNEST G.
　R—Talladega, Ala.
　B—Talladega, Ala.
　G. O. No. 59, W. D., 1919.

Colonel, Medical Corps, U. S. Army.
　As chief surgeon of the Paris district he most efficiently directed the coordination of the work of the hospitals and hospital and ambulance trains in the region of the Paris group during the Second Battle of the Marne. By his untiring zeal and his exact understanding of conditions he most ably handled the limited hospital resources of the district of Paris, permitting the clearing of the battle field of the wounded and the proper provision for their care In all these tasks he showed professional attainments of the highest order unflagging energy, and great devotion to duty.

BIRNIE, UPTON, Jr.
　R—Philadelphia, Pa.
　B—Carlisle, Pa.
　G. O. No. 27, W. D., 1920.

Colonel, Field Artillery, U. S. Army.
　As principal assistant in the operations' section, General Headquarters American Expeditionary Forces, he has by his thorough military knowledge loyalty, and devotion to duty materially assisted in attaining the success o that section of the General Staff.

BISHOP, HARRY G.
　R—Goshen, Ind.
　B—Grand Rapids, Mich.
　G. O. No. 59, W. D., 1919.

Brigadier general, U. S. Army.
　While in command of the 3d Field Artillery Brigade, during the battles of the Argonne-Meuse, and in the subsequent advance to Sedan, by his skill and able leadership, he rendered exceptionally valuable services.

BISHOP, PERCY POE.
　R—Powells, Tenn.
　B—Powells, Tenn.
　G. O. No. 18, W. D., 1919.

Brigadier general, U. S. Army.
　For services as secretary of the General Staff and in the organization and coordination of matters relating to the commissioned personnel of the Army

BISHOP, WILLIAM H.
　R—New York, N. Y.
　B—Jackport, N. Y.
　G. O. No. 38, W. D., 1922.

Lieutenant colonel, Medical Corps, U. S. Army.
　At Orleans, France. By his great ability, initiative, and tact he enlisted the sympathies of the French authorities and people, obtained buildings organized and enlarged base hospital, and contributed materially to the care of the sick and wounded during the operations of 1918. He has rendered services of much value. This efficient hospitalization was later adopted a a model by the French medical service.

BJORNSTAD, ALFRED W.
　R—St. Paul, Minn.
　B—St. Paul, Minn.
　G. O. No. 89, W. D., 1919.
　Distinguished-service cross also awarded.

Brigadier general, U. S. Army.
　As director of the Army General Staff College at Langres, he organized and conducted this institution during the first and second courses. Although he was without adequate material or personnel, by the energy and great effor he put forth he established a school which provided our armies with staf officers in a minimum of time.

BLACK, WILLIAM M.
　R—Lancaster, Pa.
　B—Lancaster, Pa.
　G. O. No. 144, W. D., 1918.

Major general, Chief of Engineers, U. S. Army.
　For services in planning and administering the engineer and military railwa; services during the war.

BLAKE, JOSEPH A.
　R—New York, N. Y.
　B—California.
　G. O. No. 59, W. D., 1919.

Colonel, Medical Corps, U. S. Army.
　As chief consultant for the district of Paris, and commanding officer of Re Cross Hospital No. 2, he efficiently standardized surgical procedures, espe cially in the recent methods of treating fractures. His remarkable talen has materially reduced the suffering and loss of life among our wounded.

BLAMER, DEWITT.
　R—Independence, Iowa.
　B—Independence, Iowa.
　G. O. No. 116, W. D., 1919.

Captain, U. S. Navy.
　For services as chief of staff of the commander, cruiser and transport fleet.

BLANCK, CARROLL T.
　R—Los Angeles, Calif.
　B—Greensburg, Pa.
　G. O. No. 53, W. D., 1921.

Lieutenant colonel, Signal Corps, U. S. Army.
　For services in connection with the control and operation of the telephone an telegraph service of the American Expeditionary Forces.

BLANDING, ALBERT H. R—Bartow, Fla. B—Lyons, Iowa. G. O. No. 118, W. D., 1919.	Brigadier general, U. S. Army. For services while commanding general of the 53d Infantry Brigade of the 27th Division throughout the entire period of active operations.
BLISS, EDWARD G. R—Fort Totten, N. Y. B—Rosemont, Pa. G. O. No. 15, W. D., 1923.	Lieutenant colonel, Corps of Engineers, U. S. Army. As executive officer in the office of the director general of transportation, American Expeditionary Forces, he was charged with the responsibility for the organization of the personnel and the administration of the Transportation Corps. His sound judgment, high administrative and executive ability, untiring energy and devotion to duty constituted highly important assets of the Transportation Corps and contributed materially to the success of that organization during its services with the American Expeditionary Forces.
BLISS, ELMER JARED. R—Boston, Mass. B—Wrentham, Mass. G. O. No. 2, W. D., 1920.	The formulation and methods adopted which gave to the U. S. Army unexcelled methods of shoe procurement and distribution were brought about largely through his efforts. As a result of the operation of these methods the efficiency and comfort of the marching soldier were greatly increased.
BLISS, TASKER H. R—Chester, Pa. B—Lewisburg, Pa. G. O. No. 136, W. D., 1918.	General, U. S. Army. For his most exceptional services as Assistant Chief of Staff, acting Chief of Staff, and Chief of Staff of the U. S. Army, in which important positions his administrative ability and professional attainments were of great value to our armies. As chief of the American section of the Supreme War Council he has taken an important part in the shaping of the policies that have brought victory to our cause.
BLOOR, ALFRED W. R—Austin, Tex. B—Pittsburgh, Pa. G. O. No. 14, W. D., 1923.	Colonel, Infantry, U. S. Army. In command of the 142d Infantry, 36th Division, including the period of its reorganization and training and during its combat operations in France, he displayed untiring energy, administrative and executive ability, and sound tactical judgment, these qualities, coupled with unremitting devotion to duty and high qualities of leadership, contributing in a conspicuous way to the success of the 36th Division in its operations against the enemy.
BOAK, SEIBERT D. R—West Virginia. B—Virginia. G. O. No. 15, W. D., 1923.	Colonel, Dental Corps, U. S. Army. As director of the dental section of the Army Sanitary School at Langres, France, from January to December, 1918, he displayed organizing and training ability and accomplishments of the highest order in successfully directing the classification and training of dental officers for field service, thereby rendering services of great value to the American Expeditionary Forces.
BOLLES, FRANK C. R—Rolla, Mo. B—Elgin, Ill. G. O. No. 95, W. D., 1919. Distinguished-service cross and oak-leaf cluster also awarded.	Colonel, Infantry, U. S. Army. He commanded, with keen tactical ability, the 39th Infantry throughout the various campaigns in which the Fourth Division participated until the early stages of the Meuse-Argonne offensive, when he was wounded. By his exceptional ability and energetic leadership he proved to be an important factor in the successes of his command during its active operations against the enemy.
*BOLLING, RAYNAL C. R—Greenwich, Conn. B—Hot Springs, Ark. G. O. No. 50, W. D., 1919.	Colonel, Air Service, U. S. Army. His service to the United States aviation was distinguished for an accurate and comprehensive grasp of aviation matters; for a sound and far-sighted conception of the measures needed to establish an efficient American air service in Europe; for initiative and resourcefulness in attacking the problems of a young air service; for brilliant capacity in arranging affairs with foreign governments; for boldness and vigor in executing determined policies. In all of these he has rendered service of great value to the Government. Posthumously awarded. Medal presented to widow, Mrs. Anna P. Bolling.
BOOTH, ALFRED J. R—Albany, N. Y. B—Albany, N. Y. G. O. No. 59, W. D., 1919.	Colonel, Adjutant General's Department, U. S. Army. As assistant to The Adjutant General, American Expeditionary Forces, he was charged with the important duty of verifying, preparing, and distributing all orders and bulletins issued from General Headquarters, American Expeditionary Forces. To his painstaking efforts are due the accuracy with which these orders were drawn and the promptness with which they were distributed. He organized and efficiently supervised the administration of The Adjutant General's printing plant at General Headquarters, American Expeditionary Forces. To his untiring zeal is largely due the success with which it handled a tremendous volume of printed matter, rendering important service to the American Expeditionary Forces.
BOOTH, EVANGELINE C. R—New York, N. Y. B—England. G. O. No. 87, W. D., 1919.	Commander of the Salvation Army in the United States. She has been tireless in her devotion to her manifold duties. The contribution of the Salvation Army toward winning the war is conspicuous, and the results obtained were due in marked degree to the great executive ability of its commander.
BOOTH, EWING E. R—Pueblo, Colo. B—Bowers Mills, Mo. G. O. No. 59, W. D., 1919.	Brigadier general, U. S. Army. He commanded, with great ability and gallantry, the 8th Infantry Brigade in the operations which forced the reluctant enemy to evacuate Bois-du-Feys, Bois-de-Malaumont, Bois-de-Peut-de-Faux, and Bois-de-Foret in September and October, 1918. His splended leadership was an important factor in these actions.

BOOTHE, EARLE‗‗‗‗‗‗‗‗‗‗‗‗‗‗‗‗‗‗‗‗
R—South Pasadena, Calif.
B—Derby, Conn.
G. O. No. 59, W. D., 1919.

Lieutenant colonel, Adjutant General's Department, U. S. Army.
He reorganized and administered with marked distinction the central records office of the American Expeditionary Forces. He handled the complex problems constantly arising with great discretion, displaying keen perception amid the maze of details involved in the reporting of casualties and changes of status of officers and soldiers. With unflagging energy and exceptional ability he performed a task of great magnitude.

BOUGHTON, EDWARD J‗‗‗‗‗‗‗‗‗‗‗‗‗‗‗‗
R—Denver, Colo.
B—Albany, N. Y.
G. O. No. 89, W. D., 1919.

Lieutenant colonel, Judge Advocate General's Department, U. S. Army.
He served with distinction as head of the international law division in the office of the Judge Advocate, American Expeditionary Forces. Through his extensive knowledge of international law and diplomatic ability, he was of the utmost assistance in handling many delicate questions involving relations between the American and allied armies.

BOWDITCH, EDWARD, Jr‗‗‗‗‗‗‗‗‗‗‗‗‗‗
R—Boston, Mass.
B—Albany, N. Y.
G. O. No. 59, W. D., 1919.

Lieutenant colonel, Infantry, U. S. Army.
At the Army General Staff College, as assistant to G-3, headquarters 1st Army Corps, he rendered service of distinction, always showing himself able in time of emergency, aggressive in action, and possessed of tact and sound judgment. As aid-de-camp to the commander in chief, American Expeditionary Forces, he displayed unflagging energy and devotion to duties of great importance. His military attainments were of marked character, proving of utmost assistance in the handling of difficult situations.

BOWEN, WILLIAM S‗‗‗‗‗‗‗‗‗‗‗‗‗‗‗‗‗‗
R—Omaha, Nebr.
B—Omaha, Nebr.
G. O. No. 9, W. D., 1923.

Lieutenant colonel (Field Artillery), General Staff Corps, U. S. Army.
From September, 1918, to June, 1919, as assistant chief of staff, G-3, 29th Division, he displayed the highest qualities of a staff officer and by his untiring energy, good judgment, and devotion to duty he contributed in a marked degree to the success of his division.

BOWLEY, ALBERT J‗‗‗‗‗‗‗‗‗‗‗‗‗‗‗‗‗‗
R—San Francisco, Calif.
B—Westminster, Calif.
G. O. No. 59, W. D., 1919.

Brigadier general, U. S. Army.
He commanded the 17th Field Artillery and later the 2d Field Artillery Brigade in the active operations from July to November, 1918. The artillery support under his direction in the engagements near Chateau-Thierry, near Soissons, those in the St. Mihiel salient, Blanc Mont Ridge, and in the Meuse-Argonne region were important factors in the great successes gained.

BOWMAN, GEORGE T‗‗‗‗‗‗‗‗‗‗‗‗‗‗‗‗‗
R—Buffalo, N. Y.
B—Buffalo, N. Y.
G. O. No. 35, W. D., 1920.

Colonel, Cavalry, U. S. Army.
As chief of a subsection of G-1 of the General Staff at General Headquarters he prepared the priority schedules for the movement of troops from the United States to France, directed replacements during active operations, prepared the order of battle data, and conserved many important and confidential records of the personnel of the American Expeditionary Forces. By his marked executive ability and loyal cooperation in all details of his important task he has given services of noteworthy consequence to the American Expeditionary Forces.

*BOYD, CARL‗‗‗‗‗‗‗‗‗‗‗‗‗‗‗‗‗‗‗‗‗‗‗
R—Adairsville, Ga.
B—Decora, Ga.
G. O. No. 59, W. D., 1919.

Colonel, Cavalry, U. S. Army.
As military attaché to the American Embassy in Paris he performed services of a most distinguished character. Later, as senior aid-de-camp to the commander in chief, he displayed remarkable ability, sound judgment, and tact in the many varied negotiations with the allied commanders and other allied officials, rendering services of inestimable value to the American Expeditionary Forces.
Posthumously awarded. Medal presented to widow, Mrs. Annie P. Boyd.

BRABSON, FAY W‗‗‗‗‗‗‗‗‗‗‗‗‗‗‗‗‗‗‗‗
R—Greenville, Tenn.
B—Greenville, Tenn.
G. O. No. 59, W. D., 1921.

Lieutenant colonel (Infantry), General Staff Corps, U. S. Army.
As an instructor of the Army General Staff College, Langres, France, May to Sept. 15, 1918, he performed exceptionally meritorious services to the Government in instructing and preparing student officers to function in the important and responsible positions as General Staff officers with troops.

BRABSON, JOE REESE‗‗‗‗‗‗‗‗‗‗‗‗‗‗‗‗
R—Greenville, Tenn.
B—Greenville, Tenn.
G. O. No. 78, W. D., 1919.

Lieutenant colonel (Field Artillery), General Staff Corps, U. S. Army.
As chief of staff of the 28th Division during the Marne-Aisne offensive he rendered conspicuous service. Later as an instructor of the fourth course at the Army General Staff College at Langres he ably assisted in the instruction of a large number of officers recommended for General Staff duty. Upon completion of his duty at the staff school he served with marked success as G-5 of the Second Army.

BRADLEY, ALFRED E‗‗‗‗‗‗‗‗‗‗‗‗‗‗‗‗‗
R—Frewsburg, N. Y.
B—Jamestown, N. Y.
G. O. No. 12, W. D., 1919.

Brigadier general, U. S. Army.
As chief surgeon, American Expeditionary Forces, he gave his utmost energy and undivided devotion to the duty of planning and organizing the work of the Medical Department in France during a period fraught with untold difficulties. To his foresight was largely due the successful operations of that department when it was called upon to meet the demands that were subsequently made upon it.

BRADLEY, JOHN J‗‗‗‗‗‗‗‗‗‗‗‗‗‗‗‗‗‗‗
R—Chicago, Ill.
B—Lake View, Ill.
G. O. No. 47, W. D., 1919.

Brigadier general, U. S. Army.
For services as chief of the training and instruction branch, War Plans Division, General Staff, in initiating and standardizing the training and instruction of the Army during its formative period.

BREES, HERBERT J‗‗‗‗‗‗‗‗‗‗‗‗‗‗‗‗‗‗
R—Laramie, Wyo.
B—Laramie, Wyo.
G. O. No. 87, W. D., 1919.

Colonel, General Staff Corps, U. S. Army.
He served with distinction as chief of staff of the 91st Division throughout its training period and during the greater part of its active operations. His marked administrative ability was reflected in the successes of this division during the first phases of the Meuse-Argonne operations. Later, as chief of staff of the 7th Army Corps, he rendered invaluable services in perfecting the necessary organization for the march into the German territory, overcoming grave difficulties in securing supplies and equipment.

DISTINGUISHED-SERVICE MEDAL

BRENNAN, CECELIA
  R—Philadelphia, Pa.
  B—Branchdale, Pa.
  G. O. No. 9, W. D., 1923.

Chief nurse, Army Nurse Corps, U. S. Army.
As chief nurse of the Toul Hospital Center, France, during the World War, she contributed largely to the successful care of over 10,000 sick and wounded by her skillful, tactful, and able direction of the work of the nurses at this center.

BRENT, CHARLES H.
  R—Buffalo, N. Y.
  B—Canada.
  G. O. No. 59, W. D., 1919.

Major, chaplain, U. S. Army.
As senior headquarters chaplain, he organized the chaplains' school and established a schematic system of religious effort, enabling all chaplains throughout France to further those excellent results which have marked their duties amongst the troops. By his loyal spirit of cooperation, his marked ability, and by his masterful attainments he has rendered services of most conspicuous merit and lasting value to the American Government.

BRETT, LLOYD M.
  R—Malden, Mass.
  B—Maine.
  G. O. No. 59, W. D., 1919.
  Medal of honor also awarded.

Brigadier general, U. S. Army.
He commanded the 160th Infantry Brigade with particular efficiency in the markedly successful operations resulting in the occupation of the Dannevoux sector in October, 1918. In the actions near Imecourt and Buzancy in November his brigade broke the enemy's resistance. Due to his masterful ability and brilliant leadership, these operations proved a crowning success.

BRETT, SERENO E.
  R—Corvallis, Oreg.
  B—Portland, Oreg.
  G. O. No. 49, W. D., 1922.
  Distinguished-service cross also awarded.

Major, Tank Corps, U. S. Army.
As chief instructor at tank center, American Expeditionary Forces, he organized and trained the 327th Battalion (Light) Tanks. Later, as commander of the 326th Battalion (Light) Tanks, he vigorously and skillfully led it in the St. Mihiel offensive over a terrain rendered most difficult through four years of enemy intrenching. Succeeding to the command of the 1st Brigade, Tank Corps, in the Meuse-Argonne offensive, he ably, devotedly, and courageously commanded his brigade from Sept. 26 to Nov. 10, 1918; during this period of 46 days his brigade supported eight of the divisions of the First Army in 18 separate attacks. By his brilliant professional attainments, technical ability, and unusual leadership he contributed in a marked manner to the success of the First Army and rendered most conspicuous services to the American Expeditionary Forces in a position of great responsibility.

BREWSTER, ANDRÉ W.
  R—Philadelphia, Pa.
  B—Hoboken, N. J.
  G. O. No. 12, W. D., 1919.
  Medal of honor also awarded.

Major general, U. S. Army.
He organized and administered with marked ability the Inspector General's Department of the American Expeditionary Forces, and his soldierly characteristics and unceasing labors influenced greatly the attainment of efficiency in the American Army in France.

BRICKER, EDWIN D.
  R—Chambersburg, Pa.
  B—Chambersburg, Pa.
  G. O. No. 78, W. D., 1919.

Colonel, Ordnance Department, U. S. Army.
As chief ordnance purchasing officer and later as ordnance representative on the general purchasing board, he conducted negotiations with marked success for material needed to supplement the supply from the United States. He worked tirelessly and with unflagging energy to the end that there would be no shortage in supplies sent to the troops at the front. At all times exercising sound judgment and discernment in times of emergency, he achieved marked successes.

BRIDGES, CHARLES H.
  R—Jerseyville, Ill.
  B—White Hall, Ill.
  G. O. No. 87, W. D., 1919.

Colonel, Infantry, U. S. Army.
As assistant chief of staff, first section of the 2d Division, and later as assistant chief of staff, first section of the 6th Army Corps, he performed creditably duties of great importance in connection with the services of supply, communication, and the movements of troops of his units, rendering services of value to the American Expeditionary Forces.

BRIGGS, RAYMOND W.
  R—Philadelphia, Pa.
  B—Beaver, Pa.
  G. O. No. 9, W. D., 1923.

Brigadier general, U. S. Army.
For services as chief of the remount service, American Expeditionary Forces; as colonel of the 311th and 304th Field Artillery, the training of which units he developed to a high degree, commanding the latter unit in action with distinction; as commanding general of the 18th and 8th Field Artillery Brigades, which units he developed to a high state of efficiency; and as commanding general of Camp Knox, Ky., during and after the period of demobilization.

BRISTOL, ARTHUR LEROY, Jr.
  R—Charleston, S. C.
  B—Charleston, S. C.
  G. O. No. 116, W. D., 1919.

Commander, U. S. Navy.
For services as flag secretary to the commander, Cruiser and Transport Fleet. His close cooperation with the Army authorities in the handling of troop ships contributed greatly to the successful outcome of our oversea operations.

BROOKE, ROGER.
  R—Sandy Spring, Md.
  B—Sandy Spring, Md.
  G. O. No. 49, W. D., 1922.

Colonel, Medical Corps, U. S. Army.
From September, 1917, until December, 1918, as senior instructor in charge of the educational training of medical officers and enlisted men of the Medical Department at the Medical Officers' Training Camp, Camp Greenleaf, Ga., he directed and coordinated the work of its several special schools with great efficiency. By his untiring efforts, devotion to his duties, and brilliant professional ability he was largely responsible for the successful training of 10,000 officers and 70,000 men, thereby rendering conspicuous service to the Government in a position of great responsibility.

BROOKINGS, ROBERT S.
  R—St. Louis, Mo.
  B—Cecil County, Md.
  G. O. No. 15, W. D., 1923.

Chairman, price fixing committee, War Industries Board.
For services in connection with the operations of the War Industries Board during the World War. As a member of the board he rendered, through his broad vision, distinguished capacity, and business ability, services of inestimable value in marshaling the industrial forces of the Nation and mobilizing its economic resources—marked factors in assisting to make military success attainable. Through his untiring efforts and devotion to duty as commissioner of finished products and later as chairman of the price fixing committee of the board he contributed markedly to the success of the supply systems of the War Department.

BROOKS, HARLOW
  R—New York, N. Y.
  B—Medo, Minn.
  G. O. No. 31, W. D., 1922.

Lieutenant colonel, Medical Corps, U. S. Army.
For services as medical consultant of the First Army and later as chief medical consultant of the Second Army by the application of principles of prevention and treatment which resulted in a marked reduction in the complications and mortality of influenza and other epidemic diseases and lessened the strain on the evacuation service already overtaxed by battle casualties, through early segregation and hospitalization within the front areas. After the armistice, Colonel Brooks, in addition to these duties, was placed in charge of all hospitals of the Second Army, where, by reorganizing the hospital service and establishing courses of instruction and clinical conferences for medical officers, he largely contributed to the betterment of the medical service of the Second Army with a consequent saving of the lives of many American and French soldiers.

BROWN, FRED R.
  R—Cornell, Ill.
  B—Streator, Ill.
  G. O. No. 56, W. D., 1922.

Colonel, Infantry, U. S. Army.
As lieutenant colonel, 313th Infantry, from July, 1917, until July, 1918, throughout its organization and training period he displayed marked efficiency. From August until December, 1918, he commanded the 368th Infantry with indefatigable energy, exceptional initiative, and resourcefulness in all its combat operations. Later, as commanding officer, 58th Infantry, as military commander of Coblenz, Germany, and as officer in charge of civil affairs in the area occupied by Third Army troops, he performed a difficult and responsible task with conspicuous success, maintaining at all times a high state of discipline and morale among the troops and civilian population, thereby contributing materially to the success of the American Expeditionary Forces, in positions of great responsibility.

BROWN, HOBART B.
  R—New York, N. Y.
  B—East Rutherford, N. J.
  G. O. No. 49, W. D., 1922.

Colonel, Infantry, U. S. Army.
From September, 1917, until April, 1918, by his broad experience and sound judgment he organized and commanded with exceptional ability the 104th Military Police. From April to October, 1918, as lieutenant colonel, 116th Infantry, and colonel, 114th Infantry, he showed himself to be resourceful and energetic and at all times equal to any emergency which arose. As deputy provost marshal general, American Expeditionary Forces, from October 1918, to February, 1919, he displayed marked ability in a position of great responsibility, thereby rendering services of great value to the American Expeditionary Forces.

BROWN, KATHARINE
  R—Philadelphia, Pa.
  B—Philadelphia, Pa.
  G. O. No. 9, W. D., 1923.

Chief nurse, Army Nurse Corps, U. S. Army.
As chief nurse of the Nantes Hospital Center, France, during the World War she supervised and directed the nursing care of more than 4,000 patients. Her good judgment, tact, foresight, and energy resulted in most successful accomplishments on the part of the nursing force of that center.

BROWN, LYTLE
  R—Nashville, Tenn.
  B—Nashville, Tenn.
  G. O. No. 47, W. D., 1919.

Brigadier general, U. S. Army.
For services as director of the War Plans Division, for his skill and good judgment in handling the many and varied questions of training, organization and policy that have been acted on by the War Plans Division during the war.

BROWN, PRESTON
  R—Lexington, Ky.
  B—Lexington, Ky.
  G. O. No. 12, W. D., 1919.

Brigadier general, U. S. Army.
As chief of staff of the 2d Division he directed the details of the battles near Chateau-Thierry, Soissons, and at the St. Mihiel salient with great credit. Later, in command of the 3d Division in the Argonne-Meuse offensive, at a most critical time, by his splendid judgment and energetic action, his division was able to carry to a successful conclusion the operations at Claire-Chêne and at Hill 294.

BROWN, WILL H.
  R—Indianapolis, Ind.
  B—Indianapolis, Ind.
  G. O. No. 15, W. D., 1923.

Lieutenant colonel, Motor Transport Corps, U. S. Army.
As chief motor transport officer, Base Section No. 1, St. Nazaire, France, he was charged with the important duty of the receipt of motor transportation arriving from overseas, the general supervision and operation of large reception parks where motor vehicles were set up and made ready for service, and for the instruction and direction of the personnel of convoys distributing vehicles to division, corps, and army troops. The grave responsibilities thus placed upon Colonel Brown were carried out by him in a signally successful way. He displayed unusual initiative, sound judgment, and high professional skill, contributing in a very material way to the successful operations of the American forces in France.

BROWN, WILLIAM C.
  R—St. Peter, Minn.
  B—St. Peter, Minn.
  G. O. No. 43, W. D., 1922.

Colonel, Cavalry, U. S. Army.
As inspector, Quartermaster Corps, American Expeditionary Forces, from November, 1917, until December, 1918, throughout the zone of operations he displayed the greatest zeal, utmost devotion to duty, and indefatigable efforts. By his long experience, marked efficiency, and tireless energy he made highly intelligent inspections and recommendations, thereby enabling the Quartermaster Corps to improve the services of supply and the saving of a large quantity of important material.

BROWNE, BEVERLY F.
  R—Accomac, Va.
  B—Accomac, Va.
  G. O. No. 9, W. D., 1923.

Brigadier general, U. S. Army.
He organized and conducted schools for artillery information service and the counter battery service in France in October and November, 1917. He participated in preparation and execution of artillery plans of First Army for the St. Mihiel offensive in September, 1918, and commanded 166th Field Artillery Brigade in October, 1918, and the corps artillery, First Army Corps, Nov. 1, to 11, 1918, during the final assault of the First Army. His high professional attainments, sound tactical judgment, and devotion to duty contributed materially to the successful operation of the American Expeditionary Forces.

BROWNING, WILLIAM S.
  R—Brooklyn, N. Y.
  B—Brooklyn, N. Y.
  G. O. No. 69, W. D., 1919.

Colonel, Field Artillery, U. S. Army.
As a member of the American section of the Supreme War Council, by his ability and his clear and sound conception of the constantly changing military situation, he has rendered invaluable aid in solving the many complex problems than have come before the Supreme War Council.

BRUFF, AUSTIN J.
  R—Detroit, Mich.
  B—New York, N. Y.
  G. O. No. 38, W. D., 1922.

Lieutenant colonel, Ordnance Department, U. S. Army.
For services in the reorganization and administration of the property and financial departments at Rock Island Arsenal, Ill., which underwent an enormous expansion in the early stages of the war. Later, he rendered unusual and highly meritorious services in developing in England the manufacture of various special and service types of small-arms ammunition, thereby securing for the American Expeditionary Forces a certain and readily available source of supply of this indispensable material.

BRYANT, MORTIMER D.
  R—Brooklyn, N. Y.
  B—Brooklyn, N. Y.
  G. O. No. 13, W. D., 1923.

Colonel, Infantry, U. S. Army.
As machine-gun officer of his division and later as colonel, 107th Infantry, he displayed rare qualities of courageous leadership, sound tactical judgment, and technical skill of a high order. His ability as an organizer and administrator and his unremitting devotion to duty enabled him to render the Government services of inestimable value in positions of responsibility.

BRYDEN, WILLIAM.
  R—Chelsea, Mass.
  B—Hartford, Conn.
  G. O. No. 19, W. D., 1921.

Brigadier general, U. S. Army.
As director of the department of field gunnery, School of Fire for Field Artillery, Fort Sill, Okla., from September, 1917, to May, 1918, and as assistant commandant of that school from May, 1918, to October, 1918, he displayed organizing ability and other professional attainments of a high order in developing and conducting a sound course of instruction in the principles of field gunnery.

BUCHAN, FRED E.
  R—Kansas City, Kans.
  B—Wyandotte, Kans.
  G. O. No. 56, W. D., 1922.

Colonel, General Staff Corps, U. S. Army.
As assistant, G-3, 2d Army Corps, and later as G-3 of that organization, he displayed military talent of a high order in the training of the organizations of the corps for battle. During operations which broke the Hindenburg line, between Cambrai and St. Quentin, he assisted in the planning and execution of operations of great moment with exceptional ability and tireless energy, and contributed to a high degree to the successes of the operations.

BUCKEY, MERVYN C.
  R—Washington, D. C.
  B—Frederick, Md.
  G. O. No. 124, W. D., 1919.

Colonel, Field Artillery, U. S. Army.
For especially meritorious and distinguished service while serving as military attaché at Rome, Italy.

BULLARD, ROBERT L.
  R—Lafayette, Ala.
  B—Youngsborough, Ala.
  G. O. No. 136, W. D., 1918.

Lieutenant general, U. S. Army.
Commander of the Second Army of the American Expeditionary Forces. In the course of this war he commanded in turn the first American division to take its place in the front lines in France, the 3d Corps, and the Second Army. He participated in operations in reduction of the Marne salient and in the Meuse-Argonne offensive. He was in command of the Second Army when the German resistance west of the Meuse was shattered.

BUNNELL, GEORGE W.
  R—Worcester, Mass.
  B—Oakland, Calif.
  G. O. No. 13, W. D., 1923.

Colonel, Corps of Engineers, U. S. Army.
As commanding officer of the 101st Engineer Regiment, from August, 1917, until April, 1919, during its organization, training, and in all its combat operations he performed all his tasks with unusual efficiency and in a manner that reflected credit of a high degree upon him. By his careful and thorough preparation, rare judgment, skillful and energetic leadership, and sound tactical and technical knowledge he contributed in a marked degree to the successes achieved by his regiment and the 26th Division.

BURGHER, EMIL H.
  R—St. Louis, Mo.
  B—Switzerland.
  G. O. No. 59, W. D., 1919.

Major, Medical Corps, U. S. Army.
As regimental surgeon of the 138th Infantry, he supervised the care of the wounded during the Argonne offensive. With untiring energy and ability of a high order, displaying personal courage under shell fire, personally rallying his men and directing them forward, he was an inspiration to all. His dressing station was placed to within a few hundred yards of the front lines whenever the terrain rendered the passage of ambulances impossible. His zeal, devotion to duty, and efficient services added greatly to the morale of all who served with him.

BURKE, Rev. JOHN J.
  R—New York, N. Y.
  B—New York, N. Y.
  G. O. No. 73, W. D., 1919.

For especially meritorious and conspicuous service as chairman of the committee on special war activities of the National Catholic War Council and as chairman of the committee of six, dealing with the subject of chaplains.

BURKHAM, ROBERT.
  R—St. Louis, Mo.
  B—Sioux City, Iowa.
  G. O. No. 19, W. D., 1920.

Lieutenant colonel, Judge Advocate General's Department, U. S. Army.
By his exceptional ability and energy he successfully organized and put into efficient practice the claims department of the rents, requisitions, and claims service. The successful handling of the many complex problems in respect to the adjustment of claims was due, in a large measure, to his high professional attainments and sound judgment. He has rendered services of signal worth to the American Expeditionary Forces.

BURNETT, CHARLES.
  R—Carlinville, Ill.
  B—Concord, Tenn.
  G. O. No. 56, W. D., 1921.

Colonel (Cavalry), General Staff Corps, U. S. Army.
As G-3 of the 30th Division during its operation in Belgium and northern France, subsequent to the armistice he functioned as chief of staff at base section No. 1 in a most creditable manner. He has rendered services of much value to the United States.

DECORATIONS, U. S. ARMY, 1862–1926

BURNETT, FRANK C.
R—Knoxville, Iowa.
B—Casey, Iowa.
G. O. No. 59, W. D., 1919.

Colonel, Infantry, U. S. Army.
He commanded with distinction a battalion of the first American regiment to occupy trenches in France, and participated in the repulse of the first raid made by the enemy upon American troops. As deputy adjutant general, General Headquarters, American Expeditionary Forces, he has performed his manifold duties with ability and sound judgment.

BURNS, JAMES H.
R—Pawling, N. Y.
B—Pawling, N. Y.
G. O. No. 56, W. D., 1922.

Colonel, Ordnance Department, U. S. Army.
First as chief of the explosives branch, design section, gun division, in which capacity he was charged with the production of sufficient explosives, propellants, and shell loading for the needs of the American Government and her allies; and later as chief of the explosives section, production division, with securing the necessary production of explosives, propellants, and assembly of ammunition to meet the needs of America in the World War.

BURNS, SOPHY M.
R—St. Francis, Wis.
B—St. Francis, Wis.
G. O. No. 9, W. D., 1923.

First lieutenant, chief nurse, Army Nurse Corps, U. S. Army.
As chief nurse of Base Hospital No. 116, at Bazoilles-sur-Meuse, France, and later, as chief nurse of Mobile Hospital No. 9, American Expeditionary Forces, in the field during the World War, she rendered conspicuous service by her unusual executive ability, tact, good judgment, and faithfulness to detail in caring for the large number of sick and wounded under her charge.

BURR, GEORGE W.
R—Sedalia, Mo.
B—Tolono, Ill.
G. O. No. 77, W. D., 1919.

Major general, U. S. Army.
For services as director of purchase, storage, and traffic, General Staff, he has had under his supervision during the last several months most important and complicated operations in relation to the cancellation of contracts, the adjustment of claims, the disposal of surplus supplies and the storage of materials that have accumulated during the war or that had been delivered by manufacturers since the armistice.

BURRELL, GEORGE ARTHUR.
R—Washington, D. C.
B—Cleveland, Ohio.
G. O. No. 77, W. D., 1919.

Colonel, Chemical Warfare Service, U. S. Army.
For services in research work pertaining to gas warfare. Colonel Burrell was in charge of the research division, and its organization was doubtless the greatest of its kind ever formed. It accomplished remarkable results of the greatest importance to our military forces.

BURTT, WILSON B.
R—La Grange, Ill.
B—Hinsdale, Ill.
G. O. No. 59, W. D., 1919.

Brigadier general, U. S. Army.
As chief of staff of the 5th Corps he displayed great tact and judgment in the organization of that command. He directed with marked ability the staff work of his corps during the St. Mihiel and Argonne-Meuse offensives and was a potent factor in insuring the successes of his organization in that campaign.

BURY, FREDERICK E.
R—Marion, Ind.
B—Miami County, Ind.
G. O. No. 53, W. D., 1921.

Lieutenant colonel, Infantry, U. S. Army.
For exceptionally meritorious and distinguished services as chief of staff, American Forces in Russia.

BUTLER, SMEDLEY D.
R—West Chester, Pa.
B—West Chester, Pa.
G. O. No. 95, W. D., 1919.

Brigadier General, U. S. Marine Corps.
He has commanded with ability and energy Pontanezen Camp at Brest during the time in which it has developed into the largest embarkation camp in the world. Confronted with problems of extraordinary magnitude in supervising the reception, entertainment, and departure of the large numbers of officers and soldiers passing through this camp, he has solved all with conspicuous success, performing services of the highest character for the American Expeditionary Forces.

BUTNER, HENRY W.
R—Stony Ridge, N. C.
B—Stony Ridge, N. C.
G. O. No. 19, W. D., 1920.

Brigadier general, U. S. Army.
He commanded, with marked distinction, the 1st Field Artillery Brigade from Aug. 18 to Nov. 11, 1918, displaying at all times keen tactical ability, initiative, and loyal devotion to duty. By his high military attainments and sound judgment he proved to be a material factor in the successes achieved by the divisions whose advances he supported.

BYLLESBY, HENRY M.
R—Chicgao, Ill.
B—Pittsburgh, Pa.
G. O. No. 38, W. D., 1922.

Lieutenant colonel, Signal Corps, U. S. Army.
As general purchasing agent for the American Expeditionary Forces at Base Section No. 3, in Great Britain, from May to December, 1918, he displayed great energy, a comprehensive knowledge of large business affairs, and executive ability of the highest order. By his broad experience, foresight, and splendid ability to cooperate with representatives of our allies, he solved many difficult problems of fuel supply with conspicuous success and in a manner which insured at critical times a plentiful supply of coal, both for our transport service and our troops in France, thereby rendering services of great value to the American Expeditionary Forces.

BYRON, JOSEPH C.
R—Hagerstown, Md.
B—Buffalo, N. Y.
G. O. No. 10, W. D., 1920.

Supply service, hides and leather.
For services in connection with the supply service of the Army during the World War, by his individual efforts he made possible the accomplishment of that portion of the supply program that depended for success upon the supply of hides and leather.

CABELL, DE ROSEY C.
R—Roseville, Ark.
B—Charleston, Ark.
G. O. No. 73, W. D., 1919.

Major general, U. S. Army.
While in command of the Arizona district of the southern department, he handled the delicate border situation there with firmness and sound judgment.

CABELL, HENRY C R—Richmond, Va. B—Richmond, Va. G. O. No. 10, W. D., 1922.	Colonel, Adjutant General's Department, U. S. Army. For services while in charge of war risk insurance matters and later in charge of the appointment division. By his untiring efforts in dealing with other departments and the public, he expedited the dispatch of official business and the solution of intricate problems arising under new laws. He rendered services of great merit.
CALL, LEWIS W R—Garrett Park, Md. B—Upper Sandusky, Ohio. G. O. No. 28, W. D., 1921.	Colonel, Judge Advocate General's Department, U. S. Army. For services as chief of the contracts and claims section, Judge Advocate General's Office, from 1917 to 1920, his knowledge of the law, sound judgment, and application enabled him to deal promptly and effectively with the many perplexing questions arising with respect to contracts, requisitions, and compulsory orders which formed the basis of claims against the Government during the war period.
CALLAN, ROBERT E R—Knoxville, Tenn. B—Baltimore, Md. G. O. No. 16, W. D., 1920.	Brigadier General, U. S. Army. As chief of staff of the Army Artillery, First Army, he exhibited ability in the organization of that unit. Later, as commanding general of the 33d Coast Artillery Brigade, he displayed high technical ability. Though confronted with innumerable difficulties, he developed the heavy artillery regiments under his command into combat units of remarkable efficiency, which units proved to be of the utmost value during the St. Mihiel and Meuse-Argonne offensives.
CAMERON, REBA G R—Taunton, Mass. B—Canada. G. O. No. 9, W. D., 1923.	First lieutenant, chief nurse, Army Nurse Corps, U. S. Army. As chief nurse of the General Hospital at Plattsburg Barracks, N. Y., during the World War, and later as chief nurse of the general hospital at Hampton, Va., during the demobilization period, her services were such as to call for special commendation. Whether by day or night, in emergency or routine work, she never failed to respond efficiently to every call. By her conscientious, unselfish devotion to duty, and cheerful, cooperative manner she was an example and an inspiration to her entire staff, and was in large measure responsible for the marked success of these special hospitals.
CAMPBELL, ROBERT M R—Owings Mills, Md. B—Owings Mills, Md. G. O. No. 124, W. D., 1919.	Lieutenant colonel, Cavalry, U. S. Army. For especially meritorious and distinguished service while serving as military attaché at Mexico City, Mexico.
CANFIELD, EDWARD, Jr R—Middletown, N. Y. B—Bath, N. Y. G. O. No. 59, W. D., 1919.	Lieutenant colonel, Coast Artillery Corps, U. S. Army. He served as assistant Chief of Staff, G-1, of the 4th Division, and organized the entire system of supply for the division. He trained and supervised the personnel and the operation of the administrative sections. He handled all problems connected with supply and transportation with such efficiency and success that the division was never short of either rations or ammunition. He proved himself to be an officer of the greatest administrative ability, exceptional foresight, and tireless energy.
CANNON, WALTER B R—Cambridge, Mass. B—Prairie du Chien, Wis. G. O. No. 49, W. D., 1922.	Lieutenant colonel, Medical Corps, U. S. Army. As director of physiological research for the American Expeditionary Forces in France, his activities in connection with the development of a standard method for the resuscitation of the wounded and in organizing, instructing, and directing the work of shock teams in hospitals at the front reflected professional skill and judgment of the highest order and resulted in saving many lives.
CARLETON, GUY R—San Antonio, Tex. B—Austin, Tex. G. O. No. 47, W. D., 1919.	Major general, U. S. Army. For exceptionally meritorious and conspicuous service as commanding general at Camp Wadsworth, S. C., in organizing and training corps and Army troops during the war.
CARSON, CLIFFORD C R—Muncie, Ind. B—North Greenfield, Ohio. G. O. No. 59, W. D., 1919.	Colonel, Coast Artillery Corps, U. S. Army. He organized and commanded the training centers for the instruction of officers for the Tractor Artillery of the American Expeditionary Forces. In this new and important field of activity he rendered conspicuously meritorious service.
CARSON, JOHN M R—Philadelphia, Pa B—Philadelphia, Pa. G. O. No. 53, W. D., 1921.	Brigadier general, U. S. Army. For services as chief quartermaster, line of communications, American Expeditionary Forces, and later as deputy chief quartermaster, American Expeditionary Forces, positions of great responsibility, due to his ability and energy he perfected and directed the organization and operation of the Quartermaster Corps of the line of communications. Later he skillfully carried out the plans and projects to make the Quartermaster Corps an unfailing auxiliary to the combatant troops of the American Expeditionary Forces. He has rendered services of much value.
CARTER, ARTHUR H R—Leesburg, Va. B—Hillsboro, Kans. G. O. No. 69, W. D., 1919.	Colonel, Field Artillery, U. S. Army. While on duty in the office of the Chief of Field Artillery, he displayed great ability in developing the organization of the Field Artillery Central Officers' Training School; he then proceeded to Camp Taylor, established this school, and administered it in an exceptionally meritorious manner during the remainder of the war.
CARTER, JESSE McI R—Farmington, Mo. B—St. Francois County, Mo. G. O. No. 25, W. D., 1919.	Major general, U. S. Army. As chief of the Militia Bureau he conceived and directed the organization of the United States Guards and utilized these and other forces most effectively in the important work of safeguarding the utilities and industries of the Nation essential to the prosecution of the war.

CARTER, WILLIAM H. R—New York, N. Y. B—Nashville, Tenn. G. O. No. 124, W. D., 1919. Medal of honor also awarded.	Major general, U. S. Army. For services as department commander, Central Department, between Aug. 26, 1917, and Mar. 13, 1918; he handled many difficult problems arising in that department with rare judgment, tact, and great skill.
CARTY, JOHN J. R—Short Hills, N. J. B—Cambridge, Mass. G. O. No. 59, W. D., 1919.	Colonel, Signal Corps, U. S. Army. He was largely instrumental in securing from the telephone and telegraph companies of the United States the best talent available to meet the urgent requirements of the Signal Corps at the outbreak of the war. He has served with marked distinction as a member of the American Expeditionary Forces, and his brilliant professional attainments and sound judgment have rendered his services of exceptional value to the Government.
CASAD, ADAM F. R—Wichita, Kans. B—Delphi, Ind. G. O. No. 78, W. D., 1919.	Colonel, Ordnance Department, U. S. Army. As deputy chief ordnance officer at General Headquarters, American Expeditionary Forces, he exercised conspicuous initiative and sound judgment in the supervision of ordnance activities. With tireless energy he organized and administered the work of the Ordnance Department in the zone of the Armies. As representative of the Ordnance Department at Chaumont, he showed wide vision and full comprehension of conditions and needs of the service, working with exceptional devotion to prevent any stoppage in the supply of ordnance material.
CASTNER, JOSEPH COMPTON. R—New Brunswick, N. J. B—New Brunswick, N. J. G. O. No. 59, W. D., 1919.	Brigadier general, U. S. Army. While in command of the 9th Infantry Brigade he displayed conspicuous tenacity of purpose and a determination to overcome all obstacles. At the Bois des Rappes, in the St. Mihiel salient and ensuing actions, his brigade effectively routed the enemy. The success of his command was in a large measure due to the splendid training and excellent leadership given it by its commander.
CATRON, THOMAS B. 2D. R—Santa Fe, N. Mex. B—New Mexico. G. O. No. 103, W. D., 1919.	Major, Signal Corps, U. S. Army. As an instructor at the Army Intelligence School he performed important duties with marked zeal and ability, aiding materially in the efficient training of a large number of officers for the intelligence service of the units of our Armies in the field.
CAVANAUGH, JAMES B. R—Olympia, Wash. B—Carrollton, Ill. G. O. No. 50, W. D., 1919.	Colonel, Engineers, U. S. Army. As commander of an Engineer regiment, he rendered great assistance in the early development of the American port at Bassens. As assistant chief of staff in charge of the administrative section of the services of supply, he exhibited rare qualities and marked ability in the solution of many problems of policy. His efforts in connection with the repatriation of American troops have been of conspicuous merit.
CHAFFEE, ADNA R. R—Manila, P. I. B—Junction City, Kans. G. O. No. 62, W. D., 1919.	Colonel, Cavalry, U. S. Army. At Army General Staff College he displayed military attainments of a high order, contributing efficiently to the training of a large number of officers. He performed tasks of great difficulty with marked distinction as G–3 of the 81st Division and later of the 7th Corps. Later, as chief of the third section, general staff, 3d Corps, he acted with sound judgment and wide comprehension of existing conditions in the discharge of the grave responsibilities connected with his office during the closing days of the Meuse-Argonne offensive, handling perplexing problems with keen energy and wise discernment.
CHAMBERLAIN, JOHN L. R—South Livonia, N. Y. B—South Livonia, N. Y. G. O. No. 25, W. D., 1919.	Major general, U. S. Army. As inspector general of the Army he has, by his highly responsible services, materially contributed to the efficiency of all departments and bureaus of the Military Establishment and to the successful execution of the military program.
CHAMBERLAIN, WESTON P. R—Bristol, Me. B—Bristol, Me. G. O. No. 10, W. D., 1922.	Colonel, Medical Corps, U. S. Army. As chief sanitary inspector of the Army within the continental limits of the United States during the World War he displayed exceptional efficiency in organizing and administering a sanitary inspection service during the periods of mobilization, active operations, and demobilization. His achievements in this capacity were of great value to the Government.
CHAMBERLAINE, WILLIAM. R—Norfolk, Va. B—Norfolk, Va. G. O. No. 2, W. D., 1920.	Brigadier general, U. S. Army. As commanding general of the Railway Artillery Reserve, he rendered valuable services to the American Expeditionary Forces in the operations of the Railway Artillery units during the Meuse-Argonne offensive.
CHAMBERLIN, STEPHEN J. R—Spring Hill, Kans. B—Spring Hill, Kans. G. O. No. 38, W. D., 1922.	Major, Infantry, U. S. Army. As acting dispatch officer and dispatch officer at port of embarkation, Hoboken, N. J., from Nov. 15, 1917, to Sept. 6, 1918, Major Chamberlin displayed marked ability in handling the movements of troops through the port, assigning units and detachments to camps, convoys, and ships, and by foresight, thorough organization, and hard work arranged for the smooth working of troop movements, prevented congestion at the camps and piers, thus enabling the transports to sail at the appointed time with the appropriate number of troops.
CHANDLER, CHARLES DEF. R—Cleveland, Ohio. B—Cleveland, Ohio. G. O. No. 50, W. D., 1919.	Colonel, Signal Corps, U. S. Army. As chief of the balloon section, Air Service, American Expeditionary Forces, from November, 1917, to February, 1919, he rendered notable service in the supply, administration, and operation of the balloon units that so thoroughly demonstrated their efficiency during all the major operations of the American Expeditionary Forces.

DISTINGUISHED-SERVICE MEDAL

CHAPIN, LINDLEY H. P.
R—New York, N. Y.
B—New York, N. Y.
G. O. No. 59, W. D., 1919.

First lieutenant, General Staff, U. S. Army. As the representative of G-4, of the American Expeditionary Forces at the D. G. C. R. A., he displayed marked ability and devotion to duty in a position of great responsibility, he handled with tact and sound judgment the involved and delicate questions continually arising in connection with our relationship with the allied armies, and rendered service of great value to the Government.

CHEATHAM, B. FRANK
R—Nashville, Tenn.
B—Beech Grove, Tenn.
G. O. No. 9, W. D., 1923.

Colonel, Quartermaster Corps, U. S. Army. As chief quartermaster, 1st Army Corps, he displayed sound judgment, great initiative, and high professional attainments. Later, as colonel, 104th Infantry, 26th Division, in operations against the enemy in the Meuse-Argonne offensive north of Verdun, Oct. 14 to Nov. 11, 1918, he rendered exceptionally valuable services, his high courage, leadership, and tactical skill proving important factors in the successful operations of the 26th Division during the second phase of the Meuse-Argonne offensive.

CHENEY, SHERWOOD A.
R—South Manchester, Conn.
B—South Manchester, Conn.
G. O. No. 108, W. D., 1919.

Brigadier general, U. S. Army. As assistant chief engineer, General Headquarters, he rendered valuable services in the organization of the Engineer Corps and its coordination with the associated services. Later, as director of the Army Transport Service, he performed eminently valuable services, achieving remarkable results in a task of great magnitude involving the expeditious return of many thousands of soldiers from the ports of France to the United States.

CHURCH, EARL D.
R—Hartford, Conn.
B—Rockville, Conn.
G. O. No. 31, W. D., 1922.

Lieutenant colonel, Ordnance Department, U. S. Army. As ordnance officer of the 80th Division, not only were ordnance and ammunition supplied at all times to members of that division, but also to thousands of men in other divisions at various times when their own supply failed. His organization of the ordnance supply system, as division ordnance officer, showed the results of exhaustive study and of determined and intelligent efforts to overcome adverse conditions. Later, as chief ordnance officer of the 9th Army Corps, he displayed high qualities of zeal, loyalty, and efficiency.

CHURCHILL, MARLBOROUGH
R—Andover, Mass.
B—Andover, Mass.
G. O. No. 73, W. D., 1919.

Brigadier general, U. S. Army. For services as chief of staff of the Army artillery of the 1st Army, American Expeditionary Forces, and for his ability, zeal, and untiring energy in building up the military intelligence division of the General Staff as director of military intelligence. He discharged these duties of great responsibility with ability, tact, and energy. He built up the intelligence service to its present high state of efficiency.

CLARK, ALBERT P.
R—Washington, D. C.
B—Washington, D. C.
G. O. No. 62, W. D., 1919.

Lieutenant colonel, Medical Corps, U. S. Army. As medical representative on, and later as General Staff member of, the first section, General Headquarters, American Expeditionary Forces, he displayed sound judgment and wide comprehension of existing conditions in the management of ocean tonnage allotments, and devised and efficiently operated a system of supply for the Medical Department of the American Expeditionary Forces. Largely through his personal efforts, energy, and farsightedness the difficulties in the procurement and shipment of medical supplies for the sick and wounded were successfully overcome.

CLARK, FRANCIS W.
R—Chicago, Ill.
B—Wichita, Kans.
G. O. No. 38, W. D., 1922.

Lieutenant colonel (Field Artillery), General Staff Corps, U. S. Army. As acting G-3 of the 3d Corps he displayed sound judgment and military attainments of the highest order. With the utmost clearness and skill he prepared the orders under which his corps operated both from the Vesle to the Aisne Rivers and during the Meuse-Argonne offensive until Oct. 14, 1918. By his marked tactical ability, loyal devotion to duty, and untiring zeal he contributed materially to the success of those operations.

CLARK, GRENVILLE
R—New York, N. Y.
B—New York, N. Y.
G. O. No. 15, W. D., 1921.

Lieutenant colonel, Adjutant General's Department, U. S. Army. For services on the committee on classification of personnel and later as a member of the committee on education and special training.

CLARK, JOSHUA REUBEN, Jr.
R—Washington, D. C.
B—Grantsville, Utah.
G. O. No. 49, W. D., 1922.

Major, Judge Advocate General's Department, U. S. Army. As special assistant to the Attorney General of the United States from June, 1917, until September, 1918, by his zeal, great industry, and eminent legal attainments, he rendered conspicuous services in the compilation and publication of an extremely valuable and comprehensive edition of the laws and analogous legislation pertaining to the war powers of our Government since its beginning. From September to December, 1918, as executive officer of the Provost Marshal General's Office, he again rendered services of inestimable value in connection with the preparation and execution of complete regulations governing the classification and later the demobilization of several million registrants.

CLARK, PAUL H.
R—Chicago, Ill.
B—Chicago, Ill.
G. O. No. 59, W. D., 1919

Lieutenant colonel, Infantry, U. S. Army. As chief of the American mission at French General Headquarters, he performed with marked distinction important duties requiring tact and judgment. His ceaseless efforts and untiring energy were of material benefit in securing the necessary cooperation with the French military authorities.

CLARK, STEPHEN C.
R—New York, N. Y.
B—Cooperstown, N. Y.
G. O. No. 56, W. D., 1922.

Lieutenant colonel, Adjutant General's Department, U. S. Army. As assistant adjutant and later as adjutant of the 2d Army Corps from August, 1918, to February, 1919, he displayed administrative ability of an exceptionally high order. During active operations of the corps his tireless energy and unceasing devotion to duty assisted materially in the successes achieved by his organization.

*CLARKE, THOMAS C R—New York, N. Y. B—Philadelphia, Pa. G. O. No. 56, W. D., 1921.	Colonel, 110th Engineers, 35th Division, U. S. Army. For services at Baulny, France, Sept. 29, 1918. He admirably established and constructed a line of resistance which he held for several days, during which time two counterattacks were repelled and severe loss inflicted upon the enemy. Later he commanded and held an advance line for two days, repelling two determined counterattacks. Posthumously awarded. Medal presented to widow, Mrs. Thomas C. Clarke
CLEMENS, PAUL B R—Superior, Wis. B—Superior, Wis. G. O. No. 9, W. D., 1923.	Lieutenant colonel (Infantry), General Staff Corps, U. S. Army. As assistant chief of staff, G-2, 32d Division, during its operations in France he displayed unusual and masterful grasp of his duties, executive ability of high order, and intense zeal and devotion to duty. His initiative, foresight and good judgment were important factors in the successes of his division and made his services of inestimable value to the Government in a position of great responsibility.
CLEVELAND, MAUDE R—Berkeley, Calif. B—Gresham, Oreg. G. O. No. 133, W. D., 1919.	American Red Cross. Chief of the home communication and casualty service of the Red Cross a Brest, France. By her unremitting efforts in caring for the sick and wounded evacuated through the port of Brest, her valuable assistance in the intermen of the dead, consummated at night under the most adverse weather conditions, her careful consideration in writing the details of the death to the nearest relative, and her supreme exertion during the distressing epidemic of influenza pneumonia from September to December, 1918, she has rendered self-sacrificing services of the highest character to the American Expeditionary Forces.
CLIFFORD, EDWARD R—Evanston, Ill. B—Virginia, Ill. G. O. No. 10, W. D., 1922.	Lieutenant colonel, Quartermaster Corps, U. S. Army. For services in organizing and administering the Army allotment system thereby enabling the War Department to make prompt payments of allotments. He rendered services of great value.
CLINNIN, JOHN V R—Chicago, Ill. B—Huntley, Ill. G. O. No. 56, W. D., 1921.	Colonel, Infantry, U. S. Army. As regimental commander of the 130th Infantry, 33d Division, by his force and energy he brought his regiment to a high state of efficiency, instilling into an aggressive spirit which proved a valuable factor in the operations of the regiment near Breuilles, Verdun, Bois-de-Chaume, Sivry, and Bois du Plat Chene. He rendered services of great merit.
CLOMAN, SYDNEY A R—Deavertown, Ohio. B—Deavertown, Ohio. G. O. No. 59, W. D., 1919.	Colonel, Infantry, U. S. Army. As chief of staff of the 29th Division, he showed himself resourceful and equa to any emergency. His sound judgment and ability, especially during th operations north of Verdun, France, in October, 1918, were of a high orde The success of these operations was in a measure due to his energy, zeal, an rare qualities of leadership.
CLOPTON, WILLIAM H., Jr R—St. Louis, Mo. B—St. Louis, Mo. G. O. No. 43, W. D., 1922.	Colonel, Tank Corps, U. S. Army. By his special knowledge of personnel matters, untiring zeal, good judgmen and administrative ability he was largely responsible for the solution of man difficult problems in the organization and operation of the personnel branch Office of the Quartermaster General, especially in the organization of th technical field units of the Quartermaster Corps. Later, as colonel, Tan Corps, he rendered conspicuous service in the establishment of tank schoo and in the training of technical troops therein, while commanding tank trail ing camps at Tobyhanna, Pa., and Camp Polk, N. C.
COCHEU, FRANK S R—Brooklyn, N. Y. B—Brooklyn, N. Y. G. O. No. 49, W. D., 1922.	Colonel, Infantry, U. S. Army. In command of the 319th Infantry, 80th Division, from August, 1917, to Octobe 1918, he displayed marked ability in its organization, training, and servic in the field. In operations against the enemy in the Artois sector and Meus Argonne offensive he rendered conspicuous service by leading his comman with exceptional judgment, unflagging energy, and tactical ability, at a times proving himself to be a skillful commander, thus enabling his regimen to always carry its tasks through to a successful end. His services wer highly meritorious and rendered in a position of great responsibility.
COCHEU, GEORGE W R—Brooklyn, N. Y. B—Brooklyn, N. Y. G. O. No. 10, W. D., 1922.	Colonel (Coast Artillery Corps), General Staff Corps, U. S. Army. As a member and later as chief of the coordination section, General Staff, position of great responsibility, he devised many methods for improving an making more efficient the administrative procedure within the War Depart ment, thereby materially facilitating the transaction of the business of th War Department and between the War Department and the Army, thu rendering service of great value to the entire military establishment.
COE, FRANK W R—Manhattan, Kans. B—Manhattan, Kans. G. O. No. 18, W. D., 1919.	Major general, U. S. Army. For services in the reorganization of the Coast Artillery, thereby enabling it t meet the great demand for oversea artillery.
COLE, HAYDN S R—Kewanee, Ill. B—Newark Valley, N. Y. G. O. No. 14, W. D., 1923.	Colonel, Quartermaster Corps, U. S. Army. For services while assistant to the general superintendent, Army Transpo Service, New York City, May 1 to Nov. 1, 1917; general manager of th Hoboken Shore R. R., July 1 to Nov. 1, 1917; and in full charge of operatio at Bush Terminal System, Brooklyn, N. Y., until January, 1919. He di played rare administrative and executive ability, sound judgment, an rendered services of immeasurable value to the Government.

COLE, WILLIAM E R—Willard, Utah. B—Willard, Utah. G. O. No. 38, W. D., 1922.	Brigadier general, U. S. Army. As commanding officer of the 351st Field Artillery, 92d Division, from November, 1917, to August, 1918, by his rare judgment and exceptional ability he organized and trained his regiment to a high standard of efficiency under the most adverse circumstances. As brigade commander from August, 1918, until December, 1918, he again displayed resourcefulness and unusual ability in the successful organization and training of the 11th and 20th Field Artillery Brigades. As commanding general at Camp Jackson, S. C., from January, 1919, to April, 1919, he rendered most valuable and distinguished service in the demobilization of great numbers of troops and immense quantities of material.
COLEMAN, FREDERICK W R—Washington, D. C. B—Baltimore, Md. G. O. No. 49, W. D., 1922.	Colonel (Infantry), General Staff Corps, U. S. Army. As G–1, 91st Division, from August to October, 1918, due to his unusual foresight, indefatigable zeal, exceptional executive and administrative ability, he so organized the supply and administrative services of the division as to insure complete coordination and a regular flow of supplies of all kinds, notwithstanding a shortage of transportation and despite grave and tremendous difficulties because of road congestion, thereby rendering conspicuous service in a position of great responsibility to the American Expeditionary Forces.
COLES, ROY H R—Warren, Ind. B—Warren, Ind. G. O. No. 59, W. D., 1919.	Lieutenant colonel, Signal Corps, U. S. Army. He served as assistant to and executive officer for the chief signal officer, American Expeditionary Forces, and at all times he performed his most exacting duties in an especially meritorious manner. By his exceptional executive ability, tireless energy, and sound judgment he successfully met every demand that was made upon him.
COLLADAY, EDGAR B R—Dunn, Wis. B—Dunn, Wis. G. O. No. 27, W. D., 1922.	Lieutenant colonel (Coast Artillery Corps), General Staff Corps, U. S. Army. As executive officer of the cable section, General Staff, during the World War, his sound judgment, his marked ability, his untiring energy, and his willingness to accept grave responsibilities, contributed greatly to the successful operation of the cable business during the World War. Later, as executive officer of the statistics branch, General Staff, he assisted materially in collecting and compiling valuable statistics pertaining to the World War.
COLLINS, CHRISTOPHER C R—Lynchburg, Va. B—Lynchburg, Va. G. O. No. 4, W. D., 1923.	Colonel, Medical Corps, U. S. Army. As corps surgeon, 2d Army Corps, from February, 1918, to February, 1919, he displayed professional attainments of a high order in the training of the organization of the corps for subsequent operations. During active operations the efficiency of his organization and arrangements for the care of the sick and wounded and their evacuation contributed in high degree to the success of the operations of the corps.
COLLINS, EDGAR T R—Williamsport, Pa. B—Williamsport, Pa. G. O. No. 16, W. D., 1920.	Colonel (Infantry), General Staff Corps, U. S. Army. As assistant to G–5, General Headquarters, and later as Chief of Staff of the 6th Army Corps, he demonstrated rare military attainments, performing his difficult tasks with unremitting zeal, rendering services of conspicuous worth to the American Expeditionary Forces.
COLLINS, JAMES L R—New Orleans, La. B—New Orleans, La. G. O. No. 59, W. D., 1919.	Lieutenant colonel, Field Artillery, U. S. Army. As aide-de-camp to the commander in chief, as line officer on duty with troops, and as secretary of the General Staff of the American Expeditionary Forces, he displayed a thorough knowledge of every duty with which he was intrusted. With tireless energy, keen perception, and able execution of his manifold duties he rendered especially meritorious services to the American Expeditionary Forces.
COLLINS, OWEN G R—Chicago, Ill. B—Chicago, Ill. G. O. No. 59, W. D., 1919.	Colonel, Quartermaster Corps, U. S. Army. Under his administration the supply of troops, care of property, and the operation of the Quartermaster Depot at Gievres, showed an excellent degree of efficiency. The great improvement and development of the organization of this important depot under his direction was largely due to his administrative ability and untiring zeal.
COLLINS, ROBERT L R—Wellesley Hills, Mass. B—Lancaster, Mass. G. O. No. 9, W. D., 1923.	Colonel, Cavalry, U. S. Army. He served as assistant chief of staff, G–1 and G–2, 33d Division, from June 13 to Oct. 2, 1918, and assistant chief of staff, G–2, 37th Division, from Oct. 25 to Nov. 7, 1918; assistant chief of staff, G–2, 84th Division, Oct. 2–25, 1918; assistant chief of staff and chief of staff, general headquarters, Tank Corps, from Nov. 8, 1918, to June 30, 1920. He displayed sound judgment and exceptional ability in the administration and operation of all the staff sections of the units with which he served and by his initiative, tireless energy, and military attainments of a high order he contributed in a marked degree to the successes achieved by those forces against the enemy.
COMMISKEY, ARCHIBALD F R—Brooklyn, N. Y. B—Brooklyn, N. Y. G. O. No. 39, W. D., 1920.	Colonel, Field Artillery, U. S. Army As regimental commander of the 77th Field Artillery, 4th Division, and during the Meuse-Argonne offensive from Oct. 3 to 11, 1918, as commander of an artillery grouping consisting of the 77th and 16th Field Artillery, he demonstrated marked ability and good judgment in the direction of his units in support of the 4th Division during its attack. From Nov. 1 to 11, 1918, his regiment supported, with marked success, the advance of the 5th Division. He kept his elements close to the attacking units and gave valuable assistance to them. He has rendered services of considerable value to the American Expeditionary Forces.

CONGER, ARTHUR L............
R—Akron, Ohio.
B—Akron, Ohio.
G. O. No. 35, W. D., 1920.

Colonel, Infantry, U. S. Army.
As a member of the second section, General Staff, General Headquarters, his marked professional attainments, his zeal, and his sound judgment contributed largely to the successful operation of this section. As chief the second section, General Staff, of the 2d Division, during active ope tions, and later as commander of a brigade of the 28th Division during Argonne-Meuse offensive, he demonstrated his great energy and his cl conception of tactics.

CONLEY, EDGAR T............
R—Fairland, Md.
B—Fairland, Md.
G. O. No. 56, W. D., 1921.

Colonel (Infantry), Adjutant General's Department, U. S. Army.
As chief of the prisoners of war division, the Provost Marshal General's l partment, he had charge of and was responsible for all matters concern the prisoners of war labor companies, escort companies, and inclosures. sound judgment, marked ability, and devotion to duty resulted in the h dling of the delicate prisoner of war questions in such a manner as to prod only commendation. His services were exceptionally valuable to the G ernment.

CONNELL, KARL............
R—New York, N. Y.
B—Omaha, Nebr.
G. O. No. 56, W. D., 1922.

Major, Medical Corps, U. S. Army.
In the Chemical Warfare Service, practically alone and unaided and at a gr personal risk of his life, he exposed himself unhesitatingly to the high concentrations of deadly gases while working with experimental models masks. Major Connell invented, tested out, and perfected a new type gas mask superior to any then in existence, thereby rendering service of estimable value to the American Expeditionary Forces.

CONNER, FOX............
R—Slate Spring, Miss.
B—Slate Spring, Miss.
G. O. No. 12, W. D., 1919.

Brigadier general, U. S. Army.
As assistant chief of staff in charge of the operations section he has show masterful conception of all the tactical situations which have confron the American forces in Europe. By his high professional attainments a sound military judgment he has handled with marked skill the many det of the complex problems of organization and troop movements that w necessitated by the various operations of the American Expedition Forces.

CONNER, LEWIS A............
R—New York, N. Y.
B—New Albany, Ind.
G. O. No. 10, W. D., 1922.

Colonel, Medical Corps, U. S. Army.
As chief of the internal medicine division of the Surgeon General's Office position of great responsibility, to him is due, in a large measure, the pansion and successful administration of that division. By his powe influence he induced many eminent internists to remain in the base hospi after the signing of the armistice until the sick from overseas had been ta care of.

CONNER, WILLIAM D............
R—Clinton, Iowa.
B—Rock, Wis.
G. O. No. 12, W. D., 1919.

Brigadier general, U. S. Army.
As assistant chief of staff and head of the coordination section of the Gen Staff, American Expeditionary Forces, he showed unusual ability and t less energy. As chief of staff of the 32d Division in the trench operation the Belfort sector and later as commander of the 63d Infantry Brigade in advance to the Vesle he displayed particular ability as a leader of troo He also performed valuable services as commander of a base port and as c of staff of the services of supply.

CONRAD, CASPER H., Jr............
R—Fort Randall, S. Dak.
B—Columbus, Ohio.
G. O. No. 2, W. D., 1920.

Colonel, Infantry, U. S. Army.
As commander of advance embarkation section, S. O. S., by his marked exe tive ability and energetic efforts displayed in the transportation of tro from the area of the Army of Occupation to the base ports, and the man ment of troop trains which were comfortably equipped, safely operated, sanitarily maintained, he has rendered services of great worth.

*COOK, CHARLES F............
R—Richmond Hill, N. Y.
B—Knoxboro, N. Y.
G. O. No. 89, W. D., 1919.

Major, Ordnance Department, U. S. Army.
While serving in the Ordnance Department he was instrumental in organiz the divisions dealing with the procurement of ordnance material. W serving on the General Staff he worked out a plan for the consolidation o articles of standard commercial circulation in single purchasing units throu out the War Department upon which basis was built the organization of present division of purchase, storage and traffic of the General Staff. In various assignments he gave himself whole-heartedly and self-sacrificingl the work of the Government.
Posthumously awarded. Medal presented to sister, Mrs. Blanche Seavey

COOPER, HARRY L............
R—Philadelphia, Pa.
B—Philadelphia, Pa.
G. O. No. 4, W. D., 1923.

Colonel, Infantry, U. S. Army.
He commanded the 2d Army Corps School at Chatillon, France, from A 15, 1918, to May 19, 1919. He so organized and coordinated the various ac ities at these schools that 1,800 to 2,500 students were constantly un going instruction. He was primarily responsible for the excellent syster training given, that training as received at these schools exercised a str influence toward the efficiency of the whole body of American troop France. By his sound administrative and superior technical ability, unti zeal, and splendid judgment in reorganizing and expanding the schools produced an organization of the highest efficiency. He rendered service signal worth to the American Expeditionary Forces in a position of g responsibility.

COOPER, WIBB E............
R—Nashville, Tenn.
B—Mount Pleasant, Tenn.
G. O. No. 103, W. D., 1919.

Colonel, Medical Corps, U. S. Army.
He commanded with notable success Base Hospital No. 8, at Savenay, wl under his efficient administration became the nucleus of a large hosp center, which developed into the largest classification and evacuation pital in France for patients returning to the United States. By his mar ability in directing the numerous activities under his control he rend services of conspicuous worth to the American Expeditionary Forces.

COOTES, HARRY N..................... | Colonel (Cavalry), General Staff Corps, U. S. Army.
R—Staunton, Va.
B—Staunton, Va.
G. O. No. 43, W. D., 1922.

As chief of staff, 78th Division, during its organization and training period and later during the St. Mihiel offensive he displayed tact, sound judgment, and military attainments of the highest order. Due to his ability in coordinating all of the various staff agencies into a harmonious machine, and by his loyalty and untiring energy in carrying out the policies of the division commander, he rendered services of great value to the American Expeditionary Forces.

CORDIER, CONSTANT..................... | Colonel (Infantry), General Staff Corps, U. S. Army.
R—Flagstaff, Ariz.
B—New Orleans, La.
G. O. No. 25, W. D., 1919.

While on duty as liaison officer between the War Department and the foreign military missions he displayed the greatest discretion and ability and contributed materially to the successful conduct of military-diplomatic relations between the War Department and the allied military missions.

CORLETT, CHARLES H..................... | Lieutenant colonel, Signal Corps, U. S. Army.
R—Monte Vista, Colo.
B—Burchard, Nebr.
G. O. No. 62, W. D., 1919.

As deputy to the Chief Signal Officer of the line of communications he displayed marked ability for organization and administration in the establishment of important Signal Corps undertakings, laying the foundation of the Signal Corps work in the American Expeditionary Forces. Later, as director of supplies in the Office of the Chief Signal Officer, he performed exacting duties with unusual ability, solving with sound judgment perplexing problems, enabling a steady flow of signal supplies to be maintained to the troops in the field.

COUGHLIN, EDNA M..................... | Reserve nurse, Army Nurse Corps, U. S. Army, attached to Emergency Medical Team No. 142, American Expeditionary Forces.
R—Chicago, Ill.
B—Chicago, Ill.
G. O. No. 10, W. D., 1920.

As a member of an emergency medical team during an extended period of active operations she served the nontransportable wounded of six divisions during the advances at Glorieux, Fromereville, Bethincourt, Septsarges, Bantheville, and Dun-sur-Meuse. She courageously administered to the gravely wounded in the advanced area under the fire of shells and aerial bombs, rendering a service of particular value to the American Expeditionary Forces.

COWARD, JACOB M..................... | Colonel, Coast Artillery Corps, U. S. Army.
R—Trenton, N. J.
B—Allentown, N. J.
G. O. No. 60, W. D., 1920.

As a member of the American section of the Supreme War Council by his high professional qualifications and sound military judgment he rendered invaluable aid in solving the many complex problems that came before the Supreme War Council.

COX, ALBERT L..................... | Colonel, Field Artillery, U. S. Army.
R—Raleigh, N. C.
B—Raleigh, N. C.
G. O. No. 9, W. D., 1923.

As commanding officer of the 113th Field Artillery, 30th Division, during its organization, training, and active operations in the St. Mihiel and Meuse-Argonne offensives he displayed tireless energy, great resourcefulness, and military attainments of a high order. By his skillful and energetic handling of his regiment he rendered the maximum support to the Infantry to which he was attached so effectively that he aided materially in the successes achieved by our troops in those important engagements.

COX, CREED F..................... | Colonel, Field Artillery, U. S. Army.
R—Saddle, Va.
B—Bridle Creek, Va.
G. O. No. 15, W. D., 1923.

As commander of one or more detachments of the 4th Artillery Brigade in addition to his own regiment, the 77th Field Artillery, in the Aisne Marne, St. Mihiel, and Meuse-Argonne operations he rendered conspicuously valuable services. In the Meuse-Argonne offensive in charge of the barrage groupings of the 4th Artillery Brigade his high technical skill contributed in a marked way to the successful operations of the American forces. His untiring energy and devotion to duty served as a stimulus to the officers and men under his command.

COXE, ALEXANDER B..................... | Colonel (Cavalry), General Staff Corps, U. S. Army.
R—St. Paul, Minn.
B—Santa Fe, N. Mex.
G. O. No. 2, W. D., 1920.

He assisted in the production of an efficient intelligence service, and in organizing and sending to France the required intelligence personnel. His excellent judgment and pronounced knowledge of intelligence principles added greatly to the efficiency of the intelligence service.

CRAIG, CHARLES F..................... | Colonel, Medical Corps, U. S. Army.
R—Danbury, Conn.
B—Danbury, Conn.
G. O. No. 10, W. D., 1922.

For services as the organizer and administrator of Army schools for the development of laboratory personnel, thereby contributing one of the most important measures for the prevention and control of epidemic diseases throughout the Army.

CRAIG, DANIEL F..................... | Brigadier general, U. S. Army.
R—Garnett, Kans.
B—Mahaska County, Iowa.
G. O. No. 103, W. D., 1919.

He served with distinction as commanding officer of the 302d Field Artillery, 76th Division, and later, upon being promoted to the grade of brigadier general, as commanding general of the 157th Field Artillery Brigade, 82d Division, his service was equally conspicuous. Due to his aggressive leadership, his batteries were at all times close behind the advancing Infantry. The accurate support which they furnished was largely due to his management and technical skill as an artillerist.

CRAIG, MALIN..................... | Brigadier general, U. S. Army.
R—Philadelphia, Pa.
B—St. Joseph, Mo.
G. O. No. 12, W. D., 1919.

He served in turn as chief of staff of a division, a corps, and an army, in each of which capacities he exhibited great ability. His personal influence, aggressiveness, and untiring efforts were repeatedly displayed in the operations of the 1st Corps in the vicinity of Chateau-Thierry, on the Ourcq, and the Vesle during the St. Mihiel and Argonne-Meuse offensives.

CRAIN, JAMES K.
R—Cuero, Tex.
B—Hallettsville, Tex.
G. O. No. 78, W. D., 1919.

Colonel, Coast Artillery Corps, U. S. Army.
Successively as ordnance officer of the 42d Division, 1st Army Corps and Army, he displayed exceptional ability in the organization and administration of work of great magnitude. Encountering unforeseen and perplex problems, he solved them with initiative and sound judgment, showing a understanding of existing needs and conditions of the service. He was tire in energy and resourceful, proving at all times devoted to his important dut

CRAVATH, PAUL D.
R—New York, N. Y.
B—Berlin Heights, Ohio.
G. O. No. 46, W. D., 1919.

Representative of the Treasury Department.
With great ability, energy, and patience, he cooperated in international matt involving the interests of the American Expeditionary Forces. Establish and maintaining the most cordial relations with the British authorities, greatly contributed to the establishment of their effective cooperation w the military board of allied supply and in many other matters of extre importance.

CRAVENS, RICHARD K.
R—Muskogee, Indian Territory.
B—Fort Smith, Ark.
G. O. No. 19, W. D., 1920.

Colonel, Coast Artillery Corps, U. S. Army.
Both as adjutant and as assistant chief of staff, G-1, of the Headquarters Ar Artillery, 1st Army, American Expeditionary Forces, he exhibited milit attainments and ability of a high order. By his clear conception of his ft tion, his untiring energy, and in his proper exercise of initiative, he cont uted in a large measure to the successful employment of the Army Artil of the 1st Army during the St. Mihiel and Meuse-Argonne offensives.

CRENSHAW, RUSSELL SYDNOR.
R—Richmond, Va.
B—Richmond, Va.
G. O. No. 116, W. D., 1919.

Commander, U. S. Navy.
For services in connection with the Naval Overseas Transportation Ser and convoy system for cargo of transport fleet.

CRILE, GEORGE W.
R—Cleveland, Ohio.
B—Chili, Ohio.
G. O. No. 50, W. D., 1919.

Colonel, Medical Corps, U. S. Army.
By his skill, researches, and discoveries he saved the lives of many of wounded soldiers. His tireless efforts to devise new methods of treatn to prevent infection and surgical shock revolutionized Army surgery met with the greatest success.

CRONKHITE, ADELBERT.
R—Arizona.
B—Litchfield Center, N. Y.
G. O. No. 12, W. D., 1919.

Major general, U. S. Army.
He commanded the 80th Division during the Argonne-Meuse offensive, w he demonstrated great ability as a leader and proved himself a command initiative and courage.

CROOKSTON, WILLIAM J.
R—Pittsburgh, Pa.
B—Irwin, Pa.
G. O. No. 62, W. D., 1919.

Colonel, Medical Corps, U. S. Army.
As division surgeon he displayed marked ability of organization and adm tration throughout the service of the 28th Division in France. With judgment he supervised the location of dressing stations and field hosp and used remarkable discretion in directing the entire work of evacuati a large number of casualties. By constant vigilance and unceasing effo provided for the health and treatment of the troops with whom he ser displaying professional attainments of a high order.

CROWDER, ENOCH H.
R—Trenton, Mo.
B—Edinburg, Mo.
G. O. No. 144, W. D., 1918.

Major general, U. S. Army.
For services as provost marshal general in the preparation and operation o draft laws of the Nation during the war.

CRUIKSHANK, WILLIAM M.
R—Washington, D. C.
B—Washington, D. C.
G. O. No. 59, W. D., 1919.

Brigadier general, U. S. Army.
He commanded with ability the artillery of the 3d Division on the M during the German attack on July 15. Subsequently, during the adv on July 18, due to his tactical knowledge and successful placing of the ﬁ he greatly assisted in the repulse of the enemy. Later he rendered valt services as commander of the artillery of the 4th Army Corps.

CRUSAN, CLYDE B.
R—Pittsburgh, Pa.
B—Kellys Station, Pa.
G. O. No. 59, W. D., 1919.

Colonel, Quartermaster Corps, U. S. Army.
He was charged with the important duty of administering the supplies div of the Quartermaster Department of the American Expeditionary Fc where he exhibited organizing ability of the highest order. His efforts foresight had a marked influence on the successful delivery of rations, clot and other quartermaster supplies to combat troops.

CUBBISON, DONALD C.
R—Kansas City, Kans.
B—Harrisville, Pa.
G. O. No. 56, W. D., 1922.

Colonel, Field Artillery, U. S. Army.
Serving in turn as director, 2d Corps Artillery School, from January to ﬁ 1918; chief of staff of the artillery of the 1st and 4th Army Corps from M September, 1918; chief of field artillery section, Office of Chief of Arti American Expeditionary Forces, from September, 1918, to March, 19] performed his duties in a conspicuously meritorious manner at all times. his great energy, sound judgment, marked ability, and high profess attainments he contributed materially to the successes achieved again: enemy, rendering invaluable services to the American Expeditionary F

CULBERSON, WILLIAM L.
R—Hillsboro, Tex.
B—Clifton, Tex.
G. O. No. 78, W. D., 1919.

Lieutenant colonel, Infantry, U. S. Army.
He displayed extraordinary qualities of leadership and ability for organiz While engaged upon another mission he discovered six companies of inf which had been ordered to relieve a front-line unit, lost and confused, (the misdirection of the guides, who had lost their way. Coming upon companies when the men were beginning to straggle from the ranks, he r them, and by his personal efforts alone succeeded in bringing them tc position just before daylight and in time to take part in the pending tion.

DISTINGUISHED-SERVICE MEDAL   693

CULKIN, JOSEPH R.
  R—Rochester, N. Y.
  B—Oswego, N. Y.
  G. O. No. 126, W. D., 1919.

Major, Medical Corps, U. S. Army.
For services when in charge of Camp Hospital No. 1, at Camp Upton, N. Y., during the serious epidemic of influenza at this camp in September and October, 1918. Due to his great energy and good will and unwillingness to meet defeat in any form, remarkable results were obtained at this hospital.

CULVER, CLARENCE C.
  R—Milford, Nebr.
  B—Milford, Nebr.
  G. O. No. 69, W. D., 1919.

Colonel, Air Service, U. S. Army.
To Colonel Culver's untiring energy, close application, and perseverance is due the credit for having completed the coordination of the chain of events leading from the earliest conception of the radio telephone to the successful accomplishment of voice-commanded flying carried through to full fruition.

CURTIS, FRANK R.
  R—Mount Vernon, N. Y.
  B—Mount Vernon, N. Y.
  G. O. No. 3, W. D., 1921.

Colonel, Signal Corps, U. S. Army.
For services while on duty in the office of the Chief Signal Officer of the Army in the organization and training of technical troops of the Signal Corps.

CUSHING, HARVEY.
  R—Brookline, Mass.
  B—Cleveland, Ohio.
  G. O. No. 15, W. D., 1923.

Colonel, Medical Corps, U. S. Army.
As senior consultant of neurological surgery, American Expeditionary Forces and in direct charge of the treatment of gunshot wounds of the head in hospitals of the 1st Army, American Expeditionary Forces, during the Meuse-Argonne offensive, he performed conspicuous and distinguished service to the Government, and through his individual efforts in that capacity saved the lives of many severely wounded soldiers.

CUSHMAN, MRS. JAMES S.
  R—New York, N. Y.
  B—Ottawa, Ill.
  G. O. No. 73, W. D., 1919.

For services as chairman of the war work council of the Young Women's Christian Association of the United States of America.

CUTCHEON, FRANKLIN WARNER M.
  R—Locust Valley, Long Island, N. Y.
  B—Dexter, Mich.
  G. O. No. 89, W. D., 1919.

Lieutenant colonel, Infantry, U. S. Army.
As chairman of the Board of Contracts and Adjustments he supervised and conducted important negotiations with allied governments and their citizens with marked success. His complete knowledge of legal and financial matters coupled with his capacity for work were important factors in the successful management of the Army's fiscal affairs in Europe, rendering services of great value to the American Expeditionary Forces.

CUTCHINS, JOHN A.
  R—Richmond, Va.
  B—Richmond, Va.
  G. O. No. 49, W. D., 1922.

Lieutenant colonel, General Staff Corps, U. S. Army.
As G-2, 29th Division, from September, 1917, until January, 1918, and from July to December, 1918, he displayed sound judgment and exceptional ability in the organization and administration of that section of the division staff. Later as G-4, liaison officer, American section, Permanent International Armistice Commission, he rendered highly meritorious services in a position of great responsibility.

CUTHELL, CHESTER WELDE.
  R—New York, N. Y.
  B—New York, N. Y.
  G. O. No. 126, W. D., 1919.

As special representative of the Secretary of War he built up and supervised an organization to liquidate the claims of the United States against the European allied governments growing out of the purchases of war materials by these governments in the United States, and, by reducing to accurate and clear statements vast and intricate transactions, brought about agreements with the representatives of the allied governments which not only promoted and maintained harmonious feeling, but settled difficult financial relation happily, speedily, and justly, leaving on all sides a sense of appreciation of the accuracy and fair dealing of the Government of the United States in its business relations with the allied and associated governments.

CUTLER, ELLIOTT C.
  R—Brookline, Mass.
  B—Bangor, Me.
  G. O. No. 19, W. D., 1922.

Major, Medical Corps, U. S. Army.
As director of surgical teams and chief of the surgical service in hospital formations at the front during our activities on the Marne and the St. Mihiel and Meuse-Argonne offensives.

CUTLER, HARRY.
  R—Providence, R. I.
  B—Russia.
  G. O. No. 73, W. D., 1919.

Colonel, National Guard, Rhode Island (retired).
For services as chairman, executive committee of the Jewish Welfare Board.

DALEY, EDMUND L.
  R—Worcester, Mass.
  B—Worcester, Mass.
  G. O. No. 95, W. D., 1919.

Colonel, Corps of Engineers, U. S. Army.
He served with distinction as division engineer of the 3d Division and as commanding officer of the 6th Engineers. Due to his energy and resourcefulness, he accomplished arduous tasks with marked success. With remarkable skill he directed the laying out of the defense scheme of the positions taken in the Meuse-Argonne offensive, rendering services of inestimable value to the American Expeditionary Forces.

DALTON, ALBERT C.
  R—Clarkshill, Ind.
  B—Thorntown, Ind.
  G. O. No. 38, W. D., 1922.

Brigadier general, U. S. Army.
For services as general superintendent, Army transport services, and quartermaster, port of embarkation, Hoboken, N. J., from Nov. 1, 1917, to Nov. 5, 1918. Colonel Dalton displayed marked ability as an organizer and administrator, having under his supervision thousands of employees and subordinates. By his energy, capacity, and ability to get results he rendered services of great value to the Government.

DALY, CHARLES P.
  R—Junction City, Kans.
  B—St. Louis, Mo.
  G. O. No. 38, W. D., 1922.

Colonel, Quartermaster Corps, U. S. Army.
In aiding and improving the service of supply in the United States while on duty in the office of the Quartermaster General during the period when the development of supply methods in the United States was in process of initiation, his experience and knowledge of administrative, legal, and executive matters were of immense value to the Government. Later he rendered exceptionally meritorious service in the organization and operation of the general supply depot at New Orleans, La.

DALY, JOSEPH J.
R—New York, N. Y.
B—New York, N. Y.
G. O. No. 56, W. D., 1921.

Lieutenant colonel, Ordnance Department, U. S. Army.
For services as division ordnance officer, 27th Division, a position of great responsibility, involving many difficulties of supply and administration. With marked ability he adapted the American supply system to that used by the British units with which his division operated. He accomplished a great task and rendered services of eminent worth.

DANFORD, ROBERT M.
R—New Boston, Ill.
B—New Boston, Ill.
G. O. No. 47, W. D., 1919.

Brigadier general, U. S. Army.
While on duty in the office of the Chief of Field Artillery he displayed marked ability in planning the organization of field artillery replacement depots; he then proceeded to Camp Jackson, S. C., established this depot, and administered it during the remainder of the war with rare ability and judgment.

DARNALL, CARL ROGER
R—Milford, N. J.
B—Collin County, Tex.
G. O. No. 69, W. D., 1919.

Colonel, Medical Corps, U. S. Army.
He has rendered especially meritorious and distinguished service in organizing developing, and administering the supply division of the Medical Department, and it is due to his foresight, and ability that new sources of medical supplies were developed in this country so that adequate quantities of material were always available for use with the sick and wounded of the Army.

*DAVIDSON, FRED LINCOLN.
R—Cincinnati, Ohio.
B—Bucksport, Me.
G. O. No. 59, W. D., 1921.

Lieutenant colonel, Infantry, U. S. Army.
For services as division machine-gun officer, 3d Division. By his supervision and dispositions, he contributed materially to the success of the 7th Machine Gun Battalion at Chateau-Thierry in May, 1918, and that of the machine-gun units of the division in the repulse of the enemy offensive across the Marne July 15 to 18, 1918, and during the Meuse-Argonne campaign. He displayed at all times energy and excellent judgment under difficult conditions, and his work deserves high commendation.
Posthumously awarded. Medal presented to widow, Mrs. Fred L. Davidson.

DAVIE, PRESTON
R—Tuxedo Park, N. Y.
B—Louisville, Ky.
G. O. No. 111, W. D., 1919.

Lieutenant colonel, Quartermaster Corps, U. S. Army.
He organized the fuel and forage division of the War Department and also assisted in reorganizing the salvage service upon a most efficient basis to meet war conditions. By his sound judgment, marked legal and administrative ability, and unselfish devotion to duty he rendered conspicuous service in reorganizing and developing the real estate service of the War Department.

DAVIS, ABEL
R—Chicago, Ill.
B—Germany.
G. O. No. 9, W. D., 1923.
Distinguished service cross also awarded.

Colonel, Infantry, U. S. Army.
As commanding officer, 132d Infantry, 33d Division, he displayed in a marked degree the many and varied qualifications of a successful commanding officer of troops. In the organization and training of his regiment he brought it to a notably high state of efficiency and morale with great thoroughness and in a remarkably short time. Afterward he handled it in all its actions against the enemy with marked success, displaying courage, resourcefulness, tactical skill, and military leadership of the highest order.

DAVIS, CHARLES G.
R—Geneseo, Ill.
B—Geneseo, Ill.
G. O. No. 53, W. D., 1921.

Colonel, Field Artillery, U. S. Army.
For services while in command of the 123d Field Artillery, 33d Division, during the St. Mihiel and Meuse-Argonne offensives.

DAVIS, EDWARD
R—Chicago, Ill.
B—Litchfield, Ill.
G. O. No. 124, W. D., 1919.

Colonel, Cavalry, U. S. Army.
For services while serving as military attaché at The Hague, Netherlands.

DAVIS, EDWIN G.
R—Samaria, Idaho.
B—Samaria, Idaho.
G. O. No. 111, W. D., 1919.

Colonel, Judge Advocate General's Department, U. S. Army.
As chief of the disciplinary division of the office of the Judge Advocate General of the Army he contributed a most helpful means of avoiding serious errors in in the administration of military justice during the war.

DAVIS, JOSEPH R.
R—Lowell, Ark.
B—Springdale, Ark.
G. O. No. 95, W. D., 1919.

Colonel, Field Artillery, U. S. Army.
He commanded the 15th Field Artillery throughout all the major operations in which the Second Division participated, at all times proving himself an officer of unusual ability and sound judgment. Inspiring the members of his command by his aggressive spirit, he kept his regiment at all times in closest proximity to the infantry units which it supported, thereby contributing materially to the successes achieved by his division against the enemy.

DAVIS, MILTON F.
R—McCoy, Oreg.
B—Milton, Minn.
G. O. No. 15, W. D., 1923.

Colonel, Signal Corps, U. S. Army.
As chief of the schools section, division of military aeronautics, his work in perfecting a system of training was thorough and complete. His soundness of judgment, fairness in dealing with all the boards of officers and branches of the service, and unusual executive ability made his work a decisive factor in the successful production of trained air personnel. He rendered service of the highest order to the Government in a position of great responsibility

DAVIS, RICHMOND P.
R—Statesville, N. C.
B—Statesville, N. C.
G. O. No. 19, W. D., 1922.

Brigadier general, U. S. Army.
For services as acting chief of the 9th Corps Artillery, in which position his direction of Artillery employment and his intelligent comment on its employment by subordinate commanders was conspicuous.

DAVIS, ROBERT C.
R—Lancaster, Pa.
B—Lancaster, Pa.
G. O. No. 12, W. D., 1919.

Brigadier general, U. S. Army.
As adjutant general of the American Expeditionary Forces he has performed his exacting duties with high professional skill and administrative ability. The exceptional efficiency of the Adjutant General's Department under his direction was a material factor in the success of the staff work at General Headquarters.

DISTINGUISHED-SERVICE MEDAL 695

DAVIS, WILLIAM C
    R—McGrawville, N. Y.
    B—McGrawville, N. Y.
    G. O. No. 59, W. D., 1919.

Brigadier general, U. S. Army.
In command of the Artillery support of the Fifth Corps in November he rendered services of the highest order. Through his energy, intelligence, and skill his guns were ever ready for an emergency. The successes of the operations between the Meuse and the Argonne Forest were in a measure due to his strong support of the attacking Infantry.

*DAVIS, WILLIAM D
    R—Neosho, Mo.
    B—Duplain, Mich.
    G. O. No. 98, W. D., 1919.
    Distinguished service cross also awarded.

Colonel, Infantry, U. S. Army.
He served with marked success as commanding officer of the 361st Infantry, displaying military attainments of a high order. Inspiring his men by his faithful devotion to duty, he proved a potent factor in the achievements of the 91st Division. While ably directing his regiment in action during the early part of November he was killed by an enemy shell.
Posthumously awarded. Medal presented to widow, Mrs. Abbie Greene Davis.

DAVISON, HENRY P
    R—New York, N. Y.
    B—Troy, Pa.
    G. O. No. 95, W. D., 1919.

As chairman of the war council, American Red Cross, he assumed general direction of the war measures of that society, and by the exercise of rare tact and consummate powers of construction and direction brought it to a perfection of organization which made it possible to extend relief promptly and bountifully to our armies and to those of the allied nations. His dynamic qualities as a financier and his forceful personality assured to the soldier in the field and to the inhabitants of the devastated countries of Europe systematized measures of relief beyond the limits of specific statement.

DAWES, CHARLES G
    R—Evanston, Ill.
    B—Marietta, Ohio.
    G. O. No. 12, W. D., 1919.

Brigadier general, U. S. Army.
He rendered most conspicuous services in the organization of the general purchasing board as general purchasing agent of the American Expeditionary Forces and as the representative of the U. S. Army on the military board of allied supply. His rare abilities, sound business judgment, and aggressive energy were invaluable in securing needed supplies for the American armies in Europe.

DAY, LEE GARNET
    R—New York, N. Y.
    B—New York, N. Y.
    G. O. No. 59, W. D., 1919.

Major, Quartermaster Corps, U. S. Army.
In command of the regulating station at St. Dizier, France, he displayed extraordinary ability in the promptness with which he organized and assured a steady flow of supplies to the 1st Army in the advance against the St. Mihiel salient and in the Argonne offensive. It was largely due to his splendid efforts in a time of great emergency that our troops were provided with necessary ammunition and supplies.

DEAN, ELMER A
    R—Centerville, Tenn.
    B—Centerville, Tenn.
    G. O. No. 89, W. D., 1919.

Colonel, Medical Corps, U. S. Army.
He came to France with a base hospital unit, which he established. Later he organized and commanded the first large hospital center at Bazoilles. The success of this center in caring for a large number of sick and wounded was due in a large measure to his high professional attainments, zeal, and extraordinary executive ability.

DEARMOND, EDWARD H
    R—Butler, Mo.
    B—Greenfield, Mo.
    G. O. No. 31, W. D., 1922.

Brigadier general, U. S. Army.
As chief of staff of the 32d Division during the period of its training in the United States and in France, he contributed largely to the organization and efficiency of that division. As chief of the Field Artillery Section of the office of the Chief of Artillery, American Expeditionary Forces, he perfected the field artillery training system in France, and by his marked ability for organization and his able supervision of that training, rendered services of great value.

DEBEVOISE, CHARLES I
    R—Brooklyn, N. Y.
    B—Brooklyn, N. Y.
    G. O. No. 89, W. D., 1919.

Brigadier general, U. S. Army.
He served with credit as commander of trains and military police of the 27th Division. Later, in command of the 107th Infantry, 27th Division, he proved himself to be an energetic and resourceful leader during the operations against the Hindenburg line and those on the La Selle River. After being promoted to brigadier general he continued to render valuable services to the American Expeditionary Forces as commander of the 53d Infantry Brigade, rendering conspicuous services to the American Expeditionary Forces.

DEEMS, CLARENCE, Jr
    R—Baltimore, Md.
    B—Charlottesville, Va.
    G. O. No. 87, W. D., 1919.

Colonel, Field Artillery, U. S. Army.
He served creditably as commanding officer of the 321st Field Artillery, 82d Division, giving proof of conspicuous military attainments. Through his tireless energy and technical skill as an artillerist his regiment gave most effective assistance to the infantry which it supported, and at all times furnished whole-hearted cooperation to the infantry in the operations against the enemy.

DELAFIELD, JOHN ROSS
    R—New York, N. Y.
    B—New York, N. Y.
    G. O. No. 47, W. D., 1921.

Colonel, Ordnance Department, U. S. Army.
For services as chairman of the War Department board of contract adjustment.

DELANEY, JOHN T
    R—New York, N. Y.
    B—New York, N. Y.
    G. O. No. 56, W. D., 1922.

Lieutenant colonel, Field Artillery, U. S. Army.
As regimental commander of the 104th Field Artillery, 27th Division, he demonstrated professional attainments and ability of the highest order. By his sound tactical judgment and superior knowledge of artillery he most successfully directed his units in support of the 157th Infantry Brigade in the operations north of Verdun, Nov. 4 to 11, 1918. By keeping his elements close to the attacking Infantry he contributed in no small measure to the success of the Infantry brigade in these operations. He rendered services of conspicuous merit and signal worth to the American Expeditionary Forces.

DeLaney, Matthew A R—Waymart, Pa. B—Waymart, Pa. G. O. No. 43, W. D., 1922.	Colonel, Medical Corps, U. S. Army. As commanding officer, Base Hospital No. 10, at Le Treport, France, from May 6, 1917, to March, 1918, he displayed tireless energy and military attain ments of a high order in the efficient operation of this important hospital on the western front. By his marked devotion to duty and splendid ad ministrative abilities, great numbers of our own and allied sick and wounded were cared for, resulting in the saving of many lives. His services were of great value to the American Expeditionary Forces.
Delano, Frederic Adrian R—Washington, D. C. B—China. G. O No. 47, W. D., 1921.	Colonel, Transportation Corps, U. S. Army. For services as deputy of the Director General of Transportation, American Expeditionary Forces, in connection with the evacuation of American troops to the ports of embarkation, France, and later in connection with the work of the liquidation commission.
*Delano, Jane A R—Washington, D. C. B—Watkins, N. Y. G. O. No. 61, W. D., 1919.	Director, Department of Nursing, American Red Cross. She applied her great energy and used her powerful influence among the nurses of the country to secure enrollments in the American Red Cross. Through her great efforts and devotion to duty 18,732 nurses were secured and trans ferred to the Army Nurse Corps for service during the war. Thus she was a great factor in assisting the Medical Department in caring for the sick and wounded. Posthumously awarded. Medal presented to American Red Cross.
Dengler, Frederick L R—Hot Springs, Ark. B—Hot Springs, Ark. G. O. No. 15, W. D., 1923.	Colonel (Coast Artillery Corps), General Staff Corps, U. S. Army. As a member of the intelligence section of the General Staff, American Expedi tionary Forces, he efficiently organized and directed with rare ability the operation of the subsection dealing with the enemy's man power, war material, economic conditions, prisoners and documents, including the enemy press. Later he was sent to the United States to expedite the organization and train ing of the intelligence personnel of the division selected for overseas service and also to assist in the coordination of the work of the Intelligence Section of the American Expeditionary Forces with that of the War Department. In all these positions he displayed rare judgment, great initiative, and unremit ting devotion to duty.
Denson, Eley P R—High Point, N. C. B—Trinity, N C. G. O. No. 14. W. D., 1923.	Lieutenant colonel (Infantry), General Staff Corps, U. S. Army. For services as assistant chief of staff, G–3, 28th Division, from Sept. 15 to Nov. 15, 1918. In this position he displayed untiring energy, sound pro fessional judgment and tactical skill, and unremitting attention to duty thus contributing extremely valuable services to the 28th Division in it operations against the enemy.
Derby, Richard R—New York, N. Y. B—New York, N. Y. G. O. No. 39, W. D., 1920.	Lieutenant colonel, Medical Corps, U. S. Army. As sanitary inspector of the 2d Division, and in charge of the front-line hospi talization and evacuation of the wounded during the active operations of the division in the Marne area, and later as division surgeon during the Meuse Argonne offensive, he demonstrated high professional attainments, excellen judgment, and gallantry in the execution of his important duties. Due to his energy, the sanitary units under his control were amply provided with facilities for the proper care of the sick and wounded in the field. He has given services of significant worth to the American Expeditionary Forces.
de Tarnowsky, George R—Chicago, Ill. B—France. G. O. No. 27, W. D., 1922.	Lieutenant colonel, Medical Corps, U. S. Army. In organizing and commanding American Red Cross Military Hospital No. 8 American Expeditionary Forces. Notwithstanding the serious deficiency in personnel and material, Colonel de Tarnowsky, by his energy and efficien administration, received and treated great numbers of wounded evacuated to the Paris district during June and July, 1918.
Devol, Carroll A R—Waterford, Ohio. B—Waterford, Ohio. G. O. No. 73, W. D., 1919.	Major general, U. S. Army, retired. General Devol, first as depot quartermaster and later as zone supply officer in San Francisco, handled the service of supply and service of transportation on the Pacific coast during the war, being responsible for the supply of troop serving in the Philippines, Hawaii, Siberia, and Alaska and the camps on the Pacific coast. He handled this large responsibility with ability, good judg ment, and conspicuous success.
Dewey, Bradley R—Pittsburgh, Pa. B—Burlington, Vt. G. O. No. 47, W. D., 1919.	Colonel, Chemical Warfare Service, U. S. Army. As chief of the gas defense production division in achieving under most try ing circumstances remarkable results in supplying the American Expedition ary Forces with sufficient number of gas masks of high grade and of improved design.
DeWitt, John L R—Fort Monroe, Va. B—Sidney, Nebr. G. O. No. 59, W. D., 1919.	Colonel (Infantry), General Staff Corps, U. S. Army. He organized the supply section of the General Staff of the 1st Army and suc cessfully administered this important section during all the operations of that command. The results obtained by his untiring efforts and brilliant profes sional ability had a marked influence on the successes attained by the 1s Army.
Dickman, Joseph T R—Wapakoneta, Ohio. B—Dayton, Ohio. G. O. No. 27, W. D., 1920.	Major general, U. S. Army. For services as commander of the 3d Army, American Expeditionary Forces He commanded the 3d Division and contributed in large measure to succes in hurling back the final enemy general attack commencing July 14, 1918 He participated in the offensive operations northward to Vesle River; com manded the 4th Army Corps from Aug. 18 to Oct. 11, 1918, including th operation of the reduction of the St. Mihiel salient, and the 1st Army Corp during the Meuse-Argonne operations from Oct. 12 until after the armistice Later he commanded the 3d Army of Occupation at Coblenz, Germany.

DISTINGUISHED-SERVICE MEDAL 697

DICKSON, ROBERT A.
R—Waterford, N. Y.
B—Lansingburg, N. Y.
G. O. No. 4, W. D., 1923.

Lieutenant colonel, Sanitary Corps, U. S. Army.
As officer in charge of the administrative division in the office of the chief surgeon, American Expeditionary Forces, by his foresight, executive ability, and unusual knowledge of administrative details he successfully organized and directed a record system which functioned on a highly efficient basis throughout the World War, thereby rendering, in a position of great responsibility, conspicuous services to the American Expeditionary Forces.

DILLARD, JAMES B.
R—New Orleans, La.
B—Norfolk, Va.
G. O. No. 69, W. D., 1919.

Colonel, Ordnance Department, U. S. Army.
For services as chief of the Heavy Artillery section of the carriage division of the office of the Chief of Ordnance, in which capacity he was charged with the design and development of all railway and other heavy artillery; and later as chief of the engineering division of the office of the Chief of Ordnance, in which capacity he was charged with the design and development of all articles of ordnance supplied to the U. S. Army.

DILLON, THEODORE H.
R—Bedford, Ind.
B—Center Valley, Ind.
G. O. No. 59, W. D., 1921

Colonel, Corps of Engineers, U. S. Army.
For services as assistant chief engineer, 1st Army, a position of great responsibility. During the St. Mihiel and Meuse-Argonne operations he administered the first engineer troops and the organization, plans, and field work of the engineer plans, operations, and information section and other engineer enterprises conducted in the 1st Army. By his energy and keen application he rendered services of much worth.

DISQUE, BRICE PURSELL.
R—Cincinnati, Ohio.
B—California, Ohio.
G. O. No. 69, W. D., 1919.

Brigadier general, U. S. Army.
For services rendered in connection with the organization and administration of the spruce production activities of the Bureau of Aircraft Production while serving as officer in charge of the spruce production division and president of the United States Spruce Production Corporation.

DODD, TOWNSEND F.
R—Waukegan, Ill.
B—Anna, Ill.
G. O. No. 50, W. D., 1919.

Colonel, Air Service, U. S. Army.
He organized the aviation training school at Issoudon and successfully conducted the negotiations for the first purchase of aeroplanes from allied governments for the use of the American Expeditionary Forces. He later served with distinction as chief of the supply section, Air Service, American Expeditionary Forces, and as technical adviser and information officer of the Chief of the Air Service, 1st Army.

DODDS, WILLIAM H., jr.
R—Detroit, Mich.
B—Detroit, Mich.
G. O. No. 38, W. D., 1922.

Colonel, Field Artillery, U. S. Army.
As commander of the 6th Field Artillery, 1st Division, he handled the regiment so brilliantly under severe conditions throughout the St. Mihiel operation, Sept. 12-13, 1918, and the Meuse-Argonne operations, Sept. 30 to Nov. 11, 1918, that the regiment demonstrated an unusually high degree of efficiency and morale. He repeatedly displayed superior tactical judgment and knowledge of artillery, and by his exceptional ability, leadership, and devotion to duty rendered the maximum support to the Infantry of the 1st Division in effectively executing the most difficult missions assigned to him, thus rendering conspicuous services to the American Expeditionary Forces.

D'OLIER, FRANKLIN.
R—Riverton, N. J.
B—Burlington, N. J.
G. O. No. 62, W. D., 1919.

Lieutenant colonel, Quartermaster Corps, U. S. Army.
He displayed marked ability in the organization and efficient administration of the American salvage depot at St. Pierre des Corps, of which he was the commanding officer. To his untiring zeal and constant devotion to duty is due the success with which this plant, the largest industrial undertaking in the American Expeditionary Forces, was operated.

DONALDSON, THOMAS Q.
R—Greenville, S. C.
B—Greenville, S. C.
G. O. No. 89, W. D., 1919.

Brigadier general, U. S. Army.
As inspector general of the services of supply, by his energy, sound judgment, and able management he organized and brought to a state of marked efficiency the Inspector General's Department in the services of supply. He proved a most potent factor in raising the standard of discipline throughout the command, rendering services of conspicuous worth.

DONAVIN, KIRKWOOD HARRY.
R—Columbus, Ohio.
B—Delaware, Ohio.
G. O. No. 116, W. D., 1919.

Commander, U. S. Navy.
For services as chief of staff of the commander, Cruiser and Transport Fleet, Newport News division.

DONOVAN, WILLIAM J.
R—Buffalo, N. Y.
B—Buffalo, N. Y.
G. O. No. 43, W. D., 1922.
Medal of honor and distinguished-service cross also awarded.

Colonel, Infantry, U. S. Army.
As battalion commander 165th Infantry, 42d Division, during its operations in the Baccarat sector July 28-31, 1918, he demonstrated high professional attainments and marked ability. He displayed conspicuous energy and most efficient leadership in the advance of his battalion across the Ourcq River and the capture of strong enemy positions. In October, 1918, as lieutenant colonel he commanded the same regiment with marked success and distinction in the Meuse-Argonne offensive. His devotion to duty, heroism, and pronounced qualities of a commander enabled him to successfully accomplish all missions assigned to him in this important operation. From Jan. 3 to Mar. 3, 1919, as inspector instructor, Provost Marshall General's Department, he rendered services of great value to the American Expeditionary Forces.

DOREY, HALSTEAD.
R—St. Louis, Mo.
B—St. Louis, Mo.
G. O. No. 59, W. D., 1919.
Distinguished-service cross also awarded.

Colonel, Infantry, U. S. Army.
He commanded with distinction the 4th Infantry, 3d Division, during the battle of the Marne, the advance from the Marne to the Ourcq, and in the St. Mihiel and Argonne-Meuse offensives. It was his regiment that led the advance to the Ourcq, capturing Charmel, Charmel-Chateau, Villardelle Ferme, and Roncheres. The successes attained by his command were greatly influenced by the high qualities of leadership he continually displayed in all these operations.

698   DECORATIONS, U. S. ARMY, 1862–1926

DORR, GOLDTHWAITE H.
R—New York, N. Y.
B—Newark, N. J.
G. O. No. 2, W. D., 1920.

Assistant director of munitions.
His assistance to the director of munitions in procuring supplies and equipment for the Army and his subsequent activities in the settlement of the complex contractual relations resulting therefrom were of signal value to the United States and its Army.

DORSEY, FRANK M.
R—Cleveland Heights, Ohio.
B—Dresden, Ohio.
G. O. No. 69, W. D., 1919.

Colonel, Chemical Warfare Service, U. S. Army.
As a civilian and as chief of development division, Chemical Warfare Service, he has displayed fine technical skill and administrative ability in developing materials and processes which have contributed greatly to the achievements of the Chemical Warfare Service during the war.

DOWELL, CASSIUS M.
R—Terre Haute, Ind.
B—Landes, Ill.
G. O. No. 3, W. D., 1924.

Lieutenant colonel, Judge Advocate General's Department, U. S. Army.
As an assistant to the provost marshal general, Apr. 10 to Sept. 3, 1917, he assisted in the administration of the selective service law, being charged with the responsibility of the appointments of all local and district draft boards. As judge advocate, 26th Division, Sept. 3, 1917, to Jan. 2, 1918; chief of staff, 26th Division, Jan. 2, 1918, to Apr. 17, 1918; lieutenant colonel, 102d Infantry, and for part of period commanding officer of that regiment, Apr. 17 to June 13, 1918; G–3, 26th Division, Sept. 15 to Dec. 31, 1918, he displayed sound tactical judgment, administrative and executive qualities of a high order, and unremitting attention and devotion to his duties, thus rendering services of great value to his Government in positions of great responsibility.

DOYLE, LUKE C.
R—Worcester, Mass.
B—Worcester, Mass.
G. O. No. 59, W. D., 1919.

Major, Sanitary Corps, U. S. Army.
As assistant regulating officer, G–4, General Headquarters, American Expeditionary Forces, he arranged the schedules of hospital and medical supply trains with marked ability and succeeded in maintaining those schedules, despite numerous difficulties. His aggressive action in time of emergency, whereby he surmounted unforeseen obstacles, together with the excellent performance of his duties, were material factors in the alleviation of much suffering and in the saving of many lives among the wounded sent from the front.

DRAIN, JAMES A.
R—Washington, D. C.
B—Warren County, Ill.
G. O. No. 31, W. D., 1922.

Lieutenant colonel, Ordnance Department, U. S. Army.
From his experience as ordnance officer of the 1st Division during its early months in France he rendered valuable service in assisting the Chief of Ordnance, American Expeditionary Forces, in formulating the policies for the supply and maintenance of ordnance for subsequent divisions. Later he performed important work in charge of the machine gun and small arms division in the office of the Chief of Ordnance, American Expeditionary Forces, and finally rendered service of a high order in representing his Government as American member of the Anglo-American Tank Commission.

DRAKE, CHARLES B.
R—Old Forge, Pa.
B—Old Forge, Pa.
G. O. No. 18, W. D., 1919.
Distinguished-service cross also awarded.

Brigadier general, U. S. Army.
For conspicuous service in the organization of the Motor Transport Corps.

DRAKE, FRANCIS E.
R—New York, N. Y.
B—Farmington, Mich.
G. O. No. 56, W. D., 1922.

Lieutenant colonel, Corps of Engineers, U. S. Army.
He served as chief of control bureau, office of general purchasing agent, American Expeditionary Forces. Through his office, for the purpose of coordination and approval, passed all the purchases of the American Expeditionary Forces in France, and due to his highly efficient organization in connection with the supply procurement work, close and harmonious relations were sustained at all times with the French Government. His unusual tact, marked ability, and great energy in a position of great responsibility were of incalculable benefit to the supply service of the American Expeditionary Forces.

DRAVO, RALPH M.
R—Edgeworth, Pa.
B—Pittsburgh, Pa.
G. O. No. 124, W. D., 1919.

As chief of the Pittsburgh ordnance district, in which capacity he maintained at all times the greatest degree of intelligent and enthusiastic cooperation between the Ordnance Department and manufacturers in his district, thereby attaining the maximum production of munitions in a minimum time; and also as chairman of the Pittsburgh ordnance district claims board, in which capacity his services have been invaluable to the Nation in adjusting equitably the $210,000,000 worth of outstanding contracts in his district in force at the signing of the armistice.

DRISCOLL, THOMAS A.
R—San Mateo, Calif.
B—Virginia City, Nev.
G. O. No. 56, W. D., 1922.

Lieutenant colonel, Infantry, U. S. Army.
As assistant chief of staff, G–2, 91st Division, during the operations of the division in the Meuse-Argonne offensive, and during the advance from the Lys to and beyond the Scheldt River, by his keen foresight, discriminating judgment, and organizing ability he was able at all times to give to his commanding officer accurate and complete information of the enemy dispositions and to furnish valuable assistance in the preparation of all attack orders thereby rendering services of inestimable value to the success of the division

DRUM, HUGH A.
R—Boston, Mass.
B—Sault Ste. Marie, Mich.
G. O. No. 12, W. D., 1919.

Brigadier general, U. S. Army.
Upon him as chief of staff of the 1st Army devolved the important duty of organizing the headquarters of this command and of coordinating the detailed staff work in its operations in the St. Mihiel and Argonne-Meuse offensives His tact, zeal, and high professional attainments had a marked influence on the success that attended the operations of the 1st Army.

DISTINGUISHED-SERVICE MEDAL 699

DUFFY, FRANCIS P.
  R—New York, N. Y.
  B—Canada.
  G. O. No. 62, W. D., 1919.
  Distinguished-service cross also awarded.

Captain, chaplain, 165th Infantry, 42d Division, U. S. Army.
He performed with distinction his combined duties as regimental and division chaplain, stimulating the work of all with whom he came in contact. When his division was in rest areas, he was tireless and devoted in his efforts to help all with whom he served. Whether in the front-line trenches or in an attack, he was with the troops, encouraging them to greater effort, an example of fearlessness and devotion to duty, helping to care for the sick and wounded, administering to the dying, and arranging for the burial of the dead.

DUGAN, THOMAS B.
  R—Baltimore, Md.
  B—Baltimore, Md.
  G. O. No. 59, W. D., 1919.

Brigadier general, U. S. Army.
He commanded the 70th Infantry Brigade, 35th Division, during a part of the Meuse-Argonne offensive with great distinction and marked ability. By his painstaking energy, zeal, and great initiative he proved to be a material factor in the successes of the division.

DUNCAN, GEORGE B.
  R—Lexington, Ky.
  B—Lexington, Ky.
  G. O. No. 12, W. D., 1919.

Major general, U. S. Army.
Arriving in France with the first contingent of American troops, he commanded in turn a regiment, brigade, and division with conspicuous success. In the command of the 77th Division in the Baccarat sector his sound military judgment, energy, and resolution were important factors in the successes gained. Later, in command of the 82d Division in the Argonne-Meuse offensive, he proved himself a brilliant leader, with great force and energy.

DUNLAP, WILLIAM R.
  R—Pittsburgh, Pa.
  B—Dubois, Pa.
  G. O. No. 15, W. D., 1923.

Colonel, Infantry, U. S. Army.
Promoted in turn captain, major, lieutenant colonel, and colonel, while serving with the Infantry regiments of the 28th Division, he displayed unusual administrative, executive, and organizing ability and sound judgment. His brilliant leadership of his battalion in action against the enemy, and later, that of the regiment, testified to the unusual skill and soldierly qualities of this officer. Colonel Dunlap's services contributed in a marked degree to the successful operations of the 28th Division and the American forces in France.

DUNN, JOHN M.
  R—Wilmington, Del.
  B—Wilmington, Del.
  G. O. No. 73, W. D., 1919.

Colonel (Coast Artillery Corps), General Staff Corps, U. S. Army.
For services as chief of the positive branch, military intelligence division, General Staff. To his untiring energy, zeal, and ability the efficiency of the service of gathering, collating, and distributing military information is largely due.

DUNWOODY, HALSEY
  R—Scranton, Pa.
  B—Washington, D. C.
  G. O. No. 62, W. D., 1919.

Colonel (Coast Artillery Corps), Signal Corps, U. S. Army.
As chief of supply and assistant chief of Air Service, by his energy, tact, and executive ability, he built up an efficient supply service, capable of meeting the program for material, airplanes, motors, and equipment. He established and maintained excellent relations with the allied military authorities. His service was marked by exceptional administrative ability, comprehensive knowledge of the needs and conditions of the service, and whole-hearted devotion to his important tasks.

EARLE, RALPH
  R—Worcester, Mass.
  B—Worcester, Mass.
  G. O. No. 2, W. D., 1920.

Admiral, U. S. Navy.
For services as chief of the Bureau of Ordnance, Navy Department, during the World War, in which position, by his close cooperation and energetic efforts, he greatly assisted the War Department in the arming of its troop and cargo transports.

EASBY-SMITH, JAMES S.
  R—Washington, D. C.
  B—Tuskaloosa, Ala.
  G. O. No. 10, W. D., 1920.

Colonel, Judge Advocate General's Department, U. S. Army.
For services to the Government in connection with the administration of the selective service law during the war. To all of the tasks assigned him he brought an indefatigable energy and rare unselfish devotion, without which their accomplishment would have been impossible.

ECKELS, CHARLES B.
  R—Washington, D. C.
  B—Harrisburg, Pa.
  G. O. No. 38, W. D., 1922.

Lieutenant colonel, Quartermaster Corps, U. S. Army.
As assistant to the chief quartermaster, American Expeditionary Forces, from July 23, 1917, to Jan. 31, 1919. During this period he served as chief of the finance division of the chief quartermaster's office and successfully handled the numerous complex financial questions arising in the American Expeditionary Forces in France, England, and Italy. He also performed the duty of chief disbursing officer for the American Expeditionary Forces in procuring and transferring funds for disbursement by the finance officers of the several services, until the establishment of the financial requisition officer. The success with which these offices of great responsibility functioned was due largely to his exceptional ability, devotion to duty, and conspicuous services.

*EDGAR, CHARLES
  R—Essex Falls, N. J.
  B—Metuchen, N. J.
  G. O. No. 15, W. D., 1923.

Director of lumber, War Industries Board.
For services in connection with the operations of the war industries board during the World War. In his position as director of one of the sections of the board he rendered, through his broad vision, distinguished capacity, and business ability, services of inestimable value in marshaling the industrial forces of the Nation and mobilizing its economic resources—marked factors in assisting to make military success attainable. As director of lumber, he rendered through his untiring efforts and devotion to duty exceptionally valuable service to the War Department in connection with the procurement of lumber for the Army.
Posthumously awarded. Medal presented to widow, Mrs. Charles Edgar.

EDGAR, CLINTON G.
R—Detroit, Mich.
B—Detroit, Mich.
G. O. No. 15, W. D., 1923.

Colonel, Signal Corps, U. S. Army.
For services as officer in charge of the construction division, Signal Corps, aviation section. Being a trained engineer with exceptional capacity for organization and execution, he was placed in charge of the construction division, Signal Corps, and had complete charge and responsibility for all buildings constructed for the Air Service, which consisted of 27 aviation fields, 9 depots, 2 experimental stations, as well as many minor activities. He originated and installed the system of securing lands for all aviation fields, securing grants and gifts of all facilities, including water and electric lights. He was responsible for the conception, design, and production of the all-steel demountable standard hangar adopted by the Army and Navy for use in the Air Service. By his untiring energy, sound judgment, and large grasp of construction problems, he has rendered services of inestimable value to the Government in a position of great responsibility.

EDIE, ELLIOTT B.
R—Connellsville, Pa.
B—Baltimore, Md.
G. O. No. 56, W. D., 1921.

Lieutenant colonel, Medical Corps, U. S. Army.
As commander of the 305th Sanitary Train, consisting of the 317th, 318th, 319th and 320th Field Hospitals and later as division surgeon, 80th Division, a position of great responsibility, he maintained suitable dressing stations and provided for the continuous evacuation of the wounded in an exceptionally efficient manner under conditions of almost constant fire.

EDIE, GUY L.
R—Christiansburg, Va.
B—Christiansburg, Va.
G. O. No. 59, W. D., 1919.

Colonel, Medical Corps, U. S. Army.
He was placed in charge of the medical service at Brest at the time when it became the chief port of debarkation for American troops and at a period when the arrival of troops in unprecedented numbers, and with many sick overwhelmed all medical arrangements for their care. By his great resourcefulness he successfully overcame the many difficult problems that were presented.

EDWARDS, OLIVER.
R—Chesterfield, Mass.
B—Chesterfield, Mass.
G. O. No. 47, W. D., 1919.

Brigadier general, U. S. Army.
Due to his rare ability and high professional attainments he was selected to organize the machine-gun training center, the success of which was, in a large measure, due to his zealous and energetic administration.

EICHELBERGER, ROBERT L.
R—Urbana, Ohio.
B—Urbana, Ohio.
G. O. No. 56, W. D., 1922.
Distinguished-service cross also awarded.

Lieutenant colonel (Infantry), General Staff Corps, U. S. Army.
As assistant chief of staff, G-2, with the American Expeditionary Forces in Siberia, he organized and directed the intelligence service of the American Expeditionary Forces in Siberia in a most able manner and under most trying circumstances. By his keen foresight, discriminating judgment, and brilliant professional attainments, exercised through his efficiently established organization, he was able to keep his commanding general well and fully informed at all times. His tireless energy and his keen insight into local conditions gave him a masterful grasp of the situation, which contributed materially to the success of the forces in Siberia. He rendered most conspicuous services of inestimable value to the Government in a position of great responsibility.

EISENHOWER, DWIGHT D.
R—Abilene, Kans.
B—Greyson, Tex.
G. O. No. 43, W. D., 1922.

Lieutenant colonel, Tank Corps, U. S. Army.
While commanding officer of the Tank Corps training center from Mar. 2? 1918, to Nov. 18, 1918, at Camp Colt. Gettysburg, Pa., he displayed unusual zeal, foresight, and marked administrative ability in the organization, training, and preparation for overseas service of technical troops of the Tank Corps

EISENMAN, CHARLES.
R—Cleveland, Ohio.
B—New York, N. Y.
G. O. No. 47, W. D., 1919.

Vice chairman of committee on supplies, Council of National Defense.
His energy, courage, business ability, and foresight did much to enlist American industry in the service of our country and thus make possible the prompt and proper equipment of our armies with clothing and equipage.

ELLIOTT, WILLIAM.
R—San Rafael, Calif.
B—Canada.
G. O. No. 59, W. D., 1919.

Colonel, Quartermaster Corps, U. S. Army.
As quartermaster at Langres and at the regulating station at Is-sur-Tille, h energy and thorough knowledge of methods and standards of supply hav been of the greatest value to the Government, particularly while depot quartermaster at Is-sur-Tille, during a period when the successful operations o some 20 divisions were dependent upon receiving supplies from that depo

ELTINGE, LEROY.
R—Kingston, N. Y.
B—South Woodstock, N. Y.
G. O. No. 87, W. D., 1919.

Brigadier general, U. S. Army.
As a member of the operations section, General Staff, General Headquarter American Expeditionary Forces, he exhibited sound military judgment an foresight in drafting important plans. Later as deputy chief of staff of th American Expeditionary Forces throughout the period of active operation and thereafter he discharged the important and complex duties of his position with admirable efficiency and by his untiring efforts and devotion t duty rendered conspicuous service to the Government.

ELY, HANSON E.
R—Iowa City, Iowa.
B—Buffalo Grove, Iowa.
G. O. No. 46, W. D., 1920.
Distinguished service cross also awarded.

Major general, U. S. Army.
He commanded, with skill and marked ability, a regiment in trench operation north of Toul, west of Montdidier, and during the attack at Cantigny. Late as a brigade commander during the Aisne-Marne and St. Mihiel offensive and in the attack on the strong enemy position of Mont Blanc Ridge; and as division commander during the latter phase of the Meuse-Argonne offensiv he demonstrated rare qualities of leadership.

EMBICK, STANLEY D.
R—Boiling Springs, Pa.
B—Greencastle, Pa.
G. O. No. 69, W. D., 1919.

Colonel, Signal Corps, U. S. Army.
As a member of the American section of the Supreme War Council, by his hig professional qualifications, his breadth of vision, and his sound militar judgment, he has rendered invaluable aid in solving the many complex pro lems that have come before the Supreme War Council.

EMERSON, HAVEN
R—New York, N. Y.
B—New York, N. Y.
G. O. No. 3, W. D., 1922.

Lieutenant colonel, Medical Corps, U. S. Army.
As chief epidemiologist of the office of the Chief surgeon, American Expeditionary Forces, where he perfected a system of keeping daily checks on all of the many contagious diseases which afflicted the American Expeditionary Forces. Much sickness and many lives were saved by this system, the practical working of which was due to the experience and tireless energy of this officer.

EMERSON, THOMAS HENRY
R—Arcata, Calif.
B—Pittsburgh, Pa.
G. O. No. 87, W. D., 1919.

Colonel, Corps of Engineers, U. S. Army.
As assistant chief of Staff, G-3, of the operations section of the 5th Army Corps, he performed his important duties with marked zeal. By his rare technical skill in originating and developing plans for operations against the enemy he rendered services of signal worth to the American Expeditionary Forces.

EMMONS, HAROLD H.
R—Detroit, Mich.
B—Detroit, Mich.
G. O. No. 69, W. D., 1919.

Lieutenant, United States Naval Reserve Force.
For services as Chief of the Engine Production Department of the Air Service.

ENNIS, WILLIAM P.
R—New York.
B—San Francisco, Calif.
G. O. No. 31, W. D., 1922.

Brigadier general, U. S. Army.
As director of the department of matériel, school of fire, for Field Artillery at Fort Sill, Okla., from May 9, 1918, to Aug. 30, 1918, his untiring energy, devotion to duty, exceptional qualifications for the task he had to perform, were directly responsible for the splendid organization developed.

ENOCHS, BERKELEY
R—Ironton, Ohio.
B—Ironton, Ohio.
G. O. No. 56, W. D., 1922.

Colonel, Infantry, U. S. Army.
As chief of staff, 39th Division, from August, 1917, until August, 1918, by his marked efficiency, loyal devotion to duty, and high military attainments, he played an important part in the successful organization and training of that division. Later, as assistant chief of staff, G-3, 4th Army Corps, from September, 1918, until April, 1919, he performed many duties of great responsibility in a highly meritorious manner, rendering services of signal worth to the American Expeditionary Forces.

ERICKSON, HJALMER
R—Brooklyn, N. Y.
B—Norway.
G. O. No. 59, W. D., 1919.

Colonel, Infantry, U. S. Army.
As commanding officer of the 26th Infantry, 1st Division, in all the operations east of the Aire River from Oct. 1 to 11, 1918, he rendered most meritorious service by displaying marked tactical ability, courage, and resourcefulness in the handling of numerous critical situations, thus enabling his regiment to advance steadily to all its objectives.

ERSKINE, JOHN
R—New York, N. Y.
B—New York, N. Y.
G. O. No. 89, W. D., 1919.

As chairman of the educational commission, he devoted himself with tireless energy to the problem of developing educational opportunities for the American soldiers in France while they were awaiting repatriation. To his rare educational ability, breadth of vision, and initiative is due, in a large measure, the success of the educational program of the American Expeditionary Forces.

ERWIN, JAMES B.
R—Savannah, Ga.
B—Savannah, Ga.
G. O. No. 15, W. D., 1923.

Brigadier general, U. S. Army.
With sound technical skill, initiative, and untiring energy, he assisted in the organization and training of the 6th Division, and commanded with distinction the 12th Infantry Brigade during its operations in the Vosges sector, and during the Meuse-Argonne offensive, Nov. 1 to 11, 1918. His rare quality of leadership and unremitting devotion to duty were material factors in the successful operations of his division, contributing markedly to the accomplishments of the American Expeditionary Forces in France.

EVANS, ROBERT K.
R—Mississippi.
B—Jackson, Miss.
G. O. No. 4, W. D., 1923.

Brigadier general, U. S. Army, retired.
As department commander, Philippine Department, between Aug. 5, 1917, and Aug. 5, 1918, he handled many difficult problems arising in that department with rare judgment, tact, and great skill.

EXTON, CHARLES W.
R—Clinton, N. J.
B—Clinton, N. J.
G. O. No. 53, W. D., 1921.

Colonel, Infantry, U. S. Army.
As assistant G-5, General Headquarters, France, a position of great responsibility, he had complete responsibility for the control, supervision, and inspection of the detachments of American students in French Universities, which was part of the educational system of the American Forces in Germany. He performed all his duties with exceptional efficiency and rendered services of much value.

FAIR, JOHN S.
R—Altoona, Pa.
B—Dakota, Nebr.
G. O. No. 81, W. D., 1919.

Colonel, Quartermaster Corps, U. S. Army.
He organized and operated the remount service, controlled the purchasing of fuel and forage for the Army, and organized and started into operation the conservation and reclamation division. By his enthusiasm and energy valuable results were obtained.

FAISON, SAMSON L.
R—Faison, N. C.
B—Faison, N. C.
G. O. No. 59, W. D., 1919.

Brigadier general, U. S. Army.
He commanded with great credit the 60th Infantry Brigade, 30th Division, in the breaking of the enemy's Hindenburg line at Bellicourt, France, and in subsequent operations in which important captures were made, all marking him as a military commander of great energy and determination.

FARNSWORTH, CHARLES S.
R—Clarion, Pa.
B—Lycoming County, Pa.
G. O. No. 111, W. D., 1919.

Major general, U. S. Army.
In command of the 37th Division, his efficient leadership and military ability were important factors in the successful operations in the Meuse-Argonne offensive, and later proved their worth when this division served with the French and Belgian forces in Belgium.

FASSETT, WILLIAM M R—Nashua, N. H. B—Nashua, N. H. G. O. No. 59, W. D., 1919.	Brigadier general, U. S. Army. In the forcing of the crossing of the Escault River, Belgium, in November, 1918, and the establishment of a bridgehead thereat he demonstrated his ability as a leader. The successful operations of his brigade in this and in ensuing actions were greatly influenced by his efforts.
FELAND, LOGAN R—Hopkinsville, Ky. B—Hopkinsville, Ky. G. O. No. 89, W. D., 1919. Distinguished-service cross also awarded.	Colonel, U. S. Marine Corps. As lieutenant colonel and second in command of the 5th Regiment, United States Marine Corps, 2d Division, he had an important function in the training of that organization, and he participated creditably in its operations in the Aisne defensive and the fighting in the Chateau-Thierry section. Having taken command of his regiment as colonel shortly before the battle of Soissons, he led it with extraordinary skill throughout the remainder of its engagements, giving proof of the highest qualities of leadership and unceasing devotion to his important duties.
FELTON, SAMUEL M R—Chicago, Ill. B—Philadelphia, Pa. G. O. No. 18, W. D., 1919.	Director general of military railways. In supervising the supply of railway material and the organization of railway operation and construction troops, by his energetic and loyal service he has contributed materially to the success of the Army in the field.
FENTON, CHAUNCEY L R—Lowellville, Ohio. B—Edinburg, Pa. G. O. No. 15, W. D., 1921.	Colonel (Coast Artillery Corps), General Staff Corps, U. S. Army. As chief of a section of the General Staff during the period of demobilization and reorganization of the Army, he has rendered conspicuous service in the solution of intricate and important problems pertaining to the scientific utilization of the commissioned personnel of the Army.
FERGUSON, HARLEY B R—Waynesville, N. C. B—Waynesville, N. C. G. O. No. 87, W. D., 1919.	Brigadier general, U. S. Army. As chief engineer of the 2d Army Corps and later of the 2d Army, he demonstrated high professional attainments and marked initiative. Through his foresight and skill in directing important technical operations he was a notable factor in the successes of the combat troops, rendering invaluable services to the American Expeditionary Forces.
FERGUSSON, FRANK K R—Riddleton, Tenn. B—Riddleton, Tenn. G. O. No. 47, W. D., 1919.	Brigadier general, U. S. Army. As commandant of the Coast Artillery training center at Fort Monroe, Va., he rendered specially meritorious and conspicuous service in organizing and administering that center and in the preparation and execution of the plans for the organization, training, and equipment of the units of Coast Artillery for oversea service.
FIEBEGER, GUSTAV J R—Akron, Ohio. B—Akron, Ohio. G. O. No. 19, W. D., 1922.	Colonel, professor of civil and military engineering, U. S. Military Academy. As head of the department of civil and military engineering he for 26 years instructed, both personally and by textbook, the officers of the Army in the principles of warfare, principles later fruitfully applied by many of these officers as commanders in the World War.
FIFE, JAMES DOUGLAS R—Charlottesville, Va. B—Charlottesville, Va. G. O. No. 59, W. D., 1919.	Colonel, Medical Corps, U. S. Army. In command of Base Hospital No. 21, he served with distinction with the British Expeditionary Forces. He was later assigned to duty in the office of the chief surgeon in charge of hospital planning and construction, procurement of permanent buildings, establishment of hospitalization, liaison with the French authorities, the General Staff, and with the Engineers. In the performance of these multifarious duties he displayed conspicuous ability.
FINNEY, JOHN M. T R—Baltimore, Md. B—Natchez, Miss. G. O. No. 50, W. D., 1919.	Brigadier general, U. S. Army. He rendered distinguished services in the organization of surgical teams, for the purpose of affording expert surgical aid to the wounded in the immediate vicinity of the battle field. He has done much to standardize the practice of surgery in war, and giving so freely of his professional experience and skill he has in many ways rendered services of exceptional value to the Government.
FISHER, HENRY C R—Washington, D. C. B—Montgomery County, Md. G. O. No. 10, W. D., 1922.	Colonel, Medical Corps, U. S. Army. As chief sanitary inspector, American Expeditionary Forces, by the tireless application of his many years of military experience to correct abuses and secure uniformity and efficiency of hospital administration in the hospitals of the American Expeditionary Forces, he rendered services of great value to the Government.
FISHER, WILLIAM A., Jr R—Baltimore, Md. B—Baltimore, Md. G. O. No. 59, W. D., 1921.	Lieutenant colonel, Medical Corps, U. S. Army. Due to his great energy, excellent judgment, and unusual knowledge of the personnel capabilities of surgeons, he made it possible to organize surgical teams and distribute surgical personnel in a manner which made it possible for evacuation hospitals to function under the greatest difficulties in spite of personnel shortage.
FISKE, CHARLES NORMAN R—Upton, Mass. B—Jaffrey, N. H. G. O. No. 116, W. D., 1919.	Captain, Medical Corps, U. S. Navy. As force medical officer, his untiring energy, his foresight in sanitary inspection of ships, and his close cooperation with the Army authorities contributed greatly to the successful outcome of our oversea operations.
FISKE, HAROLD B R—Salem, Oreg. B—Salem, Oreg. G. O. No. 12, W. D., 1919.	Brigadier general, U. S. Army. In charge of the training section of the General Staff, this brilliant officer perfected and administered the efficient scheme of instruction through which the American Army in France was thoroughly trained for combat in the shortest possible time. By his great depth of vision, his foresight, and his clear conception of modern tactical training he has enabled our forces to enter each engagement with that preparedness and efficiency that have distinguished the American Army in each battle.

FITCH, ROGER S.
 R—Buffalo, N. Y.
 B—Buffalo, N. Y.
 G. O. No. 9, W. D., 1923.

Colonel (Cavalry), General Staff Corps, U. S. Army.
As chief of staff, 86th Division, Aug. 25, 1917, to Nov. 21, 1918, he displayed the highest professional qualifications; by his tireless energy and devotion to duty he rendered conspicuous service to the Government. While chief of staff, 86th Division, he voluntarily performed the duties of assistant chief of staff, G-3, with the 89th Division during the final advance of that division from the Bois-de-Bantheville during the Meuse-Argonne offensive. In November, 1918, he was assigned to duty as G-3, 7th Army Corps; in this position of great responsibility he rendered service of great value and contributed materially to the success of that corps.

FLAHERTY, JAMES A.
 R—Philadelphia, Pa.
 B—Philadelphia, Pa.
 G. O. No. 116, W. D., 1919.

Supreme Knight of the Knights of Columbus.
His high leadership and service rendered the Army of the United States were conspicuous.

FLASH, MRS. ALICE H.
 R—Boston, Mass.
 B—Jefferson County, Ga.
 G. O. No. 9, W. D., 1923.

Chief nurse, Army Nurse Corps, U. S. Army.
As chief nurse of the Mesves hospital center, France, during the World War, she rendered invaluable assistance and made possible the efficient nursing of over 20,000 patients at one time. Her good judgment in dealing with very difficult personnel problems, her tact, and splendid example resulted in an unusually high standard of nursing efficiency at this center, in spite of the most trying physical conditions. She displayed marked executive ability and professional qualities in directing hundreds of nurses in the care of the sick and wounded.

FLEMING, ADRIAN S.
 R—Louisville, Ky.
 B—Midway, Ky.
 G. O. No. 87, W. D., 1919.

Brigadier General, U. S. Army.
He commanded with distinction the 158th Field Artillery Brigade, 83d Division, displaying aggressive leadership and the highest professional attainments. He contributed materially to the successful operations of the Infantry units to which his brigade was attached during the Meuse-Argonne offensive by the timely and accurate artillery support furnished by his regiments.

FLETCHER, FRANK F.
 R—Oskaloosa, Iowa.
 B—Oskaloosa, Iowa.
 G. O. No. 15, W. D., 1923.

Rear admiral, U. S. Navy, Navy representative, War Industries Board.
In connection with the operations of the War Industries Board during the World War as a member of the board he rendered, through his broad vision and distinguished capacity, services of inestimable value in marshaling the industrial forces of the Nation and mobilizing its economic resources—marked factors in assisting to make military success attainable. As one of the service representatives on the board his sound judgment and wide knowledge of military and naval matters contributed markedly to the successful prosecution of the war.

FLINT, JOSEPH M.
 R—New Haven, Conn.
 B—Chicago, Ill.
 G. O. No. 59, W. D., 1919.

Lieutenant colonel, Medical Corps, U. S. Army.
When placed in a position of great responsibility as commanding officer of Mobile Hospital No. 39 at Aulnois-sous-Vertuzey, France, he used extraordinary skill and sound judgment in the organization and operation of that unit, the first of its kind in the American Expeditionary Forces. In its formative period he was faced by great and unforeseen difficulties, but with untiring energy and genius he surmounted all obstacles, making his unit a model for all those subsequently organized.

FLOOD, BERNARD A.
 R—New York, N. Y.
 B—New York, N. Y.
 G. O. No. 43, W. D., 1922.

Captain, Provost Marshal General's Department, U. S. Army.
As chief inspector of the division of criminal investigation on the staff of the provost marshal general, American Expeditionary Forces, he organized, coordinated, and directed this important office in a highly efficient manner. The successes achieved by this section are largely due to his sound judgment, untiring efforts, and exceptional ability, and were of great value to the American Expeditionary Forces.

FOGG, OSCAR H.
 R—New York, N. Y.
 B—Philadelphia, Pa.
 G. O. No. 13, W. D., 1923.

Lieutenant colonel, Ordnance Department, U. S. Army.
For services as engineer in charge of the organization, establishment, and performance of the American Ordnance Repair Arsenal in France. In this great undertaking he displayed exceptional zeal, keen foresight, and sound judgment, and by his undaunted perseverance he established these extensive and highly important repair facilities, thereby rendering service of inestimable value, contributing materially to the success of the American Expeditionary Forces in France.

FOOTE, ALFRED F.
 R—Holyoke, Mass.
 B—Mooers Forks, N. Y.
 G. O. No. 4, W. D., 1923.

Lieutenant colonel, Infantry, U. S. Army.
As battalion commander during the operations of the 104th Infantry, 26th Division, at Apremont, France, Apr. 10-13, 1918, he demonstrated unusual initiative and marked efficiency and contributed materially to the successful stand of the regiment against the enemy's repeated attacks. As regimental commander during the Champagne-Marne offensive, by his devotion to duty, courage, and superior qualities as a commander he successfully accomplished all missions assigned to him. Later, as division inspector, 26th Division, by his tact, sound judgment, and ability he assisted materially in maintaining the high morale and discipline of the division.

FORBES, CHARLES R.
 R—Burton, Vashon Island, Wash.
 B—Scotland.
 G. O. No. 59, W. D., 1919.

Lieutenant colonel, Signal Corps, U. S. Army.
As division signal officer of the 33d Division he performed his duties with marked distinction, maintaining communication at all times within the division, with adjoining units, and with the higher command. His ability and untiring devotion to duty were great factors in insuring the successes achieved by the division.

FORD, JOSEPH H.
R—Washington, D. C.
B—Washington, D. C.
G. O. No. 38, W. D., 1922.

Colonel, Medical Corps, U. S. Army.
Colonel Ford organized and commanded a hospital center of 15,000 beds at Allerey, France. Due to his great force and ability, a hospital group was prepared for the care of the sick and wounded during the St. Mihiel and Meuse-Argonne offensives, when the need of hospital beds was critical. This adequate and efficient hospitalization contributed materially to the conservation of man power and to the subsequent success of our forces.

FORD, STANLEY H.
R—Columbus, Ohio.
B—Columbus, Ohio.
G. O. No. 78, W. D., 1919.

Colonel, Infantry, U. S. Army.
As chief of staff of the 27th Division he rendered valuable services in the operations of this division. By tireless energy, good judgment, and keen foresight he proved to be an important factor in the brilliant military operations of the 27th Division.

FOREMAN, ALBERT WATSON.
R—Wilmington, Del.
B—Wilmington, Del.
G. O. No. 87, W. D., 1919.

Colonel (Infantry), General Staff Corps, U. S. Army.
As assistant chief of staff, First Section of the 5th Army Corps, by his zealous application to his important duties he ably administered the service of supply, movement of troops, and the control of communication of the 5th Corps during the active operations of that unit against the enemy, rendering meritorious services to the American Expeditionary Forces.

FOREMAN, MILTON J.
R—Chicago, Ill.
B—Chicago, Ill.
G. O. No. 1, W. D., 1926.
Distinguished-service cross also awarded.

Colonel, Field Artillery, U. S. Army.
Commanding the 122d Field Artillery, 33d Division, he gave proof of eminent technical attainments and assiduous zeal. Though handicapped by many adverse conditions due to difficult terrain and determined hostile resistance, he kept his batteries in close support of the Infantry and thereby rendered services of inestimable value during the St. Mihiel offensive and the advance to the Meuse in the last phase of the Meuse-Argonne offensive.

FOSDICK, RAYMOND B.
R—New York, N. Y.
B—Buffalo, N. Y.
G. O. No. 73, W. D., 1919.

For services as chairman of the commission on training camp activities.

FOSTER, CHARLES L.
R—Washington, D. C.
B—Starkville, Miss.
G. O. No. 56, W. D., 1921.

Colonel, Medical Corps, U. S. Army.
As surgeon at Base Section No. 1, services of supply, a position of great responsibility, due to his thorough training, energy, and ability, he rendered services of great value at this important base port.

FOSTER, CHARLES W.
R—Burlington, Vt.
B—Michigan.
G. O. No. 56, W. D., 1922.

Major (Cavalry), General Staff Corps, U. S. Army.
He served with the 3d Division as assistant G-3 during May and June, 1918; assistant chief of staff G-3 from June to September, 1918; as assistant G-3 1st and 7th Army Corps, from September to November, 1918; and assistant G-3, 3d Army, from November, 1918, to July, 1919. By his marked ability, devotion to duty, and high military attainments he contributed materially to the successes achieved by the commands with which he served

FOSTER, REGINALD L.
R—New York, N. Y.
B—China.
G. O. No. 38, W. D., 1922.

Colonel, Infantry, U. S. Army.
During the Meuse-Argonne offensive from Sept. 26, 1918, to Nov. 11, 1918, he commanded his regiment, the 52d Pioneer Infantry, with marked ability and success. By zealous application to his arduous duties, energetic efforts displayed in the construction of roads, care of enemy prisoners, police and salvage of the battle fields, and the handling of ammunition and supplies, he contributed materially to the success of the 5th Army Corps during that important operation, thereby rendering meritorious and distinguished services to the American Expeditionary Forces.

FOULOIS, BENJAMIN D.
R—Washington, Conn.
B—Washington, Conn.
G. O. No. 68, W. D., 1920.

Brigadier general, U. S. Army.
As Chief of Air Service of the American Expeditionary Forces during the early organization period, he displayed great ability and untiring energy in order to place that service on a firm and efficient basis. He conducted intricate negotiations with the French for the procurement of aircraft material of sites for Air Service installations and of schools of instruction for the Air Service personnel. Similar negotiations were made by him with the English for the assembly of night bombing planes for our Air Service and for instructions of our personnel in English shops and in English aerodromes. Later he rendered valuable assistance in connection with maintenance of Air Service squadrons at the front.

FOWLER, HAROLD.
R—New York, N. Y.
B—England.
G. O. No. 108, W. D., 1919.

Colonel, Air Service, U. S. Army.
He rendered notable aid in planning the movements of the night bombing squads of the American Air Service. Later, appointed Air Service commander of the 3d Army, he assisted largely in the joint training of air and ground troops, at all times handling his troops well and establishing liaison between the air and ground forces.

FRANKLIN, BENJAMIN A.
R—Springfield, Mass.
B—Northumberland County, Va.
G. O. No. 124, W. D., 1919.

Lieutenant colonel, Ordnance Department, U. S. Army.
As production manager and assistant chief of the Bridgeport Ordnance District, in which capacity he maintained at all times the greatest degree of intelligent and enthusiastic cooperation between the Ordnance Department and manufacturers in his district, thereby attaining the maximum production of munitions in a minimum time, and also as chairman of the Bridgeport Ordnance District Claims Board, in which capacity his services have been invaluable to the Nation in adjusting equitably the $346,000,000 worth of outstanding contracts in his district in force at the signing of the armistice.

DISTINGUISHED-SERVICE MEDAL

FRANKLIN, PHILIP A. S., Sr _____
  R—New York, N. Y.
  B—Ashland, Md.
  G. O. No. 25, W. D., 1919.

Chairman, shipping control committee.
For services in connection with the embarkation service of the Army in the division of purchase, storage, and traffic. To his fine technical knowledge and energetic action is due, in a large measure, the efficient jurisdiction over dock facilities and floating equipment which has made possible the large movement of troops and supplies overseas.

FRANKLIN, WALTER S _____
  R—Baltimore, Md.
  B—Ashland, Md.
  G. O. No. 56, W. D., 1921.

Lieutenant colonel, Army Transport Service, U. S. Army.
As officer in charge of embarkation service in the troop and cargo division of the Army Transport Service, a position of great responsibility, by his energy, tact, and initiative, arrangements were effected whereby a large share of the British ocean passenger tonnage was made available for the American use, and whereby additional allied and neutral tonnage for the return of the American Expeditionary Forces was procured. He has rendered service of much value.

FRASER, LEON _____
  R—New York, N. Y.
  B—Boston, Mass.
  G. O. No. 31, W. D., 1922.

Major, Judge Advocate General's Department, U. S. Army.
For services as assistant judge advocate of the services of supply. In this capacity he bore an important part of the responsibility consequent upon deciding a wide variety of legal and administrative questions, including the reviewing of court-martial cases, the preparation of opinions, and the solution of the many problems which grew out of the interpretation of United States Statutes, Army Regulations, General Orders, and French and international law involved in the business operations of the American Expeditionary Forces.

FRAYNE, HUGH _____
  R—Scranton, Pa.
  B—Scranton, Pa.
  G. O. No. 15, W. D., 1923.

Labor commissioner, War Industries Board.
In connection with the operations of the War Industries Board during the World War, as a member of the board he rendered, through his broad vision, distinguished capacity, and organizing ability, services of inestimable value in marshaling the industrial forces of the Nation and mobilizing its economic resources—marked factors in assisting to make military success attainable. As labor commissioner he contributed largely to the successful mobilization and conservation of man power for war industry. His untiring efforts and devotion to duty in this connection contributed markedly to the successful operations of the supply system of the Army.

FRIES, AMOS A _____
  R—Central Point, Oreg.
  B—Debello, Wis.
  G. O. No. 95, W. D., 1919.

Brigadier general, U. S. Army.
As chief of the Chemical Warfare Service he was charged with the important task of training and equipping our troops for a form of warfare in which the American Army had had no experience prior to the present war. Both in securing proper defensive measures against gas and in developing new methods for its use as an offensive agency, he performed his arduous duties with marked success, thereby rendering valuable services to the American Expeditionary Forces.

FRINK, JAMES L _____
  R—Springfield, Mo.
  B—Ida Grove, Iowa.
  G. O. No. 14, W. D., 1923.

Major (Infantry), General Staff Corps, U. S. Army.
From Oct. 19 to Nov. 11, 1918, during the Meuse-Argonne offensive, he rendered highly meritorious services as assistant chief of staff, G-3, 78th Division. In this position of great responsibility he displayed rare judgment in the selection of points in the line for attack and in the designation of forces to be used in the attack. As acting chief of staff of his division from November, 1918, until February, 1919, he displayed high professional attainments, unfailing energy, and devotion to duty, contributing in a material way to the success of his division.

FULMER, JOHN J _____
  R—Reading, Pa.
  B—Amityville, Pa.
  G. O. No. 87, W. D., 1919.

Lieutenant colonel, Infantry, U. S. Army.
As director of the Infantry Specialists' School at Langres he achieved a notable success in the efficient training of thousands of officers. He also rendered invaluable service while a member of training section of the General Staff by establishing uniform and effective methods of instruction in musketry training throughout the American Expeditionary Forces.

FUQUA, STEPHEN O _____
  R—Baton Rouge, La.
  B—Baton Rouge, La.
  G. O. No. 59, W. D., 1919.

Colonel (Infantry), General Staff Corps, U. S. Army.
In charge of the troop movement subsection of G-3, 1st Army, from its organization until he became chief of staff, 1st Division, he was responsible for and supervised the movements incident to the concentration of troops for the St. Mihiel and Meuse-Argonne offensives of the 1st Army, which involved many thousands of men and was accomplished with the greatest success. His untiring, painstaking, and energetic efforts had a marked effect on the success of these major operations.

FURLOW, JAMES WADSWORTH _____
  R—Americus, Ga.
  B—Americus, Ga.
  G. O. No. 69, W. D., 1919.

Colonel, Quartermaster Corps, U. S. Army.
While on duty in the Motor Transport Corps his brilliant conception and able administration were largely responsible for the organization and highly successful operation of the plan for upkeep and maintenance of motor vehicles during the war.

*GALBRAITH, FREDERICK W., Jr _____
  R—Cincinnati, Ohio.
  B—Watertown, Mass
  G. O. No. 59, W. D., 1921.
  Distinguished-service cross also awarded.

Colonel, Infantry, U. S. Army.
As regimental commander of the 147th Infantry, 37th Division, by his energy and ability he organized, trained, and brought his regiment to a high state of efficiency and commanded it throughout its operations in the Meuse-Argonne and in the Flanders offensives of the Lys and of the Escault River. He has rendered services of conspicuous worth.
Posthumously awarded. Medal presented to widow, Mrs. Esther G. Galbraith.

GALEN, ALBERT J R—Helena, Mont. B—Broadwater County, Mont. G. O. No. 56, W. D., 1922.	Lieutenant colonel, Judge Advocate General's Department, U. S. Army. As judge advocate of the American Expeditionary Forces in Siberia he organized this important department and administered its affairs with conspicuous efficiency. His marked legal ability, sound judgment, and untiring efforts were important factors in the splendid work of his department, and he at all times handled with great success the various military and international problems with which he was confronted. He contributed materially to the success of the forces in Siberia and rendered conspicuous services in a position of great responsibility.
GARBER, MAX B R—Marble Rock, Iowa. B—Marble Rock, Iowa. G. O. No. 35, W. D., 1920.	Lieutenant colonel, Infantry, U. S. Army. He commanded with marked distinction the 59th Infantry during the attack on the Vesle. In this command he displayed those high qualities of ability, leadership, and personal courage that marked him as a determining factor in the successes achieved by the 4th Division.
*GARDNER, AUGUSTUS PEABODY R—Hamilton, Mass. B—Boston, Mass. G. O. No. 14, W. D., 1923.	Major, Infantry, U. S. Army. Resigning as a Member of Congress to serve under his reserve commission as colonel, Adjutant General's Department, in 1917, he served first at headquarters, Eastern Department, Governors Island, N. Y., and later as adjutant, 31st Division. At his own urgent request he was appointed major, 121st Infantry, 31st Division, and commanded a battalion in that regiment until his death. His entire service was characterized by untiring zeal, devotion to duty, and marked success. His splendid example of patriotism will always serve as an inspiration to his countrymen. Posthumously awarded. Medal presented to widow, formerly Mrs. Augustus P. Gardner, now Mrs. C. C. Williams.
GARDNER, FULTON Q. C R—Fort Smith, Ark. B—Lafayette Springs, Miss. G. O. No. 73, W. D., 1919.	Colonel (Coast Artillery Corps), General Staff Corps, U. S. Army. For services as secretary of the General Staff.
GARFIELD, HARRY A R—Williamstown, Mass. B—Hiram, Ohio. G. O. No. 15, W. D., 1921.	Fuel administrator. During the progress of the war, by his conduct of the Fuel Administration, he stimulated the production, conserved the use, and supervised the distribution of those supplies of fuel necessary for the support and transportation of the Armies of the United States, the maintenance of industry, the production of war supplies, and the health and well-being of the civil population upon which the successful prosecution of military activities depended.
GASKILL, CHARLES S R—Morristown, N. J. B—Mount Holly, N. J. G. O. No. 59, W. D., 1919.	Lieutenant colonel, Corps of Engineers, U. S. Army. In charge of the locomotive and car repair shops at Nevers, he carried out the installation and operation of this plant, exhibiting rare executive ability and engineering qualifications of the highest order.
GASSER, LORENZO D R—Tiffin, Ohio. B—Likens, Ohio. G. O. No. 43, W. D., 1922.	Major, Infantry, U. S. Army. As chief of motor transportation section, office of the assistant chief of staff, G-4, American Expeditionary Forces, he showed unusual ability, tireless energy, and a comprehensive grasp of details in preparing plans for the organization and operation of a general headquarters reserve of motor transportation. Later, as deputy assistant chief of staff, G-4, at advance general headquarters at Treves, Germany, in coordinating the plans for the reception and disposition of enemy war materials, he successfully handled a problem requiring great tact and high professional attainments, thereby rendering services of great value to the American Expeditionary Forces.
GAUCHE, EDWARD E R—New York, N. Y. B—Lerado, Ohio. G. O. No. 15, W. D., 1923.	Lieutenant colonel, Adjutant General's Department, U. S. Army. Charged with the responsibility for the operation of the statistical and personnel divisions, services of supply, and for the work of all personnel adjutants functioning under the statistical section, Adjutant General's Office, General Headquarters, stationed at all base ports during the repatriation of the American Army, he displayed administrative and executive ability of a high order unusual resourcefulness, and sound professional judgment. He organized and maintained a service that covered the entire theater of operations, exclusive of the zone of the armies during the entire period of military activity By his fitness and aptitude for the grave responsibilities placed upon him his tireless energy and unceasing devotion to duty he contributed materially to the successful operations of the services of supply and the American forces in France.
GERLACH, FRANK C R—Wooster, Ohio. B—Wooster, Ohio. G. O. No. 43, W. D., 1922.	Colonel, Infantry, U. S. Army. As lieutenant colonel, 146th Infantry, 37th Division, from May, 1917, until October, 1918, he organized and developed to a high state of efficiency a training school for commissioned candidates at Camp Sheridan, Ala., and the divisional training school in the Baccarat sector, France. Later, as colonel 145th Infantry, 37th Division, he commanded his regiment with marked success during the Ypres-Lys offensive, showing at all times great energy resourcefulness, and splendid leadership, thereby contributing materially to the successes achieved in this important operation.
GEROW, LEONARD T R—Petersburg, Va. B—Dinwiddie County, Va. G. O. No. 49, W. D., 1922.	Lieutenant colonel, Signal Corps, U. S. Army. For services as officer in charge of the sales and disbursing division of the Signal Corps. With unusual ability and skill he conducted the financial affairs of the Signal Corps and handled the negotiations with such tact and energy that Signal Corps property urgently needed was secured, inspected, and delivered to depots with the minimum of delay. Later, in the negotiations connected with the disposal of Signal Corps plants and stocks, he again performed his exacting duties in a highly meritorious manner, thereby rendering services of great value to the American Expeditionary Forces in a position of great responsibility.

GHORMLEY, ROBERT LEE
R—Moscow, Idaho.
B—Portland, Oreg.
G. O. No. 116, W. D., 1919.

Commander, U. S. Navy.
For services as assistant director of Overseas Division, Naval Overseas Transportation Service.

GIBBS, ELBERT A
R—Pittsburgh, Pa.
B—Kasson, Minn.
G. O. No. 87, W. D., 1919.

Colonel, Corps of Engineers, U. S. Army.
He served with distinction as chief of the general construction section in the office of the director of construction and forestry. Charged with the supervision of important engineering construction projects, he gave proof of high professional attainments and keen foresight, rendering invaluable services to the American Expeditionary Forces.

GIBBS, GEORGE S
R—Harlan, Iowa.
B—Harlan, Iowa.
G. O. No. 59, W. D., 1919.

Brigadier general, U. S. Army.
As assistant to the chief signal officer, American Expeditionary Forces, much of the efficiency of the Signal Service in the zone of advance was due to his splendid ability and to his skill in the handling of the tactical and technical operations of the Signal Corps organizations attached to the service at the front.

GIBSON, ADELNO
R—Oskaloosa, Iowa.
B—Marysville, Iowa.
G. O. No. 9, W. D., 1923.

Lieutenant colonel (Coast Artillery Corps), General Staff Corps, U. S. Army.
As officer in charge of the personnel subsection of G-1, general headquarters from October, 1917, until August, 1918, he displayed unusual foresight, excellent judgment and resourcefulness in the conception, organization, and operation of the entire replacement system at general headquarters. By his constant devotion to duty, his great ability for original work, and his high professional attainments he materially contributed to the efficiency of the staff work at general headquarters, thereby rendering services of great value to the American Expeditionary Forces.

GIGNILLIAT, LEIGH R
R—Culver, Ind.
B—Savannah, Ga.
G. O. No. 43, W. D., 1922.

Colonel, Infantry, U. S. Army.
As G-2 of the 84th Division from Oct. 6, 1917, until Nov. 9, 1918, and of the 37th Division from Nov. 9, 1918, until Mar. 15, 1919, he displayed an unusual devotion to duty and military attainments of a high order, which enabled him to place the intelligence sections of both divisions on a high plane of efficiency. From Mar. 15, 1919, to June 27, 1919, as the United States' representative on the Interallied Food Commission, by rare tact, great energy, and marked executive ability he solved with conspicuous success many perplexing problems of supply in our occupied area.

GILCHRIST, HARRY L
R—Cleveland, Ohio.
B—Waterloo, Iowa.
G. O. No. 38, W. D., 1921.

Colonel, Medical Corps, U. S. Army.
As chief of the delousing and bathing services of the American Expeditionary Forces, by his superior administration and splendid efficiency he contributed materially to the success achieved by the Army at the ports of Brest, Bordeaux, and St. Nazaire in the return to the United States of the American Expeditionary Forces.

GIRL, CHRISTIAN
R—Cleveland, Ohio.
B—Elkhart, Ind.
G. O. No. 3, W. D., 1922.

For services rendered in the organization of the production section, motors branch, Quartermaster Corps, which designed and produced the standardized motor truck.

GLASSFORD, PELHAM D
R—Carthage, Mo.
B—Las Vegas, N. Mex.
G. O. No. 89, W. D., 1919.

Brigadier general, U. S. Army.
He served creditably at the Saumur Artillery School, at the First Corps Artillery School, and as commander of a regiment of field artillery during the Chateau-Thierry campaign. Subsequently, upon being promoted to the grade of brigadier general, he displayed high military attainments and unceasing energy as commander of the 51st Field Artillery Brigade, rendering invaluable services to the American Expeditionary Forces.

GLEAVES, ALBERT
R—Nashville, Tenn.
B—Nashville, Tenn.
G. O. No. 116, W. D., 1919.

Vice admiral, U. S. Navy.
As commander of the cruiser and transport fleet, his untiring energy, close cooperation, and wide decisions contributed greatly to the successful oversea operations of the transport fleet, resulting in the successful transportation of the United States forces abroad.

GLEAVES, SAMUEL R
R—Wytheville, Va.
B—Independence, Va.
G. O. No. 62, W. D., 1919.

Colonel (Cavalry), General Staff Corps, U. S. Army.
As G-3 of the 42d Division he displayed military attainments of a high order, being constant in devotion to his exacting duties. In the operations section, General Headquarters, American Expeditionary Forces, he handled all questions arising in that section pertaining to the arrival, location and issuance of orders for movements of units in the American Expeditionary Forces. In the solution of the perplexing problems which arose he brought to his task a high faculty for organization, coupled with sound judgment and a comprehensive grasp of service conditions.

GLENDINNING, ROBERT
R—Philadelphia, Pa.
B—Philadelphia, Pa.
G. O. No. 38, W. D, 1922.

Lieutenant colonel, Air Service, U. S. Army.
As classification officer for the Air Service in the Casual Officers' Depot, Blois, France, through his untiring energy and sound judgment he developed an efficient system of classification, which was of great assistance to the American air forces. Later, as a representative of the Air Service, American Expeditionary Forces in Italy, he was charged with many and intricate negotiations with the Italian Government, which he conducted with rare intelligence, sound judgment, and successful results.

GLENNAN, JAMES D
R—Washington, D. C.
B—Rochester, N. Y.
G. O. No. 89, W. D., 1919.

Brigadier general, U. S. Army.
In charge of the hospitalization division in the office of the chief surgeon, he directed the establishment, equipment and operation, as well as the evacuation service, of all the American hospitals in France. By his keen foresight, untiring energy, and administrative ability he solved successfully the numerous problems which confronted him, rendering services of the highest value to the American Expeditionary Forces.

GODSON, WILLIAM F. H. ————————
R—New Bedford, Mass.
B—England.
G. O. No. 124, W. D., 1919.

Colonel, Cavalry, U. S. Army.
For services while serving as military attaché at Berne, Switzerland.

GOETHALS, GEORGE W ————————
R—New York, N. Y.
B—Brooklyn, N. Y.

G. O. No. 144, W. D., 1918.

Major general, U. S. Army.
For services in reorganizing the Quartermaster Department and in organizing and administering the Division of Purchase, Storage, and Traffic during the war.

GOLDTHWAIT, JOEL E ————————
R—Boston, Mass.
B—Marblehead, Mass.
G. O. No. 59, W. D., 1919.

Colonel, Medical Corps, U. S. Army.
As a member of the Medical Corps he has, by his unusual foresight and organizing ability, made it possible to reclaim for duty thousands of men suffering from physical defects. He has thereby materially conserved for combat service a great number of men who would have been lost to the service.

GOODALL, HARRY W ————————
R—Boston, Mass.
B—Wells Beach, Me.
G. O. No. 56, W. D., 1921.

Lieutenant colonel, Medical Corps, U. S. Army.
For services while in command of the gas hospital of the Justice Hospital group from the beginning of the St. Mihiel offensive until October, 1918.

GOODRICH, ANNIE W ————————
R—New York, N. Y.
B—New Brunswick, N. J.
G. O. No. 9, W. D., 1923.

Contract nurse, Army Nurse Corps, U. S. Army.
As organizer and first dean of the Army School of Nursing, by her individual energy, ability, and breadth of vision, she enrolled, trained, and placed at the disposal of the Medical Department of the Army 1,800 selected student nurses. These young women were of inestimable assistance to the Army Nurse Corps at a time when there was a shortage of nurses and an enormous influx of patients in Army hospitals because of the influenza epidemic. Through her efforts there was put into operation a system of training of student nurses which contributed in a remarkable degree to the success of the Medical Department in the saving of hundreds of lives during the World War.

GOODRICH, CHARLES C ————————
R—Orange, N. J.
B—Akron, Ohio.
G. O. No. 15, W. D., 1923.

Lieutenant colonel, Ordnance Department, U. S. Army.
As chief representative in England of the Liquidation Commission he displayed unusual professional ability, tact, resourcefulness and sound judgment. As executive officer in the office of the chief purchasing officer, Ordnance Department, American Expeditionary Forces, he coordinated and supervised the activities of that office and maintained cordial and effective relations with the French Ministry of Armament. The grave and important duties performed by Colonel Goodrich were of immeasurable value to the Government and contributed markedly to the successful operations of the American Expeditionary Forces.

GOODRICH, DAVID M ————————
R—New York, N. Y.
B—Akron, Ohio.
G. O. No. 116, W. D., 1919.

Lieutenant Colonel (Infantry), General Staff Corps, U. S. Army.
As assistant chief of staff, G-2, of the 78th Division, he rendered excellent services; as a student at the Army General Staff College at Langres he was eminently successful; as a member of the G-2 section at American Expeditionary Forces he performed duties of great importance; and as director of the liaison section of the interallied games committee he demonstrated superior executive ability by the satisfactory management of his many tasks which insured the success of the interallied games.

GOODWIN, ROBERT E ————————
R—Concord, Mass.
B—Cambridge, Mass.
G. O. No. 56, W. D., 1922.

Colonel, Field Artillery, U. S. Army.
As commanding officer of the 101st Field Artillery, 26th Division, from Sept. 11, 1918, to Apr. 28, 1919, by his high standards, exceptional ability, and unusual grasp of the principles of artillery, he rendered conspicuous service during the St. Mihiel offensive, and later during the operations north of Verdun. His sound judgment and tact, his unflagging energy coupled with the very close cooperation he maintained with the Infantry, were of very great assistance to the Infantry in these operations. His high technical attainments and extraordinary activity contributed materially to the success of the operations of his division.

GORDON, WALTER H ————————
R—St. Landry Parish, La.
B—Wilkinson County, Miss.
G. O. No. 70, W. D., 1919.

Major general, U. S. Army.
As brigade commander of the 10th Infantry Brigade, 5th Division, he showed great energy and zeal in the conduct of his brigade during the major part of its maneuvers. Later, as division commander of the 6th Division, by his painstaking efforts, he brought his division to a marked state of efficiency, rendering services of great value to the American Expeditionary Forces.

GORGAS, WILLIAM C ————————
R—Tuscaloosa, Ala.
B—Mobile, Ala.
G. O. No. 144, W. D., 1918.

Major general, U. S. Army.
For services as Surgeon General of the Army in organizing and administering the Medical Department during the war.

GORRELL, EDGAR S ————————
R—Baltimore, Md.
B—Baltimore, Md.
G. O. No. 59, W. D., 1919.

Colonel, Air Service, U. S. Army.
He rendered most excellent service as a member of the United States Aeronautical Commission charged with the selection of types of European aeronautical material to be manufactured in the United States and as the representative of the Air Service with the General Staff, American Expeditionary Forces. In the performance of his many important tasks he displayed good judgment, great energy, and showed that he possessed ability of a high order, which have been of invaluable service to the Government.

GOSMAN, GEORGE H. R.
    R—New York, N. Y.
    B—Brooklyn, N. Y.
    G. O. No. 59, W. D., 1921.

Colonel, Medical Corps, U. S. Army.
As commanding officer of Evacuation Hospital No. 1, Colonel Gosman was confronted with the tremendous task of transporting a group of partly finished barracks into an efficient and systematic hospital. He displayed sound judgment and great organizing ability. As chief surgeon, 4th Army Corps, American Expeditionary Forces, during the St. Mihiel offensive he displayed high medical military attainments in the disposition of his units and the provision for evacuation of the wounded and for supplies.

GOSS, BYRON C.
    R—Princeton, N. J.
    B—Rochester, Ind.
    G. O. No. 3, W. D., 1924.

Lieutenant colonel, Chemical Warfare Service, U. S. Army.
As chemical adviser in the office of the Chief of Chemical Warfare Service, later as chief gas officer of the 1st Army Corps, and finally of the 2d Army, by his untiring energy, exceptional ability, and wide knowledge of gases he rendered service of great value to the American Expeditionary Forces in practically every battle in which American troops were engaged, thereby contributing materially to our success.

GOTWALS, JOHN C.
    R—Yorktown Heights, N. Y.
    B—Yerkes, Pa.
    G. O. No. 56, W. D., 1922.

Lieutenant colonel, Corps of Engineers, U. S. Army.
As chief searchlight officer, American Expeditionary Forces, he rendered conspicuous service in a position of great responsibility and in a field which was practically new to our service. By his unlimited energy, marked inventive faculties, and high technical skill, together with his ever present willingness to cooperate with our allies, he organized and directed with great success an exceedingly advanced technical service for the night protection of troop concentrations, communications, supply and manufacture establishments, in rear areas, thereby contributing materially to the success of the American Expeditionary Forces.

GOWENLOCK, THOMAS R.
    R—Chicago, Ill.
    B—Clay Center, Kans.
    G. O. No. 14, W. D., 1923.

Major (Infantry), General Staff Corps, U. S. Army.
As assistant chief of staff, G-2, 1st Division, immediately before the St. Mihiel offensive he displayed resourcefulness, ability, and devotion to duty in securing information under the most adverse circumstances, upon which the attack of the division was based. Throughout the operations of the 1st Division in the Meuse-Argonne advance, Sept. 30 to Nov. 11, 1918, Major Gowenlock demonstrated an unusually high degree of efficiency, courage, and devotion, at all times displaying superior judgment, and seized every opportunity during critical situations to sustain the morale of the command, as well as to furnish division headquarters with indispensable information. By his exceptional ability and devotion to duty he executed the most difficult missions assigned to him, thus rendering important services to the American Expeditionary Forces in the operations against the enemy.

GRAHAM, ALDEN M.
    R—San Francisco, Calif.
    B—Monmouth, Ill.
    G. O. No. 38, W. D., 1922.

Lieutenant colonel, Motor Transport Corps, U. S. Army.
As motor transport officer of the 3d Division and later of the 5th Army Corps during the entire Meuse-Argonne offensive, by his superior ability, skill, leadership, and capacity for organization he overcame most difficult conditions and maintained the transportation of the corps upon which the success of the operations so largely depended.

GRAHAM, GEORGE F.
    R—Helena, Mont.
    B—Safe Harbor, Pa.
    G. O. No. 49, W. D., 1922.

Lieutenant colonel, Quartermaster Corps, U. S. Army.
As quartermaster, 42d Division, during the entire time of its operations from May until November, 1918, by his zeal, indefatigable efforts, and unusual ability as an organizer and administrator, he solved many difficult problems under most adverse circumstances and assured the supply of the division at all times with those articles for which he was responsible, thereby rendering services of great value to the American Expeditionary Forces.

GRAHAM, JAMES H.
    R—Sound Beach, Conn.
    B—Louisville, Ky.
    G. O. No. 87, W. D., 1919.

Colonel, Corps of Engineers, U. S. Army.
In charge of all the engineer depots in France for more than six months during the initial period of our entry into the war, he performed his exacting duties with rare professional ability and unflagging zeal. Later, as supervisor of railroad and dock construction in the office of the chief engineer, he rendered services of great value in connection with development of dock facilities for the American Expeditionary Forces.

GRANT, ULYSSES S., 3d.
    R—New York, N. Y
    B—Chicago, Ill.
    G. O. No. 69, W. D., 1919.

Colonel, Corps of Engineers, U. S. Army.
As secretary of the American section, Supreme War Council, he was entrusted with the important duty of coordinating the work of the joint secretariat of the Supreme War Council and of the joint secretariat of the Military Representatives of the Supreme War Council, and as a member of the War Prisoners' Commission, Berne, Switzerland, he has rendered conspicuous service to the Government.

GRANT, WALTER S.
    R—Ithaca, N. Y.
    B—Ithaca, N. Y.
    G. O. No. 50, W. D., 1919.

Colonel (Cavalry), General Staff Corps, U. S. Army.
As deputy chief of staff of the 1st Army, by his high professional attainments and ability he rendered valuable assistance in the staff work preparatory to and during the St. Mihiel and Argonne-Meuse offensives. As chief of staff of the 1st Army Corps, he displayed the same tact, zeal, and energy which marked the previous character of his services.

GRAVES, ERNEST.
    R—Chapel Hill, N. C.
    R—Chapel Hill, N. C.
    G. O. No. 59, W. D., 1919.

Colonel, Corps of Engineers, U. S. Army.
He was charged with the construction of the Gievres storage depot and later was appointed Engineer officer of the intermediate section, services of supply, where he was placed in charge of all construction projects west of Bourges. As Engineer officer of Base Section No. 2 and of the Advance Section, S. O. S., he performed the duties with which he was intrusted in a conspicuously meritorious manner. In the many responsible capacities in which he was employed the performance of his duty was characterized by sound judgment and untiring zeal.

GRAVES, WILLIAM S.
 R—Gatesville, Tex.
 B—Mount Calm, Tex.
 G. O. No. 18, W. D., 1919.

Major general, U. S. Army.
For services as an executive assistant to the Chief of Staff and as commandi general of the American Expeditionary Forces in Siberia.

GRAY, QUINN
 R—Waco, Tex.
 B—Plantersville, Tex.
 G. O. No. 108, W. D., 1919.

Colonel, Coast Artillery Corps, U. S. Army.
As an instructor at the Army General Staff College, he displayed high m: tary attainments and unfailing energy, performing services of the great value in connection with the instruction and training of officers for gene staff duty.

GREELY, JOHN N.
 R—Newburyport, Mass.
 B—Washington, D. C.
 G. O. No. 59, W. D., 1919.

Colonel, Field Artillery, U. S. Army.
As a member of the operations section of the General Staff, 1st Division, a later as chief of that section, he showed sound judgment in the tactical oper tions before Cantigny, Soissons, and St. Mihiel. As chief of staff of t 1st Division, he was a material factor in the success of the operations agai the enemy in the Argonne-Meuse offensive, where he demonstrated ability c high order.

GREELY, WILLIAM B.
 R—Washington, D. C.
 B—Oswego, N. Y.
 G. O. No. 3, W. D., 1924.

Lieutenant colonel, Corps of Engineers, U. S. Army.
In charge of the forestry section of the Division of Construction in Forest from Sept. 1, 1918, to July 6, 1919, he supervised the operations of all forest troops in France. He rendered highly important and valuable service the Government, contributing markedly to the successes of the Americ forces in France.

GREEN, FREDERICK W.
 R—St. Louis, Mo.
 B—Rock Island, Ill.
 G. O. No. 59, W. D., 1919.

Lieutenant colonel, Army Transport Service, U. S. Army.
As superintendent of the port of Brest, he organized the task expeditiously a with great ability. Without previous organization or sufficient personnel aid him, and confronted by many serious obstacles, he, by sheer force of w supported by untiring energy, undertook a new work and created the orga zation which was competent to unload the largest ships in a surprisingly sh period of time. His service was most valuable to the American Expeditiona Forces.

GRISCOM, LLOYD C.
 R—New York, N. Y
 B—Riverton, N. J
 G. O. No. 59, W. D., 1919.

Lieutenant colonel, Adjutant General's Department, U. S. Army.
He served with marked ability as adjutant of the 77th Division during the ea days of its organization and training. As special representative of the Co mander in Chief with the Minister of War of Great Britain, he fulfilled w great distinction and credit the duties of an office requiring ability, tact, a address.

GRISSINGER, JAY W.
 R—York, Pa.
 B—Mechanicsburg, Pa.
 G. O. No. 70, W. D., 1919.

Colonel, Medical Corps, U. S. Army.
As division surgeon of the 42d Division, and later as chief surgeon of the Army Corps during its operations on the Marne and in the St. Mihiel a Meuse-Argonne offensives, he displayed qualities of leadership, high pro sional attainments, and rare judgment in energetically directing the work the sanitary units under his control in providing front-line hospitalizat and evacuation facilities for our sick and wounded in the field.

GROOME, JOHN C.
 R—Philadelphia, Pa.
 B—Philadelphia, Pa.
 G. O. No. 19, W. D., 1922.

Colonel, Signal Corps, U. S. Army.
For services as chief of the officers' leave bureau, France. By his untiring ene and devotion to duty Colonel Groome rendered a service of great value the morale of the American Army at a difficult time.

GROVE, WILLIAM R.
 R—Denver, Colo.
 B—Montezuma, Iowa.
 G. O. No. 17, W. D., 1924.
 Medal of honor also awarded.

Colonel, Quartermaster Corps, U. S. Army.
Assistant to the chief of the supply division, Quartermaster General's offi a position of great responsibility, he was charged with the procurement of subsistence supplies of the Army in the United States and in France, and him is due the organization of the subsistence division of the office of Quartermaster General. In cooperation with the Food Administration, made arrangements for the procurement of all subsistence supplies requi for the Army. He rendered services of much value.

GRUBER, EDMUND L.
 R—Cincinnati, Ohio.
 B—Cincinnati, Ohio.
 G. O. No. 69, W. D., 1919.

Colonel, Field Artillery, U. S. Army.
He displayed exceptional ability in planning the organization of Field Artill brigade firing centers; in April, 1918, established such a center as Fort S and during the remainder of the war displayed rare judgment and high p fessional attainments in the administration of this center.

GRUNERT, GEORGE
 R—White Haven, Pa.
 B—White Haven, Pa.
 G. O. No. 59, W. D., 1919.

Lieutenant colonel (Cavalry), General Staff Corps, U. S. Army.
With remarkable skill, constantly displaying zeal and high military atta ments, he performed his exacting duties as assistant chief of staff, G–1, of 1st Corps, during the successive operations at Chateau-Thierry, on Ourcq and Vesle, and in the St. Mihiel and Argonne-Meuse offensives. his untiring and painstaking efforts and unusual ability he performed most difficult tasks, rendering services of great value to the Government.

GULICK, JOHN W.
 R—Goldsboro, N. C.
 B—Goldsboro, N. C.
 G. O. No. 19, W. D., 1920.

Colonel (Coast Artillery Corps), General Staff Corps, U. S. Army.
As assistant chief of the operations section and later as chief of staff of Army Artillery of the 1st Army, he demonstrated a keen conception of al the tactical situations which confronted the artillery of the 1st Army. his high professional attainments and sound military judgment, he hand the many complex problems of the 1st Army Artillery with marked sl and thereby contributed, in no small degree, to the success of this unit in St. Mihiel and Meuse-Argonne offensives.

DISTINGUISHED-SERVICE MEDAL

GULLION, ALLEN W.
R—Carrollton, Ky.
B—Carrollton, Ky.
G. O. No. 9, W. D., 1923.

Lieutenant colonel, Judge Advocate General's Department, U. S. Army.
In the national administration of the selective service law from May 4, 1917, to Mar. 26, 1918. As chief of publicity and information under the provost marshal general he successfully conducted the campaign to popularize selective service. Later, as acting executive officer to the provost marshal general, he solved many intricate problems with firmness, promptness, and common sense. Finally, as the first chief of the mobilization division of the provost marshal general's office, he supervised all matters relating to the making and filling of calls and the accomplishment of individual inductions. To each of his varied and important duties he brought a high order of ability and remarkable powers of application. His services were of great value in raising our National Army.

GUNBY, FRANK M.
R—Boston, Mass.
B—Charleston, S. C.
G. O. No. 103, W. D., 1919.

Colonel, Quartermaster Corps, U. S. Army.
As officer in charge of the engineering branch of the construction division of the Army. The success of the engineering features of the Army building program is in large measure due to Colonel Gunby's genius for organization, his ability to judge men and inspire in them a determination to succeed. The services he rendered are of signal worth.

GURNEY, SAMUEL C.
R—Detroit, Mich.
B—England.
G. O. No. 53, W. D., 1921.

Lieutenant colonel, Medical Corps, U. S. Army.
For services in evacuating and personally caring for the wounded of the 3d Division under heavy shell and machine-gun fire daily during the defensive and offensive operations on the Marne, and great devotion under shell fire in personally establishing battalion aid stations at Chartreves, Jaulgonne, and Le Charmel between July 14 and Aug. 1, 1918.

HAAN, WILLIAM G.
R—Crown Point, Ind.
B—Crown Point, Ind.
G. O. No. 12, W. D., 1919.

Major general, U. S. Army.
This officer, in command of the 32d Division, took a prominent part in the Argonne-Meuse offensive and in the brilliant and successful attack against the Cote Dame Marie, covering several days, which deprived the enemy of the key point of the position. His clear conception of the tactical situations involved showed him to be a military leader of superior order.

HACKETT, HORATIO B.
R—Abilene, Kans.
B—Chicago, Ill.
G. O. No. 56, W. D., 1921.

Colonel, Field Artillery, U. S. Army.
For services while commanding the 124th Field Artillery, 33d Division, during the St. Mihiel and Meuse-Argonne offensives until he was severely wounded.

HAGERLING, SIDNEY A.
R—Pittsburgh, Pa.
B—Pittsburgh, Pa.
G. O. No. 38, W. D., 1922.

Lieutenant colonel, Signal Corps, U. S. Army.
As division signal officer, 28th Division, during the operations of his division on the Vesle in September, 1918, and later during the Meuse-Argonne offensive, Colonel Hagerling by his complete knowledge of his duties, his ceaseless energy, his initiative, and his devotion to duty, regardless of extreme difficulties of terrain and heavy shell fire by the enemy in open-warfare situations, maintained the telephone net of the division intact at all times, thereby enabling the division commander to communicate with all elements of the division, even the front line, and assisting very materially in the control and conduct of the division and in bringing its operations to a very successful conclusion.

HAGOOD, JOHNSON.
R—Columbia, S. C.
B—Orangeburg, S. C.
G. O. No. 12, W. D., 1919.

Brigadier general, U. S. Army.
As chief of staff of the services of supply of the American Expeditionary Forces in France his ability for organization, his energy, and his sound judgment were factors in the efficiency of this important branch. By his marked zeal and aggressiveness he greatly added to the successful administrations of the services of supply.

HALE, HARRY C.
R—Galesburg, Ill.
B—Knoxville, Ill.
G. O. No. 38, W. D., 1922.

Major general, U. S. Army.
While in command of the 84th Division during its organization and training in the United States and after the armistice in command of the 26th Division in France, by his ceaseless energy and the closest personal supervision of the training, discipline, and supply of his commands, he displayed rare qualities of leadership, organization, tact, and judgment. His brilliant professional attainments, his steadfast devotion to duty, and his loyalty to superiors were reflected in the high standards maintained throughout the divisions under his command, and he thus rendered important services to the American Expeditionary Forces and contributed conspicuously to the success of the operations.

HALE, RICHARD K.
R—Brookline, Mass.
B—Boston, Mass.
G. O. No. 56, W. D., 1922.

Colonel (Field Artillery), General Staff Corps, U. S. Army.
As assistant chief of staff, G-1, 2d Army Corps, from March, 1918, until April, 1919, he displayed exceptional ability in the organization and administration of that division of the corps staff. With rare tact he assisted in the establishment of most cordial relations with the British organizations with which the corps was serving. He showed excellent judgment and great administrative ability in the handling of important questions in the arrangements for the service of American troops with the British.

HALL, ELBERT J.
R—Oakland, Calif.
B—San Jose, Calif.
G. O. No. 69, W. D., 1919.

Lieutenant colonel, Air Service, U. S. Army.
In the designing of the Liberty engine and subsequently in the adapting of the Le Rhone engine to the American methods of production and also in pushing to completion the American adaptation of the De Haviland plane.

HALL, HARRISON
R—Dayton, Ohio.
B—Dayton, Ohio.
G. O. No. 31, W. D., 1922.

Colonel, Field Artillery, U. S. Army.
In organizing and assisting in the conduct of training camps in the United States. Later, as chief of staff of the American Embarkation Center at Le Mans and as chief of staff of the 1st Replacement Depot at St. Aignan, he assisted in the organization of a system of evacuation which insured a very satisfactory flow of personnel to ports of embarkation. In these capacities he displayed exceptional efficiency.

HALLORAN, PAUL S.
R—York, Pa.
B—Camp Wright, Calif.
G. O. No. 103, W. D., 1919.

Colonel, Medical Corps, U. S. Army.
He served with great credit as division surgeon of the 90th Division from the date of its organization throughout its service in the field, displaying sound judgment, marked professional skill, and untiring energy. By enforcing effective sanitary measures he maintained the combat strength of his division, and by his able direction of the medical services he was largely responsible for the proper care of the sick and wounded.

HALSEY, CHARLES W.
R—New York, N. Y.
B—Newark, N. J.
G. O. No. 53, W. D., 1921.

Major, Quartermaster Corps, U. S. Army.
As deputy of the chief quartermaster, in the service of the 4th section of the General Staff at General Headquarters, a position of great responsibility, in which he rendered services of marked worth in all details relative to the Quartermaster Corps.

HALSTEAD, ALEXANDER SEAMAN
R—Philadelphia, Pa.
B—Philadelphia, Pa.
G. O. No. 30, W. D., 1921.

Rear admiral, U. S. Navy.
While in command of the United States naval forces at Brest, France, by his superior administration, sound judgment, and splendid cooperation he contributed materially to the success achieved by the Army at the port of Brest in the return to the United States of the American Expeditionary Forces.

HALSTEAD, LAURENCE
R—Riverside, Ohio.
B—Riverside, Ohio.
G. O. No. 49, W. D., 1922.

Colonel, Infantry, U. S. Army.
As officer in charge of quartermaster schools and assistant to officer in charge of administrative division, office of the Quartermaster General, from April to August, 1917, he rendered valuable service in the organization and operation of these schools. As chief of staff, 84th Division, from August, 1917, to November, 1918, by his marked efficiency, loyal devotion to duty, and high military attainments, he played an important part in the successful organization, training, and operations of that division. Later as assistant chief of staff, G-3, 1st Army, from November, 1918, to April, 1919, he performed many tasks of great responsibility in a highly meritorious manner.

HALYBURTON, EDGAR M. (42848)
R—Taylorsville, N. C.
B—Stony Point, N. C.
G. O. No. 72, W. D., 1920.

Sergeant, Company F, 16th Infantry, 1st Division, U. S. Army.
Sergeant Halyburton, while a prisoner in the hands of the German Government from November, 1917, to November, 1918, voluntarily took command of the different camps in which he was located and under difficult conditions established administrative and personnel headquarters, organized the men into units, billeted them systematically, established sanitary regulations and made equitable distribution of supplies; he established an intelligence service to prevent our men giving information to the enemy and prevent the enemy introducing propaganda. His patriotism and leadership under trying conditions were an inspiration to his fellow prisoners and contributed greatly to the amelioration of their hardships.

HAM, SAMUEL V.
R—Warrington, Ind.
B—Markleville, Ind.
G. O. No. 13, W. D., 1923.
Distinguished-service cross also awarded.

Colonel, Infantry, U. S. Army.
As colonel, 109th Infantry, 28th Division, he displayed in combat rare qualities of leadership, unusual tactical judgment, and devotion to duty. Severely wounded in action, he returned to duty as commanding officer of troops at Is-sur-Tille, a position of great responsibility, in which he acquitted himself with great credit, contributing materially to the proper functioning of the services of supply, American Expeditionary Forces.

HAMBLETON, THOMAS EDWARD
R—Lutherville, Md.
B—Baltimore, Md.
G. O. No. 59, W. D., 1919.

Colonel, Adjutant General's Department, U. S. Army.
He displayed unusual skill and untiring zeal in organizing and administering the statistical division of The Adjutant General's Office. With no precedent to guide or assist him, he showed marked initiative in this most difficult task, creating a wonderful record of achievement, which is a tribute to his ability and clear-sightedness amid a maze of details. Self-sacrificing in his devotion to duty, he achieved excellent results in all his endeavors.

HAMILTON, GEORGE L.
R—Boston, Mass.
B—Covington, Ky.
G. O. No. 47, W. D., 1921.

Lieutenant colonel, Postal Express Service, U. S. Army.
For services in organizing and administering the motor dispatch service of the American Expeditionary Forces.

HAMILTON, WESLEY W. K.
R—Dayton, Ohio.
B—Cincinnati, Ohio.
G. O. No. 27, W. D., 1922.

Colonel, Coast Artillery Corps, U. S. Army.
As adjutant, Base Section No. 3, in 1917–1918, in the initiation, development, extension, and administration of those headquarters, through whose agency vast supplies and over a million troops were forwarded to France, he rendered a service of great value.

HAMMOND, THOMAS W.
R—Ashland, Oreg.
B—Ashland, Oreg.
G. O. No. 15, W. D., 1921.

Colonel (Infantry), General Staff Corps, U. S. Army.
While a member of the General Staff in the early days of the war his judgment and ability were applied to the solution of intricate problems concerning the distribution of the draft. He rendered meritorious service in France both as a line and as a staff officer. The services rendered by him, pertaining to the preparation and development of the reorganization act of June 4, 1920, have been of great value to the Army.

HAND, DANIEL W.
R—Oakmont, Pa.
B—St. Paul, Minn.
G. O. No. 19, W. D., 1921.

Lieutenant colonel, Field Artillery, U. S. Army.
For services as assistant director and director of the department of firing in the School of Fire for Field Artillery, Fort Sill, Okla., from October, 1917, to October, 1918.

HANNER, JOHN W.
R—Franklin, Tenn.
B—Franklin, Tenn.
G. O. No. 89, W. D., 1919.

Colonel, Medical Corps, U. S. Army.
As commanding officer of Evacuation Hospital No. 1 he displayed high professional attainments and loyal devotion to duty. Subsequently, as chief surgeon, 4th Army Corps, by his able supervision of the medical and sanitary units under his direction he rendered invaluable services in connection with the care of many sick and wounded.

HANNUM, WARREN T.
R—Pottsville, Pa.
B—Pottsville, Pa.
G. O. No. 89, W. D., 1919.

Colonel, Corps of Engineers, U. S. Army.
As a member of the training section, General Staff, he efficiently supervised the technical and tactical training of engineer, gas, and tank troops and the operation of the schools for those services. In the performance of his manifold duties he displayed military attainments of a high order, rendering service of importance to the American Expeditionary Forces.

HANSON, MARCUS H.
R—San Antonio, Tex.
B—Stow, Mass.
G. O. No. 56, W. D., 1921.

Lieutenant colonel, Quartermaster Corps, U. S. Army.
As assistant to the Chief Quartermaster, American Expeditionary Forces, in charge of the administrative division, a position of great responsibility, in which he rendered services of conspicuous worth.

HARBORD, JAMES G.
R—Council Grove, Kans.
B—Bloomington, Ill.
G. O. No. 136, W. D., 1918.

Major general, U. S. Army.
As chief of staff of the American Expeditionary Forces, and later as commanding general, services of supply, in both of which important positions his great constructive ability and professional attainments have played an important part in the success obtained by our armies. Commanded Marine Brigade of 2d Division, Belleau Wood, and later ably commanded 2d Division during attack on Soissons, France, July 18, 1918.

HARDEMAN, LETCHER.
R—Grays Summit, Mo.
B—Arrow Rock, Mo.
G. O. No. 38, W. D., 1922.

Colonel, Quartermaster Corps, U. S. Army.
From May 30, 1917, until Oct. 10, 1918, as principal assistant in the supply office of the Quartermaster General, he showed great executive ability, excellent judgment, and a rare understanding of supply problems. On Oct. 10, 1918, during the period of urgent demand for animals so necessary to our overseas forces, he became chief of the remount service, and by his knowledge, efficiency, and broad experience he was able to organize and perfect the system for the purchase, collection, and shipment of large numbers of animals to supply these demands. Immediately after the signing of the armistice, he again rendered conspicuous services by instituting the method by which 200,000 surplus animals were promptly and efficiently disposed of, resulting in the saving of an enormous sum to the Government.

HARDING, JOHN, Jr.
R—Dayton, Ohio.
B—Nashville, Tenn.
G. O. No. 14, W. D., 1925.
Act of Congress Feb. 25, 1925.

Second lieutenant, Air Service Reserve, U. S. Army.
Lieutenant Harding, as assistant pilot of airplane No. 4, the *New Orleans*, and assistant engineer officer of the United States Army Air Service around-the-world flight from Apr. 6, 1924, to Sept. 28, 1924, displayed sound technical skill, a high spirit of cooperation, initiative, energy, and resourcefulness. His indefatigable energy, good judgment, and personal courage contributed largely to the success of this pioneer flight of airplanes around the world. In the performance of his arduous duties he aided in the accomplishment of an undertaking bringing great credit to himself and to the Military Establishment of the United States.

HARJES, HENRY H.
R—New York, N. Y.
B—Paris, France.
G. O. No. 59, W. D., 1919.

Lieutenant colonel, Infantry, U. S. Army.
As chief liaison officer of the American Expeditionary Forces he rendered most valuable and important service in establishing and maintaining cordial relations between the French and American authorities. His efforts materially furthered that deep feeling of understanding which marks the association of the allied Armies.

HARMON, KENNETH B.
R—Altoona, Pa.
B—San Francisco, Calif.
G. O. No. 74, W. D., 1919.

Lieutenant colonel, Ordnance Department, U. S. Army.
With exceptionally sound judgment and marked initiative, he displayed a wide comprehension of existing conditions, solving perplexing problems connected with the establishment and operation of the storage system of the Ordnance Department of the American Expeditionary Forces. He opened first a base, then an intermediate depot, and later an advance depot, accomplishing these tasks in spite of numerous obstacles. At all times tireless in energy he worked to insure an adequate supply of ordnance matériel for the troops at the front.

HARRELL, WILLIAM F.
R—Marion, S. C.
B—Marion, S. C.
G. O. No. 59, W. D., 1919.
Distinguished-service cross also awarded.

Colonel, Infantry, U. S. Army.
He served through all operations of the 1st Division in this war, and at all times was conspicuous for his courage, judgment, and leadership. As battalion and regimental commander, he distinguished himself by his exceptionally energetic and efficient command of his units. During the rapid advance of the 1st Division upon Sedan he carried out a most difficult mission of the division in that he successfully covered its right flank in a night march of about 20 kilometers, across broken country, in the face of the enemy. Herein he exhibited the qualities of a most able commander.

HARRIES, GEORGE H.
R—Washington, D. C.
B—South Wales.
G. O. No. 103, W. D., 1919.

Brigadier general, U. S. Army.
As commanding general of Base Section No. 5, he successfully directed the manifold activities at the port of Brest during the time when troop arrivals were at their maximum. He overcame seemingly insurmountable obstacles in coordinating and organizing his important task. Subsequently, upon being sent on a special mission to Berlin in connection with the repatriation of allied prisoners of war, he displayed commendable tact and energy.

HARRIS, CHARLES T., Jr R—Mexia, Tex. B—Mexia, Tex. G. O. No. 77, W. D., 1919.	Colonel, Ordnance Department, U. S. Army. Chief of the American Mission of Powder and Explosive Manufacture visited England. Later, as chief of the powder and explosive sectio Engineering Division of the Office of the Chief of Ordnance, he applie methods of manufacture to United States industry so successfully only were the needs of the United States fully met, but a considerabl of these materials was rendered available for the cobelligerents aga: many.
HARRIS, PETER C R—Cedartown, Ga. B—Kingston, Ga. G. O. No. 25, W. D., 1919.	Major general, The Adjutant General, U. S. Army. During his service in the Adjutant General's Department, his zeal and judgment have been made manifest by the reforms accomp. record keeping systems in the War Department and in the Army.
HARRISON, CHARLES L R—Cincinnati, Ohio. B—Cincinnati, Ohio. G. O. No. 124, W. D., 1919.	As chief of the Cincinnati ordnance district, in which capacity he me at all times the greatest degree of intelligent and enthusiastic coo between the Ordnance Department and manufacturers in his distric by attaining the maximum production of munitions in a minimu and also as chairman of the Cincinnati ordnance district claims l which capacity his services have been invaluable to the Nation in ; equitably the $153,000,000 worth of outstanding contracts in his d force at the signing of the armistice.
HART, WILLIAM H R—Bath, S. Dak. B—Winona, Minn. G. O. No. 59, W. D., 1919.	Colonel, Quartermaster Corps, U. S. Army. While serving as quartermaster, Base Section No. 1, by his thoroug edge of methods and standards of supplying troops, his resourceful: comprehensive study of the innumerable details of the largest a important supply bases in France, he executed the important du which he was intrusted in a highly satisfactory and especially efficient
HARTE, RICHARD H R—Philadelphia, Pa. B—Rock Island, Ill. G. O. No. 9, W. D., 1923.	Colonel, Medical Corps, U. S. Army. From May, 1917, until May, 1919, as director of professional services as commanding officer, Base Hospital No. 10, surgical consultant, , Expeditionary Forces, member of the Interallied Medical and Conference, and one of the pioneer instructors in the principles surgery, by his high professional attainments, keen foresight, and energy he solved successfully many problems which confronted him, services of the greatest value to the American Expeditionary Forces
HARTMAN, CHARLES D R—Brookhaven, Miss. B—Brookhaven, Miss. G. O. No. 14, W. D., 1923.	Colonel, Quartermaster Corps, U. S. Army. As chief of the utilities section of the construction division, Quar Corps, he was charged with the direction of the manifold activities in the maintenance of all fixed properties of the War Departmen States Army cantonments. including buildings and roads, the ope all utilities, including water, sewage plants and systems, lighting, refrigeration, and power plants throughout the United States. The energy, sound professional judgment, administrative and executiv displayed by Colonel Hartman contributed in a signal way to the : operations of the Quartermaster Corps during the World War.
HARTMANN, EDWARD T R—Milwaukee, Wis. B—Chicago, Ill. G. O. No. 89, W. D., 1919.	Colonel, Infantry, U. S. Army. He organized the 357th Infantry, 90th division, and commanded it w ordinary ability during its training period and throughout its acti tions. To his energy, zeal, and high qualities of leadership were lar the consistently high standards of efficiency maintained by his regime successes which it achieved in the St. Mihiel and Meuse-Argonne :
HARTS, WILLIAM W R—Springfield, Ill. B—Springfield, Ill. G. O. No. 89, W. D., 1919.	Brigadier general, U. S. Army. In command of the important District of Paris, by his painstaking e able directorship he maintained a high standard of discipline and among his large command. By his tact and keen perception he numerous diplomatic affairs with great satisfaction, rendering s a superior value to the American Expeditionary Forces.
HARTSHORN, EDWIN S R—New York, N. Y. B—Troy, N. Y. G. O. No. 98, W. D., 1919.	Colonel (Infantry), General Staff Corps, U. S. Army. As chief of the coordination section. office of the executive assista Chief of Staff, his energy, judgment, and foresight have been of e: value to the War Department and to the Army.
HARVEY, ALVA L. (6203842) R—Cleburne, Tex. B—Cleburne, Tex. G. O. No. 14, W. D., 1925. Act of Congress Feb. 25, 1925.	Staff sergeant, Air Service, U. S. Army. Sergeant Harvey displayed unusual judgment, technical knowle initiative in the preparation of the airplanes for the United States Service around-the-world flight and as mechanician and assistar airplane No. 1, the Seattle, from Apr. 6, 1924, until Apr. 30, 1924, ` to an accident which resulted in the complete wreck of the airplar forced to abandon the flight. His foresight, perseverance, and n ability were very material factors in contributing to the successi plishment of this pioneer flight of airplanes around the world. I formance of this great task he aided in bringing great credit to th forces of the United States.
HASE, WILLIAM F R—Milwaukee, Wis. B—Milwaukee, Wis. G. O. No. 69, W. D., 1919.	Colonel, Coast Artillery Corps, U. S. Army. For services as senior assistant to the Chief of Coast Artillery in the p and execution of plans for the effective accomplishment of the duti to the Coast Artillery Corps in the operations in France.

HASKELL, WILLIAM N.
R—Albany, N. Y.
B—Bath-on-the-Hudson, N. Y.
G. O. No. 59, W. D., 1919.

Colonel (Field Artillery), General Staff Corps, U. S. Army.
He exhibited devotion, skill, and untiring energy as chief of the operations section, 4th Army Corps, during its organization and in the St. Mihiel offensive. As chief of the operations section, 2d Army, he rendered exceptionally meritorious service during the organization of that Army and in the operations north of Toul, October and November, 1918.

HATCH, HENRY J.
R—Ionia, Mich.
B—Charlotte, Mich.
G. O. No. 19, W. D., 1922.

Brigadier general, U. S. Army.
As Chief of Heavy Artillery Section, office of the Chief of Artillery of the American Expeditionary Forces in France, a position involving individual and independent responsibility, he performed services of inestimable value in connection with the organization, equipment, and training of the Artillery troops in France.

HATHAWAY, LEVY M.
R—Owensboro, Ky.
B—Owensboro, Ky.
G. O. No. 56, W. D., 1922.

Colonel, Medical Corps, U. S. Army.
As surgeon, 33d Division, throughout its organization, training, and combat operations, by his devotion to duty, untiring energy, and high professional attainments, he rendered conspicuous service, maintaining at all times a remarkable health record in the division. His handling of the wounded, involving personal exposure to heavy enemy fire during his daily inspections of the advanced dressing stations, was notable for its extraordinary efficiency. Later, as chief surgeon, 9th Army Corps, he again rendered highly meritorious service to the American Expeditionary Forces.

HAY, WILLIAM H.
R—Drifton, Fla.
B—Monticello, Fla.
G. O. No. 89, W. D., 1919.

Major general, U. S. Army.
As commander of the 184th Infantry Brigade he showed efficient leadership. Promoted to major generalship in the early part of October, 1918, he took command of the 28th Division, and by his marked ability and great energy he contributed to the successes attained by the division during the time in which he was in command. He rendered services of a high character to the American Expeditionary Forces.

HAYES, EDWARD S.
R—Waterbury, Conn.
B—Waterbury, Conn.
G. O. No. 9, W. D., 1923.
Distinguished-service cross also awarded.

Lieutenant colonel (Infantry), General Staff Corps, U. S. Army.
As assistant chief of staff, G-3, 78th Division, in the St. Mihiel and Meuse-Argonne offensives, he was an important factor in the success of the division and rendered exceptional services by the persistence and courage of his front line reconnaissances; by his originality and the soundness of his plans of relief and attack; and by the clearness and correctness of all orders written by him for the operations of the division. His work was creative and constructive to a high degree and rendered in a highly meritorious manner in a position of great responsibility.

HAYES, GEORGE B.
R—Paris, France.
B—Canandaigua, N. Y.
G. O. No. 72, W. D., 1920.

An eminent dental surgeon who placed freely the advantages of his professional attainments and the full facilities of his complete clinic at Paris at the services of the American medical personnel. By the markedly distinguished record made by him in jaw and facial surgery among the wounded of the American Expeditionary Forces, and in his able directorate of the school for instruction of dental personnel in maxillo facial and prosthetic surgery, he has rendered services of preeminent worth.

HAYES, JAMES H.
R—Atlantic City, N. J.
B—Haddon Field, N. C.
G. O. No. 49, W. D., 1922.

Lieutenant colonel, Judge Advocate General's Department, U. S. Army.
As judge advocate of the 2d Division during its organization in October, 1917, and throughout all its combat operations, he handled with unusual merit many questions confronting him. By his high order of legal ability, broad vision, excellent judgment, and a most comprehensive knowledge of discipline and morale he rendered services of exceptional value to the American Expeditionary Forces.

HAYWARD, WILLIAM.
R—New York, N. Y.
B—Nebraska City, Nebr.
G. O. No. 50, W. D., 1919.

Colonel, Infantry, U. S. Army.
As commander of a regiment that was detached from the American Expeditionary Forces and served continuously with a French division, he was charged with particularly responsible and exacting duties, in the performance of which he at all times displayed commendable tact, personal bravery, and military leadership of a high order.

HEARN, CLINT C.
R—Whitesboro, Tex.
B—Weston, Tex.
G. O. No. 59, W. D., 1921.

Brigadier general, U. S. Army.
For services while in command of the 153d Field Artillery Brigade, 78th Division, during the Meuse-Argonne offensive.

HECKEL, EDWARD G.
R—Detroit, Mich.
B—Menasha, Wis.
G. O. No. 56, W. D., 1922.

Colonel, Infantry, U. S. Army.
He served with the 125th Infantry, 32d Division, as lieutenant colonel from the organization until September, 1918, and as colonel from then until June, 1919, displaying at all times military attainments of a high order. By his initiative, force, marked ability, and untiring devotion to duty he contributed materially to the successes of his division in four major operations against the enemy, thereby rendering services of inestimable value to the American Expeditionary Forces.

HECKMAN, JAMES C.
R—Buffalo, N. Y.
B—Phillipsburg, N. J.
G. O. No. 9, W. D., 1923.

Colonel, Ordnance Department, U. S. Army.
As chief, storage operations section, supply division, Office of the Chief of Ordnance, and later as chief of supply division, he assisted in formulating the general scheme of ordnance storage depots and planned and operated with marked success those assigned to the Ordnance Department. His sound judgment, wide business experience, and administrative ability contributed in a material way to the successful operations of the Ordnance Department.

HEGEMAN, HARRY A.
  R—Brookings, S. D.
  B—Sparta, Wis.
  G. O. No. 59, W. D., 1919.

Colonel, Infantry, U. S. Army.
With technical skill and great energy he organized a large force of trained wor men for the repair of motor transports. He restored to service a great ma of accumulated dead transportation of all kinds and types, and kept in op ation much transportation by timely repair. By his untiring efforts t motor transportation was maintained at such a standard as to become important factor in the successes achieved by the American troops.

HEINTZELMAN, STUART.
  R—Washington, D. C.
  B—New York, N. Y.
  G. O. No. 12, W. D., 1919.

Brigadier general, U. S. Army.
He organized the headquarters of the 4th Army Corps and later, as chief staff of this corps, directed with great success the staff of this organizati prior to and during the St. Mihiel offensive. As chief of staff of the 2d Arm he had a prominent part in organizing it as a fighting unit. His tact, energ and military ability were important elements in the success of this comman

HELMICK, ELI A.
  R—Weir City, Kans.
  B—Quakers Point, Ind.
  G. O. No. 95, W. D., 1919.

Major general, U. S. Army.
As commanding general, Base Section No. 5, he has displayed brilliant admin trative ability in successfully directing the manifold activities under h supervision. By his energy in expediting the completion of the vario engineering projects necessitated by the enlargement of Pontanezen Can and the development of Brest as a foremost embarkation camp, he h rendered invaluable services to the American Expeditionary Forces.

HERBST, GEORGE A.
  R—St. Paul, Minn.
  B—St. Paul, Minn.
  G. O. No. 15, W. D., 1923.

Colonel (Infantry), General Staff Corps, U. S. Army.
As assistant chief of staff, G-3, 2d Division, from Dec. 28, 1917, to Aug. 3, 191 and assistant chief of staff, G-2, 2d Division, Aug. 4 to Sept. 19, 1918, G section, General Headquarters, Sept. 20 to Oct. 2, 1918, assistant chief staff, G-2, 7th Army Corps, Oct. 3, 1918, to Nov. 16, 1918, he displayed unt ing energy, sound professional judgment, and devotion to duty. He render valuable services to the Government in positions of responsibility and co tributed materially to the successful operations of the American Forces France in actions against the enemy.

HERR, JOHN K.
  R—Flemington, N. J.
  B—White House Station, N. J.
  G. O. No. 87, W. D., 1919.

Colonel, Cavalry, U. S. Army.
He showed marked ability as chief of staff of the 30th Division in the capture Voormezeele and Lock Eight in the Ypres section in Belgium in Septembe 1918, and in the breaking of the Hindenburg line at Bellicourt, France, an the operations against the Selle River and the Sambre Canal, Sept. 29–Oct. 1918. By his energy, zeal, and persistent efforts, coupled with sound tactic judgment, he materially contributed to the success of the operations.

HERRINGSHAW, WILLIAM F.
  R—Cleveland, Ohio.
  B—Cleveland, Ohio.
  G. O. No. 43, W. D., 1922.

Colonel, Motor Transport Corps, U. S. Army.
As chief motor transport officer, 1st Army, American Expeditionary Force he at all times displayed initiative and marked ability. By his high milita attainments, sound judgment, and untiring efforts in his tasks he succe fully solved the many complex problems involving the supply, conservatio and repair of the motor transportation of the 1st Army during its operatio in the St. Mihiel and Meuse-Argonne offensives. He has rendered servic of signal worth to the American Expeditionary Forces.

HERRON, CHARLES D.
  R—Crawfordsville, Ind.
  B—Crawfordsville, Ind.
  G. O. No. 59, W. D., 1921.

Colonel (Field Artillery), General Staff Corps, U. S. Army.
For services as chief of staff, 78th Division, during the Meuse-Argonne offe sive.

HERSEY, MARK L.
  R—East Corinth, Me.
  B—Stetson, Me.
  G. O. No. 62, W. D., 1919.

Major general, U. S. Army.
As a brigade commander during the latter part of the Meuse-Argonne operatic he exhibited qualities of excellent leadership and sound judgment. H brigade attacked and penetrated the strong enemy position of Bois-des Log and wrested this strong point from the enemy. The success of his briga in this engagement was in a large measure due to his able leadership. Lat he commanded with distinction the 4th Division during its operations the occupied territory.

*HETRICK, HAROLD S.
  R—Canterbury, Conn.
  B—Kansas City, Mo.
  G. O. No. 56, W. D., 1922.

Colonel (Corps of Engineers), General Staff Corps, U. S. Army.
As assistant chief of staff, G-4, 2d Army Corps, from Feb. 24, 1918, to Aug. 1918, he displayed exceptional ability in the organization and administrati of that division of the corps staff. In the supply and equipment of organiz tions of the corps under the British system and with British matériel exhibited military attainments of a high order and contributed in a mark degree to the successful preparation for subsequent operations. Posthumously awarded. Medal presented to uncle, Andrew J. Clarke.

HICKMAN, EDWIN A.
  R—Lexington, Mo.
  B—Independence, Mo.
  G. O. No. 15, W. D., 1921.

Colonel (Infantry), General Staff Corps, U. S. Army.
For services as chief of a section of the General Staff which had charge of es mates and financial matters pertaining to the conduct of the war and t support of the Army.

HILDEBRAND, JOEL H.
  R—Berkeley, Calif.
  B—Camden, N. J.
  G. O. No. 56, W. D., 1922.

Lieutenant colonel, Chemical Warfare Service, U. S. Army.
As commandant of the Chemical Warfare Service Experimental Field (Hanl Field), American Expeditionary Forces, a position of great responsibili and also of considerable personal danger, his profound knowledge of chem try, coupled with his rapid grasp of military problems, enabled him to rend services of the utmost value in determining the best means for using gas an gas materials in the field.

DISTINGUISHED-SERVICE MEDAL

HILGARD, MILOSH R.
R—Belleville, Ill.
B—New York, N. Y.
G. O. No. 62, W. D., 1919.

Colonel, Quartermaster Corps, U. S. Army.
He organized the operations of the Quartermaster Corps at the important bases of St. Nazaire and Bordeaux, and later established and operated the first American regulating station, through which he successfully supplied a great number of American troops serving in the zone of the Armies and operating at the front. The successful operation of this great station was due directly to his painstaking efforts, his zeal, and great energy.

HILL, ARTHUR D.
R—Boston, Mass.
B—France.
G. O. No. 59, W. D., 1921.

Lieutenant colonel, Judge Advocate General's Department, U. S. Army.
As assistant judge advocate, services of supply, and assistant chief finance officer, American Expeditionary Forces, positions of great responsibility, he demonstrated marked ability in performing the various tasks assigned to him. He performed important services for the rents, requisitions, and claims service, and rendered valuable assistance in dealings with the representatives of the French Government in all matters of claims in France.

HILL, JOHN PHILIP.
R—Baltimore, Md.
B—Annapolis, Md.
G. O. No. 43, W. D., 1922.

Lieutenant colonel, Judge Advocate General's Department, U. S. Army.
As judge advocate of the 29th Division from August, 1917, until December, 1918, and of the 8th Army Corps from December, 1918, until April, 1919, his marked legal ability, sound judgment, and tireless energy were important factors in the splendid work of his department. Representing his division as liaison officer at headquarters, 17th Army Corps (French), in October, 1918, during the Meuse-Argonne offensive, by his tact and constant devotion to duty he rendered conspicuous services in this important operation.

HINDS, ERNEST.
R—New Hope, Ala.
B—Red Hill, Ala.
G. O. No. 12, W. D., 1919.

Major general, U. S. Army.
As Chief of Artillery, 1st Army Corps, commanding general, Army Artillery, of the 1st American Army, and as Chief of Artillery, American Expeditionary Forces, he perfected and successfully directed the organization and training of the Artillery of the American Army in France.

HINES, FRANK T.
R—Salt Lake City, Utah.
B—Salt Lake City, Utah.
G. O. No. 144, W. D., 1918.

Brigadier general, U. S. Army.
For services as chief of embarkation in organizing and administering the embarkation service during the war.

HINES, JOHN FORE.
R—Bowling Green, Ky.
B—Kentucky.
G. O. No. 116, W. D., 1919.

Captain, U. S. Navy.
For services as chief of staff of the commander, cruiser and transport fleet, Newport News division.

HINES, JOHN L.
R—White Sulphur Springs, W. Va.
B—White Sulphur Springs, W. Va.
G. O. No. 12, W. D., 1919.
Distinguished-service cross also awarded.

Major general, U. S. Army.
As regimental, brigade, division, and corps commander he displayed marked ability in each of the important duties with which he was intrusted and exhibited in the operations near Montdidier and Soissons and in the St. Mihiel and Argonne-Meuse offensives his high attainments as a soldier and a commander.

HINKLE, CHARLES L.
R—Frankfort, Ind.
B—Pleasantville, Ind.
G. O. No. 47, W. D., 1921.

Lieutenant colonel, Transportation Corps, U. S. Army.
For services in connection with the railroad operations of the United States Transportation Corps in France.

HITT, PARKER.
R—Indianapolis, Ind.
B—Indianapolis, Ind.
G. O. No. 59, W. D., 1919.

Colonel, Signal Corps, U. S. Army.
By his sound judgment and untiring efforts he assisted in perfecting the satisfactory organization of the Signal Corps of the American Expeditionary Forces, and he displayed conspicuous merit in his capacity as signal officer of the 1st American Army.

HODGE, HENRY W.
R—New York, N. Y.
B—Washington, D. C.
G. O. No. 14, W. D., 1923.

Colonel, Corps of Engineers, U. S. Army.
As general manager of roadways, American Expeditionary Forces, he displayed sound professional judgment, technical skill, untiring energy, and devotion to duty, thus contributing in a marked degree to the successes of the American forces in France.

HODGE, S. H.
R—Chicago, Ill.
B—Murfreesboro, Tenn.
G. O. No. 2, W. D., 1920.

Placed in charge of storage procurement for the Army, he rendered invaluable service in obtaining for the use of the Army an enormous amount of storage space at a cost averaging less than the commercial rate, thereby effecting a very substantial saving and enabling the storage division to meet a most pressing need for space required to mobilize and preserve the immense quantities of supplies gathered for the use of the Army. By his technical knowledge, broad judgment, and energetic action valuable results were obtained.

HODGES, CAMPBELL B.
R—Ruston, La.
B—Youngs Point, La.
G. O. No. 27, W. D., 1922.

Colonel (Infantry), General Staff Corps, U. S. Army.
As acting chief of staff, 31st Division, he demonstrated the highest professional attainments, and through his zeal and never-failing tact he was responsible in a large measure for the development of the high efficiency of that division. Later, as a member of the War Department General Staff, he rendered most valuable service in the development of the present system of efficiency reporting and in the development of the system of classification of commissioned personnel now in use.

*HODGES, GEORGE.
R—Baltimore, Md.
B—Newark, N. J.
G. O. No. 70, W. D., 1919.

Manager of the troop movement section of the division of operations, U. S. Railroad Administration.
Mr. Hodges arranged all the details of the movement of troops from local draft boards to mobilization camps, between camps, or from mobilization camps to the ports of embarkation for shipment overseas. Troops in large numbers were moved on short notice, and he was responsible for the successful coordination and carrying out of these movements.
Posthumously awarded. Medal presented to widow, Mrs. George Hodges.

HODGES, HARRY F
R—Lincoln, Mass.
B—Boston, Mass.
G. O. No. 15, W. D., 1923.

Major general, U. S. Army.
As commanding general, Camp Devens, Mass., he displayed unusual admini trative and executive ability, sound judgment, and high professional skil He established a model system of schools and training, organized and traine the 76th Division, and in addition thereto trained for overseas service mo1 than 40,000 men of other units. His untiring energy, devotion to dut; coupled with other outstanding soldierly qualities, contributed markedly 1 the successful operations of the American forces during the World War.

*HODGES, HARRY L
R—Norfolk, Va.
B—Norfolk, Va.
G. O. No. 3, W. D., 1922.

Lieutenant colonel (Field Artillery), General Staff Corps, U. S. Army.
As chief of staff of the military board of allied supply Colonel Hodges provide important liaison between the American member of the board and the Gener. Staff, General Headquarters. His duties, which were varied and comple were ably performed, often under great difficulties and embarrassment, an they continued to include the responsibility of gathering the data and pr senting the report on the supply systems of the allied armies and in the pr sentation of this completed report, which finally received the approval of h own Government.
Posthumously awarded. Medal presented to widow, Mrs. Harry L. Hodge

HODGES, JOHN N
R—Baltimore, Md.
B—Baltimore, Md.
G. O. No. 9, W. D., 1923.

Lieutenant colonel, Corps of Engineers, U. S. Army.
While in command of the 6th Engineers, 3d Division, attached to the Britis Expeditionary Forces, from Feb. 11 to Apr. 1, 1918, during which tin the regiment was engaged in the construction of heavy bridges on the Somn and on fortification and combat duty, because of his high profession ability, his great energy, and devotion to duty he contributed materially 1 the accomplishments of the forces engaged in those operations.

*HODGSON, FREDERICK G
R—Athens, Ga.
B—Athens, Ga.
G. O. No. 38, W. D., 1922.

Colonel, Quartermaster Corps, U. S. Army.
While serving as representative of the Quartermaster Corps on the gener munitions board of the Council of National Defense from April, 1917, until h death, Aug. 5, 1917, he displayed most distinguished ability and performe his manifold duties in a most conspicuous manner in a position of great respo1 sibility at a time of gravest importance. By his tact, foresight, and exceller judgment his services in connection with the development of the vast progra1 of housing and supply for our Army were of material assistance to the succes ful prosecution of the war and were of signal worth to the Government.
Posthumously awarded. Medal presented to widow, Mrs. Ida C. Hodgson.

HOF, SAMUEL
R—Boscobel, Wis.
B—Boscobel, Wis.
G. O. No. 15, W. D., 1923.

Colonel, Ordnance Department, U. S. Army.
First, as commanding officer, Frankford Arsenal, from March 1918, to Marcl 1919, where, by his indefatigable energy, outstanding administrative abilit; and thorough technical knowledge, he brought to a successful productio basis tracer, incendiary, and armor-piercing small-arms ammunition, an supplied substantially all that was used by our troops; later, as acting chai man of the ordnance claims board, where, by his energy, tact, and busine: ability, he secured the settlement of outstanding obligations, and later, : chief of field service, Ordnance Department, where he perfected the organiz tion controlling the disposition of vast quantities of materials and plants le over from the war.

HOFFMAN, GEORGE M
R—Wilkes-Barre, Pa.
B—Wilkes-Barre, Pa.
G. O. No. 74, W. D., 1919.

Colonel, Corps of Engineers, U. S. Army.
As chief engineer of the 1st Army Corps, by his great energy and marked tecl nical ability he built up a strongly efficient organization, which made itse felt in all operations of the 1st Army Corps and in a great measure contribute to the successes achieved during the active operations of the 1st Army Cor1 at St. Mihiel and in the Argonne.

HOGAN, JOHN P
R—New York, N. Y.
B—Chicago, Ill.
G. O. No. 56, W. D., 1922.

Lieutenant colonel, Corps of Engineers, U. S. Army.
As officer in charge of the topographical sections, G-2, of the 5th Army Cor1 and the 2d Army, he contributed materially toward the success of the oper tions. Joining the 2d Army staff upon organization, he exercised such energ: judgment, and foresight that remarkable results were obtained in preparii maps for an offensive action and the subsequent occupation of the enemy territory.

HOLABIRD, JOHN A
R—Chicago, Ill.
B—Evanston, Ill.
G. O. No. 59, W. D., 1921.

Lieutenant colonel, Field Artillery, U. S. Army.
As commander of the 12th Field Artillery, 2d Division, during the period fro: August to November, 1918, a position of great responsibility, he commande his unit during the offensives of St. Mihiel, Mont Blanc, and Meuse-Argon1 with much credit. He has rendered important services to the United State

HOLBROOK, LUCIUS R
R—Sargent, Minn.
B—Arkansaw, Wis.
G. O. No. 19, W. D., 1926.

Brigadier general, U. S. Army.
As commander of the 7th Field Artillery and the 1st Field Artillery Brigac he with great distinction directed the artillery support of the 1st Division : the attacks on Cantigny and the Soissons salient. His careful judgment ar high military attainments were shown in the accuracy and timeliness of tl fire from the batteries under his direction, which, despite the difficulties i volved, contributed materially to the success of the operations.

HOLBROOK, WILLARD A
R—Arkansaw, Wis.
B—Arkansaw, Wis.
G. O. No. 47, W. D., 1919.

Major general, U. S. Army.
As commanding general, Southern Department, where his firmness and ta in handling a threatening situation on the Mexican border materially ir proved the conditions between the United States and Mexico.

HOLMAN, JESSE R
  R—Comanche, Tex.
  B—Fayette County, Tex.
  G. O. No. 59, W. D., 1919.

Colonel, Corps of Engineers, U. S. Army.
In charge of general construction in the vicinity of Bordeaux he displayed unusual judgment and great executive ability in the performance of the many duties assigned to him. In addition he rendered valuable service and advice to the other departments of Base Section No. 2 regarding construction.

HOMAN, CHARLES C
  R—Cleveland, Ohio.
  B—Williamsport, Pa.
  G. O. No. 14, W. D., 1923.

Lieutenant colonel, Motor Transport Corps, U. S. Army.
As assistant to the director, Motor Transport Corps, American Expeditionary Forces, he was charged with the assignment and distribution of motor transport to division, corps, and Army troops, the general supervision of motor transport within the zone of the services of supply, maintaining therein the difficult task of a balanced and efficient motor transport service. In these positions of grave responsibility he displayed unusual administrative and executive ability, high technical skill, and unremitting attention to duty, thus contributing markedly to the successful accomplishments of the American Expeditionary Forces.

HONOR, WILLIAM H
  R—Wyandotte, Mich.
  B—Canada.
  G. O. No. 53, W. D., 1921.

Lieutenant colonel, Medical Corps, U. S. Army.
For services in organizing and operating the medical section of the labor bureau, American Expeditionary Forces.

HOPKINS, JAY P
  R—Cassopolis, Mich.
  B—Mattawan, Mich.
  G. O. No. 62, W. D., 1919.

Colonel, Coast Artillery Corps, U. S. Army.
As chief of the Antiaircraft Artillery Service in the American Expeditionary Forces he performed arduous tasks with distinction, at all times being ceaseless in devotion to his important duties. Displaying marked scientific attainments, he handled perplexing problems with which the service was continually confronted with sound judgment, untiring energy, and a wide comprehension of the needs to be supplied and the facilities available.

HOPWOOD, LUCIUS L
  R—Des Moines, Iowa.
  B—Vinton, Iowa.
  G. O. No. 59, W. D., 1921.

Lieutenant colonel, Medical Corps, U. S. Army.
In the hospitalization division of the chief surgeon's office, a position of great responsibility, he had charge of the equipment and installation of hospitals throughout the services of supply in France, and it was due to his ability and energy that these units were so efficiently provided and maintained. He has rendered services of value to the United States.

HORSEY, HAMILTON R
  R—Tampa, Fla.
  B—Tallahassee, Fla.
  G. O. No. 56, W. D., 1922.

Lieutenant colonel, Infantry, U. S. Army.
As assistant chief of staff, G-2, 26th Division, during the St. Mihiel and Meuse-Argonne offensives, Colonel Horsey, by his complete grasp and knowledge of his duties, by his unfailing devotion to duty, and by his untiring energy, kept division headquarters at all times accurately and promptly informed as to the location of our own front lines and enemy troops, thus assisting materially in bringing the operations of the division to a successful conclusion.

HORTON, WILLIAM E
  R—Washington, D. C.
  B—Washington, D. C.
  G. O. No. 53, W. D., 1921.

Colonel, Quartermaster Corps, U. S. Army.
As chief quartermaster of the advance section, services of supply, a position of great responsibility, due to his untiring energy, the supplying of many thousands of troops in this section was successfully carried out and numerous Quartermaster Corps services and activities were organized and expeditiously administered. He has rendered services of great worth.

HOUGH, BENSON W
  R—Delaware, Ohio.
  B—Delaware County, Ohio.
  G. O. No. 47, W. D., 1921.

Colonel, Infantry, U. S. Army.
As regimental commander in the military operations of the 42d Division in the Baccarat Sector, Mar. 24 to June 21, 1918; the second Battle of the Marne, in which the 42d Division participated in the defense of the line east of Chalons, June 28 to July 21, 1918; and in the offensive against Reims, Chateau-Thierry, Soissons salient, July 24 to Aug. 3, 1918.

HOWARD, CARRIE L
  R—San Francisco, Calif.
  B—Colusa, Calif.
  G. O. No. 9, W. D., 1923

First lieutenant, chief nurse, Army Nurse Corps, U. S. Army.
As chief nurse at the port of embarkation, Hoboken, N. J., during the World War, she held a position of great responsibility. To her fell the duty of supervising the nursing departments of all the hospitals at the port of embarkation and the mobilization stations for nurses destined for overseas duty. By her efficiency, energy, and knowledge of administrative detail she added greatly to the proficiency of the Medical Department of the Army at those trying stations.

HOWARD, DEANE C
  R—Coleraine, Mass.
  B—Coleraine, Mass.
  G. O. No. 69, W. D., 1919.

Colonel, Medical Corps, U. S. Army.
In organizing and administering the division of sanitation and the sanitary inspection service of the office of the Surgeon General of the Army he contributed greatly to the efficiency of the military service.

HOWE, THORNDYKE D
  R—Lawrence, Mass.
  B—Lawrence, Mass.
  G. O. No. 59, W. D., 1919.

Colonel, Field Artillery, U. S. Army.
As chief of the Postal Express Service he organized and administered with marked ability the Postal Service of the American Expeditionary Forces. He displayed great breadth of vision and untiring zeal in overcoming the many obstacles that were encountered in the organization of the service of handling mail for our troops in Europe.

HOWELL, WILLEY
  R—Fayetteville, Ark.
  B—Austin, Ark.
  G. O. No. 59, W. D., 1919.

Colonel (Infantry), General Staff Corps, U. S. Army.
As assistant chief of staff, G-2, of the 1st Army he organized and directed the operations of this section during the entire operations of the 1st Army. The results achieved by him during the St. Mihiel and Meuse-Argonne operations had a noted influence on the successes gained by the 1st Army and showed him to be an officer of sound judgment and marked ability.

Howze, Robert L. R—Overton, Tex. B—Overton, Tex. G. O. No. 89, W. D., 1919. Medal of honor also awarded.	Major general, U. S. Army. As commander of the 3d Division on its march to the Rhine and during the occupation of the enemy territory he proved himself energetic and capable, exhibiting superb qualities of leadership. He maintained an unusually high standard of efficiency in his unit, rendering eminently conspicuous services as a division commander.
*Hoyle, Eli D. R—Haynesville, Ala. B—Canton, Ga. G. O. No. 4, W. D., 1923.	Brigadier general, U. S. Army. As department commander, Eastern Department, between Aug. 25, 1917, and Jan. 15, 1918, he handled many difficult problems arising in that department with rare judgment, tact, and great skill. Posthumously awarded. Medal presented to widow, Mrs. Eli D. Hoyle.
Hoyle, Rene E. De R. R—Governors Island, N. Y. B—West Point, N. Y. G. O. No. 38, W. D., 1922.	Colonel, Field Artillery, U. S. Army. As executive officer and later as assistant commandant of the School of Fire for Field Artillery, Fort Sill, Okla., during the period from November, 1917, to May, 1919, he displayed remarkable tact and excellent judgment, combined with executive and professional ability of a high order, in positions of great responsibility, thereby contributing materially toward bringing that school to a state of maximum efficiency in a time of great emergency.
Hubbard, Samuel T. R—New York, N. Y. B—Greenville, N. J. G. O. No. 13, W. D., 1923.	Major (Signal Corps), General Staff Corps, U. S. Army. In the intelligence section, General Staff, General Headquarters, American Expeditionary Forces, he organized and directed the operation of the battle order subsection, the section responsible for determining the effectives and tactics of the enemy and the location of enemy divisions on the western front. As director of the intelligence school, American Expeditionary Forces, Langres, France, he displayed rare efficiency and grasp of his work. His zeal and administrative and technical ability enabled him to render his Government services of great value in positions of responsibility.
Huebner, Clarence R. R—Bushton, Kans. B—Bushton, Kans. G. O. No. 56, W. D., 1922. Distinguished-service cross and oak-leaf cluster also awarded.	Lieutenant colonel, Infantry, U. S. Army. As captain, major, and lieutenant colonel of the 28th Infantry, 1st Division, throughout its training and active operations in France he successfully commanded all echelons of the regiment, participating with distinction in every engagement from Cantigny to Sedan, reorganizing his regiment after its heavy losses in the first phase of the Meuse-Argonne offensive, and inspiring it with the will and dash that carried it to the heights of Sedan. By his sound tactical judgment, his unusual leadership, and indefatigable energy he contributed in a marked manner to the various successes of his regiment and of the 1st Division and rendered to the American Expeditionary Forces most conspicuous services in a position of great responsibility.
Hughes, John C. R—New York, N. Y. B—Louisville, Ky. G. O. No. 59, W. D., 1919.	Captain, Infantry, U. S. Army. As aid-de-camp to the commander in chief, American Expeditionary Forces, he performed duties of an exacting nature with peculiar tact, ability, and untiring energy, proving himself sound in judgment and indefatigable in all tasks assigned to him. At all times he served with distinction, rendering exceptional service.
Hughes, John H. R—New York, N. Y. B—New York, N. Y. G. O. No. 89, W. D., 1919.	Colonel, Inspector General's Department, U. S. Army. As a member of the Inspector General's Department at the headquarters, services of supply, for an extended period of time, by his unflagging energy, sound judgment, and tact, he handled with conspicuous ability many difficult problems which constantly arose in the execution of his important office. He rendered services of signal worth to the American Expeditionary Forces.
Hughes, William N., Jr. R—Pittsburgh, Pa. B—Columbia, Tenn. G. O. No. 59, W. D., 1919.	Colonel (Infantry), General Staff Corps, U. S. Army. While he was serving as G-3 and as chief of staff of the 42d Division, his efforts had an important bearing on the successes gained by the division in the Baccarat sector, at the second Battle of the Marne, the operations near Chalons, Chateau-Thierry, the St. Mihiel salient, and along the Meuse. His splendid judgment and tactical ability were of the greatest value and demonstrated military knowledge of a high order.
Huidekoper, Frederic L. R—Washington, D. C. B—Meadville, Pa. G. O. No. 59, W. D., 1921.	Lieutenant colonel, Adjutant General's Department, U. S. Army. As liaison officer of the 33d Division, with the 18th French Division during the Meuse-Argonne offensive, Colonel Huidekoper did this liaison work as a volunteer and at times performed his duties in great danger of his life. This work was of exceedingly great responsibility.
Hulen, John A. R—Houston, Tex. B—Centralia, Tex. G. O. No. 56, W. D., 1921.	Brigadier general, U. S. Army. For services while commanding the 72d Infantry Brigade of the 36th Division in the Meuse-Argonne offensive Oct. 8–28, 1918.
Hull, John A. R—Des Moines, Iowa. B—Bloomfield, Iowa. G. O. No. 59, W. D., 1919.	Colonel, Judge Advocate General's Department, U. S. Army. As judge advocate of the service of supplies, he most creditably handled the questions brought before him. His sound legal training, his complete knowledge of military administration, and his clear conception of the new and difficult problems involved made his services of most exceptional value.
Hume, Edgar Erskine. R—Frankfort, Ky. B—Frankfort, Ky. G. O. No. 14, W. D., 1923.	Lieutenant colonel, Medical Corps, U. S. Army. As chief medical officer and later as commissioner of the American Red Cross in Serbia, February, 1919, to June, 1920, with untiring energy, unremitting devotion to duty, and with rare administrative and professional skill he organized and operated an American sanitary service, reorganizing hospitals dispensaries, and dressing stations for soldiers and civilians alike, and successfully combating an epidemic of typhus fever which had caused the death of 80 per cent of the Serbian doctors. From June, 1918, to February, 1919, in direct charge of an American base hospital which was later expanded by the addition of Italian hospitals into a composite hospital center in the Italian war zone, he rendered professional services of a highly conspicuous character

HUME, FRANK M _____
 R—Houlton, Me.
 B—Bridgewater, Me.
 G. O. No. 56, W. D., 1921.

Colonel, Infantry, U. S. Army.
For services while in command of the 103d Infantry, 26th Division, during the St. Mihiel and Meuse-Argonne operations.

HUMPHREY, GILBERT EDWIN _____
 R—El Reno, Okla.
 B—Abilene, Kans.
 G. O. No. 77, W. D., 1919.

Colonel, Corps of Engineers, U. S. Army.
For services while in charge of the building and organizing of the engineer depot at Norfolk, Va., and later as director of storage, purchase, storage and traffic division, General Staff.

HUNT, CHARLES A _____
 R—Nashua, N. H.
 B—Nashua, N. H.
 G. O. No. 59, W. D., 1919.

Colonel, Infantry, U. S. Army.
He commanded first a battalion of the 18th Infantry and later the regiment. He conducted his unit in every action with marked ability and skillful leadership, showing the finest qualities of good judgment, courage, and devotion to duty.

HUNT, IRVIN L _____
 R—Point Arena, Calif.
 B—Boonville, Calif.
 G. O. No. 55, W. D., 1920.

Colonel, Infantry, U. S. Army.
He served with conspicuous success as the officer in charge of civil affairs in the occupied area with the 3d Army and with the American Forces in Germany. With excellent judgment and sound adherence to well-established policies in a field of intricate problems affecting the civil population, he perfected, through his wide comprehension of conditions, an effective organization, which contributed materially to the efficiency of those forces.

HUNT, ORA E _____
 R—Point Arena, Calif.
 B—Berryessa, Calif.
 G. O. No. 95, W. D., 1919.

Brigadier general, U. S. Army.
As commander of the 6th Infantry Brigade, 3d Division, during the greater part of its active operations he achieved notable success, demonstrating high qualities of leadership. Through his exceptional tactical ability his brigade was enabled to overcome desperate hostile resistance during its participation in the Meuse-Argonne offensive. By his efforts he has contributed materially to the brilliant success of his brigade in that important operation.

HURLEY, EDWARD N _____
 R—Wheaton, Ill.
 B—Galesburg, Ill.
 G. O. No. 46, W. D., 1919.

Chairman, U. S. Shipping Board.
With tireless energy, he surmounted extreme difficulties and increased transAtlantic tonnage to an extent to allow of a steady shipment, both of troops and necessary supplies. Unselfish in devotion to duty, sound in judgment, quick to act, he rendered a service to the world.

HURLEY, PATRICK J _____
 R—Tulsa, Okla.
 B—Indian Territory.
 G. O. No. 68, W. D., 1920.

Lieutenant colonel, Judge Advocate General's Department, U. S. Army.
Assigned as judge advocate, Army Artillery, 1st Army, he rendered services of marked ability, performing, in addition to his manifold duties, the duties of adjutant general and of inspector general. Later, as judge advocate of the 6th Army Corps, he ably conducted the negotiations arising between the American Expeditionary Forces and the Grand Duchy of Luxemburg wherein he displayed sound judgment, marked zeal, and keen perception of existing conditions. He has rendered services of material worth to the American Expeditionary Forces.

HUTCHESON, GROTE _____
 R—Newtown, Ohio.
 B—Cincinnati, Ohio.
 G. O. No. 18, W. D., 1919.

Major general, U. S. Army.
For services in the administration of the port of embarkation, Newport News, Va., in connection with the shipment of troops overseas.

HUTCHINSON, JAMES P _____
 R—Philadelphia, Pa.
 B—Philadelphia, Pa.
 G. O. No. 56, W. D., 1922.

Colonel, Medical Corps, U. S. Army.
As commanding officer, American Red Cross Military Hospital No. 1, American Expeditionary Forces, he displayed exceptional ability in the organization and administration of that unit. By his devotion to duty, untiring energy, coupled with professional attainments of a high order, he rendered services of inestimable value in a position of great responsibility in the alleviation of the sufferings of our sick and wounded.

HUTTON, PAUL C _____
 R—Goldsboro, N. C.
 B—Goldsboro, N. C.
 G. O. No. 59, W. D., 1919.

Colonel, Medical Corps, U. S. Army.
As chief surgeon of the Paris group from June 2 to July 26, 1918, during which period by his good judgment and untiring energy he provided a hospitalization and evacuation system that insured prompt and excellent care and treatment of the wounded, he furnished the means of saving many lives and provided comfort for the wounded, thereby greatly adding to the morale of the combatant troops of both the American and the French engaged in the second Battle of the Marne.

HUTTON, WILLIAM H. H., Jr _____
 R—Detroit, Mich.
 B—Fort Jefferson, Fla.
 G. O. No. 95, W. D., 1919.

Colonel, Air Service, U. S. Army.
As chief of personnel service and later assistant chief of the supply section, Air Service, he was charged with duties of a varied and difficult nature. He constantly displayed marked zeal and sound judgment in the solution of the important problems of supply and transportation of the Air Service, rendering services of inestimable value to the American Expeditionary Forces.

INGRAHAM, CHARLES NELSON _____
 R—Findlay, Ohio.
 B—Oil City, Pa.
 G. O. No. 116, W. D., 1919.

Lieutenant commander, U. S. Navy.
As force transport officer his untiring energy contributed greatly to the successful oversea movement of troops and supplies.

IRELAND, MARK L _____
 R—Chesaning, Mich.
 B—Chesaning, Mich.
 G. O. No. 14, W. D., 1923.

Colonel, Motor Transport Corps, U. S. Army.
As chief of the repair division, office of the Director, Motor Transport Corps, American Expeditionary Forces, he displayed sound judgment, executive ability of a high order, and unremitting devotion to duty, thus contributing markedly to the successful operations of the Motor Transport Corps of the American Expeditionary Forces.

IRELAND, MERRITTE W.
R—Columbia City, Ind.
B—Columbia City, Ind.
G. O. No. 12, W. D., 1919.

Major general, U. S. Army.
As Chief Surgeon of the American Expeditionary Forces he supervised ar perfected the organization of the medical department in France; and to b excellent judgment, untiring efforts, and high professional attainments a largely due the splendid efficiency with which the sick and wounded of tl American Army have been cared for.

IRWIN, GEORGE LE R.
R—Chicago, Ill.
B—Fort Wayne, Mich.
G. O. No. 19, W. D., 1920.

Brigadier general, U. S. Army.
He commanded with ability the 57th Field Artillery Brigade, 32d Divisio during the Marne-Aisne, Oise-Aisne, and Meuse-Argonne offensives. A all times he displayed keen judgment, high military attainments, and loy devotion to duty. The success of the division whose advance he supporte was due, in a large measure, to his eminent technical skill and ability as a artillerist.

JACKLING, DANIEL C.
R—San Francisco, Calif.
B—Appleton City, Mo.
G. O. No. 118, W. D., 1919.

For services as director of United States Government explosive plants.

JACKSON, THOMAS H.
R—Muskegon, Mich.
B—Canada.
G. O. No. 87, W. D., 1919.

Colonel, Corps of Engineers, U. S. Army.
As a member of the division of construction and forestry he displayed untirii energy and marked ability in the performance of his important duties. H stupendous task was fraught with numerous difficulties, which he overcan with noteworthy success, rendering services of signal worth to the America Expeditionary Forces.

JACKSON, WILLIAM P.
R—Palmyra, Mo.
B—Palmyra, Mo.
G. O. No. 28, W. D., 1921.

Brigadier general, U. S. Army.
For services as brigade commander, 74th Infantry Brigade, 37th Divisio American Expeditionary Forces, in operations against the enemy in Fran and Belgium.

JACOBSON, BENJAMIN L.
R—Washington, D. C.
B—Germany.
G. O. No. 14, W. D., 1923.

Lieutenant colonel, Quartermaster Corps, U. S. Army.
As executive officer in the office of the Quartermaster General of the Arm and in addition to the duties of that office, charged with the responsibili for the operations of the administrative, personnel, and regulations divisio: of that office, he rendered highly important services to the Governmen His sound judgment, rare administrative and executive ability, and his un mitting attention to duty were contributing factors in the success of tl Quartermaster Corps in the supply of the Army.

JADWIN, EDGAR.
R—Honesdale, Pa.
B—Honesdale, Pa.
G. O. No. 59, W. D., 1919.

Brigadier general, U. S. Army.
As commanding officer of the 15th Engineers, he inaugurated the importa project at Gievres. Later, in charge of the division of construction and fc estry, he brought to this important task a splendidly trained mind ar exceptionally high skill. His breadth of vision and sound judgment infl enced greatly the successful completion of many vast construction projec undertaken by the American Expeditionary Forces.

JAMERSON, GEORGE H.
R—Martinsville, Va.
B—Martinsville, Va.
G. O. No. 15, W. D., 1923.

Brigadier general, U. S. Army.
As regimental commander, 317th Infantry, and later as brigade command of the 159th Infantry Brigade of the 80th Division, he rendered conspicuo service in the organization and training of these units, and in the commai thereof during the operations of his brigade in the Meuse-Argonne offensiv Displaying sound judgment, high professional skill, untiring energy, ai devotion to duty, he contributed in a material way to the successful operatio of his division and of the American forces in France.

*JANEWAY, THEODORE C.
R—Baltimore, Md.
B—New York, N. Y.
G. O. No. 14, W. D., 1923.

Major, Medical Corps, U. S. Army.
As chief of the division of internal medicine in the Surgeon General's Offi from June 26 to Dec. 27, 1917, he distinguished himself by his conspicuo service in the organization and development of that division. Standing one at the head of his profession in America, he was responsible for the sele tion of many prominent internists for war service, thereby rendering a servi of inestimable value to the Government in caring for the sick.
Posthumously awarded. Medal presented to widow, Mrs. Eleanor C. Janewa

JARMAN, SANDERFORD.
R—West Monroe, La.
B—Boatner, La.
G. O. No. 43, W. D., 1922.

Lieutenant colonel, Coast Artillery Corps, U. S. Army.
From Sept. 14 to Nov. 26, 1918, as G-3, and later chief of staff of the comman ing general, American Railway Artillery Reserve, with the 1st and 2d Ame can Armies during the Meuse-Argonne offensive and the offensive plann to be launched by the 2d American Army on Nov. 11, 1918, he displayed t highest qualities as an organizer, and by his untiring energy and zeal, go judgment, and general excellence, as well as great technical ability, cc tributed largely to the success of the command.

JAY, NELSON D.
R—Pelham Manor, N. Y.
B—Elwood, Ill.
G. O. No. 56, W. D., 1922.

Lieutenant colonel, Quartermaster Corps, U. S. Army.
As assistant general purchasing agent, American Expeditionary Forces, l excellent judgment, untiring energy, and broad and comprehensive knov edge of business affairs, he solved in a highly meritorious manner ma difficult and serious problems of supply which confronted our forces throuş out the war. His services were rendered with conspicuous success in position of great responsibility and were of inestimable value to the Americ Expeditionary Forces.

DISTINGUISHED-SERVICE MEDAL 723

JENKS, GLEN F.
   R—Clayville, N. Y.
   B—Deansboro, N. Y.
   G. O. No. 13, W. D., 1923.

Colonel, Ordnance Department, U. S. Army.
As chief of the Heavy Artillery Division, office of Chief Ordnance Officer American Expeditionary Forces, he displayed keen foresight and excellent judgment, combined with professional ability of the highest order, in the development of allied artillery programs and the supply and maintenance of heavy and railway artillery to the troops in France. Later, as chief ordnance inspector of artillery, American Expeditionary Forces, he organized and perfected to a high degree of efficiency the maintenance of the artillery of the 1st Army during the Meuse-Aronne operations, thereby contributing materially to the success of our forces.

JERVEY, HENRY
   R—Charleston, S. C.
   B—Dublin, Va.
   G. O. No. 144, W. D., 1918.

Major general, U. S. Army.
For services as director of operations, General Staff, and as assistant to the Chief of Staff in preparing and executing the plans involving the mobilization of personnel during the war.

JERVEY, JAMES P.
   R—Atlanta, Ga.
   B—Powhatan County, Va.
   G. O. No. 87, W. D., 1919.

Colonel, Corps of Engineers, U. S. Army.
As commanding officer of the 304th Engineers, 79th Division, he performed his exacting duties with signal ability. His high technical skill and unflagging energy were largely responsible for keeping the roads in condition for the transportation of artillery and large quantities of supplies during the attack on Montfaucon and Nantillois in the latter part of September. By his great efforts he proved a potent factor in the successes achieved during these operations.

JETT, GEORGE HENRY
   R—Baker County, Oreg.
   B—Baker County, Oreg.
   G. O. No. 116, W. D., 1919.

Lieutenant, U. S. Naval Reserve Force.
For services as repair officer on the staff of the division commander, cruiser and transport force, Newport News, Va.

JEWELL, FRANK C.
   R—Beloit, Wis.
   B—Chicago, Ill.
   G. O. No. 133, W. D., 1919.

Colonel, Coast Artillery Corps, U. S. Army.
As commander of the Railway Artillery Reserve attached to the 1st Army, American Expeditionary Forces, during the Meuse-Argonne operations, he performed his task with energy and marked ability, rendering valuable services to the American Expeditionary Forces.

JEWETT, FRANK B.
   R—Wyoming, N. J.
   B—Pasadena, Calif.
   G. O. No. 47, W. D., 1919.

Lieutenant colonel, Signal Corps, U. S. Army.
For services in connection with the development of the radio telephone and the development and production of other technical apparatus for the Army.

JEWETT, HENRY C.
   R—Buffalo, N. Y.
   B—Buffalo, N. Y.
   G. O. No. 74, W. D., 1919.
   Distinguished-service cross also awarded.

Colonel, Corps of Engineers, U. S. Army.
In command of the 182d Infantry Brigade, 91st Division, in the Argonne he displayed exceptional qualities of leadership and tactical ability in important engagements. Later, as chief of staff of the 91st Division, he planned operations with sound judgment and a comprehensive understanding of existing conditions, showing military attainments and initiative of a high order. At all times he was untiring in energy and self-sacrificing in devotion to his exacting duties.

JOHNSON, ARTHUR
   R—St. Peter, Minn.
   B—St. Peter, Minn.
   G. O. No. 59, W. D., 1919.

Brigadier General, U. S. Army.
In command of the intermediate section, services of supply, he had the responsibility of forwarding to the front great quantities of supplies and thousands of replacements for the combatant units, in which important duty he displayed untiring zeal and exceptional executive ability.

JOHNSON, HUGH S.
   R—Alva, Okla.
   B—Fort Scott, Kans.
   G. O. No. 1, W. D., 1926.

Colonel, Judge Advocate General's Department, U. S. Army.
For services in the Provost Marshal General's office in connection with the planning and execution of the draft laws.

JOHNSON, JACOB C.
   R—Benton City, Mo.
   B—Marietta, Ohio.
   G. O. No. 62, W. D., 1919.

Colonel, Inspector General's Department, U. S. Army.
As inspector general of the 1st Army Corps and later of the 1st Army, he performed exacting tasks with distinction throughout the Marne-Chateau-Thierry, St. Mihiel, and Meuse-Argonne operations. Both during the months of actual fighting and the periods of training before and after the campaign, he displayed conspicuous devotion to duty, unfailing zeal, and loyalty, acting always with sound judgment.

JOHNSON, WAIT C.
   R—Burlington, Vt.
   B—Rutland, Vt.
   G. O. No. 87, W. D., 1919.

Colonel (Infantry), General Staff Corps, U. S. Army
As athletic director, G-5, of the American Expeditionary Forces he was given the important and difficult task of planning and organizing an elaborate program of athletic training and competitions for American troops, embracing all branches of sport. By his zeal and sound judgment he carried this program to an eminently successful conclusion, thereby rendering an invaluable service in maintaining the morale and physical fitness of our troops during the trying period of repatriation.

JOHNSTON, EDWARD N.
   R—Portland, Oreg.
   B—St. Louis, Mo.
   G. O. No. 56, W. D., 1922.

Colonel, Corps of Engineers, U. S. Army.
From September, 1917, until May, 1918, as commanding officer, 23d Highway Engineer Regiment, he displayed rare qualities of leadership in the organization and training of the regiment, which later performed excellent services throughout the war. As assistant to the chief of Chemical Warfare Service in France from June until December, 1918, in charge of the offensive division he showed ability of the highest order in the general supervision of operations of all gas troops. From December, 1918, until June, 1919, as acting chief of Chemical Warfare Service abroad, his keen business ability and sound judgment were important factors in the successful closing out of all chemical warfare activities in the American Expeditionary Forces.

JOHNSTON, GORDON R—Birmingham, Ala. B—Charlotte, N. C. G. O. No. 59, W. D., 1919. Medal of honor and distinguished-service cross also awarded.	Colonel (Infantry), General Staff Corps, U. S. Army. He showed great ability while chief of staff of the 82d Division in the operations in the Argonne area. The force of his energy and his masterful leadership manifested itself in the crowning successes of the division during the operations of this campaign.
JOHNSTON, JOHN A R—Washington, D. C. B—Allegheny, Pa. G. O. No. 4, W. D., 1923.	Brigadier general, U. S. Army. As department commander, Northeastern Department, between Sept. 1 1917, and May 23, 1918, he handled many difficult problems arising in the department with rare judgment, tact, and great skill. Later, as commanding general of the 34th Division, which he took overseas, his marked efficiency unusual initiative, and military attainments of a high order were important factors in the excellent standard of training attained by the division.
JOHNSTON, WILLIAM H R—Cincinnati, Ohio. B—Cincinnati, Ohio. G. O. No. 44, W. D., 1919. Distinguished-service cross also awarded.	Major general, U. S. Army. During the Argonne-Meuse offensive he commanded with skill and ability the 91st Division in the difficult advance that resulted in the taking of Epinonville. Later, in participation with the French, he led his division with marked distinction in the attack on and capture of the important city of Audenarde in the closing operations of the war in Belgium.
JOHNSTON, WILLIAM T R—Livingston, Mo. B—Alexandria, Pa. G. O. No. 126, W. D., 1919.	Colonel (Cavalry), General Staff Corps, U. S. Army. He organized and administered the officers' training camps from the outbreak of the war until July 25, 1918, and thereafter rendered conspicuous service as chief of staff, Southern Department.
JOLY, CHARLES L R—New York, N. Y. B—New Orleans, La. G. O. No. 56, W. D., 1922.	Major, Chemical Warfare Service, U. S. Army. By displaying untiring energy and enthusiasm in the performance of his important duties, he developed efficient gas discipline in the 32d Division, resulting in the prevention of gas fatalities. He was zealous and discerning in the training of troops, achieving brilliant successes. His service was marked by self-sacrificing devotion to the welfare and protection of the men who were with him.
JONES, CLIFFORD R—Norcross, Ga. B—Cumming, Ga. G. O. No. 56, W. D., 1922.	Colonel (Coast Artillery Corps), General Staff Corps, U. S. Army. In the office of the executive assistant to the Chief of Staff during the World War and the following demobilization period, his tactfulness and initiative in meeting the varied situations presented and sound judgment in passing upon many matters of highest importance contributed materially to the successful functioning of that office during the war. During demobilization his conception and organization of the emergency discharge section of the office not only protected the War Department from impositions but served in a marked degree to preserve the morale of the civilian population during that trying period.
JONES, GLENN I R—Washington, D. C. B—Washington, D. C. G. O. No. 69, W. D., 1919.	Lieutenant colonel, Medical Corps, U. S. Army. While surgeon of the 10th Division during the epidemic of Spanish influenza in that command his farsightedness in providing hospital facilities and his energetic and exceptionally efficient action in directing the care of patients resulted in a large reduction of mortality. His services show a rare devotion to duty in that, though himself a sufferer from the disease, his efforts were unabated.
JONES, HARVEY L R—Baltimore, Md. B—Tuckerton, N. J. G. O. No. 53, W. D., 1921.	Lieutenant colonel, Provost Marshal General's Department, U. S. Army. In charge of the Military Police School at Autun, France, a position of great responsibility, due to his ability and energy, hundreds of officers and enlisted men were trained as military police for the Provost Marshal General's Department, and were afterwards distributed throughout the American Expeditionary Forces. His work was conspicuous for its thoroughness and important results. He rendered services of much value to the United States.
JONES, HILARY POLLARD R—Taylorsville, Va. B—Hanover County, Va. G. O. No. 116, W. D., 1919.	Rear admiral, U. S. Navy. As commanding officer of the Newport News division of the cruiser and transport fleet, his successful administration and close cooperation with the Army authorities resulted in the efficient joint operations of the Army and Navy at the port of Hampton Roads.
JONES, JAMES S R—Wheeling, W. Va. B—Wheeling, W. Va. G. O. No. 59, W. D., 1919.	Lieutenant colonel, Adjutant General's Department, U. S. Army. As assistant to the adjutant general at General Headquarters, American Expeditionary Forces, he displayed executive ability of the highest order in the efficient administration of the divisions successively assigned to him. Possessed of a keen mind for organization, with sound judgment, tact, and a thorough understanding of the intricate details of the office, he successfully surmounted innumerable obstacles, rendering service of signal worth to the American Expeditionary Forces and to the Government.
JONES, JOHN C R—Wynnewood, Pa. B—New York, N. Y. G. O. No. 124, W. D., 1919.	As chief of the Philadelphia ordnance district, in which capacity he maintained at all times the greatest degree of intelligent and enthusiastic cooperation between the Ordnance Department and manufacturers in his district, thereby attaining the maximum production of munitions in a minimum time; and also as chairman of the Philadelphia ordnance district claims board, in which capacity his services have been invaluable to the Nation in adjusting equitably the $271,000,000 worth of outstanding contracts in his district in force at the signing of the armistice.

JONES, PERCY L
   R—Cleveland, Tenn.
   B—Bartow Co., Ga.
   G. O. No. 59, W. D., 1919.

Colonel, Medical Corps, U. S. Army.
He served with marked distinction as commander of the United States Ambulance Service with the French Armies. By the force of his energy, zeal, and ability he brought the units of that service to a high state of perfection. The splendid record held by this service is attributable to his great devotion and untiring efforts in accomplishing his tasks.

JONES, SAMUEL G
   R—Montgomery, Ala.
   B—Montgomery, Ala.
   G. O. No. 87, W. D., 1919.

Colonel, Cavalry, U. S. Army.
As commanding officer of Winchester Camp, England, he was directly charged with the transportation of several hundred thousand American troops through England, a task of great magnitude and one involving many difficulties. By his tireless energy and keen application to his important duties he accomplished his task with marked success, rendering services of distinction to the American Expeditionary Forces.

JONES, WALTER C
   R—Quincy, Mass.
   B—Quincy, Mass.
   G. O. No. 56, W. D., 1922.

Colonel, Quartermaster Corps, U. S. Army.
As quartermaster of the intermediate section, services of supply, American Expeditionary Forces, he performed his manifold duties with marked ability and outstanding successes. He was charged with the supervision of the Quartermaster Corps personnel of over 500 officers and 10,000 enlisted men, with the responsibility for the direction and control of the vast quantity of quartermaster stores required for the intermediate section, consisting of over 270,000 troops, and with the initial supply of four replacement (depot) divisions of over 300,000 troops. He fulfilled this tremendous responsibility with conspicuous and marked efficiency, handling with tact and keen judgment the many complex problems which constantly confronted him. His service was characterized with zealousness, resourcefulness, and farsightedness, and he proved himself equal to every emergency. He rendered services of signal worth to the American Expeditionary Forces.

JORDAN, CLARENCE L
   R—Monticello, Ga.
   B—Monticello, Ga.
   G. O. No. 13, W. D., 1923.

First lieutenant, Ordnance Department, U. S. Army.
In active charge of the Army ammunition depot system of the 1st American Army, from its organization until the armistice, displaying great technical ability, sound judgment, exceptional zeal and energy, he successfully assured at all times efficient and adequate storage, protection, and issue of all classes of ammunition at the front, contributing materially to the success of the American Expeditionary Forces in France.

JORDAN, RICHARD H
   R—Haymarket, Va.
   B—Haymarket, Va.
   G. O. No. 14, W. D., 1923.

Colonel, Quartermaster Corps, U. S. Army.
As senior assistant and executive assistant to the chief of transportation service from Jan. 11, 1918, to Apr. 15, 1919, with untiring energy, rare administrative and executive ability, and unremitting devotion to duty, he rendered service of great value to the Government in perfecting the necessary organization of the movement of troops from encampments throughout the United States to ports of embarkation and thence overseas.

JOY, BENJAMIN
   R—Boston, Mass.
   B—Boston, Mass.
   G. O. No. 70, W. D., 1919.

Major, Infantry, U. S. Army.
As chief of the fiscal department in the office of the officer in charge of civil affairs in the occupied territory, he has handled problems of a delicate and complicated character with remarkable success, displaying marked administrative ability, breadth of vision, and a comprehensive knowledge of international financial questions.

JOYCE, KENYON A
   R—Chicago, Ill.
   B—Brooklyn, N. Y.
   G. O. No. 3, W. D., 1921.

Colonel (Cavalry), General Staff Corps, U. S. Army.
As chief of staff of the 2d Depot Division, Le Mans, France, in the training and sending forward of replacements and in breaking up combat divisions for replacement he displayed broad professional attainments, a high degree of leadership, and unfailing tact. Later, as chief of the classification and data section, personnel branch, General Staff, he demonstrated rare executive and planning ability in developing a system for the scientific classification of officers with a view to their suitability and availability.

JUDAH, NOBLE B., Jr
   R—Chicago, Ill.
   B—Chicago, Ill.
   G. O. No. 103, W. D., 1919.

Lieutenant colonel, Field Artillery, U. S. Army.
As assistant chief of staff, G-2, of the 42d Division during all its campaigns, by the skillful direction of the intelligence service he proved a material factor in the successes gained by his division. He at all times displayed assiduous application to his important task, rendering services of the utmost value.

JUDSON, WILLIAM V
   R—Indianapolis, Ind.
   B—Indianapolis, Ind.
   G. O. No. 11, W. D., 1921.

Brigadier general, U. S. Army.
For services while serving as chief of the American military mission to Russia and military attaché to the American embassy at Petrograd, Russia.

JUNKERSFELD, PETER
   R—Chicago, Ill.
   B—Sadorus, Ill.
   G. O. No. 89, W. D., 1919.

Colonel, Quartermaster Corps, U. S. Army.
As associate officer in charge of the building branch of the construction division of the Army, by his unremitting industry and energy, sound judgment, and knowledge of men he was of the most material assistance in the accomplishment of the construction program of the Army. He performed notable service as executive, organizer, and administrator.

KEAN, JEFFERSON R
   R—Lynchburg, Va.
   B—Lynchburg, Va.
   G. O. No. 59, W. D., 1921.

Brigadier General, U. S. Army.
As chief of the department of military relief, American Red Cross, a position of great responsibility, by his foresight, marked efficiency, and energy he organized the base hospitals, which cared for many of our wounded, and administered the United States Ambulance Service for duty with the French Army, greatly assisting our ally. He rendered services of conspicuous worth to the United States.

KEECH, FRANK BROWNE R—New York, N. Y. B—Newport, Md. G. O. No. 59, W. D., 1919.	Lieutenant colonel, Inspector General's Department, U. S. Army. As inspector general of the port of embarkation, Newport News, Va., his very able control and judgment in the management of his office t ment of troops and supplies overseas was materially aided.
KELLER, CHARLES R—Fort Sam Houston, Tex. B—Coeur d'Alene, Idaho. G. O. No. 59, W. D., 1919.	Colonel, Infantry, U. S. Army. He took command of a regiment at a critical moment after two unst assaults had been made by the brigade. He reorganized the regimer fire and made possible the taking and holding of the Bois-des-Ogons, displaying the highest order of leadership and exhibiting the masterfu ties of a commander.
KELLER, CHARLES R—New York, N. Y. B—Rochester, N. Y. G. O. No. 2, W. D., 1920.	Brigadier general, U. S. Army. As assistant to the Chief of Engineers, U. S. Army, he was instrum initiating policies which protected the channels and anchorages of ou tant harbors from obstruction by enemy aliens. As power administ behalf of the United States he organized the power section of the Wa tries Board and initiated measures as a result of which the war pro the country was successfully protected against serious delay due t shortage.
KELLER, WILLIAM L R—New York, N. Y. B—Hartford, Conn. G. O. No. 62, W. D., 1919.	Colonel, Medical Corps, U. S. Army. As director of the professional services, Medical Department, America ditionary Forces, he displayed marked ability in the organization an ment of the forces at his disposal for service in hospitals at the fron the rear areas. He was discerning in his knowledge of condition his insufficient personnel to the maximum advantage in relieving th ing of our sick and wounded, and in obtaining prompt treatment f casualties. His comprehensive grasp of the problems which p themselves resulted in the saving of many lives.
KELLEY, REGINALD H R—Berkeley, Calif. B—Fresno, Calif. G. O. No. 39, W. D., 1920.	Colonel, Infantry, U. S. Army. First as division machine-gun officer and later as commanding offic Infantry, 29th Division, he displayed sterling qualities of leadersl his high military attainments, sound judgment, and self-sacrificing to duty he proved to be a material factor in the successes achieve 29th Division in the offensive actions in which they participated.
KELLOND, FREDERIC G R—Louisville, Ky. B—Canada. G. O. No. 103, W. D., 1919.	Colonel (Infantry), General Staff Corps, U. S. Army. While in charge of the construction section of the equipment branch, Staff, he was responsible for the work of that section regarding pr great magnitude, and his services have been of great value.
KELLY, WILLIAM R—West Superior, Wis. B—New York, N. Y. G. O. No. 59, W. D., 1919.	Colonel, Corps of Engineers, U. S. Army. After serving with great credit in the field he took command of the ir ports of La Rochelle and La Pallice. By his executive ability a energy he promptly relieved congested conditions and made pos uninterrupted flow of necessary supplies toward the front.
KELLY, WILLIAM, Jr R—Brownsville, Tex. B—Brownsville, Tex. G. O. No. 69, W. D., 1919.	Colonel, Adjutant General's Department, U. S. Army. For services in The Adjutant General's Department during the war untiring energy and his sound and impartial judgment is due, i measure, the efficient action leading to the maintenance of the hig ard of commissioned personnel during the war.
KENLY, WILLIAM L R—Baltimore, Md. B—Baltimore, Md. G. O. No. 15, W. D., 1923.	Major general, U. S. Army. As Chief of Air Service, American Expeditionary Forces, by his ability, clear conception, and broad mental grasp, he was able to many obstacles and placed the training of Air Service personnel on a basis. Later, as Director of Military Aeronautics in the United successfully organized and accomplished the training of personnel seas service with a resulting high degree of morale throughout the A and the efficient performance of duties at the front. Serving at the s as a member of the Advisory Committee and Joint Army and Nav Board, he rendered services of inestimable value to the Gover positions of great responsibility.
KENNEDY, JAMES M R—Troy, S. C. B—Abbeville, S. C. G. O. No. 111, W. D., 1919.	Colonel, Medical Corps, U. S. Army. As port surgeon, port of embarkation, Hoboken, N. J., he has organ vided, and administered with conspicuous efficiency all of the required for the accommodation of our troops going overseas from as well as for the large number of our sick and wounded soldiers home.
KENNEDY, JOHN T R—Orangeburg, S. C. B—Hendersonville, S. C. G. O. No. 39, W. D., 1920. Medal of honor also awarded.	Lieutenant colonel, Field Artillery, U. S. Army. As a regimental commander during the St. Mihiel offensive and th Argonne offensive he displayed conspicuous efficiency, marked a ness, and leadership. By his exceptional technical and executive solved many perplexing problems, although much handicapped by men, material, and animals. He at all times rendered invaluabl to the attacking Infantry and proved to be a material factor in achieved.
KENNEDY, MOORHEAD C R—Chambersburg, Pa. B—Chambersburg, Pa. G. O. No. 14, W. D., 1923.	Colonel, Transportation Corps, U. S. Army. As Deputy Director General of Transportation, American Expe Forces, in Paris, France, and later in London, England, he rendere to the Government of an important and responsible character, experience as a railroad executive, sound professional and technic his untiring energy and devotion to duty contributing markedly t cessful operations of the Transportation Corps of the Americai tionary Forces.

DISTINGUISHED-SERVICE MEDAL

KERNAN, FRANCIS J.
R—Jacksonville, Fla.
B—Jacksonville, Fla.
G. O. No. 12, W. D., 1919.

Major general, U. S. Army.
He was intrusted with the important duty of organizing the services of supply of the American Expeditionary Forces in France, and the foundation then laid was later successfully carried to completion. As member of the War Prisoners' Commission, Berne, Switzerland, and of the American section of the Supreme War Council, he has rendered conspicuous services to the Government.

KERR, JAMES T.
R—Martins Ferry, Ohio.
B—Martins Ferry, Ohio.
G. O. No. 77, W. D., 1919.

Brigadier general, U. S. Army.
While in charge of the enlisted men's division of The Adjutant General's Office and of the recruitment of the Army, and later as executive assistant to The Adjutant General of the Army, his sound judgment and unremitting industry were important factors in the efficient administration of The Adjutant General's Department.

KERTH, MONROE C.
R—Cairo, Ill.
B—Cairo, Ill.
G. O. No. 56, W. D., 1922.

Colonel (Infantry), General Staff Corps, U. S. Army.
As military attaché at Petrograd, Russia, from Sept. 1, 1917, to Feb. 1, 1918, he performed his exacting duties with marked ability under most trying circumstances. As director of the Army General Staff College, American Expeditionary Forces, by his high professional attainments and unfailing energy, he rendered service of inestimable worth in connection with the instruction and training of officers for general staff duty. Later, as a member of the training and instruction branch, War Plans Division, General Staff, he demonstrated sound judgment, great breadth of vision, and keen foresight in the solution of the various difficult problems with which he was confronted.

KEVILLE, WILLIAM J.
R—Belmont, Mass.
B—Somerville, Mass.
G. O. No. 13, W. D., 1923.

Lieutenant colonel, Infantry, U. S. Army.
In command of the 101st Ammunition Train, 26th Division, throughout the period of organization, training, and operations in France. During the Aisne-Marne offensive he provided a continuous and adequate supply of ammunition for the 26th Division and to elements of the 28th, 42d, and 4th Divisions over an extensive territory and under all conditions of open warfare. Because of his high professional attainments, initiative, untiring energy, and devotion to duty he rendered extremely valuable services.

KEYSER, RALPH S.
R—Thoroughfare, Va.
B—Thoroughfare, Va.
G. O. No. 9, W. D., 1923.

Major, U. S. Marine Corps.
As Assistant Chief of Staff, 2d Division, G-2, from July 26, 1918, to July, 1919, with indefatigable zeal and excellent executive ability he so organized his section as to furnish prompt and comprehensive information of the enemy for the use of the division in its operations in the battles of St. Mihiel, Blanc Mont Ridge (Champagne), and the Meuse-Argonne, and in the march to the Rhine.

KILBOURNE, CHARLES E.
R—Portland, Oreg.
B—Fort Myer, Va.
G. O. No. 89, W. D., 1919.
Medal of honor and distinguished-service cross also awarded.

Brigadier general, U. S. Army.
As chief of staff of the 89th Division, he displayed military ability of the highest order, contributing to the successes achieved by that division during the St. Mihiel offensive. Later, upon his promotion to the grade of brigadier general, he continued to render valuable services in command of the 36th Artillery Brigade during the remainder of the campaign.

KILBRETH, JOHN W.
R—Southampton, Long Island, N. Y.
B—New York, N. Y.
G. O. No. 19, W. D., 1921.

Lieutenant colonel, Field Artillery, U. S. Army.
As director of the department of firing, School of Fire for Field Artillery, Fort Sill, Okla., from September, 1917, to May, 1918, he displayed professional attainments of the highest and most progressive order. He was primarily responsible for the excellent grounding received by thousands of officers in the principles of artillery firing, including those applicable to open warfare.

KILNER, WALTER G.
R—Syracuse, N. Y.
B—Shelby, N. Y.
G. O. No. 62, W. D., 1919.

Colonel, Signal Corps, U. S. Army.
By his personal efforts and efficient labors he organized the machinery necessary to train pilots, and successfully developed this branch of the Air Service. He overcame numerous difficulties inherent in the establishment of such an organization in a foreign country, and it was largely due to his efficiency that the Air Service was able to furnish well-trained personnel to the squadrons at the front. He at all times displayed marked devotion to duty, untiring energy, and sound judgment.

KILPATRICK, JOHN R.
R—New York, N. Y.
B—New York, N. Y.
G. O. No. 59, W. D., 1919.

Lieutenant colonel, Quartermaster Corps, U. S. Army.
In his capacity as a member of the 4th Section, General Staff, he exhibited exceptional tact and ability in promoting cooperation between the French and American services of transport and supply. He has by his energy, good judgment, and decisive action in the establishment, organization, and conduct of various regulating stations and railheads very materially assisted in insuring a steady and adequate flow of supplies to our armies in their operations.

KIMBALL, GORDON N.
R—Ogden, Utah.
B—Indianapolis, Ind.
G. O. No. 10, W. D., 1922.

Lieutenant colonel, Judge Advocate General's Department, U. S. Army.
As chief of the rents, requisitions, and claims service, advance section, services of supply, from November, 1918, to July, 1919, Colonel Kimball with exceptionally sound judgment, breadth of vision, and marked initiative organized and administered a work of great responsibility and magnitude.

KIMBALL, RICHARD H.
R—Cleburne, Tex.
B—Kimball, Tex.
G. O. No. 69, W. D., 1919.

Lieutenant colonel (Cavalry), General Staff Corps, U. S. Army.
Upon joining the operations division of the General Staff he assumed the responsibility of mobilization of the draft and classification and distribution of troops. His clear judgment, initiative, and energy have done much toward the successful accomplishment of the huge task involved in receiving and placing the drafted forces.

*KING, ALFRED K.
R—Erie, Pa.
B—Geneva, Ohio.
G. O. No. 70, W. D., 1919.

Major, Field Artillery, U. S. Army.
As munitions officer of the 5th Army Corps he performed exacting duties with untiring energy, displaying high professional attainments and a complete understanding of the needs of the troops he supplied. He personally reconnoitered roads over which transportation was to be made in order that he might keep in touch with changing conditions and be prepared to meet sudden emergencies, in order that the steady flow of munitions to the front lines might be maintained. He rendered services of signal worth.
Posthumously awarded. Medal presented to widow, Mrs. Ruth W. King.

KING, CAMPBELL.
R—Atlanta, Ga.
B—Flat Rock, N. C.
G. O. No. 59, W. D., 1919.

Brigadier general, U. S. Army.
He served with distinction as chief of staff of the 1st Division in the operations near Montdidier, the advance south of Soissons, and in the attack on the St. Mihiel salient. Later, as chief of staff of the 3d Army Corps during the Argonne-Meuse operations, by his splendid tactical judgment he rendered especially meritorious service.

KING, DAVID M.
R—Smyrna, Ohio.
B—Smyrna, Ohio.
G. O. No. 78, W. D., 1919.

Colonel, Ordnance Department, U. S. Army.
Displaying exceptional technical knowledge and comprehension of existing conditions, he ably organized, installed, and operated in the services of supply and in the Army area an extensive chain of repair facilities for the maintenance of ordnance matériel. With tireless energy and unfailing devotion to his important duties he perfected a loyal and efficient organization, capable of meeting all demands made upon it.

KING, EDWARD L.
R—Bridgewater, Mass.
B—Bridgewater, Mass.
G. O. No. 59, W. D., 1919.
Distinguished-service cross also awarded.

Brigadier general, U. S. Army.
He served, with marked distinction as chief of staff of the 28th Division. Later as brigade commander, he planned and directed the operations resulting in the capture by the 65th Infantry Brigade of Chateau d'Aulnois and Marcheville, where he displayed great tactical skill and demonstrated his abilities as a commander.

KING, EDWARD P., Jr.
R—Atlanta, Ga.
B—Atlanta, Ga.
G. O. No. 15, W. D., 1921.

Major, Field Artillery, U. S. Army.
As principal assistant to the Chief of Field Artillery, Mar. 23, 1918, to Nov. 11, 1918, he contributed largely to the successful solution of the difficult problems of expansion, organization, and training which then confronted the Field Artillery.

KING, THOMAS W.
R—Redwood City, Calif.
B—Sacramento, Calif.
G. O. No. 56, W. D., 1922.

Lieutenant colonel, Adjutant General's Department, U. S. Army.
As Adjutant General of the American Expeditionary Forces in Siberia he performed his exacting duties with high professional skill and administrative ability. The exceptional efficiency of the Adjutant General's Department under his direction was a material factor in the success of the staff work at headquarters. Possessed of a keen mind for organization, with sound judgment, tact, and a thorough understanding of the intricate details of his office, he successfully surmounted innumerable obstacles and rendered service of signal worth to the Government.

KING, VAN RENSSELAER C.
R—Wilmington, N. C.
B—New York, N. Y.
G. O. No. 10, W. D., 1922.

Colonel, Transportation Corps, U. S. Army.
As general superintendent of transportation, American Expeditionary Forces, and as transportation representative with the Armistice Commission, he organized and successfully installed a central car record and a system for distributing rolling stock which were of incalculable value to the American Expeditionary Forces.

KINGMAN, JOHN J.
R—Chattanooga, Tenn.
B—Omaha, Nebr.
G. O. No. 78, W. D., 1919.

Colonel (Corps of Engineers), General Staff Corps, U. S. Army.
As chief of staff of the 90th Division he displayed exceptional ability, planning important operations with sound judgment and wide comprehension of the conditions to be encountered. He was unflagging in energy and tireless in devotion to his exacting duties. Constantly confronted by perplexing military problems, he handled them with aggression and achieved brilliant successes.

KLEIN, HARRY T.
R—Cincinnati, Ohio.
B—Bellevue, Ky.
G. O. No. 19, W. D., 1920.

Lieutenant colonel, Judge Advocate General's Department, U. S. Army.
By his initiative, intelligence, and devotion to the study of the French laws on the subject of requisitions and billeting, he has contributed in a marked degree to the highly satisfactory results obtained by the rents, requisitions, and claims service in the conduct of a task of great magnitude. Later, as chief requisition officer, by his high professional attainments and sound judgment, furthered by a keen analytical mind, solved many intricate problems which daily confronted him, in the acquisition of property by lease, and in the requisitioning of billets for our troops.

KLOEBER, ROYALL O.
R—Washington, D. C.
B—Lynchburg, Va.
G. O. No. 108, W. D., 1919.

For services as Assistant Director of Finance. In this capacity he rendered most valuable assistance in the solution of the great financial problems which arose due to the war.

KNIGHT, GEORGE W.
R—Newark, N. J.
B—Newark, N. J.
G. O. No. 47, W. D., 1921.

Lieutenant colonel, Corps of Engineers, U. S. Army.
Near Bethincourt, France, on Sept. 25, 1918, he was assigned the task of placing foot bridges over Forges River and cutting the wire in front of the enemy positions. In this his inspiring leadership and constant supervision were conspicuous. Later he organized the regiment for the Nov. 1 offensive, which entailed the building of nine bridges, every one of which was completed in time for the Artillery to keep pace with the Infantry. His organization of the work at hand enabled the advance to proceed without delay and also enabled the Infantry to have the support of the Artillery and to keep in close touch with their transport.

KNIGHT, JOHN T R—Farmville, Va. B—Poplar Hill, Va. G. O. No. 59, W. D., 1921.	Colonel, Quartermaster Corps, U. S. Army. As chief quartermaster and superintendent of the Army Transport Service at the port of embarkation, Newport News, Va., a position of great responsibility, in which he prepared ships for convoy and executed the manifold duties of his office with conspicuous merit.
KNISKERN, ALBERT D R—Manistee, Mich. B—Monee, Ill. G. O. No. 77, W. D., 1919.	Brigadier general, U. S. Army. For services in the organization and development of the supply system in the general supply depot, Chicago, Ill.
KOCH, STANLEY R—Bozeman, Mont. B—Bozeman, Mont. G. O. No. 27, W. D., 1922.	Lieutenant colonel, Infantry, U. S. Army. As executive officer of the remount service, American Expeditionary Forces, by his zeal, efficiency, and devotion to duty, he has rendered great and beneficial service in the organization of the remount service in the American Expeditionary Forces.
KOEHLER, HERMAN J R—Milwaukee, Wis. B—Milwaukee, Wis. G. O. No. 34, W. D., 1919.	Lieutenant colonel, master of the sword, U. S. Army. At the beginning of the war he was placed in charge of the physical training in officers' training camps. These and also four divisional camps were personally visited by him. He personally instructed 200,000 officers and enlisted men of the new Army.
KRAMER, HARRY C R—West Collingswood, N. J. B—Philadelphia, Pa. G. O. No. 16, W. D., 1923.	Lieutenant colonel, Judge Advocate General's Department, U. S. Army. In the administration of the selective service law in various capacities in the office of the Provost Marshal General, and as executive officer in that office during the period of the great drafts in the early part of 1918 he displayed superior executive ability, sound judgment, and complete devotion to his duties. His service was of immeasureable value to his Government in positions of great responsibility.
KRAUTHOFF, CHARLES R R—Kansas City, Mo. B—St. Louis, Mo. G. O. No. 59, W. D., 1919.	Brigadier general, U. S. Army. His energy and thorough knowledge of methods and standards of supply have been of exceptional value, particularly in directing European purchases for the Quartermaster Corps and in the difficult and complex transactions attending the payments to allied and other foreign creditors of the American Government.
KREGER, EDWARD A R—Cherokee, Iowa. B—Keota, Iowa. G. O. No. 47, W. D., 1919. Distinguished-service cross also awarded.	Brigadier general, U. S. Army. As Acting Judge Advocate General for the American Expeditionary Forces he organized and efficiently administered his office, performing exacting duties with marked distinction. His masterful knowledge of military law, his foresight, and practical comprehension of the complex problems involved in his work enabled him to perform it with noteworthy success. His counsel was wise; his decisions were just. His services to the American Expeditionary Forces have been of great value.
KROMER, LEON B R—Grand Rapids, Mich. B—Grand Rapids, Mich. G. O. No. 62, W. D., 1919.	Colonel (Field Artillery), General Staff Corps, U. S. Army. As assistant chief of staff of the 82d Division during the St. Mihiel offensive he displayed military attainments of a high order in the planning of operations of great moment. Later as assistant chief of staff, G–3, 1st Corps, and assistant chief of staff, G–1, 1st Army, during the Meuse-Argonne operations, his initiative, sound judgment, and tireless energy solved difficult problems of traffic control and regulation, playing an important part in the successes achieved.
KRUEGER, WALTER R—Cincinnati, Ohio. B—Germany. G. O. No. 3, W. D., 1924.	Colonel (Infantry), General Staff Corps, U. S. Army. He served as assistant in the Bureau of Militia Affairs; assistant chief of staff, G–3, and acting chief of staff, 84th Division; assistant chief of staff, G–3, 26th Division; chief of staff, Tank Corps; instructor, Line School, Langres, France; assistant chief of staff, G–3, 4th Corps; and assistant chief of staff, G–3, 6th Corps. By his high professional attainments, superior zeal, loyal devotion to duty, soldierly character, and his dominant leadership, he has exercised a determining influence upon the commands with which he has served, and has contributed in a marked degree to the success of the military operations of our forces.
KRUMM, LOUIS R R—Brooklyn, N. Y. B—Columbus, Ohio. G. O. No. 59, W. D., 1919.	Lieutenant colonel, Signal Corps, U. S. Army. As supervisor of radio service of the Signal Corps in France, he organized and placed in satisfactory operation this important branch. The excellent results obtained by our telephonic interception stations are due to his masterful ability and exact scientific knowledge.
KUEGLE, ALBERT S R—Sturgis, S. Dak. B—Columbiana, Ohio. G. O. No. 89, W. D., 1919.	Lieutenant colonel (Infantry), General Staff Corps, U. S. Army. As secretary of the General Staff and of the 3d Section thereof, at General Headquarters, American Expeditionary Forces, charged with executive duties of a responsible and exacting character, he performed these duties with merited success, displaying at all times a high degree of tact, zeal, and efficiency, rendering invaluable services to the American Expeditionary Forces.
KUMPE, GEORGE E R—White Sulphur Springs, Mont. B—Leighton, Ala. G. O. No. 38, W. D., 1922.	Colonel, Signal Corps, U. S. Army. As chief signal officer of the 3d Army Corps, by his untiring energy, devotion to duty, and excellent technical attainments, Colonel Kumpe established and maintained under great difficulties of terrain and enemy shell fire such thorough signal arrangements as to enable his corps headquarters to maintain communication at all times with the divisions of the corps and adjacent units, thereby greatly contributing to the success of his corps in the Meuse-Argonne offensive.

LADD, EUGENE F.
  R—Thetford Center, Vt.
  B—Thetford Center, Vt.
  G. O. No. 47, W. D., 1919.

Brigadier general, U. S. Army.
While in charge of the officers' division of The Adjutant General's Office his comprehensive grasp of the new situations developing and his technical ability enabled him to perform the duties of his office with rare distinction, thus contributing greatly to the rapid organization of our new Army.

LAHM, FRANK P.
  R—Mansfield, Ohio.
  B—Mansfield, Ohio.
  G. O. No. 70, W. D., 1919.

Colonel, Air Service, U. S. Army.
A balloon pilot of marked ability and scientific attainments, he rendered valuable services to the American Expeditionary Forces by his untiring devotion to the innumerable problems which faced the Air Service during its organization in France. His broad experience in aeronautics played an important part in the formulation of policies of the Air Service and was reflected in its successes during the St. Mihiel offensive and subsequently in the operations of the 2d Army.

LAMONT, ROBERT P.
  R—Evanston, Ill.
  B—Detroit, Mich.
  G. O. No. 77, W. D., 1919.

Colonel, Ordnance Department, U. S. Army.
As assistant to the chief of the procurement division, later as chief of the procurement division and as a member of the claims board of the Ordnance Department, he has rendered material assistance to the Nation's industry in adjusting equitably outstanding contracts with full justice to employers and employees alike.

*LAMPERT, JAMES G. B.
  R—Oshkosh, Wis.
  B—Oshkosh, Wis.
  G. O. No. 59, W. D., 1919.

Lieutenant colonel, Corps of Engineers, U. S. Army.
He invented, developed, and superintended the production of the standard floating footbridge equipage, which was successfully used by the 1st Army in its attack east of the Meuse, near Dun. His services in connection with the organization and development of the bridge department of the Chief Engineer's office were of inestimable value. He showed ability, great foresight, and exact scientific knowledge, and his work had an important bearing on the successes achieved by our armies.
Posthumously awarded. Medal presented to widow, Mrs. James G. B. Lampert.

LANGDON, RUSSELL C.
  R—Brooklyn, N. Y.
  B—Brooklyn, N. Y.
  G. O. No. 69, W. D., 1919.
  Distinguished-service cross also awarded.

Colonel, Infantry, U. S. Army.
As commanding officer of the 127th Infantry, 32d Division, he demonstrated personal courage, marked tactical ability, and military leadership of a high order. The brilliant success he achieved in the capture of Fismes during the Aisne-Marne offensive, and in the taking of Juvigny and the subsequent advance to Terny-Sorny during the Oise-Aisne offensive, was repeated later during the operations of the Meuse-Argonne, when he was given the important task of conducting the attack on La Cote Dame Marie.

LANGFITT, WILLIAM C.
  R—Millersburgh, Ohio.
  B—Wellsburg, Va.
  G. O. No. 12, W. D., 1919.

Major general, U. S. Army.
As director of light, railways, and roads, and later as chief of utilities, he displayed great ability and marked breadth of vision. As chief engineer of the American Expeditionary Forces his brilliant professional attainments, untiring energy, and devotion to duty placed his department in a state of efficiency and enabled it to perform its important function in the most satisfactory manner.

LANGSTON, JOHN D.
  R—Goldsboro, N. C.
  B—Aurora, N. C.
  G. O. No. 56, W. D., 1922.

Lieutenant colonel, Judge Advocate General's Department, U. S. Army.
As executive officer in charge of the selective draft in North Carolina from December, 1917, until September, 1918. by his unusual executive ability, rare tact and skill, great initiative, and resourcefulness exercised at times under most trying and novel conditions which arose in connection with the administration of the selective service act, he achieved a pronounced and conspicuous success in the performance of difficult and highly responsible duties, thereby rendering services of great value to the Government.

LANZA, CONRAD H.
  R—Washington, D. C.
  B—New York, N. Y.
  G. O. No. 19, W. D., 1920.

Colonel, Field Artillery, U. S. Army.
As chief of the operations section, Army Artillery, 1st Army, American Expeditionary Forces, he exhibited a high order of ability and judgment. By his clear tactical conception of complex situations, by his exercise of initiative, by his untiring energy, and by his self-sacrificing devotion to duty, he contributed in a marked degree to the successful employment of all of the artillery of the 1st Army.

LASSITER, WILLIAM.
  R—Petersburg, Va.
  B—Petersburg, Va.
  G. O. No. 12, W. D., 1919.

Major general, U. S. Army.
As commander of the 51st Field Artillery Brigade, as Chief of Artillery of the 1st and 4th Army Corps in turn, and as Chief of Artillery, 2d Army, he showed himself to be a leader of conspicuous ability. His energy and sound judgment influenced greatly the successful operations of his commands on the Vesle, at the St. Mihiel salient, and in the Toul sector. He later commanded with skill and marked success the 32d Infantry Division.

LATHBURY, BENJAMIN B.
  R—Philadelphia, Pa.
  B—Philadelphia, Pa.
  G. O. No. 11, W. D., 1921.

Colonel, Quartermaster Corps, U. S. Army.
In the adjustment and settlement of many difficult and intricate claims problems his services were distinguished by zeal, excellent judgment, and a high comprehension of the principles involved and his success has been most marked.

LEA, LUKE.
  R—Nashville, Tenn.
  B—Nashville, Tenn.
  G. O. No. 56, W. D., 1922.

Colonel, Field Artillery, U. S. Army.
As commander, 114th Field Artillery, 30th Division, he organized, trained, and handled the regiment in a skillful manner during the St. Mihiel and Meuse-Argonne offensives. By his marked tactical judgment, knowledge of artillery, and loyal devotion to duty he rendered at all times the maximum of support to the Infantry in all tasks assigned his regiment, thereby rendering in a position of great responsibility services of great value to the American Expeditionary Forces.

LEACH, GEORGE E.
R—Minneapolis, Minn.
B—Cedar Rapids, Iowa.
G. O. No. 89, W. D., 1919.
Distinguished-service cross also awarded.

Colonel, Field Artillery, U. S. Army.
As commanding officer of the 151st Field Artillery, 42d Division, he displayed marked qualities of leadership. Maintaining a high standard of efficiency and morale, he constantly kept his regiment in close proximity to the attacking infantry, where he was able to furnish it accurate and timely assistance, which contributed materially to the successes gained.

LEARNARD, HENRY G.
R—Napoleon, Mich.
B—Wright City, Mo.
G. O. No. 18, W. D., 1919.

Brigadier general, U. S. Army.
For services in the work of reorganization and administration within The Adjutant General's Department.

LEE, BURTON J.
R—New York, N. Y.
B—New Haven, Conn.
G. O. No. 59, W. D., 1919.

Lieutenant colonel, Medical Corps, U. S. Army.
As surgical consultant attached to the 2d Division, he served continuously at the front, organizing his forces for the treatment and evacuation of the casualties with skill and marked success. He displayed unusual ability in the operations before Soissons, when in an emergency he organized, personally led, and directed surgical teams which cared for hundreds of wounded soldiers at a time when adequate hospitalization could not be established.

LEE, HARRY
R—Washington, D. C.
B—Washington, D. C.
G. O. No. 95, W. D., 1919.

Colonel, United States Marine Corps.
Having taken command of the 6th Regiment, United States Marine Corps, 2d Division, prior to the attack on the Bois-de-Belleau and Bouresches, he directed the operations of his regiment with remarkable success during all the major operations in which it participated. His ability as a tactical leader and his untiring energy were reflected in the brilliant achievements of his command.

LEE, JOHN C. H.
R—Junction City, Kans.
B—Junction City, Kans.
G. O. No. 59, W. D., 1919.

Colonel (Corp of Engineers), General Staff Corps, U. S. Army.
In the preparations for the drive on the St. Mihiel salient in September, and for the Argonne-Meuse offensive in October, 1918, he had charge of the detailed arrangements for and the subsequent execution of the operations of the 89th Division. The successes attained by this division were largely due to his splendid staff coordination, marked tactical ability, and sound judgment.

LEE, JOSEPH
R—Boston, Mass.
B—Brookline, Mass.
G. O. No. 73, W. D., 1919.

For services as president of the War Camp Community Service.

LEE, RAYMOND E.
R—Kansas City, Mo.
B—St. Louis, Mo.
G. O. No. 38, W. D., 1922.

Colonel, Field Artillery, U. S. Army.
As executive officer to the Chief of Field Artillery from Sept. 1, 1918, to the present time, Colonel Lee acted as Chief of Field Artillery for a period of about 10 days prior to the armistice during the absence of the Chief of Field Artillery. After the armistice he successfully planned and executed the demobilization of the commissioned personnel of his arm and also organized and conducted the Field Artillery section of the Officers' Reserve Corps in a most effective manner.

LEGGE, ALEX
R—Chicago, Ill.
B—Dane County, Wis.
G. O. No. 15, W. D., 1923.

Vice chairman, War Industries Board.
In connection with the operations of the War Industries Board during the World War. As a member of the board he rendered, through his broad vision, distinguished capacity, and business ability, services of inestimable value in marshaling the industrial forces of the Nation and mobilizing its economic resources—marked factors in assisting to make military success attainable. As vice chairman of the board itself and as chairman of its requirements division he rendered, through his untiring efforts and devotion to duty, exceptionally valuable service to the War Department in matters connected with the supply of raw materials and general munitions to the Army.

LEGGE, BARNWELL R.
R—Charleston, S. C.
B—Charleston, S. C.
G. O. No. 56, W. D., 1922.
Distinguished-service cross also awarded.

Lieutenant colonel, Infantry, U. S. Army.
As company, battalion, and regimental commander of the 26th Infantry throughout hostilities he successfully led his command through each of the offensives of the 1st Division. By his superior tactical judgment, manifest ability, and tireless energy, coupled with unusual leadership, he contributed in a brilliant manner to the success of the 1st Division. Later, as a division adjutant, he gave further proof of the highest qualities of military character, again demonstrating conspicuous service in a position of great responsibility.

LEHMAN, HERBERT H.
R—Washington, D. C.
B—New York, N. Y.
G. O. No. 103, W. D., 1919.

Colonel, General Staff Corps, U. S. Army.
While with the purchase, storage, and traffic division of the General Staff as chief of the purchase branch, member of the board of contract adjustment, chairman of the advisory board on sales and contract termination, member of the War Department claims board, and assistant director of purchase, storage, and traffic, General Staff, his large business experience, breadth of vision, and sound judgment have been of inestimable value in formulating and in supervising the execution of the methods and policies followed in the cancellation of war contracts and obligations and in the settlement and adjustment of terminated obligations.

LEITCH, JOSEPH D.
R—Clay Center, Nebr.
B—Montague, Mich.
G. O. No. 56, W. D., 1922.

Colonel (Infantry), General Staff Corps, U. S. Army.
As chief of staff of the American Expeditionary Forces in Siberia he gave proof of his great breadth of vision, keen foresight, sound judgment, and tact. By his brilliant professional attainments, coupled with great diplomacy, he handled most ably the many delicate situations with which he was confronted. His fine soldierly qualities were at all times outstanding, and by his masterful grasp of the situation he was able to meet successfully each new and difficult problem with which he was faced. He rendered most conspicuous services of inestimable value to the Government in a place of great responsibility and at a time of gravest importance.

LEJEUNE, JOHN A R—Pointe Coupee Parish, La. B—Pointe Coupee Parish, La. G. O. No. 12, W. D., 1919.	Major general, U. S. Marine Corps. He commanded the 2d Division in the successful operations of Thiaucourt, Massif Blanc Mont, St. Mihiel, and on the west bank of the Meuse. In the Argonne-Meuse offensive his division was directed with such sound military judgment and ability that it broke and held, by the vigor and rapidity of execution of its attack, enemy lines which had hitherto been considered impregnable.
LEONARD, GRACE E R—New York, N. Y. B—Newark, N. J. G O. No. 9, W. D., 1923.	First lieutenant, chief nurse, Army Nurse Corps, U. S. Army. As assistant director of the nursing service, American Expeditionary Forces, during the World War, she rendered invaluable assistance at the headquarters of Base Section No. 3. She supervised all nursing activities of the United States Army hospitals established in England, and in many ways promoted the general welfare of the nursing staff and the sick and wounded under their care.
LEWIS, DEAN D R—Chicago, Ill. B—Kewanee, Ill. G. O. No. 56, W. D., 1922.	Lieutenant colonel, Medical Corps, U. S. Army. As chief of the surgical service of Evacuation Hospital No. 5 during the operations on the Marne, and the St. Mihiel, Meuse-Argonne, and Ypres-Lys offensives, by his tireless energy, organizing ability, and unusual surgical skill, he successfully demonstrated that war wounds could be operated upon in large numbers in front-line hospitals with limited personnel, thus conserving many lives among combat troops, thereby rendering in a position of great responsibility conspicuous service to the American Expeditionary Forces.
LEWIS, EDWARD M R—New Albany, Ind. B—New Albany, Ind. G. O. No. 12, W. D., 1919.	Major general, U. S. Army. He commanded with distinction the 30th American Division during its successful operations in Belgium with the 2d British Army, and later, with the 4th British Army in the offensive which resulted in the breaking of the enemy's Hindenburg line. During all these operations he exhibited great ability, determined energy, and marked devotion to duty.
LEWIS, FREDERICK W R—Atlanta, Ga. B—Buffalo, N. Y G. O. No. 105, W. D., 1919.	Colonel, Adjutant General's Department, U. S. Army. As officer in charge of the publication division of The Adjutant General's Office. To his painstaking efforts, tact, energy, and zeal are due the accuracy with which publications issued to the Military Establishment through The Adjutant General of the Army were drawn and the promptness with which they were distributed.
LEWIS, GILBERT N R—Berkeley, Calif. B—Weymouth, Mass. G. O. No. 56, W. D., 1922.	Lieutenant colonel, Chemical Warfare Service, U. S. Army. By his unusual energy, marked ability, and high technical attainments he rendered extremely valuable service by securing first-hand data on the uses and effects of gas and submitting reports of such value that they became fundamentals upon which the gas-warfare policies of the American Expeditionary Forces were thereafter largely based. Later, as chief of the defense division, Chemical Warfare Service, he obtained a high state of efficiency in the protection of our officers and soldiers against enemy gas and furthered the successes of American arms by securing a better and more effective use of gas, especially mustard gas, against the enemy, thereby rendering services of great value to our Government.
LIGGETT, HUNTER R—Birdsboro, Pa. B—Reading, Pa. G. O. No. 136, W. D., 1918.	Lieutenant general, U. S. Army. As commander of the 1st Army of the American Expeditionary Forces, he commanded the 1st Army Corps and perfected its organization under difficult conditions of early service in France; engaged in active operations in reduction of the Marne salient and of the St. Mihiel salient, and participated in the actions in the Forest of Argonne; in command of 1st Army when German resistance was shattered west of the Meuse.
LINCOLN, CHARLES S R—Ames, Iowa. B—Boonsboro, Iowa. G. O. No. 28, W. D., 1921.	Colonel (Infantry), General Staff Corps, U. S. Army. For services while a member of the G-1 section of the General Staff, General Headquarters, American Expeditionary Forces, later as Deputy Chief of Staff, G-1, and later as Assistant Chief of Staff, G-1.
LINDSEY, JULIAN R R—Irwinton, Ga. B—Irwinton, Ga. G. O. No. 59, W. D., 1919.	Brigadier general, U. S. Army. The brilliant and successful attack of the 164th Infantry Brigade, 82d Division, commanded by him, in the Argonne Forest, showed a spirit of aggressiveness and leadership of a high order. The tactical advantage attained in this action, whereby St. Juvin and Grand Pre were laid open to attack, was largely due to his ability and energy.
LINDSLEY, HENRY D R—New York, N. Y. B—Nashville, Tenn. G. O. No. 59, W. D., 1919.	Colonel, Adjutant General's Department, U. S. Army. He conducted with extreme devotion to duty and marked zeal the many activities of the War Risk Insurance Bureau in France. Due to his executive ability he contributed very largely to the successful development, extension and administration of that important service.
LININGER, CLARENCE R—Wabash, Ind. B—Huntington, Ind. G. O. No. 44, W. D., 1919.	First lieutenant, 13th Cavalry, U. S. Army. Lieutenant Lininger, while in action at Parral, Mexico, Apr. 12, 1916, proceeded under fire to the rescue of a dismounted man of his command who was in danger of falling into the hands of the enemy, and, taking him up behind him (Lieutenant Lininger) on his horse, carried him to safety.
LITTELL, ISAAC W R—Elizabeth, N. J. B—Elizabeth, N. J. G. O. No. 105, W. D., 1919.	Brigadier general, U. S. Army. As chief of the cantonment division of the Quartermaster General's Office he was charged with the task of building the camps and cantonments of the Army raised in summer of 1917 under conditions imposing almost insuperable obstacles. His completion of this task is a conspicuous example of the exercise of qualities of mind and character making up the highest type of officer.

LITTLE, BASCOM.
R—Cleveland, Ohio.
B—Cleveland, Ohio.
G. O. No. 126, W. D., 1919.

Colonel, Ordnance Department, U. S. Army.
As chief of the production district in which were manufactured practically all the machine guns and automatic rifles supplied for the United States Army and later as special assistant to the Chief of Ordnance, in charge of the production of small arms, automatic rifles, machine guns, small-arms ammunition, etc., he successfully organized the industry of the country for the production of these items to meet the needs of the United States Army.

LIVERMORE, PHILIP W.
R—New York, N. Y.
B—New York, N. Y.
G. O. No. 62, W. D., 1919.

Captain, Ordnance Department, U. S. Army.
As director of regional and ministerial liaison and later as deputy for the chief liaison officer, he displayed unusual administrative ability and rare judgment. By untiring effort and devotion to duty, he was largely instrumental in placing American liaison on a sound footing. His forceful personality and keen intelligence contributed largely to the successes achieved by his department. At all times he showed marked initiative, unflagging energy, and zeal in the performance of exacting and delicate tasks.

LLEWELLYN, FRED W.
R—Seattle, Wash.
B—Hillsboro, Oreg.
G. O. No. 62, W. D., 1919.

Lieutenant colonel, Infantry, U. S. Army.
Assuming the responsibilities of the first section of the general staff of the 28th Division five days before the Meuse-Argonne offensive, he efficiently coordinated the several services. By his constant vigilance and ceaseless efforts the entire system of supply, traffic, and evacuation operated during the advance of more than 10 kilometers, in accordance with the plans he had arranged. He was tireless in his energy and devotion to important duties, displaying military attainments of high order.

LLOYD, CHARLES R.
R—San Francisco, Calif.
B—England.
G. O. No. 89, W. D., 1919.

Colonel, Field Artillery, U. S. Army.
He commanded with distinction the 10th Field Artillery, displaying marked ability as an artillerist. His unflagging zeal and sound judgment was revealed by the success achieved by his regiment in furthering the gains achieved by the 3d Division in its operations in the field.

LOCHRIDGE, P. D.
R—Rara Avis, Miss.
B—Bexar, Ala.
G. O. No. 75, W. D., 1919.

Brigadier general, U. S. Army.
For services to the allied and associated governments as Chief of Staff, American Section, Supreme War Council.

LOCKE, MORRIS E.
R—Cincinnati, Ohio.
B—Salt Lake City, Utah.
G. O. No. 95, W. D., 1919.

Colonel, Field Artillery, U. S. Army.
He commanded, with marked skill and initiative, the 102d Field Artillery, 26th Division, during the Chateau-Thierry campaign, where at all times he furnished valuable support to the advancing infantry. Later he served creditably as an instructor at the Army General Staff College at Langres, rendering important services to the American Expeditionary Forces.

LOGAN, JAMES A., Jr.
R—Bala, Pa.
B—Philadelphia, Pa.
G. O. No. 59, W. D., 1919.

Colonel (Quartermaster Corps), General Staff, U. S. Army.
His marked administrative ability enabled him to assist most ably in the direction of important operations while on duty at G-1, General Headquarters American Expeditionary Forces, as deputy chief of staff, 2d Army, and G-1, 3d Army. As American representative with the Franco-American War Affairs Commission, at Paris, he displayed unfailing tact, energy, and sound judgment in handling the intricate details of the relations between the French and American authorities, achieving signal success. His high military attainments were shown in the success with which he performed duties of vital moment.

LONERGAN, THOMAS C.
R—St. Louis, Mo.
B—St. Louis, Mo.
G. O. No. 14, W. D., 1923.

Lieutenant colonel (Infantry), General Staff Corps, U. S. Army.
As an instructor at the Army General Staff College, American Expeditionary Forces, he displayed high professional attainments and unfailing energy, performing services of inestimable worth in connection with the instruction and training of officers for General Staff duty. He prepared the "Notebook for the General Staff Officer" and the "Provisional Staff Manual," and was mainly responsible for the "Handbook of Division and Brigade Commanders," all of which proved to be most valuable books. As adjutant of the 159th Infantry Brigade, 80th Division, during the St. Mihiel offensive, and later as a member of the interallied games committee he gave further proof of his sterling ability, sound judgment, and keen foresight. In all of these positions he rendered most conspicuous services to the Government.

LONGAN, RUFUS E.
R—Sedalia, Mo.
B—Sedalia, Mo.
G. O. No. 124, W. D., 1919.

Brigadier general, U. S. Army.
For services as chief of staff, port of embarkation, Hoboken, N. J., from Dec. 15, 1917, to Dec. 16, 1918.

LONGLEY, FRANCIS F.
R—Dobbs Ferry, N. Y.
B—Chicago, Ill.
G. O. No. 59, W. D., 1919.

Colonel, Corps of Engineers, U. S. Army.
He has been in charge of the water supply service, and as commanding officer of the 26th Engineers, a water-supply regiment, since the fall of 1917. His untiring energy, unusual initiative, and good judgment have to a marked degree, been responsible for the plentiful supply of pure drinking water to the combatant troops, thereby materially assisting in maintaining the unusually low rates in sickness among our troops.

LORD, HERBERT M.
R—Rockland, Me.
B—Rockland, Me.
G. O. No. 47, W. D., 1919.

Brigadier general, U. S. Army.
As assistant to the Quartermaster General and later as Director of Finance. As such he was responsible for and had authority over the preparation of estimates, disbursements, money accounts, property accounts, finance reports, and pay and mileage of the Army. The success of the Finance Department was, in a large measure, due to his breadth of vision, executive ability, initiative, and energy.

LOREE, JAMES T R—Albany, N. Y. B—Logansport, Ind. G. O. No. 116, W. D., 1919.	Colonel, Quartermaster Corps, U. S. Army. He served in turn as assistant quartermaster of the 27th Division, as quartermaster of the 80th Division, and in the Provost Marshal General's Department, American Expeditionary Forces, in all of which capacities he displayed exceptional ability. His good judgment, combined with a knowledge of methods and high professional attainments, resulted in a superior standard of efficiency, reflecting the greatest credit upon himself and enabling him to render most valuable services.
LORENZ, WILLIAM F R—Mendota, Wis. B—New York, N. Y. G. O. No. 59, W. D., 1921.	Major, Medical Corps, U. S. Army. As commanding officer of Field Hospital No. 127, and while in personal charge of the Triage (sorting station for wounded) of the 32d Division during the combat activities of that division on the Marne, Oise-Aisne, and in the Meuse-Argonne, he so displayed indefatigable zeal and exceptionally good judgment in sorting, caring for, and evacuating thousands of wounded as to directly result in the saving of many lives.
LOTT, ABRAHAM G R—Abilene, Kans. B—Gettysburg, Pa. G. O. No. 19, W. D., 1922.	Colonel, Adjutant General's Department, U. S. Army. For services in The Adjutant General's office in connection with the procurement of commissioned personnel. Later, as chief of staff, 12th Division, and executive officer at Camp Devens, Mass., by his untiring energy, loyalty and organizing ability he aided materially in the rapid demobilization of troops passing through this camp.
LOVE, JAMES M., Jr R—Fairfax Courthouse, Va. B—Fairfax Courthouse, Va. G. O. No. 89, W. D., 1919.	Colonel, Infantry, U. S. Army. As adjutant general, 2d Army Corps, and later as commanding officer of the 319th Infantry, 80th Division, he rendered services of great credit. By his marked tactical ability and unceasing energy he contributed materially to the successes achieved by the 80th Division in the Meuse-Argonne offensive.
LUBEROFF, GEORGE R—Lexington, Ky. B—New York, N. Y. G. O. No. 108, W. D., 1919.	Lieutenant colonel, Quartermaster Corps, U. S. Army. As chief quartermaster of the 1st Army, by his great energy, complete experience, and loyal efforts, he maintained an efficient service and kept a steady flow of all necessary quartermaster supplies to the 1st Army, rendering services of great value to the American Expeditionary Forces.
LUTHER, WILLARD B R—Milton, Mass. B—Attleboro, Mass. G. O. No. 13, W. D., 1923.	Lieutenant colonel, Field Artillery, U. S. Army. As assistant chief of staff, G-3, and brigade adjutant, 51st Field Artillery Brigade, during the occupancy of the Boucq sector, the Aisne-Marne, and St. Mihiel offensives, and as assistant to assistant chief of staff, G-3, headquarters, 1st Army Artillery, during the Meuse-Argonne operations, he displayed outstanding executive ability, leadership, and technical skill of high order, these qualities coupled with unremitting devotion to duty contributing in a material way to the successful operations of the organization with which he served.
LYLE, HENRY H. M R—New York, N. Y. B—Ireland. G. O. No. 59, W. D., 1921.	Colonel, Medical Corps, U. S. Army. As director of the Army evacuation ambulance companies and sections of the 1st Army of the American Expeditionary Forces, a position of great responsibility. During the St. Mihiel and Meuse-Argonne offensives he so directed the functioning of the ambulances that, in spite of the great shortage of these, he was able at all times to transport the wounded expeditiously, thereby saving many lives and enhancing the morale of the combatant troops. By his eminent surgical skill he has devised a new practical method for the treatment of gunshot fractures. He has rendered service of much value.
LYNCH, CHARLES R—Syracuse, N. Y. B—Syracuse, N. Y. G. O. No. 111, W. D., 1919.	Colonel, Medical Corps, U. S. Army. As port surgeon, port of embarkation, Newport News, Va., his service in governing and controlling the agencies for caring for sick and wounded soldiers, protecting them against diseases, and safeguarding them prior to and during transport overseas were conspicuous.
LYNCH, GEORGE A R—Blairstown, Iowa. B—Blairstown, Iowa. G. O. No. 55, W. D., 1920.	Lieutenant colonel (Infantry), General Staff Corps, U. S. Army. As a member of the training section, General Headquarters, he was chiefly responsible for the revision of the Infantry Drill Regulations. In this important task he displayed a broad grasp of the tactical lessons of the war and showed sound judgment in adapting their principles to American needs, capabilities, and characteristics, thereby rendering services of signal worth to the American Expeditionary Forces.
LYNN, CLARK R—Chicago, Ill. B—Hartford, Ind. G. O. No. 56, W. D., 1922.	Lieutenant colonel (Infantry), General Staff Corps, U. S. Army. As assistant chief of staff, G-3, 91st Division, from July, 1918, to April, 1919, by his high professional attainments and marked ability he rendered valuable assistance in the staff work during the St. Mihiel, Meuse-Argonne, and Ypres Lys offensives, his efficiency contributing materially to the success of his division in these operations.
*LYON, LEROY S R—Richmond, Va. B—Petersburg, Va. G. O. No. 68, W. D., 1920.	Major general, U. S. Army. As brigadier general commanding the 65th Field Artillery Brigade, 40th Division, he displayed splendid qualities of leadership and organizing ability and by his enthusiasm and energy he developed his brigade to a high state of efficiency. Later, as major general, commanding the 31st Division during its training, he exhibited marked tactical judgment, and his skill and leadership were largely responsible for the success achieved in perfecting the organization and training of his division. Posthumously awarded. Medal presented to widow, Mrs. Leroy S. Lyon.

LYSTER, THEODORE C.
R—Detroit, Mich.
B—Fort Larned, Kans.
G. O. No. 34, W. D., 1919.

Colonel, Medical Corps, U. S. Army.
For duty rendered in the office of the Surgeon General as Chief of the Air Service Division.

MCADAMS, JOHN P.
R—Hawesville, Ky.
B—Hawesville, Ky.
G. O. No. 59, W. D., 1919.

Colonel (Infantry), General Staff Corps, U. S. Army.
He served with marked distinction as chief of staff of the lines of communication and as deputy chief of staff of the Services of Supply. He administered the affairs with which he was intrusted with noteworthy and conspicuous efficiency, energy, and ability.

MCAFEE, LARRY B.
R—Delphi, Ind.
B—Delphi, Ind.
G. O. No. 49, W. D., 1922.

Lieutenant colonel, Medical Corps, U. S. Army.
As chief surgeon, district of Paris, France, by his unusual executive ability, sound judgment, and high professional attainments he successfully handled a position of great responsibility presenting many difficult problems, thereby bringing comfort and health to thousands of our sick and wounded and contributing materially to the success of the American Expeditionary Forces.

MCALEXANDER, ULYSSES G.
R—McPherson, Kans.
B—Dundas, Minn.
G. O. No. 59, W. D., 1919.
Distinguished-service cross also awarded.

Brigadier general, U. S. Army.
He commanded the 38th Infantry, 3d Division, with marked distinction in repelling the German attack at Mezy, south of the Marne, in July, 1918. He exhibited particular skill and energy as a brigade commander in the operations at the St. Mihiel salient and in the Argonne-Meuse offensive. The successful accomplishment of the missions of his brigade in all cases were in a large measure due to his sound judgment and leadership.

MCANDREW, JAMES W.
R—Scranton, Pa.
B—Hawley, Pa.
G. O. No. 136, W. D., 1918.

Major general, U. S. Army.
As Chief of Staff of the American Expeditionary Forces, the development of the Army schools in France is largely due to his marked ability as an organizer and to his brilliant professional attainments. As Chief of Staff of the American Expeditionary Forces during the period of active operations, he has met every demand of his important position; by his advice and decisions he has materially contributed to the success of these forces; and he has at all times enjoyed in full the confidence of the Commander in Chief.

MCANDREW, JOSEPH A.
R—Bentonville, Ark.
B—Osage Mills, Ark.
G. O. No. 87, W. D., 1919.

Lieutenant colonel, Infantry, U. S. Army.
He served with distinguished ability as an instructor in the use of infantry weapons at the 1st Corps School and also as director of the Infantry Specialists' School at Langres. Later, as a member of the training section of the General Staff, he supervised the instruction at the various corps schools and was directly responsible for the maintenance of sound tactical training, securing especially brilliant results in the training of infantry, rendering services of marked merit to the American Expeditionary Forces.

MCANDREWS, JOSEPH R.
R—Chicago, Ill.
B—Chicago, Ill.
G. O. No. 47, W. D., 1919.

Colonel (Cavalry), General Staff, U. S. Army.
As senior officer in the small group of the operations division, General Staff, designated as the section in charge of priorities of equipment and shipment, he was charged with the handling of the whole matter of preparing units for movement to the ports for oversea service, and is now engaged in the reverse process of moving returning units from the ports to camps for demobilization, all of which has been marked by conspicuous ability and meritorious service to the Government.

MACARTHUR, DOUGLAS.
R—Milwaukee, Wis.
B—Little Rock Barracks, Ark.
G. O. No. 59, W. D., 1919.
Distinguished-service cross and oak-leaf cluster also awarded.

Brigadier-general, U. S. Army.
He served with credit as chief of staff of the 42d Division in the operations at Chalons and at the Chateau-Thierry salient. In command of the 84th Infantry Brigade he showed himself to be a brilliant commander of skill and judgment. Later he served with distinction as commanding general of the 42d Division.

MCARTHUR, JOHN C.
R—Aberdeen, S. Dak.
B—Plainview, Minn.
G. O. No. 15, W. D., 1923.

Colonel, Infantry, U. S. Army.
As commanding officer, 326th Infantry, 82d Division, from the date of its organization and during its occupancy of the Somme, Toul, Nancy, and Argonne sectors, May 10, 1918, to Nov. 19, 1918, he displayed brilliant leadership, sound tactical judgment, unremitting attention and devotion to duty, these qualities inspiring the officers and men of his command, bringing their morale to a high pitch and inciting them to a rare devotion to duty. His services as a regimental commander contributed in a very marked way to the successful operations of the 82d Division and of the American Expeditionary Forces in France.

MCCAIN, HENRY P.
R—Jackson, Miss.
B—Carroll County, Miss.
G. O. No. 18, W. D., 1919.

Major general, The Adjutant General, U. S. Army.
In administering the Adjutant General's Department during the early period of the war, through his efficient management this department was able to meet the excessive burdens placed upon it.

MCCAW, WALTER D.
R—Richmond, Va.
B—Richmond, Va.
G. O. No. 12, W. D., 1919.

Colonel, Medical Corps, U. S. Army.
His counsel and advice in the earlier stages of the operations of the American Expeditionary Forces were of particular benefit to the effective work of the Medical Department. As chief surgeon of the American Expeditionary Forces, in the later operations in the field, he maintained the splendid efficiency of that department at a critical time and solved each new problem presented with wisdom and marked ability.

McCleave, Edward G. R—Berkeley, Calif. B—St. Louis, Mo. G. O. No. 56, W. D., 1922.	Lieutenant colonel (Infantry), General Staff, U. S. Army. Serving as assistant to the assistant chief of staff, G–4, Paris group and 1st Arm: from January to December, 1918, he displayed great initiative, devotion duty, and executive ability during the operations in and around Chatea Thierry in June and July, while the divisions of the American Army we serving with the 6th French Army and during the St. Mihiel and Meus Argonne operations of the 1st Army, assisted in the organization of the sectic and in a position of great responsibility contributed materially to the succes ful accomplishments of the supply of the troops engaged in those operation
McCleave, Robert. R—California. B—Fort Union, N. Mex. G. O. No. 116, W. D., 1919.	Colonel (Infantry), General Staff Corps, U. S. Army. As G–3 of the 1st Army from July 25 to Oct. 15, 1918, during the Chatea: Thierry, St. Mihiel, and Meuse-Argonne operations, he displayed marke ability. Later, in the midst of operations, he was appointed chief of sta of the 3d Division. In gaining immediate and complete control of a difficu situation and in coordinating the work of the new staff, he showed co: spicuous ability, and by his inspiring example of energy and zeal, he w: largely responsible for the successes achieved by the 3d Division at Clair Chenes Wood and the Bois-de-Foret.
McClellan, Benjamin F. R—Tallulah, La. B—Paulding Plantation, Miss G. O. No. 87, W. D., 1919.	Lieutenant colonel, Infantry, U. S. Army. Attached to the 5th Section of the General Staff, he displayed high profession attainments and marked executive ability in the general supervision of tl entire group of army schools. As an inspector-instructor of infantry, h influence was an important factor in securing the correct tactical trainir of that arm, rendering creditable services to the American Expeditiona: Forces.
McCloskey, Manus. R—Pittsburgh, Pa. B—Pittsburgh, Pa. G. O. No. 53, W. D., 1920.	Colonel, Field Artillery, U. S. Army. While in command of the 12th Field Artillery during all its operations with tl 2d Division, until Aug. 16, 1918, he displayed marked ability and efficienc He especially distinguished himself during the operations of the 2d Divisio at the Bois-de-Belleau and Bouresches, when he commanded in addition his own regiment, the 37th Field Artillery, French Army. By this servi he contributed in no small measure to the success of the Infantry brigade these operations. Later, as commanding general, 152d Field Artillery B: gade, he rendered able support to the attacking Infantry of the 77th Divisio
McCord, James H. R—St. Joseph, Mo. B—Savannah, Ga. G. O. No. 56, W. D., 1922.	Lieutenant colonel, Inspector General's Department, U. S. Army. As executive officer in charge of the selective draft in Missouri, by his unust executive ability, rare tact and skill, great initiative, and resourcefulness times under most trying and novel conditions which arose in connectic with the administration of the selective service act, he achieved a pronounc and conspicuous success in the performance of difficult and highly responsit duties, thereby rendering services of great value to the Government.
McCormick, Chester B. R—Lansing, Mich. B—Petrolia, Pa. G. O. No. 3, W. D., 1922.	Colonel, Field Artillery, U. S. Army. For services while commanding the 119th Field Artillery and at times t 57th Artillery Brigade during the Meuse-Argonne offensive. During the operations he displayed marked judgment and devotion to duty, and l the skillful handling of his command contributed materially to the success the 57th Artillery Brigade in supporting the 32d and at other times five oth divisions.
McCormick, Robert R. R—Chicago, Ill. B—Chicago, Ill. G. O. No. 15, W. D., 1923.	Colonel, Field Artillery, U. S. Army. As commander of the 1st Battalion, 5th Field Artillery, in the Ansauville sect and in the Cantigny sector, France, between Jan. 18 and May 28, 1918, a: as lieutenant colonel, 122d Field Artillery, 33d Division, May 13 to July : 1918, and colonel, 61st Field Artillery, July 30 to Dec. 31, 1918, he display rare leadership and organizing ability, unusual executive ability, and sou technical judgment. By his ceaseless energy and his close supervision training, discipline, and command in action against the enemy he contribut materially to the successful operations of the Artillery of the American Expe: tionary Forces.
McCoy, Frank R. R—Lewistown, Pa. B—Lewistown, Pa. G. O. No. 12, W. D., 1919.	Brigadier general, U. S. Army. As secretary of the General Staff, American Expeditionary Forces, his servic were of particular value in the original organization of the forces in Fran Later, in command of the 165th Infantry, 42d Division, in the Baccarat sect and then in command of the 63d Infantry Brigade in the difficult fighting e: of Reims, he had a prominent part in the successes achieved.
McCoy, John C. R—Paterson, N. J. B—New York, N. Y. G. O. No. 126, W. D., 1919.	Lieutenant colonel, Medical Corps, U. S. Army. He served with conspicuous success as commanding officer of American R Cross Hospital No. 111, at Jouy-sur-Morin and Chateau-Thierry from Ju to August, 1918. Though he was hampered by insufficient personnel a equipment, he nevertheless succeeded in caring for a large number of wound from the Marne offensive, rendering invaluable services to the Americ Expeditionary Forces.
McCoy, Robert B. R—Sparta, Wis. B—Kenosha, Wis. G. O. No. 69, W. D., 1919.	Colonel, Infantry, U. S. Army. In command of the 128th Infantry throughout all the major operations in whi the 32d Division participated, he proved himself a leader of sound judgme and exceptional ability. During the Oise-Aisne offensive he skillful handled the delicate maneuver of straightening and changing the front the left bank of his brigade during the attack on Terny-Sorny and later duri the Meuse-Argonne offensive. In the attack on the Kremhilde-Stellung performed another tactical operation of a high order in a flank moveme which resulted in the taking of the town of Romagne.

McCREA, JAMES A.
R—Woodmere, N. Y.
B—Philadelphia, Pa.
G. O. No. 59, W. D., 1919.

Colonel, Corps of Engineers, U. S. Army.
He rendered especially efficient services to the American Expeditionary Forces while acting as general manager of the transportation service and later as deputy director general of transportation in the advance section. He handled his duties in a most efficient manner, showing marked ability, great zeal, and energy.

McCULLAGH, SAMUEL.
R—New York, N. Y.
B—Philadelphia, Pa.
G. O. No. 49, W. D., 1922.

Lieutenant colonel, Medical Corps, U. S. Army.
As chief of the evacuation branches, G-4, Paris group, and G-4, 1st Army, he was charged with the supervision, coordination, and control of evacuation and hospitalization of the sick and wounded. By his great foresight, initiative, judgment, devotion to duty, and the helpful cooperation exercised by him, he played an important part in the successful treatment and evacuation of many thousands of sick and wounded under the most adverse conditions, performing this important and responsible duty with conspicuous ability, thereby contributing materially to the success of the American Expeditionary Forces.

McDONALD, JOHN B.
R—Athens, Ala.
B—Athens, Ala.
G. O. No. 59, W. D., 1919.
Distinguished-service cross also awarded.

Brigadier general, U. S. Army.
While commanding the 181st Infantry Brigade during the advance of the 91st Division from Foret-de-Hesse, Argonne, France, in September, 1918, he was instrumental in the successes achieved. He directed the attack in person, and by his example of personal courage and by his sound tactical orders he so inspired his brigade that it was enabled to capture and hold a most important position.

MacDONNELL, JOHN G.
R—Gordon, Wash.
B—Spencer, Mass.
G. O. No. 9, W. D., 1923.

Major, Cavalry, U. S. Army.
As provost marshal, 1st Army, during the Meuse-Argonne offensive, he was responsible for the maintenance of order in the extensive Army area in rear of corps areas, for the apprehension of stragglers and wrongdoers in that area, for the military police of areas relinquished by each corps as a consequence of the rapid advance of the corps of the 1st Army after Nov. 1, 1918. Due to his tact, resourcefulness, and marked efficiency he accomplished all of his missions in a highly meritorious manner, thereby contributing materially to the successes of the 1st Army.

*McDONOUGH, JOHN.
R—Beech Grove, Ind.
B—Plattsmouth, Nebr.
G. O. No. 59, W. D., 1921.

Major, Transportation Corps, U. S. Army.
As general foreman of the St. Nazaire Locomotive Erection Shops, he managed this plant from its organization in September, 1917, until June, 1918, when he was appointed superintendent, and thence performed the important duties of this later office until his death in November, 1918. It is due to his energy, ability, and devotion to duty that such a great number of American locomotives erected in France were turned out with record speed. He has rendered services of much value.
Posthumously awarded. Medal presented to widow, Mrs. John McDonough.

MacDOWELL, CHARLES H.
R—Chicago, Ill.
B—Lewistown, Ill.
G. O. No. 15, W. D., 1923.

Director of the Chemicals Division, War Industries Board.
In connection with the operations of the War Industries Board during the World War, in his position as director of one of the sections of the board he rendered, through his broad vision, distinguished capacity, and business ability, services of inestimable value in marshaling the industrial forces of the Nation and mobilizing its economic resources—marked factors in assisting to make military success attainable. As director of chemicals, he rendered, through his untiring efforts and devotion to duty, exceptionally valuable service to the War Department in connection with the procurement of chemicals, particularly those elements used in the manufacture of explosives for the Army.

McDOWELL, RALPH W.
R—Altoona, Pa.
B—Altoona, Pa.
G. O. No. 38, W. D., 1921.

Lieutenant commander, Medical Corps, U. S. Navy.
For services as sanitary inspector and surgeon of the Arrondissement of Tours, France.

McFADDEN, GEORGE.
R—Villanova, Pa.
B—Philadelphia, Pa.
G. O. No. 46, W. D., 1919.

Representative in France of the War Trade Board.
He represented in France with high ability the War Trade Board of the State Department. In close liaison with the General Purchasing Board of the American Expeditionary Forces, he had a guiding influence in determining the methods of the invaluable cooperation of the War Trade Board in the supply-procurement efforts of the Army in France and in neutral and other allied countries. With untiring energy, sound judgment, great ability, and devoted purpose he cooperated in many matters of vital importance to the American Expeditionary Forces.

McFADDEN, JAMES FRANKLIN.
R—Rosemont, Pa.
B—Philadelphia, Pa.
G. O. No. 56, W. D., 1922.

Lieutenant colonel, Air Service, U. S. Army.
As officer in charge of the leave bureau at headquarters, services of supply, Tours, France, from Dec. 14, 1918, until June, 1919, by his energy, loyal devotion to duty, unusual executive and administrative ability he was largely responsible for the successful organization and most efficient functioning of that highly important bureau which provided transportation, quarters, subsistence, recreation, and amusement for over 400,000 men on leave from the front in 19 different leave areas in southern France. In a position of great responsibility he rendered conspicuous services to the American Expeditionary Forces.

McFarland, Earl R—Topeka, Kans. B—Topeka, Kans. G. O. No. 38, W. D., 1921.	Colonel, Ordnance Department, U. S. Army. First in charge of the design, development, and production of all machine guns, automatic rifles, and accessories thereto for the Army of the United States, for service in organizing the industries of the country to meet the unprecedented demands for automatic arms created after the entrance of the United States into the World War, and later as special assistant to the Chief of Ordnance in charge of all matters pertaining to small arms, automatic arms, and equipment.
McGlachlin, Edward F., Jr. R—Stevens Point, Wis. B—Fond du Lac, Wis. G. O. No. 12, W. D., 1919.	Major general, U. S. Army. As commander of the Artillery of the 1st Army in its organization and subsequent operations he solved the difficult problems involved with rare military judgment. In the St. Mihiel and Argonne-Meuse offensives his qualities as a leader were demonstrated by the effective employment of Artillery that was planned and conducted under his direction. He later commanded with great ability and success the 1st Infantry Division of the American Expeditionary Forces.
McGuire, Stuart R—Richmond, Va. B—Staunton, Va. G. O. No. 59, W. D., 1921.	Lieutenant colonel, Medical Corps, U. S. Army. As commanding officer of Base Hospital No. 45 he received and cared for a very large number of wounded evacuated in that hospital during the Battle of the Argonne, in September and October, 1918. By his administrative and professional skill he has reflected credit upon the Medical Department of the Army.
*McIndoe, James F R—Lonaconing, Md. B—Lonaconing, Md. G. O. No. 56, W. D., 1921.	Colonel, Corps of Engineers, U. S. Army. He rendered valuable services in bringing this unit to a high state of discipline and training which manifested itself later in all operations in which it participated. Later, as director of military engineers, a position of great responsibility, he rendered services of much worth. Posthumously awarded. Medal presented to widow, Mrs. Irene McIndoe.
McIntyre, Frank R—Montgomery, Ala. B—Montgomery, Ala. G. O. No. 25, W. D., 1919.	Major general, U. S. Army. As executive assistant to the Chief of Staff, his breadth of view and sound judgment have contributed materially to the formulation and carrying out of policies essential to the operation of the military establishment.
McKean, Josiah Slutts R—Canal Dover, Ohio. B—Mount Hope, Ohio. G. O. No. 116, W. D., 1919.	Rear admiral, U. S. Navy. As acting Chief of Naval Operations, his advice and assistance greatly tended to the successful outcome of the many problems requiring the close cooperation of the Navy and Army.
McKernon, James F R—New York, N. Y. B—Cambridge, N. Y. G. O. No. 59, W. D., 1919.	Colonel, Medical Corps, U. S. Army. He has, by his tireless devotion to duty and his willingness to work in any capacity, not only placed his remarkable ability freely and fully at the disposition of the wounded, but in addition he has set so high a standard of professional efficiency as to serve as an inspiration to all with whom he has come in contact.
McLean, Angus R—Detroit, Mich. B—St. Clair, Mich. G. O. No. 56, W. D., 1922.	Colonel, Medical Corps, U. S. Army. As director of the professional services and later as commanding officer of Base Hospital No. 17 and surgical consultant in hospital formations at the front, by his tireless energy, great resourcefulness, and brilliant professional attainments he rendered services of inestimable value in the care of the sick and wounded of the American, British, and French Armies, thereby contributing materially to the success of the American Expeditionary Forces.
McLeer, Edward, Jr. R—Brooklyn, N. Y. B—Brooklyn, N. Y. G. O. No. 16, W. D., 1923.	Lieutenant colonel, Infantry, U. S. Army. With untiring energy and unremitting devotion to duty he supervised the instruction and training and commanded in action against the enemy the machine-gun organizations of the 27th Division. During the operations of the division against the Hindenburg line, Sept. 25-30, 1918, and in the Le Selle River campaign Oct. 15-20, 1918, in direct command of 14 machine-gun companies he displayed outstanding leadership, sound tactical judgment, and indomitable determination and courage, these qualities being reflected in the morale and high efficiency of the machine-gun organizations of this division. He rendered extremely valuable and important services to the Government in a position of great responsibility.
McMahon, Edmund J. R—St. Louis, Mo. B—St. Louis, Mo. G. O. No. 56, W. D., 1921.	Colonel, Infantry, U. S. Army. As commanding officer of the camp at St. Sulpice, France, a position of great responsibility, he demonstrated rare executive ability. The efficient operation and growth of this important base section was due, in a great measure, to his energy and capacity for handling a task of considerable magnitude.
McManus, George H R—Hudson, Iowa. B—Hudson, Iowa. G. O. No. 69, W. D., 1919.	Brigadier general, U. S. Army. As executive officer and troop movement officer, port of embarkation, Hoboken N. J., through his very able organization and administration of these important offices the transport of troops and supplies overseas was materially aided
MacMillan, William T. R—Mahanoy City, Pa. B—Girard Manor, Pa. G. O. No. 4, W. D., 1923.	Lieutenant colonel (Infantry), General Staff Corps, U. S. Army. As assistant chief of staff, G-1, 78th Division, from July, 1918, until June, 1919 by his indefatigable zeal, keen foresight, exceptional executive and administrative ability he successfully organized and directed the supply and administrative services of the division so as to insure at all times an ample supply of rations and ammunition, overcoming many difficult obstacles under most trying circumstances, thereby rendering conspicuous services to the American Expeditionary Forces in a position of great responsibility.

DISTINGUISHED-SERVICE MEDAL 739

McNAIR, LESLEY J.
   R—Bemidji, Minn.
   B—Verndale, Minn.
   G. O. No. 59, W. D., 1919.

Brigadier general, U. S. Army.
As the senior Artillery officer of the training section, General Staff, he displayed marked ability in correctly estimating the changing conditions and requirements of military tactics. He was largely responsible for impressing upon the American Army sound principles for the use of artillery and for improving methods for the support of Infantry, so necessary to the proper cooperation of the two arms.

McNAIR, WILLIAM S.
   R—Tecumseh, Mich.
   B—Tecumseh, Mich.
   G. O. No. 49, W. D., 1922.

Major general, U. S. Army.
Serving in turn as commander of the 1st Field Artillery Brigade, 1st Division, and the 151st Field Artillery Brigade, 76th Division, as chief of artillery, 1st Army Corps, during the latter part of the Meuse-Argonne offensive and as chief of artillery of the 1st Army from Nov. 18, 1918, until April, 1919, by his marked ability, sound judgment, and thorough knowledge of artillery he rendered conspicuous services in a position of great responsibility to the American Expeditionary Forces.

McNEELY, JOHN D.
   R—St. Joseph, Mo.
   B—St. Joseph, Mo.
   G. O. No. 56, W. D., 1921.

Colonel, Infantry, U. S. Army.
As deputy director, rents, requisitions, and claims service, a position of great responsibility, in which he discharged important administrative functions with noteworthy ability and displayed good judgment and tact while attached to the British Claims Commission.

McNEIL, EDWIN C.
   R—Alexandria, Minn.
   B—Alexandria, Minn.
   G. O. No. 19, W. D., 1922.

Colonel, Judge Advocate General's Department, U. S. Army.
As assistant judge advocate, American Expeditionary Forces, by his excellent administrative ability and sound judgment he rendered a service which enabled his department to expeditiously handle many questions of great moment.

McRAE, DONALD MARION.
   R—Boston, Mass.
   B—Fort Snelling, Minn.
   G. O. No. 56, W. D., 1922.

Lieutenant colonel, Infantry, U. S. Army.
As assistant chief of staff, G-2, 78th Division, from November, 1917, until December, 1918, he displayed military attainments of a high order. By his great energy, sound judgment, and efficient administration of his section he was able to secure complete and valuable information of the enemy, thereby contributing materially to the successful operations of his division.

McRAE, JAMES H.
   R—Lumber City, Ga.
   B—Lumber City, Ga.
   G. O. No. 12, W. D., 1919.

Major general, U. S. Army.
He commanded with great credit the 78th Division in the Argonne-Meuse offensive and had an important part in that operation which forced the enemy to abandon Grandpre. In this and other campaigns his personal influence on the result obtained showed a rich quality of military leadership.

McROBERTS, SAMUEL.
   R—New York, N. Y.
   B—Malta Bend, Mo.
   G. O. No. 72, W. D., 1920.

Brigadier general, U. S. Army.
As chief of the procurement division of the office of the Chief of Ordnance, in which capacity he was charged with the procurement, by purchase or manufacture, of all articles of ordnance supplied to the United States Army, and the execution of the necessary contracts in connection therewith.

MABEE, JAMES I.
   R—Rockwood, Mich.
   B—Gasport, N. Y.
   G. O. No. 9, W. D., 1923.

Colonel, Medical Corps, U. S. Army.
He served with the 1st Division as sanitary inspector from June 6, 1917, to July, 1918, and as division surgeon from July 4, 1918, to Feb. 10, 1919, and then as chief surgeon, 3d Army Corps. By his high professional ability, his ability for organization and for securing cooperation of his subordinates, and his tireless efforts, he effected the successful evacuation of many casualties suffered by the 1st Division in the Soissons, St. Mihiel, Meuse-Argonne, and Sedan attacks. At all times he rendered services of great value to the American Expeditionary Forces in positions of great responsibility.

MACNAB, ALEXANDER, J., Jr.
   R—Salmon, Idaho.
   B—Salmon, Idaho.
   G. O. No. 62, W. D., 1919.

Colonel, Infantry, U. S. Army.
He installed an extensive system of target ranges in France and perfected methods for the training of marksmen, personally supervising the instruction of 200,000 Infantry replacements. As a member of the training section he applied his methods to the instruction of the Infantry of the American Expeditionary Forces with extraordinary success.

MACRAE, DONALD, Jr.
   R—Council Bluffs, Iowa.
   B—Council Bluffs, Iowa.
   G. O. No. 19, W. D., 1922.

Colonel, Medical Corps, U. S. Army.
As commanding officer of Mobile Hospital No. 1, at Coulommiers and Chateau-Thierry, from June to August, 1918, Colonel Macrae promptly arranged his hospital under the most difficult conditions and inadequate equipment and personnel.

MADDOX, GEORGE W.
   R—Owenton, Ky.
   B—Rogers Gap, Ky.
   G. O. No. 56, W. D., 1922.

Lieutenant colonel (Infantry), General Staff Corps, U. S. Army.
As assistant chief of staff, G-1, 82d Division, from June until September, 1918, and of the 81st Division from then until June, 1919, he rendered highly meritorious services. Due to his unusual foresight, great energy, and marked ability, he directed the supply and administrative services of those divisions so as to insure at all times a proper supply of food and munitions, often under great difficulties and lack of transportation, thereby rendering conspicuous services in a position of great responsibility to the American Expeditionary Forces.

MADDUX, HENRY C.
   R—Orange, Va.
   B—Harrisonburg, Va.
   G. O. No. 59, W. D., 1921.

Lieutenant colonel, Medical Corps, U. S. Army.
In organizing and constructing the hospital center at Toul. His work in this showed a force, initiative, and character that contributed in an unusual way to the ability of the Medical Department and care for the sick and wounded of the American Expeditionary Forces.

MADDUX, RUFUS F.
   R—Newport, Ky.
   B—Cincinnati, Ohio.
   G. O. No. 14, W. D., 1923.

Lieutenant colonel, Chemical Warfare Service, U. S. Army.
As commanding officer and organizer of the officers' reclassification depot at Blois, France, from April to July, 1918, by his tact, judgment, and untiring energy he made it a model of efficient organization. Later as gas officer of the 5th Army Corps from Aug. 5 to Oct. 13, 1918, he displayed a great resourcefulness, marked efficiency, exceptional initiative, tireless efforts in successfully meeting the unusual demands relating to gas defense of the troops in the St. Mihiel and Meuse-Argonne offensives, thereby rendering service of great value to the American Expeditionary Forces.

MAGRUDER, BRUCE.
   R—Washington, D. C.
   B—Washington, D. C.
   G. O. No. 87, W. D., 1919.

Lieutenant colonel (Infantry), General Staff Corps, U. S. Army.
As executive officer of the intelligence section at General Headquarters, by his marked ability and zeal he performed duties of a most exacting nature, in connection with the administration and development of the section, with conspicuous merit, rendering services of great value to the American Expeditionary Forces.

MAGRUDER, LLOYD B.
   R—Washington, D. C.
   B—Washington, D. C.
   G. O. No. 60, W. D., 1920.

Lieutenant colonel, Coast Artillery Corps, U. S. Army.
As inspector of the district of Paris, he conducted many intricate and delicate investigations with noteworthy ability and solved many involved problems arising among the American Expeditionary Forces with sound judgment. The zealous and able manner with which he pursued the manifold details of his office was an important factor in raising the morale of the American Expeditionary Forces in Paris. He has performed services of special significance for the American Expeditionary Forces.

MAJOR, DUNCAN K., Jr.
   R—New York, N. Y.
   B—New York, N. Y.
   G. O. No. 89, W. D., 1919.

Colonel (Infantry), General Staff Corps, U. S. Army.
As chief of staff of the 26th Division he proved to be a capable and energetic staff officer of marked executive ability. At all times he exhibited rare qualities of military leadership. He rendered invaluable services to the American Expeditionary Forces.

MALONE, PAUL B.
   R—New York, N. Y.
   B—Middletown, N. Y.
   G. O. No. 24, W. D., 1920.
   Distinguished-service cross also awarded.

Brigadier general, U. S. Army.
He demonstrated marked ability in the important duty of organizing the military training and educational system of the American Army in France. Later, in active operations against the enemy, he commanded with distinction a regiment in the trench operations of the Sommedieue sector, in the Aisne defensive, the operations near Chateau-Thierry, and in the Aisne-Marne offensive, and a brigade in the St. Mihiel and Meuse-Argonne offensives. In all of these capacities the merit he displayed was conspicuous.

MALONE, WILLIAM B.
   R—Memphis, Tenn.
   B—Brownsville, Tenn.
   G. O. No. 38, W. D., 1922.

Major, Medical Corps, U. S. Army.
As chief of surgical teams in hospital formations at the front through all the combat activities of the American Expeditionary Forces from the Cantigny offensive to the close of the Meuse-Argonne offensive, with rare technical skill and high professional attainments he rendered service of a most conspicuous nature in a position of great responsibility and at a time of gravest importance.

MALONY, HARRY J.
   R—Dundee, N. Y.
   B—Lakemont, N. Y.
   G. O. No. 78, W. D., 1919.

Lieutenant colonel, Ordnance Department, U. S. Army.
He successfully organized and administered the many complex and difficult operations connected with the arming and equipping of airplanes for services at the front, displaying sound judgment and acting with energy and initiative in times of emergency. He worked self-sacrificingly and devotedly that there might be no delays, overcoming serious obstacles by the exercise of good judgment and thorough understanding of conditions in the American Expeditionary Forces.

MANCHESTER, PERCIVAL.
   R—Chicago, Ill.
   B—Chicago, Ill.
   G. O. No. 126, W. D., 1919.

Major, Ordnance Department, U. S. Army.
As base ordnance officer in Base Section No. 1, at St. Nazaire, France, he ably organized and administered important work with exceptional success. As commanding officer of Intermediate Ordnance Depot No. 2, at Gievres, he conducted important activities with sound judgment and marked devotion to duty, working with tireless energy for the improvement of the Ordnance Service.

MANLY, CLARENCE J.
   R—New York, N. Y.
   B—Georgetown, Ky.
   G. O. No. 103, W. D., 1919.

Colonel, Medical Corps, U. S. Army.
He organized and commanded with signal ability the hospital center at Beaune, taking charge of it when it was in an unfinished state and at a time when increased facilities were urgently needed. Overcoming numerous adverse conditions, he expedited its completion, and rendered invaluable services in furnishing effective medical treatment for large numbers of sick and wounded of the American Expeditionary Forces.

MANN, CHARLES R.
   R—Summitt, N. J.
   B—Orange, N. J.
   G. O. No. 124, W. D., 1919.

As chairman of the advisory board of the committee on education and special training, he gave invaluable service in the development of the training of technicians and mechanics for the Army, and in the organization of the Students' Army Training Corps.

MARCH, PEYTON C.
   R—Easton, Pa.
   B—Easton, Pa.
   G. O. No. 4, W. D., 1919.
   Distinguished-service cross also awarded.

General, U. S. Army.
As commanding general of the Army Artillery of the 1st Army from Oct. 4, 1917 to Jan. 31, 1918, initiated and prepared the plans for the organization of the Artillery of the American Army in France; as Acting Chief of Staff of the U. S. Army from Mar. 2, 1918, to May 20, 1918, and as Chief of Staff of the U. S. Army (General, U. S. Army), after May 20, 1918, he performed with intelligence, zeal, and patriotic devotion, duties of inestimable value in the development, the direction and the carrying into effect of the military program of the United States.

MARKEY, DAVID JOHN.
  R—Frederick, Md.
  B—Frederick, Md.
  G. O. No. 31, W. D., 1922.

Major, Infantry, U. S. Army.
While in action with the 58th Infantry Brigade, 29th Division, north of Verdun, 1918, in the absence of a regularly detailed brigade adjutant he performed the exacting duties of that office in addition to his duties as commander of the machine-gun battalion under circumstances requiring exceptional courage, tactical judgment, initiative, and endurance, all of which he displayed to a marked degree. By his brilliant professional attainments, his untiring energy and keen foresight he contributed largely to the subsequent successes of his brigade and division. He handled with rare skill and in a masterful manner the multifarious duties devolving upon him in a position of great responsibility.

MARSHALL, FRANCIS C.
  R—Darlington, Wis.
  B—Galena, Ill.
  G. O. No. 38, W. D., 1922.

Brigadier general, U. S. Army.
In command of the 2d Infantry Brigade, 1st Division, during the Meuse-Argonne offensive from Oct. 20 to Nov. 11, 1918, when, by his energy, professional skill, and his pronounced qualities of leadership, especially in the attack of the 1st Division on the line of the Meuse, Nov. 6, 1918, and the subsequent operations against Sedan, Nov. 6–7, 1918, he contributed in large measure to the success of his division.

MARSHALL, GEORGE C., Jr.
  R—Uniontown, Pa.
  B—Uniontown, Pa.
  G. O. No. 116, W. D., 1919.

Colonel (Infantry), General Staff Corps, U. S. Army.
He has performed the duties of assistant chief of staff, G–3, 1st Division, from June 26, 1917, to July 12, 1918. He served in the G–3 section, General Headquarters, American Expeditionary Forces, from July 13, 1918, to Aug. 19, 1918; in G–3 section, 1st Army, from Aug. 20, 1918, to Oct. 16, 1918; as assistant chief of staff, G–3, of the 1st Army, from Oct. 17 to Nov. 19, 1918; and as chief of staff of the 8th Army Corps from Nov. 20, 1918, to Jan. 15, 1919, during which period the 1st Division served in the Toul sector and at the Cantigny attack and the 1st Army operations in the St. Mihiel and Meuse-Argonne offensives. By untiring, painstaking, and energetic efforts he succeeded in all these undertakings. His efforts had a marked influence on the successes achieved by the units with which he served.

MARSHALL, RICHARD C., Jr.
  R—Portsmouth, Va.
  B—Portsmouth, Va.
  G. O. No. 25, W. D., 1919.

Brigadier general, U. S. Army.
In the construction division of the Army, his zeal, judgment, and exceptional administrative ability have enabled serious difficulties to be overcome and the construction necessary for a great army to be provided.

MARSHALL, WALDO H.
  R—New York, N. Y.
  B—Boston, Mass.
  G. O. No. 77, W. D., 1919.

First, as assistant to the chief of the production division of the Office of the Chief of Ordnance, in which capacity he was of material assistance in securing the production of all articles of ordnance supplied to the United States Army, and later as special assistant to the Chief of Ordnance, in which capacity he successfully organized the industry of the country for the production of artillery, artillery ammunition, etc.

MARTIN, CHARLES H.
  R—Carmi, Ill.
  B—Albion, Ill.
  G. O. No. 87, W. D., 1919.

Major general, U. S. Army.
As commander of the 90th Division during the greater part of its service with the Army of Occupation, by his ceaseless energy he performed his duties with the utmost efficiency, giving the closest personal supervision to the training, discipline, and equipment of his division. His brilliant professional attainments and steadfast devotion to duty were reflected in the high standards maintained throughout the organizations under his command, rendering important services to the American Expeditionary Forces.

MARTIN, FRANKLIN H.
  R—Kenilworth, Ill.
  B—Xenia, Wis.
  G. O. No. 3, W. D., 1922.

Colonel, Medical Corps, U. S. Army.
As chairman of the committee on medicine and sanitation of the Council of National Defense, a position of great responsibility, by his tireless energy and marked ability, he so coordinated the civil medical resources of the Nation as to meet the needs of the Government medical service. He rendered valuable assistance in solving the important medical problems of the war.

MARTIN, FREDERICK L.
  R—Liberty, Ind.
  B—Liberty, Ind.
  G. O. No. 14, W. D., 1925.
  Act of Congress Feb. 25, 1925.

Major, Air Service, U. S. Army.
As commanding officer of the U. S. Army Air Service around-the-world flight and as pilot of Airplane No. 1, the *Seattle*, from Apr. 6, 1924, until Apr. 30, 1924, when, due to an accident which resulted in the complete wreck of his airplane, he was obliged to relinquish command of the expedition. Major Martin by his tireless energy, foresight, and thorough technical knowledge assisted materially in completing arrangements and developing the special equipment installed in the airplanes, and so perfected and organized the command that each unit would become self-sustaining and automatic in its operations in the event of separation from or disaster to the others. In the performance of this great task he aided in bringing great credit to the military forces of the United States.

MASON, CHARLES H.
  R—St. Paul, Minn.
  B—Fort Sanders, Wyo.
  G. O. No. 9, W. D., 1923.

Colonel (Infantry) General Staff Corps, U. S. Army.
While serving as chief of MI–2, information section, military intelligence division, General Staff, he originated and put into practical application an exceedingly scientific and highly technical system of handling all positive intelligence received in the division, including its dissemination to all branches of the War Department and other coordinating branches of the Government. From Sept. 16 to Dec. 12, 1918, as assistant chief of staff, G–2, 36th Division, he displayed sound judgment and exceptional ability in the administration and operation of that section of the division staff. Later, when on duty with the American Peace Mission at Paris, France, he rendered services of great value to the Government.

MASTELLER, KENNETH C. R—Bakersville, Calif. B—Pella, Iowa. G. O. No. 89, W. D., 1919.	Colonel (Coast Artillery Corps), General Staff Corps, U. S. Army. As chief of the negative branch of the military intelligence division of the eral Staff, in building up and developing the counterespionage service in country, the plant protection service, the detection of fraud and graft, the development battalion system.
MATTHEWS, HUGH. R—Louisville, Tenn. B—Tennessee. G. O. No. 59, W. D., 1921.	Lieutenant colonel, U. S. Marine Corps. As assistant chief of staff, G-1, 2d Division, a position of great responsib in which he functioned with marked ability during the St. Mihiel, I Mont, and Argonne offensives.
MAUBORGNE, JOSEPH O. R—New York, N Y B—New York, N Y G O. No. 81, W. D., 1919.	Lieutenant colonel, Signal Corps, U. S. Army. As head of the engineering and research division of the Signal Corps he dered conspicuous service in connection with coordinating the design supply of new technical apparatus for the Signal Corps. He was la responsible for the high type of radio equipment developed for our A and rendered unusual service in connection with cipher telegraphy.
MAUS, LOUIS M. R—Rockville, Md. B—Montgomery County, Md. G. O. No. 96, W. D., 1918.	First lieutenant, assistant surgeon, U. S. Army. For services on the Belle Fourche River, N. Dak., on Nov. 5, 1877, in while serving with a detachment suddenly surrounded by an overwhel force of hostile Sioux Indians he succeeded in extricating the party fr most perilous position.
MAXFIELD, HOWARD HOYT. R—Elizabeth, N. J. B—Bloomfield, N. J. G. O. No. 19, W. D., 1922.	Colonel, Corps of Engineers, U. S. Army. As general superintendent of motor power of the Transportation C American Expeditionary Forces, by his sound judgment and energy played in the organizing and administering of the activities of the mecha department he rendered services of great value to the American Ex tionary Forces.
MAYER, BRANTZ. R—Davenport, Iowa. B—Baltimore, Md. G. O. No. 116, W. D., 1919.	Lieutenant commander, U. S. Navy. For services as supply officer, Newport News division, cruiser and tran force.
MAYES, JAMES J. R—Springfield, Mo. B—Amsterdam, Ohio. G. O. No. 89, W. D., 1919.	Colonel, Judge Advocate General's Department, U. S. Army. He served with marked ability as deputy judge advocate of the Ame Expeditionary Forces. Fitted for his important duties by wide exper and conspicuous legal attainments, he solved ably and expeditiously the questions of great moment with which his department was called up deal.
MAYO, CHARLES H. R—Rochester, Minn. B—Rochester, Minn. G. O. No. 27, W. D., 1920.	Colonel, Medical Corps, U. S. Army. In addition to the manifold service to the Surgeon General by furni needed advice and counsel, he distinguished himself by exceptionally m rious service to the Government in his work in the organization of su service and his invaluable assistance in the reorganization of the M Department on the scale demanded by the war.
MAYO, WILLIAM JAMES. R—Rochester, Minn. B—Le Sueur, Minn. G. O. No. 69, W. D., 1919.	Colonel, Medical Corps, U. S. Army. In addition to the manifold service to the Surgeon General by furnishing n advice and counsel, he distinguished himself by exceptionally merit service to the Government in his work in the organization of surgical s and his invaluable assistance in the reorganization of the Medical Depart on the scale demanded by the war.
MAYO-SMITH, RICHMOND. R—Norwood, Mass. B—Easthampton, Long Island, N. Y. G. O. No. 56, W. D., 1922.	Lieutenant colonel, Chemical Warfare Service, U. S. Army. As chief of the supply section, Chemical Warfare Service, by his tireless en foresight, and marked executive ability, he built and administered a s organization consisting of 12 seaport, intermediate, and front-line d which fully met at all times the demands for chemical warfare supplie active operations brought upon the service, thereby rendering servi great value to the American Expeditionary Forces.
MEARS, FREDERICK. R—St. Paul, Minn. B—Fort Omaha, Nebr. G. O. No. 89, W. D., 1919.	Colonel, Corps of Engineers, U. S. Army. He served with distinction as commanding officer of the 31st Railway Engi and later as assistant general manager and general manager railway d ment, Transportation Corps. Due to his remarkable executive abilit skill as an organizer the railways of the American Expeditionary Force operated with rare success, and the huge transportation problem, inv the carrying of tremendous quantities of supplies from the base ports front, was satisfactorily solved.
MENOHER, CHARLES T. R—Johnstown, Pa. B—Johnstown, Pa. G. O. No. 12, W. D., 1919.	Major general, U. S. Army. In command of the 42d Division from Chateau-Thierry to the conclus the Argonne-Meuse offensive, including the Baccarat sector, Reims, V and at the St. Mihiel salient, this officer with his division participa all of those important engagements. The reputation as a fighting u the 42d Division is in no small measure due to the soldierly qualities an military leadership of this officer.
MERCHANT, BERKELEY T. R—Watervliet, N. Y. B—New York, N. Y. G. O. No. 108, W. D., 1919.	Lieutenant colonel, Quartermaster Corps, U. S. Army. While on duty in the remount service, he performed his tasks effici Later, appointed Chief Veterinarian of the American Expeditionary F he administered, with marked success, the veterinary service, providi effective means of evacuation of sick and wounded animals from the and in placing the personnel of the Veterinary Corps on an efficiently fur ing basis.

DISTINGUISHED-SERVICE MEDAL 743

ERRILL, DANA T
R—East Auburn, Me.
B—East Auburn, Me.
G. O. No. 43, W. D., 1922.

Colonel (Infantry), General Staff Corps, U. S. Army.
As chief of staff, 37th Division, during its organization, training, and entire combat period he displayed unflagging energy and marked ability. To his zeal, initiative, and military attainments was due in great measure the success of the division in both the Meuse-Argonne and Ypres-Lys offensives.

ETCALFE, RAYMOND F
R—Buffalo, N. Y.
B—West Salamanca, N. Y.
G. O. No. 15, W. D., 1921.

Colonel, Medical Corps, U. S. Army.
As division surgeon, 36th Division, in August and again in September, 1918, during serious epidemics of Spanish influenza, his farsightedness and his energetic and efficient action in personally directing the handling of these epidemics resulted in a very large reduction in the mortality.

ETTS, JOHN VAN B
R—Wilmington, N. C.
B—Wilmington, N. C.
G. O. No. 55, W. D., 1920.

Colonel, Infantry, U. S. Army.
He commanded with marked distinction the 119th Infantry, 30th Division, from the time of its organization and early training period to the completion of the active combat operations in the Ypres-Lys and Somme offensives. He especially distinguished himself while in command of his regiment on Sept. 29, 1918, during the assault on the Hindenburg line, near Bellicourt, France, where he displayed marked ability and sound judgment. He has rendered services of signal worth to the American Expeditionary Forces.

EYER, VINCENT
R—Brooklyn, N. Y.
B—New York, N. Y.
G. O. No. 39, W. D., 1920.

Major, Field Artillery, U. S. Army.
As a member of the supply section of the General Staff in charge of the munitions branch, he ably controlled and handled the details of ammunition supply for the 1st Army during the period of the St. Mihiel and Meuse-Argonne operations. In this important task he displayed marked initiative and energy, and assured by his skill and prompt action a steady supply of ammunition under most difficult conditions. His efforts were a contributing factor to the success of the supply service during these important operations.

IDDLETON, TROY H
R—Georgetown, Miss.
B—Hazelhurst, Miss.
G. O. No. 95, W. D., 1919.

Colonel, Infantry, U. S. Army.
As a battalion and a regimental commander of the 47th Infantry, 4th Division, he gave proof of conspicuous energy and marked tactical ability. He achieved notable successes in the operations near Sergy, along the Vesle River, and during the fierce fighting in the Boise-du-Fays and Bois-de-Foret of the Argonne-Meuse offensive, rendering invaluable services to the American Expeditionary Forces.

LES, PERRY L
R—Columbus, Ohio.
B—Westerville, Ohio.
G. O. No. 89, W. D., 1919.
Distinguished-service cross also awarded.

Colonel, Infantry, U. S. Army.
As commander of the 371st Infantry, 93d Division, which, during its active operations, was attached to the French forces, he conducted his regiment with conspicuous success, by his admirable tact and sound judgment he maintained at all times harmonious relationship with the allied forces to which his unit was attached, rendering valuable services to the American Expeditionary Forces.

LLER, ORRIN DAVID
R—Oakland, Calif.
B—Boonville, N. Y.
G. O. No. 56, W. D., 1921.

Lieutenant colonel, Transportation Corps, U. S. Army.
As executive officer of the Army Transportation Service, a position of great responsibility, throughout the whole period of existence of the service, by his untiring devotion to duty, loyalty, and marked ability, he proved a material factor in the success of the operation of the Army Transportation Service.

LLER, REUBEN B
R—Millington, Ill.
B—Canada.
G. O. No. 69, W. D., 1919.

Colonel, Medical Corps, U. S. Army.
In the reorganization and administration of the personnel branch of the office of the Surgeon General of the Army during the present war, he thereby contributed greatly to the proper care of the sick and wounded and thus increased the efficiency of the Army.

LLER, TROUP
R—Macon, Ga.
B—Perry, Ga.
G. O. No. 56, W. D., 1922.

Lieutenant colonel (Field Artillery), General Staff Corps, U. S. Army.
He served as adjutant, 82d Division, from December, 1917, until March, 1918; assistant chief of staff, G-1, 82d Division, from April to June and from September to December, 1918; assistant chief of staff, G-1, 1st Army Corps December, 1918, until February, 1919; and assistant chief of staff, G-4, 1st Army, from February to April, 1919, and then as G-4, intermediate section, services of supply. By his marked ability, sound judgment, and high military attainments he rendered meritorious services in positions of great responsibility, contributing in a large measure to the success attained by all the units with which he served.

LLIKEN, SAYRES L
R—Morgantown, W. Va.
B—Brownsville, Pa.
G. O. No. 9, W. D., 1923.

Captain, assistant superintendent, Army Nurse Corps, U. S. Army.
As chief nurse of the base hospital at Camp Sevier, S. C., during the early part of the World War, she was responsible for the nursing care of thousands of patients under most trying and difficult circumstances. Her tact, energy, and ability were greatly instrumental in saving many lives, particularly during the influenza epidemic. Her services were characterized by zeal and excellent judgment, and her achievements have been conspicuous. Later, while serving as assistant superintendent, Army Nurse Corps, in the office of the Surgeon General, her administrative ability and professional experience were of inestimable value to the Medical Department in providing proper nursing care for the sick and wounded.

LLIKIN, JOHN
R—Danville, Ind.
B—Danville, Ind.
G. O. No. 46, W. D., 1920.

Lieutenant colonel (Cavalry), General Staff Corps, U. S. Army.
As executive officer and assistant director of the Army General Staff College, at Langres he rendered conspicuous services. Later, as chief of the Military Police Corps Division of the Provost Marshal General's Department, American Expeditionary Forces, by his ability, untiring zeal, and sound judgment, he aided in a material way in producing an efficient organization. He has rendered services of great value to the American Expeditionary Forces.

102444°—27——48

MILLING, THOMAS DEW
R—Franklin, La.
B—Winnfield, La.
G. O. No. 50, W. D., 1919.

Colonel, Air Service, U. S. Army.
First, as chief of staff and later as commander, he organized and conducted operations of the Air Service of the 1st Army during the entire operation that Army. By untiring, painstaking, and energetic efforts he succeeded raising the efficiency of his command and insuring the proper cooperat with the land units. He exhibited professional attainments of the high order and exercised a marked influence on the success of the 1st Army.

MINER, ASHER
R—Wilkes-Barre, Pa.
B—Wilkes-Barre, Pa.
G. O. No. 89, W. D., 1919.
Distinguished-service cross also awarded.

Colonel, Field Artillery, U. S. Army.
He served with notable success as commanding officer of the 109th Field A lery, 28th Division, giving proof of high qualities of leadership. Inspi his men by his self-sacrificing devotion to duty he maintained a credit standard of efficiency in his regiment and constantly furnished the n effective artillery support to the attacking Infantry.

MINNIGERODE, FITZHUGH L.
R—Washington, D. C.
B—Oatlands, Va.
G. O. No. 126, W. D., 1919.
Distinguished-service cross also awarded.

Second lieutenant, 8th Infantry, U. S. Army.
For bravery and presence of mind in going to the rescue of drowning mer Iloilo, Panay, Philippine Islands, Sept. 10, 1907.

MINOR, SIDNEY W.
R—Durham, N. C.
B—Granville Co., N. C.
G. O. No. 55, W. D., 1920.

Colonel, Infantry, U. S. Army.
As commander of the 120th Infantry, 30th Division, from the time of its org zation and training to the completion of active combat operations in Ypres-Lys and Somme offensives, he displayed at all times initiative sound judgment. During the attack on the Hindenburg line, near B court, France, Sept. 29, 1918, and during the subsequent advance, he han his regiment with distinction, capturing several towns, numerous can and many prisoners. He has rendered services of material worth to American Expeditionary Forces.

MITCHELL, JAMES B.
R—Syracuse, N. Y.
B—Syracuse, N. Y.
G. O. No. 53, W. D., 1921.

Colonel, Inspector General's Department, U. S. Army.
As inspector general, and as chief of staff, Base Section No. 3, services of sup American Expeditionary Forces, positions of great responsibility, he sho great engery and good judgment in the organization of Base Section N and in providing for the American troops at the base and for those pas through England. H rendered services of much value.

MITCHELL, WILLIAM
R—Milwaukee, Wis.
B—France.
G. O. No. 87, W. D., 1919.
Distinguished-service cross also awarded.

Brigadier general, U. S. Army.
As Air Service commander, first of the zone of advance and later of the Army Corps, by his tireless energy and keen perception he performed du of great importance with marked ability. Subsequently as comman Air Service, of the 1st Army, and, in addition, after formation of the 2d A as commander of Air Service of both armies, by his able direction of t vitally important services he proved to be a potent factor in the succe achieved during the operations of the American armies.

MITCHELL, WILLIAM A.
R—Columbus, Ga.
B—Seale, Ala.
G. O. No. 89, W. D., 1919.

Colonel, Corps of Engineers, U. S. Army.
Having taken command of the 2d Engineers, 2d Division, just prior to battle of Soissons, he served with distinction as the leader of this regin until the close of hostilities. Under his skillful direction his regiment cessfully accomplished all the important technical missions assigned t His high military attainments were reflected by its efficiency in combat of tions. Subsequent to the armistice he continued to render important s ices to the American Expeditionary Forces as chief of engineers of the Army Corps.

MOLLOY, JANE G.
R—San Francisco, Calif.
B—Kingston, N. Y.
G. O. No. 9, W. D., 1923.

First lieutenant, chief nurse, Army Nurse Corps, U. S. Army.
As chief nurse of the base hospital at Camp Devens, Mass., during the W War, although greatly hampered by lack of personnel and equipment, displayed unusual talent for organization. By her untiring, painstak and energetic efforts in the distribution of her staff and her personal ca the sick she rendered great service to the Army, particularly during th fluenza epidemic, when the lives of many patients were saved through efforts.

MONCRIEF, WILLIAM H.
R—Atlanta, Ga.
B—Greensboro, Ga.
G. O. No. 59, W. D., 1921.

Colonel, Medical Corps, U. S. Army.
In organizing and commanding the hospital center at Mesves, he took po sion of the center in its unfinished condition and by great force and ab prepared a hospital group for the care of sick and wounded at a time w the need of hospital beds was critical.

MONTGOMERY, HENRY G.
R—New York, N. Y.
B—Washington, D. C.
G. O. No. 14, W. D., 1923.

Captain, Field Artillery, U. S. Army.
On his own initiative and with great vision, patriotism, and determinatio developed, with funds provided by public-spirited citizens, the arm motor tank car which was adopted by the American Government, trai at the same time a corps of technical experts who rendered important se in the Ordnance Department of the Army. Subsequently, as offic Field Artillery in France, he was charged with the responsibility of n taining while in action the mechanical efficiency of the newly issued Fr material forming the heavy artillery of the 33d and 79th Divisions du the St. Mihiel and Meuse-Argonne operations. In this work he displ technical skill of the highest order, reducing to a minimum the fire loss his brigade, and contributed markedly to the success of his artillery bri in these offensives.

DISTINGUISHED-SERVICE MEDAL 745

ONTGOMERY, JOHN C
R—Elizabethtown, Ky.
B—Elizabethtown, Ky.
G. O. No. 70, W. D., 1919.

Colonel (Infantry), General Staff Corps, U. S. Army.
Serving successively as division inspector, 2d Division; assistant chief of staff, G–3, 1st Army Corps; and assistant chief of staff, G–3, 3d Army, he has been charged with duties of a most important nature, in the performance of which he has at all times manifested steadfast loyalty and military ability of a high order, rendering services of signal worth.

ONTGOMERY, WALTER C
R—New York, N. Y.
B—New York, N. Y.
G. O. No. 22, W. D., 1920.

Lieutenant colonel Medical Corps, U. S. Army.
He served with marked distinction as division surgeon of the 27th Division. When confronted with a shortage of personnel, he displayed marked initiative and resourcefulness in organizing additional sanitary personnel. During the action along the Hindenburg line, Sept. 25 and 30, 1918, by his high professional attainments, sound judgment, and loyal devotion to duty he so conducted the personnel at his disposal as to provide successfully for the evacuation of 4,000 casualties in four days.

OODY, LUCIAN B
R—Huron, S. Dak.
B—Huron, S. Dak.
G. O. No. 30, W. D., 1921.

Colonel, Ordnance Department, U. S. Army.
For services as assistant to the chief ordnance officer, American Expeditionary Forces in France, and chief ordnance officer, Army of Occupation in Germany.

OORE, HUGH B
R—Texas City, Tex.
B—Huntland, Tenn.
G. O. No. 89, W. D., 1919.

Lieutenant colonel, Quartermaster Corps, U. S. Army.
He served creditably as superintendent, Army Transport Service, at Brest, and later, director of the Army Transport Service, he successfully supervised the activities of this service in 40 ports. Actuated by self-sacrificing devotion to duty, he achieved marked success in expediting the movement of troops, rendering services of inestimable value to the American Expeditionary Forces.

OORHEAD, JOHN J
R—New York, N. Y.
B—New York, N. Y.
G. O. No. 56, W. D., 1921.

Lieutenant colonel, Medical Corps, U. S. Army.
As commanding officer of American Red Cross Hospital No. 110, at Coincy, France, from June to November, 1918, he operated his hospital under the most difficult conditions and with inadequate personnel and equipment.

OORMAN, FRANK
R—Edwardsville, Ill.
B—Eureka, Mich.
G. O. No. 59, W. D., 1919.

Colonel (Coast Artillery Corps), General Staff Corps, U. S. Army.
In a position of the greatest responsibility, he displayed peculiar genius, combined with exact scientific knowledge, in organizing, training, and operating the radio intelligence service of the intelligence section. Charged with the duty of intercepting and deciphering the radio messages of the enemy, he acted with initiative and foresight, achieving brilliant results.

ORENO, ARISTIDES
R—Birmingham, Ala.
B—New York, N. Y.
G. O. No. 59, W. D., 1919

Lieutenant colonel (Infantry), General Staff Corps, U. S. Army.
As a member of the intelligence section, he efficiently organized and directed the operations of the counter-espionage service in the American Expeditionary Forces, displaying marked talents in a position of great responsibility. His unusual powers of discernment, his tact, and sound judgment made possible effective cooperation with corresponding services of the allied armies. Due to his zeal and untiring devotion, the counter-espionage service attained exceptional proficiency.

ORGAN, CASEY BRUCE
R—New York.
B—Augusta, Ga.
G. O. No. 116, W. D., 1919.

Captain, U. S. Navy.
For services as force transport officer. His untiring energy contributed greatly to the successful movement of troops and supplies.

ORGAN, JOHN M
R—Minersville, Ohio.
B—Minersville, Ohio.
G. O. No. 89, W. D., 1919.

Colonel, Infantry, U. S. Army.
As commanding officer of the 309th Infantry, 78th Division, during the last two months of hostilities he displayed marked qualities of leadership and unflagging energy. By the skillful manner in which he conducted his regiment during the advance through the Bois-de-Loges in the first part of November he contributed materially to the successes of his division in its operations in the Meuse-Argonne offensive.

ORRISON, JOHN F
R—Schoharie, N. Y.
B—Summit, N. Y
G. O. No. 47, W. D., 1919.

Major general, U. S. Army.
For services as department commander, Western Department, in handling with great skill, tact, and sound judgment many difficult problems arising in his department.

ORROW, CHARLES H
R—Somerset, Ky.
B—Somerset, Ky.
G. O. No. 3, W. D., 1922.

Colonel, Infantry, U. S. Army.
In command of American forces in the Baikal sector, Siberia, Colonel Morrow with great energy, tact, and force handled a situation fraught with serious possibilities and rendered a service of great worth.

ORROW, DWIGHT W
R—Englewood, N. J.
B—Huntington, W. Va.
G. O. No. 46, W. D., 1919.

Member of the American Shipping Mission.
He was responsible for the first intelligent epitomization of the complete allied tonnage situation, and his able presentation of the situation to the allied countries materially affected the tonnage policy, resulting in all possible economy. By his tact and good judgment in matters affecting the establishment of the military board of allied supply he helped materially in the splendid results obtained by that organization.

ORROW, FRANK J
R—Omaha, Nebr.
B—Fort Douglas, Utah.
G. O. No. 49, W. D., 1922.

Colonel, Infantry, U. S. Army.
From September, 1917, to March, 1918, in the organization and operation of the 1st Division and 1st Corps Schools, he rendered valuable and unusual services under very great difficulties. From April to December, 1918, as a member of the training and instruction branch of the war-plans division, General Staff, and in direct supervision of the field officers' schools in the combat divisions, and the War College course for instruction of divisional staff officers, his zeal, marked ability, and high military attainments were important factors in successfully standardizing the training and instruction of a great many senior officers. Later, while in direct charge of the organization of the Reserve Officers' Training Corps, he again rendered invaluable services in building up this important branch of civilian military training along sound and enduring lines.

MORROW, HENRY M R—Omaha, Nebr. B—Niles, Mich. G. O. No. 49, W. D., 1922.	Colonel, Judge Advocate General's Department, U. S. Army. As judge advocate, Philippine Department, by his legal ability and soun advice in the solution of unusual and highly important military and int national problems, he contributed in a marked degree to the successful a ministration of military and civil affairs in the Philippines and China. Lat as judge advocate of the 2d Army in France from October, 1918, until Api 1919, and then as judge advocate of the district of Paris until August, 1919, displayed great zeal, marked legal training, and sound judgment in ma difficult problems which confronted him and solved them with conspicuo success.
MORROW, WILLIAM M R—Fort Sidney, Nebr. B—Niles, Mich. G. O. No. 126, W. D., 1919. Distinguished-service cross also awarded.	Colonel, Infantry, U. S. Army. He served with conspicuous success as commanding officer of the 7th Infantr 3d Division, succeeding in all of the difficult missions assigned to him. F sound judgment and untiring energy proved important factors in the succe ful operations of his division against the enemy.
MORSE, CHARLES F R—Montpelier, Vt. B—Montpelier, Vt. G. O. No. 14, W. D., 1920.	Colonel, Medical Corps, U. S. Army. As director of the Veterinary Corps, by displaying exceptional energy, zeal, a good judgment he organized and administered with marked success a vete nary service capable of meeting every need in home territory and in t theater of operations. He provided effective means for the treatment of si and wounded animals, for the prevention of disease among well animals, the inspection of meat and dairy products used by the Army, and, throu the establishment of schools of instruction, placed the personnel of the Vete nary Corps of the Army on a high plane of efficiency.
MORSE, ERNEST C R—Neeham, Mass. B—Lebanon, N. H. G. O. No. 3, W. D., 1921.	Director of Sales, Supply Division, War Department, General Staff. Charged with the very important duty of organizing and training a compete force for the entirely novel functions of supervising, coordinating, and dire ing the disposal, according to law, of the vast War Department surplus supplies, materials, and properties of every description, and with the forn lation and development of sales policies, he performed his manifold dut with marked ability, energy, and judgment, with the result that the Unit States disposed of great quantities of supplies at exceptionally advantagec prices.
MORTON, CHARLES G R—Brookline, Mass. B—Cumberland, Me. G. O. No. 12, W. D., 1919.	Major general, U. S. Army. He commanded the 29th Division from the date of its organization until the e of hostilities, and led this division with skill and ability in the success operations east and northeast of Verdun, which forced the enemy to ma tain this front with strong forces, thus preventing an increase of host strength between the Argonne and the Meuse.
MOSELEY, GEORGE V. H R—Evanston, Ill. B—Evanston, Ill. G. O. No. 12, W. D., 1919.	Brigadier general, U. S. Army. For services as Assistant Chief of Staff. He handled with great executive abil and rare understanding all problems of equipping and supplying the la number of American troops arriving and operating in France, and by large grasp of supply problems and tireless energy he has conspicuously aic the successful administration of the supply department.
MOSES, ANDREW R—Strickling, Tex. B—Strickling, Tex. G. O. No. 38, W. D., 1922.	Brigadier general, U. S. Army. Commanding the 316th Field Artillery, 81st Division, from August, 1917, a the 156th Field Artillery Brigade, 81st Division from June, 1918, until it v demobilized, he exhibited qualities of excellent leadership and milit attainments of a high order. Later, as chairman of a joint board of revic he occupied a position of great responsibility, having full charge and con of the redelivery of all ships allocated to the War Department during World War. By his administrative ability, excellent judgment, energy, a tact, he rendered conspicuous services in bringing about speedy and accur settlements with the shipowners, which resulted in a large saving to Government.
MOTT, JOHN R R—Montclair, N. J. B—Livingston Manor, N. Y. G. O. No. 73, W. D., 1919.	For services as general secretary of the national war work council of Young Men's Christian Association of the United States.
MOTT, T. BENTLEY R—Leesburg, Va. B—Leesburg, Va. G. O. No. 59, W. D., 1919.	Colonel, Field Artillery, U. S. Army. As chief liaison officer of the Commander in Chief, American Expedition Forces, at Allied General Headquarters, he performed the important du with which he was charged with marked ability, and by his tact and sou judgment he materially assisted in insuring close cooperation between French and American Armies.
MOUNT, JAMES R R—Kansas City, Kans. B—Kansas City, Kans. G. O. No. 59, W. D., 1919.	Colonel, Medical Corps, U. S. Army. Arriving in France with the first American troops, he undertook the task creating a medical supply depot and administering a medical supply ser for the American Expeditionary Forces. Using his limited resources v great skill and judgment, he displayed unusual talent for organization : laid the foundation of an efficient medical supply service.
MOUNTFORD, FREDERICK A R—East Liverpool, Ohio. B—England. G. O. No. 56, W. D., 1922.	Lieutenant colonel, Coast Artillery Corps, U. S. Army. As assistant to the Chief of Coast Artillery and in charge of the matériel sect in that office he displayed excellent judgment and a thorough knowledg the involved and intricate details in connection with matériel, ther rendering highly meritorious service in the preparation and executio plans for the effective accomplishment of the duties assigned to the Cc Artillery Corps in the operations in France.

DISTINGUISHED-SERVICE MEDAL

MUDGETT, CHARLES F
R—Valley City, N. Dak.
B—Ravenna, Mo.
G. O. No. 38, W. D., 1922.

Lieutenant colonel, Adjutant General's Department, U. S. Army.
As officer in charge of the enlisted division, Adjutant General's Office, General Headquarters, American Expeditionary Forces, he demonstrated the highest order of efficiency, and by his tact and sound judgment he handled in a masterful manner the many difficult problems that arose. During the demobilization he carried to successful completion the various projects relative to the discharge and return of enlisted personnel. By his splendid attainments and professional zeal he contributed materially to the success of the work of The Adjutant General's Office at General Headquarters, American Expeditionary Forces.

MUIR, CHARLES H
R—Erie, Mich.
B—Erie, Mich.
G. O. No. 12, W. D., 1919.
Distinguished-service cross also awarded.

Major general, U. S. Army.
As division and corps commander, commanding the 28th Division during the Argonne-Meuse offensive, and especially in the difficult operations which resulted in the clearing of the Argonne Forest, he proved himself to be an energetic leader of the highest professional attainments. As a corps commander he displayed the same fine qualities that characterized his service with a division.

MULLALLY, THORNWELL
R—San Francisco, Calif.
B—Columbia, S. C.
G. O. No. 49, W. D., 1922.

Colonel, Field Artillery, U. S. Army.
He projected, recruited, organized, and mobilized the 144th Field Artillery, 40th Division, as an additional regiment of the California National Guard. Later, as colonel of that regiment, his sound judgment and marked ability as a leader were largely responsible for the successful training of his regiment both in the United States and France and in the development in that unit of over 168 officers for our Army.

MUNSON, EDWARD L
R—New Haven, Conn.
B—New Haven, Conn.
G. O. No. 34, W. D., 1919.

Brigadier general, U. S. Army.
He developed the scheme of field training for officers and enlisted men of the Medical Department, directed the organization and administration of the medical officers' training camps, and organized and administered the Morale Branch of the General Staff.

MURPHY, FRED T
R—St. Louis, Mo.
B—Detroit, Mich.
G. O. No. 59, W. D., 1919.

Colonel, Medical Corps, U. S. Army.
As director of Base Hospital No. 21, as supervisor of the evacuation of the sick and wounded of the 1st Army, and later as director of the Bureau of Medicine and Surgery of the American Red Cross he rendered most valuable assistance to the American Expeditionary Forces. Throughout his service he displayed unusual administrative ability and professional skill, combined with a genius for organization that contributed greatly to the efficiency of the Medical Service of the Army. Untiring in zeal and enthusiastic in his duty, he was an inspiration to those associated with him.

MURPHY, GRAYSON M. P
R—New York, N. Y.
B—Philadelphia, Pa.
G. O. No. 59, W. D., 1919.

Lieutenant colonel (Infantry), General Staff Corps, U. S. Army.
He organized the work of the American Red Cross in Europe, and to his foresight, wisdom, and untiring efforts are largely due the splendid work performed for the American Expeditionary Forces by that institution. Later he displayed marked ability as assistant chief of staff of the 42d Division during the operations of that unit.

MURPHY, JOHN B
R—Notre Dame, Ind.
B—Fort Robinson, Nebr.
G. O. No. 39, W. D., 1920.

Colonel, Coast Artillery Corps, U. S. Army.
As commanding officer of the 44th Artillery Regiment, Coast Artillery Corps, by his marked ability, energy, and resourcefulness, he organized, equipped, and trained a regiment of 8-inch howitzers in an extraordinarily brief period of time, thus enabling them to reach the front in time to be of valuable service during the critical days of April, 1918. Later, as a member of the operations section at General Headquarters, he rendered services of great value to the American Expeditionary Forces.

MURRAY, ARTHUR
R—Bowling Green, Mo.
B—Bowling Green, Mo.
G. O. No. 4, W. D., 1923.

Major general, U. S. Army.
As department commander, Western Department, between August 29, 1917, and May 14, 1918, he handled many difficult problems arising in that department with rare judgment, tact, and great skill.

MURRAY, MAXWELL
R—Fort Totten, N. Y.
B—West Point, N. Y.
G. O. No. 9, W. D., 1923.

Colonel, Field Artillery, U. S. Army.
As commander of the 5th Field Artillery, 1st Division, he handled the regiment so brilliantly under severe conditions during the assault and capture of Cantigny, May 28, 1918, and during the Aisne-Marne offensive in the assault southeast of Soissons, July 18-25, 1918, that the regiment demonstrated an unusually high degree of efficiency and morale. He repeatedly displayed superior tactical judgment and knowledge of artillery and by his exceptional ability, leadership, and devotion to duty, he rendered the maximum of support to the Infantry of the 1st Division in effectively executing the most difficult missions assigned to him, thus rendering important services to the American Expeditionary Forces.

MURRAY, PETER
R—Visalia, Calif.
B—Visalia, Calif.
G. O. No. 3, W. D., 1922.

Colonel (Quartermaster Corps), General Staff Corps, U. S. Army.
As chief, training and instruction branch, War Plans Division, General Staff, during 1919, under Colonel Murray's direction the foundation for the existing system of Army education and training was established and ways and means evolved to apply to peace training the lessons learned in the World War.

MURY, EDITH A. (now Mrs. EDITH A. KERSHAW).
R—Oakland, Calif.
B—Wadsworth, Nev.
G. O. 9, No. W. D., 1923.

Assistant superintendent, Army Nurse Corps, U. S. Army.
As chief nurse on duty at the nurses' mobilization station, Ellis Island, N. Y., during the early period of the World War, she rendered invaluable assistance to the Medical Department by instructing newly appointed chief nurses before embarkation for overseas, and through her untiring energy and unusual capabilities set a splendid example for all who came in contact with her. Later, as assistant superintendent, in the office of the Surgeon General, she contributed services of high value in supervising the demobilization of the Army Nurse Corps.

MYER, EDGAR A R—Troy, N. Y. B—Fort Richardson, Tex. G. O. No. 89, W. D., 1919.	Colonel, Infantry, U. S. Army. Having taken command of the 129th Infantry, 33d Division, at a critical period during active operations, he displayed marked ability as a military leader by the successful manner in which he conducted his regiment. Constantly maintaining a high grade of morale among his command, he was able to accomplish with marked success all missions assigned to his unit.
MYERS, HU B R—Shelbyville, Tenn. B—Shelbyville, Tenn. G. O. No. 95, W. D., 1919.	Colonel (Infantry), General Staff Corps, U. S. Army. As assistant chief of staff, G-3, and chief of staff, 2d Division, during its final operations, he performed his exacting staff duties with conspicuous ability. To his brilliant military attainments and untiring zeal were due, in a large measure, the successes achieved by his division in its attack on Massif du Mont at St. Etienne-a-Arnes, when the 2d Division served with the 4th French Army, and again during its advance from Landres-et-St. Georges to the Meuse during the final phase of the Meuse-Argonne offensive.
NAYLOR, WILLIAM K R—St. Paul, Minn. B—Bloomington, Ill. G. O. No. 59, W. D., 1919.	Brigadier general, U. S. Army. While chief of staff of the 33d Division he exhibited conspicuous ability in the operations north of Verdun, France, in September and October, 1918. He frequently visited the front-line positions under heavy enemy artillery fire, and by his personal efforts and skillful dispositions was in a large measure responsible for the successes gained.
NELSON, ERIK H R—New York, N. Y. B—Sweden. G. O. No. 14, W. D., 1925. Act of Congress, Feb. 25, 1925.	First lieutenant, Air Service, U. S. Army. Lieutenant Nelson, as pilot of Airplane No. 4, the *New Orleans*, and engineer officer of the U. S. Army Air Service around-the-world flight from Apr. 6, 1924, to Sept. 28, 1924, displayed sound technical skill, initiative, untiring energy, and resourcefulness and succeeded in piloting his airplane throughout the voyage. His sound judgment, indefatigable energy, and courageous conduct in the face of extraordinary perils contributed largely to the success of this pioneer flight of airplanes around the world. In the efficient performance of his arduous duties he aided in the accomplishment of an exploit which brought great credit to himself and to the Army of the United States.
NEVILLE, WENDELL C R—Portsmouth, Va. B—Portsmouth, Va. G. O. No. 59, W. D., 1919.	Brigadier general, U. S. Marine Corps. While in command of the 5th Regiment, U. S. Marine Corps, and later of the 4th Infantry Brigade, 2d Division, he participated in the battles of Chateau-Thierry, the advance near Soissons, and the operations of St. Mihiel, Blanc Mont Ridge, and the Argonne-Meuse. In all of these he proved himself to be a leader of great skill and ability.
NICHOLSON, WILLIAM J R—Washington, D. C. B—Washington, D. C. G. O. No. 50, W. D., 1919. Distinguished-service cross also awarded.	Brigadier general, U. S. Army. He commanded with distinction the 157th Infantry Brigade, 79th Division, from its organization to the time of the armistice—at all times with credit to himself and to his command.
NOBLE, ROBERT E R—Anniston, Ala. B—Rome, Ga. G. O. No. 73, W. D., 1919.	Major general, U. S. Army. He had immediate charge of the personnel division of the Surgeon General's Office and solved the problem of getting medical officers into the Army during an increase from 1,500 at the beginning of the war to 30,000. He also had charge of the hospital division of the Surgeon General's Office, handling both of these large responsibilities with conspicuous success.
NOLAN, DENNIS E R—Akron, N. Y. B—Akron, N. Y. G. O. No. 12, W. D., 1919. Distinguished-service cross also awarded.	Brigadier general, U. S. Army. He organized and administered with marked ability the intelligence section of the General Staff of the American Expeditionary Forces. His estimates of the complex and everchanging military and political situation, his sound judgment, and accurate discrimination were invaluable to the Government, and influenced greatly the success that attended the operations of the American armies in Europe.
NUTTMAN, LOUIS M R—Newark, N. J. B—Newark, N. J. G. O. No. 89, W. D., 1919.	Brigadier general, U. S. Army. As a regimental commander of the 89th Division he displayed marked military ability, providing his regiment with efficient training which showed its effects by the excellent conduct of the regiment in combat. Later, when promoted to the grade of brigadier general, he demonstrated great executive ability in the organization and administration of the combat officers' replacement depot at Gondrecourt.
O'BRIEN, MICHAEL J R—New York, N. Y. B—Ireland. G. O. No. 31, W. D., 1922.	Lieutenant colonel, Adjutant General's Department, U. S. Army. As officer in charge of the officers' division, Adjutant General's Office, General Headquarters, American Expeditionary Forces, he demonstrated the highest professional attainments in the discharge of his multifarious duties. By his zeal, good judgment, and never-failing tact he was responsible in a large measure for the development of the high efficiency of his division. During the demobilization of the American Expeditionary Forces, working without regard to hours, by his tireless energy and exceptional ability he carried to successful completion the various and difficult projects that arose. Later, in charge of the American Expeditionary Forces records in Washington, D. C., he maintained that same high standard of efficiency which marked his work in the Adjutant General's Office, General Headquarters, American Expeditionary Forces.

O'DONNELL, JOHN L.
  R—Chicago, Ill.
  B—Chicago, Ill.
  G. O. No. 62, W. D., 1919.

First lieutenant, chaplain, 132d Infantry, 33d Division, U. S. Army.
As regimental chaplain he was ceaseless in his efforts to better the welfare of the men, and during the period of operations accompanied the attacking waves in every action in which the regiment took part. Exposing himself to artillery and machine-gun fire to care personally for the wounded, organizing parties of stretcher bearers, going without a thought of personal danger wherever he was needed, he set an example of courage and heroism, appreciably raising the morale of those with whom and for whom he worked.

OGDEN, HENRY H.
  R—Woodville, Miss.
  B—Woodville, Miss.
  G. O. No. 14, W. D., 1925.
  Act of Congress, Feb. 25, 1925.

Second lieutenant, Air Service, U. S. Army.
Lieutenant Ogden, as assistant pilot of Airplane No. 3, the *Boston*, and assistant supply officer of the U. S. Army Air Service around-the-world flight from Apr. 6, 1924, to Sept. 28, 1924, displayed to a marked degree technical skill, courage, energy, and resourcefulness in carrying out his supply duties, in addition to alternate piloting of Airplane No. 3 during the voyage. His foresight, perseverance, and mechanical ability were very material factors in contributing to the successful accomplishment of this pioneer flight of airplanes around the world. In the efficient performance of his arduous duties he aided in the accomplishment of an undertaking bringing great credit to himself and to the military forces of the United States.

OGDEN, HUGH WALKER.
  R—Brookline, Mass.
  B—Bath, Me.
  G. O. No. 74, W. D., 1919.

Lieutenant colonel, Judge Advocate General's Department, U. S. Army.
As judge advocate and inspector of the 42d Division he rendered valuable services. He exhibited ability of a high order throughout the operations of the division. Later, assigned to the bureau of civil affairs for the Third Army, he performed his task with marked success.

OLIVER, LLEWELLYN W.
  R—Escanaba, Mich.
  B—Escanaba, Mich.
  G. O. No. 59, W. D., 1921.

Colonel (Infantry), General Staff Corps, U. S. Army.
As chief of staff, port of embarkation, Hoboken, N. J., from Jan. 21, 1919, to Feb. 26, 1920, he occupied a position of great responsibility. The details of arrangements for demobilization and for handling the sick and wounded fell largely upon his shoulders. His energy, excellent judgment, and administrative ability were of greatest value to the Government.

OLIVER, ROBERT T.
  R—Indianapolis, Ind.
  B—Indianapolis, Ind.
  G. O. No. 103, W. D., 1919.

Colonel, Dental Corps, U. S. Army.
As chief dental surgeon he displayed remarkable ability in the performance of his numerous and exacting duties. He directed the personnel, equipment, and operations of his department with sound judgment, showing resourcefulness in solving new problems which confronted him.

OLMSTED, EDWARD.
  R—Elizabeth, N. J.
  B—San Francisco, Calif.
  G. O. 22, W. D., 1920.

Lieutenant colonel, Infantry, U. S. Army.
As assistant chief of staff, G-1, of the 27th Division, by his high military attainments, zeal, and keen perception of his manifold duties the technical services of the division were so promptly and effectively coordinated and supervised that the front-line units were at all times completely supplied with all necessities. He has rendered services of particular worth to the American Expeditionary Forces.

O'NEILL, JOHN.
  R—Newburyport, Mass.
  B—Newburyport, Mass.
  G. O. No. 49, W. D., 1922.

Lieutenant colonel, Transportation Corps, U. S. Army.
From November, 1917, until November, 1919, at Base Section No. 5, Brest, France, while serving in succession as chief of stevedores, assistant general superintendent in charge of the operations and troop and cargo divisions, and finally as superintendent of that port, by virtue of his marked ability, indomitable energy, and his capacity for inspiring his men he overcame all difficulties and met every demand made upon his force. His remarkable achievements in the quick turn-around of large vessels carrying troops and supplies were of inestimable value to the American Expeditionary Forces.

ORD, JAMES B.
  R—San Diego, Calif.
  B—Mexico.
  G. O. No. 96, W. D., 1918.

Second lieutenant, 6th Infantry, attached to 13th Cavalry, U. S. Army.
While in action at Parral, Mexico, Apr. 12, 1916, after being himself wounded, he dismounted from his horse under heavy fire, placed a wounded man on a horse, and assisted him from the field.

ORTON, EDWARD, Jr.
  R—Columbus, Ohio.
  B—Chester, N. Y.
  G. O. No. 69, W. D., 1919.

Lieutenant colonel, Motor Transport Corps, U. S. Army.
His untiring energy and spendid judgment were displayed in the efficient organization of the Engineering Division of the Motor Transport Corps in bringing about standardization of equipment and supplies and in efficiently directing the forces of the motor industry to the mutual advantage of the Army and the industry itself.

O'RYAN, JOHN F.
  R—New York, N. Y.
  B—New York, N. Y.
  G. O. No. 12, W. D., 1919.

Major general, U. S. Army.
As commander of the 27th Division in its successful operations with the British in France in the autumn of 1918 he displayed qualities of skill and aggressiveness which mark him as a leader of ability. In the breach of the Hindenburg line between St. Quentin and Cambrai the name of his division is linked with the British in adding new laurels to the allied forces in France.

OURY, WILLIAM H.
  R—Lincoln, Nebr.
  B—Smyth County, Va.
  G. O. No. 78, W. D., 1919.

Colonel, Infantry, U. S. Army.
Placed in command of the 157th Infantry Brigade, 79th Division, during the Montfaucon drive, he displayed exceptional qualities of leadership and marked tactical skill. Continuing at the same time in command of his regiment, the 314th Infantry, he directed the men of his command, and by his dauntless determination carried them forward under heavy enemy fire. He proved himself untiring in energy and possessed of great initiative, sound judgment, and military attainments of high order.

OVENSHINE, ALEXANDER T.
R—Philadelphia, Pa.
B—Fort Leavenworth, Kans.
G. O. No. 31, W. D., 1922.

Colonel, Inspector General's Department, U. S. Army.
While serving as inspector general, 3d Army Corps, during the Meuse-Argonne offensive, Colonel Ovenshine was charged with many important reports and investigations, which service was performed with marked ability and good judgment, and aided his corps and his Army commanders in decisions culminating in the success of this offensive. Later, as inspector general, 2d Army, he rendered distinguished service of a similar nature in connection with the operations of the 2d Army from Oct. 12, 1918,, to the day of the armistice.

PAEGELOW, JOHN A.
R—Chicago, Ill.
B—Germany.
G. O. No. 95, W. D., 1919.

Lieutenant colonel, Air Service, U. S. Army.
As commander of balloon service of the 1st Army Corps and 1st Army, he was well fitted for his important position both by long experience in aeronautics and by noted organizing ability. Through his untiring energy an efficient system of supply and transportation was developed in spite of the numerous difficulties which assailed him. The successes achieved by the balloon service in the second Battle of the Marne and in the St. Mihiel offensive are a tribute to the high character of services rendered by him to the American Expeditionary Forces.

PALMER, BRUCE.
R—Harrison, Ill.
B—Fort Wallace, Kans.
G. O. No. 50, W. D., 1919.

Colonel (Cavalry), General Staff Corps. U. S. Army.
As a member of the General Staff of the American Expeditionary Forces, on duty with the 1st section, first as chief of the tonnage division during a period of stress, befraught with difficulties, and later as deputy assistant chief of staff, he performed duties of great responsibility with marked ability, fidelity, and success, invariably displaying personal and professional attainments of a high order.

PALMER, FREDERICK.
R—New York, N. Y.
B—Pleasantville, Pa.
G. O. No. 16, W. D., 1923.

Lieutenant colonel, Signal Corps, U. S. Army.
Charged with the responsibility of drafting regulations covering the mail and press censorship, as well as formulating plans for the guidance of press correspondents with the American forces in France, he rendered conspicuously valuable services. Having served in all the zones occupied by the allied forces, his information, of far reaching value, was placed at the disposal of our Government. His broad experience with many armies, his outstanding skill as an observer, his untiring energy and devotion to duty contributed markedly to the successful operations of the American Expeditionary Forces.

PALMER, JOHN McA.
R—Springfield, Ill.
B—Carlinville, Ill.
G. O. No. 12, W. D., 1919.

Colonel, Infantry, U. S. Army.
In the organization of the operations section of the General Staff, American Expeditionary Forces, this officer displayed sound tactical judgment and breadth of vision, and the ultimate success of the American plan of campaign was largely due to his detailed plans. As commander of the 58th Infantry Brigade, 29th Division, during the severe fighting north of Verdun, in the Argonne-Meuse offensive, his services were conspicuous and his brigade successful.

PARK, RICHARD.
R—Warren, N. H.
B—Malden, Mass.
G. O. No. 69, W. D., 1919.

Colonel, Corps of Engineers, U. S. Army.
To his energy and good judgment may be largely attributed the rapid development and successful administration of the Engineer Training School and mobilization camp at Camp A. A. Humphreys, Va. His utilization of labor of troops to supplement construction forces is a fine example of initiative in meeting a critical situation.

PARKER, CORTLANDT.
R—Newark, N. J.
B—Fort Apache, Ariz.
G. O. No. 49, W. D., 1922.

Colonel, Field Artillery, U. S. Army.
He organized and conducted the training camp for Field Artillery at Camp Coetquidan and later, at the office of the Chief of Artillery, American Expeditionary Forces, by his superior professional attainments, his zeal, and keen foresight, he contributed in a marked manner to the successful conduct of Field Artillery training. As regimental commander of the 6th Field Artillery, 1st Division, in the Cantigny sector and in the Aisne-Marne offensive, he repeatedly displayed superior tactical judgment and knowledge of artillery, and by his exceptional ability. leadership, and devotion to duty he rendered the maximum support to the Infantry of the 1st Division in effectively executing the most difficult missions assigned to him, thus rendering in a position of great responsibility most important services to the American Expeditionary Forces.

PARKER, EDWIN B.
R—Houston, Tex.
B—Shelby County, Mo.
G. O. No. 35, W. D., 1920.

As priority commissioner on the War Industries Board he formulated and directed policies for the fullest development of war industries with marked ability and foresight. Later and subsequent to the armistice he, as chairman of the United States Liquidation Commission, War Department, undertook the immense task of liquidating the mass of intricate transactions incurred between the War Department and the allied Governments during the war, and also the disposal of all surplus war stocks and property of the War Department in Europe. As directing head of this commission and by his patience, industry, and diplomacy he brought this immense task to a successful conclusion in less than one year, to the very great credit of the War Department and the United States and the continued and warm friendship of the nations involved.

PARKER, FRANK.
R—Georgetown, S. C.
B—Georgetown, S. C.
G. O. No. 59, W. D., 1919.

Brigadier general, U. S. Army.
He commanded with marked distinction the 18th United States Infantry. Later, as a brigade commander, he exhibited qualities of rare leadership, superb courage, and unusual initiative. Finally he commanded the 1st Division in the Argonne offensive in the autumn of 1918, where he showed himself to be a skilled leader of marked ability.

DISTINGUISHED-SERVICE MEDAL

PARKER, HUGH A⎯⎯⎯⎯⎯⎯⎯⎯⎯⎯
  R—Royse City, Tex.
  B—Hunt, Tex.
  G. O. No. 49, W. D., 1922.

Colonel (Infantry), General Staff Corps, U. S. Army.
He served as assistant G-3, 1st Army Corps, during June and July, 1918; G-3, 4th Division, from August to October, 1918; chief of staff, 7th Division, from November, 1918, to February, 1919; and chief of staff, American Military Mission at Berlin. By his tact, sound judgment, marked ability, and loyal devotion to duty, he contributed materially to the success of all units with which he served.

PARKER, JAMES⎯⎯⎯⎯⎯⎯⎯⎯⎯⎯
  R—Newark, N. J.
  B—Newark, N. J.
  G. O. No. 15, W. D., 1923.
  Medal of honor also awarded.

Major general, U. S. Army.
He served with great distinction as commander of the Southern Department, Fort Sam Houston, Tex., Mar. 31, 1917, to Aug. 25, 1917; and as division commander, 32d Division, from Aug. 25 to Dec. 11, 1917; division commander, 85th Division, Dec. 11, 1917, to Feb. 20, 1918, when having reached the statutory age he was retired from active service. In these positions of great responsibility he displayed rare and outstanding leadership, the organizations under command at all times showing the results of sound training, a high state of morale and discipline. His unusual professional attainments, sound judgment, and devotion to duty were material and important factors in the development of organizations of the American Army, and contributed in a signal way to their successful operations in action against the enemy.

PARKER, JOHN H⎯⎯⎯⎯⎯⎯⎯⎯⎯⎯
  R—Green Ridge, Mo.
  B—Tipton, Mo.
  G. O. No. 89, W. D., 1919.
  Distinguished-service cross and three oak-leaf clusters also awarded.

Colonel, Infantry, U. S. Army.
As an instructor in the Army Machine Gun School at Langres, by his tireless efforts he secured the necessary equipment and ably instructed a large student body in the technical handling of one of the most important fire power weapons developed in the present war, rendering services of great value to the American Expeditionary Forces.

PARSONS, JAMES K⎯⎯⎯⎯⎯⎯⎯⎯⎯⎯
  R—Birmingham, Ala.
  B—Rockford, Ala.
  G. O. No. 59, W. D., 1921.
  Distinguished-service cross also awarded.

Colonel, Infantry, U. S. Army.
He organized and commanded with energy and ability the embarkation camp at St. Nazaire, France, and handled with conspicuous success the reception, care, and departure of the large number of officers and soldiers passing through that camp en route to the United States. He demonstrated administrative abilities of a high order and performed services of great value to the American Expeditionary Forces.

PARSONS, WILLIAM BARCLAY⎯⎯⎯⎯
  R—New York, N. Y.
  B—New York, N. Y.
  G. O. No. 4, W. D., 1923.

Colonel, Corps of Engineers, U. S. Army.
He served as major, 11th Engineers (Railway), during its organization and training period; chairman of Engineering Railway Commission sent overseas to investigate and report upon railway conditions in France; lieutenant colonel and then colonel, 11th Engineers, during its combat operations. By his wide experience, sound judgment, and brilliant professional and technical attainments he handled many difficult problems which confronted him with conspicuous success, thereby rendering services of great value to the American Expeditionary Forces.

PATRICK, MASON M⎯⎯⎯⎯⎯⎯⎯⎯⎯⎯
  R—Lewisburg, W. Va.
  B—Lewisburg, W. Va.
  G. O. No. 12, W. D., 1919.

Major general, U. S. Army.
He displayed much ability and devotion to duty as director of construction and forestry, and later, as chief of the Air Service of the American Expeditionary Forces, he perfected and ably administered the organization of this important department.

PATTERSON, CHARLES H⎯⎯⎯⎯⎯⎯⎯⎯
  R—Harrisburg, Pa.
  B—Harrisburg, Pa.
  G. O. No. 15, W. D., 1921.

Colonel, Coast Artillery Corps, U. S. Army.
As an officer in the Inspector General's Department and as chief of the investigations division of that department his rare efficiency and good judgment in the investigation and treatment of difficult and intricate problems have materially facilitated the administration of the office of the Inspector General, and have been of great value to the War Department and to the Army.

PATTERSON, HANNAH J⎯⎯⎯⎯⎯⎯⎯⎯
  R—Pittsburgh, Pa.
  B—Smithton, Pa.
  G. O. No. 73, W. D., 1919.

Council of National Defense.
She devoted herself throughout the whole period of the war to executive work of the Women's Committee of the Council of National Defense, devoting herself with great ability and energy to the organization of the activities and interests of the women throughout the United States in the interest of the successful prosecution of the war and, by her efforts, contributed to the splendid cooperation on the part of the women of the country in the great national emergency.

PATTERSON, PAUL M⎯⎯⎯⎯⎯⎯⎯⎯⎯⎯
  R—Kansas City, Kans.
  B—Anthony, Kans.
  G. O. No. 9, W. D., 1923.

Captain, Medical Corps, U. S. Army.
As evacuation officer of the 1st Army in the St. Mihiel and Meuse-Argonne offensives he directed the routing of all battle casualties into Army hospitals at the front, supervised the daily supply of those hospitals, and so skillfully and energetically classified and coordinated the constant flow of evacuations to the rear by timely calls for and expeditious loading of hospital trains that beds were always available for thousands of sick and wounded of the 1st Army. He rendered services of inestimable value to the American Expeditionary Forces in a position of great responsibility.

PATTERSON, ROBERT U⎯⎯⎯⎯⎯⎯⎯⎯
  R—Baltimore, Md.
  B—Canada.
  G. O. No. 13, W. D., 1923.

Colonel, Medical Corps, U. S. Army.
As commanding officer, Base Hospital No. 5, United States Army, serving with the British Expeditionary Forces at Dannes-Camiers and Boulogne, France, he displayed tireless energy and military attainments of a high order in the efficient operation of this hospital. By his marked devotion to duty and administrative ability great numbers of our own and allied sick and wounded were treated, resulting in the saving of many lives. His services were of material value to the American Expeditionary Forces.

PATTON, GEORGE S., Jr.
R—San Gabriel, Calif.
B—San Gabriel, Calif.
G. O. No. 103, W. D., 1919.
Distinguished-service cross also awarded.

Colonel, Tank Corps, U. S. Army.
By his energy and sound judgment he rendered very valuable services in his organization and direction of the tank center at the Army schools at Langres. In the employment of Tank Corps troops in combat he displayed high military attainments, zeal, and marked adaptability in a form of warfare comparatively new to the American Army.

PAULES, EARL G.
R—Marietta, Pa.
B—Marietta, Pa.
G. O. No. 95, W. D., 1919.

Colonel, Corps of Engineers, U. S. Army.
As a member of the American Military Commission of Italy from April to July, 1918, he displayed tact and diplomacy in making a preliminary investigation of the Czechoslovak situation. Later, as commanding officer of the 7th Engineers, he participated creditably in the St. Mihiel and Meuse-Argonne offensives, materially aiding in the operations of the 5th Division by his skill in constructing bridges across the Meuse River in the face of desperate hostile resistance.

PEABODY, PAUL E.
R—Los Angeles, Calif.
B—Chicago, Ill.
G. O. No. 22, W. D., 1920.

Major, Infantry, U. S. Army.
As an assistant chief of staff, G-1, 1st Division, during the attack on Soissons, he displayed marked ability. Later, as G-1, during the St. Mihiel and Meuse-Argonne offensives, by his extraordinary ability, his capacity for organization, and his brilliant execution of all details pertaining to administration of supply he overcame unusual difficulties and thereby contributed in a marked degree to the success of the operations of the 1st Division.

PEARCE, EARLE D'A.
R—Thomaston, Ga.
B—Thomaston, Ga.
G. O. No. 56, W. D., 1922.

Colonel, Field Artillery, U. S. Army.
As commanding officer of the 319th Field Artillery, 82d Division in the organization and training of the regiment and in its very successful operations against the enemy in the Aisne-Marne, St. Mihiel, and Meuse-Argonne offensives, he displayed tireless energy, keen devotion to duty, and eminent technical skill as an artillerist, gave most effective support to the Infantry of the 82d and 80th Divisions, and very materially contributed to the successes attained by those units.

PECK, ALLEN STEELE
R—Stottville, N. Y.
B—West Barre, N. Y.
G. O. No. 78, W. D., 1919.

Lieutenant colonel, Corps of Engineers, U. S. Army.
As an officer of the Forestry Service he displayed exceptional tact and sound judgment in securing public and private grants for large quantities of timber from the French Government. At all times he pursued his task with great energy, achieving signal success. He organized and administered a project for the production of fuel wood, which proved entirely successful. In these endeavors he rendered valuable service to the American Expeditionary Forces.

PECK, CHARLES H.
R—New York, N. Y.
B—Newton, Conn.
G. O. No. 59, W. D., 1919.

Lieutenant colonel, Medical Corps, U. S. Army.
As director of Base Hospital No. 15, which he had organized most efficiently, he displayed unusual skill and very marked ability in the conduct of that unit. Later, as senior consultant in general surgery for the American Expeditionary Forces, his professional attainments, wide experience, and sound advice proved of inestimable value in increasing the efficiency of the Medical Department of the United States Army.

PECK, ROBERT H.
R—San Diego, Calif.
B—San Francisco, Calif.
G. O. No. 95, W. D., 1919.
Distinguished-service cross also awarded.

Colonel, Infantry, U. S. Army.
He rendered services of signal worth as commanding officer of the 47th Infantry, 4th Division, and subsequently of the 11th Infantry, 5th Division, successfully accomplishing all missions assigned to the regiment under his command during the active operations in which it participated. Constantly displaying unremitting zeal and tactical ability of a high order, he proved himself invaluable to the American Expeditionary Forces.

PEEK, ERNEST D.
R—Oshkosh, Wis.
B—Oshkosh, Wis.
G. O. No. 72, W. D., 1920.

Colonel, Corps of Engineers, U. S. Army.
He organized and conducted the operations of the standard gauge and light railways of the 1st Army during its active operations, resulting in the reduction of the St. Mihiel salient and the recovery of the extensive Meuse-Argonne area. Although handicapped by lack of personnel and material, he pushed the enterprise to success. By untiring, painstaking, and energetic efforts in the use of the inadequate means at his disposal, he displayed unusual talent for organization and masterful execution.

PEEK, GEORGE N.
R—Moline, Ill.
B—Polo, Ill.
G. O. No. 15, W. D., 1923.

Commissioner of Finished Products, War Industries Board.
In connection with the operations of the War Industries Board during the World War. As a member of the board he rendered, through his broad vision, distinguished capacity, and business ability, services of inestimable value in marshaling the industrial forces of the Nation and mobilizing its economic resources—marked factors in assisting to make military success attainable. As commissioner of finished products, it was largely through his untiring efforts and devotion to duty that the supply bureaus of the War Department were able to maintain a constant flow of munitions as well as supplies of a general character to the Army.

PEIRCE, WILLIAMS S.
R—Burlington, Vt.
B—Burlington, Vt.
G. O. No. 25, W. D., 1919.

Brigadier general, U. S. Army.
While in charge of the Springfield Arsenal his exceptional ability contributed materially to increasing the output of small arms. As Assistant Chief of Ordnance he has rendered conspicuous service.

PENNELL, RALPH McT.
R—Belton, S. C.
B—Belton, S. C.
G. O. No. 31, W. D., 1922.

Colonel, Field Artillery, U. S. Army.
As assistant to the Chief of Field Artillery from Apr. 16, 1918, to Sept. 4, 1918, he planned and executed those measures which provided a balanced production of different types of field artillery matériel and equipment and the selection of the types to be produced, and which determined the priorities of distribution of the same.

DISTINGUISHED-SERVICE MEDAL 753

PENNER, CARL
  R—Milwaukee, Wis.
  B—Milwaukee, Wis.
  G. O. No. 47, W. D., 1921.

Colonel, 120th Field Artillery, 32d Division, U. S. Army.
He commanded his regiment during the Marne-Aisne, Oise-Aisne, and Meuse-Argonne offensives. His devotion to duty and skillful handling of his command proved a material factor in the success of the 57th Field Artillery Brigade while supporting the 32d Division, and at other times five other divisions.

PEPPER, SAMUEL D.
  R—Lansing, Mich.
  B—Canada.
  G. O. No. 56, W. D., 1922.

Lieutenant colonel, Judge Advocate General's Department, U. S. Army.
From August, 1917, until June, 1919, he served in turn as judge advocate of the 32d Division, 5th Army Corps, and advance section, Services of Supply. By his marked legal ability, excellent judgment, and thorough knowledge of discipline and morale, he rendered services of signal worth to all the units with which he served, thereby contributing materially to the success of the American Expeditionary Forces.

PERKINS, ALBERT T.
  R—St. Louis, Mo.
  B—Brunswick, Me.
  G. O. No. 59, W. D., 1919.

Colonel, Corps of Engineers, U. S. Army.
As deputy and later as manager of light railways, he undertook the task of organizing a light railway service for the American Expeditionary Forces. His long and complete railroad experience and knowledge assured the success of these lines. By his foresight in promptly gathering from the United States a generous supply of railway material he quickly brought the light railway service to a high degree of efficiency.

PERKINS, FRED MILTON
  R—Salem, Oreg.
  B—Salem, Oreg.
  G. O. No. 116, W. D., 1919.

Commander, U. S. Navy.
As flag secretary to the commander, cruiser and transport fleet, his close cooperation with the Army authorities in the handling of troop ships contributed greatly to the successful outcome of our oversea operations.

PERKINS, JAMES H.
  R—Greenwich, Conn.
  B—Milton, Mass.
  G. O. No. 50, W. D., 1919.

Lieutenant colonel, Quartermaster Corps, U. S. Army.
He was in charge of the work of the American Red Cross in Europe for a period of time, and by his great energy and untiring efforts maintained that institution at a high state of excellence and rendered valuable assistance to the American Expeditionary Forces. While in the military service he displayed marked ability in the performance of the various duties with which he was intrusted.

PERSHING, JOHN J.
  R—Laclede, Mo.
  B—Linn County, Mo.
  G. O. No. 111, W. D., 1918.

General, U. S. Army, Commander in Chief, American Expeditionary Forces.
As a token of the gratitude of the American people to the commander of our armies in the field for his distinguished services, and in appreciation of the success which our armies have achieved under his leadership.

PERSONS, ELBERT E.
  R—Chicago, Ill.
  B—Prouts, Ohio.
  G. O. No. 49, W. D., 1922.

Colonel, Medical Corps, U. S. Army.
He organized the United States Army Ambulance Service Training School at Camp Crane, Allentown, Pa., and as its commanding officer from June, 1917, to May, 1918, by his great energy, marked executive ability, and wide professional knowledge, succeeded in rapidly training, equipping, and dispatching overseas ambulance units where they rendered excellent service with the French armies and later with our own forces. From June to December, 1918, he commanded the American Ambulance Service, serving on the Italian front, where he again rendered conspicuous service in a position of great responsibility.

PETERSON, VIRGIL L.
  R—Mannsville, Ky.
  B—Raywick, Ky.
  G. O. No. 56, W. D., 1922.

Colonel, Corps of Engineers, U. S. Army.
As commanding officer, Engineer Officers' Training Camp at Camp Lee, Va., from April to August, 1918, and director of training at Camp Humphreys, Va., until October, 1918, he displayed marked foresight, rare ability, and sound judgment in the reorganization and standardization of the instruction for engineer troops. By his organizing and training ability, indefatigable efforts, and high military attainments he successfully directed the training of 4,500 engineer officers and 20,000 enlisted men, thereby rendering services of great value to our Government in positions of great responsibility.

PEYTON, EPHRAIM G.
  R—Columbus, Miss.
  B—Gallatin, Miss.
  G. O. No. 59, W. D., 1919.

Colonel, Infantry, U. S. Army.
As the commanding officer of the 320th Infantry Regiment, 80th Division, in all its operations, by careful and painstaking preparations and skillful leadership, he enabled his regiment to carry always its tasks through to a successful end. At all times he displayed a high order of leadership and exhibited superb qualities as a commander.

PEYTON, PHILIP B.
  R—Charlottesville, Va.
  B—Nashville, Tenn.
  G. O. No. 59, W. D., 1919.

Colonel, 61st Infantry, 5th Division, U. S. Army.
He took command of a regiment which had undergone six days of shell fire and commanded it with such unusual skill as to enable the regiment to capture Aincreville, Bois-de-Bablemont, Doulcon, and, after crossing the Meuse, to capture Hill No. 292, Dun-sur-Meuse, Milly-devant-Dun, Lion-devant-Dun, Cote St. Germain, Chateau Charmois, and Mouzay, thereby displaying the highest order of leadership and exhibiting the masterful qualities of a commander.

PHILLIPS, ALBERT E.
  R—New Orleans, La.
  B—New Orleans, La.
  G. O. No. 19, W. D., 1922.

Colonel, Ordnance Department, U. S. Army.
In the development and operation of machine-gun centers, in the design and development of machine-gun equipment, and later he rendered invaluable service in the preparation of machine-gun manuals.

PICKERING, RICHARD R.
  R—Uniontown, Ala.
  B—Uniontown, Ala.
  G. O. No. 19, W. D., 1922.

Lieutenant colonel, Infantry, U. S. Army.
As commanding officer of the large embarkation camp at Camp Mills, Long Island, N. Y., from Apr. 5, 1918, to Sept. 13, 1918, and from Dec. 11, 1918, to May 8, 1919, he displayed executive ability of the highest order in a position of great responsibility. His work marked Colonel Pickering as an exceptional officer in his capacity as organizer and administrator, and by his energy and excellent judgment contributed in a notable degree to the success of troop movements at the port of embarkation, Hoboken, N. J.

PIERCE, CHARLES C.
R—Germantown, Pa.
B—Salem, N. J.
G. O. No. 59, W. D., 1919.

Lieutenant colonel, Quartermaster Corps, U. S. Army.
Serving as assistant to the chief quartermaster, American Expeditionary Forces, in the capacity of chief of Graves Registration Services since December, 1917, he displayed unusual ability and conscientious care in the performance of his exacting duties. Under his skillful administration the service functioned efficiently. He at all times showed great energy and performed his important task with exceptional success.

PIERCE, JUNNIUS.
R—Brooklyn, N. Y.
B—Gainesville, Tex.
G. O. No. 59, W. D., 1921.

Major, Quartermaster Corps, U. S. Army.
As chief quartermaster, adjutant general, chief of staff, and later commanding officer, Base Section No. 3, England, he served in these various capacities with great credit. As commanding officer of Base Section No. 3 he had charge of evacuation of troops and liquidation of American interests in England. By his energy, ability, and tact he conducted American Expeditionary Forces affairs in England to a successful conclusion.

PIERCE, PALMER E.
R—Traer, Iowa.
B—Savanna, Ill.
G. O. No. 56, W. D., 1922.

Brigadier general, U. S. Army.
His zeal, intelligence, and effective work in the preliminary organization of our industries for war contributed substantially to the progress made. From May, 1917, until March, 1919, he commanded the 54th Infantry Brigade, 27th Division, in a highly meritorious manner during all the operations of his division against the Hindenburg line. His sound judgment, marked ability, and skillful leadership were important factors in the successes attained by his division against the enemy.

PIERSON, ROBERT H.
R—Syracuse, N. Y.
B—Fayettesville, N. Y.
G. O. No. 95, W. D., 1919.

Colonel, Medical Corps, U. S. Army.
He served as division surgeon of the 5th Division from its organization until the close of hostilities, when he became chief surgeon of the 6th Army Corps. Due to his sound judgment and efficient direction of medical personnel, gas casualties in his division were reduced to a minimum. By his resourceful methods in combating disease he prevented the firing lines from being depleted at a critical time, maintaining a high standard of combat strength efficiency.

PIKE, SHEPARD L.
R—Plattsburg, N. Y.
B—Plattsburg, N. Y.
G. O. No. 103, W. D., 1919.

Lieutenant colonel, Infantry, U. S. Army.
As commandant of the Army Candidates' School at Langres, France, he organized an important institution and developed it to a high state of efficiency. His services in capably directing the training of more than 5,000 candidates for active duty at the front were of the utmost value to the American Expeditionary Forces.

PILLOW, JEROME G.
R—Helena, Ark.
B—Columbia, Tenn.
G. O. No. 9, W. D., 1923.

Lieutenant colonel (Cavalry), General Staff Corps, U. S. Army.
As assistant chief of staff, G-3, 32d Division, he displayed marked ability, high professional attainments, rendering immeasurably valuable services in the operations of his division in the offensives of Aisne-Marne, Oise-Aisne, the Meuse-Argonne, and during the march to the Rhine.

PILLSBURY, GEORGE B.
R—Tewksbury, Mass.
B—Lowell, Mass.
G. O. No. 56, W. D., 1922.

Colonel, Corps of Engineers, U. S. Army.
As corps engineer, 2d Army Corps, from October, 1918, to January, 1919, he displayed professional qualifications of an exceptionally high order. During operations which broke the Hindenburg line between Cambrai and St. Quentin his tireless energy and highly efficient work contributed in a marked degree to the success of the operations of the corps.

PLUNKETT, CHARLES PERSHALL.
R—Washington, D. C.
B—Washington, D. C.
G. O. No. 59, W. D., 1919.

Rear admiral, U. S. Navy.
He supervised the production, transportation to Europe, and the placing in action on the western front of the United States Naval Gun Battalion of five 14-inch guns on railway mounts, the most powerful artillery weapons brought into action against Germany and her allies during the war. In this stupendous undertaking the successful accomplishment of which had an important bearing on the outcome of the war, he displayed technical knowledge of a high order, combined with practical knowledge of the needs of the service and the difficulties to be encountered. He worked with unceasing zeal and devotion, rendering a service of rare distinction to the American Expeditionary Forces.

POILLON, ARTHUR.
R—New York, N. Y.
B—New York, N. Y.
G. O. No. 124, W. D., 1919.

Lieutenant colonel, Cavalry, U. S. Army.
For services while serving as military attaché at The Hague, Netherlands.

POOL, EUGENE H.
R—New York, N. Y.
B—New York, N. Y.
G. O. No. 49, W. D., 1922.

Lieutenant colonel, Medical Corps, U. S. Army.
As surgical consultant with the 4th Army Corps, 5th Army Corps, and then the 1st Army, he displayed unusual organizing ability, excellent judgment, and professional attainments of the highest order in directing the work of surgical teams in the care of large numbers of wounded in various hospitals at the front during the St. Mihiel and Meuse-Argonne offensives, thereby rendering services of great value to the American Expeditionary Forces.

POORE, BENJAMIN A.
R—Fitchburg, Mass.
B—Center, Ala.
G. O. No. 59, W. D., 1919.
Distinguished-service cross also awarded.

Brigadier general, U. S. Army.
He commanded with distinction and ability the 7th Infantry Brigade, 4th Division, in the numerous engagements of the Argonne-Meuse campaign. By his energy and ability his brigade drove the enemy from Ruisseau-des-Forges and from the Bois-du-Fays. In these engagements important captures of many prisoners and much material were made by the troops of his command.

POPE, FRANCIS H
  R—St. Louis, Mo.
  B—Fort Leavenworth, Kans.
  G. O. No. 3, W. D., 1921.

Colonel, Quartermaster Corps, U. S. Army.
As chief of the Motor Transport Service, American Expeditionary Forces, he developed a rational organization for the operation and maintenance of the motor transport of the American Expeditionary Forces, and as Deputy Chief, Motor Transport Corps, American Expeditionary Forces, was largely instrumental in further developing and applying this organization, thereby rendering exceptionally meritorious and distinguished service to the United States.

POPE, WILLIAM R
  R—Pulaski, Tenn.
  B—Pulaski, Tenn.
  G. O. No. 4, W. D., 1923.

Colonel, Infantry, U. S. Army.
Having taken command of the 113th Infantry, 29th Division, shortly before the beginning of the Meuse-Argonne offensive, held it with signal ability throughout the period of its engagement in that operation. By his energy and resourcefulness in overcoming the numerous adverse conditions which confronted his regiment, he proved an inspiration to his men and an important factor in the successes of his division. As provost marshal general of the embarkation center at Le Mans, France, from December, 1918, until June, 1919, he displayed tact, marked efficiency, and executive and administrative ability of the highest order, thereby rendering highly conspicuous services in a position of great responsibility.

PORGES, GUSTAVE
  R—New York, N. Y.
  B—Bohemia.
  G. O. No. 39, W. D., 1920.

Colonel, Quartermaster Corps, U. S. Army.
He gave markedly able assistance in the establishment of the American Expeditionary Forces depot at Nevers and the Engineer camp at Vierzon. Later, when placed in charge of the purchase of subsistence, clothing, equipage, forage, and bedding, by his valuable knowledge of commercial conditions and by his persistent efforts and able negotiations, he secured much needed supplies from allied and neutral countries. He originated the manufacture in Europe of necessary items of food, clothing, and cloth for the use of the American Expeditionary Forces. Subsequently he rendered valuable assistance in the liquidation of the American Expeditionary Forces surplus supplies. At all times he showed remarkable energy in all matters affecting the welfare of the troops in the American Expeditionary Forces.

POSTON, ADELE S
  R—White Plains, N. Y.
  B—Springdale, Ark.
  G. O. No. 9, W. D., 1923.

Chief Nurse, Army Nurse Corps, U. S. Army.
As chief nurse of Base Hospital No. 117 (psychiatric unit), at La Fauche, France, during the World War, she performed very difficult and exacting duties with marked skill and distinction. By her professional efficiency, untiring energy, and tact, she made a large contribution to the success of this novel and highly important hospital of the American Expeditionary Forces.

POTTER, WILLIAM CHAPMAN
  R—Old Westbury, N. Y.
  B—Chicago, Ill.
  G. O. No. 118, W. D., 1919.

He reorganized the equipment division of the Signal Corps and organized and developed the Bureau of Aircraft Production.

POWER, NEAL
  R—San Francisco, Calif.
  B—Washington, D. C.
  G. O. No. 89, W. D., 1919.

Lieutenant colonel, Judge Advocate General's Department, U. S. Army.
As head of the special disciplinary division in the office of the judge advocate, American Expeditionary Forces, he was charged with duties of an exceptionally arduous and responsible nature, in the performance of which he displayed high professional attainments and notable devotion to duty.

*POWERS, CHARLES A
  R—Denver, Colo.
  B—Lawrence, Mass.
  G. O. No. 3, W. D., 1924.

Major, Medical Corps, U. S. Army.
As a surgeon, first with the French armies and later with the American Red Cross Military Hospital No. 1, he displayed untiring energy and surgical ability of the highest order. By his professional skill he revolutionized the surgical treatment of faces mutilated by war wounds, demonstrating to the world how to restore them to a normal condition, thereby rendering conspicuous service, by this great contribution, in saving the lives of many French and American soldiers.
Posthumously awarded. Medal presented to stepfather, Dr. A. J. Stevens.

PRATT, JOSEPH H
  R—Chapel Hill, N. C.
  B—Hartford, Conn.
  G. O. No. 56, W. D., 1922.

Colonel, Corps of Engineers, U. S. Army.
He commanded the 105th Engineers during its organization and training period in the entire operation of the 30th Division near Ypres, Belgium, and during the breaking of the Hindenburg line and the advance beyond. He displayed forceful energy, exceptional ability, and remarkable foresight in the solution of all engineer tasks, including the construction of railways and roads, as well as the location and destruction of mines and traps, thereby contributing materially to the success of the operations.

PRATT, WILLIAM VEAZIE
  R—Belfast, Me.
  B—Belfast, Me.
  G. O. No. 116, W. D., 1919.

Captain, U. S. Navy.
As assistant to the Chief of Naval Operations, his untiring energy and close cooperation with the Army in connection with its oversea movements of troops and supplies, and especially in the making up and routing of convoys, resulted in the successful movement of over 2,000,000 men without material loss of life.

PRENTISS, AUGUSTIN M
  R—Barnwell, S. C.
  B—Chapel Hill, N. C.
  G. O. No. 56, W. D., 1922.

Major, Chemical Warfare Service, U. S. Army.
As officer in charge of the ordnance section, Chemical Warfare Service, he displayed great energy, untiring devotion to duty, and high technical skill. Due to his thorough knowledge of ordnance supplies and material, especially shells and guns, he rendered invaluable assistance in the proper choice of gases, gas shells, and other materials used both by the gas troops and artillery throughout the war, thereby contributing materially to the successes of the American Expeditionary Forces.

PRICE, HOWARD C.
R—Chester, Pa.
B—Chester, Pa.
G. O. No. 89, W. D., 1919.

Colonel, Infantry, U. S. Army.
He organized, trained, and commanded in active operations the 360th Infantry 90th Division, which under his capable leadership was eminently successf as a combat unit. At all times he inspired a notable spirit among the member of his command. He displayed military attainments of a high order in the capture of the Foret-du-Bois le Pretre during the St. Mihiel offensive and the assault on the Freya Stellung in the Argonne-Meuse operations, rendering merited services to the American Expeditionary Forces.

PRICE, WILLIAM G., jr.
R—Chester, Pa.
B—Chester, Pa,
G. O. No. 103, W. D., 1919.

Brigadier general, U. S. Army.
He commanded the 53d Field Artillery Brigade, 28th Division, with marked distinction, proving himself a tactical leader of extraordinary ability. Through the formidable assistance which his brigade furnished to the attacking Infantry during the engagement of the 91st Division from the Lys to the Scheldt, the rapid advance of the Infantry was insured and the success made more brilliant.

PRICE, XENOPHON H.
R—Bay City, Mich.
B—Saginaw, Mich.
G. O. No. 87, W. D., 1919.

Lieutenant colonel, Corps of Engineers, U. S. Army.
He organized and was continuously in charge of all map-room data of the Section, General Staff, at General Headquarters, American Expeditiona Forces. Through his energy, ability, and sound military judgment ma showing accurately the situation on the battle fronts were constantly availabl for outlying projected operations, and the data compiled by him is of inca culable historical value in preserving a record of the achievements of the American Expeditionary Forces.

PURINGTON, GEORGE A.
R—Fort Sheridan, Ill.
B—Cleveland, Ohio.
G. O. No. 59, W. D., 1919.

Lieutenant colonel, Cavalry, U. S. Army.
He was engaged in keeping roads open and traffic moving in the advance of t 1st Army between the 26th of September and the 30th of Sepember, 1918, the battle west of the Meuse. Due to his tireless effort and determinati the supply of ammunition and food of the 3d and 5th Corps was insure Although confronted with a most difficult task, he overcame all obstacles a crowned his efforts with great success.

PUSEY, FRED TAYLOR.
R—Lima, Pa.
B—Philadelphia, Pa.
G. O. No. 38, W. D., 1922.

Lieutenant colonel, Quartermaster Corps, U. S. Army.
As division quartermaster, 28th Division, he displayed exceptional ability a zeal in developing the personnel and in handling the endless duties of office, both in training and in combat, and constantly maintained the supp of food and equipment to the command and its various units under mo difficult circumstances, thereby contributing materially to the success of th division during its active operations in France.

QUAKEMEYER, JOHN G.
R—Yazoo City, Miss.
B—Yazoo City, Miss.
G. O. No. 59, W. D., 1919.

Lieutenant colonel, Cavalry, U. S. Army.
As chief of the American Mission at British General Headquarters, he adm istered the duties of the office with tact and ability, promoting cordial relatio between members of the Allied Armies with whom he came in contact. aide-de-camp to the Commander in Chief, he has performed his importa duties with marked distinction and sound judgment.

RAFFERTY, WILLIAM A.
R—Chicago, Ill.
B—Fort Wingate, N. Mex.
G. O. No. 56, W. D., 1922.

Major (Infantry), General Staff Corps, U. S. Army.
While in charge of the supply branch, 4th (Supply) Section, General Staff, Army, American Expeditionary Forces, he displayed great initiative, zeal, a devotion to duty, and by his excellent judgment, forethought, and coope tion materially assisted in the solution of many difficult problems concerni the supply of the troops during the St. Mihiel and Meuse-Argonne offensiv thereby contributing in a marked degree to the successful accomplishme of the supply of the troops engaged in those operations.

RALSTON, FRANCIS W.
R—Philadelphia, Pa.
B—Philadelphia, Pa.
G. O. No. 59, W. D., 1919.

Colonel, Coast Artillery Corps, U. S. Army.
His marked military attainments rendered his services most valuable wh serving as adjutant of the 42d Division. As commandant of General He quarters, American Expeditionary Forces, he performed exacting duties w distinction. By his unflagging energy, zeal, and sound judgment he solv difficult problems of administration, achieving most satisfactory results.

RAND, WILLIAM.
R—New York, N. Y.
B—Chicago, Ill.
G. O. No. 15, W. D., 1923.

Colonel, Judge Advocate General's Department, U. S. Army.
As principal assistant in the office of the Acting Judge Advocate General for American Expeditionary Forces in Europe and as a member of the board review to which was referred records of trial by courts-martial in the Ameri army operating on foreign soil, he performed duties of an important and reaching character and grave responsibility. His broad learning, his com hensive grasp of the problems with which he had to deal, coupled with tiring industry and energy contributed markedly to the accomplishment the office of the Judge Advocate General and of the American Expedition Forces.

READ, ALVAN C.
R—Baton Rouge, La.
B—Lewisburg, Tenn.
G. O. No., 108, W. D., 1919.

Colonel, Infantry, U. S. Army.
As inspector general for the armies during their operations in the St. Mihiel Meuse-Argonne offensives, by his keen observations of the conduct of u and leadership displayed by commanders he was able at all times to p valuable information as to the morale and efficiency of troops and their c manders. By the able handling of his important duties, prompt and adequ means were always provided for improving conditions as to these import factors in the conduct of operations. Later, as chief inspector of the Arm Occupation, he continued to render the same superior quality of service wh marked that given by him prior to the armistice.

DISTINGUISHED-SERVICE MEDAL

READ, GEORGE W.
  R—Des Moines, Iowa.
  B—Indianola, Iowa.
  G. O. No. 12, W. D., 1919.

Major general, U. S. Army.
He commanded with distinction the 30th Division, and organized and commanded the 2d Army Corps in its operations with the British forces in France. He displayed qualities of leadership and professional attainments of a high order, and to his efforts are largely due the brilliant success achieved.

RECKORD, MILTON A.
  R—Bel Air, Md.
  B—Harford County, Md.
  G. O. No. 89, W. D., 1919.

Colonel, Infantry, U. S. Army.
He served with distinction as commanding officer of the 115th Infantry, 29th Division at all times showing qualities of high military leadership and great tactical ability. Inspiring his men by his aggressive spirit and fervent devotion to his task, he led them with noted success through three weeks of constant action against the enemy during the operations north of Verdun.

REECE, B. CARROLL.
  R—Butler, Tenn.
  B—Butler, Tenn.
  G. O. No. 59, W. D., 1919.

First lieutenant, Infantry, U. S. Army.
He showed energy, initiative, and military ability of a high order while serving as second lieutenant in the 102d Infantry, 26th Division, in command of a company and later a battalion. He led his company brilliantly in the attack upon the St. Mihiel salient and during the operations of the 26th Division north of Verdun. Confronted later by a task of great difficulty when placed in command of a battalion, which suffered heavy casualties and became badly disorganized, he displayed marked ability and determination in reorganizing his command and molding it into a good fighting unit, able under his leadership to achieve valuable results.

REED, DAVID A.
  R—Pittsburgh, Pa.
  B—Pittsburgh, Pa.
  G. O. No. 56, W. D., 1922.

Major, Field Artillery, U. S. Army.
As battalion commander, 311th Field Artillery, 79th Division, he displayed exceptional ability as an organizer, instructor, and leader. By his professional attainments and tireless energy he was instrumental in bringing his command to a high state of efficiency. Later, as the Field Artillery member of the United States section of the Inter-Allied Armistice Commission at Spa and as acting chief of staff thereof, by his exceptional ability and insight into affairs requiring delicate and diplomatic treatment, he rendered conspicuous service to the American Expeditionary Forces.

REED, WALTER L.
  R—Washington, D. C.
  B—Fort Apache, Ariz.
  G. O. No. 10, W. D., 1922.

Lieutenant colonel, Inspector General's Department U. S. Army.
In the organization and administration of the Inspector General's Department at Camp Pontanezen, Brest, France, thereby enabling that department to meet the excessive demands made upon it during the return of the American Expeditionary Forces through the port of Brest.

REES, ROBERT I.
  R—Houghton, Mich.
  B—Houghton, Mich.
  G. O. No. 25, W. D., 1919.

Brigadier general, U. S. Army.
For services with the committee charged with education and special training in the Army. To his initiative and breadth of vision are largely due the successful measures for training of enlisted men for special services and the establishment of the Student Army Training Corps.

REEVES, IRA L.
  R—Chicago, Ill.
  B—Jefferson City, Mo.
  G. O. No. 59, W. D., 1921.

Colonel, Infantry, U. S. Army.
As president of the American Expeditionary Forces University in France his fine ability as an organizer made possible the expeditious establishment of this institution, and to his initiative, energy, rare tact, and good judgment is due, in a large measure, the successful operation of the university.

REEVES, JAMES H.
  R—Center, Ala.
  B—Center, Ala.
  G. O. No. 87, W. D., 1919.
  Distinguished-service cross also awarded.

Colonel, Infantry, U. S. Army.
He organized the 353d Infantry, 89th Division, and commanded it with distinction during all but one month of its active service. The high qualities of leadership and unfailing devotion to duty displayed by him were responsible for the marked esprit and morale of his command. To his marked tactical ability and energy are largely due the brilliant successes achieved by his regiment during its operations against the enemy.

*REGISTER, EDWARD C.
  R—Georgetown, S. C.
  B—Rose Hill, N. C.
  G. O. No. 9, W. D., 1923.

Lieutenant colonel, Medical Corps, U. S. Army.
While a member of the Polish Relief Expedition, volunteering for service at Tarnopol, Poland, the entire city being prostrate from the effects of typhus fever, 45 doctors having sacrificed their lives within the preceding two months. Upon arrival at Tarnopol he assumed entire charge of the situation, organized and established a 1,500-bed hospital equipped with supplies which had been concealed from enemy forces and found by him. Fifteen days after his arrival in the city he contracted typhus fever and died from its effects on January 3, 1920.
Posthumously awarded. Medal presented to widow, Mrs. Edward C. Register.

REILLY, HENRY J.
  R—Winnetka, Ill.
  B—Fort Barrancas, Fla.
  G. O. No. 108, W. D., 1919.

Colonel, Field Artillery, U. S. Army.
In command of the 149th Field Artillery, 42d Division, he participated with credit in the operations of the 42d Division. Through his tireless energy and technical skill as an artillerist, his regiment gave most effective assistance to the Infantry which it supported.

REINHART, STANLEY E.
  R—Polk, Ohio.
  B—Polk, Ohio.
  G. O. No. 70, W. D., 1919.

Major, Field Artillery, U. S. Army.
In command of a battery and subsequently a battalion of the 17th Field Artillery, 2d Division, he gave proof of high qualities of leadership and military attainments, notably during the operations near Soissons in July, 1918, when he skillfully maneuvered his battalion in front of the infantry under machine-gun fire from the enemy with but few casualties to his command. Later he rendered valuable and loyal service as chief of staff to the chief of artillery, 6th Army Corps.

REPLOGLE, J. LEONARD
R—New York, N. Y.
B—Bedford County, Pa.
G. O. No. 15, W. D., 1923.

Director of steel, War Industries Board.
In connection with the operations of the War Industries Board during the World War. As a member of the board he rendered through his broad vision, distinguished capacity, and business ability, services of inestimable value in marshaling the industrial forces of the Nation and mobilizing its economic resources—marked factors in assisting to make military success attainable. As director of steel, he rendered, through his untiring efforts and devotion to duty, exceptionally valuable service to the War Department in connection with the procurement and supply of steel and iron for the Army

REPP, WILLIAM F.
R—Philadelphia, Pa.
B—Philadelphia, Pa.
G. O. No. 59, W. D., 1919.

Lieutenant colonel, Signal Corps, U. S. Army.
With his valuable assistance the Signal Corps was enabled originally to plan for the immense network of the United States Army telegraph and telephone lines now existing in France. To him is attributable the exceptionally high standard of efficiency attained by the telephone and telegraph service. As chief signal officer, advance section, services of supply, his services have been marked by a character of exceptional excellence.

RETHERS, HARRY F.
R—San Francisco, Calif.
B—San Francisco, Calif.
G. O. No. 59, W. D., 1919.

Colonel, Quartermaster Corps, U. S. Army.
He distinguished himself by his extraordinary ability and exceptional skill in organizing the work of the Quartermaster Corps at Base Section No. 3. His good judgment, combined with tact, knowledge of methods, and high professional attainments, resulted in a superior standard of efficiency, reflecting the greatest credit upon himself and enabling him to render most valuable services to the Government.

REYBOLD, EUGENE
R—Delaware City, Del.
B—Delaware City, Del.
G. O. No. 3, W. D., 1921.

Colonel, Coast Artillery Corps, U. S. Army.
As director of the department of enlisted specialists, Coast Artillery School where, by his excellent judgment, energy, and foresight, he enabled the department to meet the demands made upon it in an effective manner.

REYNOLDS, CHARLES R.
R—Elmira, N. Y.
B—Elmira, N. Y.
G. O. No. 89, W. D., 1919.

Colonel, Medical Corps, U. S. Army.
As division surgeon of the 77th Division, as chief surgeon, 6th Army Corps and later as chief surgeon, 2d Army, he displayed qualities of leadership, high professional attainments, and rare judgment in energetically directing the work of the sanitary units under his control. By his foresight in providing front-line hospitalization and evacuation facilities for the sick and wounded in the field, he rendered services of signal merit to the American Expeditionary Forces.

REYNOLDS, FREDERICK P.
R—Elmira, N. Y.
B—Elmira, N. Y.
G. O. No. 30, W. D., 1921.

Colonel, Medical Corps, U. S. Army.
As surgeon of the advance section, services of supply, American Expeditionary Forces, he displayed rare judgment, unusual executive ability, and high professional attainments in the institution of sanitary measures and in providing and supervising hospitalization and evacuation facilities for the sick and wounded flowing into the advanced areas from the principal centers of combat activity.

REYNOLDS, STEPHEN C.
R—St. Louis, Mo.
B—Louisiana, Mo.
G. O. No. 87, W. D., 1919.

Lieutenant colonel (Infantry), General Staff Corps, U. S. Army.
As assistant chief of staff, G-1, of the 5th Division, by his keen application to his task he overcame almost insurmountable difficulties in maintaining communications and securing supplies for his division during the 27 days when it was advancing against the enemy north of Verdun. In the performance of his many duties he displayed indefatigable zeal and showed exceptional administrative ability, rendering valuable services to the American Expeditionary Forces.

RHEA, JAMES C.
R—Strawn, Tex.
B—Hamburg, Iowa.
G. O. No. 59, W. D., 1919.
Distinguished-service cross also awarded.

Colonel (Cavalry), General Staff Corps, U. S. Army.
In charge of the operations section, and later as chief of staff and brigade commander of the 2d Division, he played a conspicuous part in the successful engagements at the St. Mihiel salient, Blanc Mont Ridge, and in the Argonne Meuse, revealing traits of military knowledge and attainments of a high order

RHOADS, THOMAS L.
R—Fort Worth, Tex.
B—Boyertown, Pa.
G. O. No. 62, W. D., 1919.

Colonel, Medical Corps, U. S. Army.
As division surgeon of the 80th Division, he had charge of the Medical Department's work of that unit throughout its combat activities. Due to his skillful administration, it functioned smoothly and with precision at all times, caring properly for a large number of the sick and wounded. As chief surgeon of the 1st Army Corps, and later of the 1st Army, he displayed executive ability high order, being constant and zealous in devotion to his arduous tasks.

RHODES, CHARLES D.
R—Delaware, Ohio.
B—Delaware, Ohio.
G. O. No. 89, W. D., 1919.
Distinguished-service cross also awarded.

Major general, U. S. Army.
As commander of the Artillery brigade in support of the 82d Division, during the offensive operations of the St. Mihiel salient and again in command of Artillery brigade during the Meuse-Argonne offensive, by his marked ability shown in the conduct of his units he contributed in a noted degree to the successes attained. Later he served with distinction as a member of the Inter allied Commission at Spa, rendering conspicuous services to the American Expeditionary Forces.

DISTINGUISHED-SERVICE MEDAL

RHODES, MARIE B. (now Mrs. CLARENCE CASH).
R—Pittsburgh, Pa.
B—Pittsburgh, Pa.
G. O. No. 9, W. D., 1923.

Nurse, Army Nurse Corps, U. S. Army.
As chief of the nurses' equipment bureau of the military department, American Red Cross, in Paris, France, during the World War, she rendered invaluable service to the Army. She organized and developed a department which was able not only to supply and replace nurses' equipment but to transport the material all over France, even to rapidly moving units and teams at the front. By her remarkable business acumen and integrity, unusual resourcefulness, and initiative she made a contribution to the welfare, efficiency, and conduct of the American Expeditionary Forces nursing forces which can not be measured. In addition to her most arduous duties during the day she frequently spent part of the nights during the emergency giving her services as an anesthetist in the Army hospitals in Paris.

RICE, JOHN H.
R—Webster Groves, Mo.
B—St. Louis, Mo.
G. O. No. 62, W. D., 1919.

Brigadier general, U. S. Army.
As chief of the engineering division of the office of the Chief of Ordnance, he performed with peculiar ability his arduous duties in connection with the design and development of all articles of ordnance supplied to the United States Army. Later as Chief Ordnance Officer, American Expeditionary Forces, he was charged with the procurement and supply of all ordnance to our forces in France, which duties he performed with exceptional success, displaying untiring energy and zeal. He handled perplexing problems of supply with sound judgment, achieving most valuable results.

RICE, MERVYN A.
R—Montclair, N. J.
B—Rockland, Me.
G. O. No. 56, W. D., 1922.

Lieutenant colonel, Ordnance Department, U. S. Army.
As corps ordnance officer of the 2d Army Corps from February to October, 1918, he displayed exceptional ability in the organization and administration of the system used in equipping with ordnance the American troops serving on the British front. Later, his great tact and business ability assisted to a marked degree in the satisfactory settlement of important claims arising out of this service.

RICE, SEDGWICK.
R—St. Paul, Minn.
B—St. Paul, Minn.
G. O. No. 96, W. D., 1918.

Second lieutenant, 7th Cavalry, U. S. Army.
For services against hostile Indians near the Catholic Mission on White Clay Creek, S. Dak., Dec. 30, 1890.

RICHARDSON, LORRAIN T.
R—Janesville, Wis.
B—Janesville, Wis.
G. O. No. 56, W. D., 1922.

Colonel, Infantry, U. S. Army.
As commander of the 322d Infantry, 81st Division, during its organization, training, and in all its combat operations he displayed marked efficiency, tireless energy, and military attainments of the highest order. By his sound judgment and skillful and energetic leadership he contributed materially to the successes achieved by the regiment against the enemy.

RICHARDSON, ROBERT C., Jr.
R—Charleston, S. C.
B—Charleston, S. C.
G. O. No. 87, W. D., 1919.

Colonel (Cavalry), General Staff Corps, U. S. Army.
He organized and conducted with great efficiency the important strategical and tactical liaison service of the 3d Section, General Staff, General Headquarters, American Expeditionary Forces. During the Meuse-Argonne operations he gave proof of notable military attainments and untiring devotion to duty by the efficient manner in which he organized and administered the advanced General Headquarters, rendering services of distinction to the American Expeditionary Forces.

RICHARDSON, WILDS P.
R—Paris, Tex.
B—Hunt County, Tex.
G. O. No. 19, W. D., 1922.

Brigadier general, U. S. Army.
As commanding general of the American Expeditionary Forces in North Russia, by his skillful handling of the many difficult situations which arose, he rendered a signal service to the United States Government.

RICKARDS, GEORGE C.
R—Oil City, Pa.
B—Philadelphia, Pa.
G. O. No. 38, W. D., 1922.

Colonel, Infantry, U. S. Army.
As commanding officer of the 112th Infantry, 28th Division, he proved himself a forceful and capable military leader. Maintaining at all times a high degree of efficiency in his regiment through his personal magnetism, heroism, zeal, and energy, he contributed materially to the successes achieved by the 28th Division in its operations against the enemy, rendering services of distinction to the American Expeditionary Forces.

RIGGS, KERR T.
R—Cynthiana, Ky.
B—Harrison County, Ky.
G. O. No. 19, W. D., 1922.

Colonel (Cavalry), General Staff Corps, U. S. Army.
As G-2, 2d Army Corps, he displayed exceptional ability in the organization and administration of that division of the corps staff. He also showed great ability and rare tact in his relations with the intelligence branch of the staffs of the British organizations with which the 2d Army Corps served. By his tireless energy and unceasing devotion to exacting duties, he contributed to a marked degree to the successes achieved by his organization.

RIVERS, WILLIAM C.
R—Pulaski, Tenn.
B—Pulaski, Tenn.
G. O. No. 89, W. D., 1919.

Brigadier general, U. S. Army.
As commander of the 76th Field Artillery, 3d Division, he was a material factor in stemming the tide of the enemy's advance during the second Battle of the Marne. Subsequently, upon being promoted to the grade of brigadier general, he displayed marked leadership and high military attainments in command of the 5th Field Artillery Brigade, 5th Division, in the Meuse-Argonne offensive.

ROBERTS, CHARLES D.
R—Fort D. A. Russell, Wyo.
B—Cheyenne Agency, S. Dak.
G. O. No. 59, W. D., 1919.
Medal of honor also awarded.

Colonel (Infantry), General Staff Corps, U. S. Army.
He displayed unusual ability as chief of staff of the 81st Division in its organization, and in the conduct of its operations in the St. Die Sector, on Nov 9, 10, and 11, 1918, near Verdum, where the division was enabled to advance some 5½ kilometers over marshy ground under heavy fire.

ROBERTS, GEORGE J.
R—East Orange, N. J.
B—Charlotte County, Va.
G. O. No. 124, W. D., 1919.

As chief of the New York ordnance district, in which capacity he maintaine at all times the greatest degree of intelligent and enthusiastic cooperatio between the Ordnance Department and manufacturers in his district, thereb attaining the maximum production of munitions in a minimum time; an also as chairman of the New York ordnance district claims board, in whic capacity his services have been invaluable to the Nation in adjusting equ tably the $525,000,000 worth of outstanding contracts in his district in force a the signing of the armistice..

ROBERTS, OSCAR E.
R—Taylor, Tex.
B—Milan County, Tex.
G. O. No. 15, W. D., 1923.

Colonel, Infantry, U. S. Army.
As colonel commanding the 144th Infantry, 36th Division, he displayed untirin energy, initiative, and resourcefulness both during the period of organizatio and training and during the combat operations of his regiment in Franc His leadership, sound judgment, and devotion to duty were material factor in the successes of his regiment, brigade, and division in action against th enemy.

ROBERTS, THOMAS A.
R—Springfield, Ill.
B—Springfield, Ill.
G. O. No. 50, W. D., 1919.

Colonel, Cavalry, U. S. Army.
As commander of an American regiment on duty with the French Arm although confronted with many difficult situations, he handled all question with marked success. His tasks were performed with ability, in a manne that reflected the greatest credit upon him; his preparations were careful, h leadership skillful. The excellent results achieved by his regiment are in measure attributable to his sound judgment and military knowledge.

ROBERTSON, ASHLEY HERMAN.
R—Ashmore, Ill.
B—Ashmore, Ill.
G. O. No. 116, W. D., 1919.

Rear Admiral, U. S. Navy.
As force transport officer, his untiring energy contributed greatly to the su cessful oversea movement of troops and supplies.

ROBERTSON, SAMUEL ARTHUR.
R—San Benito, Tex.
B—Fort Benton, Mont.
G. O. No. 59, W. D., 1919.

Lieutenant colonel, Corps of Engineers, U. S. Army.
As general superintendent of construction of the light railways he managed a the intricate details of complex organization and classification of tasks wit a master hand. With untrained personnel he established a record for spee in tracklaying of the 60-centimeter lines, exciting the admiration of our allie During the advance of the 1st Army, by his ceaseless activity, tireless energ and great knowledge he performed his duty with marked credit to the Go ernment.

ROBINS, THOMAS MATTHEW.
R—Snow Hill, Md.
B—Snow Hill, Md.
G. O. No. 77, W. D., 1919.

Colonel, Corps of Engineers, U. S. Army.
For services while in charge of the engineer depot established in connection wit the port of New York, and subsequently included in the port of embarkatio at Hoboken, N. J.

ROBINSON, DONALD A.
R—Seattle, Wash.
B—Chippewa Falls, Wis.
G. O. No. 56, W. D., 1922.

Lieutenant colonel (Cavalry), General Staff Corps, U. S. Army.
As chief of the executive division, fourth section, General Staff, Headquarter Services of Supply, American Expeditionary Forces, from Apr. 25, 1918, Feb. 19, 1919, he was charged with the immediate coordination of maj supply activities, including the difficult and gravely responsible task adjusting priority of shipments and determining the order in which movements of supplies from the base ports of the American Expeditiona Forces should proceed. In a position of great responsibility, in which lar powers were delegated to him, he displayed to an unusual degree rare tac excellent judgment, and the faculty of firm and prompt decision. By h successful handling of difficult supply situations of the most critical charact directly affecting important operations in the field, he rendered services of t highest value to the American Expeditionary Forces.

ROBINSON, FRED J.
R—Miami Beach, Fla.
B—Detroit, Mich.
G. O. No. 124, W. D., 1919.

As chief of the Detroit Ordnance District, in which capacity he maintain at all times the greatest degree of intelligent and enthusiastic cooperatio between the Ordnance Department and manufacturers in his district, thereb attaining the maximum production of munitions in a minimum time; a also as chairman of the Detroit Ordnance District Claims Board, in whi capacity his services have been invaluable to the Nation in adjusti equitably the $271,000,000 worth of outstanding contracts in his district force at the signing of the armistice.

ROCKENBACH, SAMUEL D.
R—Boonville, Mo.
B—Lynchburg, Va.
G. O. No. 78, W. D., 1919.

Brigadier general, U. S. Army.
As quartermaster of Base Section No. 1, St. Nazaire, from June to Decemb 1917, he rendered especially valuable services. Confronted with a proble of great magnitude, befraught with serious difficulties, he went about task with keen determination, and by his energy and great zeal organiz and efficiently operated the first American base in France. Later, as ch of the Tank Corps, by his tireless energy and keen determination he esta lished schools of training for tank personnel and laid the foundation for t organization of the tank units. He ably directed the operations of the tan with the First Army and contributed in a measure to the success attained.

ROGERS, HARRY L.
R—Orchard Lake, Mich.
B—Washington, D. C.
G. O. No. 12, W. D., 1919.

Major general, U. S. Army.
He has organized, perfected, and administered with great efficiency the qu termaster department in France. He was able to meet each emergency times fraught with untold difficulties, and by his energy and untiring z he has insured to our troops a prompt and constant supply of quartermas stores, without which the ultimate success of our Army could not have be obtained.

ROGERS, HENRY H.
R—Tuxedo, N. Y.
B—New York, N. Y.
G. O. No. 47, W. D., 1921.

Lieutenant colonel, Field Artillery, U. S. Army.
While commanding the 2d Corps Artillery Park which operated with the 5th Army Corps, in spite of great difficulties he delivered large quantities of ammunition to the troops, and by his resourcefulness, courage, and leadership he maintained his command in a high state of efficiency and morale, thereby contributing to the success of the operations of the corps.

ROGERS, JOSEPH A.
R—Mullin, Tex.
B—Cameron, Tex.
G. O. No. 4, W. D., 1923.

Lieutenant colonel, Field Artillery, U. S. Army.
He commanded the 1st Battalion, 18th Field Artillery, 3d Division, from July 1 to Oct. 3, 1918, and the 124th Field Artillery, 33d Division, from Oct. 4 until Nov. 17, 1918, at all times proving himself to be an officer of exceptional ability. By his sound tactical judgment, loyal devotion to duty, and great skill he supported the Infantry, to which attached, so effectively that he aided materially in the successful operations of several divisions in many important engagements.

RONAYNE, JAMES.
R—New York, N. Y.
B—Ireland.
G. O. No. 59, W. D., 1919.

Colonel, U. S. Army.
He served as assistant commandant of the Army schools for eight months. By his energy, perseverance, and good judgment, in all matters connected with the Army schools, he exhibited high professional attainments and military qualities of a superior order.

ROOP, JAMES CLAWSON.
R—Upland, Pa.
B—Upland, Pa.
G. O. No. 56, W. D., 1922.

Lieutenant colonel, Corps of Engineers, U. S. Army.
He served as assistant to the general purchasing agent, American Expeditionary Forces. His marked ability and tact were important factors in numerous negotiations with the allied armies and governments, involving critical matters of supply to our Army. In the organization of the work of the general purchasing board and general purchasing agent, Colonel Roop throughout its existence was an indispensable factor in a position of great responsibility. He rendered most distinguished service in connection with important supplies of all kinds for the Army as well as in the organization of the general system of coordination between the supply services of the American Expeditionary Forces and the allied armies.

ROOSEVELT, THEODORE, Jr.
R—New York, N. Y.
B—Oyster Bay, Long Island, N. Y.
G. O. No. 2, W. D., 1927.
Distinguished-service cross also awarded.

Lieutenant colonel, Infantry, U. S. Army.
As battalion and regimental commander, 26th Infantry, he displayed consistent gallantry, conspicuous energy, and marked efficiency in the operations around Cantigny, Soissons, and during the Meuse-Argonne offensive. By his devotion to duty, pronounced tactical ability, and brilliant qualities of leadership he contributed materially to the successes of his regiment and of the 1st Division. He rendered services of signal worth to the Government in a position of great responsibility at a time of gravest importance.

ROSE, WILLIAM H.
R—Refton, Pa.
B—Safe Harbor, Pa.
G. O. No. 25, W. D., 1919.

Brigadier general, U. S. Army.
While in charge of the engineer depot he was charged with the system of purchase of supplies. His exceptional ability, judgment, and resourcefulness are apparent in the efficient solution of the many difficult problems involved and in the success attained in supplying the vast quantities of engineering supplies to the Army overseas.

RUCKER, WILLIAM H.
R—Los Angeles, Calif.
B—Fort Riley, Kans.
G. O. No. 95, W. D., 1919.

Lieutenant colonel, Field Artillery, U. S. Army.
As commander of the 107th Field Artillery, 28th Division, and of a French artillery regiment during the operations of the 32d Division on the Vesle River, he displayed consummate skill as an artillerist and showed notable qualities of leadership. Subsequently he commanded the 16th Field Artillery, 4th Division, and acted as group commander of French and American artillery units, where he furnished effective support to the Infantry during the St. Mihiel and Argonne-Meuse operations.

*RUCKMAN, JOHN W.
R—Sidney, Ill.
B—Sidney, Ill.
G. O. No. 1, W. D., 1926.

Major general, U. S. Army.
As department commander, Southern Department, between Aug. 30, 1917, and May 4, 1918, and department commander, Northeastern Department, between May 23, 1918, and July 20, 1918, he handled many difficult problems arising in these departments with rare judgment, tact, and great skill.
Posthumously awarded. Medal presented to widow, Mrs. John W. Ruckman.

RUFFNER, ERNEST L.
R—Buffalo, N. Y.
B—Fort Leavenworth, Kans.
G. O. No. 59, W. D., 1919.

Colonel, Medical Corps, U. S. Army.
He served as surgeon of the intermediate section, Services of Supply, having under his supervision 39 base hospital units. He performed his strenuous and exacting duties in an unusually efficient manner, displaying rare judgment and professional attainments of the first order.

RUGGLES, COLDEN L'H.
R—Poughkeepsie, N. Y.
B—Omaha, Nebr.
G. O. No. 73, W. D., 1919.

Brigadier general, U. S. Army.
The conception and construction of the Aberdeen Proving Ground and its operation during the early and most difficult period of its history are a monument to his sagacity and unremitting labor.

RUGGLES, FRANCIS A.
R—Washington, D. C.
B—St. Paul, Minn.
G. O. No. 49, W. D., 1922.

Colonel, Field Artillery, U. S. Army.
As a battalion commander during the Aisne-Marne offensive, July 18-25, 1918, and as a regimental commander during the St. Mihiel offensive, Sept. 13-19, 1918, and the Meuse-Argonne offensive, Sept. 30, 1918, to Nov. 8, 1918. In all of these offensives he displayed conspicuous efficiency, marked aggressiveness, and unusual leadership. By his exceptional technical and executive ability he solved with sound judgment many perplexing problems, and although much handicapped by severe losses in men, matériel, and animals he at all times so commanded his regiment as to render invaluable support to the attacking Infantry, thus materially adding to the success of the operations of the 1st Division.

RULON, BLANCHE S.
  R—Pittsburgh, Pa.
  B—Waretown, N. J.
  G. O. No. 9, W. D., 1923.

Captain, Army Nurse Corps, U. S. Army.
As chief nurse of Base Hospital No. 27, at Angers, France, during the World War, and later as assistant to the director of the Nursing Service, American Expeditionary Forces, at Tours, France, she displayed qualities of leadership and organizing ability of the highest order. Through her skillful management and untiring energy she developed the nursing force at Base Hospital No. 27 to a high degree of proficiency and was of material assistance in establishing and maintaining a reputation for unusual efficiency for that hospital, which had the unique distinction of caring for the largest numer of patients of any single hospital at any one time in the American Expeditionary Forces. Upon her return to the United States she had charge of the claim department of the Army Nurse Corps in the office of the Surgeon General, and the efficiency, sound judgment, and knowledge of the principles involved displayed by her in that capacity made a signal contribution to the demobilization work of the Government.

RUMBOLD, FRANK M.
  R—St. Louis, Mo.
  B—Meeker Grove, Wis.
  G. O. No. 56, W. D., 1922.

Colonel, Field Artillery, U. S. Army.
As assistant to the chief, Militia Bureau, during the inception of the World War, in which office of great responsibility his genius and ability were applied to the organizing, training, and expansion of the National Guard, the success of which was due, in a large measure, to his zeal, devotion to duty, and unquestionable competency, For his marked ability in the organizing, training and disciplining of the 128th Field Artillery Regiment, 35th Division, the successful functioning of which unit during the war may be attributed in large part to Colonel Rumbold's indefatigable efforts. For his untiring and successful efforts throughout his entire service to secure close cooperation between the National Guard and the Regular Army in order that these two elements for the national defense might function successfully as the Army of the United States.

RUSSEL, EDGAR.
  R—Kingston, Mo.
  B—Pleasant Hill, Mo.
  G. O. No. 12, W. D., 1919.

Brigadier general, U. S. Army.
As Chief Signal Officer, American Expeditionary Forces, he has shown great ability in the organization and administration of his department and the results attained are largely due to his zeal and energy. The Signal Corps in France stands out as one of the masterful accomplishments of the American Expeditionary Forces, and to General Russell is due the credit for its foundation and organization.

RUSSELL, EDMUND A.
  R—Lake Forest, Ill.
  B—Athens, N. Y.
  G. O. No. 124, W. D., 1919.

As chief of the Chicago Ordnance District, in which capacity he maintained at all times the greatest degree of intelligent and enthusiastic cooperation between the Ordnance Department and the manufacturers in his district, thereby attaining the maximum production of munitions in a minimum time; and also as chairman of the Chicago Ordnance District Claims Board, in which capacity his services have been invaluable to the Nation in adjusting equitably the $325,000,000 worth of outstanding contracts in his district in force at the signing of the armistice.

RUSSELL, FREDERICK F.
  R—Brooklyn, N. Y.
  B—Auburn, N. Y.
  G. O. No. 69, W. D., 1919.

Colonel, Medical Corps, U. S. Army.
He organized and directed the division of laboratories and infectious diseases of the Surgeon General's Office during the present war and thereby contributed in great measure to the efficiency of the military forces.

RUSSELL, GEORGE M.
  R—Plymouth, N. H.
  B—Plymouth, N. H.
  G. O. No. 103, W. D., 1919.

Colonel (Field Artillery), General Staff Corps, U. S. Army.
As assistant chief of staff, G-2, of the 5th Army Corps, he directed the activities of the intelligence section with marked skill and untiring energy. By effecting the collection and dissemination of timely and accurate information, he was an important factor in the successes achieved by his corps.

RYAN, LILLIAN J.
  R—Denver, Colo.
  B—Ireland.
  G. O. No. 9, W. D., 1923.

First lieutenant, Army Nurse Corps, U. S. Army.
As chief nurse of the base hospital at Camp Merritt, N. J., during the World War, she rendered signal service. By the display of excellent judgment, energy, and example under unusual difficulties she so directed her staff as to enable it to meet in an efficient manner all the demands made upon it, thus making a large contribution to the saving of lives. By her great organizing ability and untiring efforts she played an important part in the successful aftercare of thousands of tuberculous soldiers during the demobilization period.

RYAN, WILLIAM B.
  R—Greensburg, Pa.
  B—Fairfield, Vt.
  G. O. No. 103, W. D., 1919.

Lieutenant colonel, Corps of Engineers, U. S. Army.
In charge of the tonnage section of G-1, General Headquarters, he performed services of great value to the American Expeditionary Forces. Later, as supervisor of cargo and supplies at the port of Marseilles, by his zeal and energy he ovecame all obstacles and successfully accomplished his important task.

SAFFARRANS, GEORGE C.
  R—Paducah, Ky.
  B—Memphis, Tenn.
  G. O. No. 56, W. D., 1922.

Colonel, Infantry, U. S. Army.
As provost marshal of the district of Paris from Jan. 3, 1918, to May 3, 1918, and subsequently in command of this important district during a period of grave import and charged with most important duties, he labored unceasingly and succeeded in attaining excellent results. Aided by his superior tact and keen perception, he performd his difficult duties with sound judgment and handled numerous diplomatic affairs with great satisfaction, thereby rendering important service to the American Expeditionary Forces in positions of great responsibility.

ST. JOHN, FORDYCE B.
R—Hackensack, N. J.
B—Hackensack, N. J.
G. O. No. 59, W. D., 1921.

Major, Medical Corps, U. S. Army.
As commanding officer of Mobile Hospital No. 2, at Coincy, France, from June to August, 1918, he commanded his hospital under most difficult and trying conditions with inadequate equipment and personnel. Later he served continuously at the front, taking a most active part in the Medical Service of our military efforts. Due to his unusual organizing ability and his indomitable will, his unit was always close to the firing line.

SALMON, THOMAS W.
R—West New Brighton, N. Y.
B—Lansingburg, N. Y.
G. O. No. 87, W. D., 1919.

Colonel, Medical Corps, U. S. Army.
He has, by his constant, tireless, and conscientious work, as well as by his unusual judgment, done much to conserve man power for active front-line work. Of special value was his demonstration that war neurosis could be treated in advanced sanitary units with greater success than in base hospitals.

SALTZMAN, CHARLES MCK.
R—Des Moines, Iowa.
B—Panora, Iowa.
G. O. No. 47, W. D., 1919.

Colonel, Signal Corps, U. S. Army.
While assigned to duty in the Air Service he voluntarily undertook and successfully accomplished the difficult task, in the face of many obstacles, of preparing an organization for the procurement and supply of Signal Corps equipment for the Army.

SAMPLE, WILLIAM R.
R—Fort Smith, Ark.
B—Memphis, Tenn.
G. O. No. 39, W. D., 1920.

Brigadier general, U. S. Army.
In command of the advance section, Services of Supply, throughout the campaigns in France in 1918, by his skillful management of the supply of the Army, involving many emergency orders to be promptly met, he showed himself to be, under those difficult conditions, an officer of great ability and resource.

SANBORN, JOSEPH B.
R—Chicago, Ill.
B—Manchester, N. H.
G. O. No. 89, W. D., 1919.
Distinguished-service cross also awarded.

Colonel, Infantry, U. S. Army.
He commanded the 131st Infantry, 33d Division, during all its campaigns against the enemy, displaying military leadership of a high order. His unremitting zeal and tactical skill were largely responsible for the success of his regiment in combat.

SANDS, ALFRED L. P.
R—Pittsburgh, Pa.
B—Pittsburgh, Pa.
G. O. No. 56, W. D., 1922.

Colonel, Field Artillery, U. S. Army.
Serving in turn as a battalion and regimental commander, he rendered exceptionally efficient services, and at all times was conspicuous for his courage, leadership, and high military attainments. As commanding officer of the 7th Field Artillery, 1st Division, and a group of attached French Artillery at Cantigny, in May, 1918, and later at Soissons in July, 1918, he displayed unusual ability, and by his high professional attainments and great tactical skill supported the Infantry, to which he was attached, so effectively that he aided materially in the successful operations of that brigade in those important engagements. Later, by his tireless energy, great resourcefulness, and efficiency, he organized and trained, in a highly satisfactory manner, the 67th Field Artillery.

SAUNDERS, EDWIN O.
R—Sharpsburg, Ky.
B—Sharpsburg, Ky.
G. O. No. 49, W. D., 1922.

Lieutenant colonel, Judge Advocate General's Department, U. S. Army.
As chief of the criminal investigation division of the Provost Marshal General's Department, American Expeditionary Forces, he had charge of and was responsible for the investigation of crime and bringing to trial of criminals. His remarkable skill as an organizer, his untiring efforts, and his sound judgment were mainly responsible for the reduction and prevention of crime in the American Expeditionary Forces, and the recovery of thousands of dollars of Government and private property. His services were of very great value to the American Expeditionary Forces.

SCHELLING, ERNEST H.
R—Bar Harbor, Me.
B—Belvidere, N. J.
G. O. No. 14, W. D., 1923.

Major, Infantry, U. S. Army.
While serving as assistant military attaché at the American Legation in Switzerland from September, 1917, to October, 1919, his great tact, initiative, resourcefulness, sound judgment and unremitting devotion to duty contributed markedly to the successful operations of the American and Allied forces during the World War.

SCHLEY, JULIAN L.
R—Savannah, Ga.
B—Savannah, Ga.
G. O. No. 4, W. D., 1923.

Colonel, Corps of Engineers, U S. Army.
As commanding officer of the 307th Engineers and division engineer officer, 82d Division, and later as corps engineer, 5th Army Corps, during the St. Mihiel and Meuse-Argonne offensives, he displayed excellent qualities of leadership and command while serving with his regiment in the battle line, as well as superior technical attainments as an engineer, together with great zeal and devotion to duty. By the high degree of efficiency with which he performed his manifold duties, he contributed materially to the success of the operations of the commands with which he served. Later, as Director of Purchase, in the Purchase, Storage, and Traffic Division of the General Staff, and as a member of the War Department Claims Board, by his good judgment and keen foresight in undertakings of great difficulty and magnitude he rendered conspicuous service.

SCHMITT, WILLIAM J.
R—St. Paul, Minn.
B—St. Paul, Minn.
G. O. No. 19, W. D., 1921.

Second lieutenant, Quartermaster Corps, U. S. Army.
While serving in the regulating stations at Creil, Noisy-le-Sec, St. Dizier, and Metz, France, he showed untiring application in his devotion to duty. He remained continually on duty during nightly bombardments at Creil, performing ably the important tasks assigned to him. During the battle of Chateau-Thierry and during the St. Mihiel and Argonne-Meuse offensives by his energetic action he aided materially in the maintenance of a steady flow of supplies to the troops at the front, at all times showing marked ability and initiative when faced with difficult problems of transportation arising from the evacuation of the wounded. He rendered valuable service to the Government.

764 DECORATIONS, U. S. ARMY, 1862–1926

SCHOEFFEL, FRANCIS H
R—Rochester, N. Y.
B—Rochester, N. Y
G. O. No. 14, W. D., 1923.

Lieutenant colonel, Inspector General's Department, U. S. Army.
As inspector general, port of embarkation, Hoboken, N. J., from Aug. 1, 19 to Apr. 1, 1919, he was charged with inspection of troops, troop transports a trains, money accounts of disbursing officers, and duties of a similar natu all of which he performed in a highly efficient and successful manner. W untiring energy, sound judgment, and unusual professional skill and w unremitting attention and devotion to duty he rendered extremely valua services to the Government in a position of great responsibility.

SCHULL, HERMAN W
R—Watertown, S. Dak.
B—England.
G. O. No. 9, W. D., 1923.

Colonel, Ordnance Department, U. S. Army.
As assistant chief and acting chief of the inspection division, Ordnance Depa ment. His broad-minded policy, zeal, and technical ability contributed a conspicuous way to the success of the Ordnance Department in the procu ment of munitions in the United States and Canada during the World Wa

SCHULTZ, THEODORE
R—St. Louis, Mo.
B—Orville, Ohio.
G. O. No. 10, W. D., 1924.

Captain, 9th Cavalry U. S. Army.
At Naco, Ariz., Oct. 9–10, 1914, he commanded the most important and m exposed outposts of the American troops engaged in preserving order on international boundary line. Although his troops were constantly expo to fire from Mexican attacking forces, by his firmness, tact, and courage actions he handled in a highly efficient manner a threatening situation, the by preventing serious international complications and contributing materia to the preservation of law and order on the Mexican border.

SCHULZ, JOHN W. N
R—Wheeling, W. Va.
B—Wheeling, W. Va.
G. O. No. 56, W. D., 1922.

Colonel, Corps of Engineers, U. S. Army.
As representative of the Chemical Warfare Service at General Headquar he rendered valuable services in the solution of many important proble relating to the offensive use of gas and also in planning more effective meth for the issue of equipment and for training in gas warfare. Later, as c gas officer of the 1st Army, he was charged with the entire responsibilit the gas warfare in that army during the St. Mihiel and Meuse-Argonne of sives. By great ability and untiring energy, his efforts resulted in the prev tion of large numbers of casualties and fatalities from enemy gases as wel increasing the use of gas against the enemy, thereby contributing to the suc of the American arms.

SCOTT, ERNEST D
R—De Witt, Nebr.
B—Canada.
G. O. No. 15, W. D., 1923.

Colonel, Field Artillery, U. S. Army.
He commanded the American and allied light artillery in the Toul sector p to and after its occupation by the 1st Division, and was largely responsible the instruction and training of the 66th Field Artillery Brigade and of briga of Coast Artillery in their training areas. As Heavy Artillery comman 1st Army Corps, in the Champagne-Marne and the Aisne-Marne operati and as brigade and grouping commander of the 66th Field Artillery Brig and numerous French units in the operations of the 5th Army Corps in St. Mihiel offensive, and in the operations of the Army artillery in the Me Argonne offensive, he performed his duties with great efficiency and dist tion.

SCOTT, FRANK A
R—West Mentor, Ohio.
B—Cleveland, Ohio.
G. O. No. 69, W. D., 1919.

In assisting in organizing and as chairman of the munitions standards board the general munitions board. He was later first chairman of the War In tries Board. He thus contributed greatly in developing the War Dep ment's programs.

SCOTT, HUGH L
R—Princeton, N. J.
B—Danville, Ky.
G. O. No. 47, W. D., 1919.

Major general, U. S. Army.
As Chief of Staff in advocating and persistently urging the adoption of selective service law and as Commanding General, Camp Dix, N. J organizing and training the divisions and miscellaneous troops committe his care during the war.

SCOTT, WALTER DILL
R—Evanston, Ill.
B—Cookesville, Ill.
G. O. No. 69, W. D., 1919.

Colonel, U. S. Army.
In originating, organizing, and putting into operation the system of classi tion of enlisted personnel now used in the United States Army.

SCOTT, WALTER J
R—Mount Morris, Ill.
B—Brownsville, Tenn.
G. O. No. 9, W. D., 1923.

Lieutenant colonel (Cavalry), General Staff Corps, U. S. Army.
As assistant chief of staff, G-1, 89th Division, due to his unusual fores indefatigable efforts, and great executive ability, he was able to keep a stant flow of supplies and ammunition for the troops under extremely dif combat conditions, thereby contributing materially to the success of the sion and the American Expeditionary Forces.

SCOWDEN, FRANK F
R—Albany, N. Y.
B—Meadville, Pa.
G. O. No. 14, W. D., 1923.

Lieutenant colonel, Motor Transport Corps, U. S. Army.
As executive officer in the office of the director, Motor Transport Corps, Ai can Expeditionary Forces, he discharged with rare distinction duties of g responsibility. His sound judgment, tact, administrative and tech ability contributed in a marked degree to the successful functioning o Motor Transport Corps of the American Expeditionary Forces.

SCREWS, WILLIAM P
R—Montgomery, Ala.
B—Montgomery, Ala.
G. O. No. 19, W. D., 1920.

Colonel, Infantry, U. S. Army.
He commanded, with courage, resourcefulness, and great skill the 167th I try, 42d Division, from the time of its organization and early training thro out the successive phases of sector warfare, offensive combat in the batt the Champagne and Ourcq, and in the St. Mihiel and Meuse-Argonne o sives. By his high military attainments, sound judgment, and devoti duty he has contributed, in no small degree, to the successes achieved b 42d Division.

DISTINGUISHED-SERVICE MEDAL

SEAMAN, A. OWEN
   R—Greenville, Ill.
   B—Greenville, Ill.
   G. O. No. 77, W. D., 1919.

Colonel, Infantry, U. S. Army.
In the very efficient operation of the Motor Transport Corps, War Department General Staff, and in accomplishing the standardization of motor vehicles in the Army.

SEAMAN, GILBERT E.
   R—Milwaukee, Wis.
   B—Alpena, Mich.
   G. O. No. 116, W. D., 1919.

Colonel, Medical Corps, U. S. Army.
After serving with conspicuous success as division surgeon of the 32d Division, he became chief surgeon, 6th Army Corps, and in this capacity was an important factor in the establishment of effective measures for treating numerous sick and wounded. Fitted for his exacting duties by wide experience and unusual ability, he rendered services of great value to the American Expeditionary Forces.

SEWELL, JOHN S.
   R—Gantts Quarry, Ala.
   B—Butlers Landing, Tenn.
   G. O. No. 59, W. D., 1919.

Colonel, Corps of Engineers, U. S. Army.
In command of a regiment of Engineers and later as commander of the base port at St. Nazaire he displayed high engineering skill and long practical experience in the management of men. His genius together with his great energy and devotion to duty, contributed largely to the successful development and efficient operation of that base.

SHALLENBERGER, MARTIN C.
   R—Alma, Nebr.
   B—Osceola, Nebr.
   G. O. No. 89, W. D., 1919.

Lieutenant colonel (Infantry), General Staff Corps, U. S. Army.
As assistant chief of staff, G-1, of the 3d Army Corps, during the Argonne-Meuse offensive, by his tireless efforts, marked organizing ability, and keen application to his numerous duties, he contributed in a large measure to the successes attained by his corps, rendering valuable services to the American Expeditionary Forces.

SHANKS, DAVID C.
   R—Salem, Va.
   B—Salem, Va.
   G. O. No. 18, W. D., 1919.

Major general, U. S. Army.
For services in the administration of the port of embarkation, Hoboken, N. J., in connection with the shipment of troops overseas.

SHANNON, EDWARD C.
   R—Columbia, Pa.
   B—Phoenixville, Pa.
   G. O. No. 10, W. D., 1920.

Colonel, Infantry, U. S. Army.
As commanding officer of the 111th Infantry, 28th Division, he proved himself a forceful and capable military leader. Maintaining at all times a high degree of efficiency in his regiment, he contributed materially to the successes achieved by the 28th Division in its operations against the enemy, rendering services of distinction to the American Expeditionary Forces.

SHARP, GEORGE A. (1623188)
   R—Breckenridge, Colo.
   B—Victor, Colo.
   G. O. No. 88, W. D., 1918.

Sergeant, Company A, 115th Engineers, 40th Division, U. S. Army.
For his bravery in entering a dangerous surf at Ocean Beach, Calif., on May 5, 1918, and rescuing three men and assisting in the rescue of Corporal Stein, Company B, 115th Engineers, at the risk of his own life.

SHAUGHNESSY, EDWARD H.
   R—Chicago, Ill.
   B—Chicago, Ill.
   G. O. No. 95, W. D., 1919.

Lieutenant colonel, Transportation Corps, U. S. Army.
Serving successively as general superintendent, general manager, and acting deputy director general of transportation, by his energy, zeal, and able management he rendered services of the highest type to the Transportation Corps of the American Expeditionary Forces. In the performance of his manifold duties he constantly displayed marked enthusiasm, originality, and sound judgment.

SHAW, ANNA HOWARD
   R—Moylan, Pa.
   B—England.
   G. O. No. 69, W. D., 1919.

As chairman of the woman's committee of the Council of National Defense, she coordinated the mobilization and organization of women throughout the country in every phase of war work, including the securing of women for some of the various branches of the Army.

SHAW, HENRY A.
   R—Worcester, Mass.
   B—Salem, Mass.
   G. O. No. 56, W. D., 1921.

Colonel, Medical Corps, U. S. Army.
As surgeon of Base Section No. 2, Services of Supply, a position of great responsibility. Due to his ability and energy, he brought the medical service of the port of Bordeaux and the hospitalization of the same to a high degree of efficiency. He has rendered services of much value.

SHEARMAN, LAWRENCE H.
   R—Roslyn, N. Y.
   B—Washington, D. C.
   G. O. No. 46, W. D., 1919.

Member of American Inter-Allied Maritime Council.
As civilian member of the 1st Section of the General Staff, American Expeditionary Forces, he placed his mature experience and his extensive technical and business knowledge of the shipping industry at the disposal of the American Expeditionary Forces during a period of several months when tonnage and shipping problems were of the most vital importance. His clear vision, sound advice, and unfailing energy and loyalty were of the greatest value to his country and to the allied cause.

SHEDD, WILLIAM E., Jr.
   R—Danville, Ill.
   B—Danville, Ill.
   G. O. No. 56, W. D., 1922.

Colonel, Coast Artillery Corps, U. S. Army.
He served with marked efficiency as instructor and then as director of the Heavy Artillery School in France. As assistant in the office of the Chief of Artillery, American Expeditionary Forces, and later chief of the Heavy Artillery section in that office, he rendered services of inestimable value in connection with the organization, equipment, and training of the Heavy Artillery troops in France.

SHEEHAN, MARY E.
   R—Syracuse, N. Y.
   B—Cortland County, N. Y.
   G. O. No. 9, W. D., 1923.

First lieutenant, Army Nurse Corps, U. S. Army.
As chief nurse of the Vichy Hospital Center, France, during the World War, she organized the nursing service of that center, and by her tact, good judgment, energy, and personal devotion to duty contributed largely to the successful care and well-being of 11,000 sick and wounded.

SHEEN, HENRY H R—Norfolk, Va. B—Quincy, Mass. G. O. No. 56, W. D., 1922. Distinguished-service cross also awarded.	Colonel, Infantry, U. S. Army. As quartermaster, 39th Division, from September, 1917, until October, 19 and acting chief of staff, same division, from October until December, 19 he rendered highly meritorious services. As chief quartermaster, int mediate section, Services of Supply, he displayed sound judgment in 1 disposal of property valued at many millions of dollars. Later, as ch quartermaster and acting chief of staff, G-4, American Forces in Germai he displayed marked ability and initiative in many large undertakings a perplexing problems confronting him, resulting in immense savings to 1 Government.
SHELBY, EVAN R—Washington, D. C. B—Fayette County, Ky. G. O. No. 89, W. D., 1919.	Colonel, Quartermaster Corps, U. S. Army. As chief of the contracts branch of the Office of the Chief of Construction Di sion, in following up contracts, aiding in their interpretation, adjust: differences between the contractors and the Government, and advising matters of procedure and the rights of the parties involved, he has display sound judgment, marked professional attainments, and extraordini capacity for sustained and unremitting labor.
*SHELTON, GEORGE H R—Seymour, Conn. B—Seymour, Conn. G. O. No. 53, W. D., 1921.	Brigadier general, U. S. Army. While commanding the 51st Infantry Brigade, 26th Division, during the Mihiel and Meuse-Argonne offensives. Posthumously awarded. Medal presented to widow, Mrs. Bernice Sheltor.
SHELTON, NENA R—Kansas City, Mo. B—Lexington, Ky. G. O. No. 9, W. D., 1923.	First lieutenant, Army Nurse Corps, U. S. Army. As assistant to the director of nursing service, American Expeditionary For in Paris, France, during the World War, she contributed largely to the succ of that force of over 10,000 nurses. Her zeal, good judgment, and ene added greatly to the efficiency with which the sick and wounded of American Expeditionary Forces were cared for. Her faithfulness to de and unfailing devotion to duty greatly facilitated the work of the Med Department.
SHEPARD, JOHN L R—Galesburg, Ill. B—Sheboygan, Wis. G. O. No. 15, W. D., 1921.	Colonel, Medical Corps, U. S. Army. In 1918, as surgeon of Camp Funston, Kans., and of the 89th Division, he played high administrative, technical, and constructive ability in prevent measures adopted against epidemics and in the conservation of phys defects by their segregation and development. Later he performed consp ous services in connection with hospital demobilization in France and return to the United States of the sick and wounded.
SHEPHERD, WILLIAM E., Jr R—New York, N. Y. B—New York, N. Y. G. O. No. 87, W. D., 1919.	Lieutenant colonel, Field Artillery, U. S. Army. As assistant chief of staff, 3d Section, of the 5th Army Corps, and as chie staff of Artillery of that corps, by his marked military attainments and de tion to his exacting duties, he ably planned the employment of the Corp Artilley in its operations against the enemy, rendering services of great wc to the American Expeditionary Forces.
SHERMAN, WILLIAM C R—Augusta, Ga. B—Augusta, Ga. G. O. No. 56, W. D., 1922.	Lieutenant colonel (Corps of Engineers), General Staff Corps, U. S. Army. As assistant chief of staff, G-2, 1st Division and 3d Army Corps, from Februa 1918, until October, 1918, he skillfully organized and directed the servic information of the enemy which guided in the preparation of the orders ur which his division and corps achieved their many victories. Later, as c of staff, Air Service, 1st Army, from November 1 to November 11, 1918 displayed great ability and by his rare tactical conceptions rendered ceptionally meritorious service, enabling the Air Service to function highly efficient manner at all times.
SHERRILL, CLARENCE O R—Raleigh, N. C. B—Newton, N. C. G. O. No. 53, W. D., 1921.	Colonel (Corps of Engineers), General Staff Corps, U. S. Army. He organized the 302d Engineers and conducted their operations with the ' Division until he became the division chief of staff. To his initial energy, and good judgment is due much of the success of the staff funct ing of the division in its operations in the Argonne. He has rendered s ices of marked worth.
SHINKLE, EDWARD M R—Higginsport, Ohio. B—Higginsport, Ohio. G. O. No. 16, W. D., 1923.	Colonel, Ordnance Department, U. S. Army. In charge of the ammunition section of the gun division, Ordnance Departm he was responsible for the design, development, and placing of orders and tracts for all ammunition and projectiles supplied to the American Ar Later, in charge of ammunition section, engineering division, in the offi Chief of Ordnance, his technical skill, executive ability, and sound judgr were highly important factors in the successful operations of the Ordn Department during the World War.
SHIPLEY, WALTER V R—Arlington, Md. B—Cockeysville, Md. G. O. No. 56, W. D., 1922.	Lieutenant colonel, Quatermaster Corps, U. S. Army. As quartermaster and assistant chief of staff, G-1, 29th Division, from J 1917, until June, 1919, by his untiring zeal, great energy, tact, and sc judgment he was able to overcome many difficult problems of supply an: sist to a marked degree in the operations of his division, thereby rende services of great value to the American Expeditionary Forces.
SHOCKLEY, M. A. W R—Fort Scott, Kans. B—Fort Scott, Kans. G. O. No. 87, W. D., 1919.	Colonel (Medical Corps), General Staff Corps, U. S. Army. As a member of the 5th Section, General Staff, he displayed sound judg: and administrative ability in organizing, supervising, and inspecting various sanitary schools and in conducting the sanitary training of tr: He also initiated and planned the preliminary organization of school instruction in civil educational subjects, established after the cessatic hostilities, rendering invaluable services to the American Expeditio Forces.

DISTINGUISHED-SERVICE MEDAL

SHORT, WALTER CAMPBELL
R—Columbus, Ohio.
B—Columbus, Ohio.
G. O. No. 70, W. D., 1919.

Colonel (Infantry), General Staff Corps, U. S. Army.
Attached to the Fifth Section, General Staff, General Headquarters, American Expeditionary Forces, he rendered conspicuous service in inspecting and reporting upon front-line conditions pertaining to the work of his section. During the St. Mihiel and Meuse-Argonne operations of the 1st Army Corps he efficiently directed the instruction and training of machine-gun units at every available opportunity during rest periods. Later, as assistant chief of staff, G–5, 3d Army, he manifested the same assiduous devotion to duty in organizing schools, conducting necessary inspections, and carrying out the intensive training program.

SHREEVE, HERBERT E
R—Wyoming, N. J.
B—England.
G. O. No. 59, W. D., 1919.

Lieutenant colonel, Signal Corps, U. S. Army.
As officer in charge of the Division of Research and Inspection of the Signal Corps, at Paris, he rendered exceptionally valuable service, resulting in marked improvement in the efficiency of Signal Corps equipment. By his exact scientific knowledge and inventive genius he assisted in solving problems arising both at the front and in the Services of Supply.

SHULER, GEORGE K
R—Lyons, N. Y.
B—Lyons, N. Y.
G. O. No. 59, W. D., 1919.

Major, U. S. Marine Corps.
In command of the 3d Battalion, 6th Regiment, U. S. Marine Corps, 2d Division, he displayed leadership of the highest order and marked tactical ability, resulting in the capture by his command of large numbers of prisoners and machine guns in the battles at Blanc Mont and St. Etienne, France. In the advance to the north from Sommerance he showed rare judgment in maneuvering his battalion in a difficult position, making important captures of field artillery. Fearless, aggressive, and able, he twice accomplished missions of vital importance with brilliant success.

SHUMAN, JOHN B
R—La Crosse, Wis.
B—Espey, Pa.
G. O. No. 3, W. D., 1922.

Colonel (Infantry), Adjutant General's Department, U. S. Army.
In The Adjutant General's Department during the war and the demobilization period, his unusual initiative and splendid judgment contributed in a large measure to the successful handling of the commissioned personnel of the Army. He rendered services of great worth.

SIBERT, WILLIAM L
R—Gadsden, Ala.
B—Gadsden, Ala.
G. O. No. 18, W. D., 1919.

Major General, U. S. Army.
For services in the organization and administration of the Chemical Warfare Service, contributory to the successful prosecution of the war.

*SIGERFOOS, EDWARD
R—Arcanum, Ohio.
B—Potsdam, Ohio.
G. O. No. 103, W. D., 1919.

Brigadier general, U. S. Army.
He organized the Army School of the Line at Langres, and as its commandant displayed unceasing energy and marked military and executive ability in directing its activities. Through the thorough instruction furnished by this school, he contributed materially to the combat efficiency of line troops, thereby rendering services of inestimable value to the American Expeditionary Forces.
Posthumously awarded. Medal presented to widow, Mrs. Edward Sigerfoos.

SILER, JOSEPH F
R—Opelika, Ala.
B—Orion, Ala.
G. O. No. 59, W. D., 1919.

Colonel, Medical Corps, U. S. Army.
He has been in charge of the laboratory service of the American Expeditionary Forces. Due to his untiring zeal and high professional attainments, he has been able to render invaluable service in the prevention of the spread of infectious disease among our troops. Under his able instructions, medical officers were sent out equipped to handle the new medical and surgical problems of war in a manner not believed possible before the present war.

SIMMONS, GEORGE H
R—Chicago, Ill.
B—England.
G. O. No. 3, W. D., 1922.

Major, Medical Section, Officers' Reserve Corps, U. S. Army.
By his thorough knowledge of the medical profession and by his great esteem therein, together with his whole-hearted devotion to his task, he rendered services of a signal worth in the procurement of physicians and surgeons for the Medical Corps of the Army and in his able advising of the War Department upon the qualifications of that great body of the medical profession who entered the Army.

SIMONDS, GEORGE S
R—Cresco, Iowa.
B—Cresco, Iowa.
G. O. No. 59, W. D., 1919.

Brigadier general, U. S. Army.
He served with marked distinction as chief of staff of the 2d Army Corps during the important operations along the Hindenburg line in the region of the Sambre Canal. His great administrative ability was shown in the excellent manner in which he handled a large force of American soldiers serving with the British.

SIMPSON, JOHN R
R—Newton, Mass.
B—Richmond, Ind.
G. O. No. 56, W. D., 1921.

Colonel, Ordnance Department, U. S. Army.
While on duty in the office of the Chief Ordnance Officer, American Expeditionary Forces, in connection with the requirements and procurement of ordnance supplies, by his accurate forecasting and energetic following up of deliveries, he secured an adequate and uninterrupted flow of ordnance material for the American Expeditionary Forces.

SIMPSON, WILLIAM H
R—Aledo, Tex.
B—Weatherford, Tex.
G. O. No. 59, W. D., 1921.

Lieutenant colonel (Infantry), General Staff Corps, U. S. Army.
For services as assistant chief of staff, 33d Division, during the Meuse-Argonne offensive and later as chief of staff of this division.

SINGLETON, ASA L
R—Fort Valley, Ga.
B—Taylor County, Ga.
G. O. No. 126, W. D., 1919.

Colonel (Infantry), General Staff Corps, U. S. Army.
As chief of staff of Base Section No. 5 he displayed exceptional administrative ability. The excellent results obtained in evacuating over 700,000 men through the port of Brest are due in no small measure to the efficient organization created by him. He has rendered services of signal worth to the American Expeditionary Forces.

SINGLETON, MARVIN E
    R—St. Louis, Mo.
    B—Waxahachie, Tex.
    G. O. No. 124, W. D., 1919.

As chief of the St. Louis Ordnance District, in which capacity he maintained at all times the greatest degree of intelligent and enthusiastic cooperation between the Ordnance Department and manufacturers in his district, thereby attaining the maximum production of munitions in a minimum time and also as chairman of the St. Louis Ordnance District Claims Board, which capacity his services have been invaluable to the Nation in adjusting equitably the $122,000,000 worth of outstanding contracts in his district force at the signing of the armistice.

SINNOTT, CATHERINE G
    R—Nashville, Tenn.
    B—Middletown, Conn.
    G. O. No. 9, W. D., 1923.

Second lieutenant, Army Nurse Corps, U. S. Army.
As chief nurse of Camp Hospital No. 28, France, during the World War, th nurse exhibited marked efficiency and administrative ability. Later, chief nurse of the Nurses' Concentration Camp at Savenay, France, s managed the affairs of nearly a thousand nurses with exceptional tact, indu try, and good judgment. She performed the unusual duties assigned to h in a way not only to facilitate greatly the embarkation of nurses, but to mai tain a high state of morale and efficient organization among them. S rendered a conspicuously worthy service to the American Expeditiona Forces. Her splendid leadership, tireless energy, and unselfish devotion duty were an inspiration to all who came in contact with her.

SKINNER, GEORGE A
    R—St. Paul, Minn.
    B—Osage, Iowa.
    G. O. No. 38, W. D., 1922.

Colonel, Medical Corps, U. S. Army.
Colonel Skinner organized and commanded a hospital center of 20,000 beds Mars, France. Due to his great force and ability, a hospital group w prepared for the care of the sick and wounded during the St. Mihiel a Meuse-Argonne offensives, when the need of hospital beds was critical. Th adequate and efficient hospitalization contributed materially to the conser tion of man power and to the subsequent success of our forces.

SLADE, GEORGE T
    R—St. Paul, Minn.
    B—New York, N. Y.
    G. O. No. 50, W. D., 1919.

Colonel, Transportation Corps, U. S. Army.
He served with marked distinction as deputy director general of transportatio first with the French ministry and later with the railroad department in t zone of the services of supply. Due to his tactful negotiations and zealo efforts, the Transportation Department secured efficient cooperation w the French railroads and was enabled to meet the tremendous demands i posed upon it by the rapid advance of our armies during the Argonne-Me battles.

SLADEN, FRED W
    R—Omaha, Nebr.
    B—Lowell, Mass.
    G. O. No. 59, W. D., 1919.
    Distinguished-service cross also awarded.

Brigadier general, U. S. Army.
While commanding the 5th Infantry Brigade, 3d Division, in the Battle the Marne in July and in the Argonne operations in France, in Octob 1918, he demonstrated conspicuous qualities of ability and leadership. T successes that attended the operations of his brigade were influenced grea by his energy, skill, and courage as a commander.

SLAUGHTER, NUGENT H
    R—Washington, D. C.
    B—Danville, Va.
    G. O. No. 69, W. D., 1919.

Lieutenant colonel, Signal Corps, U. S. Army.
For services in the very successful development of the radio equipment of United States Army.

SLAVENS, THOMAS H
    R—Urbana, Mo.
    B—Portland Mills, Ind.
    G. O. No. 53, W. D., 1921.

Colonel, Infantry, U. S. Army.
As commander of the New York depot from July, 1917, to March, 1918, which he demonstrated superb energy and marked executive ability i position of great responsibility. Later, as commanding officer of the Infantry, 6th Division, from October, 1918, he showed marked ability in training of the regiment and during its operations in the Meuse-Argonne.

*SLIFER, HIRAM J
    R—Chicago, Ill.
    B—Montgomery County, Pa.
    G. O. No. 59, W. D., 1919.

Lieutenant colonel, Corps of Engineers, U. S. Army.
He was charged with active field operations and the construction and operat of the light railways of the 1st Army during the St. Mihiel and Argo Meuse offensives. His efforts were unceasing, and, due to his resourceful and exceptional executive ability, he was an important factor in the succ ful operations of the light railways, assuring for the troops of the 1st Arm steady flow of munitions and supplies.
Posthumously awarded. Medal presented to widow, Mrs. Hiram J. Sl

SLOCUM, STEPHEN L'H
    R—New York, N. Y.
    B—Cincinnati, Ohio.
    G. O. No. 124, W. D., 1919.

Lieutenant colonel, U. S. Army.
For services while serving as military attaché at London, England.

SMALLEY, HENRY R
    R—Chicago, Ill.
    B—Chicago, Ill.
    G. O. No. 56, W. D., 1922.

Major, Cavalry, U. S. Army.
As adjutant and operations officer of the 5th Infantry Brigade of the 3d Divi during its occupation of the Chateau-Thierry defensive sector, and du the Champagne-Marne defensive, the Aisne-Marne, St. Mihiel, and Me Argonne offensives, by his military knowledge, devotion to duty, excel judgment, and unhesitating assumption of responsibility he rendered inv able services and materially assisted in the success attained by the brigad its operations.

SMITH, EMERY T
    R—San Francisco, Calif.
    B—Virginia City, Nev.
    G. O. No. 56, W. D., 1922.

Colonel, Field Artillery, U. S. Army.
As commander of the group of Artillery supporting the 33d Division in attack on the east bank of the Meuse River, Oct. 8 to 13, 1918, he den strated professional attainments and ability of a high order. Later, regimental commader, by his sound tactical judgment and special knowl of Artillery, he most successfully directed his units in the support of attacking Infantry of the 79th Division in the operations north of Ver from Nov. 4 to 11, 1918. By keeping his elements close to the attacl Infantry he contributed in no small measure to the success of these op tions. He rendered services of conspicuous merit and signal worth to American Expeditionary Forces in a position of great responsibility.

SMITH, ERNEST G.
R—Wilkes-Barre, Pa.
B—Martins Ferry, Ohio.
G. O. No. 59, W. D., 1919.

Lieutenant colonel, Infantry, U. S. Army.
As chief of the casualty section, central records office, he performed with marked efficiency duties of a most exacting character. With untiring efforts, sound analytical ability, and masterful attention to detail he handled questions pertaining to casualties in the American Expeditionary Forces with noteworthy success.

SMITH, HARRY A.
R—Atchison, Kans.
B—Atchison, Kans.
G. O. No. 12, W. D., 1919.

Brigadier general, U. S. Army.
He rendered most conspicuous service as commandant of the Army schools at Langres, France, the success of which was, in a large measure, due to his vision, zeal, and administrative ability. He later showed marked executive ability as officer in charge of the administration of civil affairs in the German territory occupied by the American Army.

SMITH, LOWELL H.
R—Rockwell Field, Calif.
B—Santa Barbara, Calif.
G. O. No. 14, W. D., 1925.
Act of Congress Feb. 25, 1925.

Captain, Air Service, U. S. Army.
Lieutenant Smith, as pilot of the Airplane No. 2, the *Chicago*, and later when placed in command of the United States Army Air Service around-the-world flight from Apr. 6, 1924, to Sept. 28, 1924, displayed untiring energy, courage, and resourcefulness during the entire period that the Air Service expedition was upon its hazardous undertaking. His leadership, sound judgment, and tenacity of purpose were material factors in the success of this pioneer flight of airplanes around the world. In the performance of his great task he brought to himself and to the military forces of the United States the signal honor of an achievement which is a testimonial to American thoroughness, courage, and resourcefulness.

SMITH, PERRIN L.
R—Minneapolis, Minn.
B—Henry, Ill.
G. O. No. 105, W. D., 1919.

Colonel, Quartermaster Corps, U. S. Army.
To his great administrative ability, initiative, and tireless energy is due in great measure the very successful practical application of the regulations governing the payment of allotments made by officers and enlisted men, the handling of the various Liberty bond issues subscribed for through the Army allotment system, and other important financial matters connected with the Army during the emergency.

SMITH, WILLIAM R.
R—Nashville, Tenn.
B—Nashville, Tenn.
G. O. No. 2, W. D. 1920.

Brigadier general, U. S. Army.
As commanding general, 36th Division, by his thorough and ceaseless efforts, coupled with a keen insight into the principles of military training, he brought his division to such a high standard of discipline and proficiency as to achieve conspicuous results in a major operation without previous service under fire. The excellent conduct of his division subsequent to the signing of the armistice reflects great credit on him. His services have been of great value to the American Expeditionary Forces.

SMITH, WINFORD HENRY.
R—Baltimore, Md.
B—Scarboro, Me.
G. O. No. 3, W. D., 1922.

Colonel, Medical Corps, U. S. Army.
For services as a specialist in hospital management and construction.

SMITH, WRIGHT.
R—Holly Oak, Del.
B—New York, N. Y.
G. O. No. 95, W. D., 1919.

Colonel, Field Artillery, U. S. Army.
As commander of the 13th Field Artillery, 4th Division, he proved himself an artillerist of extraordinary skill and ability. Due to his energy and determination, he overcame seemingly insurmountable obstacles, keeping his regiment at all times on the alert in order to take its positions promptly, and rendered most effective support to the advancing Infantry units.

SMITHER, HENRY C.
R—Denver, Colo.
B—Indian Territory.
G. O. No. 50, W. D., 1919.

Colonel (Signal Corps), General Staff Corps, U. S. Army.
As assistant chief of staff, in charge of the supply section, of the General Staff of the Services of Supply, he demonstrated by his energy, zeal, and masterful efforts a high order of efficiency and ability. He organized the supply section and handled without friction the questions of priority and troop orders during the period of the arrival of American troops in France. With a rare gift of tact and address, he discharged most successfully his many important duties.

SNOW, WILLIAM J.
R—Rivervale, N. J.
B—Brooklyn, N. Y.
G. O. No. 18, W. D., 1919.

Major general, U. S. Army.
For services in planning and executing those measures responsible for the efficiency of the Field Artillery during the war.

SNYDER, FREDERIC A.
R—Williamsport, Pa.
B—Williamsport, Pa.
G. O. No. 87, W. D., 1919.

Colonel, Corps of Engineers, U. S. Army.
As division engineer officer of the 28th Division during its participation in the Aisne-Marne and the Meuse-Argonne offensives, he solved numerous and difficult problems with marked ability. By his tireless energy in the construction and maintenance of transportation routes and defensive positions he contributed in no small degree to the successes of the combat troops.

SNYDER, JOHN JACOB.
R—New Oxford, Pa.
B—Two Taverns, Pa.
G. O. No. 116, W. D., 1919.

Commander, Medical Corps, U. S. Navy.
As force medical officer, his untiring energy and close cooperation with the Army authorities contributed greatly to the successful outcome of our oversea operations.

SOLBERT, OSCAR N.
R—Worcester, Mass.
B—Sweden.
G. O. No. 124, W. D., 1919.

Colonel, Corps of Engineers, U. S. Army.
For services while serving as military attaché at Copenhagen, Denmark.

SOMERVELL, BREHON B.
R—Little Rock, Ark.
B—Little Rock, Ark.
G. O. No. 14, W. D., 1923.
Distinguished-service cross also awarded.

Lieutenant colonel, Corps of Engineers, U. S. Army.
As adjutant, 15th Engineers, during the period of organization and training; in charge of construction of the Mehun ammunition depot; in charge of the construction at Is-sur-Tille depot, including the gas depot at Poinson and the Etain engine terminal; assistant chief of staff, G-3, and assistant chief of staff, G-1, 89th Division, from October, 1918, until the division returned to the United States, when he was assigned as assistant chief of staff, G-4, 3d Army. In all these positions he displayed unusual vision, initiative, sound judgment, and high professional skill, contributing in a conspicuous way to the successful operations of the American forces in France.

SPALDING, GEORGE R.
R—Monroe, Mich.
B—Monroe, Mich.
G. O. No. 59, W. D., 1919.

Colonel, Corps of Engineers, U. S. Army.
He served with marked distinction as commanding officer of the 305th Engineers, 80th Division, as division engineer of the 80th Division, as chief engineer of the 5th Army Corps, and as chief engineer of the 1st and 3d Armies. At all times he exhibited professional attainments of the highest order in handling the difficult problems with which he was confronted.

SPAULDING, OLIVER L., Jr.
R—St. Johns, Mich.
B—St. Johns, Mich.
G. O. No. 19, W. D., 1920.

Lieutenant colonel, Field Artillery, U. S. Army.
As assistant commandant, School of Fire for Field Artillery, Fort Sill, Okla., from December, 1917, to May, 1918. His constructive and administrative ability was of great value in the remarkable and successful expansion of that school to meet the war requirements of the Field Artillery. In especial, his work in connection with the coordination and development of the course of instruction contributed materially to the excellence of the Field Artillery education received by thousands of officers.

SPEAKS, CHARLES E.
R—Akron, Ohio.
B—Washington, D. C.
G. O. No. 16, W. D., 1923.

Lieutenant colonel, Motor Transport Corps, U. S. Army.
He organized and operated with marked success the division for the procurement of motor transport supplies in the office of the director, Motor Transport Corps, American Expeditionary Forces, and by his intelligent application, wide experience, sound judgment, and devotion to duty successfully surmounted great difficulties in providing adequate motor transportation for the American Expeditionary Forces.

SPEAR, RAY.
R—Spokane, Wash.
B—Illinois.
G. O. No. 116, W. D., 1919.

Captain, Supply Corps, U. S. Navy.
As force supply officer, the efficient performance of which duties contributed greatly to the successful provisioning of ships engaged in the transportation of troops and supplies overseas.

SPENCE, CARY F.
R—Knoxville, Tenn.
B—Knoxville, Tenn.
G. O. No. 19, W. D., 1920.

Colonel, Infantry, U. S. Army.
He commanded with marked distinction the 117th Infantry, 30th Division, from the time of its organization and early training period to the completion of the active combat operations in the Ypres-Lys and Somme offensives. He especially distinguished himself while in command of his regiment on Oct. 8-9, 1918, when he advanced his line 2½ miles, capturing several towns, numerous cannon, and many prisoners.

SPENCER, EUGENE J.
R—Webster Groves, Mo.
B—St. Louis, Mo.
G. O. No. 13, W. D., 1923.

Colonel, Corps of Engineers, U. S. Army.
As colonel, 32d Engineers, he constructed, in large part, the storage camp at St. Sulpice, Bordeaux, the receiving barracks of Genicourt, the new port at Talmont, the munitions depot at St. Loubes, France. As chief engineer of Base Section No. 2, Bordeaux, France, his duties included the construction and maintenance of roads and buildings, supervision of forests and posts. His high professional skill, unremitting energy, and devotion to duty contributed markedly to the success of the American Expeditionary Forces.

SPINKS, MARCELLUS G.
R—Meridian, Miss.
B—Meridian, Miss.
G. O. No. 59, W. D., 1919.

Brigadier general, U. S. Army.
By his untiring efforts, zeal, and marked military efficiency in the performance of duties of responsibility as senior assistant of the Inspector General's Department in France he has rendered services of exceptional value to the Government.

SPRUANCE, WILLIAM C., Jr.
R—Wilmington, Del.
B—Wilmington, Del.
G. O. No. 77, W. D., 1919.

Colonel, Ordnance Department, U. S. Army.
As chief of the powder section, production division, of the office of the Chief of Ordnance. Later as special assistant to the Chief of Ordnance in charge of chemicals, propellants, and explosives, and chief of the explosives, chemicals, and loading division, office of the Chief of Ordnance, in which capacities he successfully organized the industry of the country so as to yield at all times an ample supply of powder, not only for the needs of the U. S. Army, but to some extent for the needs of the cobelligerents against Germany.

SQUIER, GEORGE O.
R—Dryden, Mich.
B—Dryden, Mich.
G. O. No. 103, W. D., 1919.

Major general, U. S. Army.
As Chief Signal Officer he has demonstrated scientific attainments of the highest order. His researches and contributions to the scientific equipment of the Signal Corps are noteworthy. The Signal Corps under him has been an extremely progressive and efficient organization.

STACKPOLE, PIERPONT L.
R—Boston, Mass.
B—Brookline, Mass.
G. O. No. 126, W. D., 1919.

Lieutenant colonel, Field Artillery, U. S. Army.
As aide-de-camp to Lieut. Gen. Hunter Liggett, U. S. Army, he rendered exceptional services during the entire time that the latter commanded the 1st Army Corps, the 1st Army, and the 3d Army. By his military attainments and pronounced ability he proved to be a most important factor in the successes of the corps and also of the armies.

STANBERY, SANFORD B.
R—California, Ohio.
B—Millersburg, Ohio.
G. O. No. 89, W. D., 1919.

Brigadier general, U. S. Army.
Having taken command of the 155th Infantry Brigade, 78th Division, prior to the attack of Nov. 1, he proved himself a forceful and capable military leader. With the tactical situation thoroughly in hand, by his zeal and good judgment he contributed to the brilliant results attained during the severe fighting in the advance toward Sedan in the final phase of the Meuse-Argonne offensive

STANLEY, DAVID S.
  R—Washington, D. C.
  B—Dakota Territory.
  G. O. No. 15, W. D., 1923.

Colonel, Quartermaster Corps, U. S. Army.
As chief quartermaster and chief of staff, Base Section No. 5, at Brest, France, by his great administrative ability, exceptional foresight, and tireless energy he handled numerous difficult problems of supply and transportation with unusual efficiency and success. In the performance of his great task he rendered services of conspicuous worth to the American Expeditionary Forces.

STANSFIELD, JAMES H.
  R—Oak Park, Ill.
  B—Bridgeport, Ill.
  G. O. No. 56, W. D., 1921.

Lieutenant colonel, 132d Infantry, 33d Division, U. S. Army.
In the Bois-de-Chaume during Oct. 9–11, 1918, when, due to his rare presence of mind and courage, he prevented the disorganization of units of regiments that had suffered heavy casualties. He personally reorganized scattered groups and caused them to hold a line which appeared untenable. He has rendered services of great value.

STANTON, CHARLES E.
  R—Salt Lake City, Utah.
  B—Monticello, Ill.
  G. O. No. 70, W. D., 1919.

Colonel, Quartermaster Corps, U. S. Army.
As chief disbursing officer in the office of the finance division, Quartermaster Corps, at Paris he performed his duties with unremitting zeal, displayed marked administrative ability and accurate judgment in solving problems of extraordinary difficulty, rendering services of marked worth.

STARBIRD, ALFRED A.
  R—South Paris, Me.
  B—South Paris, Me.
  G. O. No. 19, W. D., 1922.

Brigadier general, U. S. Army.
For services in connection with the planning, organization, and administration of the post and subposts of Brest, Base Section No. 5, thereby contributing in a very great measure to the successful operation of this base during the return of the American Expeditionary Forces.

STARK, ALEXANDER N.
  R—Norfolk, Va.
  B—Norfolk, Va.
  G. O. No. 59, W. D., 1919.

Colonel, Medical Corps, U. S. Army.
He served as chief surgeon of the 1st Army during all its offensives, charged with the organization and direction of the Medical Service, involving the treatment and evacuation of many thousands of sick and wounded under most adverse conditions. In this important capacity he performed his duties with marked ability. With good judgment, furthered by high professional attainments and tireless energy, he solved the difficult problems which arose, prevented much suffering, and saved the lives of many among the American and French wounded soldiers.

STARR, WILLIAM T.
  R—New York, N. Y.
  B—Indianapolis, Ind.
  G. O. No. 59, W. D., 1921.

Lieutenant colonel, Military Police Corps, U. S. Army.
In the organization of the Provost Marshal General's Department, American Expeditionary Forces, from Nov. 18, 1917, to Feb. 1, 1919, in which capacity he displayed marked qualities of zeal and efficiency that were of great benefit to the American Expeditionary Forces.

STAYTON, WILLIAM H., jr.
  R—Washington, D. C.
  B—New York, N. Y.
  G. O. No. 14, W. D., 1923.

Major, Adjutant General's Department, U. S. Army.
With rare vision, sound judgment, and signal ability, he organized and operated the office charged with the responsibility for the circulation of officers, soldiers, and civilians of the American Expeditionary Forces in France, and of the officers of the allied forces in the zones occupied by the American armies, maintaining active contact with British and French authorities and with the American military police throughout France with reference to such circulation. By his tact and initiative, without American precedent, he handled these activities with the utmost efficiency. Later, in charge of the appointment and promotion section of The Adjutant General's Office, American Expeditionary Forces, he displayed unusual executive and administrative ability. His services were of immeasurable value to the Government.

STEARNS, CUTHBERT P.
  R—Denver, Colo.
  B—Elizabeth, N. J.
  G. O. No. 14, W. D., 1923.

Lieutenant colonel, Air Service, U. S. Army.
As chief of staff, spruce production division, Bureau of Aircraft Production, by his loyal devotion to duty, tact, industry, and resourcefulness, he handled with conspicuous success all the military problems of organizing the division and distributing the troops and supplies, an operation which involved constant and intimate relations with 150,000 civilian lumbermen and over 500 lumber mills, extending over an extensive territory. He rendered services of great value to the Government in a position of great responsibility.

STEBBINS, HORACE C.
  R—New York, N. Y.
  B—Boston, Mass.
  G. O. No. 87, W. D., 1919.

Lieutenant colonel (Infantry), General Staff Corps, U. S. Army.
As assistant chief of staff, G–2, 3d Army Corps, he performed his important duties with merited ability and zeal. Through his efficient administration of the section, complete and timely intelligence of the enemy was promptly disseminated through the combatant troops, which aided materially in the successes of his corps.

STEESE, JAMES G.
  R—Harrisburg, Pa.
  B—Mount Holly Springs, Pa.
  G. O. No. 47, W. D., 1919.

Colonel, Corps of Engineers, U. S. Army.
As assistant to the Chief of Engineers and in charge of the personnel, equipment, construction, and maps division of the office of the Chief of Engineers, he displayed exceptional ability in handling commissioned personnel matters and developed special apparatus and methods for the production of aerial navigation maps. Since September, 1918, the solution of the many difficult problems in the organization and operation of the personnel branch, General Staff, has been due largely to his special knowledge of personnel matters, his untiring zeal, good judgment, and exceptional administrative ability.

STEPHENS, JOHN E.
  R—Brentwood, Tenn.
  B—Brentwood, Tenn.
  G. O. No. 56, W. D., 1922.

Brigadier general, U. S. Army.
As chief of the war plans branch of the war plans division of the General Staff from Oct. 4, 1917, to June 13, 1918, he was directly responsible for the preparation of plans for the organization of units of the Army and all special branches thereof. In this capacity he rendered most conspicuous services in a brilliant manner. By his keen foresight, great breadth of vision, and tireless energy he carried to successful completion the various plans and problems which confronted him. Later, as commander of the 61st Field Artillery Brigade, 36th Division, he again demonstrated these high professional attainments and splendid leadership, which at all times characterized his service.

STERNBERGER, HENRY S. R—New York, N. Y. B—New York, N. Y. G. O. No. 38, W. D., 1922.	Lieutenant colonel, Quartermaster Corps, U. S. Army. While serving as quartermaster of his division throughout the entire period of its operations in Belgium and France, by his untiring zeal, great energy, tact, and sound judgment he was able to overcome many difficult problems of supply, thereby rendering services of great value to the American Expeditionary Forces.
STETTINIUS, EDWARD R. R—New York, N. Y. B—St. Louis, Mo. G. O. No. 25, W. D., 1919.	Who, as director general of purchases for the War Department, Second Assistant Secretary of War, and special representative in France of the Secretary of War in connection with the procurement of munitions for the American Expeditionary Forces, rendered conspicuous services. His broad vision and splendid judgment have been of the greatest value to the success of the military program.
STEVENS, JOHN F. R—New York, N. Y. B—West Gardiner, Me. G. O. No. 95, W. D., 1919.	As head of the Railway Advisory Commission to Russia and special adviser of the Russian Ministry of Ways of Communication. In the midst of revolutionary conditions he has pursued his undertaking to rehabilitate Russia by the restoration of railway traffic. In a distant country, far from immediate support, he has maintained an unflagging devotion to duty which is now beginning to show the valuable results of his labor.
STEWART, MERCH B. R—Glenn Falls, N. Y. B—Mitchell Station, Va. G. O. No. 49, W. D., 1922.	Brigadier general, U. S. Army. As senior instructor at the Plattsburg Training Camp from May until August, 1917, he displayed organizing and training ability and talents of the highest order in successfully directing the training and selection of 6,000 officer candidates, thereby rendering services of inestimable value to our newly formed forces. As chief of staff, 76th Division, from August, 1917, until June, 1918, he again showed tireless energy, practical resourcefulness, and military attainments of the highest order. Later, as commander of the 175th Infantry Brigade, 88th Division, he performed his duties with marked ability and excellent judgment.
STEWART, REDMOND C. R—Eccleston, Md. B—Baltimore County, Md. G. O. No. 56, W. D., 1922.	Major, Judge Advocate General's Department, U. S. Army. He served with the 1st Division as division judge advocate throughout the entire hostilities. At all times, by his high-minded sense of duty, his personal example of energy, loyalty, and courage, he was a powerful and consistent influence for promoting the morale, harmony, spirit, and the high standards of the 1st Division. His superior professional attainments and his loyal devotion to duty contributed materially to the success of his division and made him a conspicuous figure in a position of great responsibility.
STILWELL, JOSEPH W. R—Yonkers, N. Y. B—Palatka, Fla. G. O. No. 78, W. D., 1919.	Lieutenant colonel (Infantry), General Staff Corps, U. S. Army. As assistant chief of staff, G-2, 4th Army Corps, during the St. Mihiel offensive and later during the operations in the Woevre, he displayed military attainments of a high order. With great energy and zeal he pursued the developments of the enemy activities on the corps front, securing invaluable information which assisted in a marked degree in the planning of the operations. He contributed by the excellent performance of his task to the success of these operations.
STIMSON, JULIA C. R—St. Louis, Mo. B—Worcester, Mass. G. O. No. 70, W. D., 1919.	Chief nurse, Army Nurse Corps, U. S. Army. As chief nurse of Base Hospital No. 21 she displayed marked organizing and administering ability while that unit was on active service with the British forces. Her devotion to duty was exceptional while she was chief nurse of the American Red Cross in France. Upon her appointment as director of nursing service of the American Expeditionary Forces, she performed exacting duties with conspicuous energy and achieved brilliant results. Thousands of sick and wounded were cared for properly through the efficient service she provided.
STIVERS, DANIEL G. R—Butte, Mont. B—Fort Davis, Tex. G. O. No. 56, W. D., 1921.	Lieutenant colonel, Quartermaster Corps, U. S. Army. As quartermaster of the 3d Division during the Aisne-Marne, St. Mihiel, and Meuse-Argonne offensives, in maintaining an excellent system of quartermaster supplies and utilities under the greatest difficulties of active service, his superb efforts contributed in a marked degree to the success of this division throughout its operations.
STOKES, MARCUS B. R—Early Branch, S. C. B—Colleton, S. C. G. O. No. 49, W. D., 1922.	Colonel, Infantry, U. S. Army. As commander of the 311th Infantry, 78th Division, during its organization, training, and in all of its operations, he handled all of his tasks with marked efficiency and in a manner that reflected great credit upon him. By his most careful and thorough preparations, sound judgment, skillful and energetic leadership, he contributed in a large measure to the successes achieved by his regiment against the enemy.
STONE, DAVID L. R—Greenville, Miss. B—Stoneville, Miss. G. O. No. 59, W. D., 1919.	Colonel (Quartermaster Corps), General Staff Corps, U. S. Army. As assistant chief of staff, G-1, 3d Division, as G-1 of that organization, and later as G-1, 2d Army, he performed with distinction his important duties. In the action from July 5 to Aug. 2, 1918, near Chateau-Thierry, and in the advance to the Ourcq River, he displayed tireless energy and ability of an unusually high order in supplying troops under most difficult conditions. Aggressive and resourceful, he proved equal to every emergency.
STONE, EDWARD R. R—Spencer, Mass. B—Spencer, Mass. G. O. No. 89, W. D., 1919. Distinguished-service cross also awarded.	Colonel, Infantry, U. S. Army. As second in command of the 9th Infantry, 2d Division, he participated with credit in the Aisne defensive, the operations in the Chateau-Thierry sector, and in the Aisne-Marne offensive. Subsequently, upon being placed in command of the 23d Infantry, 2d Division, he led it with marked ability in the St. Mihiel offensive, and by his skillful leadership was largely responsible for the successes gained by this regiment in the Battle of Blanc Mont Ridge and the Meuse-Argonne offensive.

DISTINGUISHED-SERVICE MEDAL 773

*Straight, Willard D.
  R—New York, N. Y.
  B—Oswego, N. Y.
  G. O. No. 50, W. D., 1919.

Major, Adjutant General's Department, U. S. Army.
In the service of the organization, development, and administration of the War Risk Bureau his efforts resulted in marked efficiency in the handling of the large volume of insurance, as well as the numerous applications for allotments and allowances which covered almost the entire personnel of the American Expeditionary Forces. As an assistant in the first section of the general staff of the 1st Army he rendered particularly valuable services to the Government by his great energy and high ability.
Posthumously awarded. Medal presented to widow, Mrs. Donley Straight.

Strong, George V.
  R—Helena, Mont.
  B—Chicago, Ill.
  G. O. No. 38, W. D., 1922.

Lieutenant colonel (Judge Advocate General's Department), General Staff Corps, U. S. Army.
While on staff duty with Headquarters, 4th Army Corps and Headquarters, 2d Army, American Expeditionary Forces, he was in charge of all troop movements preparatory to the St. Mihiel attack and immediately following this attack, and was also in charge of all troop movements from the 4th Army Corps in the Toul sector to the Argonne front. By his tireless energy, keen foresight, and sound judgment he perfected the multifarious duties whereby all of these movements were carried to successful completion. During this period his services were conspicuously efficient and contributed materially to the success of these operations.

Strong, Richard P.
  R—Cambridge, Mass.
  B—Fortress Monroe, Va.
  G. O. No. 70, W. D., 1919.

Lieutenant colonel, Medical Corps, U. S. Army.
Possessed of the highest professional qualifications and actuated by zealous devotion to duty, he has rendered services of inestimable value to the American Expeditionary Forces, notably as president of a board appointed to investigate the cause of trench fever, a disease which had caused serious losses to the effectives of the allied armies. The scientific research of this board under his skillful direction led to the discovery of the means by which trench fever is transmitted and in the establishment of effective measures for its prevention.

Sultan, Daniel I.
  R—Oxford, Miss.
  B—Oxford, Miss.
  G. O. No. 56, W. D., 1922.

Colonel (Corps of Engineers), General Staff Corps, U. S. Army.
As chief of the personnel section in the office of the executive assistant to the Chief of Staff of the Army during the war and the demobilization, he formulated policies covering commissioned personnel and handled with marked ability many complex questions of grave importance to the War Department and to the entire Army. His work was characterized by conspicuous breadth of vision and keen foresight. His splendid judgment and the sound policies initiated by him contributed in a large measure to the successful handling of the commissioned personnel of the Army. He rendered service of signal worth to the Government in a position of great responsibility.

Summerall, Charles P.
  R—Astatula, Fla.
  B—Lake City, Fla.
  G. O. No. 12, W. D., 1919.
  Distinguished-service cross also awarded.

Major general, U. S. Army.
He commanded in turn a brigade of the 1st Division in the operations near Montdidier, the 1st Division during the Soissons and St. Mihiel offensives and in the early battles of the Argonne-Meuse advance, and the 5th Army Corps in the later battles of this advance. In all of these important duties his calm courage, his clear judgment, and his soldierly character had a marked influence in the attainment of the successes of his commands.

Summers, Leland L.
  R—Whitestone, N. Y.
  B—Cleves, Ohio.
  G. O. No. 15, W. D., 1923.

Technical advisor, War Industries Board.
In connection with the operations of the War Industries Board during the World War, as a member of the board he rendered through his broad vision, distinguished capacity, and business ability, services of inestimable value in marshaling the industrial forces of the Nation and mobilizing its economic resources—marked factors in assisting to make military success attainable. As technical advisor of the board and later as representative on the interallied munitions board he rendered, through his untiring efforts and devotion to duty, exceptionally valuable service to the War Department in connection with the procurement and supply of explosives for the Army.

*Sumner, Edwin Vose, Jr.
  R—Milton, Mass.
  B—Fort Niobrara, Nebr.
  G. O. No. 62, W. D., 1919.

Lieutenant colonel, Air Service, U. S. Army.
As commanding officer of the Air Service production and assembly center at Romorantin, he displayed peculiar administrative ability in coordinating the work of the many different elements at the largest Air Service project in the American Expeditionary Forces. The satisfactory results obtained at Romorantin were due largely to his tireless energy and skill in supervising and directing its operation. His example established a spirit of teamwork and accomplishment which were most marked.
Posthumously awarded. Medal presented to widow, Mrs. Edwin V. Sumner.

Sunderland, Archibald H.
  R—Delavan, Ill.
  B—Delavan, Ill.
  G. O. No. 47, W. D., 1919.

Brigadier general, U. S. Army.
As commandant of the Coast Artillery School and in the reorganization and administration of that institution, he thereby enabled it to meet effectively the demands made upon it for training candidates for commissions in the Coast Artillery Corps.

Sweeney, Walter C.
  R—Wheeling, W. Va.
  B—Wheeling, W. Va.
  G. O. No. 59, W. D., 1919.

Colonel (Infantry), General Staff Corps, U. S. Army.
As chief of staff of the 28th Division he rendered conspicuously valuable services in the Argonne-Meuse offensive. In the capture of the strong enemy positions at le Chene Tondu, Apremont, Chatel-Chehery, and Hill No. 244, by his marked ability and tactical knowledge he proved a material factor in the successes achieved during these important operations.

SWEET, ETHEL E. (now Mrs. THEODORE FALCONER).
R—Canada.
B—Detroit, Mich.
G. O. No. 9, W. D., 1923.

Chief nurse, Army Nurse Corps, U. S. Army.
As chief nurse of the nurses' mobilization stations in New York City, she contributed largely to the rapid and successful embarkation of over 10,000 nurses for overseas duty during the World War. She displayed exceptional zeal, foresight, and good judgment in organizing the separate staffs of this large group of nurses, and by her efficiency, industry, and tact made possible the transfer to Europe of this large contingent of women, an unusual and difficult feat performed under the most trying and perplexing conditions.

SWOPE, GERARD.
R—New Brunswick, N. J.
B—St. Louis, Mo.
G. O. No. 10, W. D., 1920.

Assistant to the Director of Purchase, Storage, and Traffic, War Department.
As one of the principal advisers and assistants to the Director of Purchase, Storage and Traffic he accomplished the task of working out the detailed plan for bringing under one head the direction and supervision of procurement, storage, and issue of all commodities and articles of equipment and supply needed for the Army. It was due to his foresight, ability, energy, and loyal cooperation that the procurement program for the great Army of 1918 was successfully planned, and he assisted materially in carrying it into effect, thereby contributing directly to the success of the military program.

SYMMONDS, CHARLES J.
R—Kenosha, Wis.
B—Holland, Mich.
G. O. No. 59, W. D., 1919.

Colonel, Cavalry, U. S. Army.
He commanded for many months the important intermediate storage depot at Gievres. He successfully administered a large personnel and supervised the growth of Gievres as a storage depot. He organized the system of supply from that station so efficiently that there were no shortages, either of food or material, at the regulating stations dependent upon Gievres for supply during all the active operations.

TAYLOR, BRAINERD.
R—Newtonville, Mass.
B—Malden, Mass.
G. O. No. 89, W. D., 1919.

Colonel, Motor Transport Corps, U. S. Army.
Serving as chief motor transport officer of the advance section, S. O. S., he gave proof of excellent judgment and untiring energy in the performance of his duties. By his success in overcoming numerous obstacles involved in the transportation of supplies and troops, he rendered conspicuous services to the American Expeditionary Forces.

TAYLOR, HARRY.
R—Tilton, N. H.
B—Tilton, N. H.
G. O. No. 50, W. D, 1919.

Brigadier general, U S. Army.
Arriving in France June 11, 1917, as Chief Engineer, American Expeditionary Forces, he organized and administered the Engineer Department, which included the construction of wharves, depots, railways, barracks, and shelters throughout the theater of operations. He continued these duties with most marked and conspicuous ability, building a complete and efficiently functioning institution.

TAYLOR, JAMES D.
R—Lake City, Fla.
B—Lake City, Fla.
G. O. No. 108, W. D., 1919.

First lieutenant, Infantry, U. S. Army.
While commanding the station of Pantabangan, Luzon, P. I., in January, 1901, by his discretion and excellent judgment he obtained possession of the correspondence which made known the whereabouts of the insurgent chieftain, Aguinaldo, thus making possible the expedition resulting in his capture.

TEBBETTS, HARRY H.
R—Haverhill, Mass.
B—Great Falls, N. H.
G. O. No. 53, W. D., 1921.

Colonel (Infantry), General Staff Corps, U. S. Army
As assistant chief of staff, G-1, of the Services of Supply, he demonstrated marked energy and executive ability in the management of troop evacuation from France, and especially subsequent to the armistice in the repatriation of the American Expeditionary Forces, when several hundred thousand men were returned to the United States each month. He has rendered services of great value.

TEFFT, William H.
R—Belmont, N. Y.
B—Belmont, N. Y.
G. O. No. 103, W. D., 1919.

Colonel, Medical Corps, U. S. Army.
As commanding officer of Evacuation Hospital No. 7 at Chateau Montomglaust, he performed his exacting duties with unflagging energy and marked executive ability. Overcoming grave difficulties due to inadequate personnel and equipment, he succeeded in receiving, treating, and evacuating a large number of wounded from the Marne offensive with notable success, thereby rendering services of the utmost value to the American Expeditionary Forces.

TENNEY, CHARLES H.
R—Longmeadow, Mass.
B—Everett, Mass.
G. O. No. 9, W. D., 1923.

Colonel, Ordnance Department, U. S. Army.
First as chief of the financial and accounting divisions of the Ordnance Department, in which position he was charged with effecting the disbursement of all ordnance funds and with accounting for all ordnance property; next as special representative of the Chief of Ordnance to coordinate the financial and accounting operations of the Ordnance Department in the United States with those in France; and finally, as chairman and organizer of the ordnance salvage board, in which capacity he was charged with the duty of perfecting the organization and outlining the procedure of that board and with reviewing its recommendations with respect to the disposition of great quantities of surplus stores. He performed all his duties with zeal, sound judgment, and exceptional ability, thereby rendering services of great value to the Government.

TERRELL, JOHN P.
R—Yonkers, N. Y.
B—Yonkers, N. Y.
G. O. No. 56, W. D., 1922.

Colonel (Coast Artillery Corps), General Staff Corps, U. S. Army.
As assistant G-4, and later as G-4, 2d Army Corps, from July, 1918, to January, 1919, he displayed exceptional ability in the administration of that division of the corps staff. During the operations which broke the Hindenburg line between Cambrai and St. Quentin his great energy and able handling of matters of supply and transportation for the organizations of the corps contributed in a marked degree to the success of the operations.

THAYER, WILLIAM S.
    R—Baltimore, Md.
    B—Milton, Mass.
    G. O. No. 50, W. D., 1919.

Brigadier general, U. S. Army.
As chief consultant in medicine of the American Expeditionary Forces, with untiring zeal he devoted his time, energy, and high professional talents in promoting the organization of eminent medical officers for the prosecution of efficient treatment among the sick and wounded of the American Expeditionary Forces. Largely through his individual efforts, the treatment of the sick was so standardized, coordinated, and proficiently perfected as to result in a direct saving of many lives and a consequent conservation of man power and morale of these forces.

THELEN, MAX.
    R—Berkeley, Calif.
    B—Rising City, Nebr.
    G. O. No. 10, W. D., 1920.

Assistant to the Director of Purchase, Storage and Traffic, War Department.
As chief of the purchase branch of the Purchase, Storage, and Traffic Division he was responsible for the initiation of the purchase policy and the supervision of all contracts. His constructive ability and exceptional foresight are responsible for the results attained in the settlement of war contracts.

THOMAS, JOHN R., Jr.
    R—Chicago, Ill.
    B—Metropolis, Ill.
    G. O. No. 59, W. D., 1919.

Colonel (Infantry), General Staff Corps, U. S. Army.
As chief of the aviation division of the Intelligence Section, he displayed unusual energy and skill in the collection and dissemination of information regarding the enemy's air forces. During part of the period covered by the Argonne-Meuse offensive operations he acted as head of the Intelligence Section and performed the duties of that position with marked ability and sound judgment.

THOMPSON, CHARLES F.
    R—Jamestown, N. Dak.
    B—Jamestown, N. Dak.
    G. O. No. 59, W. D., 1919.

Lieutenant colonel (Infantry), General Staff Corps, U. S. Army.
As assistant chief of staff, G-2, of the 1st Army he aided in its organization by his skill and sound judgment, participating in the preliminary preparations and operations at the St. Mihiel salient. The successes achieved by his section are largely due to his high military attainments, his great energy, and painstaking devotion to duty. He served with equal ability as G-2 of the 2d Army in September, 1918, at all times showing great skill and accomplishing results of exceptional value.

THOMPSON, DORA E.
    R—Cold Spring, N. Y.
    B—New York, N. Y.
    G. O. No. 108, W. D., 1919.

Superintendent, Army Nurse Corps, U. S. Army.
To her accuracy, good judgment, and untiring devotion to duty is due the splendid management of the Army Nurse Corps during the emergency.

THOMPSON, JOHN T.
    R—Newport, Ky.
    B—Newport, Ky.
    G. O. No. 34, W. D., 1919.

Colonel, Ordnance Department, U. S. Army.
As chief of the small arms division of the office of the Chief of Ordnance, in which capacity he was charged with the design and production of all small arms and ammunition thereby supplied to the United States Army, which results he achieved with such signal success that serviceable rifles and ample ammunition therefor were at all times available for all troops ready to receive and use them.

THOMPSON, MELVILLE WITHINGTON
    R—Spy Rock, N. Y.
    B—Washington, D. C.
    G. O. No. 14, W. D., 1920.

Lieutenant colonel, Air Service, U. S. Army.
As governor of the War Credits Board, he was untiring in his efforts, and his good judgment in solving the many complex questions confronting the board added materially to the proper discharge of its many responsibilities.

THORNE, ROBERT J.
    R—Lake Forest, Ill.
    B—Chicago, Ill.
    G. O. No. 18, W. D., 1919.

Assistant to Acting Quartermaster General, U. S. Army.
For services in the reorganization of the service of supply, thereby enabling the heavy demands due to an increased Army to be met.

TILLMAN, SAMUEL E.
    R—Shelbyville, Tenn.
    B—Shelbyville, Tenn.
    G. O. No. 77, W. D., 1919.

Brigadier general, U. S. Army.
For services as superintendent, U. S. Military Academy, during the period of the emergency.

TINLEY, MATHEW A.
    R—Council Bluffs, Iowa.
    B—Council Bluffs, Iowa.
    G. O. No. 78, W. D., 1919.

Colonel, Infantry, U. S. Army.
He displayed exceptional qualities of leadership in command of the 168th Infantry, 42d Division, which under his able leadership fulfilled every mission assigned to it. He was untiring in energy and devotion to his important duties, acting with sound judgment and initiative in times of emergency. His conduct was an inspiration to the men of his command, whom he led repeatedly in successful engagements.

TOBIN, WILLIAM H.
    R—San Francisco, Calif.
    B—Middleboro, Mass.
    G. O. No. 19, W. D., 1920.

Colonel, Coast Artillery Corps, U. S. Army.
As commander of the Army Artillery Park of the 1st Army, American Expeditionary Forces, by his broad grasp of the problems of ammunition supply he contributed in a marked degree to the solution of this most difficult problem and also to the success of the artillery of the 1st Army during the St. Mihiel and Meuse-Argonne offensives.

TOD, ROBERT E.
    R—New York, N. Y.
    B—Scotland.
    G. O. No. 49, W. D., 1922.

Commander, U. S. Navy, port officer, and later utilities officer at Base Section No. 5, Brest, France.
For conspicuously successful and cooperative industry in matters essential to the handling of transports and cargo ships of the United States; for the exercising of well-balanced business judgment in dealing with emergencies and for untiring and self-sacrificing effort to the end that ships be speedily turned around; for his subordination of all personal consideration in time of stress and for his helpfulness in all that concerned army troops, thereby rendering most conspicuous services to the American Expeditionary Forces in a position of great responsibility.

TODD, HENRY D., Jr R—Philadelphia, Pa. B—Clauverick, N. Y. G. O. No. 24, W. D., 1920.	Brigadier general, U. S. Army. As commanding general of the 58th Field Artillery Brigade, 33d Division, demonstrated marked skill as an artillery officer in the preparations for attack of the 5th Corps on the Kriemhilde Stellung on Nov. 1, 1918, and in support of the 89th Division in its further advance and crossing of the Me River from Nov. 6 to 11, 1918. The brigade which he commanded effectiv supported the 1st, 91st, 32d, and 89th Divisions, during the period of operations in which it served with them. His services have been of particu value to the American Expeditionary Forces.
TOLMAN, EDGAR B R—Chicago, Ill. B—British India. G. O. No. 56, W. D., 1922.	Major, Infantry, U. S. Army. As executive officer in charge of the selective draft in Illinois, by his unus executive ability, rare tact and skill, great initiative and resourcefuln exercised at times under most trying and novel conditions which arose connection with the administration of the selective service act, he achie a pronounced and conspicuous success in the performance of difficult highly responsible duties, thereby rendering services of great value to Government.
TOMPKINS, FRANK R—Governors Island, N. Y. B—Washington, D. C. G. O. No. 96, W. D., 1918.	Major, 13th Cavalry, U. S. Army. At Columbus, N. Mex., Mar. 9, 1916, having requested and received autho to pursue a superior force of bandits into Mexico, carried on, after be wounded, a running fight with said bandits for several miles, inflicting he losses upon the bandits and only stopping the pursuit when men and ho were exhausted and ammunition reduced to a few rounds per man.
TOOMBS, LOUIS A R—Meridian, Miss. B—Pickens, Miss. G. O. No. 59, W. D., 1921.	Lieutenant colonel, Adjutant General's Department, U. S. Army. As provost marshal in Italy, a position of great responsibility, during critical situation arising from the decision of the peace conference on the Fiu question, by the means of good judgment and tact, he so managed the situa as to prevent all friction between the American Expeditionary Forces and Italian populace. Due to his efficiency the military police of Italy were to a high state of military training and discipline. He has rendered servic much value.
TOULMIN, HARRY A., Jr R—Dayton, Ohio. B—Springfield, Ohio. G. O. No. 38, W. D., 1922.	Lieutenant colonel, Air Service, U. S. Army. As head of the coordination section of the staff of the Chief of Air Serv American Expeditionary Forces, he was charged with the responsibility outlining and developing an organization to handle the many and gr problems of administration, mobilization, supply, and armament. In performance of this duty he displayed rare intelligence, great initiative, br vision, and an ability to obtain results, thus contributing materially to success of the American Expeditionary Forces.
TOWNSHEND, ORVAL P R—Shawneetown, Ill. B—Shawneetown, Ill. G. O. No. 11, W. D., 1921.	Lieutenant colonel, Infantry, U. S. Army. For services in connection with the mobilization, organization, and trainir Porto Rico's quota of troops in the World War.
TRACY, EVARTS R—Plainfield, N. J. B—New York, N. Y. G. O. No. 3, W. D., 1922.	Major, Corps of Engineers, U. S. Army. As the pioneer camouflage officer in the United States Army, by his mar ability he ably assisted in recruiting and organizing personnel for this im tant work and in preparing lists of equipment and necessary material for carrying out of this enterprise. He served as chief instructor in camoufla at the Army Engineer School at Langres from its organization until Aug 1918. To him is due the success in developing a school course and a fiel hibit that disseminated important knowledge among a large number of combat personnel of the American Expeditionary Forces.
TRACY, JOSEPH P R—Monroeton, Pa. B—Washington, D. C. G. O. No. 133, W. D., 1919.	Colonel, Coast Artillery Corps, U. S. Army. While in charge of the enlisted division of The Adjutant General's Office du the war, in which capacity his sound judgment and administrative ab were conspicuous.
TREAT, CHARLES G R—Monroe, Mich. B—Dexter, Me. G. O. No. 55, W. D., 1920.	Brigadier general, U. S. Army. As chief of the American military mission to Italy and commanding Section No. 8, by his untiring devotion to duty, loyalty, and zeal, he formed his intricate duties with marked ability and sound judgment. his cheerfulness and sound diplomatic ability he furthered those co relations which existed between the American and Italian troops, and wa important factor in maintaining the morale at a high state of efficiency du the trying days prior to the armistice.
TRIPP, GUY E R—Washington, D. C. B—Wells, Me. G. O. No. 25, W. D., 1919.	Brigadier general, U. S. Army. Who, as chief of the production division of the Ordnance Department, later as Assistant Chief of Ordnance, displayed fine technical ability broad judgment in systematizing methods and practices resulting in efficient cooperation of industries producing articles of ordnance for the A
TRIPPE, HARRY M R—Whitewater, Wis. B—Whitewater, Wis. G. O. No. 56, W. D., 1921.	Lieutenant colonel, Corps of Engineers, U. S. Army. As commanding officer of the 308th Engineers, 83d Division, a position of responsibility, much of the engineering success in facilitating the pro and supply of the 3d Army Corps during the Meuse-Argonne operation is to his efforts and ability. He rendered important services to the Ur States.

DISTINGUISHED-SERVICE MEDAL

TROTT, CLEMENT A
   R—Milwaukee, Wis.
   B—Milwaukee, Wis.
   G. O. No. 59, W. D., 1919.

Colonel (Infantry) General Staff Corps, U. S. Army.
As chief of staff of the 5th Division, through his intimate knowledge of staff duties and the requirements of troops of the line he organized a staff which insured efficient cooperation in combat. His ability was shown in sound tactical directions to his division, which insured successes in four offensive operations.

TROWBRIDGE, AUGUSTUS
   R—Princeton, N. J.
   B—New York, N. Y.
   G. O. No. 87, W. D., 1919.

Lieutenant colonel, General Staff Corps, U. S. Army.
As supervisor of the technique of flash and sound ranging, by his complete scientific knowledge and keen devotion to his important duties he rendered services of great value. Due to his good judgment and painstaking energy suitable personnel was selected and properly trained in the efficient operation of the flash and sound ranging service of the American Expeditionary Forces.

TRUESDELL, KARL
   R—Washington, D. C.
   B—Moorhead, Minn.
   G. O. No. 103, W. D., 1919.

Lieutenant colonel, Signal Corps, U. S. Army.
As signal officer of the 1st Division and the 5th Army Corps he displayed high professional attainments and unflagging zeal. By his skill in directing the construction and maintenance of extensive telephone and wireless systems he contributed materially to the success of combat operations.

TURCK, RAYMOND C
   R—Jacksonville, Fla.
   B—Gratiot County, Mich.
   G. O. No. 19, W. D., 1922.

Lieutenant colonel, Medical Corps, U. S. Army.
As division surgeon, 35th Division, during the Meuse-Argonne offensive, Colonel Turck organized the medical service of that division and provided hospitalization and evacuation facilities for the sick and wounded under conditions which rendered the service of the Medical Department unusually hazardous and difficult.

TURNBULL, SAMUEL J
   R—Monticello, Fla.
   B—Monticello, Fla.
   G. O. No. 103, W. D., 1919.

Major, Medical Corps, U. S. Army.
As commanding officer of Evacuation Hospital No. 9, he performed his exacting duties with notable success. Overcoming numerous obstacles, by his keen foresight and administrative ability he was instrumental in securing the prompt evacuation and effective treatment of a large number of sick and wounded.

TUTTLE, ARNOLD D
   R—Highland Falls, N. Y.
   B—Sturgis, S. Dak.
   G. O. No. 59, W. D., 1919.

Colonel (Medical Corps), General Staff Corps, U. S. Army.
In his capacity as assistant to the chief surgeon, and later as a member of the General Staff, American Expeditionary Forces, he supervised the preparation of hospitalization plans and their execution and assisted in the evacuation of sick and wounded from the battle fields in such manner as to greatly increase the efficiency of his department.

TWACHTMAN, JOHN ALDEN
   R—Greenwich, Conn.
   B—Cincinnati, Ohio.
   G. O. No. 9, W. D., 1923.

Colonel, Field Artillery, U S. Army.
As battalion and later regimental commander, 103d Field Artillery, 26th Division, in the Aisne-Marne, St. Mihiel, and Meuse-Argonne offensives, he was conspicuous for his courage, marked ability, and leadership qualities. At all times he displayed superior tactical judgment and knowledge of artillery, and by his devotion to duty, great resourcefulness, and high military attainments he rendered the maximum support to the Infantry to which he was attached, thereby contributing in a large measure to their successes.

TWELVETREE, HERBERT J
   R—Cleveland, Ohio.
   B—Cleveland, Ohio.
   G. O. No. 13, W. D., 1923.

Lieutenant colonel (Infantry), General Staff Corps, U. S. Army.
As assistant chief of staff, G-1, 37th Division, throughout its operations in France, he displayed unusual ability, leadership, resourcefulness, and high technical skill, thus contributing in a material way to the successful operations of his division.

TYDINGS, MILLARD E
   R—Havre de Grace, Md.
   B—Havre de Grace, Md.
   G. O. No. 16, W. D., 1923.

Lieutenant colonel, Infantry, U. S. Army.
While commanding the 111th Machine Gun Battalion, 29th Division during the Meuse-Argonne operations, north of Verdun, Oct. 8 to 30, 1918, he distinguished himself by his energy, fearlessness, and high qualifications for the gravely responsible duties devolving upon him. The exceptionally effective use made by him of the weapons at his command rendered an advance possible against formidable hostile field works. His constant personal reconnaissance of frontline positions of the Infantry made possible an effective disposal of machine guns and artillery in the support of the efforts of the Infantry to advance and contributed in a large measure to the success of the brigade which his command was supporting.

TYLER, MAX CLAYTON
   R—Fargo, N. Dak.
   B—Fargo, N. Dak.
   G. O. No. 69, W. D., 1919.

Colonel, Corps of Engineers, U. S. Army.
As executive officer and military advisor to the Director General of Military Railways, he has displayed high professional attainments and given valuable assistance in procuring personnel and equipment for the railway service abroad.

TYNDALL, ROBERT H
   R—Indianapolis, Ind.
   B—Indianapolis, Ind.
   G. O. No. 13, W. D., 1923.

Colonel, Field Artillery, United States Army.
As commander, 150th Field Artillery, 42d Division, in the Baccarat, Champagne, Aisne-Marne, St. Mihiel, and Meuse-Argonne operations, part of which time he commanded one or more additional elements of the Artillery with which he was operating. His high technical attainments, his untiring energy and devotion to duty were important factors in the successful operations of the American Expeditionary Forces.

TYNER, GEORGE P
   R—Chicago, Ill.
   B—Davenport, Iowa.
   G. O. No. 59, W. D., 1919.

Colonel (Cavalry), General Staff Corps, U. S. Army.
He served first as assistant G-4 of the 1st Army and later as G-4 of the 2 Army. He rendered devoted, skillful, and efficient service in the supply of the 1st and 2d Armies during the St. Mihiel offensive in the Forest of Argonne and in the Woevre. His painstaking and tireless energy contributed materially to the success of these operations.

DECORATIONS, U. S. ARMY, 1862–1926

TYSON, LAWRENCE D R—Knoxville, Tenn. B—Greenville, N. C. G. O. No. 89, W. D., 1919.	Brigadier general, U. S. Army. He commanded with distinction the 59th Infantry Brigade, 30th Divisio throughout its training period and during its active operations against th enemy. His determination and skill as a military leader were reflected the successes of his brigade in the attack and capture of Brancourt an Premont, where a large number of prisoners and much material fell in our hands. He rendered services of great worth to the American Exped tionary Forces.
ULIO, JAMES A R—Fort Keogh, Mont. B—Fort Walla Walla, Wash. G. O. No. 89, W. D., 1919.	Lieutenant colonel, Infantry, U. S. Army. As assistant chief of staff, G–1, of the 4th Army Corps, he showed marke organizing and administrative ability. By his tireless efforts and ceasele energy he contributed in a large degree to the successes achieved by the 4t Army Corps in the Toul sector and in the battles of the St. Mihiel salien Later he handled with great success the evacuation and feeding of Frenc civilians in the occupied territory recovered from the enemy, rendering i valuable services to the American Expeditionary Forces.
UPHAM, JOHN S R—Los Angeles, Calif. B—Fort Walla Walla, Wash. G. O. No. 14, W. D., 1923.	Lieutenant colonel (Infantry), General Staff Corps, U. S. Army. As assistant chief of staff, G–3, and acting chief of staff, 36th Division, durin the organization and training of the division in the United States and France. In these positions of great responsibility he displayed sound jud ment, high professional skill, executive and administrative ability, an devotion to duty, his services contributing greatly to the successes of t 36th Division in its operations with the American Expeditionary Forces.
UPTON, LAROY S R—Big Rapids, Mich. B—Decatur, Mich. G. O. No. 59, W. D., 1919. Distinguished-service cross also awarded.	Brigadier general, U. S. Army. He commanded with conspicuous ability the 9th Infantry in the trench sect south of Verdun and in all its operations before Chateau-Thierry. In t campaign north of Verdun, in October, as commander of the 57th Infant Brigade, 29th Division, he exhibited qualities of brilliant leadership, succes fully participating in the battles at Molleville Farm, Grand Montagr Etraye, and in those east of the Meuse. At all times he remained near l front lines, personally directing the attacks and serving as a constant inspir tion to his men.
VAN CISE, PHILIP S R—Denver, Colo. B—Deadwood, S. Dak. G. O. No. 56, W. D., 1922.	Lieutenant colonel (Infantry), General Staff Corps, U. S. Army. As assistant chief of staff, G–2, 81st Division, from September, 1918, un June, 1919, he displayed exceptional ability in the administration and oper tion of that section of the division staff. By his keen foresight, sound juc ment, and military attainments of a high order he was able at all times secure valuable information of the enemy and to keep his commandi general well informed, thereby contributing materially to the successi operations of his division.
VAN DEMAN, RALPH H R—Delaware, Ohio. B—Delaware, Ohio. G. O. No. 73, W. D., 1919.	Colonel (Infantry), General Staff Corps, U. S. Army. As chief of the military intelligence branch, General Staff, in organizing t Intelligence Service of the Army in the United States, to his ability, untiri zeal, and devotion to duty the building up of a very efficient Intelligen Service of the Army was largely due.
VANDERBILT, CORNELIUS R—New York, N. Y. B—New York, N. Y. G. O. No. 118, W. D., 1919.	Brigadier general, U. S. Army. As commanding officer, 102d Engineers, and as Engineer officer of the 27 Division, his marked qualities of leadership and thorough training a instruction developed a high state of military efficiency in his command, demonstrated throughout its entire service.
VANDERVORT, LYNNETTE L R—Denver, Colo. B—La Salle, Ill. G. O. No. 9, W. D., 1923.	Chief nurse, Army Nurse Corps, U. S. Army. As chief nurse of the Mars Hospital Center, France, during the World W: she was largely responsible for the nursing care of thousands of sick a wounded at that center. Her work was characterized by great efficienc tact, and good judgment. Later, as chief nurse of the Nurses' Embarkati Center at Vannes, France, she had under her care at one time as ma as 1,100 nurses for whom she was responsible. Her efforts in this capaci to facilitate the work of demobilization, and to improve the general welfa of the nurses, contributed largely not only to the success of their concent tion and organization for transfer to the United States but also to their hi morale and physical well-being.
VAN HORN, ROBERT O R—Fort D. A. Russell, Wyo. B—Whipple Barracks, Ariz. G. O. No. 38, W. D., 1921.	Colonel, Signal Corps, U. S. Army. On the night of Nov. 3, 1918, he led his regiment, the 9th Infantry, 2d Divisi against the enemy position in the edge of the Bois de Belval. The regime passed through the woods and the enemy lines and took up a position 6 ki meters in rear of the enemy, capturing many prisoners and much war ma rial. At daylight, Nov. 4, his regiment was heavily counterattacked l not dislodged. The effect of night penetration of the enemy lines cau the enemy on the right and left of the 2d Division sector to fall back to east bank of the Meuse River.
VAN NATTA, THOMAS F., Jr R—St. Joseph, Mo. B—Atchison, Kans. G. O. No. 124, W. D., 1919.	Lieutenant colonel, Cavalry, U. S. Army. For services while serving as military attaché at Habana, Cuba.
VAN VOORHIS, DANIEL R—Zanesville, Ohio. B—Zanesville, Ohio. G. O. No. 69, W. D., 1919.	Colonel (Cavalry), General Staff Corps, U. S. Army. As chief of staff at the port of embarkation, Newport News, Va., his servi in governing and controlling the troop-movement branch at the port embarkation materially aided in the efficient transport of troops and suppl overseas.

VAUCLAIN, SAMUEL MATTHEWS
   R—Rosemont, Pa.
   B—Philadelphia, Pa.
   G. O. No. 69, W. D., 1919.

He assisted in organizing the munitions standards board and was chairman of a subcommittee of that board which later became a subcommittee of the War Industries Board. He rendered valuable assistance in developing the War Department's program as to artillery and rifles.

VAUGHAN, VICTOR C.
   R—Ann Arbor, Mich.
   B—Mount Airy, Randolph County, Mo.
   G. O. No. 69, W. D., 1919.

Colonel, Medical Corps, U. S. Army.
During his service in the office of the Surgeon General his contributions of advice and information have been of great value to the Army in connection with the control of communicable diseases. During the recent epidemic of influenza, in particular, his work was of extreme value.

VERDI, WILLIAM F.
   R—New Haven, Conn.
   B—Italy.
   G. O. No. 27, W. D., 1922.

Major, Medical Corps, U. S. Army.
As surgical consultant and specialist in surgery of the chest in hospital formations at the front during the operations on the Marne and the St. Mihiel and Meuse-Argonne offensives.

VIDMER, GEORGE
   R—Mobile, Ala.
   B—Mobile, Ala.
   G. O. No. 16, W. D., 1920.
   Distinguished-service cross also awarded.

Colonel, Infantry, U. S. Army.
As commander of the 306th Infantry, 77th Division, he demonstrated marked ability as a military leader. His sound judgment and tireless energy were largely responsible for the successes which his regiment gained in its operations against the enemy.

VINCETT, GEORGE H.
   R—Butler, Pa.
   B—Syracuse, N. Y.
   G. O. No. 59, W. D., 1919.

Lieutenant colonel, Corps of Engineers, U. S. Army.
As chief of construction and operation of the car-erecting plant at La Rochelle he performed with credit a task of great magnitude. By his skill in organizing labor and ability in imbuing the men with enthusiasm, he was enabled to increase greatly the output of his plant. The persistent high quality of the duty performed by him greatly facilitated the major operations of the American armies in the field.

VORIS, ALVIN C.
   R—Neoga, Ill.
   B—Neoga, Ill.
   G. O. No. 74, W. D., 1919.

Colonel, Signal Corps, U. S. Army.
As chief signal officer, successively, of the 1st Division, the 1st Army Corps, and the 3d Army, he rendered conspicuous services. With tireless energy and indefatigable zeal he performed a task of great magnitude, insuring at all times the installation and maintenance of communications throughout the Marne and Argonne-Meuse offensives, contributing in a marked degree to the successes attained.

WADE, LEIGH
   R—Cassopolis, Mich.
   B—Cassopolis, Mich.
   G. O. No. 14, W. D., 1925.
   Act of Congress Feb. 25, 1925.

First lieutenant, Air Service, U. S. Army.
Lieutenant Wade, as pilot of airplane No. 3, the *Boston*, and supply officer of the United States Army Air Service around-the-world flight from Apr. 6, 1924, to Sept. 28, 1924, displayed to a remarkable degree courage, energy, and resourcefulness in carrying out these duties, in addition to actually piloting his airplane throughout the voyage. His sound judgment and foresight were material factors in contributing to the successful achievement of this pioneer flight of airplanes around the world. He has assisted materially in bringing a signal honor to himself and to the military forces of the United States.

WADHAMS, SANFORD H.
   R—Torrington, Conn.
   B—Torrington, Conn.
   G. O. No. 59, W. D., 1919.

Colonel, Medical Corps, U. S. Army.
In his capacity as assistant to the Chief Surgeon, American Expeditionary Forces, and later as a member of the General Staff he ably supervised the hospitalization and evacuation activities of the Medical Corps in advanced areas. By his timely anticipation of requirements he assisted in a marked degree the support of our operations against the enemy.

WADSWORTH, ELIOT
   R—Boston, Mass.
   B—Boston, Mass.
   G. O. No. 95, W. D., 1919.

As vice chairman of the central committee, American Red Cross, he brought the great problem of systematized relief for our armies, those of the Allies, and for the stricken people of Europe to an eminently successful solution. By earnest, unselfish concentration of high faculties of organization and control he helped most materially to conserve life and reconstitute the wastage of war in the devastated areas, and made it possible to express the generosity of the American people in terms of substantial helpfulness.

WAHL, LUTZ
   R—Milwaukee, Wis.
   B—Milwaukee, Wis.
   G. O. No. 15, W. D., 1923.

Brigadier general, U. S. Army.
In command of the 58th Infantry, 4th Division, from Aug. 6, 1917, to Feb. 1, 1918, he demonstrated leadership of a high order, untiring energy, and sound judgment. As chief of the operations section, General Staff, War Department, from Feb. 4, 1918, to May 12, 1918, he displayed rare professional attainments, initiating and developing many valuable ideas in the organization of the operations section. As brigadier general commanding the 14th Infantry Brigade, 7th Division, from May 19, 1918, to Nov. 3, 1919, he again displayed unusual gifts of organization, leadership, and tactical judgment, both during the period of organization and training of his brigade, as well as in combat operations in France.

WAINER, MAX R.
   R—Delaware City, Del.
   B—Russia.
   G. O. No. 59, W. D., 1919.

Lieutenant colonel, Quartermaster Corps, U. S. Army.
As assistant to the quartermaster at Nevers, by his zeal and rare talent for organization he contributed in a large measure to the prompt and efficient operation of the first advance supply depot of the American Expeditionary Forces. Later he proved himself sound in judgment and of exceptional ability when he organized and operated the classification depot at Blois. He showed marked discernment and determination in the reclassification and assignment of commissioned personnel, performing most exacting duties with brilliant success.

WAINWRIGHT, JONATHAN MAYHEW R—Rye, N. Y. B—New York, N. Y. G. O. No. 55, W. D., 1920.	Lieutenant colonel, Inspector General's Department, U. S. Army. As division inspector and more especially as an acting general staff officer of the 27th Division in the Dickebusch sector in Belgium, the Ypres-Lys offensive, and the battle of the La Selle River, in France, by his energy, efficient coordination of details, and persistent application to his task, he regulated all movements of the division, involving the evacuation of wounded, the relief of units of the line, the supplying of rations and ammunition, and the control of communications, with such marked success as incurred a minimum of loss in each operation.
WAINWRIGHT, JONATHAN M. R—Chicago, Ill. B—Fort Walla Walla, Wash. G. O. No. 19, W. D., 1922.	Lieutenant colonel (Cavalry), General Staff Corps, U. S. Army. As assistant chief of staff, 82d Division, first assistant to the assistant chief of staff, G-3, 3d Army, and later as assistant chief of staff, G-3, American Forces in Germany, by his untiring energy, devotion to duty, and exercise of initiative he contributed in a large measure to the success attained by the commands with which he served.
WAITE, HENRY M. R—Dayton, Ohio. B—Toledo, Ohio. G. O. No. 22, W. D., 1920.	Colonel, Corps of Engineers, U. S. Army. As deputy director general of transportation, headquarters, services of supply, later as constructing engineer of the Transportation Corps and deputy director general of transportation, Zone of the Armies, he displayed marked technical ability, initiative, and judgment of a high order. Subsequently, as a member of the bridgehead commission of the 3d Army, as chief motor transport officer of the 3d Army, and as advisor to the officer in charge of civil affairs at advanced general headquarters, he displayed those same high qualities which characterized his previous distinguished service.
WAITE, SUMNER R—Portland, Me. B—Highland Lake, Me. G. O. No. 56, W. D., 1922.	Major (Infantry), General Staff Corps, U. S. Army. As assistant chief of staff, G-2, 37th Division, from Aug. 15, 1918, to Oct. 13, 1918, he organized and developed a splendid intelligence system by which he kept his division commander constantly well informed of the enemy on his front. By the skillful direction of the intelligence service he proved a material factor in the successes gained by his division. Aggressive and resourceful, he proved equal to every emergency. Later, as assistant chief of staff, G-3, of the same division, he demonstrated high professional attainments, sound tactical judgment, and keen farsightedness. He at all times displayed assiduous application to each important task, rendering services of signal worth and conspicuous merit in a position of great responsibility.
WALDRON, WILLIAM H. R—Welch, W. Va. B—Huntington, W. Va. G. O. No. 19, W. D., 1922. Distinguished-service cross also awarded.	Colonel (Infantry), General Staff Corps, U. S. Army. As chief of staff, 80th Division, during the Meuse-Argonne offensive his extraordinary energy, initiative, and ability contributed largely to the success of the operations of the division.
WALES, BOYD R—Howard, S. Dak. B—Brownville, Nebr. G. O. No. 59, W. D., 1921.	Colonel, Field Artillery, U. S. Army. As commander of the 147th Regiment of Field Artillery of the 57th Field Artillery Brigade, 32d Division, he commanded his regiment with marked ability throughout the campaign of the Aisne-Marne, Oise-Aisne, and Meuse-Argonne. By his energy and devotion to duty he contributed materially to the success of the 57th Field Artillery Brigade during its support of the 32d Division, and at other times its support of five other divisions. He has rendered service of much value.
WALKE, WILLOUGHBY R—Norfolk, Va. B—Norfolk, Va. G. O. No. 133, W. D., 1919.	Colonel, Coast Artillery Corps, U. S. Army. As commanding officer of the Middle Atlantic Coast Artillery District during the war, his services were conspicuous in the administration of that command and in the execution of all projects coming within his control for the organization and training of Coast Artillery Corps units for overseas service.
WALKER, GEORGE R—Baltimore, Md. B—York, S. C. G. O. No. 15, W. D., 1923.	Colonel, Medical Corps, U. S. Army. As a member of Base Hospital No. 18, in the prevention of the spreading of diseases at the base ports, and later as clinical chief of genito-urinary section of the Medical Department in France, he rendered services of inestimable value to the Government. His untiring energy and unremitting devotion to duty, coupled with his technical knowledge as a professional urologist, were of material value and contributed markedly to the successful operations of the American forces in France.
WALKER, JOHN B. R—New York, N. Y. B—Lodi, N. J. G. O. No. 31, W. D., 1922.	Colonel, Medical Corps, U. S. Army. As commanding officer of Base Hospital No. 116, American Expeditionary Forces, and later as consultant in the United States during the period of demobilization. The services rendered by Colonel Walker in standardizing and supervising the treatment of the wounded suffering from gunshot fractures were of inestimable value to the Government and a material contribution to the rehabilitation of the disabled.
WALKER, KENZIE W. R—Schulenburg, Tex. B—Pin Oak, Tex. G. O. No. 15, W. D., 1923.	Colonel, Finance Department, U. S. Army. As assistant to the Chief of Finance, charged with the responsibility for the settlement of many thousands of claims of officers and men of the National Army, he displayed extraordinary administrative and executive ability, sound business judgment, unflagging energy, and devotion to duty. The services rendered the Government were of immeasurable value in a position of great responsibility.

DISTINGUISHED-SERVICE MEDAL

.LKER, MERIWETHER L
R—Lynchburg, Va.
B—Lynchburg, Va.
G. O. No. 78, W. D., 1919.

Brigadier general, U. S. Army.
As chief of the Motor Transport Service he rendered services of much value. With tireless energy he assailed an important task, and by his zealous efforts met all difficulties arising from irregular shipments and lack of adequate material, successfully organizing the Motor Transport Service, and brought it to a high state of efficiency, thereby materially assisting in the solution of the important problem of transportation in the American Expeditionary Forces.

\LKER, WILLIAM H
R—Cambridge, Mass.
B—Pittsburgh, Pa.
G. O. No. 69, W. D., 1919.

Colonel, Chemical Warfare Service, U. S. Army.
His extraordinary technical ability, untiring industry, and great zeal have enabled remarkable results to be achieved in the Production Division of the Chemical Warfare Service in the face of many obstacles encountered.

\LLACE, FRED C
R—McMinnville, Tenn.
B—McMinnville, Tenn.
G. O. No. 38, W. D., 1922.

Lieutenant colonel, Field Artillery, U. S. Army.
As inspector-instructor for the Chief of Field Artillery from Apr. 16, 1918, to Oct. 16, 1918, he rendered valuable service in raising the efficiency of Field Artillery brigades and in recommending the measures needful to be taken to prepare these brigades for service overseas.

\LLACE, WILLIAM B
R—Marquette, Mich.
B—Canada.
G. O. No. 69, W. D., 1919.

Lieutenant colonel, Infantry, U. S. Army.
As a member of the American section, Supreme War Council, he has rendered invaluable service in handling with especial ability and good judgment matters of the greatest importance to all the allied and associated Governments.

ALSH, JAMES L
R—Brookline, Mass.
B—Boston, Mass.
G. O. No. 38, W. D., 1922.

Colonel, Ordnance Department, U. S. Army.
First as chief of the personnel division, office of the Chief of Ordnance, which he organized and administered with conspicuous success during the first nine months of the war, a critical period during which all ordnance activities depended upon the successful handling of the personnel problem, and later as personal and executive assistant to the Chief of Ordnance, in which capacity his breadth of vision, tact, sound judgment, and loyalty were invaluable to the Government in the numerous highly confidential matters entrusted to his care. In each of these positions his services to the Government were exceptionally conspicuous and meritorious.

ALSH, ROBERT D
R—Redwood City, Calif.
B—Alleghany, Calif.
G. O. No. 59, W. D., 1919.

Brigadier general, U. S. Army.
In command of the important base ports of St. Nazaire and Bordeaux, France, and as deputy director general of transportation, his services have been characterized by exceptional ability, energy, and devotion to duty.

ARBURTON, BARCLAY H
R—Wyncote, Pa.
B—Philadelphia, Pa.
G. O. No. 38, W. D., 1922.

Major, Field Artillery, U. S. Army.
While serving as military attaché at Paris, France, by his devotion to duty, intelligent cooperation, and indefatigable efforts he rendered invaluable assistance and conspicuous service to the military representative of the United States on the Supreme War Council.

ARD, CABOT
R—New York, N. Y.
B—New York, N. Y.
G. O. No. 59, W. D., 1919.

Lieutenant colonel (Air Service), General Staff Corps, U. S. Army.
As assistant chief of staff, in charge of the intelligence section of the Services of Supply, he has rendered services of the most valuable character. He has handled with great efficiency the important task of counterespionage throughout the American Expeditionary Forces and in the neighboring neutral countries. In this service he showed marked ability, combined with superior military knowledge.

ARD, FRANKLIN W
R—Albany, N. Y.
B—Philadelphia, Pa.
G. O. No. 118, W. D., 1919.

Colonel, Infantry, U. S. Army.
For services as division adjutant and acting chief of staff of the 27th Division and as commanding officer of the 106th Infantry. As commanding officer, 106th Infantry, his personal courage, determination, and thoroughness in the handling of his regiment under heavy fire during the battle of the LeSelle River in the Somme offensive of October, 1918, were conspicuous.

ARD, RALPH T
R—Denver, Colo.
B—Fayette, Mo.
G. O. No. 59, W. D., 1921.

Colonel (Corps of Engineers), General Staff Corps, U. S. Army.
As chief of the operations subsection G-3, 1st Army, Colonel Ward was given the responsibility of drawing up plans, preparing orders, making personal reconnaissances, and insuring mutual relations with adjacent armies. He fulfilled these functions with exceptional ability, and his work was largely responsible for the successes achieved during the St. Mihiel and Meuse-Argonne offensives.

ARFIELD, AUGUSTUS B
R—Buffalo, N. Y.
B—Prattsburg, N. Y.
G. O. No. 9, W. D., 1923.

Colonel, Field Artillery, U. S. Army.
As commanding officer of the 322d Field Artillery, 83d Division, from August 22, 1917, until February 15, 1919, he displayed untiring energy, unusual administrative ability, and an unfailing dependability, these qualities being reflected in the excellence of his regiment. His outstanding ability as an organizer, his leadership and his devotion to duty were material factors in the successful operations of his division.

ARREN, CHARLES B
R—Detroit, Mich.
B—Bay City, Mich.
G. O. No. 10, W. D., 1920.

Colonel, Judge Advocate General's Department, U. S. Army.
In connection with the administration of the selective-service law during the war, in all of his varied and important duties he displayed unselfish devotion, tireless energy, and extraordinary executive ability

WARREN, CHARLES ELLIOT R—New York, N. Y. B—Brooklyn, N. Y. G. O. No. 27, W. D., 1922.	Lieutenant colonel, Ordnance Department, U. S. Army. While in charge of finances of the small arms division, Ordnance Office, where his eminent ability as a financier and as an executive of large affairs, and also his previous military training, were invaluable in the early organization of the division. Later, as chief of the small-arms section, procurement division, Ordnance Office, and as one of the members and vice governor, the war credits board, Office of the Secretary of War, he rendered conspicuous service in the conduct of its immense affairs.
WASHBURN, FREDERIC A R—Boston, Mass. B—New Bedford, Mass. G. O. No. 59, W. D., 1921.	Lieutenant colonel, Medical Corps, U. S. Army. As commanding officer of Base Hospital No. 6, American Expeditionary Forces, and as surgeon of Base Section No. 3, positions of great responsibility, by his ability, energy, and whole-hearted devotion to duty he has rendered services of great value.
WATKINS, LEWIS H R—Franklin, Tenn. B—Nashville, Tenn. G. O. No. 62, W. D., 1919.	Colonel (Corps of Engineers), General Staff Corps, U. S. Army. As assistant chief of staff, G–5, 1st Army, he performed exacting duties with marked energy and ability, achieving valuable results. Notwithstanding his many duties, he arranged to aid G–3, 1st Army, in the preparation of plans for important operations. By his especial ability, military attainments, and painstaking devotion to the tasks assigned to him he contributed in a marked degree to the successes achieved by our troops.
WATSON, ERNEST E R—St. Paul, Minn. B—Augusta, Ky. G. O. No. 53, W. D., 1921.	Major, Infantry, 341st Machine Gun Battalion, 89th Division, U. S. Army. For services near Romagne, France, in October, 1918, in organizing the machine gun defense of the 89th Division sector.
WATT, DAVID A R—Hasbrouck Heights, N. J. B—Sandusky, Ohio. G. O. No. 16, W. D., 1923.	Lieutenant colonel, Adjutant General's Department, U. S. Army. As adjutant, port of embarkation, Hoboken, N. J., Sept. 3, 1917, to Sept. 10 1918, and Jan. 6, 1919, to Feb. 28, 1920, his untiring energy, resourcefulness and devotion to duty, coupled with administrative and executive ability of an exceptionally high order, were of immeasurable value to the Government in a position of great responsibility.
WEBB, GEORGE H R—Detroit, Mich. B—Dubuque, Iowa. G. O. No. 59, W. D., 1919.	Colonel, Corps of Engineers, U.S. Army. He was intrusted with the execution of some of the largest construction enter prises in France. Confronted by difficulties of labor, material, and equipment he set about his task with ceaseless energy, and by his resourcefulness, initia tive, and skill he overcame all obstacles and completed these difficult projects with great success.
WEED, FRANK W R—Baltimore, Md. B—Baltimore, Md. G. O. No. 9, W. D., 1923.	Lieutenant colonel, Medical Corps, U. S. Army. In August, 1917, as sanitary inspector at Camp Funston, Kans., he initiated and perfected the organization and establishment of a standardized type of detention and quarantine camp, the successful operation of which resulted in the installation of similar camps in all large cantonments throughout the United States during the war. This original and constructive work of his had a marked influence in controlling epidemic diseases, then prevalent, and greatly facilitated the rapid mobilization and training of urgently needed man power. From January until August, 1918, as general sanitary inspector Surgeon General's Office, he rendered services of the highest order. Later while on duty in the hospital division of the chief surgeon's office, American Expeditionary Forces, as transportation officer in charge of hospital trains ambulances, and the movement of sick and wounded within the American Expeditionary Forces to the United States during the period from January to July, 1919, he directed the evacuation of over 100,000 sick and wounded to the United States.
WEEKS, ALANSON R—San Francisco, Calif. B—Allegan, Mich. G. O. No. 16, W. D. 1923.	Major, Medical Corps, U. S. Army. During the World War, as surgical consultant and director of surgical teams in hospital formations at the front during the operations on the Marne, the St Mihiel, and Meuse-Argonne offensives, and later in command of Base Hos pital No. 30, by his loyal devotion to duty, sound judgment, and brillian professional attainments, he rendered services of great value in the care of th sick and wounded of the American troops, thereby contributing materially to the success of the American Expeditionary Forces.
WEEMS, FONTAINE CARRINGTON R—Washington, D. C. B—Houston, Tex. G. O. No. 14, W. D., 1920.	Lieutenant colonel, General Staff Corps, U. S. Army. As chief of the foreign relations section of the Purchase, Storage and Traffi Division of the General Staff, he foresaw the necessity of the preservation of accurate data affecting the international relations of the War Department in the matter of purchase of supplies by the allied Governments in the Unite States, and by his prevision and care prevented the loss of information essentia to just and speedy liquidation. Thereafter, in association with those charge with the settlement of widely ramifying, intricate, and involved busines relations, by his judgment, industry, and knowledge he made possible speed and just settlements, reflecting a high degree of credit upon the America Army for its accuracy and fairness in business transactions with its allies.
WEIGEL, WILLIAM R—New Brunswick, N. J. B—New Brunswick, N. J. G. O. No. 12, W. D., 1919.	Major general, U. S. Army. As commander of a brigade of the 28th Division in the fighting on the Vesle of August, 1918, he inspired confidence by his constant activities and his aggre sive pressing of the enemy at every opportunity, which resulted in drivin the hostile forces across the Vesle northward toward the Aisne.

NELBORN, IRA C.
    R—Mico, Miss.
    B—Mico, Miss.
    G. O. No. 18, W. D., 1919.
    Medal of honor also awarded.

Colonel, Tank Corps, U. S. Army.
For services in the organization and administration of the Tank Corps.

WELCH, WILLIAM H.
    R—Baltimore, Md.
    B—Norfolk, Conn.
    G. O. No. 69, W. D., 1919.

Colonel, Medical Corps, U. S. Army.
From his rich experience in scientific medicine, sanitation, public health, and medical education he helped materially in guiding the medical profession both in and out of the Army safely through the many difficulties of war.

WELD, DE WITT C., Jr.
    R—Brooklyn, N. Y.
    B—Brooklyn, N. Y.
    G. O. No. 56, W. D., 1922.

Colonel, Field Artillery, U. S. Army.
As regimental commander of the 105th Field Artillery, 27th Division, he demonstrated professional attainments and ability of the highest order. By his sound tactical judgment and superior knowledge of artillery, he most successfully directed his units in support of the 158th Infantry Brigade in the operations north of Verdun, Nov. 4 to 11, 1918. By keeping his elements close to the atttacking Infantry he contributed in no small measure to the success of the Infantry brigade in these operations. He rendered services of conspicuous merit and signal worth to the American Expeditionary Forces.

WELLES, EDWARD M., Jr.
    R—New York, N. Y.
    B—Addison, N. Y.
    G. O. No. 14, W. D., 1923.

Lieutenant colonel, Medical Corps, U. S. Army.
In the office of the Chief Surgeon, American Expeditionary Forces, for nearly two years and embracing the entire period of combat activities, he was charged with all details concerning the reception and distribution and the classification and assignment of all officers, nurses, and enlisted men of the Medical Department serving overseas, a force aggregating approximately 250,000 individuals. In this position of great responsibility he displayed exceptional ability and rendered conspicuous service to the Government by directing with the greatest economy the distribution of all available personnel during periods of stress and threatened shortage, thereby materially contributing to the success of our forces in the field.

WELLS, BRIANT H.
    R—Salt Lake City, Utah.
    B—Salt Lake City, Utah.
    G. O. No. 62, W. D., 1919.

Brigadier general, U. S. Army.
As chief of staff of the 4th Army Corps while it was in the front line in the Woevre he displayed military attainments of a high order in the planning of operations. Both then and subsequently, during the march to the Rhine and the occupation of German territory, his service was marked by tireless zeal, excellent judgment, and whole-hearted devotion to the performance of important tasks.

WELLS, FREDERICK B.
    R—Minneapolis, Minn.
    B—France.
    G. O. No. 69, W. D., 1919.

Colonel, Quartermaster Corps, U. S. Army.
In the organization and operation of the entire storage system for the Army he has displayed marked ability, energy, and application, to which are due, in a large measure, the satisfactory results attained.

*WELSH, ROBERT S.
    R—Sault Ste. Marie, Mich.
    B—Canada.
    G. O. No. 50, W. D., 1919.

Colonel, Field Artillery, U. S. Army.
He commanded the 314th Field Artillery, 80th Division, which later became part of the 3d Army Corps. He rendered exceptionally efficient service with the 80th Division, taking part in all operations of that division. He displayed a high order of leadership and exhibited those masterful qualities of a commander which insure success. Later, assigned to the 3d Army Corps, his devotion to duty and high professional attainments were again revealed. Posthumously awarded. Medal presented to widow, Mrs. Eleanor E. Welsh.

WELSH, WILLIAM E.
    R—Hanover, Pa.
    B—Hanover, Pa.
    G. O. No. 15, W. D., 1923.

Brigadier general, U. S. Army.
As colonel, 346th Infantry, 87th Division, from September, 1917, to June, 1918, he demonstrated unusual leadership, organizing and training his regiment to a high state of efficiency and morale; as brigadier general, General Staff, and inspector-instructor of Infantry, training section, General Headquarters, American Expeditionary Forces, he displayed marked tactical ability and by his general supervision shared largely in the responsibility for the training in that arm. His duties of very great importance were carried out with conspicuous success.

WELSHIMER, ROBERT R.
    R—Neoga, Ill.
    B—Neoga, Ill.
    G. O. No. 3, W. D., 1921.

Colonel, Coast Artillery Corps, U. S. Army.
As senior instructor at the Coast Artillery School, and later as commandant of that school in the organization and administration of that institution so as to result in effective accomplishment of its object.

WENTZ, DANIEL B.
    R—Philadelphia, Pa.
    B—Jeddo, Pa.
    G. O. No. 15, W. D., 1923.

Lieutenant colonel, Quartermaster Corps, U. S. Army.
While in charge of the fuel branch, office of the chief quartermaster, American Expeditionary Forces, a position of great responsibility, he displayed extraordinary ability in the promptness with which he procured and forwarded a steady flow of fuel to the American Expeditionary Forces.

WESSON, CHARLES M.
    R—Centerville, Md.
    B—St. Louis, Mo.
    G. O. No. 49, W. D., 1922.

Colonel, Ordnance Department, U. S. Army.
As commanding officer, Watertown Arsenal, Mass., from January to October, 1918, by his indefatigable energy, great administrative ability, and thorough technical knowledge he planned, erected, equipped, and brought to a highly efficient working basis a new factory for the manufacture of 240-mm. howitzer carriages, as well as a new forging plant for large-caliber guns—a definite contribution to the military power of the Nation. From November, 1918, until August, 1919, as commanding officer of the ordnance base repair shops at Mehun-sur-Yevre, France, he again rendered highly meritorious service in a position of great responsibility in salvaging ordnance matériel valued at millions of dollars and prepared it properly for shipment to the United States.

784 DECORATIONS, U. S. ARMY, 1862–1926

WESTERVELT, WILLIAM I
   R—Corpus Christi, Tex.
   B—Corpus Christi, Tex.
   G. O. No. 59, W. D., 1919.

Brigadier general, U. S. Army.
As assistant to the Chief of Artillery, through his initiative, organizing abi
and comprehensive knowledge of the technique and tactics of Artillery i
its branches, and particularly through his complete knowledge of Artil
material, he has rendered services of exceptional value to the Governmer

*WESTNEDGE, JOSEPH B
   R—Kalamazoo, Mich.
   B—Kalamazoo, Mich.
   G. O. No. 70, W. D., 1919.

Colonel, Infantry, U. S. Army.
With signal ability he commanded the 126th Infantry, 32d Division, from
date of its organization to its final engagement during the Meuse-Argo
offensive, inspiring the members of his command by his personal cou
and indefatigable zeal; he kept his regiment efficiently organized at all ti
as demonstrated by the successful results obtained in its operations age
the enemy. During his service at the front he contracted a disease w
subsequently proved fatal.
Posthumously awarded. Medal presented to widow, Mrs. Eva M. Westne

WESTOVER, OSCAR
   R—Bay City, Mich.
   B—Bay City, Mich.
   G. O. No. 14, W. D., 1923.

Lieutenant colonel, Air Service, U. S. Army.
He served in turn as signal officer, port of embarkation, Hoboken, N. J.,
of storage department, Signal Corps, and chief of storage and traffic divi
Bureau of Aeronautical Production, Air Service. By his great initia
painstaking attention to details, exceptional ability, and untiring effort
installed and developed with conspicuous success at all ports of embarka
a complete system of keeping records of shipment of Signal Corps and
Service property for overseas. His services were of inestimable valu
the Government in a position of great responsibility.

WHALEY, ARTHUR M
   R—Sault Sainte Marie, Mich.
   B—Canada.
   G. O. No. 56, W. D., 1922.

Colonel, Medical Corps, U. S. Army.
He served with marked ability as surgeon, 30th Division, from the time
organization and early training period to the completion of the Ypres
and Somme offensives. The care and evacuation of the wounded du
the active operations of the division were conducted with the greatest sm
ness and efficiency, and it was due to the great energy and conspic
ability displayed by him that his services were of the utmost value to
division.

WHEELER, CHARLES B
   R—Fergus Falls, Minn.
   B—Mattison, Ill.
   G. O. No. 56, W. D., 1922.

Brigadier general, U. S. Army.
He initiated, organized, and developed the plans for the successful opera
of the supply division in the office of the Chief of Ordnance, which div
received, transported, warehoused, issued, and maintained all items of
nance stores and equipment manufactured and purchased for issue to
Army during the war. With fine business acumen and with the full
ception of the magnitude and intricacy of the complex problems invol
he brought to full and complete fruition a well-balanced and successful w
ing organization. By his wide vision and full comprehension of condi
and the needs of the service and by his unflagging energy to insure con
supply of ordnance materials, he rendered service of signal worth to the
ernment in a position of great responsibility.

WHEELER, RAYMOND A
   R—Peoria, Ill.
   B—Orchard Mines, Ill.
   G. O. No. 68, W. D., 1920.

Colonel, Corps of Engineers, U. S. Army.
As active regimental commander of the 4th Engineers, 4th Division, d
the Aisne-Marne, the St. Mihiel, and the Meuse-Argonne offensive
ably supported the 4th Division in these operations by the promptness
skill with which he constructed bridges across the Vesle, destroyed e
wire, and built and maintained roads during the attacks in the M
Argonne offensive. His able and expeditious support of the 3d an
Army Corps by constructing roads through the Argonne was a material f
in the rapid advance and ultimate success of the units of those corps di
this important operation.

WHIPPLE, SHERBURNE
   R—Springfield, Mass.
   B—Cold Spring, N. Y.
   G. O. No. 49, W. D., 1922.

Lieutenant colonel, Infantry, U. S. Army.
As assistant chief of staff, G–1, of the 80th Division from June until Decen
1918, he performed his duties with marked ability in connection with the
ice of supply and communications for his division. By his tireless en
exceptional administrative ability, initiative, and sound judgment he
cessfully solved many perplexing problems, maintaining at all tim
adequate supply of food and ammunition for the troops, thereby rend
valuable services to the American Expeditionary Forces.

WHITE, HERBERT A
   R—Plymouth, Iowa.
   B—Worth County, Iowa.
   G. O. No. 15, W. D., 1921.

Colonel, Judge Advocate General's Department, U. S. Army.
As acting Judge Advocate General for the American Expeditionary F
and later for the American Forces in Germany and France he perfo
very difficult and exacting duties with marked skill and distinction
connection with the vast civil business of the War Department which p
through his hands he displayed a singular force of decision and s
judgment.

WHITE, HERBERT H
   R—Boise, Idaho.
   B—Boston, Mass.
   G. O. No. 59, W. D., 1919.

Lieutenant colonel (Field Artillery), General Staff Corps, U. S. Army.
As executive officer of the 4th Section, General Staff, General Headqua
American Expeditionary Forces, he was intimately associated wit
organization of the Services of Supply and their direction. By his e
ability, and good judgment in the discharge of important and arduous
he greatly assisted in the successful operations of the Services of Sup
support of the forces in the field.

WHITEHEAD, HENRY C
   R—Hemphill, Tex.
   B—Hemphill, Tex.
   G. O. No. 59, W. D., 1919.

Colonel, Signal Corps, U. S. Army.
During the period of organization of the American Expeditionary For
rendered service of a superior order in the planning and the organizat
the Air Service. As chief of staff, Air Service, he displayed sound judg
and great ability in solving the many problems with which he was confro
Throughout the entire duration of the war his high professional attain
and untiring zeal have materially promoted the efficiency of the Air Se

DISTINGUISHED-SERVICE MEDAL

WHITFIELD, ROBERT⎯⎯⎯⎯⎯⎯⎯⎯⎯
R—Milledgeville, Ga.
B—Milledgeville, Ga.
G. O. No. 89, W. D., 1919.

Colonel (Infantry), General Staff Corps, U. S. Army.
While on duty with the operations branch of the operations division, General Staff, he was charged with a multitude of exacting and very responsible duties, all of which he performed with conspicuous accuracy and thoroughness.

WHITLEY, FRANKLIN L⎯⎯⎯⎯⎯⎯⎯⎯⎯
R—St. Louis, Mo.
B—St. Louis, Mo.
G. O. No. 27, W. D., 1922.

Lieutenant colonel, Infantry, U. S. Army.
In 1917, before instruction pamphlets were issued, Colonel Whitley prepared combat drill formations, suitable for war strength companies armed with new weapons. As battalion commander during the operations near Chateau-Thierry, he rendered valuable service. Due to his initiative and personal leadership, 39 days of constant contact with the enemy failed to break the morale of his organization. After the armistice, as chief of the decorations division, General Headquarters, American Expeditionary Forces, by his sound judgment, professional knowledge, and exceptional ability, this officer performed his manifold and responsible duties with the utmost efficiency. He has rendered services of material worth to the American Expeditionary Forces.

WHITMAN, WALTER M⎯⎯⎯⎯⎯⎯⎯⎯⎯
R—New York, N. Y.
B—New York, N. Y.
G. O. No. 89, W. D., 1919.
Distinguished-service cross also awarded.

Colonel, Infantry, U. S. Army.
He commanded with marked distinction the 325th Infantry, 82d Division, throughout its period of service in France. An able and aggressive leader, he achieved eminent success in all the missions assigned to him, contributing materially to the achievements of his division.

WHITSON, MILTON J⎯⎯⎯⎯⎯⎯⎯⎯⎯
R—Seattle, Wash.
B—Scott County, Iowa.
G. O. No. 89, W. D., 1919.

Colonel, Quartermaster Corps, U. S. Army.
While officer in charge of the building branch of the construction division of the Army, Colonel Whitson's task was of staggering magnitude, and its successful accomplishment was in a great measure due to his qualities of organization, leadership, technical knowledge, and untiring energy.

WICKERSHAM, CORNELIUS W⎯⎯⎯⎯⎯⎯⎯⎯⎯
R—Cedarhurst, Long Island, N. Y.
B—Greenwich, Conn.
G. O. No. 38, W. D., 1921.

Major (Infantry), General Staff Corps, U. S. Army.
As acting assistant chief of staff, G–3, 4th Army Corps, and as assistant to the assistant chief of staff, G–3, 4th Army Corps, in the preparation and execution of the 4th Army Corps attack at St. Mihiel. Subsequently he was one of the principal officers to organize the 2d Army Headquarters.

WICKES, FORSYTH⎯⎯⎯⎯⎯⎯⎯⎯⎯
R—Tuxedo Park, N. Y.
B—New York, N. Y.
G. O. No. 62, W. D., 1919.

Major, Infantry, U. S. Army.
He showed rare ability in the preliminary organization of the American liaison service and wide comprehension of the importance of forward interallied liaison. While attached to French divisions in liaison with the 1st American Division he performed exacting duties of a delicate nature with energy and tact, achieving signal success. He aided materially in the maintenance of cordial relations between the French and American military authorities, his service being continuously marked by ability, sound judgment, and devotion to duty.

WIGMORE, JOHN H⎯⎯⎯⎯⎯⎯⎯⎯⎯
R—Chicago, Ill.
B—San Francisco, Calif.
G. O. No. 10, W. D., 1920.

Colonel, Judge Advocate General, U. S. Army.
In connection with the administration of the selective-service law during the war, he originated and put into execution an excellent system of classification of registrants and his sound judgment and ability for analysis contributed materially to the success of the department.

WILBY, FRANCIS B⎯⎯⎯⎯⎯⎯⎯⎯⎯
R—Arlington, Mass.
B—Detroit, Mich.
G. O. No. 14, W. D., 1923.

Colonel, Corps of Engineers, U. S. Army.
As assistant in charge of military engineering in the office of the Chief Engineer, American Expeditionary Forces, and later as division engineer of the 1st Division, he displayed unusual ability and professional attainments of a high order. As editor of the Engineer Field Notes, and as the author of a large number of them, his clear conception of the functions and duties of Engineer troops was most firmly impressed upon the combat engineers and contributed in a signal manner to their marked efficiency. By his rare technical skill and knowledge, keen adaptability to all conditions, he contributed materially to the success of the 1st Division in a position of great responsibility and in times and circumstances of the gravest importance.

WILGUS, WILLIAM J⎯⎯⎯⎯⎯⎯⎯⎯⎯
R—New York, N. Y.
B—Buffalo, N. Y.
G. O. No. 50, W. D., 1919.

Colonel, Corps of Engineers, U. S. Army.
As delegate of the special railway commission, Director General of Military Railways and Deputy Director General of Transportation. In all of these positions he has demonstrated exceptional ability and untiring energy. The foundation of the Army Transportation Service was largely due to his vision and remarkable judgment. He has shown a degree of devotion to duty far above any calls which would have been made upon him by military authority.

WILKINS, HARRY E⎯⎯⎯⎯⎯⎯⎯⎯⎯
R—Victor, Iowa.
B—Genesee, Ill.
G. O. No. 77, W. D., 1919.

Brigadier general, U. S. Army.
For services while in charge of the general supply depot, New York City.

WILLCUTT, JOSEPH N⎯⎯⎯⎯⎯⎯⎯⎯⎯
R—Cohasset, Mass.
B—Cohasset, Mass.
G. O. No. 95, W. D., 1919.

Colonel, Quartermaster Corps, U. S. Army.
As officer in charge of the construction of the National Guard camps he displayed qualities of leadership, energy, administrative ability, and devotion to duty which rendered possible the housing of the National Guard troops in an incredibly short space of time. Later he served with conspicuous success as chief of the procurement branch of the Construction Division of the Army.

WILLIAMS, ALEXANDER E _____
R—Little River Academy, N. C.
B—Cumberland, N. C.
G. O. No. 43, W. D., 1922.

Colonel, Quartermaster Corps, U. S. Army.
As chief quartermaster, Army of Occupation, he displayed untiring zea administrative ability of the highest order in the organization and oper of the supply system of the 3d Army. By his sound judgment, initi and resourcefulness he solved many perplexing problems of supply finance in a most satisfactory manner, thereby effecting a great savir the United States.

WILLIAMS, CLARENCE C _____
R—Nacoochee, Ga.
B—Nacoochee, Ga.
G. O. No. 12, W. D., 1919.

Major general, U. S. Army.
An officer of high professional attainments, who rendered particularly val services in the organization of the Ordnance Department of the Am(Expeditionary Forces and exhibited unusual ability in arranging fo procurement of ordnance material and ammunition for the American . in Europe.

WILLIAMS, EZEKIEL J _____
R—Barnesville, Ga.
B—Sparks, Ga.
G. O. No. 89, W. D., 1919.

Colonel (Infantry), General Staff Corps, U. S. Army.
He served with distinction as chief of staff of the 36th Division from the of its organization to the date of departure from France. He perfc his manifold duties with unflagging energy and notable ability, renc services of striking value to the American Expeditionary Forces.

WILLIAMS, HARRY C _____
R—New Town Landing, Miss.
B—New Town Landing, Miss.
G. O. No. 56, W. D., 1922.

Colonel, Field Artillery, U. S. Army.
As commanding officer, 320th Field Artillery, 82d Division, in the organi: and training of the regiment and in its very successful operations a; the enemy in the Aisne-Marne, St. Mihiel, and Meuse-Argonne offer he displayed tireless energy, keen devotion to duty, and eminent tecl skill as an artillerist, gave most effective support to the Infantry of th and 80th Divisions, and very materially contributed to the successes att by those units.

WILLIAMS, HERBERT O _____
R—Tupelo, Miss.
B—Fulton, Miss
G. O. No. 103, W. D., 1919.

Brigadier general, U. S. Army.
As an officer of the Inspector General's Department his rare efficiency lessness, and good judgment in the inspection of large commands and investigation and solution of intricate problems presenting unusual culties have been of the greatest value and have materially facilitate operations of the War Department and of the Army during the emerg

WILLIAMS, RICHARD H _____
R—Jersey City Heights, N. J.
B—Jersey City, N. J.
G. O. No. 62, W. D., 1919.

Colonel (Coast Artillery Corps), General Staff Corps, U. S. Army.
As G-2, 1st Army Corps, he displayed rare ability in the organizatio: administration of that section, being tireless in the energy with whi handled each problem during successive offensives. Later as G-2, 3d he achieved brilliant successes when confronted with duties of a most ex: and difficult nature, accomplishing all by his zeal and ability.

WILLIAMS, RICHARD H., Jr. _____
R—Mendham, N. J.
B—New York, N. Y.
G. O. No. 19, W. D., 1922.

Lieutenant colonel, Quartermaster Corps, U. S. Army.
In the remount service, American Expeditionary Forces, through hi sightedness he saw the necessity for and by his untiring effort succeec expediting the obtaining of animals for the American Expeditionary I that were of vital importance for our Army.

WILLIAMSON, SYDNEY B _____
R—New York, N. Y.
B—Lexington, Va.
G. O. No. 15, W. D., 1923.

Colonel, Corps of Engineers, U. S. Army.
As section engineer, intermediate section west, Services of Supply, F he constructed hospitals, depots, camps, and miscellaneous structures displayed rare technical skill, broad vision and business experience, ur energy and devotion to duty, contributing in a material way to the suc(operations of the American forces in France.

WILLIFORD, FORREST E _____
R—Bayle City, Ill.
B—Coffeen, Ill.
G. O. No. 56, W. D., 1922.

Colonel, Coast Artillery Corps, U. S. Army.
He served with marked efficiency as director of the trench artillery sch Langres and commandant of the trench artillery center at Vitrey. as chief of the trench artillery section in the office of the Chief of Art American Expeditionary Forces, he initiated the plans of and cont the training of this important branch of the Artillery arm with excep ability, rendering services of inestimable value to the American E tionary Forces.

WILLS, DAVIS B _____
R—Charlottesville, Va.
B—Charlottesville, Va.
G. O. No. 62, W. D., 1919.

Major, U. S. Marine Corps.
As chief paymaster of the United States Marine Corps, he performed ar and complex duties under most trying conditions. Displaying rare ini and administrative ability, he organized and conducted his departm such a manner as to relieve combat units of a mass of detail and ad trative work. He was tireless in devotion to duty, able in its executic

WILLS, VAN LEER _____
R—Grand Rapids, Mich.
B—Davidson County, Tenn.
G. O. No. 15, W. D., 1923.

Colonel (Infantry), General Staff Corps, U. S. Army.
As assistant chief of staff, G-3, 92d Division, from Sept. 9 to Nov. 9, 1! deputy chief of staff, 1st Army, American Expeditionary Forces, from N 1918, to Apr. 20, 1919, and as acting chief of staff for various periods, his involving the direction of reequipment and supply of the 1st Army which marched into Germany with the 3d American Army; the direc' the policing of the 1st Army's battlefields and the withdrawal of the 1st to rest areas; planning and supervising the training, recreation, and voc: training of the 1st Army while in rest areas awaiting transportation ho assistant to chief of staff, G-4, Services of Supply, from April, 1919, to A 1919, and assistant chief of staff, G-4, Services of Supply, from August to October, 1919, he supervised the liquidation and disposal of the va: plies involved in the dissolution of the Services of Supply. He display(initiative, outstanding administrative and executive ability, and unren devotion to duty in these positions of grave responsibility, contri signally to the successful repatriation of the American Army and the p and effective liquidation of the affairs of the American Expeditionary I

WILMER, WILLIAM H.
　R—Washington, D. C.
　B—Powhatan County, Va.
　G. O. No. 59, W. D., 1919.

Colonel, Medical Corps, U. S. Army.
As surgeon in charge of medical research laboratories, Air Service, American Expeditionary Forces, since September, 1918, he has rendered most distinguished service. His thorough knowledge of the psychology of flying officers and the expert tests applied efficiently and intelligently under his direction have done much to decrease the number of accidents at the flying schools in France and have established standards and furnished indications which will be of inestimable value in all future work to determine the qualifications of pilots and observers. The data collected by him is an evidence of his ability, his painstaking care, and of his thorough qualifications for the important work intrusted to him. The new methods, instruments, and appliances devised under his direction for testing candidates for pilots and observers have attracted the attention and been the subject of enthusiastic comment by officers of the allied services and will be of great importance in promoting the safety and more rapid development of aerial navigation.

WILSON, GEORGE K.
　R—Pueblo, Colo.
　B—Denver, Colo.
　G. O. No. 50, W. D., 1919.

Colonel, Infantry, U. S. Army.
As assistant chief of staff in charge of the administrative section of the General Staff, first of a division, later a corps, and finally of an army, he displayed marked ability in every capacity in which he was employed. By his thorough knowledge and grasp of his duties he became a material factor in the successful operations of his several departments.

WILSON, HENRY B.
　R—Camden, N. J.
　B—Camden, N. J.
　G. O. No. 56, W. D., 1921.

Vice admiral, U. S. Navy.
While stationed at Brest, in the capacity of commander of the United States Naval Forces in France, where he showed a keen appreciation of the necessity for the closest cooperation between the military and naval services, his valuable cooperation has to a great extent made possible the prompt functioning of the port of Brest.

WILSON, JAMES S.
　R—Baltimore, Md.
　B—San Francisco, Calif.
　G. O. No. 56, W. D., 1922.

Colonel, Medical Corps, U. S. Army.
As Chief Surgeon of the American Expeditionary Forces in Siberia, he organized, supervised, and perfected the organization of the Medical Department in Siberia so as to meet successfully the complex sanitary conditions confronting the American troops. To his excellent judgment, untiring efforts, and high professional attainments is largely due the splendid efficiency which characterized the work of the Medical Department under his control. He handled in a masterful manner the organization of available sanitary forces to combat a threatened typhus epidemic in eastern Siberia. He rendered conspicuous service of signal worth to the Government in a position of great responsibility.

WILSON, LOUIS B.
　R—Rochester, Minn.
　B—Pittsburgh, Pa.
　G. O. No. 27, W. D., 1922.

Colonel, Medical Corps, U. S. Army.
As assistant to the director of laboratories and infectious diseases, American Expeditionary Forces, he organized most efficiently a pathological service throughout the American Expeditionary Forces in France that was of inestimable value to the medical and surgical services.

WILSON, WALTER K.
　R—Nashville, Tenn.
　B—Nashville, Tenn.
　G. O. No. 18, W. D., 1919

Colonel (Coast Artillery Corps), General Staff Corps, U. S. Army.
In the organization and administration of the cable service of the War Department in the United States, thereby enabling that service to meet the excessive demands made upon it during the war.

WILSON, WILLIAM H.
　R—Cincinnati, Ohio.
　B—Mount Vernon, N. Y.
　G. O. No. 62, W. D., 1919.

Colonel (Coast Artillery Corps), General Staff Corps, U. S. Army.
He displayed extensive scientific knowledge, together with a keen practical grasp of conditions, as artillery inspector with the first battalion of American Railway Artillery in action against the enemy. As a member of the training section, he was at all times energetic and tactful in the supervision of training of railway, tractor, trench, and antiaircraft artillery. As its executive officer, he organized and conducted an item of the general system of the training section, being tireless in devotion to his important duties.

WINANS, EDWIN B.
　R—Hamburg, Mich.
　B—Hamburg, Mich.
　G. O. No. 59, W. D., 1919.

Brigadier general, U. S. Army.
He showed marked efficiency and excellent judgment while commanding the 64th Infantry Brigade, 32d Division, in the actions at the second Battle of the Marne, in the attack and capture of Juvigny, and in the operations at Bois-de-la-Morine, Bois-de-Chene Sec, and Bantheville Woods. In these actions, by his tactical ability, he was always master of the situation and executed his plans with a confidence that was an inspiration to his troops.

WINGATE, GEORGE ALBERT.
　R—Brooklyn, N. Y.
　B—Brooklyn, N. Y.
　G. O. No. 126, W. D., 1919.

Brigadier general, U. S. Army.
In command of the 52d Field Artillery Brigade, 27th Division, he served with marked distinction in the St. Mihiel operation, displaying military attainments of a high order. In the Meuse-Argonne offensive he proved himself possessed of exceptionally tactical ability, working with untiring energy that the Infantry might have all the advantages of Artillery support. With sound judgment, unusual foresight, and wide comprehension of conditions and facilities available, he conducted operations in that offensive with brilliant success, repeatedly solving the difficult problems incident thereto.

WINN, CHARLES D.
　R—Paris, Ky.
　B—Winchester, Ky.
　G. O. No. 89, W. D., 1919.

Colonel, Field Artillery, U. S. Army.
As commanding officer of the 306th Field Artillery, 77th Division, he displayed high qualities of leadership. Maintaining a high standard of efficiency and morale in his regiment, he constantly kept his command in close proximity to the attacking infantry, furnishing it accurate and timely support, furthering its rapid advance, and contributing to the successes gained.

WINN, FRANK L. R—Winchester, Ky. B—Winchester, Ky. G. O. No. 62, W. D., 1919.	Major general, U. S. Army. As commander of the 177th Infantry Brigade and later of the 89th Division, he displayed military attainments of a high order and achieved signal successes. In the St. Mihiel and Meuse-Argonne offensives he accompanied the assaulting battalions and placed them on their objectives, inspiring all by his personal courage and gaining their confidence by his exceptional tactical skill and ability as a leader. At all times he was tireless in energy, showing keen judgment and initiative in handling difficult situations.
WINSHIP, BLANTON R—Macon, Ga. B—Macon, Ga. G. O. No. 19, W. D., 1920. Distinguished-service cross also awarded.	Colonel, Judge Advocate General's Department, U. S. Army. He served with distinction as judge advocate of the 42d Division and of the 1st Army. As commanding officer of the 110th Infantry, 28th Division, he displayed marked qualities of leadership. Later, as judge advocate of the Services of Supply, and as chief of the rents, requisitions, and claims service, he displayed professional attainments and judgment of a high order, contributing, in no small degree, to the success of the operations during the war and afterwards in the liquidation of our affairs in France.
WINSLOW, E. EVELETH R—Boston, Mass. B—Washington, D. C. G. O. No. 47, W. D., 1919.	Colonel, Corps of Engineers, U. S. Army. While in charge of the military section of the office of the Chief of Engineers during the early period of the war his services were marked by the energy, zeal, and good judgment which were essential to the procurement of personnel and equipment and the organization and training of engineer organizations for oversea service.
WINTER, FRANCIS A R—St. Louis, Mo. B—St. Francisville, La. G. O. No. 59, W. D., 1919.	Brigadier general, U. S. Army. As chief surgeon of the lines of communication, American Expeditionary Forces, from June to December, 1917, he organized medical units at the base ports and in camps in France. He established large supply depots, from which medical supplies were distributed to the American Expeditionary Forces, and by keen foresight and administrative ability made these supplies at all times available for our armies.
WISE, FREDERIC MAY R—Baltimore, Md. B—Brooklyn, N. Y. G. O. No. 39, W. D., 1920.	Colonel, U. S. Marine Corps. He commanded with skill, ability, and gallantry the 59th Infantry, 4th Division, from Sept. 4, 1918, to Jan. 23, 1919. During the St. Mihiel offensive he personally directed the attack of his regiment against Manheulles and Fresnes-en-Woevre, which resulted in the capture of the enemy's line in this area. On Sept. 28, 1918, he directed the attack of his regiment which resulted in the capture of the Bois-de-Brieulles. From Sept. 26 to Oct. 21, 1918, his personal courage and aggressive attitude was an important factor in the successful operations of the 8th Infantry Brigade against Bois-de-Brieulles, Bois-du-Fays, Bois-de-Malaumont, Bois-de-Peut, and Bois-de-Foret. He has rendered services of signal worth to the American Expeditionary Forces
WITTENMYER, EDMUND R—Dunbarton, Ohio. B—Buford, Ohio. G. O. No. 12, W. D., 1919.	Major general, U. S. Army. He served with marked distinction as brigade commander in the Argonne Meuse offensive and as division commander in the final operations in the Toul sector, and in both capacities, by his untiring efforts and breadth of vision, proved himself to be an able leader.
WOLF, PAUL A R—Kewanee, Ill. B—Kewanee, Ill. G. O. No. 59, W. D., 1919.	Brigadier general, U. S. Army. In the attacks on Bois-de-Forges, St. Hilaire, Bois-de-Warville, and Bois-des Hautes-Epines, France, in September and October, 1918, the conspicuous success of the brigade was due to his splendid leadership and skill
WOLFE, EDWIN P R—New York, N. Y. B—Page County, Iowa. G. O. No. 69, W. D., 1919.	Colonel, Medical Corps, U. S. Army. He systematized and controlled the distribution of medical supplies with so much foresight and good judgment that his service was able to meet promptly all the emergencies in the United States as they occurred.
WOLFE, SAMUEL H R—New York, N. Y. B—Baltimore, Md. G. O. No. 43, W. D., 1922.	Colonel, Quartermaster Corps, U. S. Army. As officer in charge of insurance matters, cantonment division, Quartermaster General's Office, by his unusual constructive ability, foresight, and familiarity with large financial problems he rendered conspicuous service resulting in the saving of large sums to the Government. As a member of the committee on labor of the advisory commission of the Council of National Defense, he again rendered invaluable services in the preparation of necessary legislation to provide for the dependents of enlisted personnel of the Army and Navy, which later became the war risk insurance act. In October, 1917, he demonstrated exceptional ability and resourcefulness in the organization and operation of the War Risk Insurance Bureau in France and England. Later, as assistant director and executive officer in the office of the Director of Finance, his thorough knowledge of financial problems proved of the greatest assistance to the Director of Finance and of inestimable value to the Government.
WOOD, LEONARD R—Boston, Mass. B—Winchester, N. H. G. O. No. 47, W. D., 1919. Medal of honor also awarded.	Major general, U. S. Army. As a department, division, and camp commander during the war, he has displayed qualities of leadership and professional attainments of a high order in the administration and training of his various commands, and has furthered in every way during the war the system of officers' training schools.
WOOD, ROBERT E R—Kansas City, Mo. B—Kansas City, Mo. G. O. No. 19, W. D., 1919.	Brigadier general, U. S. Army. For services in connection with the reorganization and operation of the Service of Supply of the Army.

DISTINGUISHED-SERVICE MEDAL   789

WOOD, WILLIAM T.
   R—Danville, Ill.
   B—Irving, Ill.
   G. O. No. 77, W. D., 1919.

Brigadier general, U. S. Army.
For services as senior assistant to the Inspector General of the Army.

WOOD, WINTHROP S.
   R—Farmington, Me.
   B—Washington, D. C.
   G. O. No. 38, W. D., 1922.

Colonel, Quartermaster Corps, U. S. Army.
In charge of the general supply depot, Jeffersonville, Ind., from April, 1917, to May, 1918, the successful organization, development, and administration of the system at that important depot for the supply of clothing and general equipment were largely due to his great energy, foresight, and marked executive ability. Later, as quartermaster, Base Section No. 6, American Expeditionary Forces, from August, 1918, to January, 1919, by his administrative ability and untiring zeal he rendered conspicuous services in the improvement and development of the organization of the supply system at this important depot.

WOODRUFF, JAMES A.
   R—Burke, Vt.
   B—Fort Shaw, Mont.
   G. O. No. 59, W. D., 1919.

Colonel, Corps of Engineers, U. S. Army.
He organized and commanded the 10th Forestry Engineers with marked ability. In spite of the difficult situations confronting him he developed the Forestry Service to a marked degree of excellence. By his great energy and devotion to duty he rendered service of the highest character to the Government.

WOODS, ARTHUR
   R—New York, N. Y.
   B—Boston, Mass.
   G. O. No. 15, W. D., 1923.

Colonel, Air Service, U. S. Army.
As inspector of schools, Signal Corps, and then as chief of Personnel, Division of Military Aeronautics, Air Service, by his executive ability, clear conception, and broad mental grasp, he handled with conspicuous success many perplexing problems in the organization and administration of the system for assigning personnel. From November, 1918, until January, 1919, as assistant director of military aeronautics, in the solution of many new and intricate problems concerning demobilization and reorganization his work was characterized by sound judgment and untiring zeal. Later as special assistant to the Secretary of War in matters pertaining to securing employment for discharged soldiers he rendered valuable service in placing great numbers of these men in lucrative positions.

WOODS, GILBERT F.
   R—Chicago, Ill.
   B—Clarksville, Mo.
   G. O. No. 16, W. D., 1920.

Director of Real Estate Service.
He rendered invaluable service to the War Department in the acquisition, either by purchase, condemnation, requisition, donation, or lease, of all real estate required for the use of the Army during the World War, also in the disposal of such real estate as was no longer required. By his technical knowledge, broad judgment, and energetic action valuable results were obtained.

WOOLDRIDGE, JESSE W.
   R—San Francisco, Calif.
   B—Hopkinsville, Ky.
   G. O. No. 35, W. D., 1920.
   Distinguished-service cross also awarded.

Captain, Infantry, U. S. Army.
Near Mezy, France, July 15, 1918, when attacked by portions of three enemy regiments, Captain Wooldridge, by exceptional skill and ability, so inspired his company that he defeated these units and drove them by successive counter attacks from the sectors of his regiment and that of an adjoining regiment. After his company had suffered a loss of 70 per cent by casualties, he organized a platoon from cooks, mess attendants, runners, and Stokes mortar men, and led it in attack upon the last enemy assault wave, which he defeated. During these successive encounters his company captured over 400 of the enemy and broke the strong enemy attempt to cross the Marne in this sector.

WOOTEN, WILLIAM P.
   R—La Grange, N. C.
   B—La Grange, N. C.
   G. O. No. 95, W. D., 1919.

Colonel, Corps of Engineers, U. S. Army.
He served with credit as commanding officer of the 14th Railway Engineers during the operations of that regiment on the British front. Subsequently, while corps engineer of the 3d Army Corps, by his energy, foresight, and skill in accomplishing important engineering works, he contributed materially to the successful operations of his corps. Later, when appointed engineer of the 3d Army, he performed important duties in a most creditable manner.

WORCESTER, PHILIP H.
   R—Portland, Me.
   B—Norfolk, Va.
   G. O. No. 60, W. D., 1920.

Colonel, Coast Artillery Corps, U. S. Army.
As ordnance officer, Army Artillery, 1st Army, during the St. Mihiel and Meuse-Argonne offensives, by his untiring energy and loyal devotion to duty he organized and successfully administered the ammunition and ordnance supplies of the Army Artillery. He at all times displayed sound judgment and military attainments of a high order. He has rendered services of signal worth to the American Expeditionary Forces.

WRIGHT, JOHN W.
   R—Washington, D. C.
   B—Kirkwood, Mo.
   G. O. No. 103, W. D., 1919.

Colonel (Infantry), General Staff Corps, U. S. Army.
As assistant chief of staff, G-3, at Headquarters, Services of Supply, he was charged with the important duty of directing the movement of troop arrivals, billeting, and the supply of initial equipment to units. He at all times displayed indefatigable zeal and administrative ability of a high order, rendering services of inestimable value to the American Expeditionary Forces.

WRIGHT, WILLIAM M.
   R—Newark, N. J.
   B—Newark, N. J.
   G. O. No. 12, W. D., 1919.

Major general, U. S. Army.
He commanded in turn the 35th Division, the 3d, 5th, and 7th Army Corps, under the 8th French Army in the Vosges Mountains, and later commanded the 89th Division in the St. Mihiel offensive and in the final operations on the Meuse River, where he proved himself to be an energetic and aggressive leader.

WYLLIE, ROBERT E.
   R—Sanford, Fla.
   B—India.
   G. O. No. 47, W. D., 1919.

Colonel (Coast Artillery Corps), General Staff Corps, U. S. Army.
In assisting in organizing the first group of General Staff officers that ultimately developed into the operations branch and the equipment branch of the operations division of the General Staff. As chief assistant and later as head of the equipment branch his services were conspicuously useful to the Government and to the Army.

YARDLEY, HERBERT O.
  R—Washington, D. C.
  B—Worthington, Ind.
  G. O. No. 56, W. D., 1922.

Major (Signal Corps), General Staff Corps, U. S. Army.
For services as chief of the communication section of the Military Intelligenc
Division, War Department General Staff, during the World War.

YEATMAN, POPE.
  R—Philadelphia, Pa.
  B—St. Louis, Mo.
  G. O. No. 15, W. D., 1923.

Director of the nonferrous metals section, War Industries Board.
In connection with the operations of the War Industries Board during th
World War, in his position as director of one of the sections of the board h
rendered, through his broad vision, distinguished capacity, and busines
ability, services of inestimable value in marshaling the industrial forces o
the Nation and mobilizing its economic resources—marked factors in assist
ing to make military success attainable. As director of nonferrous metal
he rendered, through his untiring efforts and devotion to duty, exceptionall
valuable service to the War Department in connection with the procuremen
and supply of copper, lead, zinc, and other nonferrous metals for the Army.

YOUNG, HUGH HAMPTON.
  R—Baltimore, Md.
  B—San Antonio, Tex.
  G. O. No. 50, W. D., 1919.

Colonel, Medical Corps, U. S. Army.
He has, by his constant application, tireless energy, and foresight, lowered th
nonefficiency rate of combat organizations, due to certain contagious disease
far below prewar anticipations, and has thereby aided in the conservation c
man power to a degree never before attainable.

YOUNGBERG, GILBERT A.
  R—Cannon Falls, Minn.
  B—Bellcreek, Minn.
  G. O. No. 59, W. D., 1919.

Colonel (Corps of Engineers), General Staff Corps, U. S. Army.
He served as representative of the Engineer Department and later as the prin
cipal assistant to the chief of the 4th Section, General Staff, American Ex
peditionary Forces. He performed duties of the greatest importance i
connection with construction projects of the Army. By his high professions
attainments and tireless energy, his sound judgment and logical recommend
tions on questions of construction, supply, and transportation he materiall
assisted in the successes of our forces in the field. In all matters he displaye
remarkable ability and rendered services of the highest character to th
Government.

YOUNGER, JOHN.
  R—Columbus, Ohio.
  B—Scotland.
  G. O. No. 2, W. D., 1920.

For services as advisory engineer in the designing and production of standar
motor vehicles adopted by the United States of America.

ZALINSKI, MOSES GRAY.
  R—Rochester, N. Y.
  B—Seneca Falls, N. Y.
  G. O. No. 56, W. D., 1921.

Colonel, Quartermaster Corps, U. S. Army.
As quartermaster, Base Section No. 2, Bordeaux, a position of great respons
bility, due to his long quartermaster experience, marked ability, an
knowledge of the methods and standards of supply, he performed the nume
ous duties of his important office with great success. He has rendered servic
of much value to the United States.

ZANETTI, JOAQUIN E.
  R—New York, N. Y.
  B—San Domingo, West Indies.
  G. O. No. 56, W. D., 1922.

Lieutenant colonel, Chemical Warfare Service, U. S. Army.
As chief liaison officer of the Chemical Warfare Service with the French force
his untiring energy, thorough familiarity with the French language an
methods, and his superior technical ability enabled him to gather an enormou
amount of detailed information concerning the manufacture, handling, an
use of gases, which were of inestimable value to our Government in the manu
facture and supply of chemical warfare materials in the United States.

ZIEGAUS, IRVIN W.
  R—Olympia, Wash.
  B—Sharon, Wis.
  G. O. No. 56, W. D., 1922.

Captain, Infantry, U. S. Army.
As executive officer in charge of the selective draft in Washington, by his un
usual executive ability, rare tact and skill, great initiative and resourcefu
ness exercised at times under most trying and novel conditions which aro
in connection with the administration of the selective service act, he achieve
a pronounced and conspicuous success in the performance of difficult an
highly responsible duties, thereby rendering services of great value to th
Government.

ZINSSER, HANS.
  R—New York, N. Y.
  B—New York, N. Y.
  G. O. No. 10, W. D., 1922.

Lieutenant colonel, Medical Corps, U. S. Army.
While acting as sanitary inspector of the 2d Army he organized, perfected, an
administered with extraordinary and exceptional success a plan of militar
sanitation and epidemic-disease control.

BELGIANS

[Awarded for exceptionally meritorious and distinguished services in a position of great responsibility, under the provisions of the act of Congress approved July 9, 1918]

ALBERT.
R—Belgium.
G. O. No. 121, W. D., 1919.

King of the Belgians.
To this distinguished soldier, Commander in Chief of the Belgian Army, this medal is presented as an expression of the high regard of the people of the United States and of their Army for the distinguished and patriotic service which he has rendered to the common cause on the battle fields of Europe.

ARNOULD, HENRY.
R—Belgium.
G. O. No. 87, W. D., 1919.

Lieutenant general, Belgian Army.
He served with marked distinction as chief of artillery of the Belgian Army, rendering invaluable service in the conduct of operations against the enemy. At all times he showed zeal and devotion to duty, his high military attainments having marked effect in the successes achieved by the allied armies.

BARBIER, PHILIPPE.
R—Belgium.
G. O. No. 29, W. D., 1919.

Lieutenant, Belgian Army.
For services rendered the United States Army while serving as acting military attaché to the Belgian Legation, Washington, D. C.

BERNHEIM, LOUIS.
R—Belgium.
G. O. No. 87, W. D., 1919.

Lieutenant general, Belgian Army.
In command of the 1st Belgian Army Division he achieved most valuable results by his brilliant leadership. He prosecuted the operations against the enemy with judgment and vigor and his service was marked by signal success.

BIEBUYCK, A.
R—Belgium.
G. O. No. 45, W. D., 1919.

Lieutenant general, commanding the 6th Belgian Army Corps, Belgian Army.
For services rendered to the American Expeditionary Forces and to the cause in which the United States has been engaged.

CABRA, ALPHONSE F. E.
R—Belgium.
G. O. No. 3, W. D., 1922.

Lieutenant general, Belgian Army.
For services with the American forces in Germany.

CORNELLIE, EMILE F.
R—Belgium.
G. O. No. 126, W. D., 1919.

Colonel, Belgian Army.
As commander of the Belgian naval base in Antwerp, Belgium, he has rendered conspicuous service to the United States. His great energy and sound judgment has been an important factor in the success of the operations of American Base Section No. 9, at Antwerp.

CUMONT, EUGENE F. M. H.
R—Belgium.
G. O. No. 45, W. D., 1919.

Major, Belgian Army, Belgian representative on the Military Board of Allied Supply.
For services rendered to the American Expeditionary Forces and to the cause in which the United States has been engaged.

DE CEUNINCK, ARMAND.
R—Belgium.
G. O. No. 87, W. D., 1919.

Lieutenant general, Belgian Army.
In command of the 4th Belgian Army Division he conducted operations against the enemy with signal success, displaying remarkable qualities of leadership and untiring devotion to his manifold duties. His services were of inestimable value.

DE GOLS, ISADORE.
R—Belgium.
G. O. No. 126, W. D., 1919.

Major, Belgian Army.
As a member of the Interallied Commission on the Repatriation of Prisoners of War he has rendered highly meritorious service to the United States and allied Governments in connection with the repatriation of American and allied prisoners released by the armistice. He always displayed a cheerful and active interest in all that pertained to their welfare and rendered sympathetic and practical cooperation.

DELOBBE, H.
R—Belgium.
G. O. No. 87, W. D., 1919.

General major, Belgian Army.
As chief of a staff section at Belgian General Headquarters he rendered most distinguished services. He displayed the highest military attainments and great zeal in the direction of operations against the enemy.

DE PAGE, ANTOINE.
R—Belgium.
G. O. No. 72, W. D., 1920.

Colonel, surgeon, Belgian Army.
A distinguished surgeon and one of the pioneers in developing the modern treatment of battle casualties, he placed his eminent talents and extensive experience at the disposition of the medical department of the American Expeditionary Forces, and at all times lent his cooperation toward improving the treatment of the wounded. At his hospital at Le Panne, Belgium, he took an active personal interest in training medical officers of the American Army in the advances being made in battle surgery. Under his able supervision and guidance the observation and experience gained by these officers eventually resulted in saving the lives of many American wounded.

DEVEZE, ALBERT J. C.
R—Belgium.
G. O. No. 19, W. D., 1922.

Captain, Belgian Army.
For services rendered to the allied cause and to the American forces in Germany.

D'OULTREMONT, GUY D. R—Belgium. G. O. No. 126, W. D., 1919.	Commandant, Belgian Army. The same high character of services rendered by him from 1914 to 1918 w the Belgian Artillery in the field were again revealed during the period wh he was attached to the Belgian Mission at American General Headqu ters. As principal assistant to the chief of the Belgian Mission at Ameri General Headquarters he rendered services of great value to the Ameri Expeditionary Forces. By able advice and sound judgment, coupled w loyal support, he assisted us in all problems presented to him.
DRUBBEL, HONORE. R—Belgium. G. O. No. 87, W. D., 1919.	Lieutenant general, Belgian Army. In command of the 2d Belgian Army Division he showed eminent quali of leadership, at all times using his genius for military tactics to the l advantage in the operations against the enemy. His brilliant achievem(had an important bearing upon the successful conduct of the war.
DU BOIS, AUGUSTO, D. J. A. M. R—Belgium. G. O. No. 30, W. D., 1921.	Colonel, Belgian Army, Chief of Staff, Belgian Army of Occupation. For services rendered to the allied cause and to the American forces in Germs
GILLAIN, C. C. V. R—Belgium. G. O. No. 111, W. D., 1919.	Lieutenant general, Belgian Army, Chief of the General Staff of the Bel; Army. As an expression to him of the high regard of the people of the United St and of their Army for the distinguished and patriotic services which he rendered to the common cause in which he has been associated on the b; fields of Europe.
GREINDL, LEON M. R—Belgium. G. O. No. 87, W. D., 1919.	General major, Belgian Army. As chief of a staff section at Belgian General Headquarters he rendered in uable service in the direction of the most important engineering operati Confronted by stupendous tasks he performed all with distinction, shov exact scientific knowledge and great zeal in the performance of his ardu duties.
HEMELEERS-SHENLEY, LEON A. H. R—Belgium. G. O. No. 126, W. D., 1919.	Captain, Belgian Army. As principal assistant to the chief of the Belgian Mission at American Ger Headquarters he rendered services of great value to the American Ex; tionary Forces. By able advice and sound judgment, coupled with l support, he assisted us in all problems presented to him. Zealous in efforts and wholehearted in cooperation, he at all times promoted the frier relations between the Belgians and Americans.
JACQUES, JULES M. A. R—Belgium. G. O. No. 17, W. D., 1919.	Lieutenant general, Belgian Army, in command of the 3d Belgian A Division. For services rendered to the American Expeditionary Forces and to the ca in which the United States has been engaged.
JUNGBLUTH, HARRY. R—Belgium. G. O. No. 87, W. D., 1919.	Lieutenant general, Belgian Army. As Adjutant General, Chief of the Military Household of the King he c pied with distinction one of the most important offices in the Belgian Ar He displayed the highest military attainments and his sound advice w; inestimable value in the prosecution of the war against the enemy.
LEMAN, GEORGES. R—Belgium. G. O. No. 39, W. D., 1920.	Lieutenant general, Belgian Army. To this distinguished officer this medal is presented as an expression of high regard of the people of the United States and of their Army for distinguished and patriotic services which he has rendered to the com cause on the battle fields of Europe.
MAGLINSE, HENRY H. R—Belgium. G. O. No. 87, W. D., 1919.	General major, Belgian Army. As chief of a staff section at Belgian General Headquarters he rendered ir uable services in the direction of operations against the enemy. At all t he displayed the highest military attainments, untiring energy, and ze the performance of his distinguished duties.
MAHIEU, LOUIS. R—Belgium. G. O. No. 126, W. D., 1919.	General major, Belgian Army. As Military Governor of the Province of Antwerp he has rendered conspic service to the United States. His hearty cooperation was of the gre value to our forces in the establishment of American Base Section No.
MERCHIE, SYLVIAN. R—Belgium. G. O. No. 87, W. D., 1919.	General major, Belgian Army. As chief of staff in the office of the Belgian Secretary of War he rendered : important service in the prosecution of operations against the enemy. high professional attainments furthered his rapid promotion in active se: with troops, fitting him for the distinguished duties to which he was c later.
MICHEL, AUGUSTIN E. R—Belgium. G. O. No. 87, W. D., 1919.	Lieutenant general, Belgian Army. In command of the Belgian Army of Occupation he performed his impoi duties with the greatest distinction, at all times displaying marked qua of leadership and sound judgment at critical periods.
OSTERRIETH, LEON. R—Belgium. G. O. No. 11, W. D., 1919.	Major, Belgian Army. For services rendered the United States Army while serving as chief o Belgian Military Mission to the United States and acting military att to the Belgian Legation, Washington, D. C.

RUQUOY, L. H. R—Belgium. G. O. No. 17, W. D., 1919.	Lieutenant general, Belgian Army, in command of the 5th Belgian Army Division. For services rendered to the American Expeditionary Forces and to the cause in which the United States has been engaged.
SEGERS, PAUL R—Belgium. G. O. No. 15, W. D., 1923.	Minister of Transportation, Belgium. Instrumental in the cession by the Belgian Government of steam motive power at a time when the lack of locomotives was a grave and serious handicap to the successful operations of the American Expeditionary Forces, he assisted in an important and conspicuous way in the rapid and efficient functioning of the lines of communication of the American Army.
TILKENS, AUGUST R—Belgium. G. O. No. 87, W. D., 1919.	Colonel, Belgian Army. After serving with distinction in the command of troops he rendered most valuable services as aide-de-camp to the King of the Belgians. As member of the King's military household he showed high military attainments, and his advice proved uniformly sound.
TINANT, JULES T. A. E. L. R—Belgium. G. O. No. 45, W. D., 1919.	Major, Belgian Army, Chief, Belgian Mission, General Headquarters, American Expeditionary Forces. For services rendered to the American Expeditionary Forces and to the cause in which the United States has been engaged.
VAN DE VYVERE, A. R—Belgium. G. O. No. 9, W. D., 1923.	Minister of Finance, Belgium. A grave situation having arisen with reference to a lack of steam motive power for the American Expeditionary Forces, Mr. Van de Vyvere succeeded in providing the American forces through the Belgian Government with a large number of locomotives, thus contributing in a conspicuous way to the successful operations of the allied cause.
WARNANT, URSMAR A. R—Belgium. G. O. No. 59, W. D., 1921.	Captain, Belgian Army. For services as chief of the Belgian Mission attached to the American forces in France.

BRITISH

[Awarded for exceptionally meritorious and distinguished services in a position of great responsibility, under the provisions of the act of Congress approved July 9, 1918]

ADYE, JOHN.
R—England.
G. O. No. 14, W. D., 1920.
: Major general, British Army.
His services were of conspicuous merit as a member of the committee on return of prisoners of war. His large experience in the Near East, combined with rare judgment and quiet forcefulness, made his work especially valuable in securing the rapid return of American and allied prisoners and in alleviating their condition.

ALLENBY, EDMUND H. H.
R—England.
G. O. No. 126, W. D., 1919.
: General, British Army.
The American Army will ever remember his valiant services as commander of the 3d British Army in France from 1914 to 1917 and for his marvelous successes in Palestine, rendering services of distinction to the allied cause.

ANDERSON, STUART M.
R—England.
G. O. No. 126, W. D., 1919.
: Brigadier general, British Army, Royal Artillery, 1st Australian Division, British Expeditionary Forces.
The accurate and highly efficient support by the Artillery under his command contributed materially to the successful assaults on the Hindenburg line by the 30th U. S. Division, Sept. 29, 1918. The part played by him in achieving that success has won for him the deepest gratitude and admiration on the part of the American officers and soldiers with whom he was cooperating during the great advance.

ATKINSON, CHARLES F.
R—England.
G. O. No. 45, W. D., 1919.
: Major, British Army, instructor, Army Intelligence School, American Expeditionary Forces.
For services performed for the American Expeditionary Forces and to the cause in which the United States has been engaged.

AULD, SAMUEL J. M.
R—England.
G. O. No. 45, W. D., 1919.
: Major, 4th Battalion, Royal Berkshire Regiment, British Army.
For services rendered the U. S. Army while serving as liaison officer between the British and American Chemical Warfare Services.

BALFOUR, ALFRED G.
R—England.
G. O. No. 46, W. D., 1920.
: Brigadier general, British Army.
As commander of the embarkation area of the port of Southampton, by his earnest spirit of cooperation with the American authorities at the port of Southampton, he rendered valuable assistance, offering them every facility at his command for the proper handling of the important problem of troop shipments.

BEADON, ROGERS H.
R—England.
G. O. No. 45, W. D., 1919.
: Colonel, British Army, British section, Supreme War Council.
For services rendered to the American Expeditionary Forces and to the cause in which the United States has been engaged.

BESSELL-BROWNE, ALFRED J.
R—England.
G. O. No. 126, W. D., 1919.
: Brigadier general, British Army, 5th Australian Division, British Expeditionary Forces.
The relations of the American and Australian forces, cooperating with each other, were always marked with the utmost harmony, but never was the spirit more clearly manifested than during the period from Oct. 16 to 19, 1918 when the 30th U. S. Division went forward in attack against the enemy supported by artillery under his command. To his consummate technical skill and unflagging energy is due much credit for the successful results attained in these operations.

BETHELL, HUGH K.
R—England.
G. O. No. 126, W. D., 1919.
: Brigadier general, British Army.
He commanded with distinction the 66th British Division, with which the 27th American Division was affiliated during its training period. By his broad-minded policy, personal interest, and careful supervision he gave great assistance to the division, enabling the American troops to readily adapt themselves to the methods and conditions of service with a foreign army.

BIRCH, JAMES F. N.
R—England.
G. O. No. 45, W. D., 1919.
: Lieutenant general, British Army, chief of artillery, British Expeditionary Forces.
For services rendered to the American Expeditionary Forces and to the cause in which the United States has been engaged.

BIRDWOOD, WILLIAM R.
R—England.
G. O. No. 17, W. D., 1919.
: General, British Army, commanding 5th Army, British Expeditionary Forces.
For services rendered to the American Expeditionary Forces and to the cause in which the United States has been engaged.

BLAKE, DAVID V. J.
R—England.
G. O. No. 45, W. D., 1919.
: Major, British Army, commanding officer, 3d Squadron, Australian Flying Corps, British Expeditionary Forces.
For services performed for the American Expeditionary Forces and to the cause in which the United States has been engaged.

BOND, FRANCIS G.
R—England.
G. O. No. 45, W. D., 1919.
: Major general, director of quarterings, British Army.
For services performed for the American Expeditionary Forces and to the cause in which the United States has been engaged.

BONHAM-CARTER, CHARLES.
R—England.
G. O. No. 87, W. D., 1919.

Brigadier general, British Army.
As general officer in charge of training at British General Headquarters during the period the 2d American Corps was in the British Expeditionary Forces, he rendered exceptional service to the U. S. Army. His knowledge of training methods was extensive, and with loyal cooperation he gave us the benefit of his experience.

BOWDLER, BASIL W. B.
R—England.
G. O. No. 126, W. D., 1919.

Lieutenant colonel, British Army.
While he was on duty in the intelligence section at British General Headquarters and as chief of the information section, his assistance and advice in inspecting and training American officers were of distinct advantage to the American Expeditionary Forces. He displayed military attainments of a high order, and at all times cooperated with the American military authorities whole-heartedly.

BOWLBY, ANTHONY A.
R—England.
G. O. No. 124, W. D., 1919.

Major general, British Army.
An eminent consulting surgeon, and while serving with the British Expeditionary Forces in France, with untiring zeal he devoted his time and energy toward cooperating with and unreservedly placing at the disposal of the American Expeditionary Forces his eminent talents, broad experience, and knowledge of general conditions in preventing wastage among our forces from wounds and disease. His research work in wound bacteriology and evacuation resulted in the saving of many lives among our sick and wounded.

BOYCE, CHARLES E.
R—England.
G. O. No. 45, W. D., 1919.

Major, British Army, attached as staff officer, units of Royal Field Artillery, serving with the 2d Army Corps, American Expeditionary Forces.
For services performed for the American Expeditionary Forces and to the cause in which the United States has been engaged.

BRIDGES, GEORGE T. M.
R—England.
G. O. No. 11, W. D., 1919.

Lieutenant general, British Army.
For services rendered the U. S. Army while serving as the military representative of the British Mission to the United States (April, 1917), and later (1918) as chief of British Military Missions to the United States.

BURGESS, WILLIAM L. H.
R—England.
G. O. No. 126, W. D., 1919.

Brigadier general, British Army.
He commanded with distinction the 4th Australian Artillery Division while it was in support of the 27th American Division during the operations near St. Souplet, east of the La Selle River. His consummate skill as an artillerist and forceful determination in keeping his batteries well to the front were most potent factors in the successes achieved. The services which he rendered to the American Expeditionary Forces were of inestimable value.

BURTCHAELL, CHARLES H.
R—England.
G. O. No. 87, W. D., 1919.

Lieutenant general, British Army.
As Director General of Medical Service, British Expeditionary Forces, he displayed untiring zeal, eminent talents, and broad experience in providing adequate hospitalization and evacuation facilities for the sick and wounded of the American troops serving with the British Armies. His individual efforts counted largely in enabling the American Medical Service to function efficiently.

BUSH, W. A.
R—England.
G. O. No. 87, W. D., 1919.

Captain, British Army, instructor, American Expeditionary Forces Gas Defense School, Hanlon Field, France.
At the request of the American Expeditionary Forces he was detailed as instructor in gas defense, and rendered services of extraordinary merit at the school at Hanlon Field. Largely as the result of his energy, skill, and exact knowledge the school accomplished a most important mission, providing a course of instruction which, when put in practice in the field, prevented many casualties.

BUTLER, RICHARD H. K.
R—England.
G. O. No. 45, W. D., 1919.

Lieutenant general, British Army, commanding 3d Army Corps, British Expeditionary Forces.
For services rendered to the American Expeditionary Forces and to the cause in which the United States has been engaged.

BYNG, JULIAN H. G.
R—England.
G. O. No. 17, W. D., 1919.

General, British Army, commanding 3d Army, British Expeditionary Forces.
For services rendered to the American Expeditionary Forces and to the cause in which the United States has been engaged.

CAMPBELL, RONALD B.
R—England.
G. O. No. 45, W. D., 1919.

Lieutenant colonel, British Army, deputy inspector of bayonet and physical Training, British Expeditionary Forces.
For services performed for the American Expeditionary Forces and to the cause in which the United States has been engaged.

CARTER, EVAN E.
R—England.
G. O. No. 45, W. D., 1919.

Major general, British Army, Director General of Forage and Supplies, British Expeditionary Forces.
For services performed for the American Expeditionary Forces and to the cause in which the United States has been engaged.

CASSEL, FELIX.
R—England.
G. O. No. 46, W. D., 1920.

As Judge Advocate General of the British forces, he ably assisted the American authorities with whom he came in contact. By his sound advice and able counsel on all questions affecting military justice he rendered services of great value to the American Expeditionary Forces.

CHARTERIS, JOHN.
R—England.
G. O. No. 126, W. D., 1919.

Colonel, British Army, bureau of intelligence, British Expeditionary Forces.
As brigadier general of intelligence at British General Headquarters he rendered most valuable service to the American Expeditionary Forces during the early period of the organization of the staff by placing every facility at the disposal of the American staff officers who were sent to British General Headquarters for the purpose of instruction. He displayed military attainments of a high order, tireless energy, and marked zeal in the performance of his exacting duties. He was at all times tactful and proved himself a loyal friend.

CHURCHILL, WINSTON
R—England.
G. O. No. 62, W. D., 1919.

He rendered the Allied cause service of inestimable value. As British Minister of Munitions, he was confronted with a task of great magnitude. With ability of a high order, energy, and marked devotion to duty, he handled with great success the trying problems with which he was constantly confronted. In the performance of his great task he rendered valuable service to the American Expeditionary Forces.

CLARKE, TRAVERS E
R—England.
G. O. No. 45, W. D., 1919.

Lieutenant general, British Army, quartermaster general, British Expeditionary Forces.
For services rendered to the American Expeditionary Forces and to the cause in which the United States has been engaged.

CORNWALL, JAMES H. M
R—England.
G. O. No. 126, W. D., 1919.

Lieutenant colonel, British Army.
While a member of the intelligence section at British General Headquarters he rendered us very valuable and distinguished services by his hearty cooperation in placing at the disposal of the American officers sent to British General Headquarters his experience and profound knowledge regarding the work of intelligence. He was at all times tactful and helpful, proving himself a loyal friend.

COVELL, FRANK C
R—England.
G. O. No. 126, W. D., 1919.

Captain, British Army.
As liaison officer at general headquarters, Base Section No. 3, in London, he performed his duties with great tact, skill, and indefatigable zeal. The harmony which constantly characterized the relations of the American authorities with the British War Office was due, in no small degree, to his faithful services.

COWANS, JOHN S
R—England.
G. O. No. 45, W. D., 1919.

General, quartermaster general to the forces, British Army.
For services performed for the American Expeditionary Forces and to the cause in which the United States has been engaged.

CRAVEN, FRANCIS W
R—England.
G. O. No. 27, W. D., 1919.

Lieutenant, British Navy, commanding His Majesty's destroyer Mounsey.
For rescuing 7 officers and 313 men of the American forces at sea on Oct. 16, 1918.

CROOKSHANK, SYDNEY D'A
R—England.
G. O. No. 2, W. D., 1920.

Major general, British Army.
The services General Crookshank rendered as Director General of Transportation of the British forces were of great merit. He heartily cooperated with the American authorities and gave much assistance to our Transportation Corps. He lent every effort to further those friendly relations which characterized the transportation services of the British and American Armies.

CUNINGHAME, THOMAS A. A. M
R—England.
G. O. No. 45, W. D., 1919.

Lieutenant colonel, British Army, instructor, Army Staff College, American Expeditionary Forces.
For services performed for the American Expeditionary Forces and to the cause in which the United States has been engaged.

CURRIE, ARTHUR W
R—England.
G. O. No. 17, W. D., 1919.

Lieutenant general, British Army, commanding Canadian Corps, British Expeditionary Forces.
For services rendered to the American Expeditionary Forces and to the cause in which the United States has been engaged.

CURRY, PHILIP A
R—England.
G. O. No. 69, W. D., 1919.

Major, British Army.
As director of transports for the British Ministry of Shipping at the port of New York during the movement of troops overseas.

DAVIDSON, GILBERT
R—England.
G. O. No. 87, W. D., 1919.

Lieutenant colonel, British Army, forage and supplies, British Expeditionary Forces.
He extended whole-hearted cooperation to our supply procurement agencies, rendering very valuable services to the American Expeditionary Forces. By his efforts and devotion to the American interests, great quantities of necessary supplies were made available for our troops.

DAVIDSON, JOHN H
R—England.
G. O. No. 45, W. D., 1919.

Major general, British Army, general staff operations, British Expeditionary Forces.
For services performed for the American Expeditionary Forces and to the cause in which the United States has been engaged.

DAVIES, FRANCIS J
R—England.
G. O. No. 46, W. D., 1920.

Lieutenant general, British Army.
As Secretary of the British War Office and member of the Army Council, by his great energy and marked military attainments, he rendered services of signal worth to the common cause.

DAWNAY, GUY
R—England.
G. O. No. 126, W. D., 1919.

Lieutenant colonel, British Army.
As head of the staff duties section of the General Staff at General Headquarters American Expeditionary Forces, he was an important factor in the victorious termination of the war by his brilliant military attainments and unremitting zeal. He constantly manifested the utmost consideration for the American units attached to the British Armies, aiding materially in their training and thereby rendering invaluable services to the American Expeditionary Forces.

DEEDES, CHARLES P
R—England.
G. O. No. 46, W. D., 1920.

Brigadier general, British Army.
As Deputy Director of Staff Duties of the British Army, by his tact, marked ability, and spirit of wholehearted cooperation with American officers on duty with the British Army staff, ably assisting them in every endeavor, he rendered services of great value to the American Expeditionary Forces.

DELANO-OSBORNE, OSBORNE H
R—England.
G. O. No. 45, W. D., 1919.

Brigadier general, director of movements (transportation), British Army.
For services performed for the American Expeditionary Forces and to the cause in which the United States has been engaged.

DRAKE, JOHN R—England. G. O. No. 126, W. D., 1919.	Lieutenant colonel, British Army. As chief of the intelligence bureau section at British General Headquarters he at all times cooperated with the officers of the U. S. Army, and by his sound advice and cooperation rendered most valuable services to the American Expeditionary Forces. He was tireless in his devotion to his important duties, proving tactful and ready to come to our assistance at all times.
ELLES, HUGH J. R—England. G. O. No. 45, W. D., 1919.	Major general, British Army, commanding Tank Corps, British Expeditionary Forces. For services performed for the American Expeditionary Forces and to the cause in which the United States has been engaged.
EWART, RICHARD. R—England. G. O. No. 126, W. D., 1919.	Major general, British Army. As senior British member of the Interallied Commission on the Repatriation of Prisoners of War he has rendered conspicuous service to the United States and the allied Governments in connection with the sustenance, care, and homeward transportation of American and allied prisoners released by the armistice. He has at all times displayed a personal interest and supervising influence which resulted in speedy and comfortable repatriation of prisoners of war.
FORBES, ARTHUR W. R—England. G. O. No. 46, W. D., 1920.	Brigadier general, British Army. As commander of the embarkation area of the port of Liverpool he gave important assistance to the American Expeditionary Forces. At all times he exhibited a spirit of zealous cooperation with the American authorities, placing all the facilities of his important office at their disposal. He rendered service of conspicuous worth to the American Expeditionary Forces.
FORD, REGINALD. R—England. G. O. No. 45, W. D., 1919.	Major general, British Army, British representative, military board of allied supply. For services performed for the American Expeditionary Forces and to the cause in which the United States has been engaged.
FOULKES, CHARLES H. R—England. G. O. No. 45, W. D., 1919.	Brigadier general, British Army, director British Chemical Warfare Service. For services performed for the American Expeditionary Forces and to the cause in which the United States has been engaged.
FOWKE, GEORGE H. R—England. G. O. No. 45, W. D., 1919.	Lieutenant general, British Army, Adjutant General, British Expeditionary Forces. For services rendered to the American Expeditionary Forces and to the cause in which the United States has been engaged.
FOWLER, JOHN S. R—England. G. O. No. 126, W. D., 1919.	Major general, British Army. As Director of Signals of the British Expeditionary Forces he constantly rendered us valuable assistance in connection with the supply of needed material at critical times. He aided us very materially in promoting the efficiency of our electrical communications, displaying at all times military and scientific attainments of a high order. He was energetic in our behalf, proving himself a loyal friend of the American Expeditionary Forces.
FURSE, WILLIAM T. R—England. G. O. No. 45, W. D., 1919.	Lieutenant general, British Army, Master General of the Ordnance, British Expeditionary Forces. For services performed for the American Expeditionary Forces and to the cause in which the United States has been engaged.
GEIGER, GERALD J. P. R—England. G. O. No. 46, W. D., 1920.	Major, British Army. As liaison officer of the British with the American Army, and later as chief of the British Mission at the Headquarters of the 3d Army, he has, by his tact, loyalty, and painstaking efforts, earnestly cooperated with the American authorities in handling the difficult problems which constantly arose, rendering services of great worth to the American Expeditionary Forces.
GELLIBRAND, JOHN. R—England. G. O. No. 126, W. D., 1919.	Major general, British Army. During the operations against the Hindenburg line near Ronssoy, in September, 1918, he commanded with brilliant leadership the 3d Australian Division, operating in close liaison with the 27th American Division. The fine spirit of comradeship prevailing between the officers and soldiers of these two divisions was in no small measure a reflection of the warm spirit of cooperation which he constantly manifested and his willingness to aid the American Expeditionary Forces in every way possible.
GILES, EDWARD D. R—England. G. O. No. 45, W. D., 1919.	Lieutenant colonel, British Army. As advisor to the training and instruction branch, war plans division, he rendered invaluable assistance in making possible the inception and successful conduct of war-time instruction at the Army War College.
GLYN, RALPH G. R—England. G. O. No. 45, W. D., 1919.	Major, British Army, instructor, Army Staff College, American Expeditionary Forces. For services performed for the American Expeditionary Forces and to the cause in which the United States has been engaged.
GOLIGHER, HUGH G. R—England. G. O. No. 126, W. D., 1919.	Brigadier general, British Army. Serving as a financial officer of the British Expeditionary Forces in France by his broad experience and extraordinary administrative ability he proved a notable factor in the success of the allied cause. He was at all times at the service of the American officers, who were charged with questions of supply and finance, and by his sound advice, unfailing courtesy, and loyal spirit of cooperation rendered services of the utmost value to the American Expeditionary Forces.

GOODWIN, THOMAS H. J. C.
R—England.
G. O. No. 87, W. D., 1919.

Lieutenant general, British Army.
As Surgeon General of the British Army, he placed at the disposal of the Ameri can divisions serving with the British forces all the evacuation and hospita zation facilities at his command. His eminent skill, ability, and bro experience enabled him to extend most useful cooperation.

GREEN, ARTHUR F. U.
R—England.
G. O. No. 14, W. D., 1920.

Colonel, British Army.
He has done conspicuous service as chief of staff of the British Mission. I sound judgment, sympathetic understanding, and steadfastness of purp contributed in large measure to the furtherance of Anglo-American und standing and to the execution of the terms of the armistice.

GUTHRIE, CONNOP.
R—England.
G. O. No. 103, W. D., 1919.

British Ministry of Shipping.
As a member of the shipping control committee his services in connection w negotiations for British tonnage in the interchange of tonnage by the V Department and the British Government have been conspicuous.

HAIG, DOUGLAS.
R—England.
G. O. No. 111, W. D., 1918.

Field Marshal, British Army, commander in chief of the British Armies France.
As an expression to him of the high regard of the people of the United Sta and of their Army, for the distinguished and patriotic services which he rendered to the common cause in which he has been associated on the bat fields of Europe.

HAKING, RICHARD C. B.
R—England.
G. O. No. 14, W. D. 1920.

Lieutenant general, British Army.
He rendered conspicuously meritorious service as chief of the British Missi standing shoulder to shoulder with the chief of the American Mission in questions of policy, aiding with rare tact and a genial personality the core relations between the English-speaking missions. He saw 52 months' se ice in the field, commanded the XI Army Corps, and is the hero of the re of Lille in 1918.

HARINGTON, CHARLES H.
R—England.
G. O. No. 45, W. D., 1919.

Major general, deputy chief of the Imperial General Staff, British Army.
For services performed for the American Expeditionary Forces and to cause in which the United States has been engaged.

HEADLAM, JOHN E. W.
R—England.
G. O. No. 11, W. D., 1919.

Major general, British Army.
For services rendered the United States Army while serving as chief of British Artillery Mission to the United States.

HEATH, GERARD M.
R—England.
G. O. No. 126, W. D., 1919.

Major general, British Army.
As Engineer in Chief of the British Expeditionary Forces he performed, w conspicuous success, highly responsible duties in the struggle against common enemy. He gave unfailing support to the American units serv with the British Armies, and in spite of his numerous other tasks sou every opportunity to aid in developing their efficiency, thereby render services of the utmost value to the American Expeditionary Forces.

HOLLAND, HENRY W.
R—England.
G. O. No. 45, W. D., 1919.

Lieutenant colonel, censorship and publicity section, British Army.
For services performed for the American Expeditionary Forces and to cause in which the United States has been engaged.

HONE, THOMAS N.
R—England.
G. O. No. 126, W. D., 1919.

Captain, British Army.
As assistant to the chief of the British Mission at American General He quarters from December, 1917, to June, 1919, by his complete knowledg the intelligence service, fostered by an earnest spirit of cooperation, he g much valuable aid to our second section of the General Staff, offering t every facility at his command.

HORNE, HENRY S.
R—England.
G. O. No. 17, W. D., 1919.

General, British Army, commanding 1st Army, British Expeditionary For
For services rendered to the American Expeditionary Forces and to the ca in which the United States has been engaged.

HUTCHINSON, HUGH M.
R—England.
G. O. No. 126, W. D., 1919.

Lieutenant colonel, British Army.
As instructor at the Gondrecourt schools, he rendered service of exceptio value in the training of a large number of officers of the American Exp tionary Forces. He was tireless in devotion to his important duties displayed military attainments of high order. Tactful and forceful in presentation of important subjects, he gave us very valuable assistance

HUTCHISON, ROBERT.
R—England.
G. O. No. 45, W. D., 1919.

Major general, Director of Organization, British Army.
For services performed for the American Expeditionary Forces and to cause in which the United States has been engaged.

JACK, EVAN M.
R—England.
G. O. No. 126, W. D., 1919.

Lieutenant colonel, British Army.
As officer in charge of maps in British General Headquarters he rendered v able and distinguished services to the American Expeditionary For making available to us all the information at his command. He provi for the instruction of American officers on the British front, and supplie with special technical equipment that could not be obtained elsewhere.

JACOB, CLAUD W.
R—England.
G. O. No. 45, W. D., 1919.

Lieutenant general, British Army, commanding 2d Army Corps, Bri Expeditionary Forces.
For services performed for the American Expeditionary Forces and to cause in which the United States has been engaged.

JONES, ROBERT R—England. G. O. No. 124, W. D., 1919.	Major general, British Army. An eminent orthopedic surgeon and chief of the division of orthopedic surgery in the British Army, he placed at the disposal of the medical service of the American Expeditionary Forces his eminent talents and broad experience in standardizing methods of treatment for the sick and wounded and took an active personal interest in class instruction of American medical officers in this very important branch of surgery.
JURY, EDWARD C R—England. G. O. No. 126, W. D., 1919.	Lieutenant colonel, British Army. As principal assistant to the chief of the British Mission attached to the American General Headquarters of the period, January, 1918, to March, 1919, by his brilliant military ability and his earnest spirit of wholehearted cooperation with the personnel of our fourth and fifth sections of the General Staff, he gave much valuable assistance to these sections during the period of their organization and development, rendering services of inestimable value to the American Expeditionary Forces.
KNAPP, KEMPSTER K R—England. G. O. No. 87, W. D., 1919.	Brigadier general, British Army. In command of the British artillery supporting the 2d American Corps during the operations from Sept. 27, 1918, to Oct. 21, 1918, he proved of invaluable assistance to our Infantry. He showed himself an indefatigable worker, a brilliant tactician, and a loyal friend.
LAMB, MALCOLM H. M R—England. G. O. No. 126, W. D., 1919.	Major, British Army. As chief of intelligence, line communications, British Expeditionary Forces, he assisted most ably in the organization, instruction, and working of the American intelligence section in the Services of Supply. Due to his advice, experience, and aid many of the difficult problems confronting our Services of Supply during its preliminary organization were successfully overcome. The services which he rendered the American Expeditionary Forces were most valuable.
LAWRENCE, HERBERT A R—England. G. O. No. 17, W. D., 1919.	Lieutenant general, British Army, Chief of Staff, British Expeditionary Forces. For services rendered to the American Expeditionary Forces and to the cause in which the United States has been engaged.
LAWRENCE, RICHARD C. B R—England. G. O. No. 126, W. D., 1919.	Brigadier general, British Army, commanding the British base at Marseille, France. When the American base was established at Marseille he was of the utmost assistance in its development and maintenance by the practical aid and valuable advice he gave. Always ready, in case of need, to place at our disposition the valuable facilities acquired by the British base, during four years of operation, he made possible an increased supply to the American troops. By his fervent spirit of cooperation he rendered service of inestimable value to the American Expeditionary Forces.
LEISHMAN, WILLIAM B R—England. G. O. No. 60, W. D., 1920.	Major general, Royal Army Medical Corps, British Army. By his marked energy and zealous cooperation with the Medical Service of the American Expeditionary Forces in important research work, he promoted the efficient treatment of the American sick and wounded. His remarkable achievements in the domain of preventive medicine and wound bacteriology resulted in the saving of many lives among our wounded. His services were of great consequence to the American Expeditionary Forces.
LIDBURY, CHARLES A R—England. G. O. No. 45, W. D., 1919.	Major, British Army, attached to the 2d Army Corps, American Expeditionary Forces. For services performed for the American Expeditionary Forces and to the cause in which the United States has been engaged.
LIVESAY, ROBERT O'H R—England. G. O. No. 126, W. D., 1919.	Brigadier general, British Army. As instructor at the American Army General Staff College, he rendered services of exceptional value to the American Expeditionary Forces in connection with the efficient training of our officers. He displayed military attainment of high order in the performance of his exacting duties, working always wholeheartedly in our interests. He proved himself sound in judgment, tactful, and a loyal friend.
LYNDEN-BELL, ARTHUR L R—England. G. O. No. 126, W. D., 1919.	Major general, British Army. As Director of Staff Duties at British General Headquarters he performed with distinction the important duties of his high office. In the midst of his manifold and exacting tasks he interested himself repeatedly in behalf of the American Expeditionary Forces, rendering us service of exceptional value. Through his instrumentality masses of information requested by us of the British Mission at Washington, Versailles, and at American General Headquarters have been made available. Most helpful at all times, he has proved himself a loyal friend.
MACDONOGH, GEORGE M. W R—England. G. O. No. 45, W. D., 1919.	Lieutenant general, adjutant general to the forces, British Army. For services performed for the American Expeditionary Forces and to the cause in which the United States has been engaged.
MCLACHLAN, JAMES D R—England. G. O. No. 11, W. D., 1919.	Major general, British Army. For services rendered the U. S. Army while serving as military attaché to the British Embassy, Washington, D. C.

McNamee, John T. R—England. G. O. No. 126, W. D., 1919. Distinguished-service cross also awarded.	Captain, Royal Field Artillery, British Army, attached to the 1st Battali(1st Gas Regiment, American Expeditionary Forces. As instructor with the 1st Gas Regiment, American Expeditionary Forces, worked unceasingly in developing aggressive forms of gas attack. He v tireless in his devotion to duty, showing particularly valuable ability personally supervising the liaison and conduct of the gas operations in Meuse-Argonne drive.
MacPherson, William G. R—England. G. O. No. 56, W. D., 1921.	Major general, British Army. As Deputy Director General of Medical Services of the British Armies in Fra he displayed exceptional energy, initiative, and good judgment in direct and supervising in the most expeditious manner possible the organizati equipment, and training of medical department units of the 2d Corps, Am(can Expeditionary Forces, serving with the British Expeditionary Forc It was largely through his cooperation and individual efforts that the Medi Service of the 2d Corps, American Expeditionary Forces, was prepared time to proficiently discharge its duties to the sick and wounded in comb
Maud, Harry. R—England. G. O. No. 87, W. D., 1919.	Colonel, British Army, forage and supplies, British Expeditionary Forces. He gave most valuable assistance to the American Expeditionary Forces in procurement of necessary supplies for our troops. He rendered tactful a most willing service, affording whole-hearted cooperation in his import; duties.
May, Reginald S. R—England. G. O. No. 45, W. D., 1919.	Major general, British Army, Deputy Quartermaster General, British Expe tionary Forces. For services performed for the American Expeditionary Forces and to the ca in which the United States has been engaged.
Miller, Walter. R—Canada. G. O. No. 29, W. D., 1919.	Major, Canadian forces. For services rendered the U. S Army while serving as the liaison officer betw the British Embassy, the Ministry of Militia and Defense, Dominion Canada, and the War Department.
Milne, George F. R—England. G. O. No. 62, W. D., 1919.	Lieutenant general, British Army. As British Minister of War he displayed military attainments of a high ord achieving a brilliant success. Untiring in devotion to his important dut he was aggressive and capable, rendering service of inestimable value to American Expeditionary Forces and the allied cause.
Monash, John. R—England G. O. No. 4, W. D., 1919.	Lieutenant general, British Army, commanding Australian Army Co1 British Expeditionary Forces. For services rendered to the American Expeditionary Forces and to the ca in which the United States has been engaged.
Montgomery, Archibald A. R—England. G. O. No. 126, W. D., 1919.	Major general, British Army. As chief of staff of the 4th British Army he directed the operations of the American Army Corps with distinguished ability, displaying military tainments of the highest order. The officers and soldiers of the 27th, 3(and 33d U. S. Divisions are justly proud of having served with their Eng comrades against the common foe and of having shared with them in successes which were due, in no small degree, to his capable direction.
Nash, Philip A. M. R—England. G. O. No. 87, W. D., 1919.	Major general, British Army. The service he rendered the American Expeditionary Forces as Inspe(General of Transportation for the British Army and as a member of Interallied Transportation Council was of the greatest value. He lent ev possible assistance to the American military authorities, giving us so1 advice and important information.
Needham, Henry. R—England. G. O. No. 45, W. D., 1919.	Lieutenant colonel, British Army, instructor at the Army General Staff (lege, American Expeditionary Forces. For services performed for the American Expeditionary Forces and to cause in which the United States has been engaged.
Overton, George C. R. R—England. G. O. No. 45, W. D., 1919.	Lieutenant colonel, British Army, liaison officer, American Rest Camp, V chester, England. For services performed for the American Expeditionary Forces and to cause in which the United States has been engaged.
Pakenham, Hercules A. R—England. G. O. No. 29, W. D., 1919.	Lieutenant colonel, General Staff, British Army. For services rendered the U. S. Army while serving as the liaison officer tween the British and American Military Intelligence Services.
Parsons, Harold D. E. R—England. G. O. No. 87, W. D., 1919.	Major general, British Army. As Director of Equipment and Ordnance Stores of the British Expeditior Forces he was able to render assistance of the greatest value to the Amer Expeditionary Forces. He aided us most markedly in the procuremer artillery material and ammunition from British sources, at all times gi loyal cooperation.
Peal, Edward R. R—England. G. O. No. 45, W. D., 1919.	Lieutenant colonel, British Army, in charge of British Aviation Office at P; France. For services performed for the American Expeditionary Forces and to cause in which the United States has been engaged.

DISTINGUISHED-SERVICE MEDAL 801

PHILLIPS, OWEN F_____
R—England.
G. O. No. 126, W. D., 1919.

Brigadier general, British Army, 2d Australian Division, British Expeditionary Forces.
Commanding the artillery in support of the 30th American Division in its operations of Oct. 8–11, 1918, he aided greatly in the successes achieved at that time during these operations. He displayed military ability of the highest order and a spirit of earnest cooperation which made the members of the American units proud to be associated with him in their operations against the common foe.

PLAYFAIR, PATRICK H. L_____
R—England.
G. O. No. 45, W. D., 1919.

Lieutenant colonel, British Army, commanding 13th Wing, Royal Air Forces.
For services performed for the American Expeditionary Forces and to the cause in which the United States has been engaged.

PLUMER, HERBERT C. O_____
R—England.
G. O. No. 17, W. D., 1919.

General, British Army, commanding 2d Army, British Expeditionary Forces.
For services rendered to the American Expeditionary Forces and to the cause in which the United States has been engaged.

PRITCHARD, CLIVE G_____
R—England.
G. O. No. 126, W. D., 1919_____

Brigadier general, British Army, chief of artillery, 4th Army, British Expeditionary Forces.
The valuable services which he rendered to the American Expeditionary Forces in supplying our divisions with artillery while he was serving as deputy chief of artillery, 4th British Army, will ever be remembered. Giving us the benefit of his brilliant experience as an artillerist he made an extended tour of American Artillery camps and thereby aided materially in bringing this branch of our arms up to the standard required for effective combat.

PUCKLE, FREDERICK K_____
R—England.
G. O. No. 126, W. D., 1919.

Lieutenant colonel, British Army.
With the British Mission at Washington and later in France, he rendered services of inestimable value in the training of officers for the U. S. Quartermaster Corps and in the preparation of that department for oversea service. He gave us great assistance also in connection with the preliminary arrangements for the supply of our forces. He was tireless in the performance of his exacting duties, tactful at all times, and a loyal friend.

RADCLIFFE, PERCY P. deB_____
R—England.
G. O. No. 45, W. D., 1919.

Major general, British Army, Director of Military Operations, British War Office.
For services performed for the American Expeditionary Forces and to the cause in which the United States has been engaged.

RAWLINSON, HENRY S_____
R—England.
G. O. No. 17, W. D., 1919.

General, British Army, commanding 4th Army, British Expeditionary Forces.
For services rendered to the American Expeditionary Forces and to the cause in which the United States has been engaged.

RENNISON, WILLIAM_____
R—England.
G. O. No. 45, W. D., 1919.

Major, British Army, instructor, Army School of the Line, American Expeditionary Forces.
For services performed for the American Expeditionary Forces and to the cause in which the United States has been engaged.

ROBERTSON, WILLIAM R_____
R—England.
G. O. No. 45, W. D., 1919.

General, British Army, commander in chief, Great Britain.
For services performed for the American Expeditionary Forces and to the cause in which the United States has been engaged.

RUDOLPH, FREDERICK_____
R—England.
G. O. No. 45, W. D., 1919.

Lieutenant general, British Army, commanding 10th British Army in Italy.
For services performed for the American Expeditionary Forces and to the cause in which the United States has been engaged.

SACKVILLE-WEST, CHARLES J_____
R—England.
G. O. No. 75, W. D., 1919.

Major general, British Army.
For services to the allied and associated Governments as permanent military representative, British section, Supreme War Council.

SALMON, GEOFFREY N_____
R—England.
G. O. No. 123, W. D., 1919

Lieutenant colonel, British Army.
Detailed as an instructor to the school at Chatillon-sur-Seine, France, he displayed military attainments of a high order, and rendered very valuable services to the American Expeditionary Forces in connection with the training of its officers. He was tireless in devotion to his important duties, and at all times tactful and energetic in the presentation of important subjects.

SALMOND, JOHN M_____
R—England.
G. O. No. 87, W. D., 1919.

Major general, British Army.
As general officer commanding the British Royal Air Forces in the field, he distinguished himself by the exceptionally valuable services he performed. He aided and furthered the training of the units of the U. S. Air Service attached to his command. He organized the training in the field of squadrons, pilots, ground officers, and mechanics of the American Air Service, rendering us most valuable assistance at all times.

SARGENT, HARRY N_____
R—England.
G. O. No. 87, W. D., 1919.

Brigadier general, British Army.
As chief of the British Military Mission, Headquarters, Services of Supply, he provided for prompt and satisfactory procurement of enormous amounts of supplies from England, thereby contributing greatly to the successes achieved by the American Expeditionary Forces.

SINCLAIR-MACLAGAN, EWEN G_____
R—England.
G. O. No. 126, W. D., 1919.

Major general, British Army, Commanding 4th Australian Division, British Expeditionary Forces.
The 27th and 30th U. S. Divisions profited by the wide experience and brilliant military attainments which he displayed as commander of the Australian division, when he served with the 2d American Army Corps and so ably assisted in the direction of the operations. The officers of these organizations count it a high privilege to have been associated with him during the final phases of the struggle with the common enemy, in which he and his forces played such a splendid part.

STUDD, HERBERT W. R—England. G. O. No. 75, W. D., 1919.	Brigadier general, British Army. For services to the allied and associated Governments as chief of staff, British section, Supreme War Council.
SYKES, FREDERICK H. R—England. G. O. No. 46, W. D., 1920.	Major general, British Army. As chief of staff of the British Air Forces, by his willing spirit of cooperation with the American authorities in all matters pertaining to the Air Service and its operation, he rendered service of great worth to the American Expeditionary Forces.
THOMAS, GEORGE P. R—England. G. O. No. 126, W. D., 1919.	Captain, British Army. He rendered valuable services to the American Expeditionary Forces in connection with the training of American Artillery officers. He displayed high military attainments and a keen comprehension of conditions in the field. His service was continuously marked by devotion to duty, tireless energy and tact.
THOMPSON, HARRY N. R—England. G. O. No. 124, W. D., 1919.	Major general, British Army. An eminent medical officer, and as Director of the Medical Service, 1st British Field Army in France, he placed his time and energy at the disposal of the American Expeditionary Forces. The sanitary school maintained in his army for teaching front-line medical requirements was utilized for the instruction of the American medical officers sent to him by classes. The observation and experience gained by these student officers under his able supervision and guidance eventually resulted in the saving of lives of many American wounded.
THORNTON, HENRY W. R—England. G. O. No. 87, W. D., 1919.	Major general, British Army. As Paris representative of the Director General of Movements and Railways in London he rendered the greatest assistance to the American Expeditionary Forces in the procurement of hospital trains and supplies. He furnished us with information which proved most important in the development of the American Transportation Corps.
THWAITES, WILLIAM. R—England. G. O. No. 45, W. D., 1919.	Major general, British Army, Director of Military Intelligence, British War Office. For services performed for the American Expeditionary Forces and to the cause in which the United States has been engaged.
TRENCHARD, HUGH M. R—England. G. O. No. 45, W. D., 1919.	Major general, British Army, chief of Air Service, British Expeditionary Forces. For services performed for the American Expeditionary Forces and to the cause in which the United States has been engaged.
TROTTER, GERALD F. R—England. G. O. No. 11, W. D., 1919.	Brigadier general, British Army. For services rendered the U. S. Army while serving as chief of the British Military (or Advisory) Mission to the United States.
TWINING, PHILIP G. R—England. G. O. No. 126, W. D., 1919.	Major general, British Army. As Director of the Royal Engineers, by his active interest in behalf of the needs of the American services in both France and England, he has given valuable services to the American Expeditionary Forces. Always manifesting an aggressive spirit in furthering our efforts, he handled many important questions of supply with marked tact and diplomacy.
WAGSTAFF, CYRIL M. R—England. G. O. No. 45, W. D., 1919.	Brigadier general, British Army, chief, British Mission, General Headquarters, American Expeditionary Forces. For services rendered to the American Expeditionary Forces and to the cause in which the United States has been engaged.
WALLACE, CUTHBERT S. R—England. G. O. No. 124, W. D., 1919.	Major general, British Army. An eminent consulting surgeon, and while serving with the British Expeditionary Forces in France, with untiring zeal he devoted his time and energy toward promoting standard methods for efficient treatment of American sick and wounded, and unreservedly placed at the disposal of the medical service of the American Expeditionary Forces his eminent talents, broad experience, and knowledge of general conditions, with a view to assisting in the prevention of wastage among our forces from wounds and disease.
WATTS, HERBERT E. R—England. G. O. No. 45, W. D., 1919.	Lieutenant general, British Army, commanding 19th Army Corps, British Expeditionary Forces. For services rendered to the American Expeditionary Forces and to the cause in which the United States has been engaged.
WELLESLEY, WILLIAM R. R—England. G. O. No. 46, W. D., 1920.	Lieutenant colonel, British Army, Undersecretary of State for War. In his capacity of Undersecretary of State for War, he manifested a constant desire to assist the American Expeditionary Forces in every possible way. The cordial spirit of cooperation and harmony which has marked the relations between the British and American forces during their struggle against the common enemy has been due, in large measure, to his zealous efforts.
WILSON, HENRY H. R—England. G. O. No. 45, W. D., 1919.	General, British Army, chief of the Imperial General Staff, British War Office. For services performed for the American Expeditionary Forces and to the cause in which the United States has been engaged.

WINTERBOTHAM, HAROLD ST. J. L. R—England. G. O. No. 126, W. D., 1919.	Lieutenant colonel, British Army. His practical advice, constructive criticism, and keen personal interest influenced greatly the organization and methods of training for topographic and ranging work in the American Expeditionary Forces. He personally furnished us with a large amount of important topographic data and information on survey and ranging work in the British and German Armies which could not have been obtained elsewhere and which proved of the greatest value to us.
WORTHINGTON, EDWARD S. R—England. G. O. No. 2, W. D., 1920.	Colonel, British Army. For services demanding the fullest of his time and energy. He exerted himself to such good purpose in behalf of medical officers of the U. S. Army that large numbers of them were sent for special and intensive instruction to the various special medical and hospital centers in the British Isles, where they received at the hands of Great Britain's most eminent instructors the lessons learned from three years of war, thereby enabling the American surgeons to apply the knowledge acquired, with the result that many lives and limbs were conserved in the American Expeditionary Forces.
WEIR, ANDREW R—England. G. O. No. 62, W. D., 1919.	British Surveyor General of Supplies. He displayed ability of a high order, untiring devotion to duty, and zeal in the performance of his exacting duties. At all times he worked with singleness of purpose for the good of the allied cause, rendering service of exceptional value to the American Expeditionary Forces.
WEIR, WILLIAM R—England. G. O. No. 62, W. D., 1919.	British Secretary of State for the Royal Air Forces. In the performance of his important duties he displayed great energy and ability of a high order. He handled difficult situations with tact and aggressiveness, achieving brilliant results. At all times he was zealous to the best interests of the American Expeditionary Forces.

FRENCH

[Awarded for exceptionally meritorious and distinguished services in a position of great responsibility, under the provisions of the act of Congress approved July 9, 1918]

ALBY, HENRI M. C. E. R—France. G. O. No. 45, W. D., 1919.	Major general, Chief of Staff, French Army. For services performed for the American Expeditionary Forces and to the cause in which the United States has been engaged.
ALCAN, ADRIEN H. R—France. G. O. No. 126, W. D., 1919.	Captain of infantry, French Military Mission at General Headquarters, American Expeditionary Forces. While on duty with the French Military Mission at General Headquarters, American Expeditionary Forces, he rendered service of exceptional value to the U. S. Army. His ability, tact, loyalty, and untiring efforts on our behalf proved of inestimable assistance in the successful execution of many important negotiations with the French Army. He went far beyond the bounds of duty to help us, proving himself a willing and devoted friend to our interests.
ALERME, MARIE M. E. R—France. G. O. No. 126, W. D., 1919.	Lieutenant colonel of Colonial Infantry, French Army. As assistant chief of the cabinet of the Minister of War, charged with the management of Franco-American affairs, by his tact, good judgment, and loyal spirit of cooperation with the American authorities he has rendered important service to the American Expeditionary Forces.
ALEXANDRE, GEORGES R. R—France. G. O. No. 126, W. D., 1919.	Brigadier general, French Army, chief of artillery, 5th Army Corps, American Expeditionary Forces. As chief of artillery of the 5th Army Corps he performed invaluable services to the American Expeditionary Forces. To his consummate skill as an artillerist was due in a large measure the success of the artillery in the operations of the 5th Army Corps in the St. Mihiel offensive and in the first phase of the Meuse-Argonne offensive. The loyal spirit of cooperation which he constantly manifested will ever be held firm in memory by his American colleagues.
ALEXANDRE, MARIE N. G. R—France. G. O. No. 126, W. D., 1919.	Lieutenant colonel of artillery, 3d Bureau, French Army. Possessed of military attainments of a high degree, he placed these at our disposal, rendering very valuable services to the American Expeditionary Forces by the advice he has given us in connection with artillery operations. At all times he was devoted to the best interests of the allied cause. He displayed tireless energy and ceaseless vigilance in our behalf, proving himself loyal to our service.
ALLAIN, EMILIEN. R—France. G. O. No. 126, W. D., 1919.	Captain, 315th Regiment of Infantry, French Army. By his able adaptation of the French combat formations to the American units and by the thorough instructions he gave the students of the Army Candidates' School in the technique of the combat formation, he has given valuable service to the American Expeditionary Forces. Later, as liaison officer between the marshal commanding the allied armies and American General Headquarters, by his courteous efforts and good judgment, he has rendered much valuable assistance to the American Army.
ALPHANDERY, LEVY. R—France. G. O. No. 126, W. D., 1919.	Captain of infantry, French Army, mayor of Chaumont, France. By his whole-hearted spirit of cooperation with the authorities at American General Headquarters in all matters concerning the American personnel at General Headquarters, he rendered services of great value to the American Expeditionary Forces.
ANDLAUER, JOSEPH L. M. R—France. G. O. No. 126, W. D., 1919	Brigadier general, commanding the 18th Division of Infantry, French Army. As commander of the 18th French Division he displayed conspicuous military attainments and the most loyal devotion to the allied cause. By his cordial spirit of cooperation and careful supervision of the training of the 1st, 2d 26th, and 42d American Divisions during the time in which they were attached to his command, he rendered invaluable services to the American Expeditionary Forces.
ANDRIOT, MAURICE. R—France. G. O. No. 87, W. D., 1919.	Lieutenant colonel of infantry, French Army. As regulating officer for the French railroads at American Headquarters Services of Supply, he displayed remarkable efficiency in meeting the needs of the American forces for railroad transportation. By his untiring energy and technical ability he satisfied all sudden calls made upon him for railroad facilities.
ARDON, PIERRE R. I. R—France. G. O. No. 45, W. D., 1919.	Lieutenant commander, French Army, instructor, Valdahon Training Camp American Expeditionary Forces School of Fire Triangulation, Langres France. For services performed for the American Expeditionary Forces and to the cause in which the United States has been engaged.

DISTINGUISHED-SERVICE MEDAL 805

ARMENGAUD, PAUL F. M.
R—France.
G. O. No. 126, W. D., 1919.
Distinguished-service cross also awarded.

Major, Air Service, French Mission, General Headquarters, American Expeditionary Forces.
Throughout the entire organization and operation of the American Air Service in France, he rendered us services of exceptional value. He displayed most marked tactical conception of aerial activities, his advice proving of inestimable worth during the St. Mihiel and Meuse-Argonne offensives. Out of his wide experience he gave us his best, proving at all times devoted to our interests and going far beyond the bounds of his duties, as a member of the French Mission, to assist us.

BADRE, LOUIS H. J.
R—France.
G. O. No. 45, W. D., 1919.

Major of infantry, French Army, forestry officer, attached to the French Military Mission at General Headquarters, American Expeditionary Forces.
For services performed for the American Expeditionary Forces and to the cause in which the United States has been engaged.

BARRAUD, CLAUDIUS E.
R—France.
G. O. No. 45, W. D., 1919.

Interpreter officer of 1st class, French Army, instructor, Army Intelligence School, American Expeditionary Forces.
For services performed for the American Expeditionary Forces and to the cause in which the United States has been engaged.

BARRILLON, PAUL C.
R—France.
G. O. No. 45, W. D., 1919.

Major of engineers, French Army, chief of Service for Military Development of Ports, Minister of Public Works.
For services performed for the American Expeditionary Forces and to the cause in which the United States has been engaged.

BATAILLARD, FÉLICIEN F.
R—France.
G. O. No. 45, W. D., 1919.

Captain of gendarmes, French Army, provost marshal with the 1st Army Corps, American Expeditionary Forces.
For services performed for the American Expeditionary Forces and to the cause in which the United States has been engaged.

BEAUDENOM DE LAMAZE, LOUIS E. M. J. I.
R—France.
G. O. No. 126, W. D., 1919.

Brevet lieutenant colonel of infantry, French Army.
As chief of the personnel section of the Army General Staff, by his able executive ability and good judgment, he has rendered most distinguished service to the Allies. He has always shown a keen interest in the American Army and lent them every assistance which he could furnish. His services have been of great value to the American Expeditionary Forces.

BECQ, RAYMOND.
R—France.
G. O. No. 45, W. D., 1919.

Lieutenant colonel of engineers, chief of the telegraphic service of the 2d French Army.
For services performed for the American Expeditionary Forces and to the cause in which the United States has been engaged.

BELIN, EMILE E.
R—France.
G. O. No. 75, W. D., 1919.

Major general, French Army.
For services to the allied and associated Governments as permanent military representative, French section, Supreme War Council.

BELLOT, LEON H. A.
R—France.
G. O. No. 126, W. D., 1919.

Lieutenant colonel of artillery, Geographic Service of the French Army.
As a member of the Geographic Service of the army, he, by his sound practical advice and good judgment, proved of the utmost assistance to the American Expeditionary Forces. Due largely to his personal efforts, the closest cooperation existed between his army and our own Topographic Service. Just prior to the Meuse-Argonne he personally arranged for the Geographic Service to extend and enlarge its facilities, so as to assist the 1st American Army in every way possible. His services were of inestimable value.

BERDOULAT, PIERRE E.
R—France.
G. O. No. 126, W. D., 1919.

Major general, commanding the 20th Army Corps, French Army, with the 1st and 2d Divisions, American Expeditionary Forces.
His gallant and conspicuous services are connected with the deeds of the 1st and 2d United States Divisions in the counterattack south of Soissons, July, 1918.

BERGASSE, GASTON L. E. E.
R—France.
G. O. No. 3, W. D., 1922.

Medical inspector, director of medical service of the 20th Army Area, French Army.
For services in the organization of American hospital centers. In addition to his official cooperation in the larger affairs, his influence exerted in innumerable ways has been a material factor in the successful installation and operation of the activities of the medical department of Base Section No. 2.

BERGER, MICHEL D.
R—France.
G. O. No. 87, W. D., 1919.

Major, French Army, chief of D. T. M. A., detailed at French General Headquarters.
While serving in the D. T. M. A. he was in personal charge of practically all of the movements of troops and hospital trains. He was tireless and careful in supervising the transportation of our troops through France and in providing railroad facilities for the shipment of supplies. He accomplished with brilliant success a most arduous and important task.

BERNARD, FREDERIC.
R—France.
G. O. No. 87, W. D., 1919.

Quartermaster, French Navy.
With extraordinary heroism he achieved the seemingly impossible in rescuing 70 members of the crew of the U.S. Army transport Jinsen Maru, when that vessel foundered at Ile d'Yeu, France, Dec. 4, 1918. Braving the rocky surf, he got a line to the ship when other efforts had failed, and by that line sent all the members of the crew one by one to shore, being himself the last man to leave the ship. Displaying personal bravery of the highest order, he voluntarily jeopardized his life to perform this courageous service.

BERTHELOT, HENRI M. R—France. G. O. No. 17, W. D., 1919.	Major general, French Army, chief of the French Military Mission with Rumanian Armies, commanding the French forces in the Orient. For services rendered to the American Expeditionary Forces and to the ca in which the United States has been engaged.
BERTHIER, EMILE J. R—France. G. O. No. 126, W. D., 1919.	Major of artillery, French Army. By his brilliant military attainments and steadfast devotion to duty he rende invaluable services to the American Expeditionary Forces as an instructo the army schools at Langres. Subsequently, upon being attached to the American Army as liaison officer, he capably performed duties of the utn importance in maintaining effective liaison between the French and Am can Armies of Occupation, doing much to promote the harmonious relati which prevailed among the two allied forces.
BERTIN, JEAN M. A. R—France. G. O. No. 126, W. D., 1919.	Second lieutenant of the 5th Regiment of Engineers, French Army, liaison. As liaison officer between the D. T. M. A. of the French Army and the Dep Director General of Transportation at American General Headquarters, his tactful, capable, and untiring efforts to assist the American Army, he rendered services of great value to the American Expeditionary For Loyal to the American Army, he at all times showed a friendly interes all our needs.
BLETRY, CAMILLE L. C. R—France. G. O. No. 59, W. D., 1921.	Major of artillery, French Army. For services while conducting all coal negotiations between the French Gov ment and the American Expeditionary Forces. His unfailing respons every demand made upon him and his friendship and energy have m times proved of inestimable value to our Armies.
BLONDLAT, ERNEST J. R—France. G. O. No. 126, W. D., 1919.	Major general, commanding the 2d Colonial Army Corps, French Army. It was under his command that the 2d Colonial Corps performed such glor deeds as part of the 1st American Army during the St. Mihiel offensive.
BOQUET, ERNEST. G. O. No. 87, W. D., 1919.	Colonel of engineers, French Army. As director of Military Transports Service with the Armies he extended he cooperation to the American military authorities, aiding us greatly in sol transportation problems. He displayed marked ability in handling intricate details of his important work and went far beyond the bound duty to render vital assistance to the American Expeditionary Forces.
BORDEAUX, JOSEPH P. E. R—France. G.O. No. 126, W. D., 1919.	Brigadier general, commanding the 18th Division of Infantry, French Arn In command of the 18th French Division he displayed superb military att ments and unfailing devotion to the allied cause. By his cordial spir cooperation and careful supervision of the instruction of the American u which were attached to his command during their training periods he dered invaluable services to the American Expeditionary Forces.
BORELLI, GEORGES M. R—France. G. O. No. 45, W. D., 1919.	Captain of artillery, French Army, commissariat general of the Franco-Ar can military affairs, liaison officer with the 158th Field Artillery Brig 83d Division, American Expeditionary Forces, and operations officer, Field Artillery Brigade, 30th Division, American Expeditionary Forces. For services performed for the American Expeditionary Forces and to cause in which the United States has been engaged.
BOUCHER, MARCEL A. F. R—France. G. O. No. 87, W. D., 1919.	Major of air service, French Army. As commander of the air service of the 4th French Army, he displayed a l interest in the welfare and training of the American officers serving with French squadrons. He imparted to them freely of his wide experience knowledge of air-service offensive tactics. He showed himself at all t: tactful, able, and possessed of complete technical attainments.
BOULANGER, EDOUARD. R—France. G. O. No. 24, W. D., 1920.	As Chief of Interministerial Service of Expenditures he rendered great sei to the United States.
BOULANGER, PIERRE. R—France. G. O. No. 87, W. D., 1919.	Lieutenant of the air service, French Army. As chief of the American Bureau of the French Aeronautic Ministry, secretary of the Interallied Aviation Committee, he displayed tact, ex tive ability, and wide experience in aviation matters, rendering invalu assistance to the American Air Service. He evinced the keenest int in our success and an exceptional understanding of our needs, proving self at all times most loyal to our interests.
BOURGEOIS, MAURICE J. R—France. G. O. No. 126, W. D., 1919.	Captain of the air service, French Army. As aide-de-camp to Marshal Pétain, he, through his careful and promp tion, rendered valuable service to the allied cause. His constant and ti efforts brought about the consolidation and thorough regulation of the Cross and other benevolent organizations, which proved to be of great w to the comfort of the American and other allied soldiers.
BOURGEOIS, JOSEPH E. R. R—France. G. O. No. 87, W. D., 1919.	Major general, French Army. As Director of the Geographic Service of the Army he afforded most l cooperation to the American Expeditionary Forces. He rendered excepti service by placing at our disposal the various departments under his cor including the use of maps and optical instruments that proved of inestim value in the planning and execution of important military operations.

OUSQUET, ACHILLE R.
R—France.
G. O. No. 87, W. D., 1919.

Captain of the General Staff, French Army.
As assistant to the American regulating officers of Creil, Le Bourget, Noisy-le-Sec, St. Dizier, and Metz, France, he rendered invaluable services during successive military operations of the greatest importance. He labored unceasingly under most trying conditions in order that the supply of American combat troops might not be interrupted, thus ably furthering the American operations.

OUVARD, HENRI.
R—France.
G. O. No. 46, W. D., 1920.

Brevet major of infantry, French Army.
As an aide to Marshal Pétain, he served with distinction in a position of great responsibility. He displayed military attainments of a high order, and was constant in his devotion to the best interests of the allied cause. In the midst of his exacting duties, he found time to render very valuable service to the American Expeditionary Forces, being ever ready to assist us by his sound judgment and wide knowledge of constantly changing conditions.

BREART DE BOISANGER, JOSEPH M. H.
R—France.
G. O. No. 126, W. D., 1919.

Colonel of infantry, French Army.
As chief of the French Mission with the 2d American Army, he worked loyally in the interests of the allied cause, proving always both energetic and tactful in the performance of his exacting duties. He aided materially in the maintenance of cordial relations between the French and American military authorities. He at all times cooperated with us most helpfully, proving himself an able and loyal friend.

BREUCQ, HENRI A.
R—France.
G. O. No. 126, W. D., 1919.

Brevet major of infantry, French Army.
As a member of the Franco-American Bureau, Army General Staff, by his sound judgment, tact, and keen interest in the American Army, he has handled many delicate problems affecting the American Expeditionary Forces with marked ability and in a most satisfactory manner. The services he has given us have been of great value.

BRUNON, LOUIS E. P.
R—France.
G. O. No. 126, W. D., 1919.

Brevet major of artillery, French Army.
As assistant chief of the 2d Bureau at French General Headquarters, he, by his wholehearted cooperation and sound advice, was of the greatest assistance to the various officers of the American Expeditionary Forces with whom he came in contact. At all times he gladly extended to us every facility available to aid in the successful operations of our forces. He was tactful and loyal, proving himself a true friend.

BRUNOT DE ROUVRE, ANTOINE C. P. C. M.
R—France.
G. O. No. 87, W. D., 1919.

Lieutenant colonel of artillery, French Army.
As regulating commissioner at St. Dizier, France, he labored unceasingly in the interests of the American Expeditionary Forces during the St. Mihiel and Argonne offensives. Notwithstanding that the responsibility of supplying two French armies rested upon him, the facilities at his command were put unreservedly at our service. Without his loyal cooperation the supply of our combat troops would have been most complicated.

BRUSSAUX, EDOUARD O. J.
R—France.
G. O. No. 126, W. D., 1919.

Brevet major of infantry, French Army.
While he was on duty at the 2d Bureau, French General Headquarters, he cooperated in every way possible with American military authorities, placing at their disposal the facilities at his command. He thereby rendered service of great value to the American Expeditionary Forces, proving himself at all times a helpful, able, and loyal friend.

BUAT, EDOUARD A. L.
R—France.
G. O. No. 17, W. D., 1919.

Major general, French Army, chief of staff to Marshal Pétain.
For services rendered to the American Expeditionary Forces and to the cause in which the United States has been engaged.

BUCAILLE-LITTINÈRE, HENRI.
R—France.
G. O. No. 87, W. D., 1919.

Captain of artillery, French Army.
In connection with the supply and maintenance of automatic arms and machine guns he rendered service of inestimable value to the American Expeditionary Forces. When assigned as assistant to the chief inspector of machine guns and small arms, American Ordnance Department, he displayed high professional attainments, energy, and untiring devotion to duty, cooperating with us most loyally at all times.

CAMBON, JULES.
R—France.
G. O. No. 126, W. D., 1919.

As special adviser to the French Prime Minister for Franco-American Affairs he displayed the same spirit of cooperation and warm friendship for the American people which he had manifested during his distinguished service as the French Ambassador at Washington. Ever actuated by the desire to cement the cordial relations between the two Republics, he and his staff offered us every facility which his important post commanded, thereby rendering services of inestimable value to the American Expeditionary Forces.

CAQUOT, A. T.
R—France.
G. O. No. 87, W. D., 1919.

Major of air service, French Army.
As chief of the technical section of French aeronautics, he displayed technical aviation knowledge of high order, and performed his exacting duties with untiring energy and devotion. He rendered very valuable services to the American Expeditionary Forces, gladly assisting us at all times in the solution of perplexing problems.

CARREL-BILLIARD, MARIE J. A. A.
R—France.
G. O. No. 59, W. D., 1921.

Surgeon major, 1st class, medical service, French Army.
For services in important researches and in the application of bacteriological methods of control to the dressing and closing of wounds. To him is due the discovery of the Carrell-Dakin treatment for war wounds. By his important service he has shortened the period of hospitalization of wounded men to a marked degree, and to him is due in a great measure the saving of many lives and limbs and the prevention of many disabilities among the wounded of our Army.

CARTIER, FRANCOIS R—France. G. O. No. 126, W. D., 1919.	Lieutenant colonel of engineers, French Army. As chief of the wireless-section of the French Ministry of War he rendered distinguished services to the American Expeditionary Forces by pla every facility at the disposal of the American Army and by assisting officers repeatedly with his sound advice, helping them in the solution o many technical problems which confronted our Intelligence Section.
CASTELLI, EMILE J. B. R—France. G. O. No. 87, W. D., 1919.	Surgeon major, 1st class, French Army, medical section of the Central Bure Franco-American Relations. As adviser to the Medical Service of the American Expeditionary Force assisted in the preparation of a comprehensive hospitalization program was of the greatest assistance in putting this plan into effect. Realizing importance of liaison between the French and American Medical Serv he organized the medical section of the Central Bureau of Franco-Amer Relations, which proved of the greatest mutual benefit to the French American Armies.
CHARET, CHARLES E. R—France. G. O. No. 14, W. D., 1920.	Colonel of artillery, French Army. He rendered service of conspicuous merit as chairman of the committe material. In securing the rapid, early, and complete delivery by the mans of all the artillery and airplane material required by the armistice te the achievement of his committee was noteworthy.
CHARREYRE, EUGÈNE J. R—France. G. O. No. 126, W. D., 1919.	Brevet major of infantry, French Army. As chief of the 3d Bureau, General Staff of the group of French Armies o East, he has rendered great assistance in the placing of the 1st Amer Division in the Camp de Lorraine and in furthering their rapid instructio combat. During the American operations of St. Mihiel and the M Argonne he again ably assisted us in furnishing additional artillery sup during the attacks. At all times he assured the best conditions of lii between the staffs of the French and the American Armies.
CHEVALIER, LOUIS J. G. R—France. G. O. No. 87, W. D., 1919.	Major general, French Army. As inspector general of the Forest Service, Minister of Munitions and Manufactures, he directed the French civil agencies in obtaining stan timber and manufactured forest products required by the allied ar With great administrative ability he superintended the supply of lumb the American Expeditionary Forces, at all times doing everything withi power to further our needs, affording most loyal cooperation.
CHICOYNEAU DE LAVALETTE DE COË-LOSOUET, CHARLES O. M. R—France. G. O. No. 126, W. D., 1919.	Lieutenant colonel of infantry, French Army. In his capacity as chief of the French Geographic Bureau he went far be the bounds of duty to render valuable services to the American Expeditio Forces. He placed a fund of valuable information at our disposal, being ready to give us the benefit of his wide knowledge. At all times he pr himself devoted to our interests and a most loyal friend.
CLAUDEL, HENRI E. R—France. G. O. No. 45, W. D., 1919.	Major general, French Army, commander of the 26th and 79th divis American Expeditionary Forces. For services rendered to the American Expeditionary Forces and to the c in which the United States has been engaged.
CLAUDON, JOSEPH P. H. R—France. G. O. No. 11, W. D., 1919.	Brevet colonel of infantry, French Army. For services rendered the United States Army while serving as chief o French Military Information Mission to the United States.
CLAVEILLE, ALBERT. R—France. G. O. No. 62, W. D., 1919.	As French Minister of Public Works he rendered service of immense val the Transportation Corps of the American Expeditionary Forces, sho himself at all times willing to go to any lengths to assist us. He displ broad vision, a keen grasp of the essentials and great energy in overco difficulties in times of emergency.
CLAVEL, JEAN. M. G. R—France. G. O. No. 126, W. D., 1919.	Colonel of engineers, French Army, at Base Section No. 2, American Ex tionary Forces, Bordeaux, France. Through his wide experience and eminent technical ability he was of th most assistance in connection with the establishment of Base Section I at Bordeaux. Not only did he conduct the negotiations for placing a disposal the indipensable Bassens dock, but he made possible the enlarge of our port facilities by the construction of railroad terminals. In num other ways he furnished us material aid by his sound advice and w hearted spirit of cooperation, rendering services of a high character t American Expeditionary Forces.
CLEMENSON, LOUIS. R—France. G. O. No. 87, W. D., 1919.	Lieutenant colonel, of infantry, French Army. As regulating commissioner at Is-sur-Tille, France, he rendered invalu assistance in the organization and operation of the American regulating st and depots at that point. His hearty cooperation and genius for organiz aided materially in the achievement of most satisfactory results an development of an efficient service.
COCHET, MAURICE D. R—France. G. O. No. 126, W. D., 1919.	Lieutenant colonel of engineers, French Army. In his capacity as a member of the French Mission attached to the Ame General Headquarters from June, 1917, to April, 1918, he gave us muc sistance in all matters of organization of units, and especially those affe the organization of artillery. By his good judgment and willing spirit operation, coupled with his high military attainments, he rendered ser of particular worth to the American Expeditionary Forces.

DISTINGUISHED-SERVICE MEDAL   809

EC, FREDERIC M. M
—France.
O. No. 126, W. D., 1919.

Brigadier general, French Army.
As director of artillery, Ministry of War, during the formative period of our Artillery, he has given most valuable service to our Artillery personnel in the solution of the difficult problems of organization and training. He placed at our disposal the means of instruction and training for our Artillery. Through his efforts the Saumur Artillery School was opened to us, the instruction camps at Coetquidan, Meucon, Souge, and Valdahon, France, were prepared as centers of training, and the facilities of the Tractor Artillery School at Vincennes were opened to us. The services he has rendered to the American Expeditionary Forces have been of great value.

ARDET, LOUIS
—France.
O. No. 11, W. D., 1919.

Colonel of infantry, French Army, military attaché, French Embassy, Washington, D. C., United States of America.
For services rendered the United States Army while serving as military attaché to the French Embassy and chief of French Military Missions to the United States.

NNA-CECCALDI, MARIE
—France.
O. No. 87, W. D., 1919.

Brevet lieutenant colonel of infantry, French Army.
As chief of the French Mission in Base Section No. 2, American Expeditionary Forces, he furthered the combining of French and American resources and interests, aiding materially in the success of the American Expeditionary Forces and the allied cause. He displayed untiring energy, devotion to duty, and great tact in the performance of his manifold duties.

BY, LOUIS
—France.
O. No. 87, W. D., 1919.

Major general, French Army.
In command of the 12th French Region, he showed unceasing devotion to the welfare and comfort of the American troops entering that territory, at all times affording the American military authorities loyal cooperation. He exercised extraordinary personal interest in Franco-American relations and rendered invaluable service to the American Expeditionary Forces.

VISART, CHARLES P. R. V
—France
O. No. 4, W. D., 1923.

Major general, commanding the 15th Army Corps, French Army.
For services rendered to the American Expeditionary Forces and to the cause in which the United States has been engaged.

SSERGUE
R—France.
O. No. 62, W. D., 1919.

As French regulating doctor at St. Dizier, France, he rendered the American Expeditionary Forces valuable service in making possible the evacuation of the forward areas during the St. Mihiel and Argonne offensives. When the number of American hospital trains available were found insufficient, he placed at our disposition the facilities of the French, laboring personally, day and night, in order that there might be no interruption of the service.

TANCEAU, MICHEL H. M
R—France.
G. O. No. 87, W. D., 1919.

Major general, French Army.
As commanding general of the 11th French Region, he rendered the American authorities most valuable assistance, meeting them always in a spirit of cordial cooperation. Through his willing help, billeting areas and many other facilities were placed promptly at the disposal of the American Expeditionary Forces.

CHET, EUGÈNE
R—France.
G. O. No. 126, W. D., 1919.

Captain of infantry, French Army, liaison officer with the 1st Division, American Expeditionary Forces.
As liaison officer with the 1st Division during all the active operations of the division from April to October, 1918, he showed exceptional ability and tireless energy in the performance of his exacting duties. Although his task was a difficult one, he labored incessantly to our best interests, manifesting at all times a spirit of loyalty and friendship for the American Expeditionary Forces.

LET, CHARLES
R—France.
G. O. No. 24, W. D., 1920.

As chief, bureau of Franco-American Service, Administration Division, Ministry of War, he rendered great service to the United States in the adjustment of numerous and complicated accounts between the United States and France.

MADE, ALBERT G. L
R—France.
G. O. No. 126, W. D., 1919.

Major general, French Army, 10th French Region.
As general commanding the 10th Region he has displayed the same brilliant military attainments and loyal devotion to the common cause which characterized his service with combat troops at the front. By his spirit of wholehearted cooperation and earnest desire to furnish every facility to the American troops in his region, he has rendered services of the utmost value to the American Expeditionary Forces.

NTANT, GEORGES V
R—France.
G. O. No. 126, W. D., 1919.

Major general, French Army, 13th French Region.
After long and honorable service in active operations against the enemy he took command of the 13th Region, in which were subsequently located a large variety of American military activities. The unbroken harmony which characterized the relations between the French and American authorities was due in no small degree to his tact and breadth of vision, and by his constant desire to further our interests in every possible manner he rendered services of inestimable value to the American Expeditionary Forces.

RMAU DE POUYDRAGUIN, LOUIS
I. G.
R—France.
G. O. No. 17, W. D., 1924.

Major general, French Army.
He commanded with distinction the 67th Chasseurs Division, with which a large number of American troops had the honor of serving. He continually showed every consideration for the Americans in his command, and by his skill in directing their training for effective combat he rendered services of the highest value to the American Expeditionary Forces.

D'AUVIN, FRANCOIS R.
R—France.
G. O. No. 126, W. D., 1919.

Major general, French Army.
His brilliant military attainments and forceful leadership were an important factor in the combat training of the American units which were attached to his command in the Chemin des Dames and Vosges Sectors. Later, as aide major general for personnel at French General Headquarters, he continued to display a desire to aid the American Army with all the important facilities at his disposal, thereby rendering services of the utmost value to the American Expeditionary Forces.

DEBAINS, FREDERIC H.
R—France.
G. O. No. 87, W. D., 1919.

Colonel of cavalry, French Army.
As chief of staff in the 18th French Region he gave invaluable assistance and cooperation in the operation of Base Section No. 2, American Expeditionary Forces. His efficient and painstaking efforts assisted most materially in the results achieved by the American military authorities. At all times he showed tact and a most valuable comprehension of existing conditions and our needs.

DE BARESCUT, MAURICE.
R—France.
G. O. No. 17, W. D., 1924.

Brigadier general, French Army.
As aide major general for operations at French General Headquarters, he gave us information and advice of the greatest importance. At all times he extended whole-hearted cooperation to the American military authorities. He showed himself a tireless worker, brilliant tactician, and loyal friend.

DE BAZELAIRE, GEORGES.
R—France.
G. O. No. 45, W. D., 1919.

Major general, commanding the 7th Army Corps, French Army, with the 42d Division, American Expeditionary Forces.
For services rendered to the American Expeditionary Forces and to the cause in which the United States has been engaged.

DE BEAUMONT, MARIE J.
R—France.
G. O. No. 87, W. D., 1919.

Colonel of infantry, F ench Army.
As chief of the French Mission at Headquarters of Base Section No. 1, American Expeditionary Forces, he discharged his duties with tact, zeal, and distinguished ability. He contributed very largely by his personal efforts to creating conditions which made it possible for Base Section No. 1 to maintain a steady flow of supplies to the American troops.

DEBENEY, MARIE E.
R—France.
G. O. No. 17, W. D., 1919.

Major general, commanding the 1st French Army.
For services rendered to the American Expeditionary Forces and to the cause in which the United States has been engaged.

DE BOISSOUDY, ANTOINE P. T. J.
R—France.
G. O. No. 17, W. D., 1919.

Major general, commanding the French Army of Belgium.
For services rendered to the American Expeditionary Forces and to the cause in which the United States has been engaged.

DE CHAMBRUN, JACQUES A.
R—France.
G. O. No. 45, W. D., 1919.

Lieutenant colonel, 40th Regiment of Artillery, French Army.
For services rendered to the American Expeditionary Forces and to the cause in which the United States has been engaged.

DE COINTET, LÉON E.
R—France.
G. O. No. 126, W. D., 1919.

Brevet lieutenant colonel of artillery, French Army.
As head of the 2d Bureau, French General Headquarters, he placed every facility in his power at the disposal of officers of the American Expeditionary Forces. The cooperation he extended to us was hearty and sincere. He rendered us distinguished and valuable service and played an important part in our successes. At all times he acted with tact and energy and showed himself a loyal friend.

DE CURIERES DE CASTELNAU, NOËL M. J. E.
R—France.
G. O. No. 17, W. D., 1919.

Major general, French Army, commanding the Group of Armies of the East.
For services rendered to the American Expeditionary Forces and to the cause in which the United States has been engaged.

DE FAUCIGNY-LUCINGE ET COLIGNY, AYMON J.-B.-M.
R—France.
G. O. No. 19, W. D., 1922.

Captain of cavalry, detached, French Army, head of Franco-American section, G. S., 15th Region.
For services rendered to the American Expeditionary Forces.

DEGOUTTE, JEAN M. J.
R—France.
G. O. No. 17, W. D., 1919.

Major general, French Army, commanding the group of the Armies of Flanders.
For services rendered to the American Expeditionary Forces and to the cause in which the United States has been engaged.

DE LA FERRONAYS.
R—France.
G. O. No. 87, W. D., 1919.

Major, French Army.
As personal liaison officer between the French Minister of War and the American Commander in Chief, he showed great tact and energy in the performance of his duties. He rendered service of exceptional value to the American Expeditionary Forces, laboring incessantly for the common cause, and doing much to promote the cordial relations between the French and American authorities.

DE LAGRANGE, AMAURY.
R—France.
G. O. No. 126, W. D., 1919.

Captain of air service, French Army.
His broad knowledge of the conditions of modern warfare, gained through creditable service at the front, coupled with his loyalty and friendship for the United States and the American Army, fitted him admirably for his important service as a member of the French Mission at Washington. Later upon his return to France, as chief of the aeronautical section of the French Mission at Tours, he assisted materially in the establishment of schools and training systems for our Air Service, thereby rendering services of the utmost value to the American Expeditionary Forces.

ALAIN, JOSEPH L. P.
R—France.
G. O. No. 87, W. D., 1919.

Lieutenant colonel of infantry, French Army.
As chief of staff of the communication zone of the French Army he was charged with the study and development of many of the most important projects affecting the American Expeditionary Forces. He displayed untiring energy in carrying out many delicate problems, and as supervising head of the whole work of the communication zone continually rendered valuable services to our armies.

ASSUS, GEORGES A.
R—France.
G. O. No. 87, W. D., 1919.

Major of air service, French Army.
As chief of the 1st Bureau, Office of the French Undersecretary of State for Aeronautics, he rendered services of especial value to the American Expeditionary Forces. Through his energetic efforts the American balloon companies in France were at all times supplied with the equipment necessary to efficient operation.

AUNAY, M. L.
R—France.
G. O. No. 27, W. D., 1922.

Captain of infantry, French Army.
For services while serving in the capacity of liaison officer with the 78th Division, American Expeditionary Forces.

L'ESPÉE, JEAN F. M. H.
R—France.
G. O. No. 126, W. D., 1919.

Major general, French Army.
In command of the 5th Region he performed his important duties with marked success. At all times he manifested the utmost consideration for American interests in the territory under his jurisdiction. By his generous action in placing at our disposal many French barracks and cantonments in the Department of Loire-et-Cher and at other places, he rendered services of the highest value to the American Expeditionary Forces.

L'ESTRADE, JACQUES E.
R—France.
G. O. No. 126, W. D., 1919.

Captain of air service, pilot, French Army, attached to Air Service headquarters, American Expeditionary Forces, Paris, France.
During his connection with our Air Service headquarters in Paris he was of the greatest assistance in solving many problems relating to supply through his wide practical experience and intimate knowledge of French factory and industrial methods, particularly in connection with the repair of airplanes and the procurement of spare parts. Ever displaying a desire to further the interests of the Air Service of our Army in every possible way, he rendered services of high character to the American Expeditionary Forces.

IGNY, HENRI V.
R—France.
G. O. No. 87, W. D., 1919.

Major general, French Army.
In command of the 3d French Region at the time of the formation of American Base Section No. 4, he gave most helpful attention to the needs of the American Expeditionary Forces, affording us his unhesitating support. His tireless efforts in our behalf assured the success of important projects in the base section, contributing largely to the achievements of our armies.

MARENCHES, CHARLES C. M.
R—France.
G. O. No. 45, W. D., 1919.

Captain of infantry, French Army, liasion officer between the commander in chief, American Expeditionary Forces, and Marshals Foch and Pétain.
For services rendered to the American Expeditionary Forces and to the cause in which the United States has been engaged.

MARGUERY.
R—France.
G. O. No. 87, W. D., 1919.

Admiral, French Navy.
As French naval representative at the port of Nantes, he cooperated at all times with the American authorities, showing ability of the highest order and tact in the performance of his duties. He gave us the greatest possible assistance in times of emergency, far exceeding the bounds of his duties to render important services to the American Expeditionary Forces.

MAUD'HUY, LOUIS E.
R—France.
G. O. No. 45, W. D., 1919.

Major general, French Army.
For services rendered to the American Expeditionary Forces and to the cause in which the United States has been engaged.

MONTAL, LÉOPOLD P.
R—France.
G. O. No. 29, W. D., 1919.

Major, French Army.
For services rendered the U. S. Army while serving as the liaison officer between the embassy, the High Commission of France, and the War Department.

NEUFLIZE, ANDRÉ P.
R—France.
G. O. No. 49, W. D., 1922.

Lieutenant, General Staff, French Army.
As liaison officer between the French Ministry of Armament and the American services in France and later as chief of the armament section of the French High Commission in the United States, he rendered valuable services to the American Army. To his efforts may be attributed, in a great measure, the success which the American Government had in obtaining from French sources artillery matériel and ammunition needed to complete the equipment for American troops arriving in France.

NEUVILLE, SEBASTIEN H.
R—France,
G. O. No. 24, W. D., 1920.

Lieutenant of cavalry, French Army.
As chief of the sales and purchases section, French Mission, with the American service at Paris, he rendered great service to the United States.

NNERY.
R—France.
G. O. No. 62, W. D., 1919.

French inspector general of the telephone service of the Department of Posts, Telephones, and Telegraphs.
He rendered the American Expeditionary Forces service of the greatest value in securing much-needed supplies and personnel for the Signal Corps. He was devoted in his efforts to secure all grants from the French Posts, Telephones, and Telegraphs administration to the best interests of our service.

De Pelacot, Jacques M. G. J.
R—France.
G. O. No. 126, W. D., 1919.

Lieutenant colonel of infantry, French Army.
As chief liaison officer with the 5th Army Corps from the date of its organizatio until a period subsequent to the suspension of hostilities, he performed important duties with distinguished ability and a spirit of whole-hearte cooperation. At all times he assured efficient liaison between the Americ troops and adjacent French units. Subsequently, while he was a memb of the French Mission attached to the 1st Army, he continued to render i valuable services to the American Expeditionary Forces.

Dercle, Charles U.
R—France.
G. O. No. 59, W. D., 1921.

Surgeon colonel, service of military health, French Army.
For services as liaison officer and adviser to the Surgeon General. By thorough knowledge he gave much needed and excellent advice upon medic military subjects, which was of great assistance in the solution of importa problems confronting the Surgeon General. He has rendered services great value.

d'Esperey, Louis F. M. F.
R—France.
G. O. No. 17, W. D., 1919.

Major general, French Army, commander in chief of the Allied Armies of t Orient.
For services rendered to the American Expeditionary Forces and to the cau in which the United States has been engaged.

De St. Quentin, Marie C. A. G.
R—France.
G. O. No. 87, W. D., 1919.

Major of artillery, French Army.
He took upon his own shoulders the complete reorganization of the Fren delivery services, that the American Air Service might be supplied in a tin of great need with airplanes, motors, and a large number of spare parts. H foresight was marked, and he acted at all times with keen judgment ar energy, rendering most valuable services to the American Expeditiona Forces.

Desticker, Pierre H.
R—France.
G. O. No. 17, W. D., 1924.

Brigadier general, French Army.
As aide major general of Marshal Foch's staff, he collaborated with wholehearte interest with officers of the American Expeditionary Forces, and brought their aid his sound judgment and military attainments in the solution perplexing and intricate problems. At all times he was unswerving in dev tion to his important and exacting duties, and proved a loyal friend. T services which he rendered us were of inestimable value.

De Valdner de Freundstein, Maurice F.
R—France.
G. O. No. 59, W. D., 1921.

Reserve captain of cavalry, French Army.
For services rendered to the American Expeditionary Forces.

Dhe, Paul.
R—France.
G. O. No. 87, W. D., 1919.

Colonel of air service, French Army.
As Military Director of French Aeronautics he displayed untiring attentio to the problems of the American Air Service, and by his earnest and whol hearted cooperation did much to render possible of execution the air progra of the American Expeditionary Forces. In all of his relations with the Amer can Air Service he acted in a broad-minded manner, showing a spirit of willir helpfulness at all times.

Dive, Gabriel A.
R—France.
G. O. No. 15, W. D., 1923.

Subintendant of the 3d class, French Army.
As a member of the staff of the inspector general of supply, French Army, l was charged with the responsibility for the cooperation of his section of t French General Staff with the American Expeditionary Forces with referen to supply problems. The rare technical skill, resourcefulness, tact and spir of cooperation displayed by Colonel Dive, coupled with sound judgmer and unremitting devotion to duty contributed markedly to the successfu operations of the American forces in France.

Domejean, Raymond X.
R—France.
G. O. No. 87, W. D., 1919.

Major of artillery, French Army.
He rendered service of inestimable value to the American Expeditionary Forc in connection with the supply and maintenance of artillery matériel. Throug out the offensive of the 1st American Army, in the St. Mihiel and Meus Argonne operations, he commanded with great distinction the importar artillery repair and supply establishment at Souhesmes.

Doumenc, Joseph E. A.
R—France.
G. O. No. 87, W. D., 1919.

Major of artillery, French Army.
As chief of the French Automobile Service, he was intimately associated an uniformly helpful in the development of the American motor transportatio system in France. With extraordinary foresight he organized the interallie motor reserve. His exceptional ability and personal efforts made possible th transport of large numbers of American troops at times when the success c operations depended on rapid transportation.

Dubail, Augustin Y. E.
R—France.
G. O. No. 87, W. D., 1919.

Major general, French Army, Military Governor of Paris, France.
Through his distinguished efforts one of the largest hospitals in Paris was mad available for the use of the American Expeditionary Forces, rendering possibl the hospitalization there of hundreds of the sick and wounded of the Americas armies.

Duchene, Joseph C.
R—France.
G. O. No. 126, W. D., 1919.

Lieutenant colonel of artillery, French Army.
In his capacity as chief of Marshal Pétain's cabinet he extended to us mos helpful cooperation, far exceeding the bounds of his important duties t render us valuable assistance. Possessed of military attainments of a hig order, he aided the allied cause greatly, and by the advice and informatio he so willingly furnished rendered very valuable services to the America Expeditionary Forces.

DUFFOUR, GASTON C. G. A. R—France. G. O. No. 126, W. D., 1919.	Lieutenant colonel of infantry, French Army. In command of troops in the field and as chief of the French Operations Bureau he rendered services of inestimable value in the prosecution of the war. He gave us very material assistance by imparting to the chief of the American Military Mission at French General Headquarters information as to the plans of his bureau. At all times he afforded us whole-hearted cooperation, going far beyond the bounds of duty to render service to the American Expeditionary Forces.
DUFIEUX, JULIEN C. M. S. R—France. G. O. No. 17, W. D., 1924.	Brigadier general, French Army. As assistant chief and chief of the French Operations Bureau he was always ready to cooperate with the American military authorities. He willingly furnished us with valuable information and wise advice. Able, tactful, and helpful, he rendered very valuable services to the American Expeditionary Forces.
DUMAS, CHARLES F. E. R—France. G. O. No. 126, W. D., 1919.	Lieutenant, French Army. On duty with the French mission attached to the 4th American Army Corps, and later with the 2d American Army, he rendered most valuable assistance to both the G-1 and G-3 sections of the staff in the preparations for and during the St. Mihiel offensive. He prepared the orders for the movements of French troops operating in this offensive, and saw that they were properly executed. He also gave us great assistance in solving problems of traffic control and billeting, working cheerfully day and night performing arduous tasks and going far beyond the bounds of duty to render service to the American Expeditionary Forces.
DUMESNIL, M. J. L. R—France. G. O. No. 62, W. D., 1919.	French Undersecretary of State for Aviation, president of the interallied aviation committee. With persistent effort and determination he supplied each American division going into the line with the same aviation equipment as was given to corresponding French units. He performed a task of tremendous magnitude with remarkable success, working at all times with great zeal for the American Expeditionary Forces.
DUMONT, GEORGES A. L. R—France. G. O. No. 19, W. D., 1922.	Colonel, French Army. For services in connection with the supply and transportation of the American Expeditionary Forces.
DUPONT, CHARLES. R—France. G. O. No. 126, W. D., 1919.	Brigadier general, French Army. As President of the Interallied Commission on the Repatriation of Prisoners of War he has rendered highly meritorious service to the United States and allied Governments in connection with the repatriation of American and allied prisoners released by the armistice. He always displayed a cheerful and active interest in all that pertained to their welfare and rendered sympathetic and practical cooperation.
DUPORT, PIERRE G. R—France. G. O. No. 126, W. D., 1919.	Major general, French Army, commanding the 37th and 77th Divisions, American Expeditionary Forces. It was under his brilliant command that the 37th and 77th United States Divisions first entered the zone of operations and engaged the enemy at Baccarat and Badonvillers.
DURETTE, CLÉMENT. R—France. G. O. No. 19, W. D., 1922.	Major of artillery, French Army. For services as head of the French Field Artillery Mission at the School of Fire for Field Artillery, Fort Sill, Okla., from September, 1917, to May, 1918. His knowledge of field artillery, tireless effort, unfailing tact, and loyal cooperation were largely responsible for the great value of the services of this mission to that school and to the Field Artillery.
DUTEY, HENRI. R—France. G. O. No. 49, W. D., 1922.	Lieutenant, French Army. For services while serving as liaison officer with the 15th Field Artillery, 2d Division, American Expeditionary Forces.
DUVAL, MAURICE. R—France. G. O. No. 87, W. D., 1919.	Brigadier general, French Army. As aide-major general of Air Service he cooperated in every way possible with the chief of the U. S. Air Service in the organization and development of the American air units at the front. He placed French units at our disposal during important offensive operations and at all times showed himself a most loyal friend. His service to the American Expeditionary Forces was most valuable.
EBENER, CHARLES. R—France. G. O. No. 87, W. D., 1919.	Major general, French Army. As Military Governor of Lyon, France, and general commanding the 14th French Region, he served with distinction. Amid his manifold responsibilities and duties he at all times lent us his valuable assistance, greatly furthering the interests of the American Expeditionary Forces. He was in command of a region in which were located large American military centers, and the services rendered by him were of inestimable value.
ESTIENNE, JEAN B. E. R—France. G. O. No. 126, W. D., 1919.	Major general, French Army. As chief of tank corps, French Army, he manifested a constant desire to aid our Tank Service in every possible way, assisting in the instruction of American officers at Recloses and giving us the benefit of his extensive experience by his valuable advice. He also came to our assistance at a critical time when he helped secure a large number of tanks from the French Government, thereby rendering invaluable services to the American Expeditionary Forces.

FAYOLLE, MARIE E.
R—France.
G. O. No. 17, W. D., 1919.

Major general, commanding Group of Armies of the Center, French Army.
For services rendered to the American Expeditionary Forces and to the cause in which the United States has been engaged.

FERRIÉ, GUSTAVE A.
R—France.
G. O. No. 87, W. D., 1919.

Colonel of engineers, French Army.
He rendered the American Expeditionary Forces services of exceptional value in his capacity as technical director of the military wireless. Without his counsel and unremitting devotion to our interests, it would have been exceedingly difficult to have equipped our forces with the indispensable radio apparatus which he placed so freely at our disposal.

FEVRIER, CHARLES.
R—France.
G. O. No. 59, W. D., 1921.

Medical inspector general, medical service, French Army.
For services as chief medical officer of the military government of Paris. During the period of the great offensives of Chateau-Thierry, Soissons, and the Meuse-Argonne, when the American sick and wounded were arriving in great numbers from the battle front and our hospital resources and accommodations were exhausted, he placed at the disposal of the American Medical Service the entire available space in the French military hospitals of Paris. During the development of the American hospital facilities, General Fevrier greatly assisted the American Medical Service in the location and obtaining of suitable buildings for hospitals. He has rendered service of great merit to the United States.

FILLONNEAU, ETIENNE.
R—France.
G. O. No. 87, W. D., 1919.

Brigadier general, French Army.
As chief of the French Mission at Headquarters, Services of Supply, American Expeditionary Forces, he proved assiduous, tactful, and efficient in the performance of his duties. As intermediary between the Services of Supply and the Bureau of Franco-American Relations, he was prompt and most helpful, rendering exceptional service to the American Expeditionary Forces.

FILLOUX, LOUIS J. F.
R—France.
G. O. No. 87, W. D., 1919.

Lieutenant colonel of artillery, French Army.
He designed and developed the 155-mm. Giant Power Filloux material, which proved indispensable to the American Expeditionary Forces. He rendered further valuable service by placing all his technical engineering ability and experience at our disposal for the manufacture of this material in America.

FOCH, FERDINAND.
R—France.
G. O. No. 111, W. D., 1918.

Marshal of France, commander in chief of the allied armies.
As an expression to him of the high regard of the people of the United States and of their Army, for the distinguished and patriotic services which he has rendered to the common cause in which he has been associated on the battle fields of Europe.

FORT, JULES E. L.
R—France.
G. O. No. 87, W. D., 1919.

Lieutenant colonel of infantry, French Army.
As chief of the French Mission of the 1st American Army throughout its operations he performed with distinction and success the task of coordinating the work of the American and French units. He was painstaking and untiring in his efficient efforts to maintain helpful cooperation.

FOURNIER, GASTON.
R—France.
G. O. No. 14, W. D., 1920.

Colonel, French Army.
He rendered specially meritorious service as chief of staff of the French Mission. He organized the business side of the mission, the arrangements for meetings, the editing, distributing, and filing of notes with skill, accuracy, and dispatch.

FOURNIER, PIERRE.
R—France.
G. O. No. 87, W. D., 1919.

Captain, French Army.
As chief of the 1st Bureau of the French Mission attached to General Headquarters, American Expeditionary Forces, his thorough knowledge of the French military service, unfailing tact, and spirit of cheerful cooperation greatly assisted the officers of the American General Staff, contributing to the success of the allied cause.

FRANTZ, PHILIPPE.
R—France.
G. O. No. 3, W. D., 1922.

Brigadier general, chief of staff, 2d French Army.
For services rendered the American Expeditionary Forces in connection with the Meuse-Argonne operation.

FRESOULS, EMILE S.
R—France.
G. O. No. 126, W. D., 1919.

Major of artillery, French Army.
As regulating officer at Dunkerque he occupied a particularly difficult position in being called upon to meet the needs of the British, French, Belgian, and American Armies. He, despite the complexities of situations with which he was confronted, rendered us exceptional service, lightening the task of supplying our troops in Belgium, and at all times extending whole-hearted cooperation. He brought his wide knowledge of existing conditions to bear upon difficult problems of transportation, handling them with peculiar success. At all times he displayed marked devotion to his exacting tasks. In times of need he proved himself a loyal friend of the American Expeditionary Forces.

FRID, GEORGE E.
R—France.
G. O. No. 30, W. D., 1921.

Brevet colonel, Deputy Chief of Staff, French Army of the Rhine and Allied Forces of Occupation.
For services to the allied cause and to the American forces in Germany.

GAMELIN, MAURICE G.
R—France.
G. O. No. 53, W. D., 1920.

Brigadier general, French Army.
As commander of the 9th French Division of Infantry, he displayed conspicuous military attainments and most loyal devotion to the allied cause. He assigned a large number of French officers and noncommissioned officers as instructors, prepared complete program of final training, cooperated with our personnel, and carefully supervised the training of the 32d Division during its training period from May 16 to July 21, 1918. By his important efforts he has rendered invaluable services to the American Expeditionary Forces.

DISTINGUISHED-SERVICE MEDAL

GANNE.
R—France.
G. O. No. 62, W. D., 1919.

French delegate of the Commissioner General for the Franco-American War Affairs.
He displayed untiring energy and exceptional ability in handling relations between the French and American authorities. At all times tactful and courteous, he did much to cement the feelings of friendship between the two nations, rendering services of great value to the American Expeditionary Forces.

GASCOUIN, FIRMIN E.
R—France.
G. O. No. 19, W. D., 1922.

Brigadier general, French Army.
For services rendered to the American Expeditionary Forces.

GASSOUIN, JOSEPH M. G.
R—France.
G. O. No. 126, W. D., 1919.

Brigadier general, French Army.
As director of French military railways he displayed the same administrative ability and devotion to duty which had characterized his service as a commander of a division in the field. He has at all times showed a broad-minded appreciation of the transportation needs of the American Army and by his cordial spirit of cooperation and valuable assistance in furnishing the necessary railway facilities has rendered a substantial service to the American Expeditionary Forces.

GAUCHER, LÉON M.
R—France.
G. O. No. 126, W. D., 1919.

Brigadier general, French Army.
As commander of the 164th French Division of Infantry, he displayed brilliant leadership and military attainments of a high order. The splendid successes achieved by the 4th American Division are due in no small degree to the splendid initial training in actual warfare they received under his command when they first went into the trenches in the Toul sector.

GAUTHIER, ADOLPHE F. M.
R—France.
G. O. No. 126, W. D., 1919.

Major of infantry, French Army, general staff of the 14th Region at Lyons, France.
As head of the section of the G-2, with American division, he displayed untiring zeal, energy, and devotion to his exacting duties. By his spirit of whole-hearted cooperation with our personnel in solving the many and complex problems with which we were confronted he proved himself a most efficient officer and valuable friend.

GAUTHIER, JEAN B.
R—France.
G. O. No. 24, W. D., 1920.

Military intendant, French Army.
As Assistant Director, Bureau of the Undersecretary of State for the Liquidation of Stocks, he ably discharged a difficult and important task and rendered great service to the United States in the settlement of complicated claims and the liquidation of stocks involving millions of dollars.

GAY, ANTOINE.
R—France.
G. O. No. 87, W. D., 1919.

Lieutenant, French Army, representative of the French railroads, G-4, Base Section No. 1, Services of Supply, American Expeditionary Forces.
As representative of the French railroads, he rendered the American Services of Supply invaluable assistance by obtaining for us the rolling stock necessary to forward vitally important shipments to the front. During the period of the Argonne offensive his services were of especial value.

GÉRARD, AUGUSTIN G. A.
R—France.
G. O. No. 17, W. D., 1919.

Major general, commanding the 8th French Army.
For services rendered to the American Expeditionary Forces and to the cause in which the United States has been engaged.

*GÉROME, AUGUSTE C.
R—France.
G. O. No. 87, W. D., 1919.

Major general, French Army.
In command of the 15th French Region, he rendered the American Expeditionary Forces most valuable assistance, showing himself resourceful and at all times willing to aid the American military authorities at the base port at Marseille. His tact was marked and he displayed ability of a high order, combined with energy and devotion to duty.
Posthumously awarded. Medal presented to wife, Madam Auguste C. Gérome.

GIGIDOT, JEAN R.
R—France.
G. O. No. 126, W. D., 1919.

Major of artillery, French Army.
As chief of staff to the adviser of the Prime Minister for Franco-American affairs, by his cordial spirit of whole-hearted cooperation with the American authorities he has rendered services of marked distinction. He has ably assisted the American Expeditionary Forces in many important matters which came before his office.

GILLY, EUGÈNE L.
R—France.
G. O. No. 87, W. D., 1919.

Captain, French Army.
As French Commandant of the port of St. Nazaire he cooperated whole-heartedly with the American authorities, extending them most valuable assistance. Due to his tireless efforts, facilities of the utmost importance were placed at our disposal. He showed marked ability and initiative in the performance of his arduous duties.

GIROD, LÉON A.
R—France.
G. O. No. 87, W. D., 1919

Colonel of Air Service, French Army.
In his capacity as Chief of Training of the French Aviation Schools he opened those schools to our cadets at a time when our air program was seriously retarded by lack of trained pilots. He took a personal interest in the training of our pilots, and it is due, in a large measure, to his attention that we did not incur further delay in placing our squadrons at the front. His high military attainments enabled him to render us a very valuable service, which was enhanced by the spirit of friendship and cooperation he at all times manifested.

GODART, JUSTIN.
R—France.
G. O. No. 126, W. D., 1919.

As Undersecretary of State, Chief of the Medical Department of the French Army, he exercised his influence and energy to assist in the initial hospitalization of the American Army, and by his cordial cooperation and untiring efforts expedited and facilitated that hospitalization, thus rendering valuable service to the American Expeditionary Forces.

GODEFROY, ANTOINE P.
R—France.
G. O. No. 87, W. D., 1919.

Lieutenant colonel of engineers, French Army.
As chief of the French Mission attached to Base Section No. 6, American Expeditionary Forces, he rendered invaluable assistance in the development of Marseille as an American base port. He displayed tact, energy, and foresight in a position of great responsibility, and his assistance aided markedly in the prompt forwarding of supplies to the troops operating in the advanced zones.

GORJU, EUGÈNE
R—France.
G. O. No. 126, W. D., 1919.

Captain of artillery, French Army.
As delegate from the Director of the Automobile Service, French General Headquarters, to the 1st and 2d American Armies, he displayed great foresight and sound judgment, working ceaselessly and with untiring energy in our behalf. He aided us repeatedly in the solution of perplexing problems of transportation. At all times devoted to our interests, he proved himself a loyal friend.

GOUDCHAUX, JOSEPH M.
R—France.
G. O. No. 30, W. D., 1921.

Captain of General Staff, French Army.
For services as commander of the French Mission with the 89th Division and the 9th Army Corps of the American Expeditionary Forces.

GOUIN, EDOUARD F. M. A.
R—France.
G. O. No. 126, W. D., 1919.

Lieutenant, 59th Regiment of Artillery, French Army.
He rendered services of great worth to the American Expeditionary Forces while he was attached successively to the 1st Field Artillery Brigade and 1st Division, the 5th Army Corps, and the 9th Army Corps. His earnest devotion to duty and marked tactical ability displayed in the execution of important artillery missions have earned for him the lasting respect and high esteem of the American officers with whom he served.

GOURAUD, HENRI J. E.
R—France.
G. O. No. 17, W. D., 1919.

Major general, commanding the 4th French Army.
For services rendered to the American Expeditionary Forces and to the cause in which the United States has been engaged.

GOURGUEN, LOUIS A. G.
R—France.
G. O. No. 126, W. D., 1919.

Lieutenant colonel of infantry, French Army.
As chief of the 2d Bureau, French Ministry of War, he at all times effectively collaborated with the various missions in deciding questions of policy and work to be undertaken. By his tactful and wholehearted cooperation he rendered valuable and distinguished service to the American Expeditionary Forces. He was tireless in devotion to his important duties, and at all times showed himself a loyal friend, zealous in our behalf.

GOYBET, MARIANO F. J.
R—France.
G. O. No. 17, W. D., 1924.

Brigadier general, French Army.
As commander of the 157th French Division of Infantry, he was an important factor in the successes of the Allies. By his valiant leadership and eminent tactical ability the officers and soldiers of the 371st and 372d American Infantry Regiments count it a great honor to have served as part of his command in the operations conducted by him in the Champagne and in the Vosges.

GRAZIANI, JEAN C.
R—France.
G. O. No. 3, W. D., 1922.

Major general, French Army.
For services as commander in succession of the 28th Infantry Division, the 17th Army Corps, the 12th Army Corps, the French forces in Italy, and as the French representative on the Interallied Military Mission to Hungary, positions of great responsibility, in which he rendered valuable services in the furtherance of the allied cause.

GROUT, M. G.
R—France.
G. O. No. 87, W. D., 1919.

Rear admiral, French Navy, at Base Section No. 5, American Expeditionary Forces.
He rendered services of marked distinction and value to the American Expeditionary Forces in lending his assistance during the formative period of American Base Section No. 5. Going far beyond the bounds of duty, he placed at the disposal of that base all of the facilities at his command.

GUERIN, ETIENNE F. M.
R—France.
G. O. No. 30, W. D., 1921.

Major general, French Army.
During the assault of the 5th Army Corps in the St. Mihiel offensive, Sept. 12, 1918, General Guerin commanded the 15th Division of Colonial Infantry, French Army, as a part of the 5th Army Corps. By his superior skill and leadership, his resolute execution of orders, his loyal and aggressive devotion to the operations of the 1st American Army, and his high courage in combat, he contributed in a determining manner to the assault of the 5th Army Corps.

GUILLAUMAT, MARIE L. A.
R—France.
G. O. No. 17, W. D., 1919.

Major general commanding the 5th French Army.
For services rendered to the American Expeditionary Forces and to the cause in which the United States has been engaged.

GUILLON, HENRI A.
R—France.
G. O. No. 87, W. D., 1919.

Lieutenant colonel of infantry, French Army.
As chief of the French Mission at Headquarters, Services of Supply, American Expeditionary Forces, he was zealous, tactful, and energetic in the performance of his exacting duties. At all times he displayed tact and exceptional ability. His loyal cooperation proved of great assistance to the American Expeditionary Forces.

HALLIER, EUGÈNE H.
R—France.
G. O. No. 126, W. D., 1919.

Brigadier general, French Army.
As Assistant Chief of the Army General Staff of the French Army and in his capacity as chief of the 2d Bureau of the General Staff, by his loyal cooperation in all matters concerning the American Army, he has rendered the American Expeditionary Forces eminent service. He at all times furthered those friendly relations which characterized all association of the French and American authorities.

DISTINGUISHED-SERVICE MEDAL 817

HALLOUIN, LOUIS E. A.
R—France.
G. O. No. 87, W. D., 1919.

Major general, French Army.
In command of the 18th French Region he gave the American military authorities earnest cooperation and sound advice on matters of great importance. His able assistance counted greatly in increasing the efficiency of Base Section No. 2. His tact, energy, and wide knowledge of conditions were most marked.

HALPHEN, HENRI J.
R—France.
G. O. No. 126, W. D., 1919.

First lieutenant of artillery, French Army.
As a member of the artillery section of the French Mission, during the entire period of the American activities, by his energetic policy and loyal spirit of cooperation with our Artillery personnel, he rendered valuable assistance to the American Expeditionary Forces. His advice was sound; his judgment was good.

HANAUT, HENRI S. A.
R—France.
G. O. No. 105, W. D., 1919.

Major of infantry, General Staff, French Army.
As a member of the French Military Commission he was on duty with the training and instruction branch of the war plans division of the General Staff. In this branch he was charged with teaching the higher phases of the military art, a course which only a talented and experienced officer could have conducted. His services to the United States were of inestimable value.

HANOTEAU, JEAN A.
R—France.
G. O. No. 126, W. D., 1919.

Captain of infantry, French Army.
As a member of the staff on the cabinet of the Minister of War, charged with affairs concerning American and other allied nations, by his splendid tact, good judgment, and sympathetic understanding of the American people, he has promoted that friendly spirit which has marked all dealings of the French with the American authorities.

HANOTTE, MAURICE J. V.
R—France.
G. O. No. 59, W. D., 1921.

Territorial surgeon, major of the 2d class, Medical Service, French Army.
For services as assistant to the director of the Medical Service, 9th Region, and as a member of the French Mission, Headquarters, Services of Supply. Due to his energy, devotion to his task, and keen judgment, he rendered valuable assistance to the American Expeditionary Forces in the procurement of buildings for hospitalization and in the placing of American soldiers in French hospitals. His cordial assistance and excellent advice have been of great service to the American medical officials.

HAVARD, VICTOR.
R—France.
G. O. No. 87, W. D., 1919.

Colonel of infantry, French Army.
As regulating officer at Creil and Nantes he rendered great service to the American Expeditionary Forces in connection with the supply and transportation of the American units engaged at Cantigny and Chateau-Thierry. Later he rendered exceptionally valuable assistance in relation to the St. Mihiel and Argonne offensive, at all times displaying brilliant organizing ability and a keen spirit of cooperation.

HELLET, FRÉDÉRIC E. A.
R—France.
G. O. No. 45, W. D., 1919.

Major general, French Army.
For services rendered to the American Expeditionary Forces and to the cause in which the United States has been engaged.

HENNOCOQUE, EDMOND C. A.
R—France.
G. O. No. 30, W. D., 1921.

Major general commanding the 4th Cavalry Division, French Army of the Rhine.
For services to the allied cause and to the American forces in Germany.

HERING, PIERRE.
R—France.
G. O. No. 30, W. D., 1921.

Colonel of artillery, Deputy Chief of Staff, French Army of the Rhine and Allied Forces of Occupation.
For services to the allied cause and to the American forces in Germany.

HERR, FRÉDÉRIC G.
R—France.
G. O. No. 87, W. D., 1919.

Major general, French Army.
In his capacity as Inspector General of Artillery of the French Army he rendered exceptionally valuable services to the American Expeditionary Forces in connection with the design and production of new artillery material. He gave wise advice and painstaking assistance in this task, placing all the information at his command at our disposal.

HIRSCHAUER, AUGUSTE E.
R—France.
G. O. No. 17, W. D., 1919.

Major general, commanding the 2d French Army.
For services rendered to the American Expeditionary Forces and to the cause in which the United States has been engaged.

HUBERT, XAVIER, L. M. R.
R—France.
G. O. No. 126, W. D., 1919.

Brigadier general, French Army.
As a commander of a unit at the front during a period of three years, he has given eminently distinguished service to the allied cause. Later, as commander of the 1st and 2d Subdivisions of the 18th Region, by his loyal cooperation with the American authorities and ever willing in spirit to assist them with all means at his disposal, he has rendered services of great worth to the American Expeditionary Forces.

HUE, EUGÈNE.
R—France.
G. O. No. 126, W. D., 1919.

Major of infantry, French Army.
As chief of the 2d Bureau, French Mission, General Headquarters, American Expeditionary Forces, he displayed sympathetic intelligence and untiring ardor in interpreting and sustaining the American point of view in the many delicate problems that arose. Due to his zeal, a spirit of complete cooperation existed between the French services and the American military authorities. He rendered services of great distinction to the United States and France.

HUMBERT, GEORGES L.
R—France.
G. O. No. 17, W. D., 1919.

Major general, commanding the 3d French Army.
For services rendered to the American Expeditionary Forces and to the cause in which the United States has been engaged.

JACQUEMIN, HENRI R—France. G. O. No. 126, W. D., 1919.	Major of cavalry, French Army. As a member of the Presidency of the Council, Commissariat General Franco-American War Affairs, by his thorough application to the ne the American troops and by his fervent cooperation with the Am authorities he has rendered most distinguished services to the Am Expeditionary Forces. The 28th Division will always remember his ous and efficient efforts in their behalf in all their dealings with the I authorities under his able supervision.
JOFFRE, JOSEPH J. C. R—France. G. O. No. 111, W. D., 1918.	Marshal of France. As an expression to him of the high regard of the people of the United and of their Army, for the distinguished and patriotic services which rendered to the common cause in which he has been associated on the fields of Europe.
JULLIEN, GEORGES L. E. R—France. G. O. No. 87, W. D., 1919.	Major general, French Army. As chief of engineers, he gave the American Expeditionary Forces heart port at all times, rendering especially valuable service by supplying American Army with pontoon equipages and bridge material. He pr an ample training center for our troops and in solving the problems of supply and barracks construction aided materially our engineering ations.
KLOTZ, MAURICE R—France. G. O. No. 46, W. D., 1920.	Captain of infantry, General Staff, French Army. As liaison officer with the 1st American Depot Division and the 77th An Division, he rendered services of exceptional value to the American ditionary Forces. He acted with tact and energy in handling all qu between the American military authorities, with whom he served, a French authorities, immeasurably facilitating our work. In the fi assured efficient liaison with the French units operating on the flank: 77th American Division, rendering services of inestimable worth.
KOECHLIN-SCHWARTZ R—France. G. O. No. 126, W. D., 1919.	Colonel of cavalry, French Army. As a lecturer at the American Army schools he displayed extraordin thusiasm and ability in the performance of his important duties. Fr and always working for the best interests of the allied cause, he re very valuable services to the American Expeditionary Forces in con with the training of a large number of its officers.
LABROSSE, HENRI R—France. G. O. No. 126, W. D., 1919.	Captain of cavalry, French Army. As a member of the Army General Staff, by his excellent military sound judgment, and tact, he has given most creditable service to the His interest in the American Army was shown by his ever willing s assist us by all means at his disposal. His services have been of grea to the American Expeditionary Forces.
LACAZE, MARIE J. L. R—France. G. O. No. 87, W. D., 1919.	Vice admiral, French Navy, commander in chief and prefect, 5th M Region. At a critical period of the war he performed invaluable service by givin ance in the establishment of a supplementary American port at the naval base of Toulon. He assigned docks, storage, and transport f to the American authorities, aiding them with his wise advice and ence, and thus assuring the rapid development of the American inte this port.
LACOMBE, LOUIS F. R—France. G. O. No. 75, W. D., 1919.	Major of infantry, French Army. For service to the allied and associated Governments as chief of staff, section, Supreme War Council.
LACOMBE DE LA TOUR, ALPHONSE E. E. E. X. J. R—France. G. O. No. 126, W. D., 1919.	Major general, French Army. As commander of the 5th French Cavalry Division in its operations 1st American Corps, he handled his division with ability. Zealou effort to effectively use his force, he was severely wounded while n reconnaissance of the terrain between Four de Paris and Varennes.
LASNET, ALEXANDRE B. R—France. G. O. No. 39, W. D., 1920.	Medical inspector, French Army. As chief surgeon of the 6th French Army, he placed all the facilities of plete organization at the disposal of the American Expeditionary F instruction purposes of our inexperienced medical personnel. In F 1918, when the 26th Division became a part of the 6th French Army, the most complete and detailed arrangements for the care of our wounded and assisted in every possible way in making their in: period a success. During the Chateau-Thierry offensive, when se visions of the American Expeditionary Forces were in the 6th Frenc he rendered significant aid to the American units. Later, when he chief surgeon of the group of armies of the Center, he again manife same whole-hearted spirit of cooperation and helpfulness. No were ever too great to receive his consideration and no effort was left by him to assist in meeting the many emergencies which confro medical department in the trying periods of 1918. His services were consequence to the American Expeditionary Forces.
LAVAL, EDOUARD C. R—France. G. O. No. 87, W. D., 1919.	Surgeon principal, 2d class, French Army. As a member of the 4th Bureau of French General Headquarters, he w associated with front-line medical tasks in the American Expe Forces, and by his cooperation aided us in procuring hospital facili displayed good judgment, broad experience, and unfailing courtesy, service of inestimable value in the proper care of the sick and woun

DISTINGUISHED-SERVICE MEDAL   819

LAVELLE, PAUL M. P. L.
R—France.
G. O. No. 87, W. D., 1919.

Major of infantry, French Army.
As a member of the 4th French Bureau, General Staff, he showed himself at all times willing to help the American Expeditionary Forces. To expedite the selection of sites for various American transportation projects, he traveled extensively, making a personal inspection. His wide experience, tireless energy, and loyal cooperation made his services of inestimable value.

LEBRUN, LÉONCE M.
R—France.
G. O. No. 45, W. D., 1919.

Major general, French Army, commanding the 3d French Region.
For services rendered to the American Expeditionary Forces and to the cause in which the United States has been engaged.

LECONTE, MARIE G. F.
R—France.
G. O. No. 45, W. D., 1919.

Major general, French Army, commanding the 33d French Army Corps.
For services rendered to the American Expeditionary Forces and to the cause in which the United States has been engaged.

LEFEVRE-PONTALIS, HENRI G.
R—France.
G. O. No. 126, W. D., 1919.

Lieutenant of infantry, French Army.
As a member of the special Franco-American section, Army General Staff, he has administered with marked ability many important matters concerning the American Army. Actuated at all times by a spirit of friendship for the American Forces, he has rendered them great assistance by the excellent manner in which he managed the many items which came before his bureau.

LEFORT, FERRÉOL F. G.
R—France.
G. O. No. 19, W. D., 1922.

Colonel of engineers, French Army, assistant chief of the D. M. T. A.
For services in connection with the transportation of American troops and supplies.

LEGRAND, ALBERT L.
R—France.
G. O. No. 87, W. D., 1919.

Captain, French Army.
As chief liaison officer with the American Rents, Requisitions, and Claims Service, he rendered most valuable service in conducting negotiations between the French and American authorities relative to the settlement of numerous claims and in making of agreements relative to the occupancy of French Government property by the American Expeditionary Forces. He displayed tact and zeal at all times, working unreservedly for the good of the allied cause.

LEGRAND, EMILE E.
R—France.
G. O. No. 87, W. D., 1919.

Major general, French Army.
In command of the 15th French Region at the time of the creation of Marseille as an American base port, he gave most valuable assistance and advice to the American military authorities, rendering possible the rapid organization and development of the American base. His able cooperation assisted greatly in putting the port on an efficient basis capable of supplying the needs of the troops at the front.

LEGRAND, JACQUES G.
R—France.
G. O. No. 87, W. D., 1919.

Major of artillery, French Army.
As executive member of the artillery section of the French mission at American General Headquarters during the entire period of American activities he gave himself wholly to the varied details of organization, training, and equipment of the American artillery. His services were of great value to the American Expeditionary Forces.

LE HENAFF, JOSEPH H. F.
R—France.
G. O. No. 87, W. D., 1919.

Colonel of infantry, French Army.
As representative of the French Government on the Interallied Transportation Council he evinced great vision and excellent judgment in handling questions of interallied transportation. In helping to solve problems of supply he rendered assistance of the greatest value to the American Expeditionary Forces.

LEMERRE, LOUIS A.
R—France.
G. O. No. 126, W. D., 1919.

Lieutenant colonel of infantry, French Army.
As a member of the French Military Mission attached to General Headquarters, American Expeditionary Forces, he rendered great assistance in the selection of French officers and soldiers for duty with American divisions and other American units. He at all times displayed remarkable tact and sound judgment in furthering the important tasks under his charge. Equipped, as he was, by a long period of staff training and high professional ability furthered by a keen appreciation of the importance of his task, he contributed to the maintenance of these cordial relations which had been established between the French and American forces.

LEPELLETIER, LOUIS R. V.
R—France.
G. O. No. 46, W. D., 1920.

Colonel of artillery, French Army.
As chief liason officer for the French War Office to American General Headquarters, he rendered services of a distinguished character. By his painstaking efforts and thorough understanding of conditions which the American Army had to meet, he gave valuable assistance, at all times manifesting a spirit of loyalty and friendship for the American Expeditionary Forces.

LE PELLETIER DE WOILLEMONT, BERNARD C. F. M. X. E. G.
R—France.
G. O. No. 49, W. D., 1922.
Distinguished-service cross also awarded.

Lieutenant of cavalry, French Army.
As liason officer with the 2d Division he participated in all the battles in which the division was engaged. By his loyal devotion to duty, whole-hearted spirit of cooperation, and high military attainments he rendered invaluable services to the American Expeditionary Forces.

LE ROCH, JULIEN E.
R—France.
G. O. No. 24, W. D., 1920.

Captain of infantry, French Army.
As a member of the Liquidation Commission, American Expeditionary Forces, he rendered great service to the United States in the adjustment of numerous and complicated accounts between the United States and France.

LE ROND, HENRI L. E.
R—France.
G. O. No. 126, W. D., 1919.

Brigadier general, General Staff, French Army.
In his capacity as a member of the general staff attached to the Minister of War and supervisor of all Franco-American Missions in France, by his thorough military knowledge and fervent spirit of cooperation, he gave the American authorities invaluable assistance. He placed at the disposal of our officials all the facilities that his extensive office afforded. His services have been of inestimable worth to the American Expeditionary Forces.

LESCANNE, FERNAND L. J.
R—France.
G. O. No. 19, W. D., 1922.

Major of infantry, chief of staff of the D. A., French Army.
For services rendered the American Expeditionary Forces.

L'HOPITAL, RENÉ M. M.
R—France.
G. O. No. 126, W. D., 1919.

Captain of artillery, French Army.
As a member of the Cabinet of the Minister of War, he has at all times displayed a friendly interest in the American Army, rendering it courteous consideration and assistance in all matters which came before him. His services have been of great value to the American Expeditionary Forces.

LIBAUD, EMMANUEL U.
R—France.
G. O. No. 19, W. D., 1922.

Major of infantry, staff officer, French Army.
For services rendered to the American Expeditionary Forces.

LINARD, JEAN L. A.
R—France.
G. O. No. 45, W. D., 1919.

Colonel of artillery, French Army, chief, French mission, General Headquarters, American Expeditionary Forces.
For services rendered to the American Expeditionary Forces and to the cause in which the United States has been engaged.

LOBEZ, STANISLAS J.
R—France.
G. O. No. 126, W. D., 1919.

Colonel of cavalry, French Army.
As chief of the French mission with the 32d American Division, he rendered us services of exceptional value in connection with the planning and operation of an efficient system of liason. He displayed a wide comprehension of the needs and difficulties which would be encountered and his advice proved of the greatest assistance to us. He was energetic, tactful, and tireless in his devotion to our interests.

LOMBARD, EMMANUEL E.
R—France.
G. O. No. 126, W. D., 1919.

Captain of artillery, French Army.
As senior French instructor at the American Artillery Training Camp at Valdahon he rendered services of great value to the American Artillery. At all times he exhibited a spirit of whole-hearted cooperation with the American authorities, assisting them by all means at his command.

LORAIN, ———.
R—France.
G. O. No. 62, W. D., 1919.

French director of the Telephonic Exploitation of the Department of Posts, Telephones, and Telegraphs.
He procured much-needed telephone material for the American Expeditionary Forces at critical times. His assistance was indispensable in obtaining leases for the long lines which formed the basis of our general telephone and telegraph system. Laboring unremittingly in our behalf, he rendered service of inestimable value.

LOUCHEUR, LOUIS.
R—France.
G. O. No. 62, W. D., 1919.

French Minister of Armament.
He displayed ability of high order in the performance of his important duties. In his relations with the American authorities he was tactful and zealous in our behalf, going far beyond the bounds of his duties to render valuable service and assistance to the American Expeditionary Forces.

MABILLE, MARIE J. H.
R—France.
G. O. No. 126, W. D., 1919.

Major, French Army.
While he was a member of the 2d Bureau at French General Headquarters he manifested a warm spirit of cooperation by doing all in his power to aid the members of the American Military Mission at these headquarters, placing at their disposal all the important facilities of his office, rendering invaluable service to the American Expeditionary Forces. Subsequently, as chief of the 2d Bureau of the 2d French Army, he continued to perform valiant services in the common cause.

MAISON, LÉOPOLD.
R—France.
G. O. No. 126, W. D., 1919.

Brevet colonel detached, French Army.
As commanding officer of artillery, 132d French Division, he rendered us service of exceptional value by his accurate and rapid work in directing and controlling the fire of the divisional artillery which was supporting the 37th American Division. His efficiency resulted in our infantry receiving all the advantages of constant artillery support, and he was in a large measure responsible for the success achieved. He displayed military attainments of a high order and was constant and untiring in his efforts in our behalf.

MAISTRE, PAUL A. M.
R—France.
G. O. No. 17, W. D., 1919.

Major general, Frency Army, commanding the Group of Armies of the Center.
For services rendered to the American Expeditionary Forces and to the cause in which the United States has been engaged.

MAITRE, ALPHONSE A.
R—France.
G. O. No. 87, W. D., 1919.

Colonel of artillery, French Army.
As chief of the artillery section, French mission, during the entire period of American activities, he gave himself wholly to the varied details of the organization, training, and equipment of the American Artillery. His services were of inestimable value to the American Expeditionary Forces.

MANGIN, CHARLES M. E.
R—France.
G. O. No. 17, W. D., 1919.

Major general, commanding the 10th French Army.
For services rendered to the American Expeditionary Forces and to the cause in which the United States has been engaged.

DISTINGUISHED-SERVICE MEDAL

MARCOMBE, MARIE J. P.
R—France.
G. O. No. 46, W. D., 1920.

Surgeon major, 1st class, French Army.
As regulating medical officer at Le Bourget, France, he performed highly responsible duties with conspicuous success. When the number of our wounded from the operations in the vicinity of Chateau-Thierry and Soissons became so large that our transportation facilities proved inadequate, he relieved the critical situation by placing French trains at our disposal and personally directed their operations. He also furnished supplies for American patients, cooperated in selecting advantageous evacuation points, and in numerous other ways made himself the instrumentality for saving many American lives and alleviating much suffering, thereby rendering services of incalculable value to the American Expeditionary Forces.

MARTIN-ZÉDÉ, HENRI.
R—France.
G. O. No. 126, W. D., 1919.

Lieutenant of cavalry, French Army.
As a member of the French mission attached to the American General Headquarters, he has constantly exerted himself in the interest of the American Army, rendering us every assistance which his office afforded. By his courtesy and good judgment he has done much to further the strengthening of those friendly relations which have characterized the services of the French and American forces.

MARTY, AUGUSTIN A.
R—France.
G. O. No. 46, W. D., 1920.

Paymaster general of 1st c ass, French Army, technical inspector, French Military Postal Service.
In charge of the French Military Postal Service, he gave us assistance of inestimable value in the planning and organization of our own military postal system. At all times he cooperated with us most whole-heartedly, giving us sound advice and proving at all times most helpful and tactful. The services which he rendered to the American Expeditionary Forces were of great worth to us.

MARZAC, A. JOSEPH.
R—France.
G. O. No. 87, W. D., 1919.

Major of artillery, French Army.
In command of the Aerial Gunnery school at Cazeaux he displayed exceptional zeal and technical knowledge, combined with keen interest in the training of American students detailed to this school. He enabled them to secure training which rendered them markedly efficient at the front, thus rendering most valuable services to the American Expeditionary Forces.

MATHIEU DE VIENNE, ALEXANDRE H. M.
R—France.
G. O. No. 24, W. D., 1920.

Major of cavalry, French Army.
As chief of the French mission attached to the American services in Paris, he rendered great service to the United States.

MAUGIN, JULES E.
R—France.
G. O. No. 19, W. D., 1922.

Major of infantry, French Army, assistant chief of staff of the communication zone.
For services in connection with the ammunition supply of the American Expeditionary Forces.

MAURIER, GEORGES T. P. H.
R—France.
G. O. No. 87, W. D., 1919.

Colonel of infantry detached, French Army.
As chief of the 4th French Bureau of the French General Staff he practically controlled transportation from the coast to the army zone. He rendered the American Expeditionary Forces service of great worth, assisting us most ably in handling the Army supply problem. He cooperated always most fully and unselfishly with the American authorities.

MAURIN, LOUIS F. T.
R—France.
G. O. No. 17, W. D., 1924.

Brigadier general, French Army.
As commander of the general reserve of artillery, by his earnest efforts and loyal cooperation with our forces the American Railway Artillery was always provided with suitable cantonments and equipment facilities and an ample supply of ammunition for every mission which was assigned to them. By the high quality of service he has rendered he has contributed materially to the successes achieved by our Railway Artillery during the operations against the enemy.

MAZEL, OLIVIER C. A. A.
R—France.
G. O. No. 126, W. D., 1919.

Major general, French Army.
After serving with eminent distinction at the front he was assigned to the command of the 4th Region at Le Mans, France, where he continued to perform important duties with conspicuous ability. By his warm spirit of cooperation and appreciation of American needs he was of material assistance in connection with the establishment and development of our embarkation and replacement center at Le Mans, thereby rendering valuable services to the American Expeditionary Forces.

MENARD, VICTOR R.
R—France.
G. O. No. 87, W. D., 1919.

Major of air service, French Army.
From the inception of the American Air Service he was its constant and reliable adviser, and rendered most important services in its training and development. He personally supervised the instruction of the first American pursuit squadrons. During the St. Mihiel attack the organization which he commanded was placed at our disposition, and in his personal direction of his group during the battle he showed military ability of a high order, rendering most distinguished service.

MEYER, MAURICE.
R—France.
G. O. No. 126, W. D., 1919.

Brevet lieutenant colonel, French Army.
He served with marked distinction as head of the 2d Bureau at French General Headquarters, performing duties of the utmost responsibility. At all times he manifested the most cordial spirit of cooperation and desire to assist our officers by all the means at his disposal, thereby rendering valuable services to the American Expeditionary Forces.

MICHEL, CAMILLE C. G. A.
R—France.
G. O. No. 30, W. D., 1921.

Brigadier general, chief of staff of the French Army of the Rhine and chief of staff of the Interallied Armies of Occupation in Germany.
For services to the allied cause and to the American forces in Germany.

MICHEL-LEVY, MARCEL J. B. R—France. G. O. No. 126, W. D., 1919.	Second lieutenant of infantry, French Army. He served with exceptional ability as chief of the administrative offices of the French Mission at General Headquarters, American Expeditionary Forces, displaying the same sound judgment and untiring zeal which had previously characterized his service in the field. By his admirable tact and broad sense of justice he aided materially in solving many delicate questions which arose between the American Army and the French civilians, thereby rendering services of great worth to the American Expeditionary Forces.
*MOINIER, CHARLES E. R—France. G. O. No. 87, W. D., 1919.	Major general, French Army. As military governor of Paris, France, he constantly rendered services of the greatest value to the American Expeditionary Forces, in whose interests he proved himself zealous and self-sacrificing. Occupying a position of high distinction and with a multitude of important duties claiming his attention, he yet found time to aid us with his wise advice and extended hearty cooperation to the American military authorities. Posthumously awarded. Medal presented to next of kin, Major Moinier.
MOLINIER, FRÉDÉRIC. R—France. G. O. No. 126, W. D., 1919.	Captain of cavalry, French Army. As an aide-de-camp on the staff of the marshal commanding the Armies of France, by his thorough military knowledge, tact, and keen judgment he has rendered valuable services to the allied cause. At all times he has shown an active interest in the American Army and has rendered them every assistance at his command.
MONIER, LÉON F. V. R—France. G. O. No. 126, W. D., 1919.	Major, French Army. When he became liaison officer between the military government of Paris and the office of the chief surgeon, district of Paris, he brought to this important position a broad professional experience and devoted loyalty. During the summer of 1918, when the shortage of our hospital facilities in Paris became acute, he worked with self-sacri cing energy and made available for us many additional beds in French hospitals, also securing numerous buildings which were subsequently converted into hospitals, thereby rendering invaluable services in securing proper care for the sick and wounded of the American Expeditionary Forces.
MONROE DIT ROE, MARIE L. J. R—France. G. O. No. 17, W. D., 1924.	Brigadier general, French Army. He commanded with great distinction the 69th French Infantry Division, which under his skillful leadership achieved brilliant successes in combat. The 1st American Division had a most valuable initial experience in actual warfare when it went into the trenches of the Toul sector under his supervision. He gave also equally valuable assistance in the training of other American divisions which were attached to his command.
MORDACQ, JEAN J. H. R—France. G. O. No. 87, W. D., 1919.	Major general, French Army. As chief of the military cabinet of the Minister of War, he at all times accorded most valuable assistance to the American Expeditionary Forces. In the discharge of his exacting duties he cooperated loyally with the American military authorities, and by his timely advice and wholehearted service greatly increased the efficiency of our forces.
MOREAU, FRÉDERIC P. R—France. G. O. No. 87, W. D., 1919.	Vice admiral, French Navy, at Base Section No. 5, American Expeditionary Forces, Brest, France. He rendered most valuable assistance to the American Expeditionary Forces in the solution of difficult problems arising in Base Section No. 5 at Brest. He unified the energies of the French and American authorities, working wholeheartedly in the interest of the allied cause.
MOREL, PAUL. R—France. G. O. No. 24, W. D., 1920.	As French assistant secretary of the board of finances, charged with the liquidation of stocks, he ably discharged difficult and important tasks and rendered great service to the United States in the settlement of complicated claims and the liquidation of stocks involving millions of dollars.
MORNET, CHARLES L. D. R—France. G. O. No. 87, W. D., 1919.	Rear admiral, French Navy. In command of the French Marine at Marseille he showed rare tact, judgment, and energy in the performance of his varied duties. He gave generously and untiringly of his services in furthering the interests of the American base, placing every facility at the disposal of the American authorities.
MORTIER, PIERRE F. R—France. G. O. No. 87, W. D., 1919.	Surgeon major of 1st class, French Army. As medical member of the French Mission at General Headquarters, American Expeditionary Forces, and later in the medical section of the Central Bureau of Franco-American Relations, he labored ceaselessly and with conspicuous success in the interests of the sick and wounded. He obtained for us hospital sites, hospital trains, and ambulances in times of emergency.
MOURIER, LOUIS. R—France. G. O. No. 62, W. D., 1919.	As undersecretary of state of the medical service, civilian chief of the medical department of the French Army, he placed all available resources of his great department, both in material and personnel, at the disposal of the American Expeditionary Forces. His advice was of great value, aiding us in the solution of many problems, and he rendered services of inestimable value in assisting us in securing proper evacuation and hospitalization for the sick and wounded.
MOYRAND, AUGUSTE E. M. R—France. G. O. No. 126, W. D., 1919.	Brevet lieutenant colonel, French Army. In his capacity as assistant chief, 3d Bureau, French Army, he proved himself at all times a loyal friend of the American Expeditionary Forces, being ever ready to aid us. He gave advice on important matters which proved of the greatest value in handling difficult problems which we were confronted with. At all times he afforded us most hearty cooperation in the performance of all his duties, rendering us valuable assistance.

DISTINGUISHED-SERVICE MEDAL 823

MUTEAU, PAUL J. H.
R—France.
G. O. No. 126, W. D., 1919.

Major general, French Army.
He served with notable success as commanding general of the 8th Region, in which was located our intermediate section, Services of Supply. By his sound judgment and unfailing cordiality he was of the utmost assistance in the solution of many problems which arose, thereby rendering services of distinction to the American Expeditionary Forces

NAULIN, STANISLAS.
R—France.
G. O. No. 45, W. D., 1919.

Major general, commanding the 21st Army Corps, French Army.
For services rendered to the American Expeditionary Forces and to the cause in which the United States has been engaged.

NEVEGANS, PAUL E.
R—France.
G. O. No. 105, W. D., 1919.

Captain of artillery, French Army.
As a member of the French Military Mission he was placed on duty with the training and instruction branch, war plans division of the General Staff. His brilliant mental and exceptional professional attainments, coupled with rare tact and tireless devotion to duty, caused his services to be of signal worth to the United States Army.

NIVELLE, ROBERT G.
R—France.
G. O. No. 3, W. D., 1921.

Major general, French Army, member of the Superior Council of War.
To this very distinguished soldier of the French Army this medal is presented as an expression of the high regard of the people of the United States and their Army for the distinguished and patriotic service which he has rendered to the common cause on the battle fields of Europe.

NORMAND, ANDRÉ C. J. J.
R—France.
G. O. No. 46, W. D., 1920.

Major of infantry, 4th Bureau, General Staff of the Army, (transportation), French Army.
As chief of section in charge of railroad transportation for the American Expeditionary Forces he rendered valuable services. He took an active interest in the transportation problems of our service, and by his energy, zeal, and good judgment aided us materially in solving the perplexing problems that confronted us.

NUDANT, PIERRE A.
R—France.
G. O. No. 14, W. D., 1920.

Major general, French Army.
As a commander, he rendered notable service in the field in command of the 34th Army Corps. As a diplomat, his keen sense of the situation, his tact and firmness toward the enemy, sound judgment in questions of moment, and constant devotion to the cause of the Allies made his services as president of the Permanent International Armistice Commission conspicuously meritorious.

OLIVARI, CHARLES.
R—France.
G. O. No. 87, W. D., 1919.

Major of artillery, French Army.
As chief of the French Military Mission with the 88th American Division he worked efficiently and tirelessly, both in the training area and in the front lines. His tactful and most capable direction of the efforts of the French officers assigned to the division met with exceptionally valuable results. He rendered efficient and valuable service to the American Expeditionary Forces.

OPPENHEIM, RENÉ.
R—France.
G. O. No. 24, W. D., 1920.

Major of engineers, French Army.
As assistant to the chief, Bureau of the General Commission of Franco-American War Affairs, he rendered great service to the United States.

PAGÉZY, EUGUÈNE H. J.
R—France.
G. O. No. 126, W. D., 1919.

Lieutenant colonel of artillery, French Army.
As a member of Marshal Foch's staff he cooperated with us most efficiently in the solution of many problems which presented themselves in connection with the combined operations of the French and the American forces. With sound judgment, tact, and untiring energy he managed difficult situations, rendering us services of exceptional value.

PAGÉZY, JULES E. E.
R—France.
G. O. No. 87, W. D., 1919.

Lieutenant colonel of artillery, French Army.
By his efforts in devising and developing the French system of fire control for antiaircraft artillery, adopted by our armies, and in command of the French Officers' Antiaircraft Artillery School at Arnouville les Genesse, he rendered most valuable service to the American Expeditionary Forces.

PAILLE, LOUIS J.
R—France.
G. O. No. 126, W. D., 1919

Lieutenant colonel of infantry, French Army.
As Chief of Instruction Service he rendered very valuable assistance to the American Expeditionary Forces, aiding us continually by giving us the benefit of his able advice. He displayed military attainments of a high order, and in the midst of exacting duties he never failed to come to our assistance. He cooperated with us wholeheartedly, proving himself at all times a loyal friend.

PASSAGA, FÉNELON F. G.
R—France.
G. O. No. 45, W. D., 1919.

Major general, commanding the 32d Army Corps, French Army.
For services rendered to the American Expeditionary Forces and to the cause in which the United States has been engaged.

PAULINIER, MARIE J. A.
R—France.
G. O. No. 45, W. D., 1919.

Major general, commanding the 40th Army Corps, French Army.
For services rendered to the American Expeditionary Forces and to the cause in which the United States has been engaged.

PAYOT, CHARLES.
R—France.
G. O. No. 45, W. D., 1919.

Brigadier general, French Army, Director General of Communication and Supply for the Armies.
For services rendered to the American Expeditionary Forces and to the cause in which the United States has been engaged.

PENET, HIPPOLYTE A.
R—France.
G. O. No. 45, W. D., 1919.

Major general, commanding the 12th Division of Infantry, French Army.
For services rendered to the American Expeditionary Forces and to the cause in which the United States has been engaged.

PERIA, JEAN V. H. R—France. G. O. No. 126, W. D., 1919.	Controller of 1st class of the administration of the army, French Army. As controller of the administration of the army and chief of the Franco-Americ: Service of the Direction of Control, he rendered very valuable services to t. American Expeditionary Forces in connection with the organization of t. American Rents, Requisitions, and Claims Service. He aided us material in the matter of negotiations for the installation of American projects throug out France, proving tactful, energetic, and wholeheartedly devoted to t. interests of the allied cause.
PERRIN, CHARLES E. F. R—France. G. O. No. 30, W. D., 1921.	Brevet lieutenant colonel, French Army, chief of the Interallied Bureau Operations, Interallied Armies of Occupation. For services to the allied cause and to the American forces in Germany.
PESSON-DIDION, MAURICE. R—France. G. O. No. 126, W. D., 1919.	Captain of infantry, French Army. As a member of the French Mission in Paris he gave invaluable aid and assis: ance to the American authorities on numerous occasions when it was necessa to obtain material quickly in order to further the operations of the Americ: Army. At all times he showed earnest cooperation with all the America authorities in all the activities in which he was associated with them.
PÉTAIN, HENRI P. B. O. J. R—France. G. O. No. 111, W. D., 1918.	Marshal of France, commander in chief of the French Armies of the North ai Northeast. As an expression to him of the high regard of the people of the United Stat and of their Army, for the distinguished and patriotic services which he h rendered to the common cause in which he has been associated on the bat: fields of Europe.
PETIT, PAUL A. J. R—France. G. O. No. 87, W. D., 1919.	Surgeon major of 2d class, Medical Service, French Army. Attached to the medical section of the Central Bureau of Franco-Americ: Relations and later at G-4, General Headquarters, American Expeditiona Forces, he gave whole-hearted assistance and cooperation at all times. F advice and distinguished ability materially aided us in the prompt evacuati and hospitalization of casualties.
PIARRON DE MONDESIR, JEAN F. L. R—France. G. O. No. 45, W. D., 1919.	Major general, commanding the 36th Army Corps, French Army. For services rendered to the American Expeditionary Forces and to the cau in which the United States has been engaged.
PICARD, FRANCOIS. R—France. G. O. No. 46, W. D., 1920.	Captain of cavalry, French Army. He served with marked distinction in his capacity as aide to Marshal Péta and rendered very valuable service to the allied cause. He was at all tim energetic and tactful in behalf of the American Expeditionary Forces, and l the sound advice and accurate information with which he furnished proved of very material assistance. At all times he cooperated with us who heartedly, and showed himself a loyal friend.
PIKETTY, PAUL. R—France. G. O. No. 126, W. D., 1919.	Major of artillery, French Army. As Chief of the 3d Division of Artillery, by his able advice and assistance t vocation of the organization and training centers for the heavy artillery the American Expeditionary Forces was decided upon and the equipme and organization of these training centers were accomplished. He display: great personal interest in the solution of the details of his task, at all tim exhibiting an energetic spirit in furthering the general plan and in securi grants from the Ministry of War. His services have been of a high order.
POMPÉ, DANIEL. R—France. G. O. No. 3, W. D., 1922.	Lieutenant colonel of artillery, French Army. For services rendered to the American Expeditionary Forces.
PONT, FERDINAND A. R—France. G. O. No. 87, W. D., 1919.	Major general, French Army. He served with marked distinction throughout the war and in positions great responsibility rendered invaluable service to the American Expe tionary Forces. As Deputy Chief of Staff of the French Army he display brilliant military genius and was at all times ready to afford us most lo} cooperation.
POUPART, HARMAN. R—France. G. O. No. 126, W. D., 1919.	Major of infantry, 158th Regiment of Infantry, French Army. In command of front-line troops he performed valiant and faithful service the allied cause. When he became an assistant to the members of t American Military Mission at French General Headquarters his wi practical experience fitted him admirably for his important duties, and his zeal in promoting the interests of our Army he rendered services of t highest value to the American Expeditionary Forces.
POUPINEL, RAYMOND J. E. R—France. G. O. No. 46, W. D., 1920.	Major of infantry, French Army. As head of the allied armies section of the French General Staff and later the same position under the supreme Interallied Commander, he labo: unceasingly in the interests of the American Expeditionary Forces. Throu his tact and unswerving devotion many problems of great difficulty w solved carefully and expeditiously. He rendered most distinguished servi
POUY, JEAN F. R—France. G. O. No. 39, W. D., 1920.	Medical inspector, French Army. As chief of the hospitalization section of the undersecretary of state for 1 Medical Service, he collaborated with the Medical Service of the Ameri(Expeditionary Forces in the preparation of a comprehensive hospitalizat: program. Through his wide knowledge of the possible hospital resour of France and his persistent efforts to insure adequate care for Americ soldiers, the trying period preceding combat operations was successfu bridged. He met all demands made for the delivering of French hospit to the American Expeditionary Forces, even to the extent of burdening own service. By his broad-minded conception of our problem and his en getic assistance in a most important task, he rendered estimable services the American Expeditionary Forces.

PRESTAUT, RENÉ C. J. R—France. G. O. No. 87, W. D., 1919.	Second lieutenant of engineers, French Army. By his exceptional enthusiasm, good judgment, and untiring energy in the performance of his arduous duties as instructor at the American Army signal schools at Langres he proved himself of great value in the instruction of the Signal Corps of the American Expeditionary Forces.
PUPIER, CLAUDE F. R—France. G. O. No. 126, W. D., 1919.	Interpreter officer of the 1st class, French Army. As military secretary and chief of cabinet to the marshal commanding the allied armies he was charged with duties of a most exacting and responsible character, which duties he performed with conspicuous success. In his official capacity he was called upon to treat matters of the utmost delicacy pertaining to American affairs, in the conduct of which he displayed admirable tact, comprehension, and marked ability, thereby rendering invaluable services to the American Expeditionary Forces.
PURNOT, ALBERT. R—France. G. O. No. 126, W. D., 1919.	Captain of infantry, French Army. As a member of the cabinet of the Minister of War by his good judgment and earnest cooperation with the American authorities he has rendered services of marked distinction to the American Expeditionary Forces.
RAGENEAU, CAMILLE M. R—France. G. O. No. 45, W. D., 1919.	Brigadier general, French Army, chief, French Mission, General Headquarters, American Expeditionary Forces. For services rendered to the American Expeditionary Forces and to the cause in which the United States has been engaged.
REBOUL, JACQUES F. R—France. G. O. No. 87, W. D., 1919.	Colonel of infantry, French Army. As Chief of the Franco-American Bureau of the Army General Staff, he performed eminent and important services to the U. S. Army in deciding many essential questions in our relations with the French. That he acted with exceptional success is proven by the cordial relations which were at all times maintained.
REILLE, G. R. C. F. XAVIER. R—France. G. O. No. 55, W. D., 1920.	Lieutenant colonel of artillery, French Army. As head of the artillery section of the French Mission to the United States during the World War by his untiring efforts he aided materially in the training of the Artillery in the United States.
REMOND, LOUIS. R—France. G. O. No. 29, W. D., 1919.	Colonel of artillery, French Army. For services rendered the U. S. Army while serving as chief of the French Artillery Mission to the United States.
RENIÉ, ANDRÉ J. R—France. G. O. No. 126, W. D., 1919.	Colonel of infantry, French Army. As chief of the Personnel Bureau and as head of the 1st Bureau of the General Staff of the French Army, he placed the facilities of his important office at the service of the American authorities, lending every assistance in his power to meet the needs of the American troops. His services, rendered with a loyal spirit of cooperation, have been of great value to the American Expeditionary Forces.
REQUICHOT, HENRY L. M. J. R—France. G. O. No. 87, W. D., 1919.	Major general, French Army. As commanding general of the 9th French Region, in which were located American Headquarters, Services of Supply, he showed himself uniformly helpful, giving us willing assistance and cooperation. He went far beyond the exacting duties of his office to aid the American Expeditionary Forces in securing necessary supplies.
REQUIN, EDOUARD J. R—France. G. O. No. 29, W. D., 1919.	Brevet lieutenant colonel, French Army. For services rendered the United States Army while serving as the personal representative of Marshals Joffre and Foch and as special delegate of the French General Staff to the United States.
RICHERT, AUGUSTIN X. R—France. G. O. No. 49, W. D., 1922.	Major of infantry, French Army. For services as an instructor of the 90th Division. During the training of the division at Aignay-le-Duc he was constantly in the field, and by his unceasing work and high military attainments he materially assisted the division to acquire as quickly as possible that proficiency which enabled it to join the fighting forces at the front. His services at this period were invaluable, and later at the front his courage and coolness were an inspiration to the men who saw him.
RIEGEL, GEORGES. R—France. G. O. No. 46, W. D., 1920.	Major of engineers, French Army. As representative of the 4th Bureau, French Armies of the North and Northeast, in the office of assistant chief of staff, G-4, he was charged with the supervision of the supply of French units and personnel placed at the disposition of the 1st American Army. By his high professional attainments and interest he assured the closest liaison between the French and American authorities, contributing largely to the success of the allied cause.
RIST, EDOUARD. R—France. G. O. No. 59, W. D., 1921.	Major of the 1st class, Medical Service, French Army. For services as an eminent scientist. By his untiring zeal, devotion, and energy he promoted the efficient treatment of the American sick and wounded. In his important research work he cooperated with the Medical Service of the American Expeditionary Forces in the fullest measure of devotion to duty. To him is due much credit for the arresting of the ravages of disease and injuries among our forces. His valuable research efforts in the domain of preventive medicine and wound bacteriology resulted in the saving of many lives among our wounded soldiers. He has rendered services of signal worth,

ROTTÉE, LUCIEN R—France. G. O. No. 10, W. D., 1922.	Lieutenant of infantry, French Army. For services rendered the United States Army while serving as French liaison officer in the division of criminal investigation, American Expeditionary Forces.
ROUGET, JULES F. A. R—France. G. O. No. 39, W. D., 1920.	Medical inspector, French Army. As chief surgeon of a group of armies, and later as chief of the cabinet of the undersecretary of state for the medical service, by his broad-minded treatment of all important questions arising with regard to hospitalization, and by his earnest cooperations with our Medical Service in all matters affecting the furtherance of efficiency in the care of our sick and wounded, he has rendered services of an important character to the American Expeditionary Forces. He at all times gave ready assistance to the limit of his power, in all important medical matters which constantly came under his extensive jurisdictions. He rendered services of great consequence to the American Expeditionary Forces.
ROUX, P. R—France. G. O. No. 39, W. D., 1920.	Professor, medical inspector, French director of Pasteur Institute, Paris, France. By his untiring zeal and devotion to the promotion of efficient treatment of the American sick and wounded, and by his earnest cooperation with the medical service of the American Expeditionary Forces in important research work, the inroads of disease and infections from wounds among Americans were curtailed. By his eminent skill in scientific research in the field of preventive medicine and wound bacteriology, he achieved marvelous results in the saving of lives among our sick and wounded. He has rendered services of great consequence to the American Expeditionary Forces.
ROUX, PAUL L. R—France. G. O. No. 87, W. D., 1919.	Major of artillery, French Army. He organized schools for ordnance and artillery mechanics and inspectors in the American Field Artillery Training Camp at Valdahon and in the American Ordnance Training Center at Is-sur-Tille. In the training of officers and soldiers of our armies he showed high military attainments and achieved distinguished success.
ROZET, HENRI E. R—France. G. O. No. 126, W. D., 1919.	Lieutenant colonel of infantry, 3d Bureau, French Army. He was tireless in his efforts to keep the American Mission at French General Headquarters informed on all matters of importance to it, rendering very valuable services to the American Expeditionary Forces; he at all times afforded us most loyal cooperation, proving unflagging in his devotion to our interests. He displayed military attainments of a high order and gave us valuable advice in times of emergency.
SAINTE-CLAIRE-DEVILLE, CHARLES E. R—France. G. O. No. 87, W. D., 1919.	Major general, French Army. As inspector general of material and ammunition for the French Armies he placed at our disposal at all times the results of his wide experience and the facilities under his control. He rendered most valuable service to the American Expeditionary Forces in connection with the development of the American ordnance inspection and maintenance work.
SALAUN, H. R—France. G. O. No. 126, W. D., 1919.	Vice admiral, French Navy. As prefect maritime, governor of the place of Brest, by his splendid spirit o whole-hearted cooperation with the American authorities in all matters concerning the welfare and comfort of the large number of American troops which constantly passed through the important port of Brest, he has rendered services of signal worth to the American Expeditionary Forces. Every demand upon the facilit'es of his office received the same courteous consideration which characterized all the dealings of the Americans with him and his efficien personnel.
SCHMIDLIN, GEORGES A. R—France. G. O. No. 126, W. D., 1919.	Major of infantry, French Army. As a member of the Cabinet of the Minister of War he has always exhibited sympathetic interest in the American Army, offering them every assistance which his office afforded. His services have been of a high order and of much value to the American Expeditionary Forces.
SCHMIDT, HENRI F. E. R—France. G. O. No. 30, W. D., 1921.	Brigadier general, French Army, commanding the garrison of Mayence Germany. For services in the allied cause and to the American forces in Germany.
SELIGMAN, GERMAIN. R—France. G. O. No. 126, W. D., 1919.	Captain, 132d Regiment of Infantry, French Army, liaison officer, 1st Division American Expeditionary Forces. By his high professional attainments and wide experience he rendered invaluable services to the American Expeditionary Forces as liaison officer o the 1st Division. Both during the training period of the division an subsequently during active operations he performed his task with excellen judgment, admiralbe tact, and earnest loyalty.
SISTERON, EUGÈNE P. J. R—France. G. O. No. 19, W. D., 1922.	Major of infantry, French Army, assistant chief of staff of the communication zone. For services rendered the American Expeditionary Forces.
SORDET, HENRI. R—France. G. O. No. 24, W. D., 1920.	Captain of infantry, French Army. As chief of a section of the Franco-American Mission in Paris, his dutie required the daily handling of important matters with the Liquidatio Commission. He rendered great service to the United States in the efficien performance of these difficult tasks.

SPITZ, MARIE C. L.
R—France.
G. O. No. 126, W. D., 1919.

Colonel of infantry, Chief of Staff, 2d Division of Infantry, French Army.
He has been a most sincere and devoted friend to American interests, always willing to do more than his share to bring about a harmonious and friendly understanding between the French and American authorities. By his unfailing tact, sympathy, and understanding, and by his untiring efforts to successfully solve the many intricate problems that arose between the French and the Americans, he has rendered an invaluable service to the American Expeditionary Forces.

TARDIEU, ANDRÉ.
R—France.
G. O. No. 62, W. D., 1919.

He rendered service of great value for the American Expeditionary Forces as High Commissioner of the French Republic at Washington, D. C. Displaying tact, energy, and devotion to duties, he handled difficult problems with unswerving zeal for the good of the American Army.

THENAULT, GEORGES.
R—France.
G. O. No. 15, W. D., 1923.

Captain, Air Service, French Army.
He commanded the Lafayette Escadrille from the time of its creation in April of 1916 until it was transferred to the Air Service, American Expeditionary Forces in January, 1918. He led the squadron throughout the operations in Alsace and the Verdun offensive in 1916, later participating in the allied offensive on the Somme and the Aisne. In 1917 he continued to command the squadron which was withdrawn from the line, and participated immediately afterwards in the operations on the Chemin des Dames. During this time more than 50 American pursuit pilots served in this unit. By his initiative, force, courage, and devotion to duty he contributed mateally to the successful operations of the squadron and instilled in the Americarı pilots under his command the principles of pursuit aviation which contrıbuted materially to the success of other American pursuit organizations wherı these pilots were transferred. By his ability as a pilot and his frequent mnssions over the lines he set an admirable example to the American officers undier his command.

THOMAS, JOSEPH C. A.
R—France.
G. O. No. 87, W. D., 1919.

Lieutenant colonel of artillery, French Army.
As director of organization at the Samur Artillery School, he rendered services of inestimable value to the American artillery. By his energy, enthusiasm, and devotion, he lightened the task involved in the training of young officers for the greatly expanded artillery establishment needed for the American Army.

TINARDON, M. A.
R—France.
G. O. No. 87, W. D., 1919.

Major of engineers, French Army.
As a member of the 4th Bureau of the General Staff of the French Army he rendered invaluable service to the American Expeditionary Forces in connection with the selection of suitable sites for depots and hospitals. He gave us his time willingly, although his duties were pressing, aiding us most ably in the development of plans, and frequently furnishing us with labor and construction material in time of emergency.

TONGAS, GASTON.
R—France.
G. O. No. 87, W. D., 1919.

Colonel of engineers, French Army.
As director of telegraphic service of the 2d line, he labored most zealously and efficiently in our interests at French General Headquarters. He willingly offered wise counsel and unfailing support in our applications for service and material.

TREMBLAY, FRANCOIS L.
R—France.
G. O. No. 49, W. D., 1922.

Major of infantry, French Army.
As chief of the French officers assigned to the 90th Division during the training period and later as liaison officer of the division at the front, by his tireless efforts, willing spirit of cooperation, and his high military attainments he rendered services of great value to our troops and won the warmest admiration of both officers and men. On the front in the St. Mihiel and Meuse-Argonne offensives his conduct and courage were a marked example to the men of the 90th Division.

TUFFIER, T.
R—France.
G. O. No. 39, W. D., 1920.

Professor, French medical inspector, School of Medicine.
By his untiring zeal and devotion to the promotion of efficient treatment of the American sick and wounded, and by his earnest cooperation with the medical service of the American Expeditionary Forces in important research work, the inroads of disease and infections from wounds among Americans were curtailed. By his eminent skill in scientific research in the field oi preventive medicine and wound bacteriology, he achieved marvelous results in the saving of lives among our sick and wounded. He rendered services of great consequence to the American Expeditionary Forces.

VALDANT, HENRY C.
R—France.
G. O. No. 126, W. D., 1919.

Brigadier general, French Army.
As chief of staff to the commanding general, Military Governor of Paris, he has at all times manifested a most cordial attitude in all Franco-American relations, offering us every assistance at the command of his far-reaching office. His services to the American Expeditionary Forces have been of great value.

VALLOTTE, PAUL C. A. R.
R—France.
G. O. No. 126, W. D., 1919.

Major of cavalry, French Army.
As chief of the 2d-Bureau of Marshal Foch's staff he kept us constantly informed as to the general trend of operations as well as the situation of the enemy. He brought to bear on this important task an exact knowledge of the terrain, comprehensive understanding of the enemy movements, and the successive situations which confronted our troops. The services which he so willingly rendered to the American Expeditionary Forces were of exceptional value.

VANDENBURG, CHARLES A.
R—France.
G. O. No. 45, W. D., 1919.

Major general, commanding the 13th Army Corps, Franch Army.
For services rendered to the American Expeditionary Forces and to the cause in which the United States has been engaged.

VAN HEEMS, ROGER A. R—France. G. O. No. 19, W. D., 1922.	Major of infantry, French Army, regulating commissioner at Le Bourget, France. For services in connection with the supply and transportation of American troops during the operations at Chateau-Thierry.
VARAIGNE, HENRI A. R—France. G. O. No. 126, W. D., 1919.	Major of infantry, French Army. As chairman of the French Mission attached to the Headquarters of the American General Purchasing Board he rendered services of inestimable importance in carrying on for us negotiations with the French Government for the procurement of an immense amount of material. He was indefatigable in his efforts in our behalf, proving himself able, tactful, and possessed of a wide comprehension of existing needs and conditions. Cooperating with us at all times most whole-heartedly, he proved a loyal friend.
VERLEY, EDOUARD. R—France. G. O. No. 87, W. D., 1919.	Captain of artillery, French Army. As liaison officer with the troop movement bureau at G-4, General Headquarters, American Expeditionary Forces, he solved many difficult transportation problems incident to active operations. No task proved too large or too small for him to accept, and he accomplished with distinction and unfailing courtesy his many duties, rendering services of great value to us.
VERNAY, ROMAIN P. J. J. R—France. G. O. No. 24, W. D., 1920.	As French military intendant in the bureau of the assistant secretary of the board of finances, liquidation of stocks, he ably discharged a difficult and important task and rendered great service to the United States in the settlement of complicated claims and the liquidation of stocks involving millions of dollars.
VIDAL, PAUL. R—France. G. O. No. 87, W. D., 1919.	Major general, French Army. In command of the 7th French Region he was tireless in his devotion to our interests and to the success of our varied projects in the region of which he had charge. His relations with the American military authorities were always cordial and helpful. He always evinced personal interest in our plans and aided us materially by his sound advice.
VIDALON, JEAN. R—France. G. O. No. 17, W. D., 1924.	Brigadier general, French Army. As Assistant Chief of Staff of the French Army and as head of the 2d section of the General Staff, particularly charged with relations with foreign armies and of the special Franco-American Bureau, he successfully and most satisfactorily managed and coordinated the relations of the ministry of war with the American authorities. To him is due much credit for the able direction of all the American units in French territory. His able assistance has contributed in a large measure to the friendly spirit that has existed between the French and the Americans.
VIGNAL, PAUL. R—France. G. O. No. 11, W. D., 1919.	Brigadier general, French Army. For services rendered the United States Army while serving as military attaché to the French Embassy and chief of French Military Mssions to the United States.
VINEL, LOUIS A. R—France. G. O. No. 87, W. D., 1919.	Military intendant, French Army. As Quartermaster General of the French Army he showed ability of the highest order in handling his important duties and cooperated most loyally with the the American military authorities. In a position of great responsibility, he made special efforts to aid the American Expeditionary Forces.
WAHL, VICTOR E. R—France. G. O. No. 126, W. D., 1919.	Colonel of infantry, French Army. As commander of the 1st Brigade, Artillery of Assault, by his marked ability, initiative, and sound judgment, he gave much valuable assistance to the American armies operating in the St. Mihiel and Meuse-Argonne offensives. His earnest cooperation in carrying out the details of the plans of operations had a marked influence on the success of the Tank Corps units in those important operations.
WALCH, CAMILLE. R—France. G. O. No. 126, W. D., 1919.	Brigadier general, French Army. As chief of the French Artillery attached to the 1st Army Corps, American Expeditionary Forces, during the Meuse-Argonne offensive, he rendered us services of noteworthy distinction. His services were continuously marked by his qualities of leadership and military attainments, which were of a high order. Displaying tireless energy and devotion to his arduous duties, he strove diligently that our infantry might have all the benefits of efficient Artillery support.
WEYGAND, MAXIME. R—France. G. O. No. 17, W. D., 1919.	Brigadier general, French Army, Chief of Staff to Marshal Foch. For services rendered to the American Expeditionary Forces and to the cause in which the United States has been engaged.
WIRBEL, HENRI. R—France. G. O. No. 45, W. D., 1919.	Major general, commanding the 21st Region, French Army. For services rendered to the American Expeditionary Forces and to the cause in which the United States has been engaged.
WISSEMANS, MAURICE M. R—France. G. O. No. 39, W. D., 1920.	Medical inspector, Chief of the Medical Service, 2d French Army. When the 1st American Division went into the Verdun sector for training purposes, he collaborated with the medical service of the American Expeditionary Forces in every possible way to the end that our battle casualties should receive proper care. Later, as chief surgeon of the Group of Armies of the East, he actively participated in the preparation of the plans for the St. Mihiel and the Argonne offensives. His wide experience in battle conditions and his whole-hearted desire to be of assistance to his country's allies enabled him to render services of great value to the American Expeditionary Forces. He freely placed at the disposition of the American Expeditionary Forces all his resources as to hospitals, ambulance and train transportation, and medical material. His able advice and valuable assistance was a material factor in the provisions for the care and evacuation of our battle casualties. He rendered services of great consequence to the American Expeditionary Forces.

ITALIANS

[Awarded for exceptionally meritorious and distinguished services in a position of great responsibility, under the provisions of the act of Congress approved July 9, 1918]

ALBRICCI, CONTE ALBERICO
R—Italy.
G. O. No. 126, W. D., 1919.

Lieutenant general, Italian Army.
As commander of the 2d Italian Army Corps in France he rendered services of great distinction to the allied cause. Later as Minister of War he showed a keen spirit of cooperation with the American forces in Italy, assisting us by all means at the disposal of his extensive office. He has given services of great value to the American Expeditionary Forces.

ALLEGRETTI, LORENZO
R—Italy.
G. O. No. 45, W. D., 1919.

Major, commanding the Arditi Assault Battalion, Italian Army, while attached to the 332d Infantry, American Expeditionary Forces.
For services performed for the American Expeditionary Forces and to the cause in which the United States has been engaged.

ANGELOZZI, CAMILLO
R—Italy.
G. O. No. 126, W. D., 1919.

Lieutenant general, Italian Army.
As Director General of Engineers, Italian Army, he performed his exacting duties with eminent technical skill. At all times he was actuated by a desire to aid the American authorities by all the means at his command, thereby rendering services of the greatest value to the common cause.

APOLLONI, ENEAL
R—Italy.
G. O. No. 126, W. D., 1919.

Lieutenant colonel, Italian Army.
As liaison officer with the American Red Cross, by his admirable tact and helpful spirit of cooperation he aided materially in the effective relief work of this organization in caring for the sick and wounded of the American and Italian Armies.

AYMONINO, ALDO
R—Italy.
G. O. No. 45, W. D., 1919.

Colonel, Italian Army, chief of Group of Allied Missions of the Comando Supremo in Italy.
For services performed for the American Expeditionary Forces and to the cause in which the United States has been engaged.

BADOGLIO, PIETRO
R—Italy.
G. O. No. 17, W. D., 1919.

Lieutenant general, Deputy Chief of Staff, Italian Army.
For services rendered to the American Expeditionary Forces and to the cause in which the United States has been engaged.

BASSI, GUIDO
R—Italy.
G. O. No. 126, W. D., 1919.

Brigadier general, Italian Army.
As a member of the Interallied Commission on the Repatriation of Prisoners of War he has rendered highly meritorious service to the United States and allied Governments in connection with the repatriation of American and allied prisoners released by the armistice. He always displayed a cheerful and active interest in all that pertained to their welfare, and rendered sympathetic and practical cooperation.

BONGIOVANNI, LUIGI
R—Italy.
G. O. No. 87, W. D., 1919.

Major general, Italian Army, chief of the Italian Combat Air Forces.
In command of the Italian air forces during the time American pilots attached to Italian squadrons were on active duty at the Italian front, he exercised great ability, tact, and energy in his direction of the work of our officers. At all times he showed the highest military attainments, and his enthusiasm was an example to all. He rendered a most valuable service in his prosecution of operations against the enemy.

BUSINELLI, UGO
R—Italy.
G. O. No. 75, W. D., 1919.

Colonel, Italian Army.
For services to the allied and associated Governments as chief of staff, Italian section, Supreme War Council, Apr. 27, 1918, to Feb. 11, 1919.

CARPENTIERI, GIACOMO
R—Italy.
G. O. No. 126, W. D., 1919.

Colonel, Italian Army.
As chief of the Transportation Department, Italian Army, he displayed exceptional administrative ability and untiring energy in his important duties, thereby playing an important part in assuring the victorious termination of our struggles against the common enemy. Manifesting an earnest desire to aid the American forces in every possible way, he assisted us materially by furnishing adequate facilities for the transportation of our troops and supplies.

CAVALLERO, UGO
R—Italy.
G. O. No. 75, W. D., 1919.

General, Italian Army.
For services to the allied and associated Governments as permanent military representative, Italian section, Supreme War Council.

CAVIGLIA, ENRICO
R—Italy.
G. O. No. 126, W. D., 1919.

Lieutenant general, Italian Army.
In his capacity as Secretary of State for War, he was a potent factor in the victorious termination of our struggles against the common foe. For his unfailing courtesy and constant desire to aid in every possible way the American forces serving in Italy, he will ever be held in enduring memory by the officers and soldiers of our forces serving on Italian soil.

CHIESA, EUGENIO
R—Italy.
G. O. No. 46, W. D., 1920.

As Minister of Aeronautics for Italy, he rendered very valuable services to the American Expeditionary Forces in connection with the training of our pilots and the supply of aviation material. At all times he displayed a helpful interest in our Air Service, going far beyond the bounds of duty to render us advice and assistance. He has proved himself possessed of a wide knowledge of all matters pertaining to aviation and was always a loyal friend.

DALLOLIO, ALFREDO R—Italy. G. O. No. 126, W. D., 1919.	Lieutenant general, Italian Army. As Inspector General of Artillery, Italian Army, he performed duties of the greatest importance with conspicuous ability. Actuated by a warm spirit of cooperation, he aided materially in maintaining the cordial relations which existed between the Italian and American military authorities.
DE ANGELIS, CIRO R—Italy. G. O. No. 45, W. D., 1919.	Major general, commanding 31st Infantry Division, 3d Italian Army. For services rendered to the American Expeditionary Forces and to the cause in which the United States has been engaged.
DELLA VALLE, FRANCESCO R—Italy. G. O. No. 46, W. D., 1920.	Major general, Italian Army. Serving as surgeon general of the Italian Army he performed duties of the greatest responsibility with conspicuous merit. By his sympathetic knowledge of American needs he was of the greatest assistance in securing proper care for our sick and wounded in Italy.
DE LUCA, MARCELLO R—Italy. G. O. No. 126, W. D., 1919.	General, Italian Army. As chief of staff of a division at the outbreak of the war, he gave excellent service; later as commander of an infantry brigade, he showed great initiative and marked tactical ability; and finally as chief of staff of the Army Corps of Genoa he rendered eminent distinguished service.
DE MARCORENGO, FABRIZIO ODETTI R—Italy. G. O. No. 126, W. D., 1919.	Lieutenant general, Italian Army. As remount inspector of the Italian Army he performed his exacting duties with conspicuous success. Through his earnest desire to give the American authorities the advantage of all facilities at his disposal, he rendered services of the highest value in promoting effective cooperation between the two armies.
DEVALLE, GIOVANNI R—Italy. G. O. No. 126, W. D., 1919.	Colonel, Italian Army. He served with distinction as chief of T. A. E. A. of the Italian Army, contributing materially to the success of the common cause. At all times manifesting a cordial spirit of cooperation, he did much toward promoting the harmonious relations existing between the Italian Army and the American forces serving in Italy.
DIAZ, ARMANDO R—Italy. G. O. No. 111, W. D., 1918.	Lieutenant general, commander in chief, Italian Armies. As an expression to him of the high regard of the people of the United States and of their Army, for the distinguished and patriotic services which he has rendered to the common cause in which he has been associated on the battle fields of Europe.
DI CAMPIGLIONE, ENRICO R—Italy. G. O. No. 29, W. D., 1919.	Captain, Italian Army. For services rendered the United States Army while serving as the liaison officer between the embassy, the High Commission of Italy, and the War Department.
DI ROBILLANT, MARIO NICOLIS R—Italy. G. O. No. 75, W. D., 1919.	Lieutenant general, Italian Army. For services to the allied and associated Governments as permanent military representative, Italian section, Supreme War Council, Apr. 27, 1918, to Feb. 11, 1919.
DI SAVOIA, EMANUELE FILIBERTO R—Italy. G. O. No. 126, W. D., 1919.	Lieutenant general, Italian Army, commanding the 3d Italian Army. For services rendered the American Expeditionary Forces and to the cause in which the United States has been engaged.
GIRALDI, GUGLIELMO PECORI R—Italy. G. O. No. 126, W. D., 1919.	Lieutenant general, Italian Army. As commander of the 1st Italian Army, he rendered eminent services to the 332d U. S. Infantry, whose good fortune it was to be attached to his command during its training period, and which owes much of its successful preparation for combat to his painstaking efforts in its behalf.
GRAZIOSI, EUGENIO R—Italy. G. O. No. 126, W. D., 1919.	Brigadier general, Italian Army. As Director of Military Transportation of the Army of Italy, he rendered valuable service to the allied cause. His energy and zealous efforts were a deciding factor in the successful movement of the American forces in Italy.
GUGLIELMOTTI, EMILIO R—Italy. G. O. No. 11, W. D., 1919.	Major general, Italian Army. For services rendered the U. S. Army while serving as military attaché to the Royal Italian Embassy, Washington, D. C.
GUIDONI, ALESSANDRO R—Italy. G. O. No. 87, W. D., 1919.	Major, Italian Army. As the Italian technical delegate to the Interallied Aviation Committee, he displayed unusual technical knowledge and perfect understanding of the various problems incident to aviation. He was most helpful in giving the American Air Service the benefit of his wide experience, and rendered most valuable assistance in solving technical problems with which we were often confronted.
HUNTINGTON, CARLO H R—Italy. G. O. No. 126, W. D., 1919.	Captain, Italian Army. As principal assistant to the chief of the Italian Mission attached to American headquarters he has rendered great assistance to the various staff services at general headquarters. At all times he has manifested a zealous spirit of full cooperation with our staff personnel, furthering these cordial relations which have always prevailed between the Italian and American services.
LANZA, PAOLO R—Italy. G. O. No. 126, W. D., 1919.	Colonel, Italian Army. As Assistant Director of Transportation by his whole-hearted cooperation he rendered valuable services to the American Expeditionary Forces,

DISTINGUISHED-SERVICE MEDAL   831

LEVI, CAESER GIULIO
R—Italy.
G. O. No. 87, W. D., 1919.

General, Italian Army.
As the representative of the Italian Government on the Interallied Transportation Council he aided in the solution of difficult transportation problems, involving shipment of supplies from and to Italy. He proved an able executive and demonstrated the possession of broad vision and sound judgment.

MALLANDRA, GUISEPPE
R—Italy.
G. O. No. 126, W. D., 1919.

Major general, Italian Army.
In his capacity as general attached to the Italian War Ministry he showed a constant desire to aid the American forces in every possible way. By his helpful spirit of cooperation he did much toward the success of operations against the common enemy, rendering services of worth to the allied cause.

MARCHETTI, ODOARDO
R—Italy.
G. O. No. 126, W. D., 1919.

Colonel, Italian Army.
He performed his highly important duties as chief of the Intelligence Department of the Italian Army with conspicuous success, aiding thereby to a marked degree in the success of the operations against the common foe. Actuated by a constant desire to assist the American authorities with all the facilities of his office, he contributed materially to the harmonious relations existing between the Italian Army and the American forces in Italy.

MARIENI, GIOVAN BATTISTA
R—Italy.
G. O. No. 126, W. D., 1919.

Lieutenant general, Italian Army.
He served with distinction as Inspector General of Engineers, Italian Army, displaying technical attainments and devoted loyalty to the common cause. Ever ready to aid the American authorities with all the facilities at his command, he was a potent factor in furthering the spirit of cooperation which marked the relations of the Italian and American forces.

MERRONE, ENRICO
R—Italy.
G. O. No. 45, W. D., 1919.

Major general, Italian Army, Italian representative, Military Board of Allied Supply.
For services rendered to the American Expeditionary Forces and to the cause in which the United States has been engaged.

MODENA, ANGELO
R—Italy.
G. O. No. 126, W. D., 1919.

Major general, Italian Army.
He served with distinction as Director General of Transport and Administration of the Italian Army. He was ever ready to aid the American forces by his sound advice and cordial spirit of cooperation, thereby aiding us materially in the solution of the many problems of transportation which arose during the continued operations against the enemy.

MOLTENI, FILIPPO
R—Italy.
G. O. No. 45, W. D., 1919.

Major, Italian Army, chief of Paris section, Italian Foreign Military Aeronautical Mission.
For services performed for the American Expeditionary Forces and to the cause in which the United States has been engaged.

MOMBELLI, ERNESTO
R—Italy.
G. O. No. 10, W. D., 1922.

Major general, Italian Army.
As corps commander of the Italian Oriental Expeditionary Force during the war and as the Italian representative on the Interallied Military Mission to Hungary, positions of great responsibility, in which he rendered valuable services in the furtherance of the Allied cause.

MONTUORI, LUCA
R—Italy.
G. O. No. 126, W. D., 1919.

Lieutenant general, Italian Army.
As commanding general of the 5th Italian Army he displayed eminent military attainments in the performance of his important duties. To his brilliant leadership was due, in no small degree, the success achieved by the Italian forces against the common foe.

PAOLINI, GIUSEPPE
R—Italy.
G. O. No. 45, W. D., 1919.

Lieutenant general, Italian Army, commanding 11th Army Corps, 3d Italian Army.
For services rendered to the American Expeditionary Forces and to the cause in which the United States has been engaged.

PERELLI, IPPOLITO
R—Italy.
G. O. No. 45, W. D., 1919.

Brigadier general, Italian Army, chief, Italian Mission, General Headquarters, American Expeditionary Forces.
For services rendered to the American Expeditionary Forces and to the cause in which the United States has been engaged.

PIRAJNO, ANTONIO
R—Italy.
G. O. No. 46, W. D., 1920.

Brigadier general, Italian Army.
As Adjutant General of the Italian Army he performed his manifold duties with excellent success. At all times desirous of aiding the American forces in every possible way, he did much to further the spirit of harmony which marked the relations between the Italian and American Armies.

RAGIONI, RODOLFO
R—Italy.
G. O. No. 45, W. D., 1919.

Colonel, General Staff, Italian Army, Italian military delegate for British and American troops.
For services performed for the American Expeditionary Forces and to the cause in which the United States has been engaged.

RICALDONI, OTTAVIO
R—Italy.
G. O. No. 87, W. D., 1919.

Colonel, Air Service, Italian Army.
He furnished us with scientific and technical information needed in the development of the American Air Service in America, France, and in Italy. At all times he showed himself zealous in our behalf, going far beyond the bounds of his important duties to render us invaluable services. His judgment was sound, his advice helpful, his loyalty whole-hearted.

ROTA, ALFREDO
R—Italy.
G. O. No. 126, W. D., 1919.

Colonel, Italian Army.
By his efficient performance of his exacting duties as chief of the General Staff Department, Italian Army, he did much toward bringing about the victory which terminated our struggles against the common enemy. At all times he showed an ardent desire to give every consideration to the American forces serving in Italy, thereby furthering materially the effective cooperation of the Italian and American Armies.

RUISECCO, CLAUDIO R—Italy. G. O. No. 126, W. D., 1919.	Captain, Italian Army. In his capacity as assistant to the chief of the Italian Mission at America General Headquarters, he has constantly shown an earnest desire to fu nish our staff services with all assistance at his command. With a loy devotion to the common cause, he furthered the friendly relations betwee the two allied services.
SACHERO, GIACINTO R—Italy. G. O. No. 126, W. D., 1919.	Lieutenant general, Italian Army. As Director General of Artillery of the Italian Army he was charged wi duties of a most important nature, which he performed with marked ze and ability. He was ever ready to place the facilities of his office at t disposal of the American authorities and thereby rendered important servi in assuring the efficient cooperation of the two armies.
SCIMECA, VITO R—Italy. G. O. No. 14, W. D., 1920.	Colonel, Italian Army. His services were of distinguished merit as chief of the Italian Mission. H conscientious attention to duty presented a united allied front to the enem while his diplomatic tact cemented the cordial relations among the allies.
SCIPIONI, SCIPIONE R—Italy. G. O. No. 17, W. D., 1919.	Major general, Italian Army. For services rendered to the American Expeditionary Forces and to the cau in which the United States has been engaged.
SOGNO, VITTORIO R—Italy. G. O. No. 126, W. D., 1919.	Lieutenant colonel, Italian Army. He served with conspicuous success as chief of the 3d section of the Gener Staff Department, Italian Army, performing services of the utmost impo tance in connection with the struggle against the common enemy. T warm spirit of cooperation which he constantly displayed in his dealin with the American authorities was a potent factor in cementing the cord relations between the Italian Army and the American forces serving in Ital
TASSONI, GIULIO R—Italy. G. O. No. 126, W. D., 1919.	Lieutenant general, Italian Army. He commanded with distinction the 4th Italian Army, performing duties great importance with conspicuous success. His high military attainmer and the able leadership were an important factor in the victorious termin tion of the struggle against the common enemy.
TOMMASI, DONATO ANTONIO R—Italy. G. O. No. 126, W. D., 1919.	Lieutenant general, Italian Army. As Judge Advocate General of the Italian Army he performed his exacti duties with high conceptions of justice and loyal devotion to the comm cause. By his unfailing desire to aid the American forces in every possil way he did much to further the harmonious relations which existed betwe the two armies.
TONI, RENZO R—Italy. G. O. No. 75, W. D., 1919.	Lieutenant colonel, Italian Army. For services to the allied and associated Governments as chief of staff, Itali section, Supreme War Council.
TROIANI, ETTORE R—Italy. G. O. No. 126, W. D., 1919.	Lieutenant colonel, Italian Army. As chief of R. Section, Intelligence Department, he performed his importa duties with rare skill and untiring energy. Always ready to aid the Americ authorities with all the facilities at his command, he did much toward maki possible the efficient cooperation of the American forces with the Itali Army.
VACCHELLI, NICOLA R—Italy. G. O. No. 126, W. D., 1919.	Brigadier general, Italian Army. As Chief of General Staff Department, Italian Army, he played an importa part in bringing about the successful termination of the common strug against the Central Powers by his distinguished services in a duty of gre responsibility. Ever ready to aid the American forces in Italy by all t means at his disposal, he was an important factor in maintaining the h monious relations between the American and Italian autho-ities.
ZACCONE, VITTORIO R—Italy. G. O. No. 126, W. D., 1919.	Lieutenant general, Italian Army. He rendered invaluable services to the common cause as Quartermaster Gener Italian Army, displaying keen foresight and notable executive ability. his ardent desire to assist the American forces in every possible way he w a potent factor in fostering the spirit of cooperation which marked the relatic of the Italian and American Armies.
ZANGHIERI, GIOVANNI R—Italy. G. O. No. 126, W. D., 1919.	Lieutenant colonel, Italian Army. As Chief of P. of W. Department, he performed highly exacting duties w unflagging energy and marked executive ability. At all times he aided American authorities in every way possible, thereby assisting materially furthering the cordial relations between the Italian Army and the Americ forces serving in Italy.
ZUGARO, FULVIO R—Italy. G. O. No. 126, W. D., 1919.	Colonel, Italian Army. Charged with highly responsible duties as Chief of Organization and I mobilization Department, Italian Army, he displayed eminent administ tive ability and rendered services of great value to the common cause. his broad-minded spirit of cooperation and unfailing courtesy he did mu toward promoting the harmony which marked the relations between Italian Army and the American forces serving in Italy.
ZUPELLI, VITTORIO R—Italy. G. O. No. 126, W. D., 1919.	Lieutenant general, Italian Army. As Secretary of State for War he performed highly responsible duties w conspicuous ability and devoted loyalty, thereby meriting a large share the credit for the success of our common cause. The unbroken harmo which marked the relations of the American and Italian military authorit was in no small degree a reflection of the war spirit of cooperation which constantly manifested.

JAPANESE

[Awarded for exceptionally meritorious and distinguished services in a position of great responsibility, under the provisions of the act of Congress approved July 9, 1918]

INOUYE, KAZUTSUGU R—Japan. G. O. No. 29, W. D., 1919.	Major general, Imperial Japanese Army. For services rendered the U. S. Army while serving as military attaché to the Imperial Japanese Embassy, Washington, D. C.
MIZUMACHI, T R—Japan. G. O. No. 11, W. D., 1919.	Lieutenant colonel, Imperial Japanese Army. For services rendered the U. S. Army while serving as military attaché to the Imperial Japanese Embassy, Washington, D. C.
OTANI, KIKUZO R—Japan. G. O. No. 45, W. D., 1919.	General, Imperial Japanese Army. For services as senior allied commander in Siberia.
TANAKA, GIICHI R—Japan. G. O. No. 19, W. D., 1922.	General, Imperial Japanese Army. For services rendered the United States during the World War and in his relations with the U. S. Army while serving as vice chief of the Japanese General Staff and later as Minister of War of the Empire of Japan.
UYEHARA, Y R—Japan. G. O. No. 11, W. D., 1919.	General, Imperial Japanese Army. For services rendered in the war against Germany and in his relations with the U. S. Army while serving as Chief of the General Staff, Imperial Japanese Army.
WATARI, HISAO R—Japan. G. O. No. 29, W. D., 1919.	Captain, Imperial Japanese Army. For services rendered the U. S. Army while serving as acting military attaché to the Imperial Japanese Embassy, Washington, D. C.

CITIZENS OF OTHER COUNTRIES

[Awarded for exceptionally meritorious and distinguished services in a position of great responsibility, under the provisions of the act of Congress approved July 9, 1918]

ARGENTINIAN

CHUTRO, PIETRO
R—Argentina.
G. O. No. 2, W. D., 1920.

At his clinic in Paris, Doctor Chutro devoted himself unreservedly to teaching American medical officers the principles of the lessons learned through experience by the French and British surgeons in the first years of the war with the result that the knowledge so imparted assisted in a great measure to conserve the life and limb of thousands of American and allied wounded

RUMANIANS

RUDEANU, JOHN
R—Rumania.
G. O. No. 10, W. D. 1922.

General, Rumanian Army.
For services in connection with the American Military Mission in Hungary.

TEIUSANU, LIVIUS D
R—Rumania.
G. O. No. 87, W. D., 1919.

Major, Rumanian Army.
For services rendered the U. S. Army while serving as military attaché to the Rumanian Legation, Washington, D. C.

VASILESCU, CRISTEA
R—Rumania.
G. O. No. 10, W. D., 1922.

Lieutenant colonel, Rumanian Army.
For services in connection with the American Military Mission in Hungary.

RUSSIAN

MESTCHERINOFF, SERGE A
R—Russia.
G. O. No. 53, W. D., 1921.

Lieutenant colonel, Russian Army.
As deputy military attaché of Russia in France from March, 1917, to April 1918, he demonstrated qualities of initiative, energy, and ability. Later, as attaché to the King of Montenegro, he showed marked devotion in furthering the friendly relation of the two Governments. He has rendered valuable services to the allied cause.

SERBIAN

*MISHICH, ZHIVOYIN
R—Serbia.
G. O. No. 30, W. D., 1921.

Field marshal, Commander in Chief of Serbian Army.
For services to the allied cause during the World War.
Posthumously awarded. Medal forwarded to the military attaché, American Embassy, Belgrade, Serbia, for delivery to the next of kin.

MEMBERS OF THE ARMY, IN LIEU OF THE CERTIFICATE OF MERIT

[Distinguished-service medal issued in lieu of the certificate of merit under the provisions of the act of Congress approved July 9, 1918]

ABBOTT, GEORGE F
R—Worcester, Mass.
B—Brandon, Vt.
: Corporal, Company G, 9th Infantry, U. S. Army.
For distinguished gallantry in action at Tientsin, China, July 13, 1900.

AKERS, THOMAS P
R—Lexington, Ky.
B—Lexington, Ky.
: Sergeant, 1st class, Signal Corps, U. S. Army.
For distinguished service in the China relief expedition in China, Aug. 12, 1900.

ALBERTSON, EDWARD J
R—Sante Fe, N. Mex.
B—Corpus Christi, Tex.
: Private, Company F, 1st U. S. Volunteer Cavalry.
For distinguished service in battle on July 1, 1898, at Santiago, Cuba.

ALDRIDGE, JOHN S
R—Watauga County, N. C.
B—Mitchell County, N. C.
: Corporal, Company D, 19th Infantry, U. S. Army.
For gallant conduct in action at Mount Bud-Dajo, Jolo, P. I., Mar. 7, 1906.

ALEXANDER, JAMES
R—Monroe, Ohio.
B—Ohio.
: First sergeant, Troop A, 4th Cavalry, U. S. Army.
For distinguished service in engagement at Rio Chico Nueva Ecya, P. I., Dec. 6, 1900.

ALLEN, LUCIUS A
Near Donna, Tex., May 27, 1914.
R—St. Elmo, Tenn.
B—Buncombe County, N. C.
: Private, Company D, 12th Cavalry, U. S. Army.
For most distinguished courage and bravery beyond the call of duty in continuing his efforts to save a drowning comrade after having been seized and almost drowned himself in the Rio Grande River, near Donna, Tex., May 27, 1914.

ARNDT, ALVIN
R—NR.
B—Germany.
: First sergeant, Troop I, 4th Cavalry, U. S. Army.
For distinguished gallantry in action near Nozagaray, P. I., Feb. 15, 1899.

ASH, JOHN W
R—Chicago, Ill.
B—Henderson, Ky.
: Sergeant, Company E, 24th Infantry, U. S. Army.
For conspicuous gallantry in action against Pulajanes at Tabon-Tabon, Leyte, P. I., July 24, 1906.

ASKEW, PRESTON
R—Guthrie, Okla.
B—Sulphur Springs, Tex.
: Corporal, Company E, 24th Infantry, U. S. Army.
For distinguished gallantry in action against Pulajanes at Tabon-Tabon, Leyte, P. I., July 24, 1906.

BAKER, WILLIAM B
R—New York, N. Y.
B—New York, N. Y.
: Corporal, Astor Battery, U. S. Army.
For distinguished service in action at Manila, P. I., Aug. 13, 1898.

BANDIRA
R—Mindanao, P. I.
B—Mindanao, P. I.
: Private, 51st Company, Philippine Scouts.
For distinguished gallantry in action against hostile Moros, at Mount Bagsak, Jolo, P. I., June 15, 1913.

BARNES, WALTER K
R—Birmingham, Ala.
B—Clay Center, Kans.
: Acting hospital steward, Hospital Corps, U. S. Army.
On June 3, 1900, at Province of Bulacan, P. I., during an engagement with insurgents he went forward to the firing line and applied first-aid dresssing to a soldier who had been wounded fatally.

BARNHOUSE, JOHN L
R—Fairmount, Ind.
B—Fairmount, Ind.
: Private, Company F, 17th Infantry, U. S. Army.
For gallantry in action at Tempitan, Mindanao, P. I. on May 9, 1904.

BARRETT, MICHAEL
R—Lynn, Mass.
B—Ireland.
: Sergeant, Company A, 7th Infantry, U. S. Army.
For distinguished service in action at El Caney, Cuba, July 1, 1898.

BASSETT, DANIEL S
R—Philadelphia, Pa.
B—Philadelphia, Pa.
: Private, Company F, 21st Infantry, U. S. Army.
For distinguished service at San Felipe Church, El Deposito, Manila Province, P. I., June 22, 1899.

BEASLEY, HALBERT M
R—Kinston, N. C.
B—Granville County, N. C.
: Sergeant, Hospital Corps, U. S. Army.
Being injured himself he rendered aid to others injured in a wreck at Buckatunna, Miss., Oct. 19, 1913.

BELL, FRED
R—NR.
B—Ulster County, N. Y.
: Sergeant, Battery H, 3d Artillery, U. S. Army.
For distinguished service in the campaign near Malalos, P. I., Mar. 25–31, 1899.

BELMONT, JOHN
R—Haverhill, Mass.
B—Haverhill, Mass.
: Private, Company B, 23d Infantry, U. S. Army.
For heroic efforts to his own extreme exhaustion and danger, which resulted in saving a comrade from drowning at Galveston, Tex., June 18, 1914.

BERNHEIM, ALFRED A
R—Sacketts Harbor, N. Y.
B—Little Big Horn River, Mont.
: Sergeant, Company D, 9th Infantry, U. S. Army.
For distinguished gallantry in battle of Tientsin, China, July 13, 1900.

BIEFER, ALBERT
  R—New York, N. Y.
  B—Switzerland.
First sergeant, Company G, 13th Infantry, U. S. Army.
For distinguished service in the battle of Santiago, Cuba, July 1, 1898.

BINCKLI, FREDERIC
  R—New York, N. Y.
  B—Germany.
Private, Company H, 13th Infantry, U. S. Army.
For distinguished service in action at Santiago, Cuba, July 1, 1898.

BOWDEN, WILLIAM H
  R—Farmersville, Tex.
  B—Benton Co., Miss.
Corporal, Company C, 27th Infantry, U. S. Army.
Rescued a fellow soldier from drowning in the Wisconsin River, Wis., on June 25, 1912.

BRADFORD, CLAUDE L
  R—Port Hudson, La.
  B—Port Hudson, La.
Sergeant, Company B, 43d Infantry, U. S. Volunteers.
For coolness, bravery, and good judgment in action against bolomen near Alang Alang, Leyte, P. I., Mar. 29, 1900.

BROADUS, LEWIS
  R—Richmond, Va.
  B—Richmond, Va.
First sergeant, Company M, 25th Infantry, U. S. Army.
For coolness, presence of mind and bravery in saving lives of others at Fort Niobrara, Nebr., on July 3, 1906.

BRYAN, WILLIAM
  R—New York, N. Y.
  B—New York, N. Y.
Sergeant, 69th Company, Coast Artillery Corps, U. S. Army.
For voluntarily entering a closed place and removing sacks of powder that were in close proximity to burning powder and smoldering debris, at the risk of his own life, thereby preventing further disaster after the explosion, at Fort Monroe, Va., July 21, 1910.

BUGBEE, FRED W
  R—Tucson, Ariz.
  B—Oakland, Calif.
Private, Troop A, 1st U. S. Volunteer Cavalry.
For distinguished service in battle at Santiago, Cuba, July 1, 1898.

CAPRON, HARRY W
  R—NR.
  B—Waverly, Iowa.
Corporal, Troop B, 7th Cavalry, U. S. Army.
For extraordinary gallantry in action at Wounded Knee Creek, S. Dak, Dec. 29, 1890.

CHICK, LEON H
  R—Lynn, Mass.
  B—Rockport, Mass.
Sergeant, Battery H, 3d Artillery, U. S. Army.
For risking his life in order to check a fire at Manila, P. I., Feb. 22, 1899.

CHISUM, JENNER Y
  R—Jackson, Tenn.
  B—Jackson, Tenn.
First sergeant, Troop B, 6th Cavalry, U. S. Army.
For distinguished service in twice attempting at the risk of his own life to rescue a fellow soldier from drowning in Wild Cat Creek at Fort Meade, S. Dak., May 25, 1907.

CLARK, JOHN J
  R—White County, Ind.
  B—Tippecanoe County, Ind.
Quartermaster sergeant, 3d Infantry, U. S. Army.
For distinguished service in battle at Santiago, Cuba, July 1, 1898.

CLARK, ORION L
  R—Nemaha, Nebr.
  B—Nemaha, Nebr.
Private, Company B, 2d Infantry, U. S. Army.
For distinguished service in battle at Santiago, Cuba, July 1, 1898.

CLARKE, HENRY N
  R—NR.
  B—East Indies.
Private, Troop D, 3d Cavalry, U. S. Army.
For distinguished service in a fire in the troop stables at Fort Sam Houston, Tex., on Aug. 12, 1892.

COMBS, KENRICK B
  R—NR.
  B—Stafford County, Va.
Private, Troop F, 5th Cavalry, U. S. Army.
For gallantry in action at Milk River, Colo., Sept. 29, 1879.

COOK, WILLIAM C
  R—Owosso, Mich.
  B—Owosso, Mich.
Private, Company C, 13th Infantry, U. S. Army.
For distinguished service in battle at Santiago, Cuba, July 1, 1898.

CORBETT, JOHN E
  R—Brooklyn, N. Y.
  B—Long Island City, N. Y.
Recruit, Field Artillery, U. S. Army.
For distinguished service on June 22, 1912, at Fort Slocum, N. Y., for rescuing a fellow soldier from drowning at the risk of his own life.

COX, ROY F
  R—Junction City, Kans.
  B—Manhattan, Kans.
Corporal, Signal Corps, U. S. Army.
For highly meritorious services in voluntarily traveling about 30 miles during a severe blizzard, rescuing a civilian from freezing near Lake Minto, and dragging by sled 65 miles to Fairbanks, Alaska, Feb. 26-29, 1908.

CRAVEN, RALPH G
  R—Siler City, N. C.
  B—Beaufort, N. C.
Color sergeant, 6th Infantry, U. S. Army.
For conspicuous gallantry in action at Mount Bud-Dajo, Jolo, P. I., Mar. 7, 1906.

CROSBY, SCOTT
  R—NR.
  B—Marion County, Tenn.
Private, Company A, 24th Infantry, U. S. Army.
For distinguished service in battle at Santiago, Cuba, July 1, 1898.

CROWELL, LEON
  R—Monterey, Mexico.
  B—Portland, Ind.
Private, Company B, 4th Infantry, U. S. Army.
For conspicuous gallantry in action near Dasmarinas, Luzon, P. I., June 19, 1899.

DAVIS, EDWARD
  R—San Antonio, Tex.
  B—Nashville, Tenn.
Private, Troop H, 9th Cavalry, U. S. Army.
For distinguished service in action at Santiago, Cuba, July 1, 1898.

DISTINGUISHED-SERVICE MEDAL

DEAVEY, WILLIAM H
   R—New York, N. Y.
   B—Fort Edwards, N. Y.
: Sergeant, Company H, 3d Infantry, U. S. Army.
For distinguished service at Almacenes River, Luzon, P. I., Dec. 3, 1899.

DELANEY, MICHAEL J
   R—Portland, Me.
   B—Portland, Me.
: Private, 24th Company, Coast Artillery Corps, U. S. Army.
For bravery in rescuing a comrade from drowning at Fort McKinley, Me., on Apr. 30, 1913.

DILLMAN, WILLIAM
   R—Terre Haute, Ind.
   B—Milton, Pa.
: Quartermaster sergeant, Company A, 13th Infantry, U. S. Army.
For distinguished service in action at Santiago, Cuba, on July 1, 1898.

DONALDSON, LORENZO D
   R—Fremont County, Iowa.
   B—Fremont County, Iowa.
: Private, Company F, 32d Infantry, U. S. Volunteers.
For distinguished gallantry in action at Abucay, Luzon, P. I., May 25, 1900.

DONNELLY, JAMES
   R—Cincinnati, Ohio.
   B—Ireland.
: Private, Company G, 18th Infantry, U. S. Army.
For distinguished service at the fire at Fort Clark, Tex., Mar. 31, 1892.

DOYLE, LAWRENCE
   R—Newark, N. J.
   B—New York, N. Y.
: Corporal, Company G, 11th Infantry, U. S. Army.
For distinguished service at the Malabang River, Mindanao, P. I., Aug. 2, 1902.

DOZIER, ERNEST
   R—San Francisco, Calif.
   B—East Oakland, Calif.
: First-class sergeant, U. S. Volunteer Signal Corps.
For distinguished service in action near Manila, P. I., Aug. 5, 1898.

ELDER, ROBERT W
   R—Boston, Mass.
   B—Athol, Mass.
: First sergeant, Troop L, 14th Cavalry, U. S. Army.
For exceptional courage and daring in action at Cotto Pangpang, P. I., Feb. 14, 1904.

ELLIOTT, HENRY W
   R—Indianapolis, Ind.
   B—Indianapolis, Ind.
: Corporal, Troop H, 3d Cavalry, U. S. Army.
For distinguished service in battle at Santiago, Cuba, July 1, 1898.

EVERSOLE, JOSEPH
   R—Dutton, Ark.
   B—Perry County, Ky.
: Corporal, Company H, 8th Infantry, U. S. Army.
For saving a fellow soldier from drowning at the risk of his own life at Nagasaki, Japan, Sept. 7, 1917.

FARMER, LYLE G
   R—Grand Meadow, Minn.
   B—Mears, Mich.
: Corporal, Company I, 43d Infantry, U. S. Army.
For saving Miss Eleanor Bourgeois from drowning in the artificial lake, disregarding personal risk and danger. Place: City Park, New Orleans, La. Date: Apr. 27, 1918.

FEARINGTON, GEORGE W
   R—Durham, N. C.
   B—Durham County, N. C.
: Private, Troop I, 9th Cavalry, U. S. Army.
For excellent conduct and heroic service at Fort Duchesne, Utah, Dec. 13, 1899, when the troop barracks were destroyed by fire, having taken post on the peak of the seriously threatened building, remaining there in spite of the great heat, applying water until the danger was over.

FEARNLEY, ARTHUR
   R—Oklahoma City, Okla.
   B—Wichita, Kans.
: Corporal, 75th Company, Coast Artillery Corps, U. S. Army.
For courage and tenacity of purpose in the face of dangers both known and unknown while searching for a comrade who had been lost in the Koolan Range, Oahu, Hawaii, Apr. 8, 1914.

FELDCAMP, GEORGE
   R—Cincinnati, Ohio.
   B—Sedamsville, Ohio.
: First sergeant, Company E, 12th Infantry, U. S. Army.
For conspicuous gallantry in action against insurgents at Barrio of Mazambique, Ilocos Norte, P. I., Sept. 22, 1900.

FINERTY, WILLIAM M
   R—Napoleon, Ohio.
   B—Napoleon, Ohio
: Corporal, Company E, 2d Infantry, U. S. Army.
For most distinguished conduct at Santiago, Cuba, July 2, 1898.

FISHER, ROBERT L
   R—Augusta, Ga.
   B—Augusta, Ga.
: Private, Battery A, 1st Field Artillery, U. S. Army.
For saving a comrade from drowning in Medicine Creek, near Fort Sill, Okla., June 29, 1907.

FLACH, JOHN
   R—Effingham County, Ill.
   B—Effingham County, Ill.
: Post commissary sergeant, U. S. Army.
For distinguished service in Boston Harbor, Mass., Jan. 3, 1900.

FLANNERY, DAVID T
   R—Brooklyn, N. Y.
   B—Ireland.
: First-class private, Company E, Signal Corps, U. S. Army.
For distinguished gallantry in action at Big Bend, Luzon, P. I., Oct. 2, 1899.

FLYNN, EDWARD
   R—Cincinnati, Ohio.
   B—Ireland.
: Quartermaster sergeant, Company G, 21st Infantry, U. S. Army.
For distinguished service in battle at Santiago, Cuba, July 1, 1898.

FORTESCUE, GRANVILLE ROLAND
   At Santiago, Cuba, July 1, 1898.
   R—New York, N. Y.
   B—New York, N. Y.
: Corporal, Troop E, 1st U. S. Volunteer Cavalry.
For distinguished service in battle at Santiago, Cuba, July 1, 1898.

GANNON, WILLIAM F
   R—Lowell, Mass.
   B—Lowell, Mass.
: Musician, Company L, 8th Infantry, U. S. Army.
For conspicuous gallantry in action against Pulajanes near La Paz, Leyte, P. I., Dec. 5, 1906.

DECORATIONS, U. S. ARMY, 1862–1926

GOODE, BENJAMIN H R—Abbeville County, S. C. B—Abbeville County, S. C.	Private, Company H, 24th Infantry, U. S. Army. For most distinguished gallantry in action at Naguilian, Luzon, P. I., Dec. 7, 1899.
GOULD, CLARENCE S R—Cone, Mich. B—Cone, Mich.	First sergeant, Troop C, 1st Cavalry, U. S. Army. For gallant conduct in battle at Santiago, Cuba, July 1, 1898.
GOULD, FRED H R—Los Gatos, Calif. B—Forest Grove, Oreg.	Corporal, Company H, 9th Infantry, U. S. Army. For distinguished service in operations at Oras, Samar, P. I., January and February, 1902.
GROGAN, MICHAEL R—Haverstraw, N. Y. B—England.	Corporal, Company B, 13th Infantry, U. S. Army. For distinguished service in action at Santiago, Cuba, July 1, 1898.
GUNN, JAMES C R—Eureka, Tex. B—Eureka, Tex.	Sergeant, 1st class, Hospital Corps, U. S. Army. For distinguished service in action at Peruke-Utig, Jolo, P. I., on May 3, 1905.
HARRIS, JOHN C R—Chicago, Ill. B—Canada.	Private, Company L, 4th Infantry, U. S. Army. For distinguished service in the engagement near Dasmarinas, Luzon, P. I., June 19, 1899.
HARRISON, FRED A R—La Junta, Colo. B—Kirwin, Kans.	Private, Troop C, 6th Cavalry, U. S. Army. For distinguished service in engagement near San Nicolas, Cavite Province, P. I., Dec. 31, 1901.
HAWK, WILMER HARRISON R—New Brighton, Pa. B—New Brighton, Pa.	Cook, 69th Company, Coast Artillery Corps, U. S. Army. For voluntarily entering a closed place and removing sacks of powder that were in close proximity to burning powder and smoldering débris, at the risk of his own life, thereby preventing further disaster after the explosion, at Fort Monroe, Va., July 21, 1910.
HAWKINS, GEORGE P R—Coldenham, N. Y. B—Greenwood, Nebr.	Private, Troop K, 14th Cavalry, U. S. Army. For gallant conduct on Jan. 29, 1910, in rescuing at the risk of his own life an officer from drowning in the Quinqua River, Luzon, P. I.
HECHT, HERMAN R—Coryville, Ohio. B—Germany.	First sergeant, Company H, 4th Infantry, U. S. Army. For distinguished service in battle at El Caney, Cuba, July 1, 1898.
HEINZE, JULIUS R—Minneapolis, Minn. B—Germany.	Private, Hospital Corps, U. S. A. For distinguished service in the fight on the Gandara River, Samar, P. I., Oct. 16, 1901.
HENNECKE, FRED R—New York, N. Y. B—New York, N. Y.	Sergeant, Company L, 8th Infantry, U. S. Army. For conspicuous gallantry in action against Pulajanes, near the village of La Paz, on the island of Leyte, P. I., Dec. 5, 1906.
HERBERT, THOMAS H R—Washington, D. C. B—Montgomery County, Md.	Corporal, Troop E, 10th Cavalry, U. S. Army. For distinguished service in battle at Santiago, Cuba, July 1, 1898.
HICKEY, EDWARD J R—West Point, N. Y. B—West Point, N. Y.	Private, U. S. M. A., detachment Army Service men, Quartermaster department, U. S. Army. For rescuing the body of a drowning boy at West Point, N. Y., Nov. 28, 1904.
HICKMAN, TAYLOR B R—Knoxville, Tenn. B—Sevier County, Tenn.	Private, Company C, 9th Infantry, U. S. Army. For distinguished service in battle at Tientsin, China, July 13, 1900.
HILYARD, SAMUEL W R—Louisville, Ky. B—Louisville, Ky.	Artificer, Company E, 13th Infantry, U. S. Army. For distinguished service in battle at Santiago, Cuba, July 1, 1898.
HOGAN, JAMES E R—Chicago, Ill. B—Boston, Mass.	First-class sergeant, Signal Corps, U. S. Army. For energy and good judgment displayed in administration of relief to, and safe transportation of three badly frozen enlisted men of Signal Corps from Summit to North Fork, Alaska, Jan. 3, 4, 5, 6, and 7, 1906.
HOGAN, THOMAS R—NR. B—Wayne County, Mich.	Private, Troop E, 3d Cavalry, U. S. Army. For bravery in action with hostile Utes at Milk Creek, Colo., Sept. 29, 1879.
HOUSTON, ADAM R—Pulaski County, Va. B—Pulaski County, Va.	First sergeant, Troop C, 10th Cavalry, U. S. Army. For distinguished service in battle at Santiago, Cuba, July 1, 1898.
HOWE, CHARLES S R—Chicago, Ill. B—Brooklyn, N. Y.	Sergeant, Company D, 17th Infantry, U. S. Army. For distinguished service in the engagement near San Isidro, Luzon, P. I., July 29, 1900.
HUGHES, DAVID L R—Tucson, Ariz. B—Tucson, Ariz.	Sergeant, Troop B, 1st U. S. Volunteer Cavalry. For distinguished service in battle at Santiago, Cuba, on July 1, 1898.
HUMPHREY, CHARLES L R—W. Boylston, Mass. B—Holden, Mass.	Private, Company H, 9th Infantry, U. S. Army. For distinguished service in the battle of Tientsin, China, July 13, 1900.

DISTINGUISHED-SERVICE MEDAL 839

HUNSAKER, IRVIN L. R—Cobden, Ill. B—Cobden, Ill.	First sergeant, Company H, 18th Infantry, U. S. Army. For distinguished gallantry in battle at Jaro, Panay, P. I., Feb. 12, 1899.
HUNTER, CHARLES. R—Mansfield, Ohio. B—Mansfield, Ohio.	Sergeant, Company E, 12th Infantry, U. S. Army. For conspicuous gallantry in action against insurgents at Barrio of Mazambique, Ilocos Norte, P. I., Sept. 22, 1900.
HYATT, THADDEUS R. R—Quallatown, N. C. B—Jackson County, N. C.	Corporal, Company L, 19th Infantry, U. S. Army. For capturing two of the worst criminals in Porto Rico, Nov. 8, 1898, near Guayanilla, P. R.
JACKSON, PERRY B. R—Ozark, Ala. B—Jonesburg, Mo.	Corporal, Company K, 6th Infantry, U. S. Army. For exceptional bravery in action at Mount Bud-Dajo, Jolo, P. I., Mar. 7, 1906.
JACKSON, PETER. R—New York, N. Y. B—New York, N. Y.	Corporal, Company G, 24th Infantry, U. S. Army. For distinguished service in battle at Santiago, Cuba, July 1, 1898.
JANOWSKI, FRANK. R—Chicago, Ill. B—Germany.	Artificer, Company D, 13th Infantry, U. S. Army. For distinguished service in battle at Santiago, Cuba, July 1, 1898.
JENSEN, JULIUS. R—New York, N. Y. B—Germany.	Sergeant major, 21st Infantry, U. S. Army. For distinguished service in battle at Santiago, Cuba, July 1, 1898.
JOHNSON, SANT. R—Jackson, Ky. B—Kentucky.	Corporal, Troop G, 3d Cavalry, U. S. Army. For distinguished service at a fire at Fort Apache, Ariz., Apr. 12, 1904.
JOHNSON, THOMAS. R—Lexington, Ky. B—Woodford County, Ky.	First sergeant, Company I, 24th Infantry, U. S. Army. For pursuing and disarming an enlisted man bent on murdering his first sergeant at Camp McGrath, Batangas, P. I., Aug. 22, 1912.
JONES, FRED B. R—Nough, Tenn. B—Cocke County, Tenn.	Sergeant, 109th Company, Coast Artillery Corps, U. S. Army. For attempting to rescue a civilian from drowning at Fort Greble, R. I., May 28, 1907.
JONES, WILLIE R. R—Atlanta, Ga. B—Atlanta, Ga.	Private, Battery A, 4th Field Artillery, U. S. Army. For saving a comrade from drowning at the risk of his own life at Vera Cruz, Mexico, on Sept. 1, 1914.
JORDAN, JOSEPH K. R—New York, N. Y. B—New York N, Y.	Private, Company H, 43d Infantry, U. S. Volunteers. For distinguished service in the attack by insurgents at Calbayog, Samar, P. I., Mar. 26, 1900.
KAINE, PATRICK. R—NR. B—Ireland.	First sergeant, Company D, 3d Infantry, U. S. Army. For saving a comrade from drowning at the risk of his own life at Leech Lake, Minn., June 16, 1893.
KALBER, LOUIS. R—NR. B—Germany.	Corporal, Company G, 9th Infantry, U. S. Army. For distinguished service at Singalan, P. I., Aug. 9, 1899.
KARSTEN, CHARLES. R—NR. B—Germany.	First sergeant, Troop D, 1st Cavalry, U. S. Army. For distinguished service in battle at Santiago, Cuba, July 1, 1898.
KEISTER, GUY A. R—Marion, Ind. B—Tipton County, Ind.	Private, Company F, 8th Infantry, U. S. Army. For saving a comrade from drowning at Lakeside, Calif., May 7, 1911.
KELLY, MICHAEL. R—Lewiston, Me. B—West Minot, Me.	First sergeant, Company C, 21st Infantry, U. S. Army. For distinguished service in battle at Santiago, Cuba, July 1, 1898.
KENNEDY, CECIL W. R—Central Lake, Mich. B—Wetzel, Mich.	Private, Troop B, 12th Cavalry, U. S. Army. For distinguished conduct in passing through a zone infested with bandits and carrying a message to his troop commander after having had two horses shot from under him at Progreso, Tex., Sept. 24, 1915, while serving as private, Troop B, 12th Cavalry, U. S. Army.
KLINGENSMITH, SAMUEL. R—Greensburg, Pa. B—West Newton, Pa.	Private, Troop F, 5th Cavalry, U. S. Army. For gallantry in action at Milk River, Colo., Sept. 29, 1879.
KOENIG, EDWARD. R—New York, N. Y. B—New York, N. Y.	Private, Company G, 8th Infantry, U. S. Army. For distinguished service on July 13, 1905, at the Governors Island Dock, New York, N. Y., in saving from drowning, at the risk of his own life, a civilian who had jumped into the bay with the intention of committing suicide.
LEABACK, CHARLES C. R—Chicago, Ill. B—Reading, Pa.	First sergeant, Company F, 9th Infantry, U. S. Army. For distinguished service near Tarlac, P. I., Nov. 19, 1899.

LEAKINS, JOHN ADAM .... | Private, Company C, 13th Infantry, U. S. Army.
R—Taneytown, Md. | For distinguished service in battle at Santiago, Cuba, July 1, 1898.
B—Libertytown, Md.

LEONARD, CHARLES L .... | Hospital steward, U. S. Army.
R—Lancaster, Pa. | For distinguished gallantry in the assault on Fort Bacolod, Lake Lanao, Mindanao, P. I., Apr. 8, 1903.
B—Lancaster, Pa.

LEWIS, OLIVER .... | Sergeant, 73d Company, Coast Artillery Corps, U. S. Army.
R—Nebo, N. C. | For saving a girl from drowning at the risk of his own life at Fort Monroe, Va., July 27, 1915.
B—Nebo, N. C.

LEWIS, THOMAS .... | Private, Troop E, 3d Cavalry, U. S. Army.
R—NR. | For conspicuous bravery before hostile Utes at Milk Creek, Colo, Sept. 29, 1879.
B—Burlington, Vt.

LIESMANN, FREDERICK J .... | Corporal, Company B, 16th Infantry, U. S. Army.
R—Dixon, Mo. | For distinguished service in battle at Santiago, Cuba, July 1, 1898.
B—Pierce City, Mo. | Oak-leaf cluster.
 | Sergeant, Company M, 38th Infantry, U. S. Volunteers.
 | For most conspicuous gallantry in action near San Juan de Bocboc, **Luzon,** P. I., July 1, 1900.

LIPSCOMB, SPENCER K .... | Corporal, Company G, 14th Infantry, U. S. Army.
R—East Seattle, Wash. | For distinguished gallantry in action near Manila, P. I., on Feb. 5, 1899.
B—St. George, W. Va.

LOFTUS, JOHN .... | Private, Company C, 13th Infantry, U. S. Army.
R—Philadelphia, Pa. | For distinguished service in battle at Santiago, Cuba, July 1, 1898.
B—Ireland.

LONG, JOHN .... | Artificer, Battery F, 3d Artillery, U. S. Army.
R—Baltimore, Md. | For services rendered during fire at Fort Sam Houston, Tex., on Aug. 12, **1892.**
B—Baltimore, Md.

LONGACRE, BENJAMIN F .... | First sergeant, Troop F, 12th Cavalry, U. S. Army.
R—Lewistown, Pa. | For saving a comrade from drowning at the risk of his own life at Louisville, Colo., July 8, 1914.
B—Mifflintown, Pa.

LOOMIS, WILLIAM E .... | Corporal, Company B, 21st Infantry, U. S. Army.
R—Montrose, Pa. | For distinguished service in battle at Santiago, Cuba, July 1, 1898.
B—Forest Lake, Pa.

McBRIDE, JOHN .... | Sergeant, Troop A, 3d Cavalry, U. S. Army.
R—Boston, Mass. | For distinguished service in battle at Manimani River, Cuba, July 23, **1898.**
B—Boston, Mass.

McCOMYN, RICHARD H .... | Private, Troop A, 6th Cavalry, U. S. Army.
R—NR. | For distinguished service in engagement at San Juan, Santiago, Cuba, **July 1,** 1898.
B—Ireland.

McCUTCHEON, JAMES .... | Private, Company G, 13th Infantry, U. S. Army.
R—Washington County, Minn. | For distinguished service in battle at Santiago, Cuba, July 1, 1898.
B—Washington County, Minn.

McDONALD, FRANK R .... | Trumpeter, Troop L, 1st U. S. Volunteer Cavalry.
R—Oologah, Ind. T. | For distinguished service in battle at Santiago, Cuba, July 1, 1898.
B—Keysport, Ill.

McDONALD, JOHN .... | First sergeant, 77th Company, Coast Artillery Corps, U. S. Army.
R—Sugar Notch, Pa. | For saving from drowning an employee of the United States Engineer **Department,** at Otis Wharf, Boston, Mass., June 24, 1905.
B—Shenandoah, Pa.

McDONALD, WILBERT L .... | Sergeant, Company D, 19th Infantry, U. S. Army.
R—Huntsville, Tenn. | For gallant conduct in action at Mount Bud-Dajo, Jolo, P. I., Mar. 7, **1906.**
B—Huntsville, Tenn.

McGURTY, FRANK P .... | Private, Company E, 22d Infantry, U. S. Army.
R—New York, N. Y. | For distinguished service during the San Francisco fire and earthquake, **April,** 1906.
B—Worcester, Mass.

McMILLEN, JAMES L .... | Private, Company H, 12th Infantry, U. S. Army.
R—Fountain County, Ind. | For distinguished service at El Caney, Cuba, July 1, 1898.
B—Fountain County, Ind.

McNARNEY, FRANK T .... | Sergeant, Company H, 10th Infantry, U. S. Army.
R—Lock Haven, Pa. | For distinguished service in battle at Santiago, Cuba, July 1, 1898.
B—McElhattan, Pa.

MAHONEY, DENIS .... | Private, Company I, 36th Infantry, U. S. Volunteers.
R—New York, N. Y. | For gallantry in action near Guagua, P. I., Aug. 16, 1899.
B—Ireland.

MALONE, JOHN .... | Corporal, 47th Company, Coast Artillery Corps, U. S. Army.
R—Anacostia, D. C. | For rescuing with assistance, a comrade from drowning at Fort **Washington,** Md., Feb. 6, 1910.
B—New York, N. Y.

MERDINGER, GEORGE .... | First sergeant, Company H, 21st Infantry, U. S. Army.
R—NR. | For distinguished service in battle at Santiago, Cuba, July 1, 1898.
B—Germany.

DISTINGUISHED-SERVICE MEDAL 841

MILLER, RICHARD _____ | Sergeant, Troop F, 9th Cavalry, U. S. Army.
R—Louisville, Ky. | For distinguished service in the engagement at Tagbac, Albay, P. I., Dec. 17,
B—Madison County, Ky. | 1900.

MOLL, JULIUS _____ | Sergeant major, 6th Cavalry, U. S. Army.
R—NR. | For distinguished service in battle at Santiago, Cuba, July 1, 1898.
B—Germany.

MOORE, JOHN I _____ | Sergeant, Company C, 27th Infantry, U. S. Army.
R—Columbia, S. C. | For distinguished service in the assault on Fort Bacolod, Lake Lanao, Min-
B—Hagood, S. C. | danao, P. I., Apr. 8, 1903.

MORRISON, EDWARD W _____ | Private, 1st class, Hospital Corps, U. S. Army.
R—Colfax, Ind. | For rendering first aid to wounded comrades under fire of hostile Moros at
B—Boone County, Ind. | Mamaya Peak, P. I., Dec. 15, 1913.

MORROW, BISHOP L _____ | Sergeant, Company I, 28th Infantry, U. S. Army.
R—Mark, La. | For bravery in saving the life of a wounded comrade by defending him against
B—Osage, Mo. | the treacherous attack of three Moros, all of whom he killed or wounded, near
  | Pantar on the Iligan-Lake Lanao Military Road, P. I., May 1, 1903.

MOSELY, THOMAS _____ | Private, Hospital Corps, U. S. Army.
R—Brandenburg, Ky. | For distinguished gallantry in action against hostile Moros at Mount Bagsak,
B—Brandenburg, Ky. | Jolo, P. I., June 11, 1913.

MULHERN, BARTHOLOMEW _____ | Sergeant, Troop E, 3d Cavalry, U. S. Army.
R—NR. | For distinguished service in battle at Santiago, Cuba, July 1, 1898.
B—Ireland.

MURPHY, MICHAEL J _____ | First sergeant, Company D, 13th Infantry, U. S. Army.
R—Boston, Mass. | For distinguished service in battle at Santiago, Cuba, July 1, 1898.
B—Ireland.

MYERS, EDWIN _____ | Corporal, Signal Corps, U. S. Army.
R—Brooklyn, N. Y. | For distinguished service at Siassi, P. I., May 11, 1905.
B—Bayard, Ohio.

NAGEL, THEODORE _____ | First sergeant, Company A, 13th Infantry, U. S. Army.
R—Brooklyn, N. Y. | For distinguished service in action at Santiago, Cuba, July 1, 1898.
B—Germany.

NEAL, LOYD _____ | Musician, Battery H, 3d Artillery, U. S. Army.
R—Darlington, S. C. | For distinguished service in action near Manila, P. I., July 31, 1898.
B—Darlington, S. C.

NICHOLS, EDWARD T _____ | First sergeant, Company D, 21st Infantry, U. S. Army.
R—Boston, Mass. | For distinguished service in action at Santiago, Cuba, July 1, 1898.
B—Bangor, Me.

O'CONNOR, JOHN C _____ | First sergeant, Battery G, 3d Artillery, U. S. Army.
R—Jersey City, N. J. | For distinguished services in the campaign in the Philippine Islands, July 31,
B—Ireland. | 1898, to Jan. 1, 1901.

ODEN, GEORGE J _____ | Sergeant major, 36th Infantry, U. S. Volunteers.
R—Los Angeles, Calif. | For distinguished gallantry in action near Mangaperen, Luzon, P. I., Nov. 28,
R—Germany. | 1899.

ODEN, OSCAR N _____ | Trumpeter, Troop I, 10th Cavalry, U. S. Army.
R—San Francisco, Calif. | For distinguished service in action at Santiago, Cuba, July 1, 1898.
B—Eaton County, Mich.

ODIN, ARTHUR S _____ | Private, Company I, 9th Infantry, U. S. Army.
R—Syracuse, N. Y. | For distinguished service in the action near Zapote River, P. I., June 13, 1899.
B—Syracuse, N. Y.

O'KEEFFE, DANIEL _____ | Private, Battery B, 7th Artillery, U. S. Army.
R—New York, N. Y. | For heroic conduct in rescuing from drowning a corporal of his battery who
B—Albany, N. Y. | fell overboard from the tugboat Alert in Long Island Sound, Apr. 13, 1900,
  | while the boat was plying between New London, Conn., and the islands.

O'KEEFE, JOHN P _____ | Corporal, Company M, 2d Infantry, U. S. Army.
R—New York, N. Y. | For imperiling his life in rescuing a drowning militiaman at American Lake,
B—New York, N. Y. | Wash., Aug. 19, 1908.

OLSEN, STANLEY R _____ | Private, 1st class, Troop H, 6th Cavalry, U. S. Army.
R—Schenectady, N. Y. | For distinguished service in saving from death by drowning Private Emil A.
B—Frankfort, N. Y. | Saboslay, Troop B, 6th Cavalry, at Espia, Chihuahua, Mexico, May 17, 1916.

OLSON, ROY C _____ | Corporal, Company D, 19th Infantry, U. S. Army.
R—Kansas City, Mo. | For gallant conduct in action at Mount Bud-Dajo, Jolo, P. I., Mar. 7, 1906,
B—Kansas City, Mo. | in willingly and unhesitatingly responding to a call for a few men to occupy
  | an exposed point in advance of the line in plain view and within 25 or 30 yards
  | of the enemy, from which point he kept up a most effective fire until the
  | assault was made.

OLSSON, HENRY _____ | Corporal, Battery E, 1st Artillery, U. S. Army.
R—NR. | For distinguished service in the action at San Cristobal Bridge, P. I., July 30,
B—Springfield, Me. | 1899.

O'REILLY, JAMES F............ | Corporal, Company B, 9th Infantry, U. S. Army.
R—Westville, N. Y. | For distinguished service in action at Santiago, Cuba, July 1, 1898.
B—Westville, N. Y. |

O'ROURKE, JOHN............ | First sergeant, Company C, 17th Infantry, U. S. Army.
R—NR. | For distinguished service in action at El Caney, Cuba, July 1, 1898.
B—Ireland. |

PARKER, JESSE E............ | Artificer, Company D, 24th Infantry, U. S. Army.
R—Charleston, W. Va. | For brave and faithful conduct (assisting a wounded officer to a place of safety
B—Charleston, W. Va. | while exposed to a severe fire at Santiago, Cuba, July 1, 1898.

PARKS, CHARLES H............ | Private, 69th Company, Coast Artillery Corps, U. S. Army.
R—Gas City, Ind. | For voluntarily entering a closed place and removing sacks of powder that we
B—Grant County, Ind. | in close proximity to burning powder and smoldering débris, at the risk
 | his own life, thereby preventing further disaster after the explosion at Fo
 | Monroe, Va., July 21, 1910.

PASCHAL, JESSE J............ | Private, 14th Company, Coast Artillery Corps, U. S. Army.
R—Louisiana, Mo. | For voluntarily imperiling his own life in the rescue of fellow soldiers at Fo
B—Trenton, Mo. | Screven, Ga., July 4, 1906.

PAYNE, WILLIAM............ | Sergeant, Troop E, 10th Cavalry, U. S. Army.
R—Chattanooga, Tenn. | For distinguished service in battle at Santiago, Cuba, July 1, 1898.
B—Nashville, Tenn. |

PHILBIN, PATRICK............ | Sergeant, Company L, 15th Infantry, U. S. Army.
R—Dunmore, Pa. | For distinguished service in the action at the barrio of San Juan, P. I., De
B—Ireland. | 31, 1900.

PITTS, WILLIAM C............ | Private, Company F, 21st Infantry, U. S. Army.
R—Mineral Point, Wis. | For saving from drowning, near Florence, Ariz., a citizen of Florence, Ariz., o
B—Milwaukee, Wis. | Mar. 7, 1908.

POTTER, HARRY E............ | First sergeant, Company A, 37th Infantry, U. S. Volunteers.
R—Monticello, Me. | For distinguished conduct June 6, 1900, near Majajay, Laguna Province, Luzo
B—Penobscot, Me. | P. I., in exposing himself to the fire of the enemy at close range in order
 | remove a wounded comrade to shelter.

PRICE, WILSON C............ | Private, Company F, 9th Infantry, U. S. Army.
R—W. Philadelphia, Pa. | For distinguished gallantry in battle of Tientsin, China, July 13, 1900.
B—Philadelphia, Pa. |

PUMPHREY, GEORGE W............ | Corporal, Troop H, 9th Cavalry, U. S. Army.
R—Baltimore, Md. | For distinguished service in battle at Santiago, Cuba, July 1, 1898.
B—Anne Arundel County, Md. |

REED, JOSPEH E............ | Private, Company L, 47th Infantry, U. S. Volunteers.
R—Huntingdon, Pa. | For distinguished gallantry in action at Bulusan, Luzon, P. I., Nov. 11, 1900
B—Drafton, Pa. |

RICHARDSON, HURLEY O............ | Sergeant, Troop C, 6th Cavalry, U. S. Army.
R—Lorley, Md. | For conspicuous bravery and efficiency in action against hostile Moros o
B—Berlin, Md. | Patian Island, P. I., July 4, 1909.

RICHMOND, CHARLES C............ | First sergeant, Company L, 30th Infantry, U. S. Volunteers.
R—Toledo, Ohio. | For distinguished gallantry in action on Analaon Mountain, Luzon, P. I
B—White House, Ohio. | Mar. 26, 1900.

ROSE, FRANKLIN............ | Post commissary sergeant, U. S. Army.
R—St. Louis, Mo. | For distinguished service during the cyclone at Galveston, Tex., Sept. 8, 190
B—Fulton County, Ohio. |

ROSSER, HENRY............ | Corporal, Company A, 17th Infantry, U. S. Army.
R—Stork, N. C. | For distinguished service in the attack on Angeles, P. I., Oct. 16, 1899.
B—Chatham County, N. C. |

ROWBOTTOM, HENRY T............ | First-class private, Signal Corps, U. S. Army.
R—Valdez, Alaska. | For rescuing two soldiers clinging to a capsized canoe in the Yukon Rive
B—England. | Alaska, on July 3, 1913.

RYAN, THOMAS............ | First sergeant, Troop K, 1st Cavalry, U. S. Army.
R—Baltimore, Md. | For distinguished service in battle at Las Guasimas, Cuba, June 24, 1898.
B—Ireland. |

RYDER, WILLIAM............ | Sergeant, Company G, 13th Infantry, U. S. Army.
R—Chicago, Ill. | For distinguished service in the battle at Santiago, Cuba, July 1, 1898.
B—Canada. |

SACKNUS, HENRY W............ | Private, Troop C, 6th Cavalry, U. S. Army.
R—Cleveland, Ohio. | For exceptional gallantry in an engagement at Talisay, P. I., Mar. 29, 1901
B—Cleveland, Ohio. |

SATCHELL, JAMES............ | Corporal, Company A, 24th Infantry, U. S. Army.
R—Eastville, Va. | For distinguished service in battle at Santiago, Cuba, July 1, 1898.
B—Eastville, Va. |

SCALETTA, PAUL............ | Corporal, Company B, 159th Infantry, 40th Division, U. S. Army.
R—San Jose, Calif. | For repeatedly entering a dangerous surf and saving the lives of other soldie
B—San Jose, Calif. | at the risk of his own life at Ocean Beach, Calif., May 5, 1918.

DISTINGUISHED-SERVICE MEDAL 843

SCHUCK, WILLIAM J.   Sergeant, Company K, 6th Infantry, U. S. Army.
   R—Williamsville, N. Y.   For distinguished service in action at Bobong, Negros, P. I., July 19, 1899.
   B—Williamsville, N. Y.

SCHWARZ, ADOLPHUS A.   Private, Troop K, 3d Cavalry, U. S. Army.
   R—Edwardsville, Ill.   For excellent conduct and heroic service during the burning of a troop barracks
   B—Edwardsville, Ill.   at Jefferson Barracks, Mo., Apr. 22, 1896.

SELMIRE, GEORGE.   Sergeant, Company H, 7th Infantry, U. S. Army.
   R—Philadelphia, Pa.   For distinguished service in battle at El Caney, Cuba, July 1, 1898.
   B—Philadelphia, Pa.

SEUFERT, LOUIS P.   Corporal, Company H, 13th Infantry, U. S. Army.
   R—Buffalo, N. Y.   For distinguished service in battle at Santiago, Cuba, July 1, 1898.
   B—Germany.

SHADDEAU, HENRY D.   Corporal, Company F, 17th Infantry, U. S. Army.
   R—Swan Creek, Mich.   For exceptional and conspicuous bravery in action at Simpiton, Mindanao,
   B—Owosso, Mich.   P. I., on May 8, 1904.

SHAFFER, SAMUEL W.   Sergeant major, 7th Infantry, U. S. Army.
   R—Collington, Md.   For distinguished service in battle of El Caney, Cuba, July 1, 1898.
   B—Baltimore, Md.

SHEWBRIDGE, SMITH M.   First sergeant, Company B, 17th Infantry, U. S. Army.
   R—Cincinnati, Ohio.   For gallantry in action at Tamparan, Mindanao, P. I., Apr. 5, 1904.
   B—Charlestown, W. Va.

SILLITO, LOUIS A.   Private, Company C, 3d Infantry, U. S. Volunteers.
   R—Fort Myers, Fla.   For volunteering to nurse and nursing yellow fever patients at Guantanamo,
   B—Nashville, Tenn.   Cuba, Sept. 1, 1898.

SIMPSON, ALFRED G.   Private, Company C, 3d Infantry, U. S. Army.
   R—Columbia, Ind.   For distinguished service in battle at Santiago, Cuba, July 2, 1898.
   B—Fayette County, Ind.

SLOAN, JAMES.   Private, Company G, 16th Infantry, U. S. Army.
   R—Salt Lake City, Utah.   For distinguished service in battle at Santiago, Cuba, July 1, 1898.
   B—Meadville, Pa.

SMITH, GEORGE.   Corporal, Company A, 7th Infantry, U. S. Army.
   R—Edgefield, Tenn.   For distinguished service in battle at El Caney, Cuba, July 1, 1898.
   B—De Kalb, Tenn.

SMITH, JACK.   Lance Corporal, Company E, 21st Infantry, U. S. Army.
   R—Marksville, La.   For conspicuous bravery in action at Arroyo de Lanao, Samar, P. I., June 4,
   B—Marksville, La.   1905.

SMITH, LUCHIOUS.   Private, Troop D, 10th Cavalry, U. S. Army.
   R—Pittsburgh, Pa.   For distinguished service in battle at Santiago, Cuba, July 1, 1898.
   B—Etowah County, Ala.

SMITH, ROBERT M.   Corporal, Company B, 7th Infantry, U. S. Army.
   R—NR.   For distinguished service in battle at El Caney, Cuba, July 1, 1898.
   B—Detroit, Mich.

SMITH, WESLEY W.   Private, Company D, 21st Infantry, U. S. Army.
   R—New York, N. Y.   For distinguished service in battle at Santiago, Cuba, July 1, 1898.
   B—New York, N. Y.

SMITH, WILLIE B.   Corporal, Battery O, 1st Artillery, U. S. Army.
   R—Lockesburg, Ark.   For distinguished service during the cyclone at Galveston, Tex., Sept. 8, 1900.
   B—Union County, Ark.

SMYTH, CHARLES E.   Sergeant, Troop A, 14th Cavalry, U. S. Army.
   R—Chicago, Ill.   For manner in which he handled his detachment of 8 men while surrounded
   B—New York, N. Y.   by and under fire of almost 100 Mexican bandits at Glen Springs, Tex.,
      May 5, 1916.

STAPLES, FRANK.   Private, Company F, 27th Infantry, U. S. Army.
   R—Brooklyn, N. Y.   For distinguished gallantry in the assault on Fort Pitacus, P. I., May 4, 1903.
   B—Brooklyn, N. Y.

STEGER, EDWARD.   Private, Company C, 1st Infantry, U. S. Army.
   R—Detroit, Mich.   Assisted in rescuing a fellow soldier from drowning at the risk of his own life in
   B—Germany.   the sea near Haleiwa, Hawaii, Oct. 22, 1914.

STEVENS, JACOB W.   First sergeant, Company K, 24th Infantry, U. S. Army.
   R—Baltimore, Md.   For distinguished service in engagement near Santa Ana, P. I., Oct. 6, 1899.
   B—Franktown, Va.

STEWART, CLYDE H.   Corporal, Company F, 7th Infantry, U. S. Army.
   R—Pawnee, Okla.   For saving a child from drowning at Fort Wayne, Mich., Sept. 7, 1908.
   B—Seneca, Kans.

STOCKFLETH, HENRY.   Corporal, Battery H, 3d Artillery, U. S. Army.
   R—NR.   For distinguished service in action near Manila, P. I., July 31, 1898.
   B—Germany.

STOKES, EARNEST.
R—Wartrace, Tenn.
B—Wartrace, Tenn.

Private, Company F, 24th Infantry, U. S. Army.
For most distinguished gallantry in action at Naguilian, Luzon, P. I., Dec. 7, 1899.

STOKES, GEORGE P.
R—Rocky Ford, Colo.
B—Rogers, Ark.

Private, Company I, 21st Infantry, U. S. Army.
For marked courage and intelligence in saving a comrade from drowning at Lake Lanao, P. I., Dec. 12, 1909.

TEETER, MILO C.
R—New Albany, Pa.
B—New Albany, Pa.

Private, Company E, 19th Infantry, U. S. Army.
Rescued a comrade from drowning at Penaranda, P. I., on Feb. 22, 1912.

THORNTON, WILLIAM.
R—Great Falls, Mont.
B—Washington Court House, Ohio.

Corporal, Company G, 24th Infantry, U. S. Army.
For distinguished service in battle at Santiago, Cuba, July 1, 1898.

TOBIN, WILLIAM J.
R—NR.
B—Fort Warren, Mass.

First sergeant, Battery G, 7th Artillery, U. S. Army.
For distinguished service in Boston Harbor, Mass., Jan. 3, 1900.

TOM, JACOB W.
R—Paulding, Ohio.
B—Hancock County, Ohio.

Quartermaster sergeant, Company D, 19th Infantry, U. S. Army.
For gallant conduct in action at Mount Bud-Dajo, Jolo, P. I., Mar. 7, 1906.

TOMLINSON, FREDERICK.
R—Philadelphia, Pa.
B—Memphis, Tenn.

Corporal, 138th Company, Coast Artillery Corps, U. S. Army.
Rescued the body of a comrade from a burning launch on the Pasig River, Manila, P. I., Sept. 9, 1912.

TURNER, CLEMON.
R—Cincinnati, Ohio.
B—Gainesville, Ala.

Private, Company K, 24th Infantry, U. S. Army.
For rescuing a fellow soldier from drowning at the risk of his own life, near Camp McGrath, P. I., Nov. 12, 1914.

TURNER, VICTOR.
R—Homestead, Pa.
B—Homestead, Pa.

Musician, Company C, 17th Infantry, U. S. Army.
For meritorious conduct in saving the life of a drowning comrade at the risk of his own at Sweetwater Creek, Ga., June 29, 1909.

VAN CAMPEN, HIEL.
R—Jeffersonville, Ind.
B—Jeffersonville, Ind.

Private, Company E, 1st Infantry, U. S. Army.
For his assistance in saving a comrade from drowning at great risk of his own life near Haleiwa, Hawaiian Islands, Oct. 22, 1914.

VENUS, CHARLES.
R—Lawrenceville, Ill.
B—Lawrenceville, Ill.

Sergeant, Company I, 23d Infantry, U. S. Army.
For exceptional courage in swimming and wading to shore from a capsized boat and guiding a rescue boat to the relief of three comrades whom he had left on the upturned hull in Galveston Bay, Tex., June 29, 1914.

VILLUMSEN, HANS.
R—Philadelphia, Pa.
B—Denmark.

Sergeant, Company D, 10th Infantry, U. S. Army.
For distinguished service in battle at Santiago, Cuba, July 1, 1898.

VOLKMAR, WALTER S.
R—NR.
B—Philadelphia, Pa.

Sergeant, Signal Corps, U. S. Army.
For distinguished services in subduing a fire which threatened to destroy public property, at Fort Sam Houston, Tex., Mar. 15, 1898.

WALKER, ARTHUR L., Jr.
R—Brookline, Mass.
B—Yonkers, N. Y.

Private, Headquarters Company, 301st Infantry, 76th Division, U. S. Army.
For saving the life of a fellow soldier when the latter was thrown into the water by the capsizing of a canoe, at the risk of his own life, at Robbins Pond, Camp Devens, Mass., May 4, 1918.

WALKER, JOHN.
R—Thornhill, Va.
B—Orange County, Va.

Corporal, Troop D, 10th Cavalry, U. S. Army.
For distinguished service in action at Santiago, Cuba, July 1, 1898.

WARNER, JAMES H.
R—NR.
B—Tioga County, N. Y.

First sergeant, Company D, 4th Infantry, U. S. Army.
For distinguished service in action near Dasmarinas, P. I., June 19, 1899.

WEBER, ANTON.
R—New York, N. Y.
B—Switzerland.

Quartermaster sergeant, Company H, 13th Infantry, U. S. Army.
For distinguished service in action at Santiago, Cuba, July 1, 1898.

WEISS, GEORGE.
R—St. Louis, Mo.
B—Prussia.

Sergeant, Troop F, 4th Cavalry, U. S. Army.
For gallant conduct in action at Mount Bud-Dajo, Jolo, P. I., Mar. 7, 1906.

WHELAN, JOHN.
R—New York, N. Y.
B—Ireland.

Sergeant, Company F, 27th Infantry, U. S. Army.
For conspicuous gallantry in action at Bayang, P. I., May 2, 1902.

WHITE, JOSEPH.
R—NR.
B—New Orleans, La.

Musician, Company B, 24th Infantry, U. S. Army.
For distinguished service at the Rio Grande River, Cabanatuan, P. I., Nov. 8, 1900.

WHITNEY, PERCY M.
R—Washington, D. C.
B—Washington, D. C.

Private, Troop E, 6th Cavalry, U. S. Army.
For distinguished service in unhesitatingly plunging into the Palico River, P. I., Sept. 2, 1901, and at the risk of his own life attempting to rescue from drowning Sergt. John W. Harris, of said troop.

ῘY, DORPHIN C_____ —Pine Creek, Pa. —Pine Creek, Pa.	Private, 69th Company, Coast Artillery Corps, U. S. Army. For voluntarily entering a closed place and removing sacks of powder that were in close proximity to burning powder and smoldering débris, at the risk of his own life, thereby preventing further disaster after the explosion, at Fort Monroe, Va., July 21, 1910.
INS, GEORGE W_____ —Sioux City, Iowa. —Sioux City, Iowa.	Sergeant, Company G, 39th Infantry, U. S. Volunteers. For distinguished gallantry in action at San Cristobal River, Luzon, P. I., on Jan. 1, 1900.
'ORD, JAMES W_____ —Urbana, Ohio. —Urbana, Ohio.	Sergeant, Company G, 9th Infantry, U. S. Army. For great coolness and good judgment displayed in commanding a battery when ambushed by natives near Basey, Samar, P. I., Sept. 1, 1901.
AMS, RICHARD_____ —Dayton, Ohio. —Cincinnati, Ohio.	Corporal, Company B, 24th Infantry, U. S. Army. For distinguished service in action at Santiago, Cuba, July 1, 1898.
IAMS, THOMAS S_____ —NR. —Glasgow, Ky.	Private, Company E, 2d Infantry, U. S. Army. For most distinguished conduct at Santiago, Cuba, July 2, 1898.
ER, JOHN G_____ —San Antonio, Tex. —Waco, Tex.	Private, Troop F, 1st U. S. Volunteer Cavalry. For distinguished service in battle at Santiago, Cuba, July 1, 1898.
ERS, OSCAR F_____ —NR. —Flintstone, Md.	Corporal, Company F, 9th Infantry, U. S. Army. For distinguished service in action at Santiago, Cuba, July 2, 1898.
IG, JOHN C_____ —NR. —Canada.	Sergeant major, 3d Infantry, U. S. Army. For rescuing a comrade from drowning in Minnesota River near Fort Snelling, Minn., Nov. 19, 1896. Oak-leaf cluster. For distinguished service in battle at El Caney, Cuba, July 1, 1898.

ADDITIONAL COPIES
OF THIS PUBLICATION MAY BE PROCURED FROM
THE SUPERINTENDENT OF DOCUMENTS
GOVERNMENT PRINTING OFFICE
WASHINGTON, D. C.
AT
$1.35 PER COPY
▽

www.ingramcontent.com/pod-product-compliance
Lightning Source LLC
Chambersburg PA
CBHW070936180426
43192CB00039B/2302